"Missing from the last half century's flood of scholarship on the fourth century has been a detailed reflection on the ecclesiological visions implicit in the alliances and relationships that are so important in the Trinitarian controversies. Fr. Twomey's rich volume forces upon us a vital series of questions and a compellingly argued thesis. From his detective work emerges the possibility that an inchoate vision of the Apostolic See's pre-eminence was a concrete reality in the early fourth century. Fr. Twomey's argument has great import both for how we envisage the early growth of the papacy and for the vital and continuing dialogue between the Churches of East and West. This compelling text deserves the attention of all interested in these questions."

— LEWIS AYRES —
Durham University

"It gives me great pleasure to see Fr. Twomey's book republished under its new title. I read the book with great interest shortly after its publication in 1982, and I was impressed by both the cogency of its arguments and the clarity of its presentation of dense and difficult material. Not all historians will agree with his conclusions about Eusebius' 'original ecclesiology' and the implication that aspects of 'Eusebianism' survive into later Chalcedonian Orthodox rejection of the 'Petrine Ministry' of Rome. Such is the nature, however, of groundbreaking historical works. I hope that in this new edition Fr. Twomey's book will receive the attention it so fully deserves."

— WILLIAM J. TIGHE —
Muhlenberg College

"This new edition of Fr. Twomey's *Apostolikos Thronos* is much to be welcomed. It is a work that has helped me to see how the primacy of the Bishop of Rome was understood in the patristic era, a matter that John Henry Newman regarded as crucial for the witness of Christian unity. Fr. Twomey's analysis of the changing perspective in Eusebius' *Church History* is especially noteworthy—the danger of linking the Church's mission too closely to the structures of the earthly city is as real today as it was in the fourth century."

— MSGR. JEFFREY STEENSON —
Ordinary Emeritus of the Ordinariate of the Chair of St. Peter

APOSTOLIKOS THRONOS

APOSTOLIKOS THRONOS

Rival Accounts of Roman Primacy in Eusebius and Athanasius

Vincent Twomey

EMMAUS
ACADEMIC

Steubenville, Ohio
www.emmausacademic.com

EMMAUS
ACADEMIC

Steubenville, Ohio
A Division of The St. Paul Center for Biblical Theology
Editor-in-Chief: Scott Hahn
1468 Parkview Circle
Steubenville, Ohio 43952

The First Edition was published in 1982 by Aschendorff Münster under the original title *Apostolikos Thronos: Competing Visions of the Primacy of Rome in Eusebius and Athanasius*

Library of Congress Cataloging-in-Publication Data applied for
ISBNs: 978-1-64585-310-7 hardcover | 978-1-64585-311-4 paperback |
    978-1-64585-312-1 ebook

Layout by Julia Petersen and Allison Merrick
Cover design by Allison Merrick
Cover image: *Cathedra Petri* by Heinz-Dieter Falkenstein

✝

Dedicated to the Memory of the 265th Successor of St. Peter,
Pope Benedict XVI, in gratitude

CONTENTS

PART ONE:
THE CHURCH HISTORY OF
EUSEBIUS OF CAESAREA

PREFACE TO THE
REVISED EDITION

The Apostolic See's claim to a primacy in the universal Church has long been one of the main stumbling blocks in ecumenical dialogue. It was only when I attended the Fourth Regensburg Oecumenical Symposium in 1972—exactly fifty years ago—that I became aware of how explosive a topic it was. In Spindelhof, near Regensburg, some of the leading bishops and theologians of the Orthodox churches had come together to engage in a theological dialogue with their Catholic counterparts on the subject of intercommunion. One day, out of the blue, the rather strained politeness that marked the proceedings up to then was shattered when a bishop of one of the Eastern Rite Catholic churches happened to mention the primacy of the pope. Vocal outrage was the reaction of the Orthodox prelates. This came as a shock to someone like myself, who had absorbed the doctrine of papal infallibility with his mother's milk, to quote the reason given by Archbishop John McHale of Tuam for opposing the proclamation of the dogma of papal infallibility at the First Vatican Council. At the time, I was studying St. Athanasius. He had appealed to the Bishop of Rome in defense of his claim to the See of Alexandria, the second Apostolic See. So I asked myself, why did this Eastern bishop turn to Rome? My long search led me back to the original draft of Eusebius' *Church History* in order to discover how that "spokesman of the East" understood the generally acknowledged but still undefined preeminence of the Church of Rome at the turn of the fourth century—that is, before Constantine's epoch-making embrace of Christianity.

The most significant manifestation of the new era was, as is well known, the First Oecumenical Council called by the Roman emperor and held in the imperial palace of Nicaea, 325. Eusebius participated in the Council as bishop. Athanasius was also in Nicaea (as a deacon accompanying his bishop, Alexander of Alexandria). In different ways, Nicaea impacted both of their lives—and with profound implications for their respective attitudes to the Bishop of Rome. What I discovered was the beginnings of the emergence of two distinct ecclesiologies, which centuries later would result, tragically, in the Great Schism between East and West.

The salient features of this nascent division into Eastern and Western Christianity, initially but a fissure in the body of the universal Church, can be detected in the evolving attitudes of Eusebius and Athanasius to the Bishop of Rome's status in the Church. That, at least, is my thesis, which is up for discussion.

When I informed Pope Emeritus Benedict XVI in 2017 that Professor Scott Hahn had persuaded me to republish *Apostolikos Thronos*, his reaction was immediate: "That Emmaus Academic is preparing a new publication of your '*Apostolikos Thronos*' is for me a personal and an ecclesial joy. My hope is that your great opus can indeed help bring us a step further in the dialogue with the Churches of the East, which has taken on a new significance in this hour of Christianity."[1] That, too, is my sincere hope as we approach the seventeenth centenary of the First Oecumenical Council of Nicaea.

Donamon,
Feast of St. Gregory the Great 2022

---

[1] Pope Emeritus Benedict XVI, personal correspondance with the author: "Dass Emmaus Academic eine neue Publikation Ihres '*Apostolikos Thronos*' vorbereitet, ist eine persönliche und eine ekklesiale Freude für mich. Ich hoffe, dass Ihr großes Opus uns doch ein Stück weiterhelfen kann im Dialog mit den Kirchen des Orients, der in dieser Stunde der Christenheit neue Bedeutung erlangt hat."

INTRODUCTION TO THE
REVISED EDITION

Since this book was first published, a vast amount of scholarship has appeared devoted to two of the major ecclesiastical figures that dominated the Church in the first half of the fourth century, Eusebius of Caesarea and Athanasius of Alexandria. The same can be said of the epoch-making historical events such as the conversion of Constantine[1] and the so-called Arian crisis.[2] However, the significance of what, almost by accident, this writer discovered—first in the generally neglected texts from the pen of Athanasius (his *Apologies* and *Historia Arianorum*), and then hidden in the earliest draft of the much-celebrated *Church History* of Eusebius—has been given less attention, and so I am grateful for the opportunity to publish this revised version of the original.

But first, some general comments on interpreting Eusebius and Athanasius, remembering Gadamer's hermeneutical principle regarding *Wirkungsgeschichte* (the history of effects), namely that one must take into account the effects it produced in history, if one is to understand a text; this demands of the interpreter that he places himself within that history and enters into dialogue with it.

Modern scholarship is deeply indebted to such giants as Seeck and Schwartz for their inestimable contribution to scholarship. Their influence

---

[1] See, e.g., Ernst Dassmann, *Kirchengeschichte II/1: Konstantinische Wende und spätantike Reichskirche* (Stuttgart: Kohlhammer, 1996); Harold A. Drake, *Constantine and the Bishops: The Politics of Intolerance* (Baltimore and London: The John Hopkins University Press, 2000); Klaus M. Girardet, *Die Konstantinische Wende: Voraussetzung und geistige Grundlagen der Religionspolitik Konstantins des Großen* (Darmstadt: Wissenschaftliche Buchgesellschaft, 2007); Heinrich Schlange-Schöningen, ed., *Konstantin und das Christentum. Neue Wege der Forschung* (Darmstadt: wbg Academic in Wissenschaftliche Buchgesellschaft, 2007). Perhaps the most comprehensive and profound account is that by the Byzantinist Endre von Ivánka in his *Rhomäerreich und Gottesvolk* (Freiburg/ München: Karl Alber, 1968) (developing the insights of Christopher Dawson's *The Making of Europe: An Introduction to the History of European Unity* [London: Sheed & Ward, 1939], 103).

[2] See, e.g., Khaled Anatolios, *Retrieving Nicaea: The Development and Meaning of Trinitarian Doctrine* (Grand Rapids, MI: Baker Academic, 2018).

has been immense down to our own day. As well as editing the major texts, these scholars and their successors opened up new horizons in their interpretation of those texts. But inevitably they also brought their own particular cultural (and underlying confessional) assumptions to their studies. Their approach to the fourth century texts was necessarily from the perspective of what is today called late antiquity, an approach which is essentially antiquarian and secular rather than one taken from a theologian's faith (and existential) perspective. Accordingly, scholars of late antiquity since then find a kindred spirit in Eusebius, the accomplished scholar and imperial panegyrist, and so tend to be largely sympathetic to his writings however critical they may be.[3] Indeed, apart from anything else, we are indebted to him for all the documentary evidence (and texts) which he provides that would otherwise have been lost. On the other hand, scholars of late antiquity tend to find the vibrant faith of St. Athanasius if not repugnant then at the very least incomprehensible, and so tend to ascribe (usually self-serving) political motives to his actions.[4] They interpret his writings written in his self-defence such as his *Apologies*, to which this study is devoted, from such a negative perspective.[5] Thankfully, recent scholarship has seen a movement toward a more balanced estimate of the person of Athanasius.[6]

More significantly, Western contemporary scholars spontaneously

[3] Cf., e.g., the major study of Timothy D. Barnes, *Constantine and Eusebius* (Cambridge, MA: Harvard University Press, 1981).

[4] The origins of the widely influential, negative, scholarly attitude to Athanasius is to be found in the work of the classical philologists Otto Seeck (1850–1921) and, especially, Eduard Schwartz (1858–1940), whose contribution to Athanasian studies were phenomenal. For a detailed analysis of the scholarly interpreters of Athanasius over the past century, see Duane W.-H. Arnold, *The Early Episcopal Career of Athanasius of Alexandria* (Notre Dame, IN: University of Notre Dame Press, 1991), section 1, in particular 9–23.

[5] Cf. Timothy D. Barnes, *Athanasius and Constantius: Theology and Politics in the Constantinian Empire* (Cambridge, MA: Harvard University Press, 1993), who frankly acknowledges at the outset the presumption behind his study, namely "that Athanasius consistently misrepresented central facts about his ecclesiastical career. . ."(2). It is therefore not surprising that Barnes calls the *History of the Arians* "a systematically deceptive work" (129).

[6] See in particular Martin Tetz, *Athanasiana,* ed. W. Geerlings et al. (Berlin: Walter de Gruyter Gmbh US SR, 1995); Arnold, *Early Episcopal Career*; Khalad Anatolios, *Athanasius* (London and New York: Routledge, 2004). What Athanasius says of the writers of Scripture, could be said to apply, *mutatis mutandis*, to interpreting the writings of saintly theologians: "Without a pure mind and a life modelled on the saints, no one can apprehend the words of the saints" (Athanasius, *De incarn.*, in *Contra Gentes* and *De Incarnatione*, ed. and trans. Robert W. Thomson [Oxford: Clarendon Press, 1971], 57).

tend to view the historical events of the fourth century through the prism of their own contemporary culture. That culture has its roots in Latin Christianity, which, culminating in the Enlightenment, produced the separation of Church and State we take for granted today.[7] However, as Harold Drake has pointed out, for all parties in the early centuries "the State" as we now understand it, did not exist; what the Church confronted was the sacral Roman Empire. This insight makes the study of the transformation of the Church in the wake of the conversion of Constantine to a form of Christian monotheism more complex and, indeed, more interesting because of its inherent ambiguity.[8] Eusebius was the first to interpret theologically that epoch-making event as inaugurating a new dispensation; his influence was and is profound.

The origins of that Western cultural development characterized by the distinction between the temporal and the spiritual realms are likewise to be found in the fourth century, precisely in the battle of Athanasius contra mundum. Though acutely aware of the ambiguity of the emerging Christian Roman Empire, it has to be admitted that this writer was also affected by the same Western cultural assumptions and, as a consequence, frequently used the term "State" in the original publication when trying to highlight the *civil* authority in the Roman Empire. Though it in no way affects the main thesis, the revised text takes account of this important terminological nuance and so tries to avoid the term "State" apart from direct quotations. It was precisely the ambiguity of the Christianized sacral Empire—the dangers intrinsic to the new possibilities for the Church's flourishing under the patronage of the Christian emperor—that threatened the integrity of the apostolic and universal Church founded on the Confession of Peter (Matt 16:16–18).

A lack of adequate attention to the ecclesiological issues raised by—or, rather, intrinsic to—the disputes with regard to Trinitarian theology seems

---

[7] See Dawson, *The Making of Europe*; Marcia L. Colish, *Medieval Foundations of the Western Intellectual Tradition, 400–1400* (New Haven and London: Yale University Press, 1997).

[8] Basil Studer, *Schola Christiana: Die Theologie zwischen Nizäa (325) und Chalzedon (451)* (Paderborn-Munich, Vienna, Zürich: F. Schöningh, 1998), 41–45, limits the Imperial Church, strictly speaking to the Theodosian period (380–450), but the dangers were present from the start. Gratitude to the emperor for his unexpected support and magnanimity (building churches, financing synods, etc.) concealed the danger of becoming subservient to the emperor even in matters of faith and Church order.

to characterize most theological studies of the so-called Arian crisis.[9] The result is that the main concern of Athanasius in the immediate aftermath of the great Synod of Nicaea was assumed to be primarily in defence of the Faith of Nicaea.[10] What a close examination of the generally neglected texts of Athanasius reveals is that what preoccupied him up to and beyond the Synod of Serdica, 343, was not so much the Nicene Creed but his claim to the See of Alexandria. That claim hinged on the more immediate, ecclesiological issue of the nature and exercise of the traditional apostolic authority in the Church that was in the process of being remodelled in line with the emerging Imperial ecclesiology first articulated by Eusebius of Caesarea after Nicaea.

+ + +

It is almost a century since a Catholic scholar expressed his astonishment that: "The history of the Arians of the fourth century has sometimes been written with the Pope almost left out. St. Athanasius appealed to the Pope, obeyed the Pope's summons, and was acquitted by the Pope. The Eusebians used flattery and guile; they pretended to appeal to Pope Julius and evaded obedience. The Pope quashed their council of Tyre. The great council of Serdica instituted a new system under which metropolitans or bishops of the East, who wished to appeal to the Pope, need not appear in person in Rome, as had been till then the law. . . ."[11] The thesis of this book is that the playing down of the Bishop of Rome's role in the fourth century was

---

[9]   See, e.g., R. P. C. Hanson, *The Search for the Christian Doctrine of God: The Arian Controversy, 318–381* (Edinburgh: T. and T. Clark, 1988); Lewis Ayres, *Nicaea and its Legacy: An Approach to Fourth Century Trinitarian Theology* (Oxford: Oxford University Press, 2004); Anatolios, *Retrieving Nicaea.* Rowan Williams seems to be the exception, in so far that he is aware of some of the ecclesiological issues at stake; see his *Arius: Heresy and Tradition* (London: Darton, Longman & Todd, 1987), 81–91. There he presents the ecclesiological issues in terms of the tension between the pre-Constantinian "Catholic" and "Academic" under-standings of authority in the Church (see below, p. 190), a synthesis of which, he claims, was attempted by Constantine's development of the universal synod.

[10]   On the Synod of Nicaea, see the introduction to the texts in G. Alberigo et al., *Conciliorum Oecumenicorum Generaliumque Decreta* (Turnhout, Belgium: Brepols, 2006), 3–15, with a comprehensive coverage of the most important secondary literature.

[11]   C. Lattey, ed., *The Papacy: Papers from the Summer School of Catholic Studies Held at Cambridge, August 7–10, 1923* (London: Burns Oates & Washbourne, 1924), 35f., as quoted in Stephen K. Ray, *Upon This Rock* (San Francisco: Ignatius Press, 1999), 200.

due primarily to the failure to give due attention to the broader, ecclesiological issues that were at stake in that period of radical change in the Church's history.

This writer discovered the ecclesiological dimension to the so-called Arian crisis quite by accident, while studying Athanasius' much-derided *Historia Arianorum*. It is his self-defence written for his followers among the monks in the Egyptian desert. Its objective was to explain what he saw as the true meaning of his own excommunication by Ossius of Cordoba and Liberius of Rome (357). Both eminent bishops had, up to then, opposed the might of the emperor Constantius II in their support for Athanasius, who at the time was perceived to be identified with the Creed of Nicaea so that his excommunication amounted to a denial of Nicaea. What was surprising was to discover that Athanasius interpreted the fall of Liberius on the basis of an understanding of the role of the Bishop of Rome as Successor of St. Peter. The scholarly consensus is that such an understanding of the Bishop of Rome was the invention of Damasus of Rome in response to Canon 3 of the Synod of Constantinople, 381, claiming a primacy of honor for the "New Rome."[12] But in the *Historia Arianorum*, Athanasius made his defense on what evidently were common assumptions at the time. What is the evidence for such assumptions?

The fragmentary evidence for the position occupied by the Bishop of Rome in the universal Church in the first three centuries has been the subject of countless scholarly studies, the examination of which Ratzinger advised me to avoid. But by the time I got that sensible advice while doing research in the Bodleian Library, Oxford, I had noticed that a considerable amount of the relevant evidence is to be found in Eusebius' *Church History*, and so I opted for a more modest approach. This was to investigate Eusebius' own understanding of (or assumptions about) the nature of the Universal Church, when he set out to write a "history" of the Church before the outbreak of Diocletian's so-called Great Persecution in 303. The methodology used was, put simply, firstly, to try to identify the framework he chose to describe the Church's origins and history, and then to examine how he fitted those same texts within that overall framework: his own

---

[12] The reponse of Damasus is to be found in the text from the Synod of Rome, 382, preserved in the *Decretum Gelasianum*; cf. Eduard Schwartz, "Zum Decretum Gelasianum," *Zeitschrift für neutestamentliche Wissenschaft* 33 (1930): 161–168; Trevor Jalland, *The Church and the Papacy: A Historical Study* (London: 1944), 255–257.

principles of selection and interpretation.[13] The result was a discovery of what could be called Eusebius' original ecclesiology of the Apostolic Church founded by St. Peter, which had lain undetected under the final redaction. In the course of several revisions of the original *History* this original ecclesiology morphed into Eusebius' well-known Imperial ecclesiology that marked the final redaction. In a word, in the new dispensation (*oikonomia*) inaugurated by Constantine,[14] the Apostolic Church had been replaced by the Imperial Church. That Imperial ecclesiology was taken up by Eusebius of Nicomedia and, it seems to this writer, characterized the first stage of the so-called Arian crisis, necessitating among other things, Athanasius' appeal to Rome, when he was deposed of his own see, and climaxing at the Synod of Sardica, 343.[15]

+ + +

Contrary to what a number of criticisms of the first edition claimed, my thesis does not purport to have discovered a developed notion of papal jurisdiction in the first half of the fourth century. The primacy of the Bishop of Rome in the third and fourth centuries was still largely undetermined. It is best described as a preeminence, as I do occasionally, except that that term does not do justice to the see's real, if still somewhat vague, theological authority, an authority not confined to the West but universal. My thesis must be seen in the context of the emerging doctrinal and structural shape of the Church in the first five centuries, where canon law was in its infancy and so more elastic than in later centuries.

Many changes in the revised edition are stylistic, but some are related to the content. What Newman wrote in his "advertisement" to the third edition of his *The Arians of the Fourth Century* (1871), I can adopt, *mutatis*

---

[13] Dieter Timpe, "Was ist Kirchengeschichte? Zum Gattungscharaker der Historia Ecclesiastica des Eusebius," in *Festschrift Robert Werner zu seinem 65. Geburtstag*, ed. W. Dahlheim et al. (Konstanz: Univ.-Verl. Konstanz, 1989), 171–204, presents a profound, nuanced analysis of the originality of Eusebius' achievement in creating this particular historiographic genre; he downplays its apologetic character and criticizes Franz Overbeck's interpretation, whose analysis greatly influenced my own interpretation of the *Church History*; see also Friedhelm Winkelmann, *Euseb von Kaisareia: Der Vater der Kirchengeschichte* (Berlin: Verlags-Anstalt Union, 1991).

[14] See Raffaele Farina, *L'impero e l'imperatore Cristiano in Eusebio di Cesarea: La prima teologia politica del cristianismo* (Zürich: Pas-Verlag, 1966), 162–163.

[15] See Hamilton Hess, *The Early Development of Canon Law and the Council of Serdica*, (Oxford: Oxford University Press, 2002).

mutandis, as my own: "No change has been made anywhere affecting the opinions, sentiments, or speculations contained in the original edition—though they are sometimes expressed with a boldness or decision which now displeases him. . . ." The only exception is a passage about the alleged letter of the Synod of Arles, 314, to Sylvester of Rome, which has been removed as not being authentic and has been replaced with a new text so as to preserve the original pagination; this does not affect the main thesis. The more significant additions, mostly in the footnotes, are indicated by square brackets.

Acknowledgements are due to so many, without whose help and support this revision and related articles would not have materialized. I should like to thank, in the first place, Scott Hahn and the editorial board of Emmaus Academic for accepting this revised version for publication. My gratitude is due, in particular, to Chris Erickson for directing the painstaking process of digitalizing the original, incorporating my revisions, and, above all, for overseeing the proof-reading. (The original had been rightly criticized for the inordinate number of typos and misspellings.) Without the professional help at different times of the staff of the John Paul II University Library, Maynooth, the Staatsbibliothek Munich, the Universitäsbibliotek Passau, the Biblioteca Gregoriana, Rome, and the library of the Görres-Gesellschaft, Rome, the decades-long research needed to undertake this revision would have been impossible. My thanks also to Ephräm Lomidze and Neil-Xavier O'Donoghue, who found many texts electronically that I was unable to locate. Finally, words cannot adequately express my gratitude to Martin Trimpe and Stephan O. Horn, fellow-members of Ratzinger's Schülerkreis, for their unfailing encouragement, advice, and criticism not only during the seven years I was working on my thesis but also in the intervening forty years. Vergelt's Gott.

Donamon,
Roscommon
Feast of the Birthday of Our Lady 2022

PREFACE

The greatest obstacle to that visible unity which contemporary Christians seek, and which the Second Vatican Council made its own special concern, seems to be the teaching and jurisdictional primacy of the pope based on the Petrine Succession of the Church of Rome. On the theoretical level, many of the objections to the primacy center around the question of its historical origins and their theological justification. This study has as its subject one of the most significant stages in the historical unfolding of the Petrine Office of the Bishop of Rome, namely those developments which took place in the first half of the fourth century. Its object is to uncover the attitude of Eusebius of Caesarea and St. Athanasius of Alexandria to such developments, each of whom played a not insignificant role in them. In doing so it is hoped that the present study will in some small way contribute to the ecumenical discussion on the nature and function of the primacy. However, in the first place, this work is offered as a contribution to Eusebian and Athanasian studies; despite renewed interest in the writings of Eusebius and Athanasius in recent years, both the *Church History of Eusebius* and the "historico-apologetic" writings of Athanasius are still largely unexplored terrain.

Originally written as a doctoral dissertation for the Faculty of Catholic Theology on the University of Regensburg, the present work was completed in 1978 and handed into the faculty on October 18 of that year. Due to external circumstances, mostly in connection with the distance between Europe and Papua New Guinea where I was engaged as lecturer at the Holy Spirit Regional Seminary Bomana from March 1979 until August 1981, the publication has been delayed until now. In the intervening years no essential changes to the text have been undertaken. A small number of references to further literature have been included in the footnotes within the limits imposed by the fact that the work was already in print. During the proof-reading on my return from PNG, I had an opportunity to check and peruse recent publications as well as some older works which I was unable to consult previously; a brief discussion of the more relevant literature is included in an appendix.

Of the many who contributed to the successful completion of this work and whom I wish to thank, only a few can be mentioned here. My Superiors in the Society of the Divine Word made it possible for me to engage in the post-graduate studies and research that led to this work by freeing me from all other duties and obligations. The present Prefect of the Congregation for the Faith Cardinal Joseph Ratzinger in his former capacity as Professor of Dogmatic Theology and the History of Dogma on the University of Regensburg supervised this present work right up to its completion. My heartfelt thanks are due to him, not only for his unfailing counsel and help, but also for providing the theological basis for my research: the unique historicity of Salvation which accounts for, indeed demands, a certain development in the Church's teaching and structure and yet avoids relativism or historicism. Here I should also like to express my gratitude to my colleagues and friends, who made up Prof. Ratzinger's Doktorandenkolloquium, for their unfailing stimulation, encouragement—and criticism. Prof. S. Horn S.D.S., Augsburg, deserves my special thanks for the trouble he took to read the manuscript and for the suggestions he kindly offered, though it was not possible to take all of them into account. I also thank Alois Grillmeier, S.J., A. Hamilton, S.J., and D. S. Wallace-Hadrill for their kind assistance with regard to secondary literature. The Faculty of Catholic Theology on the University of Regensburg accepted the work as a doctoral dissertation; here I would like to express my gratitude to Prof. Wolfgang Beinert, who despite difficult circumstances and limited time kindly agreed to act as Korreferent. Bernard Kötting of the University of Münster accepted the dissertation for publication in his "MBTh" monograph series; I am most grateful for the trouble he took to see it to a successful conclusion.

Special thanks are due to the staff of the University Library in Regensburg and the Bodleian Library in Oxford for their ready co-operation, patience, and efficiency. The kind hospitality of Haus Werdenfels near Regensburg, St. Benet's Hall Oxford, St. Jakobs Priesterseminar in Regensburg, and the Divine Word House in Maynooth provided at various times the necessary milieu for study and writing. The proof-reading and compilation of the index took place in the Missionsseminar St. Augustin near Bonn. The typing of the final manuscript was mostly executed by Mrs. M. Sheehen of Maynooth Town, an extra-ordinary performance considering the poor condition of the pencil-written manuscript at her disposal and the time pressure under which she worked. I should also like to express my appreciation to the confreres and friends who spent many a boring hour checking the manuscript and the final typed version. Das Bischöfliche Ordinariat in Regensburg enabled me to survive financially by granting me a part-time Chaplaincy, while Frau Helena Müller of Kaiserslautern offered generous support during the final two years, which I acknowledge with gratitude. The publication in its present form was made possible by the generous subsidy that was readily provided by the Steyler Mission, D-5205 Sankt Augustin 1. The publishers, Aschendorff of Münster, Westphalia, have shown remarkable cooperation and considerable patience, for which I am most grateful.

This work is dedicated to my S.V.D. Confreres in Papua New Guinea, among whom I was privileged to work for a brief period.

Vincent Twomey, S.V.D.
St. Gabriel, Mödling near Vienna,
Feast of the Cathedra Petri 1982

GENERAL INTRODUCTION[*]

The primacy of the Bishop of Rome was not unaffected by the changes which occurred in that "age of constitutional transition," as one scholar described the fourth century.[1] Indications of the

---

[*] With regard to *Primary Sources*, references in Part One to the writings of Eusebius only contain the requisite abbreviations as given in the List of Abbreviations, followed by the number of the book, chapter, and verse (in that order) as well as the name of the editor of the critical text, which is placed in brackets together with the corresponding page and line number, should the latter be supplied in the critical text. In Part Two, references to the works of Athanasius follow the same pattern, apart from the fact that the numbers following on the abbreviation refer simply to chapter and (when indicated in the critical text) verse. In both Parts One and Two, references to all other primary sources, while following the same basic pattern, differ in so far as the name of the ancient author is also given. Where no modern critical text is available, primary source references contain the volume number, page and line of the Migne version, either from the *Patrologia Graeca* (= *PG*) or the *Patrologia Latina* (= *PL*). In order to promote the legibility of the footnotes, references to *Secondary Sources* have been reduced to the surname of the author, a shortened version of the title of his book or article and the page number or numbers of the work quoted. Should the discussion demand it, the date and place of publication are also given. Otherwise, full bibliographical details are to be found in the bibliography. For the sake of simplicity, Arabic numerals have been used throughout, both for primary and secondary sources, except where reference is made to the volume number of a critical text or secondary source, when large Roman numerals are used, or where the pagination of a secondary source is given in small Roman numerals.

[1] Hess, *Canons of Sardica*, 110. The awareness of the fourth century as a period of transition is of major importance for a proper understanding of the history of the time and for a just interpretation of the documents produced by the writers of that era. This in turn places a heavy burden on the theologian who wishes to come to grips with the issues raised by the events which marked that epoch-making century since he must first try to establish the date of composition of each document at his disposal and judge it within its original setting before he can attempt to trace the lines of development and (more difficult still) distinguish the constants and the variables in the process of change. He is therefore forced to enter into the specialized field of history, as much as the historian is compelled to face the discipline of theology. Both theologian and historian must refrain from any attempt to link together texts which are apparently related to the same subject, but which are in fact separated by decades or even centuries, until such time as the groundwork has been done on the individual text. Failure to take sufficient account of the nature of the changes which took place on the constitutional plane and at the level of reflection on the nature of the Church is a criticism that can be levelled in

1

developments which took place both in the exercise of the primacy and in reflection on its nature are small but significant. On the one hand, there is the first explicit articulation of the Roman primacy of Jurisdiction (at the Synod of Sardica, 343). On the other hand, the Petrine source of the preeminent authority of the Roman See was formulated for the first time explicitly by Damasus of Rome, who, at the Synod of Rome, 382, broke the apparent silence since the time of Stephan I (254–257) with regard to the association of the prerogatives of the Roman See with the Dominical promise to Peter (Mt 16,18)[2] and so began the process of reflection on the nature of the Roman primacy which reached its first climax in the theology of St. Leo the Great.

There has been no single, detailed study devoted to an examination of the causes of the development which evidently took place in the fourth century with regard to the nature and extent of the preeminent authority exercised by the Bishop of Rome within the universal Church. My object is not to fill this gap. The aim of this study is limited to an examination of the changing consciousness of the Church with regard to the preeminence of the See of Rome as it is reflected in the works of Eusebius of Caesarea and St. Athanasius the Great. These two Eastern bishops were deeply affected by the external and internal conditions of the Church in the first half of the fourth century. They also greatly influenced the response of the

particular at studies of the Roman primacy in the fourth century, such as the relatively recent work of P.-P. Joannou, *Die Ostkirche und die Cathedra Petri im 4. Jahrhundert*, Stuttgart, 1972. So too the important study of F. Dvornik, *The Idea of Apostolicity in Byzantium*, Cambridge/Mass., 1958, is based on an examination of Church organization and the idea of Apostolicity in the West and in the East before Chalcedon, which fails to do justice to the changes that took pla2ce particularly in the fourth century. T. G. Jalland's, *The Church and The Papacy: A Historical Study*, being eight lectures delivered before the University of Oxford in the year 1942 on the Foundation of the Rev. John Bampton, Canon of Salisbury, London, 1944, is an exceptional, pioneering work, which does pay attention to the process of change. See G. Kretschmar, "Der Weg zur Reichskirche," 3–6, for a comprehensive bibliography of studies relating to the major changes which took place in the fourth century; see also G. Ruhbach, ed., *Die Kirche angesichts der konstantinischen Wende*, Darmstadt, 1976.

[2] See Stockmeier, "Primat und Kollegialität im Licht der alten Kirche," 326. See also Krömer, *Die Sedes Apostolica der Stadt Rome*, 103f: and Maccarrone's illuminating article, "Cathedra Petri und die Idee der Entwicklung des päpstlichen Primats vom 2. bis 4," Jahrhundert, 278–292, where, however, the fourth century itself is not treated in detail. See also the valuable article of V. Monachino, "Communio e primato nella controversia Ariana," (originally presented at the international conference: *De historia sollicitudinis omnium Ecclesiarum*, Rome, 1967).

Church to the changed situation in which she found herself due to three interrelated factors: the Great Persecution, the Constantinian recognition of the Christian religion, and the Arian controversy. Though these events engaged the universal Church, it was in the East that the persecution was heaviest, and the relief afforded by the Church's "liberator" Constantine was greatest; it was also to the East that the emperor moved his capital—now the capital of the Christian Empire—and it was in the East that the Arian controversy arose and was most bitterly fought. It was finally in the East that these three factors most affected the consciousness of the Church with regard to the preeminence of Rome.

By the beginning of the fourth century, not only were the bishops of peninsular Italy evidently subject to the authority of the Roman See, but, as Marrou points out, "the influence of the *Cathedra Petri* was doubtless exercised well beyond these limits and already reached out to all parts of the Church."[3] The causes of this influence as well as its nature and extent, are still the subject of controversy and opinions differ greatly on all three questions.[4] Studies of

---

[3] Marrou and Daniélou, *The First Six Hundred Years*, 240. See also Bishop Timofejeff, "Die Idee des Stuhles Petri in ihrer Entwicklung in vornikäischer Zeit," 131–135.

[4] That the primacy of the Bishop of Rome was more than a primacy of honor, seems to be generally accepted, cf., e.g., Heiler, *Altkirchliche Autonomie und päpstlicher Zentralismus*, who states that it was much more "ein Primat der geistlichen, d. h. der inneren religiös-ethischen Authorität, ein Primat der universalen Seelsorge" (p. 201). According to Caspar, *Geschichte des Papsttums* I, 18, the preeminence of the Church of Rome was primarily related to teaching matters and was due in the first place to her position in the capital of the world. Even though Hastings in his article, "The Papacy and Rome's Civil Greatness," in *The Downside Review*, vol. 75 (1957), 359–382, convincingly demonstrated that the influence of the Roman See cannot be traced back to its imperial (civil) standing, yet the opinion continues to be commonly held. The inner contradiction of the theory which attributes the primacy of Rome to the political importance of the city can be seen in Stockmeier, "Primat und Kollegialität," who argues that the political greatness of the city increased the prestige enjoyed by the see, and yet goes on to claim that when its political significance declined with the removal of the imperial residence to Milan and Constantinople, the influence of the Church grew, since the Bishop of Rome moved into the political vacuum thus caused in the West (pp. 326–327). Another version of the theory was proposed by Dvornik, *The Idea of Apostolicity*, who held that the Church adopted the administrative structure of the empire, a practice inaugurated by the Apostles, within which the principal cities of Rome, Alexandria, and Antioch evidently enjoyed precedence. He admits that Rome owed its prestige not only to the fact that it was capital of the empire, but also due to the veneration in which St. Peter was held as Chief of the Apostles, whose successor the Roman bishops claimed to be—but limits this to the West. He claims that since Rome was the only see in the West which could

these problems generally concentrate on the reconstruction of the developing consciousness of the Church as reflected in the references scattered through the documents that have come down to us from the first three centuries.[5] A considerable number of these texts were preserved for posterity by Eusebius in his *Church History,* which document also provides us with the only information at our disposal concerning one of the two controversies which brought the authority of the Roman bishop to the surface (the Paschal Controversy) as well as some important, independent evidence for the other (the Baptismal Controversy). It is therefore surprising that no comprehensive study has been undertaken to examine the attitude of Eusebius to the sources he quotes and the events which touch on the question of the Roman preeminence. The only attempt was that of N. Zernov, who examined Eusebius' presentation of the Paschal controversy and concluded that Eusebius had little sympathy with the papacy.[6]

Only two scholars—both of them Old Catholics—perceived the importance of Eusebius' *History* for the consciousness of the Church with regard to the primacy of Rome at the opening of the

claim direct Apostolic origins, no other Western see could rival it; thus, it was the *sedes apostolica* and became known as such. In the East, however, the multiplicity of sees claiming direct Apostolic origins reduced the prestige of the claim to apostolicity and contributed to the easy victory gained for the principle of adaptation to the political division of the empire (see especially p. 39f.). This hypothesis of Dvornik, which he developed in an article, "Byzantium and the Roman Primacy," *AER* 144 (1961), 289–312, though subject to some criticism (cf. Lanne, "Partikularkirchen und Patriarchate") has gained some acceptance (cf. Meyendorff, *Byzantine Theology,* 99–100; and McCue, "The Roman Primacy in the Patristic Era," 72 (though he does not mention Dvornik and may have come to the conclusion on the basis of his own study): it is, in my opinion, ultimately but a variation of the theory of Harnack, *Lehrbuch der Dogmengeschichte,* vol. II, Excurs zum 2 and 3, Capitel: Katholisch und Römisch, 439–454. On the other hand, Maccarrone, "Cathedra Petri und die Idee der Entwicklung des päpstlichen Primats," (1962), demonstrates the central importance of Peter and the Petrine Succession at Rome for the development of the consciousness of the Church that the Roman See was *the* Apostolic See in the fullest sense of the term. See also the studies of Karrer, "Das Petrusamt in der Frühkirche," (1958), Scheffczyk, *Das Unwandelbare im Petrusamt,* (1971), 49f., and Grotz, "Die Stellung der römischen Kirche anhand frühchristlicher Quellen," (1975).

[5]   See the collection of documents in Mirbt-Aland, *Quellen zur Geschichte des Papsttums und des römischen Katholizismus,* vol. I, Tübingen (1967), 6th ed. See also the useful selection of Giles, *Documents Illustrating Papal Authority: AD 96–454,* London, 1952.

[6]   Zernov, "Eusebius and the Paschal Controversy," 35. See below, Chapter Three, footnote 81, for a discussion of Zernov's findings.

fourth century. Both of them, Jaskowski[7] and Katzenmayer,[8] concluded that Eusebius did not consider Peter to have exercised a primacy of jurisdiction over the other Apostles and knew nothing about a primacy of the Roman bishop. Apart from the methodological weakness of these studies due to their projection of the highly polished and developed concept of the primacy to be found in the definitions of the First Vatican Council back into the fourth century, Jaskowski and Katzenmayer are to be faulted above all for their method of interpreting the *History*, since they ignore any examination of its literary genre or the evolution of its composition. But the fundamental perception of these two scholars remains true: the *History*, composed by Eusebius at the turn of the fourth century, ought to reflect the attitude of the Church, particularly in the East, to the See of Peter in Rome. Our analysis will show that it does. Moreover, the later Revisions of the original *History*, which took place in the wake of the Great Persecution, the official recognition of the Christian Religion by the imperial authority, and the opening phase of the Arian controversy, all reflect the change that took place in the consciousness of Eusebius and, to some extent at least, of the "Eastern" Church, since Eusebius has been described as the "Spokesman for the collective voice of the East"[9]—a description which, however, needs modification, not least in the light of the views of another representative figure of the East, Athanasius.

The paths of Eusebius and Athanasius crossed at that first synod, which was in itself epoch-making since it visibly manifested the implicit universal dimension of all genuine synods—the Oecumenical Synod of Nicaea, 325. The marks of the recent persecutions were to be seen on the bodies of some of the assembled bishops—as well as on their minds and on the agenda of the synod. Nicaea was the place where the Arian controversy was in principle definitively settled but in practice truly began. It was also the occasion

[7] Jaskowski, F., "Die Kirchengeschichte des Eusebius und der Primat," *IKZ* (1909), 104–110; 322–362.

[8] Katzenmayer, H., "Petrus und der Primat des römischen Bischofs in der ἐκκλησιαστικὴ ἱστορία des Bischofs Eusebius von Caesarea," *IKZ* 38 (1948), 158–171.

[9] Kartaschow, "Die Entstehung der kaiserlichen Synodalgewalt," 138. See also Ruhbach, *Die Kirche angesichts der konstantinischen Wende*, viii. Setton, *Christian Attitude Towards the Emperor*, 42, also draws attention to the exceptional value of Eusebius as a witness to generally accepted Christian views. Commenting on the relationship between Eusebius and Athanasius, Opitz, in "Euseb von Caesarea als Theologe," observes: "Athanasius erschließt sich erst in seiner vollen Bedeutung, wenn man die von ihm bekämpfte Welt, die eben in Euseb sich am besten darstellt, recht gründlich kennt."

for the manifestation of the new, totally unexpected relationship of the empire to the Church. Nicaea is not itself part of the subject of this study, but the history of what could be called the "reception" of Nicaea is, since it left its mark on the Church's understanding of her nature in general and of the authority of the Roman See in particular.

J. A. Möhler already perceived the significance of the recourse of Athanasius to Julius of Rome.[10] This event has received due attention from the historians of the papacy; however, the emphasis has been on the attitude of Julius of Rome and his consciousness of the authority to which he apparently laid claim.[11] In a significant contribution to the study of the constitutional changes that occurred in the fourth century, this incident and its aftermath, the Synod of Sardica (343), has been analyzed by K. M. Girardet, *Kaisergericht und Bischofsgericht,* Bonn, 1975, who concludes that in the course of the lawsuit involving Athanasius' claim to the See of Alexandria (which was instigated by the Anti-Nicene party led by Eusebius of Nicomedia and Eusebius of Caesarea), the latent tendencies towards a primacy of Jurisdiction *on the part of the Roman bishop* regularly manifest themselves, especially in the Letters of Julius, and found legal expression, at least seminally, in Canon III of Sardica; as a result of that lawsuit, the Bishop of Rome was conceded the status of an oecumenical "Supplikationsinstanz" on the basis of his earlier spiritual primacy.[12] On the other hand, P.-P.

---

[10]   "In der Vertheidigung des Athanasius, des Repräsentanten der katholischen Kirche im Kampfe für die Gottheit des Erlösers, wurde also ernstlich auf das Haupt der sichtbaren Kirche (= Pope Julius) hingewiesen. So griff alles ineinander, und das Eine bedingte das Andere. Die, welche die Würde des unsichtbaren Hauptes vertheidigen, schließen sich an das sichtbare an, und wurden durch dasselbe vertheidigt; auf diese Weise wurden sie ihren Kirchen wieder gegeben, um das unsichtbare Haupt wieder vertheidigen zu können. So wurde die *Geschichte* des Athanasius ein sehr merkwürdiger Punct für die *Geschichte* des Primats, und ihre Wirkungen erstrecken sich auch in dieser Beziehung weit in die Zukunft hinein." Möhler, *Athanasius der Große*, Mainz, 1844, 366.

[11]   See, for example, Caspar, *Geschichte des Papsttums* I, 131f. Jalland, *Church and Papacy*, 181f. See also Batiffol, *La paix constantinienne*, 363f., Chapman, *Studies on the Early Papacy*, 51f.

[12]   Girardet, *Kaisergericht und Bischofsgericht*, 156. For Girardet, as we will see below, this development was a *"novum"* which replaced the *Altkirchliche Idee* of the absolute binding force of ecclesiastical (more specifically, synodal) judgements, and which found its justification in the actual *practice* of the early Church, which in fact—and so Girardet—did not treat such decisions as finally binding. See also his article, "Appellatio: Ein Kapitel kirchlicher Rechtsgeschichte in den Kanones des vierten Jahrhunderts," *Historia*, vol. 23 (1974), 98–127.

Joannou, *Die Ostkirche und die Cathedra Petri* (published posthumously
by G. Denzler, Stuttgart, 1972), presented the case of Athanasius as one
of the many incidents, which demonstrate the existence of a *general recognition* on the part of Christianity in the fourth century, of a preeminence
accorded to the Bishop of Rome in matters of Faith and discipline. Useful
though the study of Joannou is in showing the important role played
by the Bishop of Rome in the thought and life of the Eastern Churches
during the fourth century, it has been censured by de Vries on the basis of
its method and content.[13]

Both Joannou and Girardet, however, draw attention to the development of the synodal structure of the Church in the fourth century and its
significance for the primacy of Rome. But we learn little about the attitude
of Athanasius to these developments. Recently Piétri devoted a paper to
this specific topic[14] and concluded that Athanasius' attitude to Rome was
based on political expediency and changed accordingly. Earlier, Hagel[15]
gave some attention to the same topic in his examination of the broader
question concerning Athanasius' "theory" of Church-State relations, where
he claims that Athanasius, after he had had recourse to Rome, became wary
of the papal ambitions of Julius and gave no attention to the question of
Rome's supremacy during the reign of Liberius, who showed such weakness in his abandonment of the cause of Athanasius. The studies of Piétri
and Hagel will be examined in the introduction to Part Two dealing with
Athanasius.

It is the thesis of this study that both Eusebius in his *History* and
Athanasius in his historico-apologetic writings reflect a more developed
understanding of the primacy of the Roman See than is generally assumed.
It will be seen how the epoch-making events of the fourth century occasioned in Eusebius a transformation of his earlier understanding into
the ideology of the *Reichskirche*, while the reaction of Athanasius to the
embodiment of this ideology in the new synodal structures, advocated by
the Eusebian party and supported above all by Constantius II, constrained
him to penetrate to the ultimate significance of the traditional understanding of the Petrine Succession at Rome and the promise of the Lord
to Peter (Mt 16,16–18), and so anticipate the ecclesiological developments
normally associated with the pontificate of Damasus.

[13]   See de Vries, "Die Ostkirche und die Cathedra Petri im IV. Jahrhundert," in
       OrChrPer 40 (1974), 114–144.
[14]   Piétri, "La question d'Athanase vue de Rome," (1973); see below, pp. 241–243.
[15]   Hagel, *Kirche und Kaisertum*, (1933). See below, pp. 239–241.

Considered formally, this study is essentially a study in interpretation. The *History* of Eusebius and the historico-apologetic writings of Athanasius, as well as a number of other documents related to his association with Rome, are examined separately according to *Sitz im Leben,* literary genre, and internal thought-structure. The special methodological problems peculiar to Eusebius and Athanasius are discussed in the introductions to Parts One and Two (Chapters One and Six respectively). The aim of this method is to establish, as objectively as possible, the intention of the respective authors with regard to a subject, which tends more than most to engage the subjectivity of researcher and reader alike.

My interest in the question of the primacy of Rome arose out of the heated debates on the subject which literally erupted at the fourth *Regensburger oekumenisches Symposion.* (The Symposium was held at Spindelhof, near Regensburg, from July 17–24, 1972, and was devoted to the subject of "Intercommunion.") Reading Athanasius at the time, I wondered what his attitude to the question would have been. On the surface it appeared that he had little to say on the subject, but on closer examination it became evident that what he wrote was of great significance: it was but the tip of an iceberg, since it evidently presupposed a greater grasp of the subject on the part of his readers than is commonly assumed to have been present in the Eastern part of the Church. For the reasons given above, Eusebius seemed the obvious one to turn to in order to gauge the general attitude of the Church, in particular, in the East, at the beginning of the fourth century, i.e., before Athanasius became Bishop of Alexandria and embroiled in the so-called Arian crisis which occasioned his historico-apologetic writings. My original findings with regard to Athanasius were then reevaluated in the light of the totally unexpected picture revealed by my analysis of Eusebius' *History.*

In his dissertation, *Apologetik und Geschichte: Untersuchungen zur Theologie Eusebs von Caesarea* (Heidelberg 1962), G. Ruhbach pointed to the paucity of secondary literature on Eusebius,[16] and in his introduction to his collection of studies by various authors entitled *Die Kirche angesichts der konstantinischen Wende,* (Darmstadt 1976), he comments on the very general treatment meted out to the question of Church-Empire relationships in the fourth century and the need for special research on specific questions. The latter observation is confirmed by G. Kretschmar in his

---

[16]   Ruhbach, *Apologetik und Geschichte,* 5. This is no longer the case: see https://
       blogforhoi.wordpress.com/2009/03/28/origen-eusebius-and-early-christian-
       scholarship-a-bibliography-of-secondary-literature/.

review of secondary literature related to the same question, "Der Weg zur Reichskirche," in *Verkündigung und Forschung*, vol. 13 (1968), 3–44, where he observed that there is only one major monograph devoted to the theological implications of the new relationship of the empire to the Church, that of H. Berkhof, *Kirche und Kaiser* (published originally in Dutch, 1946). What can be said about the secondary literature dealing with Eusebius in general can be said *a fortiori* about the *History*—which is generally used as our major source for the history of the Church in the second and third centuries, but which has not itself been the subject of a great deal of research.[17] So too with Athanasius' historico-apologetic writings: though they provide our primary sources for a considerable part of the history of the fourth century, and are used as such, they have rarely been the subject of special analysis.[18] As our review of the state of research into the question of the Roman primacy in the fourth century has revealed, this is one specific issue that has

[17] Though, as we will see in Chapter One, there has been a marked increase of interest in the historical methodology used by Eusebius and in his general understanding of history, there is no study devoted to an analysis of the structure of the *History* and the execution of Eusebius' objectives, apart from the general treatment found in the various introductions to the text and its translations. See in particular the introduction of Schwartz to his critical edition of the text of the *History*. Among the various introductions to translations of the latter, that of H. Kraft (Munich, 1967) is exceptionally valuable. The commentary of Lawlor and Oulton (London, 1927–1928) is the most extensive, though in many ways superseded by later research.

[18] The historico-apologetic writings which will be analyzed in Part Two are i) the *Apologia* (otherwise known as *Apologia contra Arianos,* or, according to the earliest known title recovered by Opitz, *Apologia secunda*) and ii) the *Historia Arianorum ad monachos,* both of which deal with contemporary history and are generally understood to be self-defensive in character. Other such writings include the *Apologia ad Constantinum* and the *Apologia de fuga sua*, which will only be treated in passing. These four documents are described by Quasten, *Patrology* III, 34–37, as "Historico-Polemical Writings," which I feel is inaccurate and possibly prejudicial to their true value. Admittedly the use of the adjective "apologetic" is not much more precise, since the term can refer either to traditional apologetics, to which category Eusebius' original *History* belongs, or to writings of a self-defensive nature. While the relevant "apologies" are mostly written in self-defense, Athanasius is at the same time involved in a defense of the strict ecclesiastical nature of the Church and her judgements in the face of the Eusebian Imperial Church. That, at least, is my thesis. For that reason, I have decided to use the double adjective "historico-apologetic" to describe those writings of Athanasius which deal mostly with his own role in the events of his day. What is of note, is the relatively scant scholarly attention given to these texts of Athanasius in their own right—in particular—the *Historia Arianorum,* which since the time of Eduard Schwarz and Otto Seeck has been more less dismissed as a "hate-filled pamphlet"—or at best "a political satire" (Uta Heil)—and so with little to offer the historian or theologian of the fourth century.

received scant attention. These factors naturally limit the extent of our *Auseinandersetzung* with the specialized literature.

On the other hand, studies of the historical events reported in the *History* of Eusebius and, to a lesser extent in the writings of Athanasius, as well as publications on related topics such as Constantine and the Arian Controversy—in particular, the Christological and Trinitarian questions—are myriad. These are referred to only in so far as they directly affect the main subject of this study, which is the primacy of the Bishop of Rome.

PART ONE
The Church History of Eusebius of Caesarea

CHAPTER ONE

The Date, Aims, and Presuppositions of the History (Book 1)

§1 Date of Composition

The two main theories regarding the date of composition which have dominated the discussion[1] down to our day are those proposed by Eduard Schwartz and Richard Laqueur, respectively.[2] To Schwartz goes the credit for the major breakthrough in the discussion up to then.[3] This is to be found in his introduction to what still remains the standard critical edition of the text.[4] Basing himself primarily on a critical examination of the history of the text, he concluded that four separate editions were "published" by Eusebius, the first comprising Books 1–8, circulated around the end of the year 311 or the beginning of 312; the second, with the addition of Book 9, about 315; the third around 317, being noted especially for the inclusion of the Panegyric at Tyre in the form of the original Book 10; while the fourth edition, published after the defeat of

---

[1]   The discussion is summarized by Lake, *The Ecclesiastical History*, vol. I, xix–xxiv; Emonds, *Zweite Auflage*, 25–45; Wallace-Hadrill, *Eusebius*, 39–43; Moreau, "Eusèbe de Césarée de Palestine," in *DHGE* XV, col. 1453–1456.

[2]   Schwartz, *Einleitung*, lvi–lix; Laqueur, *Eusebius als Historiker*, 1f.

[3]   Regarding the previous discussion, see, for example, Lightfoot's article on "Eusebius," in *DCB*, vol. II, 322–323; McGiffert, "Prolegomena," 45.

[4]   Schwartz, GCS 9, *Eusebius Werke*, Band II, Teile I–II, Leipzig, 1903–1909. This edition also contains Mommsen's critical edition of the Latin translation of Rufinus. Schwartz also provided his readers with a condensed version of his findings in his important article on "Eusebios," *PWK* VI, col. 1395–1406. See also Emonds, *Zweite Auflage*, 25f. The critical edition of Schwartz is reproduced, together with an English translation, to both of which I am indebted, by Lake and Oulton, London, 1926 and 1932 (in The Loeb Classics series). The same text was published with a French translation and notes by Grapin, Paris, 1905–1913 and by Bardy, Paris, 1952–1955 (*Sources Chrétiennes*, 31, 41, 55), while an Italian translation by del Ton was published in 1964, again using the text as edited by Schwartz.

Licinius by Constantine in 324, was characterized by the *damnatio memo-*
riae Licinii and included Eusebius first hymn in praise of Constantine the
sole ruler of the empire. According to Schwartz the manuscript tradition
behind the MS group BDM (Parisinus 1431 and 1433, Marcianus 338),
together with S (the Syriac translation preserved in two MSS at Petersburg
and the British Museum) and L (the Latin translation of Rufinus), is to
be traced back to a copy of this final edition, while the MS group ATER
(Parisinus 1430, Laurentianus 70,7 and 70,20, Mosquensis 50) bear witness
to a tradition which developed from a later fourth century recension by a
scribe who attempted to reintegrate into a copy of the final edition, those
parts of the 3rd edition which Eusebius himself had cut out when he
published the final text of his History.[5]

Schwartz's textual analysis prepared the way for Laqueur's painstaking
and masterly reconstruction of the genesis of the text, based not only on
textual criticism but on a penetrating analysis of the content and inner
structure of both the *History* and the related work, *The Martyrs of Palestine*.
As well as such an analysis, Laqueur undertook an illuminating examination of the origin, availability and use of those sources at the disposal of
Eusebius and used by him in Books 8–10.[6] Taking up and developing with
greater precision an observation made by Harnack,[7] Laqueur demonstrated
fairly conclusively that when Eusebius originally conceived the *History*,
the Great Persecution inaugurated by Diocletian (303–311) had not yet
taken place. Since, however, Books 8–10 presuppose the persecution, the
original *History* only contained Books 1–7 and did not include Book 8 as
Schwartz had maintained. The key to this discovery was the astute observation that the last of the stated aims of Eusebius[8] which runs: τά τ'ἐπὶ
τούτοις καὶ καθ' ἡμᾶς αὐτοὺς μαρτύρια καὶ τὴν ἐπὶ πᾶσιν ἵλεω καὶ εὐμενῆ τοῦ

---

[5]   The findings of Schwartz were criticized by Lawlor, *Eusebiana*, 243 f. (See also
      Lawlor and Oulton, *The Ecclesiastical History*, vol. I, 2–11.) The basic insight of
      Lawlor was that Eusebius had begun to write his *History* at a date earlier than that
      proposed by the German scholar. In this, Lawlor anticipated Laqueur, although
      the differences between the two scholars is otherwise considerable. For a critical
      presentation of Lawlor's solution, see Lake, *The Ecclesiastical History*, xxi–xxiii.
      My own summary of Schwartz given above owes much to G. Krüger, *ZKG* 48
      (1929), 462.
[6]   Useful accounts of Laqueur, *Eusebius als Historiker*, as well as some criticism, are
      to be found in the critiques of H. Koch, *DLZ* 27 (1929), col. 1421–1424; H. von
      Campenhausen, *ThLZ* 54 (1929), col. 514–517; and that of Krüger mentioned
      in the previous footnote.
[7]   von Harnack, *Chronologie*, bd. II, 112–114.
[8]   *HE* 1,1,1–2 (Schwartz 6,1–16).

σωτῆρος ἡμῶν ἀντίληψιν . . . ,[9] must have been a later interpolation. Laqueur pointed out that the other stated aims are thematic in nature whereas this particular one is chronological and furthermore overlaps the contents of the aim immediately preceding it, the declared purpose of which is to recount the persecutions and martyrdoms. The other aims cover not a limited period but rather span the entire history.[10] Laqueur further demonstrated that instead of four "editions" as proposed by Schwartz, the *History*, while it underwent several *revisions* at the hands of Eusebius, was in fact only once "published" as a finished work by its author in the form which has come down to us through the BDMSL MSS tradition— what Schwartz held to be the fourth edition.[11] Five principal stages in the composition of the *History* have been isolated by Laqueur, the first of which, the original *History* conceived and—with the exception of later interpolations—written before 303, will form the subject of our analysis in Chapters 1–3, while the other four stages, or, more correctly, Revisions of the original *History,* will be treated together in Chapter Four.

Apart from questioning some of the details, Laqueur's thesis would appear to have found general acceptance.[12] One serious deficiency

9 Schwartz 6,14–15. See *HE* 8,16,1 = Schwartz 788,10–11, where this theme is reiterated almost verbally. The conclusion Schwartz drew from this was, that Eusebius must have conceived the *History* during the persecution, since Book 8 was evidently composed then, and published his original edition of Books 1–8 after the Edict of Toleration, 311, as a document of the *ecclesia militans et triumphans* (cf. Schwartz, *Einleitung*, lv–lvii; Laqueur, *Eusebius als Historiker*, 3).

10 See Laqueur, *Eusebius als Historiker*, 210–212; Wallace-Hadrill correctly sees in this the central point of the discussion. Emonds however fails to take cognizance of this; neither does Moreau, who follows Emonds. Overbeck, *Anfänge*, 34, 36, and 49f., had already spotted some of the contradictions involved in the declared aims of Eusebius and in the finished work. He quite rightly insisted on the essential difference between Books 1–7 (the *History* proper) and Books 8–10, and went so far as to suggest that there was no original association between them (cf. p. 52). He further pointed out (pp. 50–51) that the final aim only refers in part to the contents of the last three books of the *History*—Laqueur demonstrates how in point of fact it most probably refers to the original draft of Book 8—so that strictly speaking only Books 1–7 correspond to the original aims of Eusebius.

11 Here Laqueur's later research complements his earlier observations, first published in *Hermes* 46 (1911), 189f., according to which he noted how the introductory verses of Books 7, 8, and 10 all indicate that each of these books was intended by the author to bring the *History* to a close.

12 Apart from the critiques already mentioned above in footnote 6, attention might also be drawn to R. Helm's excellent critique of Laqueur in *HZ* 142 (1930), 328–332, which contains worthwhile criticisms. However, Emonds, *Zweite Auflage*, 40, alone appears to have entertained serious reservations.

in Laqueur's work is his exclusion of any examination of the precise composition of the original *History* conceived before 303 and now preserved
in the extant text. Since he confines himself to an analysis of Books 8–10,
he fails to examine in any detail, for example, the end of Book 7, which
evidently dates from the end of the persecution and so cannot belong to the
original *History*. Had Laqueur given more attention to this problem—and
to the question of interpolations in Book 1—then he would have been
forced to alter some of his conclusions, in particular his interpretation of
the mind of Eusebius as it developed in the course of the various Revisions.
Since they can help us understand the *changing* attitude of Eusebius, with
regard to the position in the Church held by the Bishop of Rome, then it
will be necessary to examine some passages which seem to me to be later
interpolations. This will be treated in Note I.[13] The precise determination
of the end of the text of the original *History* and the beginning of the 1st
Revision will be taken up in Chapter Four.

about Laqueur's rejection of a 4-editions' theory as proposed by Schwartz, claiming that one could be true to the existence of two separate MS traditions only
by positing their actual publication. (It should be noted that Emonds insists on
the matter of the various *publications*, not mere revisions, as is held by Laqueur).
Unfortunately, Emonds did not develop his reservations any further—indeed
he points to the theory of Laqueur as being in itself sufficient to illustrate his
own particular thesis (p. 41)—except on the one occasion when he refers to the
textual difference in the title of *The Martyrs of Palestine* as found in the MSS:
A, T, and E (cf. p. 45); yet even in this instance, Laqueur would seem to have
provided an adequate explanation on p. 33. Moreau, in his articles on Eusebius
both in the *DHGE* XV, col. 1453–1456 and in the *RAC* VI, col. 1071–1072,
unfortunately accepts Emonds as conclusive. In his masterly introduction to
the person and writings of Eusebius, which forms the preface to the recently
published German translation of the *History* (by P. Haeuser, newly revised by H.
A. Gärtner, Munich, 1967), the editor of the publication, H. Kraft, has adopted
the findings of Laqueur, though he makes no reference to the latter, due probably
to the literary genre of his *Einleitung*, which is devoid of references to sources
or to scholarly discussions on disputed points. On the other hand, Grant, "The
Case against Eusebius," in *Stud. Pat.*, Vol. XII (1975), 413–421, seems to accept
Schwartz's 4-editions' theory; he simply refers to Laqueur and Emonds in a footnote, as though they cancelled each other out, but does not discuss the question
in detail. However, in his contribution to the *Mélanges d'histoire des religions
offerts à Henri-Charles Peuch*, Paris, 1974, 209–213, he modifies his earlier stand
in the light of his own study on "Papias in Eusebius' Church History" and, in this
case at least, prefers Laqueur's solution. It should be noted that Grapin, *Eusèbe*,
xxix–xxxvii, had, already in 1905, questioned the theory of Schwartz and had
suggested that the original work of seven books had been composed before 303.
See also Bardy, *Eusèbe*, IV, 121f.

[13] See below, pp. 192–200.

§2 The Historical Method of Eusebius

Though aptly called the Father of Church History, it must be admitted that Eusebius was a historian with a purpose. The thesis of Overbeck is now generally accepted: that the historiography exemplified in the work of Eusebius is a late example of Christian apologetics, being a direct product of the old Christian Chronology, itself a child of the earlier apologetics.[14] But, one may inquire, to what extent was Eusebius' apologetic literature—specifically the *History*—the product of a tradition cut off from its original roots and dynamic source of inspiration? The contents of the main body of the original *History* presuppose an audience already familiar with the historical events, personages, allusions, and literature which are gathered together and presented within a certain schematic framework or structure. For example, the as yet implicit defense of Origen and his orthodoxy in the original form of Book 6, which could be of little interest to the enquiring *Pagan*, was evidently intended to convince those who might have thought otherwise within the Church. And yet, it will be seen from a consideration of the contents of Book 1 alone, that Eusebius is indeed preoccupied with themes derived from the earlier apologetic tradition, in particular that of the antiquity of the Christian Religion. I am left with the overall impression, that the kind of apologetic literature to which the *History* belongs is no longer that of a Justin engaged in a genuine dialogue with rival convictions; the *History*, admittedly molded by the apologetic tradition, rather belongs to that genre of (self-)defensive literature which is ostensibly aimed at those outside the fold but in fact serves to strengthen the convictions and deepen the self-identity of those within. It answers the objections of those outside the fold in order to assure its own adherents, not unlike the "apologetics" of the Catholic schools in comparatively recent times, which helped to strengthen the convictions of believers

---

[14] Overbeck, *Anfänge*, 64. See also Lightfoot on "Eusebius," *DCB*, vol. II, 323, who (it would seem) arrived at the same conclusion, independently. Nigg, in *Die Kirchengeschichtsschreibung*, develops the same basic ideas as found in Overbeck. See also Opitz, "Euseb von Caesarea als Theologe," 8; Völker, "Tendenzen," 157–180. Berkhof, *Theologie*, 61, stresses: "Dieses Buch kann man besser Eusebius' apologetisches Hauptwerk nennen." See also Ruhbach, *Apologetik und Geschichte*, 5 and 134f., whose special merit is to have perceived (and analyzed) the basic concern of Eusebius' apologetics, namely the presentation of God's work in history. See Kraft, *Einleitung*, 19f., for an excellent description of the apologetic style of Eusebius' earlier works, as well as an illuminating account of Eusebius' place within the apologetic tradition.

but apparently had little impact on those outside the Church whose objections they answered.[15]

The apologetic concerns of Eusebius were to a large extent determined by his *Sitz im Leben*. Following Laqueur, it appears that Eusebius conceived his original *History* (Books 1–7) before the outbreak of the Great Persecution in the year 303. Thus, when Eusebius sat down to write his *History*, the Church had enjoyed almost 40 years of unparalleled peace and freedom from persecution. The Edict of Gallienus in the year 261[16] had brought about a situation whereby the Church was recognized as a religious body, and so, preserved from external threats to her security, was in a position to consolidate her position in society.[17] The very attempt to write a "History" illustrates the Church's growing awareness of her self-identity as a public body, while her relative freedom and security provided the necessary conditions for the collection of the impressive amount of documents and other source materials needed for such a task.

Eusebius' basic intention is to demonstrate from the "scattered memoirs" of history, the claim of the Church to embody the true religion—to embody, that is, the most ancient and universal of all religions, and to illustrate how this Church alone enjoyed the guidance of Providence throughout her history. His conceptual framework is that understanding of the Church which he himself shared with his contemporaries and which he set out to defend as having been the same from the beginning, i.e., the Apostolic Age, down to his own day.[18] Such a conceptual framework—the implicit ecclesiology of Eusebius—this study will attempt to determine. To begin with, we will attempt to understand as fully as possible the stated aims and presuppositions of Eusebius as outlined in his own Introduction (Book 1) and then to follow his execution of the same aims through the original *History* and the Revisions.

---

[15] Since Berkhof in his study of "Euseb als Apologet"—see Berkhof, *Theologie*, 39–64—accepts Schwartz's dating of the *History*, he was unaware of the pre-Constantinian apologetics of Eusebius. It is this early concept of Eusebius that will concern us in the following Chapters Two and Three. The more complete study of Ruhbach, *Apologetik und Geschichte*, suffers from the same defect as the work of Berkhof.

[16] For the text of the *Rescript*, cf. *HE* 7,13,1 (Schwartz 666,14–23). See Berkhof, *Kirche und Kaiser*, 39; Andresen, "Der Erlaß des Gallienus," 385–398. See also Eusebius own tendentious presentation of the golden age of Gallienus in *HE* 8,1,1–6 (Schwartz 736,1–738,10).

[17] Cf. Batiffol, *La paix constantinienne*, 135–152 (see also pp. 27–45 of the same work).

[18] Eine apologetische Haltung ruht immer, bewußt oder unbewußt, auf bestimmten theologischen Voraussetzungen" (Berkhof, *Theologie*, 62).

Most scholars recognize that the *History* is, as Schwartz expressed it, primarily a collection of transmitted material.[19] The surprising thing is that, until recently, comparatively little attention has been paid to the *principle of selection,* according to which Eusebius edited and ordered his source material.[20] Due to Eusebius' ever-

[19] "Ἱστορία ist hier von E. im allgemeinsten Sinne gebraucht, etwa wie in den Titeln Παντοδαπὴ oder Ποικίλη ἱστορία, auch Porphyrius' Φιλόσοφος ἱστορία läßt sich vergleichen: es bedeutet die Sammlung von überliefertem Material, wie E. auch den in der Praeparatio evangelica und Demonstratio evangelica gesammelten Stoff mannigfaltigster Art ἱστορία nennt . . ." (Schwartz, "Eusebios," *PWK* VI, col. 1395). See also Moreau, "Eusebius," *RAC* VI, 1072; Ruhbach, *Apologetik und Geschichte*, 129f.

[20] Lawlor's opinion (*Eusebiana*, 81) to the effect that Eusebius was "an unsystematic writer" is not completely justified, though it is an opinion commonly held. Such a view was probably due to the tendency to consider the *History* as a "Straightforward Chronicle," as Milburn entitled the chapter in his book (*Early Christian Interpretations of History*, London, 1954) which is devoted to Eusebius. A more authentic appreciation of the *History* is to be found in Ruhbach, *Apologetik und Geschichte*, 129f., who rightly maintains that ". . . die Kirchengeschichte ist ein wohl geplantes, nach den wissenschaftlichen Methoden ihrer Zeit durchgestaltetes Werk, das durch die mannigfaltigen Überarbeitungen gelegentlich aus den Fugen geraten ist" (pp. 133–134). However, Ruhbach, who incidentally paid no attention to the *Entstehungsgeschichte* of the original *History,* declined to determine more precisely the contours of the work. Instead, he gave his attention to the study of the basic apologetic purpose or *tendenz* of the *History,* which he claims is "die Darstellung des Handelns Gottes in der *Geschichte*" (cf. p. 134; see also Bebis, "Eusebius and his Theology of History," 70f., who following the basic insight of La Piana, 1943, made the same point as Ruhbach, whose work was unknown to him). Kraft, *Einleitung,* 27, articulates the basic concern of Eusebius more precisely, when he states: "Der Sinn der *Geschichte* ist für ihn die Gestaltwerdung der Welt durch den Logos, genauer gesagt, durch die Stiftung Christi. Damit ist die Kirche zum Subjekt der *Geschichte* geworden: die eigentliche *Geschichte* reicht vom ersten Wirken des Logos bis zu seiner endgültigen Herrschaft." The special merit of Kraft's *Einleitung* is to draw attention to the influences that shaped Eusebius' concept of history and to distinguish its own peculiar characteristics, though what he so well describes is the mature thought of Eusebius. Since he follows Laqueur, Kraft does pay attention to the differences which mark the various revisions, but he was evidently not aware of the interpolations described below pp. 141–147 and pp. 192–200, which resulted in a certain confusion of the later mature thought of Eusebius with his earlier conception. Kraft further suggests that the present form of the *History* can be divided into four main parts, Books 1 (the Introduction), 2–4 (Apostolic and post-Apostolic period), 5–7 (the old Catholic Church), and 8–10 (the Diocletian persecution and final victory of the Church), each part distinguished from the other by a separate Proem. But the original plan of Eusebius cannot be discovered simply by examining the Introduction to the History; attention must also be paid to principle of selection used by Eusebius with regard to his sources as well as the way he presents his picture of the early Church. As far as this writer is aware, no attempt has been made to analyze the latter; and in the

present apologetic purpose, particular attention must be paid both to his tendentious use of his sources and to the way he presents the various events, personalities, and literature which form the content of the *History*. The paraphrases he composes, the way he edits, comments on, and presents the various documents at his disposal as well as his blatant omissions all combine to make up certain patterns that reveal the attitude of Eusebius on one or other related topic.

In advance it may be said, that, as Eusebius *Sitz im Leben* changes, his apologetic concerns change with it. The unexpected persecution, the new status of the Church under Constantine, the reunification of the empire under the sole rule of an emperor more than ordinarily sympathetic to the Christian Religion, the Arian Crisis, and finally the Synods of Antioch and Nicaea in 325 all leave their mark, as we will see, both on the mind of Eusebius and on the final form of the *History*.

§3 The Original Purpose of Eusebius: The Apostolic Successions (Book 1)

Book 1 was intended by Eusebius to be an Introduction[21] to the original *History*, which strictly speaking only begins with Book 2. In this introductory Book, Eusebius sets out his aims[22] and then goes on to establish the truth of those fundamental suppositions on which his whole endeavor rests, namely the divinity of Christ, the source of the Church's life[23] and the historicity of His appearance as Man.[24]

> case of the former method, the recent studies of R. M. Grant, "The Case against Eusebius" (1971) and "Eusebius and His Church History" (1972) have only examined individual topics, such as Eusebius' treatment of Chiliasm, in order to demonstrate that a pattern can be observed in Eusebius' treatment of his facts—in particular in his omissions. What Grant has attempted with regard to individual themes, we will attempt to do with the original *History*. (However, I should like to add that I have serious reservations about the rather sweeping conclusions Grant draws with regard to the basic credibility of Eusebius as a historian.)
>
> [21] Προοίμιον: cf. *HE* 2, "Proem," 1 (Schwartz 102,1). Regarding the original aims of Eusebius see the observations of Ruhbach, Bebis, and Kraft in the previous note.
>
> [22] *HE* 1,1,1–2 (Schwartz 6,1–18).
>
> [23] *HE* 1,1,7–1,4,15 (Schwartz 8,25–44,8). These and the following suppositions Eusebius will call "the primary matter" (*HE* 1,5,1 = Schwartz 44,45). Grant, "The Case against Eusebius," 415, makes the interesting suggestion that this preface to the *History* is directed against Porphyry's criticisms, to be found in the philosopher's writing: *Against the Christians* (I, 2–4).
>
> [24] *HE* 1,5,1f. (Schwartz 44,45f.). It should be noted that the actual history of the Church begins with the mission of the Apostles in Book 2.

The *History* opens with the stated aims of Eusebius as summed up in a long, unwieldy participial clause:

"I have purposed to record in writing the successions of the sacred Apostles, covering the period stretching from our Savior to ourselves,

(A) the number and character of the transactions recorded in the history of the Church;

(B) the number of those who were distinguished in her government and leadership in the provinces of greatest fame;

(C) the number of those who in each generation were ambassadors of the word of God either by speech or pen;

(D) the names, the number, and the age of those who, driven by the desire for innovation to an extremity of error, have heralded themselves as the introducers of Knowledge, falsely so-called, ravaging the flock of Christ unsparingly, like grim wolves;

(E) to this I will add the fate which has beset the whole nation of the Jews from the moment of their plot against Our Savior;

(F) moreover, the number and nature and times of the wars raged by the heathen against the divine word [or the Divine Logos] and the character of those who, for its sake, passed from time to time through the contest of blood and torture;

[(G)....]

My starting point is therefore no other than the first dispensation of God touching our Savior and Lord, Jesus Christ."[25]

The bold phrase which opens the *History*, and is so difficult to render in English, is τὰς τῶν ἱερῶν ἀποστόλων διαδοχάς. As Overbeck pointed out,[26] this is a description of the *History* as Eusebius originally conceived it. At the end of Book 7 and in the Prooemion to Book 8, the author tells his readers that he has rounded off the subject of the "successions;" he then goes on to write the *Urform* of Book 8 as a type of excursus, covering not history but rendering an account of contemporary events of a traumatic nature, which in turn was eventually expanded into the final three books with the

---

[25] Translation by Kirsopp Lake. The numeration of the different aims (A, B, C, etc.), which is not part of the original text, is inserted here to aid the exegesis of the passage. Aim G will not be considered, as it is a later interpolation (see above, pp. 14–15).

[26] Overbeck, *Die Bischofslisten*, 27. This impressive piece of scholarship—laced with unconcealed invective against his opponents—attacks the understanding of the term as outlined in Harnack's *Chronologie*, bd. I, 65–67.

result that the original title no longer could be said to apply. That development will be shown in Chapter Four below. What did Eusebius mean by the terms τὰς τῶν ἱερῶν ἀποστόλων διαδοχάς? It can be said here at the outset that a peculiar mark of Eusebius' theological methodology is to take terms and concepts well attested by tradition and to reinterpret them in accordance with his own views; this will be repeatedly seen in the course of this work. Since the type of change which took place, with regard to the terms αἱ διαδοχαὶ τῶν ἀποστόλων,[27] is so indicative of Eusebius'

[27] Harnack (see previous footnote), taking into consideration Aims C and D above, understood the Apostolic Succession quite simply to mean a continual series of bishops and orthodox teachers. But for Overbeck, "Διαδοχή hat bei dieser Auffassung nicht mehr seinen ursprünglichen konkreten Sinn der Sukzessionsfolge als solcher, sondern den übertragenden, abstrakteren der Herrscherfolge oder Dynastie als der Trägerin eines nach ihr zu bezeichnenden Komplexes von geschichtlichen Vorgängen, von denen unter anderen manche sich auch in Sukzessionsreihen im eigentlichen, strenger oder freier angewendeten Sinne des Wortes abwickeln können. Hiernach spricht aber der uns vorliegende Satz Eusebius' Absicht aus, die Geschichte der apostolischen Nachfolge (= Dynastie) zu erzählen, und zwar in ihrem Verlauf in einer fünfgliedrigen Reihe von Vorgängen: in den drei Sukzessionsreihen der Bischöfe, der Lehrer und der Irrlehrer dieser Nachfolge, gewissen sie interessierenden Erlebnissen des jüdischen Volkes und denen der Kirche, die sich darstellen in den Verfolgungen durch die Heiden" (Overbeck, *Die Bischofslisten*, 25). While agreeing with Overbeck's main insight, Schwartz modifies it by drawing attention to another parallel use of the term as found in the non-Christian literature but not considered by Overbeck: "In der heidnischen Literatur ist Διαδοχαὶ der hergebrachte Titel für 'Geschichte der Philosophen' oder besser 'Philosophenschule,' und wenn E. mit διαδοχαὶ τῶν ἀποστόλων die ersten sieben Bücher seines Werkes bezeichnet ..., so setzt er die 'wahre Philosophie' in Parallele zur heidnischen" ("Eusebios," PWK VI, col. 1396). Caspar, *Römische Bischofsliste*, 222–237, claimed that the concept of succession understood as a sequence or series (and thus primarily chronological in nature) was not the original meaning of the term but was in fact the individual interpretation of Eusebius, as indicated by the historian's almost synonymous usage of the terms διαδοχὴ and κατάλογος (cf. p. 232). It seems to me that Caspar overestimated the weight of this admittedly important observation, due most probably to his interpretation of what he considered to be the earlier, late second century conception of διαδοχὴ to mean the Apostolic Teaching in an exclusive sense (see below, footnote 31). Over a decade before Caspar's major study was published, Turner had also observed a change in the understanding of the concept as found in Eusebius, though he appears to have underestimated its implications. To Eusebius, the successions from the Apostles take on a new import, neither doctrinal, as with St. Irenaeus and the writers of whom we have so far spoken (= Hegesippus, Tertullian, Hippolytus, and Origen), nor sacramental, as in the modern conception, but primarily historical...." He continues: "... to the historian no form of succession can come wholly amiss: the successions of theologians in the Church generally, even the succession of one generation of Churchmen to another, are all factors of that complex of continuity and

thought process, according to which he took an idea well-founded in tradition but either misunderstood the original concept or, in putting it to a new use, gave it a new interpretation, and since the actual change itself is so important for an understanding of the basic conception of his *History,* it will be advantageous to reconstruct the original concept and show how Eusebius "received" it.[28] As will also be seen repeatedly in the course of this study, Eusebius himself frequently supplies us with a considerable number of the actual sources of his own ideas in the form of quotations from earlier writers. By examining these quotations in their own right, and then looking at the usage of the term peculiar to Eusebius, we can thus reconstruct the development.

The sources which enable us to understand the original concept are Hegesippus and Irenaeus.[29] Alarmed by the spread of Gnosticism, *the former* undertook a journey to many Churches but in particular to Rome in order to ascertain what was the teaching accepted by all.[30] While at Rome, Hegesippus tells us in his own words: "I covered (literally: made for myself) the succession until Anicetus, whose deacon was Eleutherius; Soter succeeded Anicetus and after him Eleutherius. In *each succession* and *in each city* the proclamation of the Law, the Prophets and the Lord is thus preserved."[31]

[28] development which is what we mean by history" (Turner, "Apostolic Succession," 132–133). From my reading of the texts, I believe that a change did occur, one not only motivated by the interests of an historian but also by the less evident apologetical and theological interests of Eusebius.

[28] The following "reconstruction" is based on the references to the term διαδοχὴ as found in the Index to Schwartz's critical edition of the text (cf. Schwartz, *Einleitung,* 168–169).

[29] For an outline of the earlier history of the term see Kraft, *Einleitung,* 32f.; see also von Campenhausen, *Kirchliches Amt und geistliche Vollmacht,* 163–194, together with Ratzinger's comments in "Primat, Episkopat und Successio Apostolica," 45–52; Javierre Ortas, "Successione apostolica e successione primaziale."

[30] καὶ ὡς ὅτι τὴν αὐτὴν παρὰ πάντων παρείληφεν διδασκαλίαν (*HE* 4,22,1 = Schwartz 368,21). This comment of Eusebius is in fact a paraphrase of Hegesippus and describes the successful end of the latter's quest, namely, to ascertain the common teaching held by all the bishops of the Churches, which was due to their Apostolic Succession.

[31] ... διαδοχὴν ἐποιησάμην μέχρις Ἀνικήτου οὗ διάκονος ἦν Ἐλεύθερος, καὶ παρὰ Ἀνικήτου διαδέχεται Σωτήρ, μεθ᾽ ὃν Ἐλεύθερος. ἐν ἑκάστῃ δὲ διασοχῇ καὶ ἐν ἑκάστῃ πόλει οὕτως ἔχει ὡς ὁ νόμος κηρύσσει καὶ οἱ προφῆται καὶ ὁ κύριος (*HE* 4,22,3 = Schwartz 370,2–6). The translation of Lake (*The Ecclesiastical History,* vol. I, 375), reproduced by Quasten, *Patrology* I, 285, is misleading: "In each list and in each city things are as the law and the prophets and the Lord preach." For a valuable outline of the earlier discussion concerning this text, in particular the phrase διαδοχὴν ἐποιησάμην (which Schwartz, *Einleitung,* ccxxv, considered to be "hoffnungslos verderbt"), see Caspar, *Römische Bischofsliste,* 234–236. Although Caspar's thesis that Hegesippus did not refer

According to Hegesippus, there were two interrelated criteria by
which the true teaching of the Church could be ascertained: (i)
by establishing what all the Churches commonly taught, which
meant in turn (ii) establishing what had been handed down and preserved by the Successions of Bishops in each Church. The key term
in this passage is οὕτως: "in this manner," i.e., as in Rome, the original

to any literary activity as such is not acceptable (cf. Kohlmeyer, "Zur Ideologie
des ältesten Papsttums," 230–243; von Campenhausen, *Kirchliches Amt und
geistliche Vollmacht*, 180–182), yet Caspar's basic insight remains true to the
extent that Hegesippus did not set out to compile a list in the post fourth-century
sense of the term. What is unacceptable is the rest of his interpretation which
understands the term διαδοχή exclusively as though it only referred to the content
of the Faith, so that the text could be taken to mean ". . . daß die reine Lehre
auch in Rom bis auf Anicet und seine Nachfolger wie in Korinth bis auf Primus
gewährt geblieben sei . . ." (p. 235). Such an interpretation (one that was also
suggested by Turner) would mean that Hegesippus had set himself up as the
final arbiter as to what is or what is not orthodox, and thus that he had undertaken his journey with the intention of inspecting the various Churches to see
if they had preserved the orthodox and Apostolic Teaching! Kohlmeyer, "Zur
Ideologie des ältesten Papsttums," 230f., argues that the concept of "succession"
was introduced at Rome through the agency of Justin, where it was linked to
the earlier concept of a collective succession attributed to office holders (in
contrast with charismatics) as found in Clemens Romanus, and where it was
given its definitive form by Hegesippus who thus produced the concept of the
monarchical-episcopal succession, which Irenaeus simply took up and worked
out more explicitly. But this reconstruction presupposes a literary dependence
between Justin, Hegesippus, and Irenaeus which has not been proven, and, more
seriously, it projects the laws of literary causality onto the very different and
very complex historical situation of the life of the Church; further, it assumes
a degree of discontinuity in the various stages of the reconstructed process that
is irreconcilable with the constitutional "conservatism" of the early Church and
her concern to preserve her identity with the Apostolic Church. The value of
Kohlmeyer's study is to remind us of the existence of a late Jewish concept of succession, which makes it superfluous to draw on parallels from secular chronology
(regarding the kings and emperors) or from the schools of philosophy in order
to show how the concept arose in the Church (without denying some influence,
naturally). With regard to Hegesippus, it is inconceivable that he could have
started out on a quest to discover the authentic Apostolic Tradition and ended
up creating his own criteria, i.e., making up a list of office-holders whom he personally designated as the principal authorities responsible for the transmission
of the Teaching from one generation to the next. It is possible that Hegesippus,
due to his Hebrew origins, would have been more appreciative of the value of
such an authoritative succession in order to establish the true Faith, but he could
not have fabricated such a "succession." When he arrived in Rome, he found that
such a succession was already in existence, whose authenticity was verifiable, as
it was in the other cities he had visited on the way. Thus, διαδοχὴν ἐποιησάμην
most probably means that Hegesippus verified the existence of such a succession
at Rome. See also Grotz, "Die Stellung der römischen Kirche," 42–45. See also
Jalland, *Church and Papacy*, 84–88.

proclamation is preserved in all Churches. Hegesippus refers here to the *way* the teaching is preserved, namely through the bishops whose succession can be verified. When he undertook his journey in order that he might establish for himself the Apostolic Tradition, he went to those Churches whose bishops enjoyed undisputed and verifiable succession from the Apostles—above all Rome—and thus could authoritatively witness to the content of the Faith.[32] The succession of bishops could be described as that which guaranteed the identity of the contemporary teaching with the teaching of previous generations and ultimately with the original Proclamation; this we shall call "temporal unanimity." The succession is, further, the *means* by which the first criterion (namely "spatial unanimity" in the contemporary Church) is justified. Implicit in the contention of Hegesippus—that to establish the true teaching, it is sufficient to find out what all the Churches taught in common—is the argument: since the various *successions of bishops* trace their origin back to the one source, the Apostles, and since they guarantee the preservation of the original Proclamation, then it follows that the same teaching *must* be found in every Church. Such an argument, only implicit in Hegesippus, is more explicitly formulated by Irenaeus.

It may be added that the bishops are here considered primarily as authoritative teachers—which does not mean that Hegesippus necessarily considered this to be their only function as bishops.[33] To the early Church, the Apostolic Teaching was not a body of truths to be expounded and defended in the abstract, as it were, but the primary means of participation in the full life of the Church which culminated in the celebration of the Eucharist. Thus, the bishop, as the one who presided over the Eucharistic community, was the one principally responsible for the preservation and transmission of the Apostolic Teaching and so was the final authority in the Church, with the corollary power to admit or refuse admittance to the Church's communion.

---

[32] Although Hegesippus does not refer to the origin of the successions in the text, yet it can be reasonably presumed that he understood it to be Apostolic. The fragments of his writings preserved by Eusebius mention Corinth and Rome explicitly, most probably because they were both renowned for their original association with the Apostles. Rome, as the terminus of his journey, would seem to have been of particular importance with regard to the subject of Hegesippus' quest.

[33] von Campenhausen, *Kirchliches Amt und geistliche Vollmacht*, 181–182, convincingly argues that Hegesippus need not be mistrusted when he asserts that he had established for himself the succession of bishops rather than, as had been proposed, merely a succession of teachers. See also Kohlmeyer, "Zur Ideologie des ältesten Papsttums," 241–242.

In a much-disputed passage,[34] *Irenaeus* assures his readers that the Tradition (= teaching) of the Apostles can be easily ascertained by having recourse to any Church where the succession of the bishops from the Apostles can be demonstrated.[35] Since it would be tedious to demonstrate the succession of bishops in every Church, Irenaeus singles out the "maximae et antiquissimae et omnibus cognitae, a gloriosissimis duobus apostolis Petro et Paulo Romae fundatae et constitutae Ecclesiae." As though to clarify precisely what this entails, Irenaeus adds: "eam quam habet ab apostolis traditionem et annuntiatam hominibus fidem per successiones episcoporum peruenientem usque ad nos indicantes," and gives as his motive: "confundimus omnes eos qui quoquo modo, uel per sibiplacentiam malam uel uanam gloriam uel per caecitatem et sententiam malam, praeterquam oportet colligunt."[36] The importance of the last clause lies in two implications to be gathered from "omnes eos qui ... praeterquam oportet colligunt." In the first place, by referring to Rome, Irenaeus tells his readers that he could confound *all* opposition. Secondly, Irenaeus is not simply attacking individual heretics but all those who, "constituent des groupements illégitimes," as the *Sources Chrétiennes* translation aptly expresses it. Irenaeus is in other words attacking those who on the basis of their teaching attempt to set up their own communion or Churches. This point in turn reminds us of the setting in which the true Apostolic Tradition is to be found, which setting is so self-evident to Irenaeus as to be presumed and not expressed explicitly: it is the sacramental community or Church presided over by a bishop who, as the successor of an Apostle, hands on and gives authoritative witness to the Apostolic Teaching.[37] In the place of such Churches, the heretics presume to set up illegitimate communities.

The much-discussed sentence which rounds off this paragraph is in part an explication of the first implication in the foregoing sentence and in part a development of the second, since in the latter case it touches on the relationship between the various genuine Churches: "ad hanc enim Ecclesiam propter potentiorem principalitatem necesse est omnem conuenire Ecclesiam, hoc est eos qui sunt

[34]   See Ortiz de Urbina, "Patres graeci," 99–103, for a concise commentary and a useful bibliography. See also Grotz, "Die Stellung der römischen Kirche," 52–55; Minnerath, "La position de l'Eglise," 154–158.

[35]   Traditionem itaque apostolorum in toto mundo manifestatam in omni Ecclesia adest perspicere omnibus que uera uelint uidere ... *Adv. haer.* 3,3,1 (Rousseau-Doutreleau 30).

[36]   *Adv. haer.* 3,3,2 (Rousseau-Doutreleau 32).

[37]   In this context, see K. Stadler, "Apostolische Sukzession und Eucharistie bei Clemens Romanus, Irenäus und Ignatius von Antiochien," in: *IKZ* 62 (1972), 231–244; 63 (1973), 100–128.

undique fideles, in qua semper ab his qui sunt undique conseruata est ea quae est ab apostolis traditio."[38] The main point of the sentence is that every Church throughout the world where the Apostolic Tradition (= teaching) has been preserved must of necessity agree with the Church of Rome. The "necesse est" indicates in the first place an *a priori*: since the source and content of the Apostolic Tradition (= teaching) is the same, then it must of necessity be the same in every Church. In the second place, the Church of Rome, due to its superior *origins*,[39] is the ultimate criterion of the Apostolic Tradition. And here it must be remembered that when Irenaeus speaks about the *Church* of Rome in this context, he is referring to the *Bishop of Rome*, successor of St. Peter and St. Paul. The Faith of the Church of Rome, as handed on by its bishops from the Apostles Peter and Paul, is by the same token—and this is the express reason why Irenaeus demonstrates the episcopal successions at Rome in the following paragraph—representative of the Faith held by the entire Church Universal, the faithful everywhere. It is not a case that his teaching should accord with that of the other Churches,[40] but the exact reverse. All must agree with the Faith of the Church of Rome, and, where the Apostolic Tradition has been preserved, all *will* of necessity agree. Spatial unanimity, then, is both a sign and an effect of temporal unanimity. It is not a cause. Eusebius also quotes the following paragraph in Irenaeus which contains his List of Roman Bishops. The paragraph ends: τῇ αὐτῇ τάξει καὶ τῇ αὐτῇ [διαδοχῇ] ἡ τε ἀπὸ τῶν ἀποστόλων ἐν τῇ ἐκκλησίᾳ παράδοσις καὶ τὸ τῆς ἀληθείας κήρυγμα κατήντηκεν εἰς ἡμᾶς.[41] (I accept Schwartz's conjecture that διαδοχή and not διδαχή was the term that originally appeared in the Irenaean text, even though the latter term is to be found in the MS tradition ATER BDΣ. The Latin translation of Irenaeus also uses the term *successione*.)

There are two sets of terms: τῇ αὐτῇ τάξει—τῇ αὐτῇ διαδοχῇ and ἡ παράδοσις—τὸ κήρυγμα. Both sets seem to be made up of interchangeable synonyms, but in fact each term has its own specific

---

[38] According to Karrer, "Das Petrusamt in der Frühkirche," 519, Irenaeus here alludes to visits of the faithful, especially bishops, to Rome, thereby securing for themselves the surest attestation of their membership of the Church through their (demonstrable) association with the Roman bishop.

[39] Here I follow the interpretation of the controverted phrase "propter potentiorem principalitatem" as proposed by Rousseau-Doutreleau in their "Notes justificatives" to the *SC* critical edition of *Adv. haer.* (= *SC* 210, pp. 228–236), which also includes a select bibliography on the subject. See also pp. 225–228 for a commentary on the first part of the same paragraph.

[40] Thus, e.g., Heiler, *Altkirchliche Autonomie*, 192.

[41] *Adv. haer.* 3,3,3 = Eusebius, *HE* 5,6,5 (Schwartz 438,26–440,2).

meaning which is meant to complement and throw light on the other. Since the heretics also seem to claim a certain διαδοχή, which consisted primarily of hidden mysteries handed down from the Apostles,[42] Irenaeus uses the word τάξις to stress the precise (historico-sacramental) order of the episcopal succession.[43] Likewise in the second set of terms, "the tradition from the Apostles in the Church" is nothing but τὸ τῆς ἀληθείας κήρυγμα: the (public) proclamation of the truth. Each term is not only related to the other partner in the set, but to the parallel term in the other set of terms. The relationship between the first and second set is determined by the case of the terms in the first set, which is the dative of cause. Thus, the whole sentence should be rendered as: "Due to this very order, the Apostolic Teaching is handed on in the Church; on account of this very succession, the proclamation of the Truth has come down to us." The succession of bishops from the Apostles is the cause of the existence of the Apostolic Teaching in the Church of Rome, as in any Apostolic Church.

It must be remembered however that the successions of bishops understood in terms of their function to establish and preserve temporal unanimity, automatically implied spatial unanimity, the universal communion of each bishop.[44] Thus the term succession implied not only successive bishops but successive *generations* of the Church, so that, e.g., when reference was made to the teaching held by a former bishop, the authority it enjoyed was not simply that of the local Church but, provided the bishop remained in communion with the rest of the Church and died within her Peace, then his teaching was recognized as a witness to the teaching of the Universal Church at that period.[45]

Eusebius, on the other hand, both in his *Chronicle* and in the *History* showed an interest in a different type of succession, that of the imperial dynasties, and it is in the light of this that he "receives" the traditional concept. In the earlier concept, the "succession" involved both a material and a formal element, the Apostolic Teaching and the Apostolic Authority, and only in a secondary sense

---

[42] Cf. *Adv. haer.* 3,3,1 (Rousseau-Doutreleau 30).
[43] Like Turner, "Apostolic Succession," 132–133, so also von Campenhausen, *Kirchliches Amt und geistliche Vollmacht*, denies the claim that Irenaeus attributes a sacramental character to the episcopate.
[44] In this connection, see also *HE* 6,11,2 (Schwartz 540,24–542,6).
[45] This appears to be the argument of Polycrates, who refers to the witness of Polycarp of Smyrna, Sagaris of Laodicaea, and Melito of Sardis. Polycrates makes particular reference to the fact that these bishops had died witnessing to the Faith. They were moreover not predecessors of his but bishops of other Churches. See *HE* 5,24,2–8 (Schwartz 490,12–492,24).

did it imply a chronological element so that the "lists" of Hegesippus and Irenaeus probably did not contain specific chronological indications. But with Eusebius, the chronological significance of the successions is given a new prominence, while the main emphasis is on their formal character: the authority guaranteed by the successions. Accordingly, when the term διαδοχή is found in his notices which make up the "lists" of bishops at Rome,[46] Jerusalem,[47] Antioch,[48] and Alexandria,[49] it is used in the primary sense of chronological *sequence*, parallel to the successions of imperial rulers. The demonstration of the successions at Rome as found in Irenaeus and used by Eusebius as the basis of his "list" of Roman bishops is designated by the historian quite simply as a κατάλογος.[50]

Whereas earlier successions "lists," such as those of Irenaeus, preserved both in their form and content clear traces of their origin in the practice of "dating" *heretics* by referring to the bishop of the time,[51] not out of any chronological interest as such but in order to contrast the novelty of the heresy in comparison with the Apostolic origins of the orthodox teaching.[52] Eusebius, even though he retains vestiges of these,[53] adopts a new type of synchronism. He develops synchronisms of orthodox writers around bishops of certain Churches, in particular Rome, who enjoyed unquestioned authority, as we will see in Chapters Two and Three below.[54] This seems in the first place to be a consequence of Eusebius' parallelism between the bishops and the imperial rulers, so that the bishops are considered not as *teachers*, but primarily as authorities who safeguarded the orthodoxy (= Apostolicity) of the teaching. Again, due to the parallel with the imperial rulers, the episcopal successions are conceived in terms of a dynasty, which, like all dynasties, is designated by its founders, the Apostles, and implies a certain chronological *period* inaugurated by them. And so, when Eusebius describes his original *History* as "the Apostolic Successions," he is in the first place talking about the various periods of the "apostolic dynasty,"[55] which periods are defined by the "reign" of the

---

46   Cf. *HE* 5,5,9 (Schwartz 438,3).
47   Cf. *HE* 5,12,1–2 (Schwartz 454,5–13).
48   Cf. *HE* 3,36,2 (Schwartz 274,18).
49   Cf. *HE* 4,4,1 (Schwartz 300,6).
50   *HE* 5,5,9 (Schwartz 438,6).
51   E.g., *HE* 4,11,2 (Schwartz 322,3–10) = *Adv. haer.* 1,27,1–2.
52   See Caspar, *Römische Bischofsliste*, 227.
53   For example, *HE* 4,30,1–3 (Schwartz 392,14–28).
54   See below, pp. 76 and 86–88.
55   It appears that Eusebius uses the term "succession" in a semi-technical sense to describe the historico-salvific periods of the Church in *HE* 1,1,1 (Schwartz

bishops who are the successors "of the most distinguished of Our Savior's Apostles in those Churches which are still renowned and commemorated to this day."[56]

The other element in the original concept of Apostolic Succession—the tradition of the Apostolic Teaching handed on from one generation to the next—was not excluded by Eusebius. And here Eusebius' reception seems to have been directly influenced by the non-Christian concept of διαδοχή as the succession of the Philosophers or Schools of Philosophy, which, as Schwartz reminded us,[57] formed the framework for the presentation of the history of philosophy. When Eusebius refers to the study of the Aristotelian διαδοχή, the organization of which Anatolius was found worthy by the citizens

6,1), *HE* 7,32,32 (Schwartz 730,16) and *HE* 8, "Proem" (Schwartz 736,1). After considering these references among others, Overbeck concluded: "Die 'apostolische Nachfolge' bezeichnet also . . . in der Kirchengeschichte des Eusebius zunächst und an und für sich nichts Anderes als die Gesamtheit der Sukzessionen der Bischöfe der Kirche, aber indem diese Gesamtheit bei Eusebius die Trägerin der historischen Manifestationen der Kirche oder der Kirche als historischer Erscheinung überhaupt geworden ist, dient sie ihm zugleich als Bezeichnung eben dieser Erscheinung; woraus sich auch die besondere Bedeutung, welche in Eusebius' Darstellung der Kirchengeschichte seine Bischofslisten habe, erklärt" (Overbeck, *Die Bischofslisten*, 41). However, it would appear that the understanding of the term "Apostolic Succession" (in the singular) to designate the totality of the episcopal successions only occurred to Eusebius after he had completed the original *History* of seven books (cf. *HE* 8, "Proem"). In the course of the original *History*, he refers to the various periods specifically as "successions" (cf. *HE* 3,3,3 = Schwartz 190,7; also *HE* 3,4,11 = Schwartz 194,17), one of which is clearly described as the first post-Apostolic period (cf. *HE* 3,37,1 = Schwartz 282,2; *HE* 3,37,4 = Schwartz 282,22). He evidently reckons Hegesippus as one who belongs to the latter period (*HE* 2,23,3 = Schwartz 166,67) while Clement of Alexandria is said to have come close to it (*HE* 6,13,8 = Schwartz 548,18).

[56] *HE* 1,1,4 (Schwartz 8,14–17). Although Eusebius uses the list of successive Roman emperors to help determine the actual chronology of the Church's history, they remain external to the presentation: their primary relevance is to help situate the story of the Church within world history. Individual emperors are only of interest in so far as they either persecute the Church, as e.g., Nero and Decius, or recognize the sublimity of the Church's teaching or knowledge, such as Philip of Arabia and (possibly) Aurelian. Intrinsic to the Eusebian presentation of the Church's history are the list of bishops: it is they who determine the continuation of the "Apostolic Dynasty" and thus it is their reign that, properly speaking, constitutes the unit of time in the *History*. According to Wallace-Hadrill, *Eusebius*, 158f., following Lawlor, the unit of time is not the year but the reign of an emperor or a bishop of repute; this, however, does not do justice to specific functions played by the two different types of list to be found in the *History*—those of the bishops and those of the emperors.

[57] See Schwartz, "Eusebios," *PWK* VI, col. 1396. See also Caspar, *Römische Bischofsliste*, 231.

of Alexandria,[58] the succession to which he refers has nothing to do with authority in the former sense but covers the traditional *teaching* of the Aristotelian School. It is against this background, it seems to me, that the text is best understood where Eusebius talks about the participation in the Apostolic Succession of Clement of Alexandria's teacher Pantaenus.[59] Eusebius would have us believe that Pantaenus was one of Clement's eminent teachers who, according to Clement, "preserved the true tradition of the beatific teaching directly from Peter, James, John and Paul, the holy Apostles, as a son receives from his father (few however were like the Fathers). . . ."[60] There is no mention that any of these were bishops. The mention of Pantaenus and Clement at any rate indicates that for Eusebius the bishops were not the only ecclesiastics entrusted with the preservation of the Apostolic Tradition.[61] The orthodox teachers,[62] who either orally or in written documents handed on the pure Apostolic Teaching from one generation to the next, shared in their own way in the Apostolic Succession.[63]

The emphasis thus given to the second element of the original concept of the Apostolic Succession is a necessary consequence of Eusebius' new conception of the bishops as primarily authorities, parallel to the imperial rulers. Originally, the office of authority and teaching were both, as it were, invested in the bishop, but now they are being almost imperceptibly separated into two "offices," to use the word anachronistically, the one reserved for the bishop and the other for the "teacher." Many of the orthodox writers Eusebius will in fact list, such as St. Irenaeus and St. Dionysius of Alexandria, were also bishops, but his greatest hero, Origen, to whom he devotes almost an entire book, did not belong to the episcopal

---

[58]   Cf. *HE* 7,32,6 (Schwartz 718,19).

[59]   Cf. *HE* 5,11,2 (Schwartz 452,12); see also *HE* 5,20,1 (Schwartz 480,23) where the same use of the term is made with respect to Irenaeus.

[60]   Cf. *HE* 5,11,5 (Schwartz 452,22–25) = quotation from Clement, *Stromata* 1,11.

[61]   Cf. *HE* 5,25,1 (Schwartz 496,28).

[62]   Cf. *HE* 3,25,6 (Schwartz 252,18); also *HE* 3,3,3 (Schwartz 190,7).

[63]   Trevijano, "The Early Christian Church of Alexandria," 471–477, argues that the representatives of Alexandrian Christianity, up to Demetrios (ca. 200), were primarily *didaskaloi*, but that under Demetrios, the "first monarchical Bishop of Alexandria," the *didaskaleion* had to surrender to the episcopate, despite Origen's futile attempts to give theoretical preeminence to the teachers. Whatever truth there might be in this opinion, it is clear that for the Origenist Eusebius no tension exists between the bishops and the teachers, whose functions in the Apostolic Tradition or Succession are indeed distinct (one could almost say separate) but are nonetheless complementary, at least in the original *History,* in such a way that the preeminent authority of the bishops is obvious. See Thomson, "Apostolic Authority," 19–31.

order. By thus singling out the orthodox teachers—among whom, it must be remembered, Eusebius himself would have liked to have been counted—the author of the *History* perhaps came closer to the original non-Christian parallel of the successions of Philosophers (or their schools of thought) than Hegesippus and Irenaeus, with their sacramental understanding of the successions, would have approved.[64] Let us now return to the stated aims outlined by Eusebius at the beginning of his *History*, and try to interpret them in the light of the above.

The general aim of Eusebius is to present the "Apostolic Successions" to his readers, that is, to present the Church as the historical manifestation of a people characterized by the Apostolic Dynasty.[65] This general objective is sub-divided into six interrelated particular aims as follows:

(A) The first is that of any historian, to relate the great *events* which distinguished this dynasty (whereby its origins and foundation would receive special attention).

(B) Next follows, quite naturally, the dynastic succession itself, the *bishops*. However, Eusebius does not intend to list all the bishops, but even at this stage limits them to the eminent bishops who presided over the sees of "greatest distinction," a limitation which is so important that he returns again to qualify it once he has set out his aims, as we also will do.

(C) The Apostolic Succession does not simply parallel the sequence of imperial rulers, but also those successions by which a school of philosophy transmits its authentic teaching; thus, it must include details of those *teachers* who, during the "reign" of eminent bishops, defended the Divine Word in speech or writing.

(D) The foregoing aim implies this one, which commits Eusebius to give some details about the teachers' adversaries, the *heretics* who are characterized as those motivated by the spirit of innovation.[66]

---

[64] What Eusebius seems to have done, was to introduce into the specific Catholic concept of "succession," which was forged in opposition to the false claims of the Gnostics, elements of the concept which the Gnostics seemingly took over from the philosophic schools and which the orthodox writers rejected.

[65] According to Farina, *L'impero*, 284–287, the title most favored by Eusebius is "the people of the Church." According to Tetz, this new People is the fulfilment of the prophecy to Abraham, cf. "Christenvolk und Abrahamsverheißung," 33–34. Eger, "Kaiser und Kirche," 102, exaggerates a little when he speaks of the Church as a kind of "Staatswesen." See also von Ivánka, *Rhomäerrich und Gottesvolk*.

[66] To what extent this emphasis on novelty, as the main characteristic of heresy, was due to the apologetic concern of writers, such as Eusebius, to demonstrate the antiquity of the Christian Religion needs to be more thoroughly examined.

(E)   This aim deals with the second type of adversaries encountered by the Church in the course of her history, the *Jewish people* (i.e., the "dynasty" of the O.T., whose succession came to an end with the birth of Christ); Eusebius will recall what happened to them as a result of their plot against Our Savior, and thus their rejection of his authority and teaching.

(F)   And finally, Eusebius mentions the Christian People's third great adversary, the non-Christian Peoples or *Nations* (specifically: the emperors). This aim designs to relate the persecutions which occurred in the successive Apostolic periods and to display the "heroic feats" of the martyrs.

The limits of this study will prevent us from tracing these various themes through the *History* in any detail. The object of this study is to examine how Eusebius treats Aims A and B in particular. Since, however, the various themes interact, it is unavoidable that in the course of this study some treatment of each theme must be undertaken, however scantily.

After setting out the above aims, Eusebius adds a comment about his own method which is of importance. He mentions the sources he will use and adds the methodological note to the effect that "we shall endeavor by means of an historical narrative, to embody (these scattered memoirs) in a unified form, being content to rescue the successions, if not of all, then most certainly of the most illustrious of Our Savior's Apostles in those Churches which are still eminent and commemorated to this day."[67] He does not intend to draw up a catena of quotations from ancient authors or give a merely chronological account of past events but, basing himself on a "judicious" use of his sources, he will attempt to see the events and details within some overriding plan or purpose.

The unifying *motif*, as will be seen, is Divine Providence, so that events mentioned in Aim (A) are only presented because of their great significance within the plan of Salvation. However, here Eusebius draws specific attention to what was but implicit in Aim B: how the episcopal successions should perform a structurally unifying function within the narrative, providing, one might say, the skeleton for the body of the work (σωματοποιῆσαι).[68] The importance of the role thus played by the list of bishops is not exhausted by such a literary device: this methodological principle itself

[67]   Cf. *HE* 1,1,4 (Schwartz 8,13–17).

[68]   *HE* 1,1,4 (Schwartz 8,13–14). It is not the list of emperors, as Nigg, *Die Kirchengeschichtsschreibung*, 22, suggests, but rather the list of bishops which form the actual framework for Eusebius' presentation of the material he had collected (cf. Turner, "Apostolic Succession," 134).

reflects the function played by the bishops of the major sees at the opening of the fourth century in providing centers of unity and authority for the universal Church. What is of particular significance to the specific topic of this study is how Eusebius limits the scope of his overall aim, which was "to record the succession of the sacred Apostles,"[69] and is now "content to rescue the successions . . . of *the most illustrious* of Our Savior's Apostles."[70] This study will indicate how Eusebius confines himself to Saint Peter and the Churches which directly or indirectly trace their origins back to him.

It is in fact the relationship between St. Peter and the four different Churches, whose list of bishops form the framework for the *History,* which, according to Eusebius, determined in historico-salvific terms the nature of the Apostolic Authority attributed in various ways to the bishops of these Churches at the time he originally conceived the *History.* Thus the Aim (B) to record "the number of those who were distinguished in her government and leadership in the provinces of greatest fame"[71] is now more sharply delineated in this methodological note when Eusebius qualifies what he means by "greatest fame:" he does not, in the first place at least, mean to speak of Churches which were renowned for their *past* glories and fame but rather of Churches "which are *still* eminent and commemorated *to this day.*"[72] By using the verb μνημονεύω in this context, the reader's attention is drawn to a further significance in what Eusebius means by "greatest fame:" it is those important sees distinguished above all the others because of their singular eminence within the universal *koinōnia* of the Church.

The *History* then intends to trace the Apostolic Succession of those Churches which, at the time of composition, enjoyed a certain eminence (yet to be more closely delineated) by reason of their specific authoritative functions within the universal communion, and whose bishops were the successors of the most illustrious of the Apostles—St. Peter. These Churches are, as will be seen, Rome, Alexandria, and Antioch; Jerusalem's eminence is of another nature.

§4 The Suppositions and Presuppositions of the *History* (Book 1)

More important in a sense than the stated aims of Eusebius are the suppositions and presuppositions on which his *History* rests, since it

---

[69]   *HE* 1,1,1 (Schwartz 6,1).
[70]   *HE* 1,1,4 (Schwartz 8,14–15).
[71]   *HE* 1,1,1 (Schwartz 6,4–5).
[72]   *HE* 1,1,4 (Schwartz 8,16–17).

is these which will eventually enable Eusebius to readjust his original aims so radically as to abandon them in effect. The remainder of the Introduction (Book 1) sketches in broad outline those suppositions which, for Eusebius, endow the Church's history with its ultimate significance. These are the divinity of Christ and His appearance in time and space, the θεολογία of the Divine Logos and his οἰκονομία towards creation and mankind.[73]

According to Ruhbach,[73a] the term οἰκονομία was perceived by Eusebius as the adequate term to express his main preoccupation, namely to present God's salvific action in history convincingly and understandably. This is certainly true with regard to the *Praeparatio* and *Demonstatio*. Although the term is not used in this semitechnical sense, the concept is indeed present in the original draft and comes more and more to the surface in the course of the Revisions. It is of note that Eusebius speaks of the activity of the Logos in Creation as the πρώτη οἰκονομία.[74] He does not inform us explicitly as to what the second dispensation precisely consists of, but in all probability, he would have thus described the relationship of the Logos to mankind—i.e., Salvation History—as such.

Also of significance is the insight of Ruhbach to the effect that in contrast with Origen who found support for his theology by having recourse to examples drawn from history, Eusebius starts with history and moves from there to formulate his theological statements.[75] However, it must be pointed out that the difference was originally one of emphasis, since Eusebius simply turned to history as a whole (and not to isolated examples) in order to prove his own theological understanding of the true religion. It would be more precise to say that this new emphasis did in fact eventually produce a new theology—or rather, to be more specific in relationship to the main subject of the *History*, a new ecclesiology— for Eusebius in the course of his Revisions (ignored by Ruhbach) did recast his original theological understanding of the Church according to his experience of, and subsequent reflection on, two epoch-making historical events: the Great Persecution and the advent of Constantine.

---

[73] Cf. *HE* 1,1,7 (Schwartz 8,25–27). For Eusebius, θεολογία refers to the Logos in Himself (His Divinity), whereas the οἰκονομία refers to His dealings with man and creation: see Eusebius *DE* 10, "Proem," 2f. (Heikel 445,5f.).

[73a] See Ruhbach, *Apologetik und Geschichte*, especially pp. 18–19 and 134–138. Discussing the translation of the term οἰκονομία, Ruhbach considers the term "Providence" as inadequate. However, as we will see below, Eusebius concept of the Divine Dispensation and his concept of God's Providence are almost identical.

[74] Ruhbach, *Apologetik und Geschichte*, 136.

[75] Ruhbach, *Apologetik und Geschichte*, 137.

This development was almost inevitable due to the profound influence of
Eusebius' apologetic aim, and its theological presuppositions.

The main apologetic concern of Eusebius is his attempt to demonstrate the *"great antiquity"* and divine character of Christianity to those
who consider it new and outlandish.[76] This was one of the main preoccupations of the Apologists, who attempted to counter the scorn of their pagan
adversaries over the alleged youth of Christianity,[77] and whose attempts
eventually led to the interest in chronologies.[78] To meet these objections
and at the same time to prove the divine character of the Christian religion, Eusebius traces its origins back to the preexistent Logos[79] who was
witnessed to by the great Moses, "the most ancient of all prophets,"[80] and
even before him by Abraham.[81] Likewise, much importance is given to the
appearances of the Lord to Abraham at the Oak of Mamre[82] "in the shape of
man,"[83] as well as His appearance to Jacob[84] and other θεοφανείας[85] such as
that to Joshua[86]—all of which preceded the "final incarnation."[87] The latter
expression is part of a later interpolation during the 4th Revision, but it
indicates clearly the direction of Eusebius' thought: the essential difference
between the O.T. theophanies and the N.T. epiphany of the Divine Word,
namely the hypostatic union as distinct from the former appearances, is
dangerously reduced in order to make the apologetic point regarding the
antiquity of the Christian religion. This in turn means that the discontinuity between the old and the new dispensations tends to be sacrificed to the
emphasis on their continuity, so that the two become but two successive
periods of the *one* dispensation differing primarily in chronology and effect
but not, however, in kind. This entire dispensation was what we described
above as the second "dispensation" of Eusebius' Theology: Salvation

[76] Cf. Kraft, *Einleitung*, 20–21.
[77] See Nigg, *Die Kirchengeschichtsschreibung*, 5–6.
[78] See Stevenson, *Studies in Eusebius*, 38–39.
[79] Cf. *HE* 1,2,2f. (Schwartz 10,11f.).
[80] *HE* 1,2,4 (Schwartz 12,9); also *HE* 1,3,1 (Schwartz 28,12).
[81] Cf. *HE* 1,2,6 (Schwartz 14,1).
[82] Cf. *HE* 1,2,7 (Schwartz 14,6–20).
[83] ἐν ἀνθρώπου ὁρώμενος σχήματι (*HE* 1,2,8 = Schwartz 14,16).
[84] Cf. *HE* 1,2,9 (Schwartz 14,24).
[85] *HE* 1,2,10 (Schwartz 16,6).
[86] Cf. *HE* 1,2,11–12 (Schwartz 16,10–18,4).
[87] τὴν ὑστάτην ἐνανθρώπησιν αὐτοῦ (*HE* 1,2,26 = Schwartz 28,6–7). See below,
      Note I.

History, which was understood by Eusebius as *essentially* the same before and after Christ.[88]

The significance of this flaw in the thought of Eusebius, as far as this immediate study is concerned, is the way in which it ultimately facilitates Eusebius to move from the second period (of the Apostolic Successions as distinct from the O.T. successions) to a third: the new era, inaugurated by Constantine, that of the Imperial Church. This occurs decisively during the 4th Revision, as we will see, during which revision, Eusebius interpolated the passage regarding the "final incarnation."

The same apologetic concern about the antiquity of the Christian religion dominates Eusebius' demonstration of "the honor shown to the very name of 'Jesus' and of 'the Christ' by those ancient God-loving prophets."[89] The term τὸ ὄνομα here refers to the person or being of the Divine Logos and not simply to the titular designation as such.[90] The honor shown to Him is deduced from the way those such as Moses, who enjoyed the religious preeminence among men,[91] recognized the High Priest,[92] the King,[93] and some prophets[94] as having become such through their anointing "types" of Christ: "since they all refer to the true Christ, the divine and heavenly Logos of the universe, the very High Priest, of all creation the only King, and of prophets the only Archprophet of the Father."[95]

Since the Christology of Eusebius[96] is of no immediate concern to us, we can pass this subject by. But attention must be drawn to the specific *typology* of Eusebius as found here, since it is part of his methodology and so is of consequence for the interpretation of the later text. The typology used here is not the traditional understanding of a *type* in the O.T., finding its realization in the *Antitype* of

---

[88] Ruhbach, *Apologetik und Geschichte*, 137, even goes so far as to ask the pertinent question as to what extent the Incarnation was still necessary within the Eusebian concept of salvation in terms of civilization—at least the later, more developed concept that Ruhbach discusses.

[89] *HE* 1,3,1 (Schwartz 28,11–13).

[90] Cf. *HE* 1,3,2 (Schwartz 28,13–22).

[91] Cf. *HE* 1,2,6 (Schwartz 12,22–23).

[92] Moses, describing the High Priest as a man invested with the greatest power, calls him Christ (cf. *HE* 1,3,2 = Schwartz 28,17–21).

[93] Joshua, the successor of Moses as ruler of the People, was called Jesus the Savior (cf. *HE* 1,3,3–4 = Schwartz 28,22–30,3; also, *HE* 1,3,7 = Schwartz 72,3–10).

[94] Cf. *HE* 1,3,8 (Schwartz 32,10–15).

[95] *HE* 1,3,8 (Schwartz 32,12–15).

[96] Concerning the Christology of Eusebius, see Berkhof, *Theologie*, 65f.; Ricken, "Die Logoslehre des Eusebios," 341–358; des Places, "Numénius et Eusèbe de Césarée," 19–29; Simonetti, *La Crisi Ariana*, 60–66.

the N.T., but rather the more "Platonic" conception of the Divine Logos as the *Prototype* to which the various figures of the O.T.—here the High Priest, King, and Prophet—are related as types in the sense of symbolic representations.[97] It seems to me that Eusebius speaks rather in terms of a prototype and the "types" as historical embodiments of the same.

Later Eusebius will speak in a similar way about the heavenly *monarchia* as though it were the "prototype" of the earthly rule of Constantine, the sole emperor.[98] Apart from this "vertical typology," as it could be termed, Eusebius also makes use of a "horizontal typology" according to which ancient figures of Salvation History likewise became prototypes. In this sense, Moses is depicted as a prototype of Constantine.[99] It will be seen how Eusebius makes use of a basically similar form of prototype and type in order to describe the successors of Peter who are presented as types or re-embodiments of the Prototype Peter.

Before he moves on to describe that part of the οἰκονομία which deals directly with the final historical manifestation of the Divine Logos in the form of man, Eusebius once again takes up the charge of novelty levelled at the Christian Religion.[100] Though he admits that the Christian "Nation" has but recently manifested itself—quickly adding that it is nonetheless the most populous of all[101]—yet he insists that it is no new invention as its religion was held from the first creation of man[102] by those such as Abraham and the lovers of God who followed him.[103] The Christian Religion or Nation is thus seen as the fulfillment of the prophecy to Abraham in Gen 12,3; 18,8.[104] Here again we observe the tendency to emphasize the continuity between the religion of Abraham and that of the Apostolic Succession at the cost of sacrificing the discontinuity between the time before and after Christ. In this particular case, Eusebius' understanding of Christianity is of particular interest:

---

[97] See also Eusebius, *ET* 3,3 (Klostermann 155,12–26); cf. Ricken, "Die Logoslehre des Eusebius," 349. Wallace-Hadrill aptly comments that Eusebius cannot in any unqualified sense be said to have made use of the classical "typology:" "Christianity was (for Eusebius) a 'reduplication of old truths,' which is not a mode of expression to be used when speaking typologically" (Wallace-Hadrill, *Eusebius*, 183).

[98] Cf. Eusebius, *LC* 3,5–6 (Heikel 201,5–202,18); see Farina, *L'impero*, 132f.

[99] Cf. 9,9,4–9 (Schwartz 828,16–832,3). See also Eusebius, *VC* 1,12 (Winkelmann 21,2–28).

[100] Cf. *HE* 1,4,1 (Schwartz 38,4–10).

[101] Cf. *HE* 1,4,2 (Schwartz 38,13–14); see Tetz, "Christenvolk," 35–36.

[102] Cf. *HE* 1,4,4 (Schwartz 40,5–7).

[103] Cf. *HE* 1,4,10 (Schwartz 42,4–8).

[104] See Wallace-Hadrill, *Eusebius*, 168–177; see Tetz, "Christenvolk."

it consists primarily in knowledge of Christ (the Divine Logos), through which man excels in "moderation and justice, self-control, manly virtue and the confession of the one God."[105] In a word, this rather stoical conception could be summarized as a type of enlightenment which leads to the cultivation of civilized virtues.

The inadequacy of this concept is perhaps best appreciated by drawing attention to the fact that in the rest of Book 1, which covers the οἰκονομία of the Logos (specifically His historical appearance and life on earth as man among men), the Passion and death of Our Savior, apart from receiving a passing mention in a passage concerned with establishing the chronological limits of His public ministry,[106] is otherwise ignored.[107] The cross of Christ, it then appears, is not the source of the Christian Religion, which for Eusebius would seem to be primarily a form of enlightenment and moral excellence. This seems to me to be the basic flaw in Eusebius' theology and the cause both of his failure to recognize the definitive character of the Incarnation, and of his inability to perceive the difference between the theophanies of the O.T. and that of the N.T., which led him to ignore the discontinuity between both and to overemphasize their continuity. The consequences of this inadequate theology only manifest themselves gradually; but by the time Eusebius revises the *History* for the last time, twenty years or more after the first draft, the effect of this lacuna in his theology can be clearly seen, particularly in his understanding of the place of martyrdom in the Church and his interpretation of the Constantinian era.

The remainder of Book 1 is, if we prescind from the later interpolations, mostly taken up with establishing the chronological details regarding the birth of Our Lord[108]—including a discussion on the genealogical tables of Mt and Lk[109]—and the date of His public ministry.[110] Apart from devoting considerable time to the punishment meted out by the Divine Justice on Herod for his crime against Christ and the Innocents,[111] the other subject which receives special attention from Eusebius is the universal fame of the Divinity

[105] *HE* 1,4,7 (Schwartz 40,19–21).
[106] Cf. *HE* 1,10,6 (Schwartz 74,20–21).
[107] Another reference (*HE* 1,11,8) occurs in a quotation from Josephus, *Antiq.* 18,64 (Niese, vol. IV, 152).
[108] Cf. *HE* 1,5,1–6 (Schwartz 44,9–46,20).
[109] Cf. *HE* 1,7,1–17 (Schwartz 52,21–62,16).
[110] Cf. *HE* 1,10,1–7 (Schwartz 72,18–76,8). See also *HE* 1,12,1–5 (Schwartz 80,15–82,20).
[111] Cf. *HE* 1,8,3–1,9,1 (Schwartz 64,10–72,2).

of Our Lord from the beginning.[112] This subject, the last in Book 1, per-forms the literary function of linking the Introduction with the actual History of the Church Universal. Eusebius demonstrates this universal fame in two ways: (i) by drawing attention to the fact that there were many more disciples than the Seventy mentioned in Lk 10,1f, as 1 Cor 15,5–7 implies[113]—the implication being that from the beginning numer-ous disciples spread the knowledge of Christ far and wide; and (ii) by relating in particular the story of Abgar of Edessa, producing the famous "correspondence" between Our Lord and Abgar[114] as documentary proof of the Lord's fame in distant lands.

Finally, it may be remarked that in this Introduction, the figure of *St. Peter* is mentioned twice. Although on both occasions the references are incidental to the main subject, they are nonetheless of interest. In the first reference,[115] the Cephas of Gal 2,11f whom Paul rebuked is said to be another disciple and not the Apostle Peter. This attempt to remove any suspicion from the name of Peter is in accord with the tendency of Eusebius to present his heroes as spotless and perfect specimens of virtue.[116] Later Eusebius will (inaccurately) refer to Peter as the one *"who due to his virtues* was leader of all the other (Apostles)"[117] and, with similarly danger-ous naivete, will refer to Constantine as "distinguished with every virtue that godliness bestows."[118] Such an approach to historical personages well illustrates the type of historiography employed by Eusebius: its disastrous consequences will be seen later.

The second reference to Peter is to be found in the quotation of 1 Cor 15,5–7, where it is related that, after the Resurrection, Jesus was first seen by Peter.[119] This description of Peter as the first witness to the Resurrection is not developed by Eusebius; he reserves his treatment of Peter until the beginning of the history proper in Book 2, where Peter plays a central role according to Eusebius' account of the foundation of the Church.

---

[112] Cf. *HE* 1,13,1 (Schwartz 82,22–84,3).

[113] Cf. *HE* 1,12,4–5 (Schwartz 82,9–20).

[114] Cf. *HE* 1,13,1–22 (Schwartz 82,21–96,9).

[115] Cf. *HE* 1,12,2 (Schwartz 82,1–5). Eusebius acknowledges that his authority here is Clement of Alexandria.

[116] Opitz, "Euseb von Caesarea als Theologe," 9, demonstrates that a similar concept of ἀρετή is to be found in Porphyry.

[117] Cf. *HE* 2,14,6 (Schwartz 138,23). This text was completely misinterpreted by Jaskowski, "Eusebius und der Primat," 323, and Katzenmayer, "Petrus und der Primat," 159, who understood it to mean that Peter's position within the school of Apostles was, according to Eusebius, due to his personal characteristics and not due to any specific office he was entrusted with by the Lord.

[118] Cf. *HE* 10,9,6 (Schwartz 900,24).

[119] *HE* 1,12,4 (Schwartz 82,12).

CHAPTER TWO
The Apostolic Age (Books 2–3)

The Apostolic Age is presented by Eusebius in Books 2 and 3 as made up of two stages: the Apostolic Age, strictly so-called, when the initial foundation was laid (Book 2), and the Apostolic Age, derivatively so-called, when that initial foundation was consolidated and completed by the other disciples and eyewitnesses of the Apostles (Book 3). This division accords with the distinction made by Eusebius in Book 1 between the Twelve, who alone of the disciples were designated Apostles by the Lord as a special privilege, and the other disciples, such as the Seventy.[1] And yet the latter also participate in the commission of the Apostles as is implied by the use of the term ἀποστολεῖν to describe their mission. The first stage (= Book 2) of the Apostolic Age ends with the martyrdom of Saints Peter and Paul. But the mention of Apostles in the second stage (= Book 3) indicates how these two stages are not conceived as two totally separate chronological periods, but that one overlaps the other.

§1 Book 2: The Foundation of the Church

The purpose of Book 1, the Introduction to the original *History*, was, as Eusebius tells us again in the Proem to Book 2, to demonstrate the Divinity of the Logos and the antiquity of the Christian teaching, as well as to recount the historical appearance of the Logos and His choice of the Apostles. Nothing in Book 1 gave any indication that Christ founded the Church. It is the mission of the Twelve, the Apostles strictly so-called, to found the Church. This foundation occurred, according to Eusebius, after the Ascension.[2] After the Divine Logos had returned to Heaven, the Apostles established on a universal scale the work of redemption—for Eusebius primarily a work of enlightenment—which the Incarnate Λόγος had inaugurated on earth by His example and teaching. Eusebius stoutly affirmed in Book 1 that the Christian Religion was not founded in some obscure corner of the earth (οὐδ' ἐπὶ γωνίας ποι γῆς ἱδρυμένον).[3] In Book 2, he indeed situates the foundation of the

---

[1] Cf. *HE* 1,10,7 (Schwartz 76,2–8).
[2] Cf. *HE* 2, "Proem," 2 (Schwartz 102,7–10). In the Praeparatio, Eusebius explicitly affirms that the Church was not established while Our Lord lived among men (*PE* 1,3,8 = Mras, vol. I,12,1).
[3] *HE* 1,4,2 (Schwartz 38,13).

Church by the Apostles, in particular by Peter,[4] not in any remote corner of
the world but right in the center of the world, Rome,[4a] and depicts its story
against the backdrop of the universal History of Salvation. The general
outline of his presentation is taken from the Acts of the Apostles, but his
sources also include Hegesippus, Clement of Alexandria, and Josephus.[5]

The Apostolic Age properly so-called, to which we now turn our
attention, is the period of transition from the Old Testament to the New,
from the religion of the Jewish Race to the universal religion of Jews and
Gentiles alike. According to Eusebius' understanding of his sources, this
period is dominated by two personalities, James, the Brother of the Lord,
and Peter, the Leader of the Apostles, and by two cities, Jerusalem and
Rome, whose divinely guided destinies span this period and give it its
inner meaning.

a) St. James the Just and the function of Jerusalem within
Salvation History

After a brief mention of Matthias' election to fill the place among the Twelve
made vacant by Judas, and a reference to the institution of the diaconate,[6] the
narrative focuses on James the Brother of the Lord, who, we are informed,
was the first to be elected to "the throne of the bishopric of the Church of
Jerusalem."[7] Our interest in James arises from the fact that, for Eusebius,
the contemporary significance of a Church is to be found in its origins, just
as the divine character of the Christian Religion is derived from its origins
in the preexistent Logos. The succession of bishops at Jerusalem traces its
origins back to James the Brother of the Lord and their special position in
the Church Universal is determined by this. Eusebius had at his disposal
two sources from which he could gather further information about the
election of James as Bishop of Jerusalem, that of Hegesippus and Clement.
According to Hegesippus, it appears that James was appointed to the See of
Jerusalem by the Lord himself.[8] Apart from one possible allusion to this in

---

[4]   For a concise but excellent account of Eusebius' treatment of St. Peter, see
      Rimoldi, *L'Apostolo san Pietro*, 201–204. See also below, Note II.
[4a] Cf. Eusebius, *DE* 3,7,22 (Heikel 144,9–12). See below, p. 223.
[5]   A similar plan to that found here is to be discerned in Lactantius, *De mort. per.*
      2 (Brandt-Laubmann, 173f.).
[6]   Cf. *HE* 2,1,1 (Schwartz 102,11–19).
[7]   *HE* 2,1,2 (Schwartz 104,2–3). Regarding the position of St. James within the
      primitive Church of Jerusalem, see Stauffer, "Petrus und Jakobus in Jerusalem,"
      366–372.
[8]   See Lawlor, *Eusebiana*, 14–18, where he draws attention to the paraphrase of
      Hegesippus in Epiphanius, *Panarion* 78,7. Lawlor points to *HE* 7,19,1 (Schwartz

Book 7, Eusebius prefers to ignore such information and chooses the version given by Clement of Alexandria.[9] Clement informs us that James the Brother of the Lord was elected to the bishopric of Jerusalem by Peter, James, and John. Later in Book 2, we are informed that the throne (θρόνος) of the bishopric of Jerusalem was entrusted to James by the Apostles,[10] once again emphasizing that James was appointed not by the Lord, but by the Apostles, a point Eusebius had previously made in the entry in his *Chronicle* which dealt with the same event.[11] Eusebius wishes to underline as strongly as possible that James was not an apostle himself—he did not belong to the Twelve and he was not elected to fill the place of Judas, but was appointed bishop by the Apostles.[12] The significance of this particular emphasis by Eusebius is that Jerusalem is, strictly speaking, not an Apostolic See as its succession does not descend from an Apostle, but, like most sees, from the Apostles in general.[13] As will be seen in Chapter Three, Jerusalem, at the time of Eusebius, held no position of authority in the Church, not even in Palestine, where it was in fact subject to the metropolitan

674,2) as evidence of Eusebius' knowledge of the same passage in Hegesippus, where the author of the *History* modifies the statement by informing us how James received the episcopate from Our Lord *and the Apostles*.

[9] Clement of Alexandria, *Hypotyposes,* Book 6 = *HE* 2,1,3 (Schwartz 104,3–8). This work of Clement is no longer extant.

[10] *HE* 2,23,1 (Schwartz 164,19–20).

[11] Eusebius, *Chronicle*, an entry under "Olymp." 203, "Abr." 2048, "Tiberius" 19, "Herod" 19 (Karst 213). Jaskowski, "Eusebius und der Primat," 325–330, would have us believe that according to the report of Eusebius, James the Just succeeded Jesus as Head of the Church.

[12] The quotation of Gal 1,19 (*HE* 2,1,5 = Schwartz 104,17–19) has as its object to demonstrate how St. Paul also mentioned James and recognized his special position in the Church of Jerusalem—and not to imply that James was considered to be an apostle by Paul.

[13] Grotz, *Die Hauptkirchen*, concludes that the "Apostolicity" of Jerusalem (or rather the Church there) which was due to the presence of the Apostles, especially St. Peter, after Pentecost, was in no way affected when James the Just functioned as bishop over the Church there. Grotz, whose prime source for this contention is the *History*, fails to detect Eusebius' purpose behind his account of the primitive Church, which was in this case to describe the special function of the Jewish-Christian community within Salvation History, whose function was other than the general mission of the Church to the (Gentile) world. Katzenmayer, "Petrus und der Primat," 159f., correctly observed that, for Eusebius, Peter was neither Bishop of Jerusalem, Antioch, or Rome; but he, together with Jaskowski, "Eusebius und der Primat," 335–336, falsely interprets the significance of this for Eusebius. As far as Eusebius was concerned, the office of apostle and the office of bishop were two distinct offices, the former being commissioned to found the Church, while the latter, as successor to the Apostles, preserved the Church's Apostolic character from one generation to the next.

See of Casearea.[14] And yet to speak again within the perspective of Eusebius, and prescinding from any discussion as to the objective historical facts, the Church of Jerusalem did have a unique function to play in the Apostolic Age. It was a θρόνος "sui generis."

It is of note that Eusebius rarely employs the term θρόνος in connection with a Church and on the few occasions when he does, he refers quite literally to the actual physical throne used by the bishop.[15] Apart from one similar type of reference to the throne at Jerusalem,[16] Eusebius uses the term in a semi-technical sense which went beyond the literal meaning, with regard to the Church there. As already mentioned above, James is twice described as having been elected to *the episcopal throne of the Church in Jerusalem*.[17] Simeon, his successor, is similarly mentioned as having succeeded to *the throne of the Church there*.[18] Simeon's successor, Justus, is likewise said to have succeeded to *the episcopal throne of the (Church) in Jerusalem*.[19] The phrase "the episcopal throne" is otherwise only found once in the *History* in a reference to Dionysius who was "entrusted with the episcopal throne of the Church of Corinth."[20] Even when Eusebius refers to the successions at Jerusalem later in the *History,* he does not use this phrase, but simply mentions that, for example, Hymenaeus succeeded to the throne,[21] alluding most probably to the physical throne, as he does in the same book, quite explicitly, with regard to that occupied by Hymenaeus'

[14] The position of the Church of Jerusalem at the beginning of the fourth century is reflected in Canon VII of the Council of Nicaea (see below, p. 212). It is worth considering that the ascendancy of Caesarea as the metropolitan see which counted Jerusalem as one of its suffragan sees may have been due to the association of Peter with the origins of the Church there (see below, p. 47, footnote 39), and not primarily to the political importance of the city, as is generally assumed. See also Eusebius, *Theoph* 4,6 (Gressmann 173,30f.), quoted below on p. 227, which claims Peter as the founder of the Church of Caesarea.

[15] For example, *HE* 6,29,4 (Schwartz 584,5), which refers to "the episcopal throne" at Rome. See also a similar usage found in the *Letter of the Synod of Antioch*, ca. 268 (*HE* 7,30,9 = Schwartz 708,24).

[16] *HE* 7,14,1 (Schwartz 668,9).

[17] *HE* 2,1,2 (Schwartz 104,3); *HE* 2,23,1 (Schwarz 164,20).

[18] *HE* 3,11,1 (Schwartz 228,4). This reference is particularly important since it represents an editorial alteration by Eusebius of his source, Hegesippus (cf. *HE* 4,22,4 (Schwartz 370,11). See Lawlor, *Eusebiana*, 26 and 47, footnote 2.

[19] *HE* 3,35,1 (Schwartz 274,10).

[20] *HE* 4,23,1 (Schwartz 374,2).

[21] *HE* 7,14,1 (Schwartz 668,9). Here Eusebius refers to the physical chair, as already mentioned.

successor, Hermo.[22] The phrase, "the episcopal throne of the Church in Jerusalem," occurs only in Books 2 and 3 and thus is reserved for the three bishops whose reigns cover the final period of Jerusalem's significance within the History of Salvation, i.e., a period that ended with the capture of Jerusalem, the destruction of the Temple, and the foundation of the new city of Aelia Capitolina in its place.[23]

Thus, the throne of Jerusalem is episcopal and not "apostolic" in the specific sense of the term; it received its unique significance within the Plan of Salvation, due to the specific role played by the Jewish-Christian Church there, up to the destruction of Jerusalem, although its succession of Hebrew bishops who, unlike their compatriots, accepted knowledge of Christ,[23a] did not fade out for some time after that event.[24]

We are told quite explicitly that both James and Simeon were related to Our Lord and on that account were elected to the episcopal throne,[25] while Justus is described as a Jew, one of the circum-

---

[22] *HE* 7,32,29 (Schwartz 730,1–2). This is not part of the original *History* but belongs to the 1st Revision (see below, p. 140f.). It is of note that Eusebius here informs us that Hemo ἀποστολιχὸν διαδέχεται θρόνον, and thus, for the first and only time, uses the term "Apostolic throne." According to Dvornik, *The Idea of Apostolicity*, 48, this singular description of the See of Jerusalem is indicative of the special significance attached to the see by Eusebius. But it should be noted that Eusebius does not use the term here in the technical sense of the later fourth and fifth centuries: he simply refers to the physical chair which was revered in Jerusalem as a type of relic. Its significance is merely antiquarian and corresponds to the change in the mentality of Eusebius that was brought about by the Great Persecution and which resulted in his eventual disillusionment with the Apostolic Church he originally set out to defend (see below, Chapter Four).

[23] This period is dealt with in Books 2 and 3.

[23a] *HE* 4,5,2 (Schwartz 304,16–17).

[24] As though to emphasize their loss of significance for the rest of the *History,* Eusebius lumps the names of all the Hebrew Bishops of Jerusalem together at the beginning of Book 4 (*HE* 4,5,3 = Schwartz 304,22–306,3) in a list which has caused some controversy as to its origins. In his criticism of Dvornik's study, *The Idea of Apostolicity*, Lanne, "Partikularkirchen und Patriarchate," 466, uses the list of bishops of Jerusalem, as preserved in Eusebius' *History,* as part of his evidence to prove that the special honor attributed to Jerusalem in the middle of the third century right into the fourth (Canon VII of Nicaea) was due to its generally recognized Apostolicity. However, my analysis of the *History* leads me to doubt the admissibility of this evidence, and yet I do accept the main point of Lanne's article to the effect that the Apostolicity of a see did have a role to play in the organization of the Churches, particularly in the pre-Constantinian era, which organization cannot be explained merely by the parallel structure of the Roman administration, as Dvornik argues.

[25] *HE* 2,1,2 (Schwartz 102,19–23); *HE* 3,11,1 (Schwartz 228,5–6).

cised.[26] But James' relationship to Our Lord was not limited to the natural level. Using a short quotation from the *Hypotyposes* of Clement, no longer extant, Eusebius informs us that "after the Resurrection the Lord handed on the Knowledge (παρέδωκεν τὴν γνῶσιν) to James the Just, John, and Peter, who handed it on to the other Apostles, who in turn handed it on to the Seventy, of whom Barnabas also was one."[27] Within the context of Book 2, this quotation is meant to imply that, though not an apostle like John and Peter, James the Just received the tradition of Knowledge directly from the Lord because of his unique mission to the Lord's own People. The Apostles on the other hand were commissioned to found the universal Church.

According to Eusebius, in the transition period between the Ascension of Our Lord and the definitive foundation of the Church Universal, a last opportunity was afforded the Jewish race, to accept the γνῶσις of the Father, which the Savior, who was of their own race, first offered to them. This last chance was incorporated in the person of James,[28] the Brother of the Lord, who was highly esteemed by his fellow Jews for his righteousness.[29] Just as Pilate experienced the Divine Vengeance for his part in the death of Our Lord,[30] and Herod felt the weight of the Divine Wrath for his persecution of the Apostles,[31] so also the Jewish race, more specifically Jerusalem, was punished for its rejection of our Savior, since, as Eusebius tells us, unrest, revolt, war, and all kinds of evil broke loose in Jerusalem after the death of Christ.[32] But in the same passage, he informs us that the *final* evil was yet to come: the siege of Jerusalem by Vespasian.

After recounting the story of James' death at the hands of the Scribes and Pharisees, as given by Hegesippus,[33] Eusebius rounds off the event with the addition of the simple sentence: "and at once Vespasian began to besiege them,"[34] a text of Hegesippus which Schwartz suggested was taken from another context and inserted

[26] *HE* 3,35,1 (Schwartz 274,11).

[27] *HE* 2,1,4 (Schwartz 104,11–16).

[28] This theme, but implicit in Book 2, is explicitly stated in *HE* 3,7,7–9 (Schwartz 214,2–24).

[29] Cf. *HE* 2,23,4–7 (Schwartz 166,4–168,2). See Torrey, "James the Just and his Name 'Oblias,'" 93–98.

[30] *HE* 2,7,1 (Schwartz 122,23–124,2).

[31] *HE* 2,10,1–10 (Schwartz 126,7–130,16).

[32] *HE* 2,6,8 (Schwartz 122,16–22). See also *HE* 2,4,1–2,6,7 (Schwartz 114,13–122,15).

[33] *HE* 2,23,4–18 (Schwartz 166,9–170,24).

[34] *HE* 2,23,18 (Schwartz 170,23–24).

here.[35] The readers of the *History* are not left in any doubt as to Eusebius' intention behind this editorial amendment, since he adds a comment which highlights the significance of the rejection of the Christian Message in the person of James the Just: "... the (more) perceptive Jews also considered this (crime) to be the cause of the siege of Jerusalem immediately after his martyrdom."[36] The theological importance of the siege of Jerusalem lies in the destruction of the city and the Temple which eventually followed it and which sealed the end of her role in Salvation History: by murdering James, the Jews rejected the last offer of grace by God and their penalty was the end of Jerusalem itself.[37]

Book 2 concludes with a summary sketch of the "catastrophe which overcame the Jewish race" especially in Jerusalem.[38] The full portrayal of that horrific event—mostly drawn from Josephus—is reserved for Book 3, where the destruction of Jerusalem and the Jewish Race form the background to the second stage of the Apostolic Age. There in Book 3, Rome moves to the center of the stage; her importance is determined by her relationship to the other major personality to feature in Book 2: St. Peter.

b) The Divine Dispensation regarding St. Peter

The universal mission of the Church is presented by Eusebius as starting not with Pentecost (which is not even mentioned) but with the conversion of Cornelius by St. Peter at Palestinian Caesarea (Acts 10),[39] which moment is synchronized with the giving of the

---

[35]   This suggestion of Schwartz is reported by Lawlor, *Eusebiana*, 32, footnote 1 (who gives no further reference to his source). Lawlor admits that there is force to Schwartz's remark that "this and the preceding sentences are alternative endings to the narrative, both of which cannot have stood in the original text." The date of James' death is generally accepted as 61–62 (cf. Lietzmann, *Geschichte*, bd. I, 185), whereas the siege of Jerusalem by Titus and Vespasian began in March 68 (cf. Beer, "Jerusalem," in *PWK* IX, col. 951). The synchronism of Eusebius is intended to highlight the *causal* connection between both events.

[36]   *HE* 2,23,19 (Schwartz 172,3–5). Eusebius supports his contention by quoting a spurious text of Josephus (*HE* 2,23,20 = Schwartz 172,9–11).

[37]   Cf. Eusebius' exegesis of Ps 106,33–34 (*LXX*) in the *Demonstratio* 6,7,5 (Heikel 257,31–258,2). The causal connection between the siege and final destruction of Jerusalem and the rejection of the final offer of grace to the Jews (as personified in the person of James the Just and his history) is expressly formulated in Book 3 (cf. *HE* 3,7,7–9 = Schwartz 214,6–23).

[38]   HE 2,26,1–2 (Schwartz 178,16–180,9).

[39]   ἀλλὰ γὰρ τῆς χάριστος ἤδη τῆς θείας καὶ ἐπὶ τὰ λοιπὰ χεομένης ἔθνη καὶ πρώτου μὲν κατὰ τὴν Παλαιστίνων Καισάρειαν Κορνηλίου σὺν ὅλῳ τῷ οἴκῳ δι' ἐπιφανείας θειοτέρας ὑπουργίας τε Πέτρου τὴν εἰς Χριστόν πίστιν

name "Christian" to the followers of Christ at Antioch.[40] In the build-up of
the narrative to this point, the author, following Acts 8,1, had emphasized
that even though all the disciples, with the exception of the Twelve,[41] were
scattered throughout Judea and Samaria after the martyrdom of Stephen
and the first persecution of the Church in Jerusalem, yet they did not dare
"to transmit the message of faith to the Gentiles, but announced it to the
Jews alone."[42] The world mission, then, was reserved to the Twelve (= the
Apostles) and to a special divine initiative which came when the time was
ripe.[43] This moment occurred when Paul was called to become an Apostle[44]
and divine Providence had arranged for the peaceful conditions within
the empire, which for Eusebius were essential for the spread of the Gospel
throughout the world.[45]

καταδεξαμένου πλείστων τε καὶ ἄλλων ἐπ' Ἀντιοχείας Ἑλλήνων, οἷς οἱ κατὰ τὸν
Στεφάνου διωγμὸν διασπαρέντες ἐκήρυξαν, ἀνθούσης ἄρτι καὶ πληθυούσης τῆς
κατὰ Ἀντιόχειαν ἐκκλησίας ἐν ταὐτῷ τε ἐπιπαρόντων πλείστων ὅσων τῶν τε ἀπὸ
Ἱεροσολύμων προφητῶν καὶ σὺν αὐτοῖς Βαρναβᾶ καὶ Παύλου ἑτέρου τε πλήθους ἐπὶ
τούτοις ἀδελφῶν, ἡ Χριστιανῶν προσηγορία τότε πρῶτον αὐτόθι ὥσπερ ἀπ' εὐθαλοῦς
καὶ γονίμου πηγῆς ἀναδίδοται (HE 2,3,3 = Schwartz 112,29–114,9).

[40] This synchronism is not to be found in the account given in Acts 11,26. Regarding
the significance of the term Χριστιανοί, see Schelkle, "Jerusalem und Rom," 133.

[41] Acts 8,1 simply reads "apostles."

[42] HE 2,1,8 (Schwartz 106,13–14).

[43] Apparently the conversion of the Ethiopian officer, "who was the *first* of the
Gentiles to receive the mysteries of the Divine Word from Philip by means of
a revelation, and who, becoming the *first-fruits* of the faithful throughout the
world, was the *first* to preach the Gospel on returning to his native land ..." (HE
2,1,13 = Schwartz 108,10–19), was either considered, by Eusebius, to be due to
an exceptional intervention (thus using the term οἰκονομία in this context not to
mean the Divine Dispensation concerning Salvation History but in its secondary
sense, cf. footnote 49) or was inserted by him at a later stage, since it contradicts
the earlier statement in HE 2,1,8, which states that the disciples were afraid to
hand on the Faith to the Gentiles, and the later statement in HE 2,3,3, which
informs the reader that Cornelius was the first (of the Gentiles) to have received
the Faith. It is also of note that the verse immediately following the description
of the Ethiopian's conversion, i.e., HE 2,1,14, might indicate that its context had
been tampered with: the verse begins with ἐπὶ τούτοις, which can only be related
with great difficulty—if at all—to the preceding sentence.

[44] HE 2,1,14 (Schwartz 108,19–24).

[45] Here Eusebius uses the account of Tertullian, who relates how Pilate reported
the death and the Resurrection of the Lord to the Emperor Tiberius, who is said
to have believed it (*Apol.* 5). Eusebius sees in this the hand of Providence, who
created the peaceful conditions which he considered to be necessary for the initial
mission of the Church to the world (HE 2,2,1–6). This is Eusebius' first allusion
to the *Pax Romana*, the (theological) significance of which he will later develop
(see below, pp. 170–173).

Then, we are told, the Scriptures were fulfilled: the voice of the inspired evangelists and Apostles went forth "to the whole earth and their words to the end of the world"[46] when the Mission to the Gentiles was inaugurated by "a divine manifestation, the ministration of Peter."[47]

After killing the other James (the brother of John), Herod arrested Peter with the intention of getting rid of him in a similar manner: this at least is how Eusebius interprets Acts 12,2f. The death of Peter, we are reminded, was prevented by a divine intervention (διὰ θείας ἐπιφανίας) to which he adds: "These things are part of the dispensation (οἰκονομία) concerning Peter."[48] The use of the term οἰκονομία, which Eusebius will later reserve almost as a terminus technicus for the relationship of the Divine Logos to mankind,[49] is here applied to Peter's role in Salvation History; this highlights the importance Peter plays in Eusebius' understanding of the origins of the universal Church. The term conveys the implication that Peter was singled out to become a special instrument of God to continue the work of the Incarnate Logos according to his special function in God's plan of Salvation. As the Instrument of God, then, Peter inaugurated the universal mission of the Church, whose inauguration was itself seen as a divine "epiphany."

Likewise, the text we are considering implies that it is not for Herod to decide the fate of Peter, as indeed he did with regard to James, the brother of John, and so Peter is released from prison through a divine intervention. But, Eusebius adds, these things are but *part* of the Divine Dispensation concerning Peter. This terse sentence is inserted into the narrative, it seems, because Eusebius, who now goes on to describe in greater detail the special mission of Peter to found the Church, recognizes that, after his miraculous release from prison, Peter vanishes from Eusebius' main source up to now, the Acts, apart from one other appearance in connection with the Council of Jerusalem.[50] In other words, Eusebius is saying: what is

---

[46] *HE* 2,3,1b (Schwartz 112,15–18).

[47] *HE* 2,3,3 (Schwartz 114,1–2).

[48] *HE* 2,9,4 (Schwartz 126,5–6).

[49] See above, p. 35. See also *HE* 6,11,1 (Schwartz 540,23), *De mart. Pal.* 11 (Schwartz 945,11), where on the other hand Eusebius uses the term in a secondary, less technical sense of any exceptional intervention of God. However, it would seem that in the clause we are now considering (καὶ τὰ μὲν κατὰ Πέτρον οὕτως εἶχεν οἰκονομίας, *HE* 2,9,4), the term is used in its primary sense and is properly translated as "the Divine Dispensation."

[50] It is of note that in Eusebius' description of the so-called Council of Jerusalem (*HE* 2,12,2–3 = Schwartz 132,9–16), St. Peter is not mentioned.

written in the *Acts* is not the whole story about Peter and his special function in God's Plan of Salvation.

c) Rome as the Place of Confrontation between Simon Peter and Simon Magus

At this stage we must give some attention to the third main character of Book 2: Simon Magus, who, as Eusebius maintains following an earlier tradition, "was the Founder (ἀρχηγός) of all heresy."[51] In the foregoing narrative the role of Peter in the world mission of the Church was contrasted with the specific mission of James to Israel.[52] Simon Magus is now opposed to Simon Peter in order to illustrate the second Petrine function, which is the perception and repudiation of heresy. The theme was already introduced at the very opening of Book 2, where the conversion of Simon Magus by Philip the Deacon was briefly mentioned (Acts 8,9–13).[53] Eusebius warned us there that Simon only simulated Faith—which is the practice of most heresiarchs, many of whom were detected in their wickedness and driven out (of the Church) just as Simon Magus, their progenitor, "was detected for what he was by Peter."[54] Heresy is for Eusebius one of the marks of the post-Apostolic age. In his highly idealized picture of the Apostolic Period, he sees the presence of the Apostles as itself a guarantee against the possibility of error entering the Church.[55] Peter, who is said to be the spokesman, and, as such, Leader of the Apostles,[56] is now depicted as confronting and detecting the father and creator of all heresy (πατὴρ καὶ δημιουργός).[57] Of further significance is the location of the decisive confrontation between the Leader (προήγορος) of the Apostles and the Founder (ἀρχηγός) of all heresy: Rome.

---

[51] *HE* 2,13,6 (Schwartz 136,8); see also *HE* 2,14,1 (Schwartz 136,24f.).

[52] The Pauline claim that Peter was divinely appointed Apostle to the Jews and he himself sent as the Apostle to the Gentiles (Gal 2,8) is here passed over in silence. But in Book 3, these two missions are alluded to in *HE* 3,1,2–3 (Schwartz 188,5–12).

[53] *HE* 2,1,10–12 (Schwartz 106,17–108,10). In this passage, Eusebius gives us his most concise description of the nature of heresy (*HE* 2,1,12).

[54] *HE* 2,1,12 (Schwartz 108,8–10).

[55] Cf. *HE* 2,14,2–3 (Schwartz 138,3–11).

[56] Cf, *HE* 2,14,6 (Schwartz 138,23). The term προήγορος conveys both the nuance of "spokesman" and "leader" (see Liddell-Scott, *Lexicon*, 1283). Katzenmayer, "Petrus und der Primat," 159, ignores the nuance of "leader" and does not do full justice to the concept of "spokesman"; see below, pp. 54–55, 65[144], 80.

[57] *HE* 2,14,1 (Schwartz 136,24–25). Irenaeus describes Simon Magus as one "from whom all sorts of heresies derive their origin" [*Adv. haer.* 1,23,2 = *ANL* transl.) but Eusebius considers Simon as the originator of *all* heresy. See article on "Simon Magus" by Lietzmann in *PWK*[2] III, A. 1., col. 180–184.

The origin of the tradition which connected Simon Magus with Rome seems to be the mistaken understanding of *Justin Martyr* (ca. 100—ca. 165) that the inscription on a statue erected between two bridges on the River Tiber and containing the words "Simon Deo Sancto" referred to Simon Magus, from which he concluded that Simon had been honored as a god.[58] But it is generally considered that the inscription probably belonged to a statue of the Sabine deity Semo Sancus.[59] When Justin made that comment, it is unlikely that there was a tradition in existence which connected Simon with Rome,[60] not to mention any meeting between the Magician and Peter. But in the *Acts of Peter*, composed about 200–225,[61] if not earlier,[62] we find a full-blown legend which not only connects Simon with Rome and provides a history of the statue to Simon,[63] but also describes an eventful encounter there between Simon Magus and Peter and the dramatic sequel to that meeting. On the other hand, Irenaeus, writing around the same time, displays no such knowledge when he treats of the history of Simon and his teaching.[64] The Bishop of Lyons, after recounting the story of Acts 8,9–23 which included the account of the original meeting between Peter and Simon in Samaria, simply repeats the information supplied by Justin. Hippolytus, even though he is evidently using Irenaeus as his source,[65] betrays some knowledge of the legend found in the *Acts of Peter*, since he refers to Simon's activities in Rome where he confronted the Apostles and was in turn opposed by Peter.[66] Later apocryphal literature, such as the *Clementine Homilies* and *Recognitions,* develops the debates between the two personages, but situates them in Palestinian Caesarea and not in Rome,[67] while the *Acts of Peter and Paul* (third century?) embellish the story of Simon's defeat by Peter in a show of (magical) strength and add an account of Simon Magus' death. *Arnobius,* writing a

---

[58] Justin, *Apol.* 1,26 (PG 6,368,A15).

[59] See Lietzmann, "Simon Magus," PWK2 III, A. 1., col. 181. See also the article on "Simon Magus" by Salmon, DCB, vol. IV (681–688), 682.

[60] O'Connor, *Peter in Rome*, 26. See, however, below footnote 72.

[61] O'Connor, *Peter in Rome*, 35f.

[62] Cf. Quasten, *Patrology* I, 133.

[63] See Ch. 10 of the *Vercelli Acts* (James, The Apocryphal New Testament, 313–314).

[64] Cf. *Adv. haer.* 1,23,1–4.

[65] O'Connor, *Peter in Rome*, 26, maintains that Hippolytus was dependent on Justin. Regarding the dependence of Hippolytus on Irenaeus, see Lietzmann, "Simon Magus," col. 180.

[66] Hippolytus, *Philosophumena*, 6,20,2 (Wendland 148,8–13).

[67] *Hom.* γ,29,1f. (Rehm 67,9f.), *Recog.* 2,1,1f. (Rehm 51,1f.).

little later than Eusebius, retains traces of a legend similar to that found in the *Acts of Peter and Paul.*[68]

Eusebius could not have known Arnobius' work and probably only knew the forerunners of the extant pseudo-Clementine writings, which he dismisses as verbose.[69] Since he fails to mention the *Philosophumena* (which contains a brief, colorless reference to the encounter between Peter and Simon Magus at Rome) in his list of the works of Hippolytus, we must conclude that it was unknown to him.[70] Even if he did know of the *Acts of Peter and Paul,* he certainly made no use of its extraordinary tale. He himself acknowledges Justin and Irenaeus alone as having provided him with information for his account, but neither of these, as we mentioned above, actually described a meeting between Simon and Peter, apart from the original encounter in Samaria.

Eusebius knew the *Acts of Peter* and pronounced them to be valueless, since they were used by none of the (ancient) "ecclesiastical" authorities.[71] But nonetheless Eusebius' comparatively sober account of Simon's journey to Rome, his activities there, together with Peter's divine mission to follow him to Rome and to counteract the Magician's activities, follow the broad outline of the story found in the *Acts of Peter.*[72] Eusebius even repeats the minor mistake of the *Acts of Peter* where he refers to the original encounter between Simon Magus and Peter as having taken place in "Judaea."[73] It appears therefore, that, even though he makes no reference to his source, Eusebius probably took the main outline of his own account of Peter's meeting with Simon Magus in Rome from the *Acts of Peter.* But even without considering the *Acts of Peter,* it is evident that the popular imagination at the time of Eusebius had been caught by the tales of Peter's show of strength over that of the Magician, some of which were said to have taken place at Rome. Eusebius reduces the story to the bare essentials and returns to the sources of the tradition, Justin and Irenaeus, in order to underpin it with respectable authorities. He also draws his own inferences—and it is these which are of interest to this present study.

[68] Arnobius, *Adv. Gentes* 2,12 (*PL* 5,828, B2–4).
[69] Cf. *HE* 3,38,5 (Schwartz 284,18).
[70] Cf. *HE* 6,22,1 (Schwartz 568,13–21).
[71] Cf. *HE* 3,3,2 (Schwartz 190,1–6).
[72] According to Peterson, *Frühkirche, Judentum und Gnosis*, 22, the Acts may be dated ca. 150. Quasten, *Patrology* I, 133, suggests around ca. 190.
[73] Compare *HE* 2,14,4 (Schwartz 138,13) with *Acta Petri* 5 (Vouaux 254). It is perhaps a little too pedantic to describe this as an error, since both could have had the Roman province of Judea (which included Samaria) in mind.

The encounter between Peter and Simon at Rome is depicted by Eusebius as the ultimate consequence of the original meeting in "Judaea:" "Immediately the above-mentioned sorcerer was detected by the Apostle Peter, as though the eyes of his mind (= his conscience) had been struck by a divine and wonderful blaze of light at the time when he was previously acting wickedly against them (= the Apostles) in Judaea, he set off on a long journey overseas and fled from the East to the West, thinking that only in this way could he live according to his mistaken judgement."[74] The adverb which opens this sentence, αὐτίκα, with its apparent chronological implications, has puzzled commentators,[75] yet the difficulty disappears once one recognizes the particular type of "historical" narrative we are dealing with, which is more interested in trying to convey the significance of an event rather than establish chronological exactitude. "Immediately" here stands for "consequently" since Eusebius wishes to link the commonly accepted tradition regarding Simon's visit to Rome (including the more recent apocryphal tradition of the confrontation between him and Peter) with the well-attested "detection" by Peter in "Judaea" as though there were a causal connection between both.[76]

In his "introduction" to the narrative description of the actual encounter, Eusebius had already sketched the salvific-historical significance of Simon's journey to the capital: Simon is but an instrument in the hands of the "enemy of man's salvation" who, "when the Faith in Our Savior and Lord Jesus Christ was already being handed on to all men, devised to capture the imperial city in advance and (so) guided the above-mentioned Simon there. . . ."[77] With this statement we are introduced, for the first time in the *History,* to the import of Rome within the universal mission of the Church[78] in contrast with Jerusalem and the mission to the original People of God, the Jews. The nature of Rome's significance within the History of Salvation is not clarified at this stage; only the *fact* that Rome's destiny is intrinsically linked with the Church's universal

---

74 *HE* 2,14,4 (Schwartz 138,11—16).
75 McGiffert, *Eusebius*, LNPF[2], 115, footnote 4, who describes the significance of the word "immediately" as "somewhat dark." He posits, unnecessarily it seems, an unknown source used by Eusebius that recounted another encounter between Peter and Simon Magus.
76 Note also the recurrence of certain *motifs* in both the Judean encounter between the two personages and their meeting in Rome, such as the theme of "light."
77 *HE* 2,13,1 (Schwartz 132,17–22).
78 Note the emphasis on the Faith being handed on "to all men" (*HE* 2,13,1 = Schwartz 132,18).

mission is affirmed, while Rome's association with heresy and error, as well as her being the center of the world which is to be converted to Christ, are faintly adumbrated. It is Peter's presence in the city which will determine the precise character of Rome's significance.[79]

Simon, though he did achieve some initial success, was not to prosper for long,[80] since "close on his heels in the same reign of Claudius, Providence, all good and benign towards the universe, guided to Rome, as towards a gigantic destroyer of life, that valiant and great one of the Apostles, Peter, who due to his virtue was leader of all the other [Apostles]; he who, shielded in divine armor for such matters like some noble General of God, brought the precious merchandise of spiritual light from the East to those in the West, proclaiming the Kingdom of Heaven, Light itself and the Saving Word for souls."[81]

The rhetorical style of this passage, which contrasts strikingly with the prosaic narrative otherwise employed, indicates the importance which Eusebius himself attached to Peter's presence in Rome, an importance which the passage explicitly affirms. The earlier reference to the special Divine Dispensation (οἰκονομία) concerning Peter,[82] which had in part been manifested in Peter's function to inaugurate the Gentile (or world) mission of the Church,[83] is now seen to be intrinsically linked with the city of Rome. The contours of that dispensation are likewise brought more sharply into focus. We have seen how Peter, the chosen instrument of God, inaugurated the world mission—that is to say, Peter was primarily responsible for the 'foundation' of the Church, since Church and Mission are identical for Eusebius; the interpretation corresponds to Eusebius' concept of Peter's primacy among the Apostles, whose office or function is to found the Church. In this text, Peter's unique office as Leader of the Apostles is further delineated: the term chosen by Eusebius to describe this leadership is προήγορος which is inadequately translated by the English terms: spokesman, advocate, or defender. The Latin version of Rufinus reads: . . . probatissimum omnium apostolorum et maximum fidei magnificentia et virtutis merito primorum principem Petrum. . . . Thus, Peter is not understood to be merely one of the Apostles, but rather occupies an

---

[79] Regarding St. Peter's actual presence in Rome, see the extensive study by O'Connor, *Peter in Rome*, New York and London, 1969.

[80] *HE* 2,14,5 (Schwartz 138,16–20); see Farina, *L'impero*, 138.

[81] *HE* 2,14,6 (Schwartz 138,20–28).

[82] *HE* 2,9,4 (Schwartz 126,6).

[83] *HE* 2,3,3 (Schwartz 114,2).

unique position within the Apostolic College as the mouthpiece of all—an allusion, possibly, to Mt 16,16–18—and, as such, Leader of the Apostles. Using the *motifs* of Light and Darkness, the Leader of the Apostles dispels the darkness of error through the light of the Gospel which he proclaims.[84] Not only does the author draw our attention to the fact that Peter's journey to Rome was due to the Divine Guidance, but he also wishes to stress that it was part of the *universal* plan of Providence. This Eusebius achieves both by his use of the adjectival phrase "all good and benign towards the *universe*" to qualify the substantive "Providence," and by his description of Peter's mission which brought him to Rome as a journey "from the East to . . . the West," i.e., a mission that encompassed the whole world.[85]

We can therefore conclude that Rome's theological significance has a positive as well as a negative aspect. The positive aspect is inextricably bound up with the universal plan of Providence to bring Light to the world and Peter's central role in that plan, while the negative aspect introduced by Simon Magus (and later elaborated with reference to the Emperor Nero) sees Rome as the center of the κόσμος where the darkness of error reigns supreme. Rome is consequently described as "a gigantic destroyer of life."[86] Since this is not simply the known world[87] but the unredeemed "world," as distinct from the redeemed, Eusebius, within the same context, reminds his readers that Peter himself referred to the city "more figuratively as Babylon, in the words, 'the elect one in Babylon greets you . . .' (1 Pet 5,13)."[88]

There is a clear parallelism between the text which describes how Simon Magus was guided to the capital by "the enemy of man's

---

[84] Compare the text *HE* 2,14,6 (Schwartz 138,26–27) regarding St. Peter with the text *HE* 2,14,3 (Schwartz 138,9) regarding the Apostles, noting in particular the use of the related concepts of φῶς and φέγγος.

[85] So too in the parallel passages regarding Simon Magus, Eusebius also indicates the universal significance of his appearance through his reference to the fact that when Simon entered the stage of Salvation History, the Faith was being handed on "to all men" (*HE* 2,13,1 = Schwartz 132,18), and through his description of his flight to Rome in terms of journeying from the East to the West (cf. *HE* 2,14,4 = Schwartz 138,15).

[86] . . . ἐπὶ τὴν Ῥώμην ὡς ἐπὶ τηλικοῦτον λυμεῶνα βίου . . . (*HE* 2,14,6 = Schwartz 138,24).

[87] Eusebius later reminds his readers that the Roman Empire is not the whole world (*HE* 3,8,10–11 = Schwartz 220,3–13).

[88] *HE* 2,15,2 (Schwartz 140,17–19). "Tatsächlich konnte das politische Rom im Bewußtsein der frühen Christenheit gar nichts anderes sein als der Hauptsitz heidnischer Greuel und die Quelle furchtbarer Drangsale. Die römische Gemeinde befand sich gleichsam 'in der Höhle des Löwen'" (Grotz, "Die Stellung der römischen Kirche," 15).

salvation," and that which portrays the guidance of Peter to Rome by the all good and benign Providence. This parallelism gives the double event a very definite emphasis. To proclaim the Good News is the principal means by which the Apostles founded the Church[89] and so it is not surprising that this theme is awarded due attention in the text which deals with Peter's journey to Rome and the purpose of his mission there: "(to bring) the precious merchandise of spiritual light from the East to those in the West, proclaiming the Kingdom of Heaven, Light itself and the Saving Word for souls." The parallelism which provides the immediate context for this theme of founding the Church in the West, as the climax of the chief apostle's mission to found the Church Universal, lends to the theme itself a very specific and important nuance. This parallelism expresses a causal connection between Peter's journey to Rome and Simon's previous flight to the capital, and so draws the reader's attention to the negative side of the Apostolic commission, which is to destroy error, here blankly equated with heresy. Such is the meaning of the confrontation in Rome between the Leader of the Apostles and the Founder of all Heresies, which had been "prototypically"—and in a sense causally—enacted in "Judaea" when Peter first detected the hidden error of Simon Magus.

We mentioned earlier how in the *History,* Eusebius' purpose behind his portrayal of the origins, both of the Church in general and the individual Churches, is to demonstrate how their present character was and is essentially determined by those very origins. It was pointed out how the divine character of the Church emanated from her origin in the preexistent Divine Logos, and how the peculiar position held by the Church of Jerusalem at the turn of the fourth century was a consequence of her origin in James the Brother of the Lord and the end of Jerusalem's significance within Salvation History. If the same is true with regard to Rome, then it must follow that the generally recognized position of the Church of Rome at the end of the third and the beginning of the fourth century must necessarily correspond to her origins as described by Eusebius. In other words, the office of the Bishop and Church of Rome must correspond to the functions of Peter and Rome in the universal Plan of Salvation, which were, respectively, to detect and repudiate error and to be the center of the new dispensation, i.e., the mission of the Church to bring the Light of the Gospel to the unredeemed world.

---

[89]   Cf. Irenaeus, *Adv. haer.* 3,1,1 (quoted in *HE* 5,8,2 = Schwartz 444,1), who seems to equate "evangelization" with the "foundation" of the Church.

d) Peter's Association with Alexandria through St. Mark and Philo

The power of Simon having been destroyed by the Divine Word, Eusebius continues his story: the hearers of Peter were not satisfied with "the unwritten teaching of the divine kerygma" but beseeched Mark, Peter's disciple, for a written account, thus occasioning the Gospel according to Mark.[90] That Mark, the author of the Gospel of the same name, was Peter's disciple and interpreter is the venerable tradition of the early Church.[91] What interests us in Eusebius' presentation of this tradition are his own embellishments on the tradition and the reason why he recalls it at this stage of the narrative.[92] Before we examine Eusebius' highly individual version, we can immediately suggest the reason for his interest in the tradition at this particular point: the reason seems to be linked with the story of the Alexandrian Church's origins related in the chapter immediately following,[93] which we will now briefly consider.

Alone in terms of the renown she enjoyed within the realm of ecclesiastical learning and Christian asceticism, the Church of Alexandria was perhaps the most distinguished of all Churches at the end of the third century. Yet it could claim no apostle as its founder. Only from the fourth century on, do we find reference to the tradition that Mark was the "founder" of that Church.[94] Eusebius, the earliest witness, does not refer to any written source for his contention that Mark "founded" the Church of Alexandria but instead

---

[90] *HE* 2,15,1–2 (Schwartz 138,28–140,19).

[91] See Papias (= Eusebius *HE* 3,39,15 = Schwartz 290,21–292,2); Irenaeus, *Adv. haer.* 3,1,1 (Rousseau-Doutreleau 217); Tertullian, *Adv. Marc.* 4,5 (CSEL XXXVII, 431,7); Clement of Alexandria, *Hypotyposes* (= Eusebius *HE* 6,14, 6–7 = Schwartz 550,24–25); Origen, *Comm. in Matt.* (= Eusebius *HE* 6,25,5 = Schwartz 576,11–15).

[92] As could be gathered from the previous note, Eusebius repeats the tradition in *HE* 3,39,15, where he quotes the version of Papias within the "natural" context of the story, namely the discussion concerning the canon of the New Testament. The versions of Irenaeus, Clement, and Origen are quoted in contexts where the story is not immediately relevant, unless it serves to remind the reader of the Peter-Mark relationship, which, as we will see, is in a sense prototypical of the relationship between the Apostolic Authority and the orthodox writers.

[93] *HE* 2,16,1–2 (Schwartz 140,20–142,1).

[94] Cf. Epiphanius, *Panarion* 51,6,10 (Holl, vol. II, 256,3–6); Damasus (= Mansi, vol. VIII, 159; cf. Grotz, *Die Hauptkirchen*, 15–16); Jerome, *De vir. ill.*, 8 (*PL* 23,621,B10–15). Against the impressive number of eminent scholars such as H. M. Gwatkin and H. I. Bell who have denied the reliability of this report, C. M. Lee tried to defend the historicity of the tradition in his spirited paper delivered to the Sixth International Patristic Conference at Oxford, 1971 (see Lee, "Eusebius on St. Mark," 422–431). See also the contribution of Trevijano to the same event (Trevijano, "Church of Alexandria," 471–477).

prefaces the story with φασί, which, for Eusebius, generally indicates an oral tradition or unwritten source.[95] In common with his contemporaries, Eusebius was concerned to explain the theological basis of Alexandria's recognized eminence. From the various traditions concerning the Alexandrian Church's Apostolic associations at his disposal, Eusebius could have mentioned those which connected either Barnabas and/or Luke with Alexandria.[96] But these he ignores and attributes the foundation of the Church of Alexandria exclusively to Mark, the disciple of Peter.[97] The key to understanding this choice is to be found in his editorial embellishments on the sources he uses for his version of the tradition concerning the relationship between Peter and Mark in Rome, as well as the way he links that relationship with the tradition which attributed the foundation of the Church of Alexandria to St. Mark.

In the course of the *History,* Eusebius includes quotations from the works of Papias, Irenaeus of Lyons, Clement of Alexandria, and Origen, which could have provided him with source material for his version of the formation of Mark's Gospel at Rome. According to St. Irenaeus, we are informed that *after the death of Peter and Paul,*[98] Mark, the disciple and interpreter of Peter, having written what was preached by Peter, handed it on to us.[99] Since Eusebius unambiguously asserts that Mark wrote his Gospel *during the lifetime of Peter,* then he either did not consult Irenaeus at the time, or, more likely, knowing of Irenaeus' version, he chose to ignore it in favor of Papias and Clement.

Neither did Eusebius adopt the version of Origen, who asserted that Mark composed his Gospel on the instruction of St. Peter.[100] According to Eusebius, it was the *hearers* of Peter who requested Mark for a written account of Peter's proclamation.[101] Eusebius himself expressly acknowledges the accounts given by Papias and

---

[95] See Lawlor, *Eusebiana*, 36.

[96] For details, see Grotz, *Die Hauptkirchen*, 25–26.

[97] Referring to the report of *HE* 2,16,1 that Mark had founded the Church of Alexandria, Grotz, *Die Hauptkirchen*, 27, comments: "Der Zusammenhang dieses Zeugnisses mit noch früheren, die von Gächter (Summa introductionis in Novum Testamentum, Innsbruck, 1938, 78ff.) angefügt werden, spricht durchaus für die Zuverlässigkeit dieser Aussage, wenn sie auch relativ spät und keineswegs kategorisch ist." (I have been unable to check Gächter.)

[98] μετὰ δὲ τὴν τούτων ἔξοδον: according to Rousseau-Doutreleau, "Notes justificatives" (*SC* 210, p. 217), ἔξοδος here refers to the death of the two Apostles; for a similar use of the term, cf. *HE* 5,1,36 (Schwartz 416,13) and *HE* 5,1,55 (Schwartz 424,9).

[99] *HE* 5,8,2–3 (Schwartz 443,26–444,3).

[100] Cf. Origen, *Comm. in Matt.* = *HE* 6,25,5 (Schwartz 576,11–15).

[101] Cf. *HE* 2,15,1 (Schwartz 140,5–10).

Clement of Alexandria.[102] Papias, in his prosaic style, merely records that Mark, who neither heard nor followed the Lord, followed Peter, noting down the latter's occasional discourses.[103] Clement of Alexandria adds to this the information that Peter proclaimed the Gospel in Rome "by the spirit" (πνεύματι) and that it was the hearers of Peter who took the initiative to persuade Mark to give Peter's proclamation its written form.[104] Even though it appears that Eusebius followed Clement more closely than Papias, yet he differs from the Alexandrian writer at one significant point. According to Clement, "On discovering this (i.e., how Mark had committed his discourses to writing), Peter neither strongly prevented it nor did he encourage it."[105] But Eusebius changes this to read: "And they say that the Apostle, knowing *by a revelation of the Spirit* what had been done, was pleased with the people's zeal and *gave his sanction* for the Scripture to be read in the Churches."[106] This version of Eusebius is introduced by the verb φασί, which for Eusebius generally indicates an oral tradition, as we have seen.[107] At face value, however, in this instance it looks more like an editorial recasting of his written source, Clement.[108]

The intention of our author is clear: he wishes to illustrate two aspects of Peter's divinely appointed function. In line with the presentation of all his other activities in Book 2, Peter is first of all portrayed as being directly inspired by God: ἀποκαλύψαντος αὐτῷ τοῦ πνεύματος. Secondly, whereas, up to now, the narrative had been largely determined by Peter's opposition to Simon Magus, thus highlighting the Petrine office of detecting and condemning heresy, here, that function is given its *positive* expression in the recognition and official approbation of Mark's Gospel to be read in the Churches—i.e., coarsely expressed, giving Peter's authority to Mark's orthodoxy. The authority of Mark's Gospel is not, according to Eusebius, derived from the written notes of Peter's sermons, nor from any personal genius of Mark,[109] but from the *sanction*

---

[102] Cf. *HE* 2,15,2 (Schwartz 140,13–15).

[103] Cf. *HE* 3,39,15–16 (Schwartz 290,21–292,4).

[104] Cf. *HE* 6,14,6–7 (Schwartz 550,19–28).

[105] *HE* 6,14,7 (Schwartz 550,24–25).

[106] *HE* 2,15,2 (Schwartz 140,10–13).

[107] See above, p. 58.

[108] It is possible that Eusebius here betrays the influence of Origen's version (see footnote 100 above).

[109] Indeed, Mark is seen as a very passive instrument: the hearers of Peter take the *initiative* to have Peter's sermons committed to writing; the *content* of his Gospel is composed of Peter's discourses; and it is Peter who gives the finished work its final *authority*.

(κυρῶσαί) of Peter. This then seems, first of all, to reflect at least the general recognition of the Bishop and Church of Rome at the end of the third century as the principal authority with regard to orthodoxy, an attitude which will be reflected in Books 4–7. Here, Eusebius wishes to stress that such is not due to the natural genius or political importance of Rome, but due solely to Divine "Inspiration." With that, however, the nuances of this passage have not been exhausted.

The close relationship between Peter and his disciple, Mark, already portrayed in the account of the origin of Mark's Gospel, is again underlined by Eusebius when he brings that narrative to a close with a reference to 1 Pet 5,13, where Peter greets Mark.[110] This leads on to the oral tradition (= φασίν), according to which Mark is said to have been the first to evangelize in Egypt, proclaiming the Gospel he had previously committed to writing (= the proclamation of Peter), and the first to organize the Church in Alexandria itself.[111] The success of Mark's mission in Alexandria was such that Philo, we are told, who was so impressed by the very zealous and phil-osophic asceticism of the first Christians there, decided to write about their way of life.[112] The narrative continues with the surprising piece of informa-tion Eusebius springs on his readers, quoting an unnamed written source (λόγος ἔχει), to the effect that "at the time of Claudius, Philo travelled to Rome in order to converse with Peter, who was preaching to the inhabi-tants there."[113] Then follows a description of Philo's *De vita contemplativa*, or rather an account of "life in the early Church" as found therein,[114] and an excursus on the literary activity of that writer, who had such a profound influence on the theological tradition of the Church of Alexandria.[115]

What is most striking about this presentation of the Alexandrian Church's origins, is the way Eusebius loses no opportunity to draw attention to the influence of Peter on those origins. Mark, the founder of the Church there, enjoyed a special relationship with

---

[110] Cf. *HE* 2,15,2 (Schwartz 140,15–19).

[111] Cf. *HE* 2,16,1 (Schwartz 140,20–22). Note the insistence of Eusebius that Mark was the *first* to evangelize in Egypt and the *first* to organize the Church in Alexandria.

[112] Cf. *HE* 2,16,2 (Schwartz 140,23–142,1).

[113] *HE* 2,17,1 (Schwartz 142,1–2).

[114] Cf. *HE* 2,16,2–2,17,24 (Schwartz 140,23–152,22). Regarding the authenticity of this work, once hotly disputed, see the "Excursus on Authorship," by F. C. Conybeare in his edition of this work, Oxford, 1895, 258–358.

[115] See Wolfson, *Philo: Foundations of Religious Philosophy*, Cambridge/Mass., 1947.

St. Peter as his disciple and interpreter. The Gospel that Mark proclaims in Alexandria, on which the Church there is founded, is the Apostolic Teaching of Peter which he had previously recorded in writing. Philo, who represents the ancient, Alexandrian literary tradition, having decided to write about the philosophical asceticism and way of life of the early Christians he encountered in Alexandria, goes up to Rome to Peter, ostensibly for the most authoritative information, though this is left unsaid. There is in fact no record of any visit of Philo to Rome at the time of Claudius, and only one at the time of his predecessor, Gaius, when Philo led an embassy of Alexandrian Jews to the emperor.[116]

The reason for this preoccupation of Eusebius with the Petrine influence on the origins of the Alexandrian Succession, and in particular her literary tradition, can only be his "aetiological" interest in explaining the significance of that Church's special position within the universal Church at the end of the third and the beginning of the fourth century in terms of her origins. As the "oldest center of sacred science in the history of Christianity,"[117] her renown was more appreciated by Eusebius than by most. Indeed, he will later devote almost an entire book to the life and works of the greatest figure to have emerged in that tradition, his hero Origen, and presents the events which fill the pages of another book through the writings of Origen's most renowned pupil, Dionysius of Alexandria. This tradition, we are told in so many words, has its roots in the preaching of Mark, the interpreter of Peter. The relationship of Mark to Peter can therefore be understood as the prototype of the later association between the Churches of Alexandria and Rome. That relationship is between the *Apostolic Teaching of Peter* on the one hand, which Mark translated into its written form and which the succession of teachers at Alexandria hand on from one generation to the next, and the *Apostolic Authority of Peter* on the other, which sanctioned the literary product of Mark as the Petrine Successions at Rome guarantees the Apostolicity of the orthodox writers.[118] In the course of Books 4–7, we will see how this scheme of things affects Eusebius' presentation.

---

[116] Cf. Eusebius, *Chronicle*, 214. See Lawlor and Oulton, *The Ecclesiastical History,* vol. II, 62 and 67.

[117] Quasten, *Patrology* II, 2.

[118] See above, pp. 28–32, regarding Eusebius' concept of the Apostolic Succession being invested in two distinct offices, that of the holders of authority and that of the teachers.

e) St. Paul.

After the report of Peter's inauguration of the universal mission of the Church[119] and the description of its climax, the "foundation" of the Church at Rome[120] as the principal authority in matters of Faith,[121] and after the account of Mark's "foundation" of the Church of Alexandria,[122] the center of Christian piety[123] and learning,[124] Eusebius now turns his attention to Paul, The Apostle, for the first time since the brief reference to Paul's unique vocation.[125] His treatment of Paul is surprisingly condensed, consisting as it does of just one sentence in which he summarizes the mission journey of Paul "from Jerusalem to Illyricum."[126] Nevertheless it does manage to fit in a passing reference to the first known contact between Paul and the Church of Rome (i.e., his meeting Priscilla and Aquila—Acts 18,18). The text describes Paul's mission in general terms as ". . . consolidating the foundations of the Churches which had just been laid by him."

f) The End of Jerusalem's Function in Salvation History

The following three chapters are devoted to the portrayal of the gradual moral rot of Jerusalem leading to riots in the Temple,[127] faction fighting among the priests and their follow-ers,[128] the presence of criminals and murderers,[129] as well as an insurrection incited by some false prophet[130]—all prior to the martyrdom of

---

[119]   Cf. *HE* 2,3,3 (Schwartz 112,29–114,3).

[120]   Cf. *HE* 2,14,6 (Schwartz 138,20–28).

[121]   Cf. *HE* 2,14,4–2,15,2 (Schwartz 138,11–140,19).

[122]   Cf. *HE* 2,16,1 (Schwartz 140,20–22).

[123]   Cf. *HE* 2,16,2–2,17,24 (Schwartz 140,23–152,22).

[124]   Cf. *HE* 2,18,1–8 (Schwartz 152,23–156,19); see also *HE* 2,15,1 (Schwartz 140,3–10).

[125]   Cf. *HE* 2,1,14 (Schwartz 108,19–24). Considering this observation alone, it is difficult to see how Katzenmayer, "Petrus und der Primat," 157–158, could come to the following conclusion: "Überblickt man das Bild, welches der gelehrte Bischof von Caesarea von dem Urapostel in seiner Kirchengeschichte gezeichnet hat, kann man sich dem Urteil nicht entziehen, daß es recht dürftig ist. Es zeigt sich immer wieder, daß Petrus Paulus gegenüber in der "Überlieferung schlecht weggekommen ist" (p. 158). His statement about Eusebius' picture of St. Peter is all the more surprising in the light of the fact that he himself informs us that Peter is mentioned forty-four times in the course of the *History* (p. 157).

[126]   Cf. *HE* 2,18,9 (Schwartz 156,20–26). See Foakes-Jackson, *Eusebius Pamphili*, 67 and 72, who also observed this lack of attention to St. Paul.

[127]   Cf. *HE* 2,19,1–2 (Schwartz 158,1–12).

[128]   Cf. *HE* 2,20,1–3 (Schwartz 158,13–15; 21–26).

[129]   Cf. *HE* 2,20,1 (Schwartz 158,16–21); *HE* 2,20,4–6 (Schwartz 158,27–160,9).

[130]   Cf. *HE* 2,21,1–2 (Schwartz 160,10–21).

James the Just.[131] His martyrdom is the "symbolic" rejection by the Jews of the final offer of the message of Christ and thus the climax of the spiritual decay previously described. But before the description of James' martyrdom, one chapter is devoted to determining the date of Paul's death in Rome.[132] The topic is introduced through a reference to Felix the Governor, under whom the insurrection of "the false prophet from Egypt" took place, and his successor Festus, before whom Paul was put on trial and sent to Rome. Eusebius argues that Paul was not martyred at Rome on that occasion, as the silence at the end of Acts might suggest, but that, according to tradition, he preached the word of God in Rome for two whole years before he was again "dispatched"[133] on a ministry of proclamation, to return a second time to Rome and to martyrdom under Nero. This discussion could, without difficulty, have been reserved for the author's treatment of Paul's martyrdom at the end of Book 2. Eusebius is clearly anxious to remove any doubt as to the time of Paul's death—not for reasons of chronological exactitude alone, but also to draw attention to Rome's importance as the center of the world mission, where Paul labored for two years and from where he started out on further missions in comparison with the waning importance of Jerusalem.

The latter concern of Eusebius is latent in the way he compares the destinies of Paul and James the Just under Festus: reechoing the different destinies of Peter and the Apostle James under Herod, though not quite as vividly presented or theologically nuanced, Paul escapes to Rome but James is murdered.[134]

The murder of James the Just "resulted" (if we are to follow Eusebius' causal interpretation of the Divine Plan) in what would automatically lead to the definitive end of Jerusalem and its Temple as the focal point of the History of Salvation, namely the siege of the city by Vespasian. Book 2 concludes with a summary picture of the catastrophe which followed this siege,[135] but the gruesome story itself is reserved for Book 3 forming as it does the backdrop to the second stage of the Apostolic Age—its definitive completion. Rome, due primarily to her association with St. Peter, but also (though less clearly) with St. Paul, has begun to emerge as the new focal point, the center of the Church Universal and of her mission

---

[131] Cf. *HE* 2,23,1–25 (Schwartz 164,16–174,17).

[132] Cf. *HE* 2,22,1–8 (Schwartz 162,3–164,15).

[133] The passive form of the verb στείλασθαι (HE 2,22,2) is of note; it probably refers to God as the Divine Agent behind Paul's mission.

[134] Cf. *HE* 2,23,1 (Schwartz 164,16–20).

[135] Cf. *HE* 2,26,1–2 (Schwartz 178,16–180,9).

to the world. The martyrdom of Peter and Paul will make this new dispensation "definitive," as the rejection of James the Just marks the decisive end of Jerusalem and her role in Salvation History.

g) The Final Source of Rome's Authority within the Church: The Martyrdom of St. Peter and St. Paul

The Emperor Nero dominates this the final phrase of the Apostolic Age strictly so called. As Simon Magus was the Father and Founder of all Heresies, so too Nero is marked out as the "first of the Emperors who showed himself to be an enemy of the divine religion,"[136] and above all the "first fighter against God raised up to slay the Apostles."[137] In a concise but vivid manner, his depravity is sketched out[138] in such a way as to leave it clear to the reader that crowning all his evil was his enmity towards God, religion, and the Apostles—all three being considered almost synonymous in the present context. The rest of Eusebius' History will deal with the victory of the Church over the progeny of Simon Magus and the successors of the Emperor Nero who waged war against the faithful through various persecutions.[139] Consequently Nero, the first Enemy of God, is, according to Eusebius' scheme of things, attributed (with Simon Magus) a salvific-historical significance. It is as such that he is presented when he confronted Peter and Paul, whose martyrdom he caused.[140]

Again, we note how, as in the case of Simon Magus, the reader's attention is drawn to Rome as the place where the chief enemy of God and the chief Apostles were engaged in battle. By means of an editorial addition to a quotation from Tertullian—interpolated into the Greek translation—Eusebius reiterates the East-West theme of Peter and Simon Magus: Nero, we are told, was the first to persecute the Message at the time, when—having subdued the East (Eusebius' interpolation)—the Message was above all victorious in Rome.[141] The progress of the Christian Religion from the

---

[136] *HE* 2,25,3 (Schwartz 176,7–8).
[137] *HE* 2,25,5 (Schwartz 176,16–17).
[138] *HE* 2,25,1–4 (Schwartz 174,21–176,15).
[139] Thus Eusebius introduces Aim F (see above, p. 21 and p. 33).
[140] Cf. *HE* 2,25,5 (Schwartz 176,17–21).
[141] Cf. *HE* 2,25,4 (Schwartz 176,10–12). Here Eusebius quotes from Tertullian, *Apol.* 5,3 (Waltzing 13), which reads: "Consulite commentarios uestros, illic reperietis primum Neronem in hanc sectam cum maxime Romae orientem Caesariano gladio ferocisse." The translation found in the *History* renders the text as follows: ἐντύχετε τοῖς ὑπομνήμασιν ὑμῶν, ἐκεῖ εὑρήσετε πῶτον Νέρωνα τοῦτο τὸ δόγμα, ἡνίκα μάλιστα ἐν Ῥώμῃ, τὴν ἀνατολὴν πᾶσαν ὑποτάξας, ὡμὸς ἦν εἰς πάντας διώξαντα. ("Consult your records, there you will

East to the West is thus conceived as a triumphal conquest which reached its climax at Rome with the martyrdom of Peter and Paul at the hands of Nero.

Rome is not simply the place where persecutions originated, but it is above all the place where the first among the victims of the State's persecutions, Peter and Paul, were, through their martyrdom, ultimately victorious.[142] Martyrdom is not capitulation to the enemy but victory over him, as the τρόπαια over the tombs of Peter and Paul signify.[143] The martyrdom of Peter and Paul at the hands of the chief enemy of God (Nero) crowns their mission to found the Church and at the same time gives to this foundation that definitive character which death alone can convey.[144] To give due emphasis to Rome as the place of the martyrdom of the Chief Apostles, Eusebius quotes from the pen of Gaius against the Montanist Proclus (ca. 200), which is the earliest documentary evidence regarding the tombs of Peter and Paul at Rome: "But I can point out the trophies of victory of the Apostles, for if you take the great road that leads to the Vatican or travel on the Ostian Way, you will find the trophies of those who founded this Church."[145] Our author

find that Nero, who was cruel towards all, was the first to persecute this Message, which, having subdued the East, was above all victorious in Rome." This translation depends on the assumption that the aorist participle ὑποτάξας qualifies δόγμα, and not Nero, as e.g., is assumed by both McGiffert and Lake. In either assumption, the case and the gender cause difficulties. If the participle were intended to qualify Nero, then it should read ὑποτάξαντα; if it was meant to qualify the Message, then it should read ὑποτάξαν. My choice of the latter is based on three considerations: the greater likelihood of a mistake by a copyist affecting but one letter rather than three and thus transcribing "g" rather than "v"; the fact that the resulting translation is closer to the original Latin; and finally, the fittingness of the reading to the general context and to the use which Eusebius makes of the text.)

[142] Cf. *HE* 2,25,5–8 (Schwartz 176,16–178,14).

[143] Cf. *HE* 2,25,7 (quotation from Gaius). Here Eusebius faithfully reechoes the traditional concept of martyrdom. But by the time he completes the Revision of the *History* in the wake of his own experience of persecution and martyrdom, his concept will have changed quite radically.

[144] "Zu eben derselben Zeit nun wie Paulus . . . , welcher auf die Kraft seines Herrn stolz war, welcher persönlich mitten in der Kaiserstadt Rom mit dem Bekenntnissiege gekrönt wurde, da er dort in herrlichem Kampfe gestritten hatte, und mit eben dem Siege, welchen Christus den siegreichen Märtyrern gibt, wurde auch Simon, das Haupt und der Erste der Jünger ebenfalls dort gekrönt . . . und litt wie unser Herr." (From the *Longer Recension of The Martyrs of Palestine*, translated from Cureton's Syriac text by B. Violet, *Die Palästinischen Märtyrer des Eusebius von Cäsarea*, T. U. 14, Leipzig, 1896, p. 2.) It is interesting that Paul's martyrdom is again used to "date" that of Peter, as in the *History*. Notice also the emphasis on Peter as the Head and the First of the Disciples.

[145] *HE* 2,25,7 (Schwartz 178,3–6). The translation follows the correction suggested

follows this up with a second witness, Dionysius of Corinth (ca. 171), who both confirms the fact of the martyrdom of Peter and Paul, and reminds us of their mission to found the Church.[146]

Eusebius has, through the medium of his particular historical presentation, outlined both the cause and the nature of Rome's preeminence within the universal mission of the Church. She derives this preeminence as *Church* of Rome primarily through her association with St. Peter and, to a lesser extent, with St. Paul, which association is "sealed" by the blood of their martyrdom and marked by the site of their tombs. Negatively speaking, as *capital* of the empire, she is attributed a theological importance as the center of the Church's mission-field, as Babylon (the world which is to be redeemed and converted), as the place where the Enemy seeks to lead the world into error and from whence the prince of this world wages war on the saints through the State's persecution of the Church. According to the Divine Dispensation, Peter is guided to Rome where he exercises the function of detecting and repudiating error (heresy), confirming orthodoxy—not through his own means but by means of divine guidance—and, with Paul, completing his primary function (to found the Church) with his "victory" over the chief enemy of God, the persecuting emperor.

There are only two explicit references to Mt 16,18 in the *History* and both of them are found in quotations: one from Origen and the second from Dionysius of Alexandria.[147] Yet it would seem that the general σκοπός of Book 2 tends in the direction of the later developed exegesis of Mt 16,18 and its relevance for the authority of the Bishop of Rome as successor to St. Peter. Book 2 affirms and illustrates how, though the Church was (generally speaking) founded by the Apostles, their Leader, Peter, was singled out by a Divine Dispensation (a) to inaugurate this foundation historically in Palestinian Caesarea and in Antioch; (b) to execute the foundation of the Church Universal by proclaiming the Gospel of Light from the East to the West, which culminated in the final witness to the

---

by Tailliez, "Notes conjointes sur un passage fameux d'Eusèbe," 431–436. For an account of the discussion concerning this text, and in particular for an excellent summary of the studies on the history of the term τρόπαιον by F. Lammert and Ch. Mohrmann, see O'Connor, *Peter in Rome*, 97–98.

[146] In a letter to Soter and the Church of Rome, Dionysius of Corinth affirms: ταῦτα καὶ ὑμεῖς διὰ τῆς τοσαύτης νουθεσίας τὴν ἀπὸ Πέτρου καὶ Παύλου φυτείαν γενηθεῖσαν Ῥωμαίων τε καὶ Κορινθίων συνεκεράσατε. καὶ γὰρ ἄμφω καὶ εἰς τὴν ἡμετέραν Κόρινθον φυτεύσαντες ἡμᾶς ὁμοίως ἐδίδαξαν, ὁμοίως δὲ καὶ εἰς τὴν Ἰταλίαν ὁμόσε διδάξαντες ἐμαρτύρησαν κατὰ τὸν αὐτὸν καιρόν (*HE* 2,25,8 = Schwartz 178,10–14).

[147] See below, Note II.

Faith—his martyrdom at Rome; and (c) to prevent the gates of hell (error and the prince of this world) from prevailing against the Church and her mission.

§2 Book 3: The Completion of the Church's Foundation and the Transition to the Post-Apostolic Age

The third book of Eusebius' *History*, covering the completion or consolidation of the foundation of the Church, describes the period of transition from the Apostolic Age (strictly so-called), which terminated with the deaths of Peter and Paul, to the Age of the Church, the post-Apostolic era which begins with Book 4. The opening sentence succinctly summarizes the principal theme of the previous book—the end of the limited dispensation to the Jewish Nation and the beginning of the world mission[148]—while the rest of the opening paragraph sketches the broad outline of that mission: Thomas, Andrew, and John now receive brief mention[149] together with Peter and Paul who are seen in their more traditional roles[150] as the Apostle to those of the Circumcised[151] and the Apostle to the Gentiles[152] respectively. Again, the world mission of both Apostles is seen as culminating in their martyrdom at Rome.[153] Within the structure of Book 3, the martyrdom of Peter and Paul at Rome provides the axis, as it were, around which the narrative revolves. We have already mentioned how their deaths at the hand of Nero provided the end of the first stage of the Apostolic Age and the foundation of the Church with its definitive character. The transition from that moment, which marks the culmination of the world mission of the Apostles, to the post-Apostolic era of the Church is characterized by two related concerns on the part of Eusebius: 1) to establish the beginning of the list of successions, i.e., of those who take "first rank in the Apostolic Succession,"[154]

---

[148] "Such was the condition of the Jews, but the holy Apostles and disciples of Our Savior were dispersed throughout the whole world . . ." *HE* 3,1,1 (Schwartz 188,1–3).

[149] Cf. *HE* 3,1,1 (Schwartz 188,3–4).

[150] Cf. Gal 2,8.

[151] Cf. *HE* 3,1,2 (Schwartz 188,5–8).

[152] Cf. *HE* 3,1,3 (Schwartz 188,8–12). More information about Paul's role in the foundation of the Church is provided in *HE* 3,4,1 (Schwartz 192,1f.).

[153] Cf. *HE* 3,1,2–3 (Schwartz 188,7–10).

[154] *HE* 3,37,1 (Schwartz 282,2). The Alexandrian list, however, began already in the previous book (*HE* 2,24,1 = Schwartz 174,18–20). This could have been due either to an attempt by Eusebius to give the list of Alexandrian bishops, whose origins do not invite too close a scrutiny (cf. Trevijano, "Church of

and 2) to establish the canon of the New Testament. In other words, Eusebius is intent on describing the origins of the succession of Apostolic Authority and Apostolic Teaching. Both of these are in turn determined by the decisive completion of the Apostolic Age. It is the martyrdom of Peter and Paul which initiates the first list of Apostolic Successions (Linus, first Bishop of Rome)[155] and the opening discussion on what constitutes the canon of the N.T.;[156] likewise, the same martyrdom is referred to when Eusebius brings down the curtain on the Apostolic Age with the recitation of the deaths of the Apostles.[157]

a) The Beginning of the Succession Lists: The Transmission of the Apostolic Authority

Towards the end of Book 3, Eusebius elucidates on what he considers to be the specific function in the Divine Plan with which the first successors of the Apostles were entrusted: "These saintly disciples of such great men built everywhere on the foundations of the Churches laid by the Apostles . . . disseminating profusely the saving

Alexandria," 471–477), an added authority or, what is more likely, to Eusebius' endeavor to upgrade the significance of the See of Alexandria by implying that the death of St. Mark took place within the Apostolic Age. Katzenmayer, "Petrus und der Primat," 161–162, comments: "Bemerkenswert ist dabei, daß an der Spitze von keiner der Bischofsreihen ein Apostel steht . . . Bemerkenswert ist ferner, daß die Tradition der alten Kirche in Alexandria, Antiochia und Rom Petruskirchen sah." With regard to the first observation, as has already been pointed out, Katzenmayer fails to appreciate both the distinction Eusebius makes between the Apostles and their successors, the bishops, and the intrinsic relationship he assumes exists between them. Concerning the second observation, Katzenmayer did not recognize that it was precisely on the basis of this ancient tradition about the Petrine origins of the three major sees that Eusebius inserted the lists of bishops of these Churches in his *History,* and not, as he maintains, because they were the three "Weltstädte." More recently, Dvornik, *The Idea of Apostolicity in Byzantium*, Harvard, 1958, argued with great erudition in a similar vein to the effect that these three sees owed their importance primarily to their prominence within the imperial administration system, though he admitted that Rome's association with Peter and Paul was not without its influence, especially with regard to the recognition of Rome's preeminence in the West. He observed that Eusebius "does not place the founders of those Churches at the head of his lists of Bishops" (p. 42), thereby missing the significance of Eusebius' description of the origins of these three sees in Book 2, as well as the relationship of the lists of bishops to these origins.

[155] Cf. *HE* 3,2,1 (Schwartz 188,13–16).

[156] Cf. *HE* 3,3,1–3,4,11 (Schwartz 188,17–194,18).

[157] Cf. *HE* 3,31,1–6 (Schwartz 264,3–266,18). Only the deaths of those Apostles are recorded where Eusebius can provide documentary evidence for the existence of their tombs.

seed[158] of the kingdom of heaven throughout the whole wide world."[159] To spread the Gospel, they gave their property to the poor, went into the world to preach to all, committed the Gospel to writing, and so passed it on.[160] "Many simply laid the foundations of the faith in foreign parts, appointed others as pastors . . ." and passed on again to other countries and peoples.[161] In this rather rhetorical passage we do not find any clear-cut definition of the office of the first successors—in fact the description would seem more suited to the Apostles themselves. Yet two interrelated aspects of their function are discernible: they are commissioned to "hand on" the Apostolic Succession of Authority and the Apostolic Teaching, both of which, as we saw in Ch. One, constitute the Apostolicity of the Church.[162]

The initial transmission of the Apostolic Succession marks the completion of the first phrase of the Church's history and the beginning of the post-Apostolic Church Universal. This is brought home to the reader not only by the description of the deaths of the Apostles, and those of the "first rank" after the Apostles, as well as the completion of the N.T. Canon, but by the generous space devoted to the horrific scenes which resulted from the destruction of Jerusalem.[163] The causal relationship between the "rejection" of Christ and His Disciples (in particular James the Just) is repeatedly referred to[164] and the specific mission of the Church of Jerusalem, as an offer of grace by the kindness of an all-benign Providence, is explicitly formulated.[165] The reader is left in no doubt that the destruction of Jerusalem and its temple ends the significance of that city within the *Heilsgeschichte*.

Rome, the place of the martyrdom of Peter and Paul and the center of the world mission of the Church takes over the function of Jerusalem in the new dispensation. The first list of bishops in the Apostolic Succession begins, consequently, with Linus, the first Bishop of

---

[158] This is a favorite expression of Eusebius to describe the spread of religion, cf. *HE* 1,2,22 (Schwartz 24,5–6).

[159] *HE* 3,37,1 (Schwartz 282,2–7).

[160] Cf. *HE* 3,37,2 (Schwartz 282,7–13).

[161] Cf. *HE* 3,37,3 (Schwartz 282,13–17).

[162] See *HE* 3,37,4 (Schwartz 282,22), where Eusebius remarked that it would be impossible to enumerate all the "pastors or evangelists" who make up the first Apostolic Succession (= the first generation of the Apostolic "Dynasty"). The distinction, "pastors or evangelists," well expresses the two "offices" of bishop and orthodox writer, which together constitute the Apostolic Succession.

[163] Cf. *HE* 3,5,1–3,12,1 (Schwartz 194,19–228,11).

[164] Cf. *HE* 3,5,2–3 (Schwartz 196,1–22); *HE* 3,7,7–9 (Schwartz 214,6–23); *HE* 3,11,1 (Schwartz 226,20–21).

[165] Cf. *HE* 3,7,7–9 (Schwartz 214,6–23).

Rome.[166] Linus, we are told, was the first *after the martyrdom of Peter and Paul* to inherit the bishopric of that Church.[167] Later he receives a second mention (together with his own successor, Clement) as being numbered among the followers of Paul; but there he is said to be "the first *after Peter* to inherit the episcopacy of the Church of the Romans."[168] On the third occasion, Linus is referred to in conjunction with Clement, who is described as occupying "the third place of those who held the office of bishop *after Paul and Peter*.[169] The three different determinations of the origins of the Roman succession are not easy to reconcile, unless one takes the third text as being synonymous with the first[170] and interprets both as referring primarily to the "chronological" determination of Linus' and Clement's episcopacy. Later, Eusebius will refer to Eleutherius of Rome as the twelfth "after the Apostles" probably with the same idea in mind.[171] However, from the context of the second reference we gather that even though both Linus and Clement were intimately associated with St. Paul as his followers, nonetheless, Eusebius unambiguously asserts that Linus is the first *after Peter* as far as the line of succession is concerned. To emphasize the fact that he is, here, quite precisely referring to the origin of the *Succession,* Eusebius uses the term κληρωθείς: Linus was the first after Peter to *inherit* the bishopric. It is therefore worthy of note that Clement, who, according to Eusebius brings the Apostolic Age to a close, is described quite uniquely as *"handing over* the office of the Bishops of Rome to Evarestos."[172] Such minimizing of St. Paul's connection with the Apostolic Succession at Rome accurately corresponds to the downgrading of his role in the foundation of the Church, as described by Eusebius in Book 2. In this respect it is significant that the entry in the Armenian version of Eusebius'

---

[166] We have seen how the story of the first "bishop" of Jerusalem was occasioned by a very specific theological reason and so included in Book 2, where it played such an important role. Likewise, the anomalous presence of the first Alexandrian bishops in Book 2 (and not in Book 3, which, as Eusebius himself tells us, is primarily devoted to the first successions) was possibly inserted there in order to enhance the prestige of the Alexandrian succession.

[167] *HE* 3,2,1 (Schwartz 236,11).

[168] *HE* 3,4,8 (Schwartz 194,6–9). Eusebius identifies Linus with the person of the same name mentioned in 2 Tim 4,21. See also *HE* 3,2,1 (Schwartz 188, 13–16).

[169] *HE* 3,21,1 (Schwartz 236,11).

[170] The unusual sequence, "Paul and Peter," may thus be due to the fact that this was the sequence of their martyrdom (cf. *HE* 2,25,5 = Schwartz 176,17–19: see also above, footnote 144).

[171] Cf. *HE* 5, "Proem," 1 (Schwartz 400,2–3).

[172] *HE* 3,34,1 (Schwartz 274,5–6).

Chronicle, which describes Linus as succeeding Peter at Rome, likewise makes no mention of Paul.[173] We may conclude that at the turn of the fourth century, the preeminence of the Church of Rome was—in the East—principally attributed to the Apostolic Succession of its bishop from the Leader of the Apostles, Peter.[174]

Let us briefly examine the structural outline of Book 3. After opening Book 3 with the notice about Linus as the first to inherit the episcopacy of the Roman Church, Eusebius immediately enters into a discussion about the canon of the New Testament.[175] The N.T. is, of course, the written record of the Apostolic Proclamation or Teaching on which the Church was originally founded. Since this particular topic is beyond the scope of our study, we can leave it aside. Only one observation needs be made with reference to the subject of this study—one which is indicative of Eusebius' basic tendency as already noted in his treatment of Book 2: it is of note that Eusebius here begins his treatment on the N.T. Canon with a discussion of the genuine and spurious works attributed to *Peter*.[176] As Peter enjoys a preeminence within the Apostolic Authority, so too his writing occupies the first place within the corpus of Apostolic Teaching. There is a certain inner logic in this attitude of Eusebius, based on his contention that, according to Book 2, the Church was primarily founded on the Proclamation of Peter.

A brief account of Paul's writings follows[177] as well as his judgement on other writings of dubious Apostolic origin. As examples of

---

[173] Entry under "Olymp." 211, "Abr." 2084, "Neron" 14, "Agripas" 24 (Karst 216). The same exclusive reduction of the list of successors back to St. Peter is to be found in the *Liberian Catalogue,* compiled by the "Chronographer of 354," as Mommsen called its author, referring thereby to its date of composition.

[174] By way of comparison, Irenaeus (*Adv. haer.* 3,3,2) speaks in a more general fashion of his List of Succession in "the most ancient and well-known Church founded and established by the two most glorious Apostles."

[175] The principles, according to which the canonicity of a work is determined, are outlined in *HE* 3,25,6–7 (Schwartz 252,8–24).

[176] Cf. *HE* 3,3,1–4 (Schwartz 188,17–190,13).

[177] Cf. *HE* 3,3,5–7 (Schwartz 190,13–27). Of special interest here is the way Eusebius pays attention to the objections of some to the inclusion of Hebrews in the N.T. Canon on the basis of its reported rejection by the Church of Rome (cf. *HE* 3,5 = Schwartz 190,14–17). Later Eusebius will admit that some *members* of the Church there do not accept the canonicity of Hebrews (cf. *HE* 6,20,3 = Schwartz 566,16–21), implying thereby that this was not the official policy of the *bishop* there. Such a discussion is only of significance in the light of the importance attached to the unique authority of the Church of Rome by the early Eusebius, who here reflects the earlier consciousness of the Church with regard to the singular influence of the Church of Rome in the formation of the N.T. Canon (cf. Grotz, "Die Stellung der römischen Kirche," 36f.).

those who occupied first place in the Apostolic Succession, a list of Paul's
successors is given.[178] Then follows a lengthy account of the siege and
destruction of Jerusalem[179] which is rounded off by a notice concerning
the end of Linus' reign and the succession of Anacletus.[180] The destruction of Jerusalem is then the major event which characterizes the reign of
Linus, Bishop of Rome. Bereft of her significance within Salvation History
because of her rejection of Christ, her history is only of consequence in
relation to the history of the new dispensation in *Salvation History*. That
dispensation is "measured" by the reigns of the Successors of St. Peter.

   An entry from the Alexandrian succession-list[181] is added to that of
Rome, indicating once again the importance of the Church of Alexandria,
second only to Rome in determining the chronology of the Apostolic
"Dynasty." No information is given about Anacletus of Rome or his
reign. Instead, the narrative jumps to the episcopacy of Clement, who
succeeded Anacletus. The rest of Book 3 concerns itself primarily with
events which, Eusebius narrates, occurred within his reign.[182] Clement's
reign covers the final phase of the transition from the Apostolic Age to
the post-Apostolic Church.[183]

b) St. Clement of Rome and the Transmission of the Apostolic Teaching
Clemens Romanus enjoyed great popularity in the early Church
due to the letter attributed to him.[184] Of this fame, Eusebius takes
full advantage. In the course of Book 3 alone, Clement is mentioned as bishop on four occasions[185] and his epistle is referred to

---

[178] Cf. *HE* 3,4,1–11 (Schwartz 192,1–194,18). It is important to note, as already
       pointed out above, that Linus, the disciple of Paul, is expressly described as the
       successor of *St. Peter*.
[179] Cf. *HE* 3,5,1–3,12,1 (Schwartz 194,19–228,11).
[180] Cf. *HE* 3,13,1 (Schwartz 228,12–17).
[181] Cf. *HE* 3,14,1 (Schwartz 228,17–19).
[182] In view of Eusebius' understanding of the bishops as the Church's equivalent to
       the imperial rulers, we are thus entitled to use the term "reign" in this context.
[183] Cf. *HE* 3,15,1–3,34,1 (Schwartz 228,20–274,8).
[184] Cf. *HE* 3,16,1 (Schwartz 230,1–7). See also Lightfoot, *Clement of Rome*, 148–164,
       for a comprehensive list of quotations and references to Clement and his epistle,
       to be found in the ecclesiastical writings of the first four centuries. Regarding the
       significance of Clemens Romanus for the early history of the Roman Primary,
       see Grotz, "Die Stellung der römischen Kirche," (1975), 14–24, where recent
       literature on the subject is critically examined and assessed.
[185] *HE* 3,4,9 (Schwartz 194,9); *HE* 3,15,1 (Schwartz 228,21); *HE* 3,21,1 (Schwartz
       236,10); *HE* 3,34,1 (Schwartz 274,6).

three times in all.[186] What is of interest to our topic is what the author of *History* has to say about this epistle and how he says it: "One great and admirable epistle of his is recognized, which he drew up for the Church of the Corinthians in the name of the Church of the Romans."[187] Lightfoot, in his commentary on the epistle, called it "the first step towards papal domination"[188]—an interpretation which itself is not free from a certain tendency. The general Catholic view is to recognize the letter as the first manifestation of Rome's primacy. The epistle itself claims to be written "by us through the Holy Spirit"[189] and even talks at one point about the "words spoken by (Christ) through us."[190] What is more, the initiative of the Church at Rome was accepted by the Church at Corinth, which responded by regularly reading the letter in Church, a practice adopted by many other Churches up to the time of Eusebius.[191] The fact that the letter merely claims to be from the Church "which sojourns at Rome"[192] and never refers to the personality of its author has been variously interpreted. Some scholars conclude from this that Rome, at this early stage, enjoyed a "primacy not of the episcopacy but of the church."[193] The significance of the author's anonymity within the letter could be interpreted to indicate the "official" nature of the document, which received its authority not from the moral standing of its writer but from the authority associated with the Church of Rome.[194] In the latter half of the following century, Dionysius of

---

[186] *HE* 3,16,1 (Schwartz 230,1–7); *HE* 3,38,1–3 (Schwartz 284,3–15); *HE* 4,23,11 (Schwartz 378, 4–10). See also the extract from the succession list of Irenaeus, *HE* 5,6,3 (Schwartz 438,15–19).

[187] *HE* 3,16,1 (Schwartz 230,1–2).

[188] Lightfoot, *Clement of Rome*, 70, refers specifically to Clemens 56; 58; 59; and 63. The "almost imperious tone" Lightfoot detects in this letter is surely greatly tempered by the modest way the writer places himself and his Church under the same admonitions as are directed towards the Corinthians (cf. §7,1).

[189] Clemens 63,2 (Schaefer 68).

[190] Clemens 59,1 (Schaefer 64).

[191] Cf. *HE* 4,23,11 (Schwartz 378,4–10) and *HE* 3,16,1 (Schwartz 230,3–5).

[192] Clemens 1, "Proem" (Schaefer 7).

[193] Lightfoot, *Clement of Rome*, 70; Altaner, "Der 1. Clemensbrief und der römische Primat," 534–539. It is beyond the terms of reference of this study to discuss the controversy regarding the existence or non-existence of a monarchical episcopate at Rome at this early stage of the Church's history. See however the apt comments of Grotz, "Die Stellung der römischen Kirche," 33–35, with regard to the implications of the debate for the question of the Roman primacy. See also Karrer, "Das Petrusamt in der Frühkirche," 517.

[194] Although the letter recalls the martyrdom of "the greatest and most righteous pillars (of the Church)," Saints Peter and Paul, it does not explicitly link this with the authority of the Church of Rome.

Corinth refers to the letter as the epistle "which was formally written to us διὰ Κλήμεντος,"[195] while Irenaeus describes it as a ἱκανωτάτην γραφήν from the Church of Rome which was sent at the time when Clement was bishop,[196] and Clement of Alexandria refers to it simply as the Epistle of the Romans to the Corinthians.[197] Thus it is the consistent tradition of the early Church that the epistle did not receive its authority from the personal fame of a highly respected writer, but from the Church of Rome.

But a process of clarification had begun which, in spite of the apparent "regression" of Clement of Alexandria, culminated in the interpretation of Eusebius. Eusebius tells us that Clement drew up the letter . . . ὡς ἀπὸ τῆς Ῥωμαίων ἐκκλησίας τῇ Κορινθίων . . .[198] which if literally translated reads: "as though from the Church of the Romans" i.e., "in the name of the Church of the Romans"[199]—later this is more precisely formulated as ἐκ προσώπου τῆς Ῥωμαίων ἐκκλησίας:[200] "on behalf of the Church of the Romans." Although Eusebius does allude to Clement's style of writing in the context of the latter quotation, it is not the literary quality of the writer that accounts for the letter's authority, nor indeed the impressive content of the letter as such, even though this is admitted (following Irenaeus) to be "great and admirable."[201] It is the *Bishop of the Romans*, who "supervised the teaching of the Divine Word" at Rome for "nine years,"[202] and not (in the first place at least) the *writer* Clement, who grants the famous epistle its great authority. Through this interpretation, Eusebius explains and develops what was only implicit in the letter itself and does so in a way consistent with the reception' of the letter in the early Church.

Clement and the epistle attributed to him are given special prominence by Eusebius for another reason: they mark the final stage of the transition between the Apostolic Age and the age of the post-Apostolic Church, forming as it were the boundary between both. The reign of Clement, who occupied "the third place of those who held the office of bishop after Paul and Peter,"[203] was marked by the outbreak of persecution by Domitian,[204] "who showed himself

---

[195] *HE* 4,23,11 (Schwartz 378,9).
[196] Irenaeus, *Adv. haer.* 3,3,3 (*HE* 5,6,3 = Schwartz 438,15–19).
[197] Clement of Alexandria, *Stromata* 5,12 (*PG* 9,117, B 13–14).
[198] *HE* 3,16,1 (Schwartz 230,2).
[199] This is the version of Lake, *The Ecclesiastical History*, vol. I, 235.
[200] *HE* 3,38,1 (Schwartz 284,4).
[201] *HE* 3,16,1 (Schwartz 230,1–2).
[202] *HE* 3,34,1 (Schwartz 274,7–8).
[203] *HE* 3,21,1 (Schwartz 236,11).
[204] *HE* 3,17,1–3,20,9 (Schwartz 230,8–236,5).

the successor of Nero's campaign of hostility to God."[205] New bishops succeeded to the See of Alexandria[206] and the successions at Antioch receive their first mention (without reference to St. Peter).[207] The story of the Apostle, John the Evangelist, is related[208] and his writings discussed,[209] which leads to the first indication of the definitive termination of the Apostolic Age: the completion of the N.T. Canon.[210] The second indication of the end of the Apostolic Age is the advent of heresy introduced by Menander, the successor of Simon Magus,[211] while the third and final indication is the death of the Apostles[212] whom Eusebius then proceeds to list, beginning with the second reference to Peter and Paul and their tombs at Rome. We will return to this reference later. After a short treatment of the persecution of Trajan,[213] Eusebius brings the Apostolic Age to an end when Clement hands over the office (παραδοὺς τὴν λειτουργίαν) of the Bishop of Rome to Evarestos and departs this life.[214] His death, together with that of Simeon of Jerusalem,[215] completes the lists of the deaths of the Apostles and their close associates who were reckoned among those of the first generation of the Apostolic Succession.[216]

This list brings the Apostolic Age to its definitive close. But Eusebius' discussion of Clement's epistle and its contents is reserved for the Post-Apostolic Age which properly began with his successor. There the epistle is synchronized[217] with the writings of Polycarp,[218] Papias,[219] and Ignatius[220] who is now described as the second in the *Petrine Succession at Antioch*,[221] which is of interest in itself, since

---

[205] *HE* 3,17,1 (Schwartz 230,12–13); transl., Lake 235.

[206] *HE* 3,21,1 (Schwartz 236,6–13).

[207] *HE* 3,22,1 (Schwartz 236,14–17).

[208] *HE* 3,23,1–19 (Schwartz 236,18–244,5).

[209] *HE* 3,24,1–18 (Schwartz 244,6–250,18).

[210] *HE* 3,25,1–7 (Schwartz 250,19–252,24).

[211] *HE* 3,26,1–3,30,2 (Schwartz 252,25–264,2).

[212] *HE* 3,31,1–5 (Schwartz 264,3–266,12). *HE* 3,31,6 explicitly refers to the end of Eusebius' description of the Apostolic Age (Schwartz 266,12–18).

[213] *HE* 3,32,1–3,33,3 (Schwartz 266,19–274,4).

[214] *HE* 3,34,1 (Schwartz 274,5–8).

[215] *HE* 3,35,1 (Schwartz 274,9–12).

[216] *HE* 3,37,1–4 (Schwartz 282,1–284,2). Quadratus is also mentioned in this description (Schwartz 280,23–24).

[217] See Schwartz, *Einleitung*, 20.

[218] *HE* 3,38,5 (Schwartz 284,23); cf. *HE* 3,36,13–15 (Schwartz 280,1–19).

[219] *HE* 3,39,1—17 (Schwartz 284,24–292,11).

[220] *HE* 3,36,3–15 (Schwartz 274,18–280,19).

[221] . . . Ἰγνάτιος, τῆς κατὰ Ἀντιόχειαν Πέτρου διαδοχῆς δεύτερος τὴν ἐπισκοπὴν κεκληρωμένος (*HE* 3,36,2 = Schwartz 274,17–19). Considerable attention is paid to his martyrdom at Rome (*HE* 3,36,3f. = Schwartz 274,18f.).

it is the first explicit reference in the *History* to the Petrine origin of the
Antiochene Succession List. Book 3, then, concludes with a discussion on
the writings of these authors, known for their orthodoxy and the war they
waged on heresy,[222] central to which is a treatment of Clement as a writer.[223]
The significance of the latter synchronism is twofold: (i) the Letter of
Clement, in spite of its great authority, is not part of the New Testament
Canon; (ii) the orthodox writers, who defended the authoritative transmission of the Apostolic Teaching, trace their origin back to Clement,
who in an unique way incorporated both the Apostolic Authority of Peter
and his Apostolic Teaching. With Clement the third of his original aims,
Aim C, is taken up. The full treatment of this theme will dominate the
following Books 4–7. In the course of Books 4–7, the reader's attention will
be drawn to the repeated occurrence of similar synchronisms, where the
orthodox writers are "synchronized" with the Bishops of Rome, especially
those renowned for their uncompromising attitude towards heretics, thus
reechoing the Peter-Mark and the Peter-Simon Magus themes of Book 2.
Due to the limits of this study, we will not examine in any detail Eusebius'
handling of Aim C, except in so far as the topic has a direct bearing on his
attitude to the Bishop of Rome.

c) *The Tombs of St. Peter and St. Paul at Rome—Their Theological
    Relevance*

To round off our examination of Book 3, a word about the significance
attached to the *tombs* of Sts. Peter and Paul by Eusebius is called for. When
discussing the third and final phenomenon that marked the definitive end
of the Apostolic Age, the deaths of the Apostles, we saw that Eusebius
referred for the third time to the martyrdom of Peter and Paul, and for the
second time to their tombs.[224] Within the same context, Eusebius refers to
the place where John's body was laid to rest,[225] as well as the final resting
place of "Philip the Apostle" and his two daughters at Hierapolis.[226]

[222] Cf. *HE* 3,36,4 (Schwartz 274,21–276,4).
[223] Cf. *HE* 3,38,1–5 (Schwartz 284,2–23).
[224] The three references to the martyrdoms are *HE* 2,25,5–8 (Schwartz 176,16–
178,14), *HE* 3,2,2–3 (Schwartz 188,5–12) and *HE* 3,31,1 (Schwartz 264,3–5).
The first reference contains the fullest description of the tombs, while the third
refers back to that description.
[225] *HE* 3,31,2 (Schwartz 264,6–10).
[226] *HE* 3,31,3 (Schwartz 264,11–19). Regarding the identity of Philip, see McGiffert,
Eusebius, LNPF², 162, footnote 6; Lawlor and Oulton, *The Ecclesiastical History*,
vol. II, 116–118.

From the writers who provided Eusebius with much of this information, we learn a little about the significance of such tombs around 200. In his Letter to Victor of Rome during the Paschal Controversy, Polycrates of Ephesus points to the tombs of those who had fallen asleep in Asia, and in particular at Ephesus, in order to support his claim for a legitimate Apostolic Tradition.[227] This is probably the same reason why Gaius pointed to the tombs of Peter and Paul at Rome in his defense of the Roman tradition, as found in his Letter to the Montanist Proclus.[228] Around the same time, Irenaeus instructed his readers to have recourse to the most ancient Churches where the Apostles once sojourned and where consequently the tradition they handed on to their successors would be found in order to settle disputes regarding major questions.[229]

The existence of the tomb (as distinct from the relics it may contain) was the most obvious evidence of the fact that an apostle had been present in that Church at the time of its foundation; it was also the most concrete sign of the final and most eloquent manifestation of the apostle's mission, which was to *found* the Church through his *witness* to the Faith.[230] It is surely no accident that the Church in the first half of the fourth century designated the building erected over the tomb of St. Peter as τὸ μαρτύριον Πέτρου τοῦ ἀποστόλου.[231] When Irenaeus referred his readers to the undisputed Apostolic Tradition of the "greatest, most ancient and well-known Church founded and established by the two most glorious Apostles Peter and Paul,"[232] which tradition had been handed down through its succession of bishops, it is not unlikely that he recalled to mind the indisputable evidence of that "foundation" which he was shown during his visit to Rome (177–178).

---

[227] Cf. *HE* 5,24,2–5 (Schwartz 490,12–492,5).

[228] Cf. *HE* 2,25,7 (Schwartz 178,3–6). Proclus had first pointed to the graves of Philip and his daughters in order to claim the authority of an Apostolic Tradition for his teaching (cf. *HE* 3,31,4 = Schwartz 264,20–266,5). See O'Connor, *Peter in Rome*, 100–101.

[229] Et si de modica aliqua quaestione disceptatio esset, nonne oporteret in antiquissimas recurrere Ecclesias in quibus apostoli conuersati sunt et ab eis de praesenti quaestione sumere quod certum et uere liquidum est? Quid autem si nec apostoli quidem Scripturas reliquissent nobis, nonne oportebat ordinem sequi traditionis quam tradiderunt his quibus committebant Ecclesias? (*Adv. haer.* 3,4,1 = Rousseau-Doutreleau 44–46).

[230] This is demonstrated by the entry in Eusebius' *Chronicle,* which records the death of the two Apostles at the hands of Nero in the 13th year of his reign: "Nero erregte zu seinem Vergehen noch obendrein als erster eine Verfolgung der Christen, unter welcher Petrus und Paulus, die Apostel, zu Rom Zeugnis ablegten" (Karst 216).

[231] Athanasius, *Hist. Arian.,* 37,1 (Opitz 204,3).

[232] Irenaeus, *Adv. haer.* 3,3,2 (Rousseau-Doutreleau 32).

Considering the use made by Eusebius of his references to the tombs
or final resting places of the Apostles, and in particular Peter and Paul,
we note how consistent he is with the earlier understanding of their significance as manifesting in the most definitive way possible, a Church's
claim both to an Apostolic foundation and to the continual presence in
that Church of the Apostolic Tradition (i.e., the Apostolic Succession of
authority and teaching). Eusebius has nevertheless added his own nuance
to this common understanding of the early Church: the tombs of Peter
and Paul at Rome, being the most tangible evidence of their martyrdom
there, manifest the unique mission of Peter and, to a lesser extent, Paul to
found the Church *Universal*, as our analysis of the conceptual framework
of Books 2 and 3 have indicated.[233]

§3 Summary

The above analysis of Books 2 and 3 was based on the understanding that
Eusebius was not a disinterested collector of extracts but an apologist
who selected *and arranged* his source material with a definite purpose
in mind. Our aim, then, was to delineate the underlying form according
to which Eusebius selected, edited, and presented the source material at
his disposal. This form or mental framework was his ecclesiology—i.e.,
his understanding of the Church and her structure—when he set out
to compose the original *History*. Eusebius' account of the origins of the
Church, her Foundation by the Apostles, concentrated on the work of
St. Peter: the Leader of the Apostles, whose mission to found the Church
led him to Rome; he presented it in contrast with the limited mission of
James the Just, the failure of which resulted in the end of Jerusalem and
her significance within Salvation History.

The account of the origins of the major Churches is in a sense aetiological in intent. This must not be taken to mean that Eusebius fabricated
legends to explain the origin of these Churches and their eminence within
the universal Church. Eusebius wishes rather to present the ecclesiastical
tradition concerning the shape of the Church as seen and experienced by his
contemporaries. Thus, he bases his presentation on written and, sometimes,
oral traditions; he does not invent them. But his selection and editorial
amendments do indicate a very definite interpretation of his sources. It

---

[233] Another nuance peculiar to Eusebius is the interest in the remains in the tombs
(cf. *HE* 3,31,1 = Schwartz 264, 3–5), reflecting a growing interest in the *relics* of
the saints.

will be necessary later to try to separate the original tradition from his own interpretation of it, but for the moment we will attempt to summarize Eusebius' own interpretation as found in Books 2 and 3. One of the four succession-lists followed by Eusebius in the course of his original *History* is that of Jerusalem. From the account of its origins in Book 2, we gather that it was included not because it was an Apostolic See, which strictly speaking it wasn't, but out of respect for its past association with Our Lord and St. James, the Brother of the Lord. James, the first bishop and the originator of the successions, was not an apostle but a bishop, albeit a bishop with a unique mission to the Jews, a mission which failed when the Jews rejected James and the last offer of grace which he held out to them. Further, according to Eusebius, it was Peter who appointed James, Bishop of Jerusalem.

In contrast with Jerusalem, the Church of Rome enjoys a succession of bishops which originated with St. Peter the Leader of the Apostles and can boast of being the place where the Apostle, St. Paul, completed his mission to the Gentiles. In Book 3, Eusebius traces the succession back to Peter in preference to Peter and Paul in accordance with his tendency in Book 2 to underplay the role of Paul in the foundation of the Church. St. Peter is presented as inaugurating the foundation of the Church Universal and completing the first stage of that foundation in Rome with his martyrdom. The city of Rome is theologically evaluated in a negative sense as being the new Babylon, the capital of darkness and error, whither Simon Magus, the father and founder of all heresy, journeyed in order to lead the world astray and from whence Nero, the first emperor, raised up by the prince of this world to do battle with the Church, inaugurates the persecution of the Church. Hence, Peter is portrayed as bringing the Light of the Gospel from the East to the West, dispelling the darkness of error by detecting and expelling Simon Magus, confirming the orthodox content of Mark's Gospel, not through his own means but by means of the Divine Guidance, and finally, through his martyrdom, conquering the forces of evil let loose by Nero.

It is important to note that the theological significance attributed to the *city* of Rome as seen by the early Eusebius as author of the original *History* is exclusively of a negative character: it is the capital of darkness and the forces of evil. However, with the advent of Constantine, the later Eusebius[234] will be able to evaluate the theological relevance of the city in a positive way as the ancient capital of the newly "Christianized" empire—in line with his developed

---

[234] See below, Chapter Four.

imperial ecclesiology which will identify the Church with the Christian Empire—and thus pave the way for the later justification of Constantinople's claim to honor as the New Rome. Such a positive theological attitude to the city of Rome and its meaning within Salvation History was as far from the mind of the early Eusebius as it was foreign to the early Church up to the beginning of the fourth century.[235]

Alexandria's list of bishops emanates from Mark. The eminence of Alexandria as the leading center of Christian asceticism and learning is depicted through the works of Philo, whose association with the city characterizes her eminence as a center of learning. The Alexandrian School owed much to Philo and so he is represented as having come into contact with Peter in Rome. But it is the writer Mark, from whom the Alexandrian successions originate, who "determines" the function of the Church of Alexandria within the Church Universal. The Church there continues the tradition of the Evangelist. His original relationship to St. Peter determines the relationship between the Church of Alexandria and the Church of Rome as that between the center of learning in the Church and the center of authority. Mark, like James, was not an Apostle: he derives his authority from Peter.

The remaining succession-list which engages Eusebius' attention in his portrayal of the "Apostolic Dynasty" (Books 2–7) is that of Antioch. And yet the only reference to its origins in Book 2 was the synchronism of the conversion of Cornelius by Peter and the growth of the Church at Antioch, where the name of "Christian" was first given. In Book 3, Eusebius traces the origins of the Antiochene successions back to Peter,[236] but it is surprising that in Book 2 in his description of the Apostolic Age strictly so-called, he makes no mention of any visit of Peter to Antioch.[237] This omission is all the more puzzling since in the *Chronicle,* or at least in the Armenian version of it, he had previously included an entry under "Olympiade," 204, to the effect that: "Petros der Apostel begibt sich, *nachdem er zunächst die Antiochener Kirche gegründet hat,* in die Römerstadt und predigt dort das Evangelium und steht dort als Leiter der Kirche vor."[238] As we saw in Chapter One, the one reference to Peter's stay at Antioch to be found in the New Testament, Gal 2,11f, was interpreted by Eusebius to refer, not to Peter, but to

---

[235] See Hastings, "The Papacy and Rome's Civil Greatness," 359–367.
[236] *HE* 3,36,2 (Schwartz 274,18).
[237] Concerning St. Peter's association with Antioch, see Downey, *History of Antioch,* 281–287, as well as his "Excursus 3," 583f.
[238] Eusebius, *Chronicle,* (Karst 214).

another disciple with the name of Cephas. It is possible that he ignored any presentation of Peter's visit to Antioch because he lacked sufficient source material. But then, why did he mention it in the *Chronicle?* Another, more plausible reason suggests itself. Since the influence of the bishops of Antioch began to diminish in the second half of the third century, as we will see in Chapter Three, and at the same time the influence of Alexandria steadily increased, Eusebius wished in the *History,* which seems to be much more tendentious than the earlier *Chronicle,* to underplay the origins of that see, which were in fact more "respectable" than those of Alexandria. While Alexandria could only claim a disciple of Peter as the founder of its Church, Antioch claimed Peter, the Leader of the Apostles. Eusebius, in common with his contemporaries, recognized Antioch's special eminence due to its Petrine origins and so included its succession-list which originated with Peter, but he excluded any further details of Antioch's origins other than the synchronism in the general notice to the effect that, immediately after Peter inaugurated the world mission, many Greek converts were made at Antioch, where many of the brethren gathered, including Paul and Barnabas, and where the name of Christian was first given.[239] For Eusebius, then, this seems to mean that even though the bishops and Church of Antioch enjoy an eminence within the Church Universal due to the fact that Peter founded the Church there, yet this eminence is not clearly defined: there is no divinely-ordained event recorded in the Apostolic Age strictly so-called that could more precisely determine the Church's specific function within the universal Church, other than a generally recognized participation in the unique Petrine authority.

In conclusion, it may be observed that all three major sees, Rome, Alexandria, and Antioch, which are singled out by Eusebius to represent the Apostolic "Dynasty" with their successions of bishops, trace their origins one way or another back to St. Peter. These three Churches were recognized as three major centers of the universal *Koinōnia,* and as such, according to Eusebius, reflect their unique origins. They did not enjoy equal rank, however, since Rome enjoyed a real primacy, Alexandria occupied the second place, while Antioch's position is left somewhat indeterminate, corresponding to the vagueness of her Petrine origins and the decline of her influence. Later it will be seen that the decline of Antioch's influence, after the deposition of Paul of Samosata, would eventually

---

[239] Cf. *HE* 2,3,3–4 (Schwartz 112,29–114,12).

corrode the appreciation in the East of the Petrine authority in general, and so ultimately the authority of Rome.

Book 3 described the transition from the Apostolic Age to the post-Apostolic Church. The final destruction of Jerusalem, and with it the end of Jerusalem's significance in Salvation History, forms the background to the story of how the foundation of the Church was consolidated by those who held the first place in the Apostolic Succession and how the Apostolic Authority and Teaching was transmitted to the succeeding generations. Here Rome plays the leading part. It is within the *reign* of Linus that the destruction of Jerusalem takes place, while the *reign* of Clement is characterized by the definitive termination of the Apostolic Age with the completion of the N.T. Canon, the advent of heresy, and the deaths of the Apostles. The Authority of Peter is "inherited" by Linus and Anacletus, which authority Clement in turn hands over to his successor. The Apostolic Teaching, preserved in the N.T. and "begun" by St. Peter, is defended in the face of the heretical teaching of Simon Magus' successors by the orthodox writers who follow in the tradition of Clement of Rome. Clement combined in a unique way the authority of Peter and the literary charism of Mark. With him, Eusebius begins his treatment of Aim C, which will dominate the rest of the original *History*, Books 4–7.

CHAPTER THREE
The Age of the Apostolic Church (Books 4–7)

Books 4–7 offer a vast amount of material for commentary. Therefore, to keep within the limited aims we have set ourselves in this analysis of the *History*, we must, even more than in our previous examination of Books 1–3, concentrate simply on those parts which enable us to understand the mind of Eusebius with regard to his attitude to the Church of Rome and the preeminence of the Bishop of Rome within the universal Church. As in the analysis of Books 1–3, so too our object here is not so much to discover the historical truth of the events he records, which would call for a study in itself, but rather to examine the way Eusebius interprets them and presents them to his readers.[1] Our aim in this chapter,

---

[1]   This, of course, will involve some perfunctory examination of the major events relating to the question of the primacy of Rome. But it is not the aim of this study to enter into the many discussions sparked off by these events and their related documents, except in so far as this is demanded by our analysis of the text of Eusebius.

therefore, is to uncover Eusebius' theological understanding of the nature and function of the Bishop of Rome, as it is reflected in the way he reconstructs and presents the history of the first two centuries of the post-Apostolic Church, using the material at his disposal: the written and oral traditions which he had collected. We will be particularly interested in finding out to what extent Eusebius' highly idealized concept of the Church of Rome's origins is in turn reflected in the role she and her bishops play within the *History* of the first two centuries.

The (post-) Apostolic Church is in Eusebius' scheme of things, characterized by two phenomena: (i) the persecution of the Church by the State, with its resultant martyrdoms, and (ii) the rise of heresy, with the consequent defense of the Apostolic Teaching by the orthodox writers. In his treatment of the first phenomenon, Eusebius fulfills Aim F of his original objectives as set out in his Introduction. Since his coverage of this aim is primarily of significance in order to appreciate the change which takes place in the mind of Eusebius in the course of the four Revisions that were undertaken after the Great Persecution, we will reserve our examination of it to the following chapter, when we take a closer look at those Revisions. This chapter will concentrate on the second phenomenon, the battle for orthodoxy, and the way Eusebius fulfils Aims C and D, which of course automatically involves Aim B. Aim C (= the orthodox writers) and Aim D (= the heretics) will be seen to relate to Aim B (the successive reigns of the bishops of the major sees) in such a way as to follow the pattern of the Peter-Mark prototype worked out in the previous books as well as the Peter-Simon prototype also found there.

One of the most striking features of these four Books (4–7) is the predominant role played by the Bishops of the Roman Church. This is best illustrated by the determining function they exercise within the *History*. The chronology of events is primarily ordered according to the successive reigns of the Roman bishops, who in turn impart, to a particular period, its character as "apostolic" or orthodox, though not in any exclusive sense. It will be seen in the course of the *History* how at times Eusebius finds it difficult to reconcile his rather rigid concept of the Apostolic Authority invested in the Bishop of Rome, due to the distinctive Petrine origins of that see, with his knowledge of the events he is recording for posterity, and how in the Revisions he undertook after the persecution this difficulty turns into a major crisis for Eusebius when his ideal crumbles in the face of contemporary events and his own personal predicament. Meanwhile we will examine each book separately and trace

this development step by step, beginning each section with a brief examination of the way Eusebius arranges his "succession-lists."

§1 Book 4: The Defense of the Apostolic Teaching against the Successors of Simon Magus

In Book 4, we find references to the successions in the various sees "of
greater distinction" on six occasions, five of which are headed by the
Bishop of Rome.[2] The only exception is a reference to Alexandria at the
beginning of Book 4, which precedes that of Rome,[3] due possibly to the
tendency already observed in Books 2 and 3 to further the "respectability"
of Alexandria or to the more obvious fact that Book 4 goes on to relate the
story of the sufferings of the rebellious Jews at Alexandria, and in the rest
of Egypt, immediately afterwards.[4] But even there, Eusebius distinguishes
between the succession at Alexandria, which Primus held as "fourth from
the *Apostles*," and that of Alexander of Rome, "fifth from *Peter and Paul*."[5]

As we noticed in the Introduction, to establish the successions of
the major sees is one of the principal objectives of the original *History,* if
not the primary aim as the very title of the original *History,* the Apostolic
Successions, implies. It also has the function of providing the framework
around which the historical events are grouped and presented. The lists
help to unify Eusebius' historical presentation, enabling him to order his
material under the successive reigns of the Apostolic "Dynasty." Thus,
in the reign of Alexander of Rome and Primus of Alexandria, the Jews
approached the climax of their tribulations[6] and Quadratus defended the
Apostolic and orthodox Faith,[7] while under their successors, Telesophorus
and Eumenes[8] (of Rome and Alexandria respectively); the Jewish

---

[2]   *HE* 4,4,1 (Schwartz 304,7–11); *HE* 4,5,5 (Schwartz 306,5–10); *HE* 4,10,1
      (Schwartz 320,9–17); *HE* 4,11,6–7 (Schwartz 324,1–10); *HE* 4,19,1–4,20,1
      (Schwartz 368,4–11).
[3]   *HE* 4,1,1 (Schwartz 300,1–6). Notice, however, that in the list of the contents for
      Book 4, Rome is mentioned first, followed by Alexandria (Schwartz 294,3–4).
[4]   *HE* 4,2,1–5 (Schwartz 300,7–11). This is part of Eusebius' treatment of Aim E,
      concerning the fate of the Jews, which aim he completes in *HE* 4,6,1–4.
[5]   *HE* 4,1,1 (Schwartz 300,3–6).
[6]   *HE* 4,2,1 (Schwartz 300,8–9).
[7]   *HE* 4,3,1–3 (Schwartz 302,12–304,6).
[8]   *HE* 4,5,5 (Schwartz 306,5–10). Eusebius knew nothing which he could report
      for the reigns of Sixtus of Rome and Justus of Alexandria (*HE* 4,4,1 = Schwartz
      304,7–11).

Nation was finally wiped out[9] and with it the special mission of the Church of Jerusalem, now renamed Aelia Capitolina and composed no longer of Jews but of Gentiles.[10] To signify the end of the special significance of the Jewish-Christian Church at Jerusalem, Eusebius prefaces the account of the final liquidation of the Jewish Nation and its capital, Jerusalem, with a list of fifteen bishops, all Hebrew in origin, who made up the succession there,[11] and concludes the narrative with a reference to the first Bishop of the Gentile Church of Aelia, namely Marcus.[12]

After the persecutions had abated, the enemy of truth devised new means of attacking the Churches, which, the reader is informed, were by now spread throughout the world like brilliant lamps[13] in contrast with the Jewish nation which was extinguished. The new attacks came through the agency of the heretics, the successors of Simon Magus,[14] who in turn were later combated by the orthodox writers[15] such as Hegesippus[16] and Justin Martyr.[17]

The reign of Telesophorus (ca. 127—ca. 137)[18] concluded with the Roman bishop's death as a martyr, which won him fame.[19] Under his successor Hyginus (ca. 137—ca. 140), two infamous heresiarchs, Valentinus and Cerdo, came to Rome,[20] where they were excommunicated from the Church;[21] their errors were (later) exposed by Irenaeus.[22] Here Eusebius repeats the original type of synchronism associated with the successors of bishops, according to which, the novelty of a heresy was contrasted with the recognized Apostolicity of a bishop's teaching as guaranteed by the Apostolic

---

[9]   *HE* 4,6,1–4 (Schwartz 306,11–308,13).
[10]   *HE* 4,6,4 (Schwartz 308,11–13).
[11]   *HE* 4,5,1–4 (Schwartz 304,12–306,5).
[12]   *HE* 4,6,4 (Schwartz 308,11–13).
[13]   *HE* 4,7,1 (Schwartz 308,14–17).
[14]   *HE* 4,7,3f. (Schwartz 302,28f.). See also *HE* 4,7,1–2 (Schwartz 308,17–27) for a description of the new situation in which the post-Apostolic Church found itself when the enemy attacked the Church by means of heresy.
[15]   Cf. *HE* 4,7,12–15 (Schwartz 312,16–314,6).
[16]   *HE* 4,8,1–2 (Schwartz 314,6–16).
[17]   *HE* 4,8,3f. (Schwartz 314,17f.).
[18]   The dates given here, and for the subsequent Bishops of Rome, have been taken from *ODCC* 1515.
[19]   *HE* 4,10,1 (Schwartz 320,14).
[20]   *HE* 4,10,1 (Schwartz 320,15–17). Cerdo's links with Simon Magus are noted in another quote from Irenaeus, *Adv. haer.* 1,27,1 (*HE* 4,11,2 = Schwartz 322,3).
[21]   *HE* 4,11,1 (Schwartz 320,18–24) = *Adv. haer.* 3,4,3.
[22]   *HE* 4,11,3 (Schwartz 322,11–13). Eusebius also mentions another heretic, Marcus, in association with Valentinus and Cerdo (*HE* 4,11,4–5).

Succession.[23] The reign of Hyginus' successor, Pius, was uneventful, since
only the successions at Alexandria within his reign are mentioned in connection with it.[24] But the reign of Anicetus of Rome (ca. 154–ca. 166) and
Celadion of Alexandria was marked by the impressive figure of St. Justin
Martyr, who we are told was then at the height of his fame,[25] as well as the
visits to Rome by Hegesippus[26] and Polycarp[27] and many martyrdoms, the
two most famous being that of Polycarp[28] and Justin,[29] which are related
in detail.

The reign of Soter, Bishop of Rome (ca. 166–ca. 175), brings Book
4 to a close.[30] It is marked by a type of synchronism[31] which is peculiar to
Eusebius, one, that is, which groups *orthodox* writers around the Bishop
of Rome, as distinct from the traditional synchronism mentioned above
which "dates" the novelty of a heresy by referring to the successor of the
Apostles who lived at the time of the heretic. We have already seen one
example of the Eusebian synchronism at the end of Book 3, where the
orthodox writers of the first post-Apostolic generation were grouped
around Clement of Rome.

Here, a number of writers, all famous for their defense of orthodoxy, are grouped together under the reign of Bishop Soter of Rome:[32]
Hegesippus,[33] Dionysius of Corinth,[34] and Theophilus of Antioch,[35] as
well as Pinytos of Knossos,[36] Philip of Gortyna,[37]

---

[23]   Cf. *HE* 4,11,1–2 (Schwartz 320,18–322,10), where Eusebius quotes Irenaeus. *Adv.
       haer.* 3,4,3 and 1,27,1–2.
[24]   *HE* 4,11,6 (Schwartz 324,1–6).
[25]   *HE* 4,11,8 (Schwartz 324,10). The writings of Justin are covered in *HE* 4,18,1–10.
[26]   *HE* 4,11,7 (Schwartz 324,8–9).
[27]   *HE* 4,14,1f. (Schwartz 332,3f.).
[28]   Cf. *HE* 4,15,1–45 (Schwartz 334,21–352,13). Regarding the discussion concer-
       ning the date of Polycarp's martyrdom, see Lawlor and Oulton, *The Ecclesiastical
       History*, vol. II, 131–133.
[29]   *HE* 4,16,1–9 (Schwartz 354,15–358,16).
[30]   *HE* 4,19,1–4,30,3 (Schwartz 368,4–392,28).
[31]   See Schwartz, *Einleitung*, 26, for a concise account of this synchronism.
[32]   *HE* 4,21,1 (Schwartz 368,12–17).
[33]   Hegesippus visited Rome during the reign of Anicetus (ca. 154–166) and remai-
       ned there up to the time of Eleutherius (175–189). He journeyed to the major
       sees, particularly Rome, in order to establish the true doctrine and wrote five
       "books" against the Gnostics (cf. *HE* 4,22,1f.); see Quasten, *Patrology* I, 284–286.
[34]   Dionysius of Corinth corresponded with Soter of Rome (cf. *HE* 2,25,8 =
       Schwartz 178,7–14 and *HE* 4,23,1–13 = Schwartz 374,1–378,21).
[35]   Theophilus "the sixth after the Apostles" at Antioch is said to have reigned at the
       time of Soter of Rome (cf. *HE* 4,20,1 = Schwartz 368,8–11) and was famous as
       an orthodox writer (*HE* 4,24,1 = Schwartz 378,22–380,20).

Melito of Sardis,[38] Apolinarius of Hierapolis,[39] Musanus,[40] Modestus,[41] and above all Irenaeus.[42] Each of these bishops was famous in Eusebius' own day, as a writer and defender of orthodoxy. With the exception of Hegesippus, who lived in Rome at the time of Soter, Dionysius, who corresponded with him, and Theophilus, who was Bishop of Antioch during his reign, the relationships of all the others with Bishop Soter (or even his reign) is at the best tenuous—the most famous of all, Irenaeus, having no known contact with him. The "relationships" of both Hegesippus and Dionysius to Soter is characterized, each in its own way, by some allusion to the authority of Rome. Hegesippus, as we have already seen, journeyed to Rome, visiting many Churches on the way in order to ascertain from them the Apostolic Tradition and so combat the heresies with the true doctrine to be found there.[43] According to Eusebius,[44] he lived in Rome during the entire reign of Soter, thus indicating to us Hegesippus' appreciation of the Apostolic Teaching which Soter, as Bishop of Rome, preserved. On the other hand, Dionysius not only praises the admonition which Soter on behalf of the Church of the Romans sent to the Church of the Corinthians, claiming that it would, like Peter and Paul, bind both Churches even closer together[45] but, as Eusebius reminds us in this context, arranged to have it read out in Church on Sundays as was the custom with the epistle formerly sent to them by his predecessor Clement.[46] This synchronism, which recalls the synchronism of orthodox writers under Clement,

---

[36]   Pinytos of Knossos in Crete had no known contact with Soter of Rome, but with Dionysius of Corinth, with whom he corresponded (cf. *HE* 4,23,7–8 = Schwartz 376,2–13). Eusebius praises his orthodoxy and learning.

[37]   Philip of Gortyna, Crete, wrote against Marcion (cf. *HE* 4,25,1 = Schwartz 380,14–20).

[38]   Melito of Sardis was one of the "great luminaries" of Ephesus, according to Polycrates of Ephesus (cf. *HE* 5,24,5 = Schwartz 492,3–5); an account of his writings is to be found in *HE* 4,26,1–14 (Schwartz 380,21–388,9).

[39]   Apolinarius of Hierapolis, whose works (cf. *HE* 4,27,1 = Schwartz 388,10–16) are no longer extant, had no known contact with Soter.

[40]   Musanus wrote a discourse against the Encratites (cf. *HE* 4,28,1), otherwise nothing is known of him.

[41]   The only thing we know about Modestus is that he wrote against Marcion (cf. *HE* 4,25,1 = Schwartz 380,16–17).

[42]   Cf. *HE* 4,21,1 (Schwartz 368,15–16). Although Eusebius includes Irenaeus in this synchronism, he clearly does not belong to the reign of Soter. As a presbyter, he appears on the stage of history during the reign of Soter's successor, Eleutherius, and comes to the fore during the Paschal controversy under Victor I.

[43]   See above, pp. 23–25.

[44]   Cf. *HE* 4,22,3 (Schwartz 370,3–4).

[45]   *HE* 2,25,8 (Schwartz 178,10–14).

[46]   *HE* 4,23,11 (Schwartz 378,1–10).

helps to stamp the reign of Soter with its particular characteristic: it is one during which the defense of the orthodox Faith flowered in the writings of so many famous men.[47] But it also illustrates the unique authoritative role played by Rome in "determining" this orthodoxy, due to her particular Petrine Succession.[48]

By "determining" we do not mean to imply any kind of authoritarian intervention by the Church of Rome, by which she dictated to other Churches what was and what was not the orthodox Faith or the Apostolic Teaching. Eusebius must have been fully aware of the rather marked lack of initiative which characterized the early history of the Church of Rome—which enabled him to appreciate all the more the few occasions where he found evidence for some initiative: the Epistle of Clement to the Corinthians, the letter from Soter to the same Church, which was read to them "for their admonition," and the controversial action of Victor in the Easter dispute.[49] These, it would seem, were the exceptions. The more general way by which the Church of Rome "determined" the orthodox Faith was indicated by Irenaeus: in matters of dispute over serious questions regarding the Faith, then recourse should be made to those Churches which were regarded as possessing the Apostolic Tradition, in particular the Church "founded and established at Rome by the two most glorious Apostles, Peter and Paul." This recourse to Rome was best illustrated by the journey of Hegesippus. Rome was not the only Church he visited in his search to establish the content of the Apostolic Teaching, but it was the Church to which he finally made recourse and where, according to Eusebius, he settled down. A little earlier, Eusebius drew attention to the visit of Polycarp who "came to converse with Anicletus,"[50] which visit, despite

---

[47]   Cf. *HE* 4,21,1 (Schwartz 368,15–16). The reign of Soter ends with the interesting story of Bardesanes the Valentinian, who later tried to free himself from the errors of that heresy but did not quite succeed (*HE* 4,30,1–3 = Schwartz 392,14–28).

[48]   Alexandria and Antioch also receive mention, which also reflects their authority as second to that of Rome. There are no allusions in the immediate context which would throw further light on the precise nature or degree of this authoritative function, as there are for Rome.

[49]   However, the third century saw an increase in the initiative exercised by the Church of Rome, as seen, particularly in the action of Pope Stephen in the Baptismal dispute as well as the involvement of Dionysius of Rome in the Sabellian discussions in Egypt and the Pentapolis.

[50]   ... εἰς ὁμιλίαν τῷ Ἀνικήτῳ ἐλθεῖν... (*HE* 4,14,1 = Schwartz 332,5). The formulation is almost identical with that used to describe Philo's visit to Rome to visit Peter (cf. *HE* 2,17,1 = Schwartz 142,2). Regarding the actual visit, and the subject of the dialogue, see von Campenhausen, "Ostertermin oder Osterfasten," 114f.

some difference of opinion, culminated in reciprocal communion.[51] Later our author will single out the visit of Irenaeus to Rome and his recommendation to Bishop Eleutherius by the confessors of Lyons.[52] When defending Origen's orthodoxy, Eusebius will not fail to mention the visit of the great Alexandrian writer to Rome at the time of Bishop Zephyrinus, who is portrayed by Eusebius as having been renowned for his severity towards the heterodox.[53] The significance of this is only realized if one remembers that unless the visitor was explicitly denied communion, or his teaching condemned, then his visit to a Church implied his acceptance by the Church and the acknowledgement of his orthodoxy.[54]

Both the synchronism under Soter and the emphasis placed on the various "visits" of orthodox writers to Rome illustrate the recognition by Eusebius of Rome's unique authoritative role in preserving the orthodox Faith. In accordance with his concept of the Apostolic Succession as consisting of two complementary "offices" which preserved and handed on the Apostolic Tradition, the "office" of authority and that of teaching, Eusebius understands the Bishops of Rome in particular as those who exercise the first "office" (though not exclusively, since the orthodox writers he lists are also bishops), while the famous writers exercise the second "office" (again not exclusively, since Soter, like Clement before him, is one of the few Bishops of Rome whose writing was renowned). Further, due to his broader concept of the Apostolic Successions as the history of a "dynasty," Eusebius presents his history of the first century of the post-Apostolic Church according to the periods marked off by the reigns of the Bishops of Rome, the seat of the principal "authority." Although the bishops of Alexandria are singled out at the opening of Book 4, they become secondary to those of Rome in the course of the book. The successions at Antioch receive but one

---

51 Cf. "Letter of Irenaeus to Victor," *HE* 5,24,17 (Schwartz 496,15–19).
52 *HE* 5,4,1–2 (Schwartz 432,27–434,6).
53 *HE* 6,14,10 (Schwartz 552,9–13). We have no other details of Origen's visit to Rome, nor of its cause or the circumstances surrounding it.
54 Karrer, "Das Petrusamt in der Frühkirche," 519, has the following comment to make on Irenaeus, *Adv. haer.*, 3,2: "Neben den hier von Irenäus angedeuteten *Römerfahrten* der Gläubigen (besonders Bischöfe) 'von überallher' sind bemerkenswert auch die von verdächtigten oder von wirklichen Häretikern. Die Voraussetzung und der Sinn sind ohne weiteres einleuchtend: wer mit dem römischen Bischof in Beziehung stand, hatte damit die zuverlässigste Beglaubigung seiner Kirchengliedschaft." The same basic idea was shared by Eusebius.

mention,[55] where four bishops are listed together without any significance, except for Theophilus, who is inserted into the synchronism under Soter.

§2 Book 5: The Paschal Controversy and the St. Peter/ Simon Magus Prototype

Again, in Book 5, historical events are presented as occurrences under the reigns of the Roman bishops, Eleutherius, Victor, and Zephyrinus. The succession of Eleutherius, who is described as the twelfth from the Apostles,[56] opens the book. Within the reign of Eleutherius, "whose times we are now discussing,"[57] the successions at Alexandria are mentioned some nine chapters later[58] by way of introduction to the history of the famous School of Alexandria, to be followed by a notice about the successions at Jerusalem.[59] As in the previous book, the bishops at Jerusalem are here listed *en bloc,* since their reigns do not have any real significance for the universal Church. To remind us of the end of the earlier dispensation granted to the Church at Jerusalem, Eusebius again refers to the Gentile composition of that Church which once received a special mission to the Circumcised.[60] At the end of the very detailed account of Eleutherius' reign, for which Eusebius evidently had considerable material at his disposal, he makes a passing reference to the succession at Antioch—in a subordinate clause.[61]

The second half of the book is mostly dedicated to a description of the succession of Bishop Victor of Rome, whose reign is introduced by a general notice of the successions in the other major sees, Alexandria and Antioch, together with a mention of the bishops of Palestinian Caesarea, Jerusalem, Corinth, and Ephesus in that order, all of whom were prominent in the Paschal Controversy.[62] The Paschal Controversy is the main event of Victor's reign, though not the only one. Book 5 ends with a short account of

---

55   Cf. *HE* 4,20,1 (Schwartz 368,8–11).
56   Cf. *HE* 5, "Proem," 1 (Schwartz 400,2–3).
57   *HE* 5,5,9 (Schwartz 438,5).
58   Cf. *HE* 5,9,1 (Schwartz 450,7–11).
59   Cf. *HE* 5,12,1–2 (Schwartz 454,3–14).
60   Cf. *HE* 5,12,1 (Schwartz 454,5–8).
61   Cf. *HE* 5,19,1 (Schwartz 478,21–23). However, it is possible that, as Schwartz, *Einleitung*, 30, suggests, Serapion is mentioned here simply in connection with the refutation of the Montanist heresy. His succession to the See of Antioch as such is mentioned in *HE* 5,22,1.
62   Cf. *HE* 5,22,1 (Schwartz 486,20–488,6).

Zephyrinus' reign,[63] without reference to any of the other successions. Instead of an outline of the events which marked the reigns of Eleutherius, Victor, and Zephyrinus, which would be rather unwieldly, we will instead concentrate on the way Eusebius handles Irenaeus and the Paschal Controversy under Victor, where the Bishop of Lyons played such an important part.

Both in the treatment of the Montanist heresy to be found in the first half of the book, and in the Paschal Controversy, which occupies much of the second half, the personality of *Irenaeus of Lyons* dominates the scene. Obviously, an admirer of this great writer, Eusebius is also indebted to him for much of his source material for the history of the second century. From the selection Eusebius makes of the plentiful material which Irenaeus supplies, together with the way he presents the person of this giant of the early Church, we can gather how he has interpreted Irenaeus' own attitude to Rome. In Chapter One, we already noted how Eusebius, who apparently used the "lists" of successions to be found in the *Adv. haer.* 3,3,3 as the basis of his own list of Roman bishops, and indeed singles it out for special reference here in Book 5 where he quotes it almost in its entirety,[64] nonetheless interprets and makes use of the "list" in a way not originally intended by Irenaeus.[65] As mentioned above, Eusebius gives the "list" a new chronological significance and treats bishops as the ecclesiastical parallels to the successions of rulers in imperial dynasties. While retaining vestiges of the original synchronism of heretics, he creates a new type of synchronism, that of the orthodox writers grouped around certain Roman bishops, such as Soter. According to his new understanding of the concept of "Apostolic Succession," the bishops (specifically, the bishops of the Petrine Succession at Rome) are not so much authoritative teachers as authorities who guarantee the orthodoxy (or Apostolicity) of those writers who in a more narrow sense fulfil the "office" of teachers. Eusebius retains, indeed sharpens, Irenaeus' understanding of the preeminence of Rome within the Church Universal in authoritatively deciding the content of the Apostolic Tradition. This we will see again below.

At the opening of Book 5, Eusebius introduces the reader to the personality of Irenaeus by recalling how the young presbyter was numbered among the representatives from the Church in Gaul who were sent to Eleutherius, Bishop of the Romans, with letters

---

[63] Cf. *HE* 5,28,7 (Schwartz 502,8–10).
[64] Cf. *HE* 5,6,1–5 (Schwartz 438,7–440,2).
[65] See above, pp. 26–28.

containing their judgement on the Montanist heresy for the sake of the peace of the Churches,"[66] i.e., to receive confirmation of their judgement from the Bishop of the Romans through his acceptance of these *Letters of Communion*.[67] Irenaeus was further singled out for commendation to the Bishop of Rome.[68] The significance of this, as the context suggests, is to introduce Irenaeus, as a writer who, from the outset of his career, enjoyed a special association and communion with the Bishop of the Romans. We recall how Irenaeus was previously included in the synchronism under Soter of Rome for a similar and complementary reason. Thus, it is not surprising to find that, when Eusebius recounts the succession of Irenaeus to the See of Lyons, he immediately goes on to quote the Bishop of Lyons' list of Roman successions, once more drawing attention to the close connection between Irenaeus and the See of Rome,[69] the principal authority within the Apostolic Succession or Dynasty. Such an emphasis on the relationship between the great orthodox writer and the preeminent Apostolic Authority was probably intended by Eusebius to influence the reader's interpretation of the later intervention of Irenaeus in the Paschal Controversy so as to eliminate any misrepresentation of that intervention as an attack on Rome's authority.

Before enumerating his succession of bishops at Rome, Irenaeus makes the bold and much discussed statement (which Eusebius does *not* quote): "ad hanc enim Ecclesiam propter potentiorem principalitatem necesse est omnem *conuenire* Ecclesiam, hoc est eos qui sunt undique fideles, in qua semper ab his qui sunt undique conseruata est ea quae est ab apostolis traditio."[70] What the precise meaning of *propter potentiorem principalitatem* may be does not concern us here—as stated above, I accept Rousseau's interpretation of these terms to refer to the superior origin of the Roman See, which, as we saw in Chapter Two, was also the reason for Rome's preeminence in the eyes of Eusebius. But what does interest us is how, during the Paschal Controversy under Victor of Rome, the nature of the "*conuenire*" (the *agreement* of all Churches with the Church of Rome) came under scrutiny. This controversy marks the first moment in the history of the Church when the question as to *what constitutes the nature of the Church's unity* at the level of the

---

66   *HE* 5,3,4 (Schwartz 432,26).
67   Regarding the significance of such *Letters of Communion*, see the now classic study of L. Hertling, "Communio und Primat," especially p. 103f.
68   Cf. *HE* 5,4,1–2 (Schwartz 432,27–434,6).
69   Cf. *HE* 5,5,9 (Schwartz 438,3–6).
70   *Adv. haer.* 3,3,2 (Rousseau-Doutreleau 32).

Church Universal was broached. Before examining the text of Eusebius, let us first take a look at the prehistory of the question. From the beginning, the Church knew her mission to be universal but her manifestation as the ἐκκλησία to be in the first place local,[71] whose focal point was the εὐχαριστία.[72] Not limited to any one people or nation, as in the old dispensation, these local Churches, though scattered throughout the world, each with its bishop, presbytery, and diaconate, constituted the one Church, the one Body of Christ,[73] not as quantitative parts which added together or grouped under some central administration made up some multi-national corporation, but as a communion (κοινωνία).[74] This universal communion, rooted in the union of the baptized in Christ, was likewise understood to be determined by the εὐχαριστία which in various ways shaped its concrete expressions. Tertullian, whose writings Eusebius was familiar with, summed this up when, talking about the Apostolic origins of all (local) Churches, he wrote: ". . . tot ac tantae ecclesiae una est illa ab apostolis prima, ex qua omnes. Sic omnes primae et apostolicae, dum una omnes. Probant unitatem communicatio pacis et appellatio fraternitatis et contesseratio hospitalitatis, quae iura non alia ratio regit quam eiusdem sacramenti una traditio."[75] The *communicatio pacis*, which culminated in the Eucharist, presupposes adherence to the one Apostolic Tradition,[76] that is to the Apostolic Teaching as handed on through the Apostolic Succession. It is the bishops of the local Churches, who, presiding over the Eucharist and acting together with their presbyters and deacons, embody the Apostolic Succession and hand-on the Teaching. Their agreement with each other manifests the unity of the Church Universal: their bonds of hospitality, title of brother, and interchange of the Pax—all of which are regulated by the one Apostolic Faith. As Irenaeus maintained, the Church of Rome due to her greater eminence as the Church founded by Peter and Paul, was the principal Church to which one had recourse in disputes about major questions (concerning the Apostolic Teaching) and with which all must, of necessity, be in agreement.

---

[71] See Ratzinger, *Volk Gottes*, 123f.
[72] See Hertling, "Communio und Primat," 91f.
[73] See Ratzinger, *Volk Gottes*, 75–89; 97–99.
[74] See Hertling, "Communio und Primat," 91–125; see also the study of McDermott, "The Biblical Doctrine of ΚΟΙΝΩΝΙΑ," 64–77; 219–233, regarding the scriptural background of this term.
[75] Tertullian, *De praescriptione haereticorum*, 20 (CSEL 70, Kroymann, 24,25–30).
[76] See Kelly, *Early Christian Doctrine*, 35–41, for an outline of Irenaeus' and Tertullian's concept of "tradition."

As mentioned above, Eusebius did not quote the disputed statement about all Churches necessarily being in agreement with the Church of Rome, although he does quote the text immediately following this sentence, which is Irenaeus' list of Roman successions.[77] This was not due to any difficulty with regard to accepting the clause referring to *propter potentiorem principalitatem*, since, as we have seen and will continue to see in the original *History* at least, Eusebius accepted the preeminence of that Church on *account of her superior origins*. If there was any more profound reason for not quoting this text other than the obvious one, that it was not immediately relevant,[78] then it could only have been on account of his perplexity in interpreting the main point of that passage: ad hanc enim Ecclesiam . . . necesse est omnem *conuenire* Ecclesiam . . . Eusebius, like Irenaeus, was in no doubt as to the necessity of agreement. He would have no difficulty in accepting the contention of the Bishop of Lyons that "having received this preaching and this Faith (= the Apostolic Teaching he has just outlined in a credal formula) . . . the Church, though dispersed throughout the whole world, keeps it carefully as dwelling in one house; and she believes these doctrines as though she had one soul and one heart, and preaches and teaches them, and hands them down as if she had one mouth. For although there are different languages in the world, the force of tradition is one and the same. . . ."[79] But if disagreement should arise and both parties claim the support of an Apostolic Tradition, as happened in the Paschal Controversy,[80] to what or to whom should they have recourse? The Church of Rome would have

---

[77] Cf. *HE* 5,6,1f. (Schwartz 438,7f.).

[78] For the same reason, Eusebius (*HE* 5,6,1–5) edits *Adv. haer.* 3,3,3 and removes all material that is superfluous to his immediate needs (namely to quote the Irenaean list of Roman bishops in order to illustrate Irenaeus' known association with the See of Rome). The only piece of apparently superfluous information that Eusebius retains is the minor excursus of Irenaeus on Clement of Rome; and, as we will see, he does so for a specific purpose.

[79] *Adv. haer.* 1,10,2 (*PG* 7,552,A10–B5), transl. Greenslade.

[80] See Sozomen, *HE* 7,19,1 (Bidez-Hansen 330,2–9) and Socrates, HE 5,22,21 (Hussey II, 627). Schmidt, "Die Passahfeier," 582, commenting on Victor's action, states: "Die sedes apostolica stand im Hintergrund, vor allem müssen die übrigen Provinzialkirchen auf ihre παράδοσις ἀποστολική gepocht haben." See also Brox, "Tendenzen und Parteilichkeiten im Osterfeststreit," 293–295, for a concise discussion of the question. Brox draws attention to the real difficulty for dogmatic reflection produced by this clash of two "Apostolic Traditions." It seems to me that a similar situation arose during the Montanist Controversy between Gaius and Proclus (cf. *HE* 2,25,7), but there the issues were more clear-cut, since the Montanist aberrations from the Apostolic Teaching were more easily perceived for what they were.

been the answer—but one of the parties was that very Church and its tradition. This was not just any Church, or even any Church which in its own special way claimed direct Apostolic origins, but the "most ancient Church" in which the Apostles lived, with which all must, of necessity, be in agreement. It is within this context that the institution of the Synod of Bishops—as distinct from the synod of a local Church made up of its bishop, presbytery, deacons, and the faithful—makes its first appearance in history, probably as a consultative body made up of neighboring bishops who came together on a more or less informal basis to help establish unanimity on a disputed topic.

For Eusebius, the Paschal Controversy was not simply a past event to be considered with detachment and relative indifference, but an issue which continued to engage the bishops and theologians of the Church long after the original *History* was composed before 303. It is to be expected, then, that in his presentation of the history of its origins, Eusebius will arrange his source material according to his own judgement on the issues involved. Apart from the actual question about the celebration of the Easter Mystery and the Fast which led up to, and which indeed were an intrinsic part of, the Feast, the controversy also brought to a head the question of authority in the Church. Our purpose here is not to examine in any detail the subject of the controversy as such,[81] but to understand the

---

[81] Since the only extant, contemporary documents relating to the Paschal Controversy are embedded in Eusebius' version of the event as found in the *History,* then any study of the issues involved must first of all examine the nature of those preferences of Eusebius which helped to determine the way the historian edited and arranged the source material at his disposal. Basing himself on the reconstruction of the dispute by G. La Piana, "The Roman Church at the End of the Second Century," in *HThR* 18 (1925), 201–277, N. Zernov was the first scholar to examine in some detail the tendencies present in Eusebius' account. The result of his findings, published under the title, "Eusebius and the Paschal Controversy," in *ChQR* 116 (1933), 24–41, were in principle accepted by Jalland, *Church and Papacy*, 115–122, by Lohse, *Das Passafest*, 134–136, and more recently by McCue, "The Roman Primacy in the Second Century," 161–196. It is unfortunate that criticism of Zernov, by the Abbot of Downside in his article, "Eusebius and St. Victor," *The Downside Review* 69 (1951), 393–410, has been practically ignored by subsequent scholars. (I am grateful to D. S. Wallace-Hadrill for bringing it to my attention.) The Abbot of Downside argued that the main "tendency" discovered by Zernov—namely that Eusebius' view of the Pastoral Controversy was primarily determined by his support for Constantine's policy of uniformity—was groundless, since Eusebius' account of the dispute "almost certainly antedates Eusebius' alliance with Constantine." It may be said in parenthesis that the Abbot bases his criticism on Schwartz's theory that the original *History*, to which the account

attitude Eusebius takes to the action of Victor of Rome in the course of the dispute. At the outset it must be emphasized that Eusebius could in no way have been influenced by Constantine or his policy of uniformity, since the account of Eusebius predates Constantine's arrival on the stage of Church history—or even his appearance in profane history—a fact that has been generally overseen.[82] Since the Church at Caesarea observed the same practice as the Roman Church,[83] then we can expect Eusebius to be sympathetic to the stand taken by Victor regarding the issue itself, the celebration of Easter. But how did Eusebius view the reaction of Victor to the refusal of the Asian Churches to conform to the custom followed by the Roman Church? It is the attitude of Eusebius to this specific issue which will occupy our attention in the following analysis.

We have already noted how in the reign of Eleutherius, the history of Irenaeus was introduced as that of one who recognized the value of Rome's preeminent authority and who in turn enjoyed communion with Rome from the beginning of his ecclesiastical career. This communion involved the recognition of Irenaeus' writings by the Roman Church, as the synchronism under Soter and his reception at Rome by Eleutherius implied. When Eusebius quoted the list of successions found in *Adv. haer.* 3,3,3 in association with Irenaeus' election to the episcopate at Lyons, he edited the text so as to retain the first part of Irenaeus' fairly long note in it, concerning the famous epistle which was sent by the Church of Rome at the time of Clement, when "no little dissension arose among the brethren at

of the Paschal dispute belongs, was written before 311; the earlier dating of Laqueur gives even more force to his argument. Mohrmann, "Le conflit pascal au IIe siècle," 158–159, simply affirms that the presentation of Eusebius reflects the controversy as it raged in his own day. This statement, together with that of Lohse mentioned above, was rejected by Huber, *Passa und Ostern*, 30, on the ground that such a contention lacked sufficient historical demonstration. The criticism of Huber was accepted by Brox, "Tendenzen und Parteilichkeiten im Osterfeststreit," who attempted to uncover first the complex, personal situation Irenaeus of Lyons (Eusebius' principal source) found himself in as the mediator in the dispute between Rome and Asia Minor, then to reconstruct the text of Irenaeus' letter behind a key paraphrase made by Eusebius, and finally to test the account of Eusebius in the light of the reconstructed views of Irenaeus. Brox concludes that, for Irenaeus, only the Asian custom was in fact of Apostolic origin, while the Roman was not. Regarding the interpretation of Brox, see von Campenhausen, "Ostertermin oder Osterfasten," 123f.

[82] Regarding the gradual development of Eusebius' interest in Constantine, see below, Chapter Four, where it will be seen that Eusebius' alliance with the Emperor Constantine really only began at the very earliest in the year 325, with the experience of the Great Synod of Nicaea.

[83] See *HE* 5,25,1 (Schwartz 496,25–498,6).

Corinth."[84] This text served as a reminder to Eusebius' readers of the first of the three known interventions by the Church of Rome in the first century or so of her history, the justice of which intervention no one ever questioned, and prepares his readers to be more sympathetic to the very controversial action of Victor of Rome during the heated debate on the Paschal question. Another sign of Eusebius' tendentious arrangement of the narrative, to suit this purpose, appears in his presentation of the other great controversy of Book 5, the *Montanist heresy* in Asia Minor.[85]

As Schwartz observed,[86] Eusebius endeavors to link the Montanist heresy with other schisms or heresies in Rome which bore no relation to it; these are the heresies of Blastus,[87] a Quartodeciman,[88] and that of his fellow presbyter at Rome, Florinus, a Gnostic of Valentinian tendencies.[89] The reference to Blastus is also the first explicit mention of the Quartodeciman or Paschal Controversy concerning the different traditions in East (especially Asia Minor) and West (in particular Rome) with regard to the date of Easter. By linking it to the Montanist heresy in Asia Minor—its activities in Africa are ignored—Eusebius has introduced the Easter question in the most unfavorable light as far as the tradition of Asia Minor is concerned by associating their custom concerning Easter with the "Cataphrygian"[90] heresy of the same provenance which all, East and West, condemned. At the same time he has gained as much sympathy as possible from his Eastern readers for the later Roman excommunications, since he informs us that Blastus (and Florinus) were dismissed from the presbytery of the Church of Rome.[91] Immediately after this "expulsion," the attack on the Montanist heresy by Apolinarius of Hierapolis is related.[92] Apolinarius was not only a native of Asia Minor, but he was also, to judge from fragments of his work on Easter (Περὶ τοῦ πάσχα), preserved in the *Chronicon paschale*, an anti-Quartodeciman.[93] Again at the end of this section covering the Montanist heresy,

---

[84] *HE* 5,6,3 (Schwartz 438,16).
[85] Cf. *HE* 5,14,1–5,19,4 (Schwartz 458,16–480,15).
[86] See Schwartz, *Einleitung*, 29.
[87] Cf. *HE* 5,15,1 (Schwartz 458,24). McGiffert, *Eusebius*, LNPF2, 237, footnote 2, suggests that Blastus had Montanist leanings, but we have no proof apart from the context of Eusebius' presentation.
[88] See article by F. J. A. Hort in *DCB*, vol. I, 319; also, that by Jülicher in *PWK* III, 559.
[89] Cf. *HE* 5,15,1 (Schwartz 458,23); *HE* 5,20,1–8 (Schwartz 480,14–484,21).
[90] *HE* 5,16,1 (Schwartz 458,28).
[91] Cf. *HE* 5,15,1 (Schwartz 458,22–25).
[92] Cf. *HE* 5,16,1–5,19,4 (Schwartz 458,28–480,15).
[93] See Quasten, *Patrology* I, 229.

Eusebius returns to Blastus and Florinus, "who were discarding the sound ordinance of the Church" in Rome,[94] this time informing his readers that Irenaeus had written to Blastus on Schism, as well as two Letters to Florinus. On both occasions where Blastus is mentioned, he is not the main character but is overshadowed by Florinus, whose Gnostic views are pilloried by Irenaeus on the second occasion.[95] But the association of the Quartodeciman with heresy is all that Eusebius is interested in at this stage, apart from inferring (unjustly) that Irenaeus was anti-Quartodeciman since he attacked the views of Blastus.

Mention has already been made of the list of bishops which introduces the Paschal Controversy. There Victor received the first mention, as the Roman bishop under whose reign the event occurred, and his opponent in the debate about Easter, Polycrates of Ephesus, occupies the last place.[96] In the build-up of the narrative to this point, the allusion to the intervention of the Church of Rome under Clement as well as her action in excluding Blastus from the presbyterate at Rome, and so in effect "excommunicating" him, have helped to "prejudice" the reader in favor of the drastic action of Victor. The healthy state of the Church at Rome, where many wealthy people were zealous in piety to the extent of suffering martyrdom, is described in the chapter[97] which immediately precedes the account of the Paschal Controversy, as though to further enhance the "image" of the Roman Church as the place where everything was in order.

The province of Asia, we are told, observed the Lord's Passover on the "14th day after the (new) moon," coinciding with the Jewish feast of the old dispensation, "as though it were a *more ancient tradition*; on that day they ended the fast. On the other hand, the Churches "throughout the rest of the whole world" held on to the custom which they kept according to the "*Apostolic Tradition*" which decreed that the fast end on no other day than the day of the Lord s Resurrection.[98] Through his presentation, Eusebius emphasizes

---

[94] *HE* 5,20,1 (Schwartz 480,16).
[95] Cf. *HE* 5,20,1–8 (Schwartz 480,16–484,21).
[96] *HE* 5,22,1 (Schwartz 486,20–483,3).
[97] Cf. *HE* 5,21,1–5 (Schwartz 484,23–486,19).
[98] *HE* 5,23,1 (Schwartz 488,7–17). Both Zernov ("Eusebius and the Paschal Controversy," 33) and Brox ("Tendenzen und Parteilichkeiten im Osterfeststreit," 309) draw attention to the partisanship of Eusebius in the opening of his account of the controversy, as seen in the contrast between the "more ancient tradition" of the Asian community and the "Apostolic Tradition" of the Churches throughout the world. A similar tendency is to be found behind the formulation of *HE* 5,24,1 (Schwartz 490,7–9). However, any precise evaluation

that the Asian custom is very much a *local* one, while the "rest of the whole world" were unanimous (μιᾷ γνώμῃ)[99] in their support for the custom sanctioned by Apostolic Tradition. This unanimity found expression in "synods and gatherings of bishops" which literally "happened."[100] The phraseology of this clause would indicate that these first synods of bishops were of an "ad hoc" nature. It is of note that, according to the Letter of Polycrates of Ephesus to "Victor and the Church of Rome,"[101] it was the Bishop of Rome who instructed Polycrates to summon his neighboring bishops to consult on the matter.[102] Once the various gatherings of bishops—it would perhaps be incorrect to call them synods in the strict sense of a semi-permanent institution—had reached agreement, they conveyed their unanimous agreement in letters, just as the bishop of a local Church had previously communicated the Faith of that Church's synod over which he presided, through the *Letters of Communion*. These were no casual letters but the ecclesiastical teaching

of such an apparent tendentious presentation must take into consideration the fact that, for Eusebius, antiquity as such possessed an almost absolute value (see above, p. 36f.). In this case, it seems that the "more ancient" practice or tradition of the Asian communities surely refers to the Jewish background of the Quartodeciman custom, as the context of *HE* 5,23,1 implies, so that what Eusebius says in effect is, that the Asians claimed to follow a custom which went back beyond Apostolic times and celebrated the Feast on the day the Jews were instructed (by prophetic utterance) to sacrifice the Lamb. (This is also the interpretation of Socrates, *HE* 5,22,19 = Hussey II, 627.) The fact that Eusebius included the defense of the Apostolicity of the Asian custom, made by Polycrates of Ephesus in his Letter to Victor, should be sufficient to demonstrate the fact that Eusebius had no intention of going so far as denying the Apostolic sanction for the practice of the Quartodecimans. In truth, the partisanship of Eusebius is as complex as that of Irenaeus—and almost as subtle—since he too attempted to reconcile various principles which he knew ought to be in harmony with one another. But Eusebius cannot be seen, at this stage at least, as a propagandist for the later "Constantinian" solution—if such is an adequate description of the Nicene decision. One must agree with Brox with regard to the specific Eusebian nuance behind *HE* 5,23,1: "Die Formulierungen für die Asiaten in V,23,1 . . . scheinen eine fast sektiererische Vorliebe für (wenn auch alte) Teilüberlieferungen charakterisieren zu wollen" (p. 309).

99 *HE* 5,23,2 (Schwartz 488,18).
100 σύνοδοι δὴ καὶ συγκροτήσεις ἐπισκόπων ἐπὶ ταὐτὸν ἐγίνοντο (*HE* 5,23,2 = Schwartz 488,17–18). The Abbot of Downside, "Eusebius and St. Victor," 396–397, correctly rejects Zernov's interpretation of this passage as though it implied a spontaneous movement which suddenly spang up inside the Catholic Church.
101 *HE* 5,24,1 (Schwartz 490,9).
102 . . . οὓς (= the Asian bishops) ὑμεῖς ἠξιώσατε μετακληθῆναι (*HE* 5,24,8 = Schwartz 492,20). See Roethe, *Synoden*, 22.

(ἐκκλησιαστικὸν δόγμα),[103] which due to the authority of the bishops was
binding on all.

The relationship of the Bishop of Rome to these "gatherings" was
unique, not only in so far as he could take the initiative to instruct that
the bishops of Asia Minor should assemble to discuss the debated issue,
but also, according to the presentation of Eusebius, in the way the letter
issued by the "synod" held at Rome apparently carried his name: Eusebius
tells us that the writing of those who assembled in Palestine under the dual
presidency of the bishops of the preeminent Church there (Caesarea) and
the highly respected Church of Jerusalem was still extant; so too was a letter
from the bishops of Pontus, over whom the oldest bishop, Palmas, presided;
one from the communities of Gaul, which Irenaeus supervised as well as
a writing from the bishops of the Osrhoene, were also in his possession;
but the extant letter from those who convened at Rome is not described
as a letter from the bishops but rather as one which "bears the name of
Bishop Victor:" ἐπίσκοπον Βίκτορα δηλοῦσα.[104] According to Roethe,[105] the
Synod of Rome in the third and fourth centuries was distinguished from
all other synods of bishops by the fact that the Bishop of Rome was not
considered to be of equal rank, but rather to be superior to the neighboring
bishops who came together with him and acted primarily in an advisory
capacity. Eusebius' accurate report of the synods assembled to discuss the
Paschal Feast confirms the essential veracity of this observation—indeed
it underlines the fact that such was true from the very inception of the
episcopal synods at the end of the second century—and at the same time
demonstrates how the unique relationship of the Bishop of Rome to the
synod was not merely of local import but was also recognized in the East,
at least at the end of the third and the beginning of the fourth centuries.

Even though the various "synodal gatherings" communicated their

---

[103] πάντες τε μιᾷ γνώμῃ δι' ἐπιστολῶν ἐκκλησιαστικὸν δόγμα τοῖς πανταχόσε
διετυποῦντο... (HE 5,23,2 = Schwartz 488,18–19). The use of the term διατυπόω,
which when used in the passive conveys the meaning of "to deal by edict (cf.
Lampe, Lexicon, 362), is to be noted, as also the use of the term ὅρος to describe
the same unanimous decision of the bishops in HE 5,23,4 (Schwartz 490,6).

[104] HE 5,23,3–4 (Schwartz 488,22–490,6). Mention is also made of letters from
individual bishops, such as Bacchyllus of Corinth, which were of equal importance, apparently, as the letters that issued from the synodal gatherings. What is
of note, with regard to the assembly at Rome, is that its decisions were issued in
the name of the Bishop of Rome.

[105] See Roethe, G., *Zur Geschichte der römischen Synoden im 3. und 4. Jahrhundert*,
1937.

"decrees" to the faithful everywhere,[106] Polycrates, writing on behalf of
the Churches in Asia Minor, addressed himself, according to Eusebius,
to Victor and the Church of Rome.[107] He defends the Asiatic custom on
the basis of its sanction by the Apostolic Succession, which succession
was "proved" by pointing to the great luminaries who had "fallen asleep"
(and were buried) in Asia, such as the Apostles Philip and John as well as
many famous martyrs. The Apostles and Witnesses to the Faith had kept
(the custom of) "the fourteenth day" and yet never swerved from the
"Rule of Faith."[108] He also defends his orthodoxy and the legitimacy of the
practice he holds by pointing to his communion with brethren from all
parts, and declares his own good conscience on the matter after his study of
Scripture.[109] To emphasize the last point, the aged Bishop of Ephesus quotes
the words of Peter before the High Priest's Council: "One must obey God
rather than men" (Acts 5,29), prefacing them with a courageous affirmation of his lack of fear for "such panic-stricken measures" (= the threat of
excommunication by Victor).[109a] This usage of Acts 5,29 prompted, most
probably by Victor's claim to speak in the name of Peter or at least on the
authority of the Petrine Succession, reverberates with irony—gently but
effectively accusing Victor of changing places with his predecessor: Peter
had become the High Priest. But it also brings to the surface the role
of conscience (or personal responsibility) on the part of the bishop in
determining that unanimity which guarantees the truth of the Apostolic
Teaching. Unanimity is not simply majority rule, but, as Irenaeus expresses
it, a union of soul and heart.[110] As was seen in Chapter One, "spatial unanimity" or consensus among the bishops is, for Hegesippus and Irenaeus,
both a sign and an *effect* of that "temporal unanimity" or adherence to the
Apostolic Teaching passed on from one generation to the other by the
Apostolic Succession; it is not a cause. Unfortunately, Eusebius on the
other hand tends to stress the numerical or quantitative majority[111] to the
detriment of Irenaeus' concept of unanimity as a union of soul and heart.

---

[106] *HE* 5,23,2 (Schwartz 488,19).
[107] *HR* 5,24,1 (Schwartz 490,9).
[108] *HE* 5,24,2–6 (Schwartz 490,12–492,8).
[109] *HE* 5,24,7 (Schwartz 492,12–14).
[109a] *HE* 5,24,7 (Schwartz 492,15–16). Regarding the attitude of Polycrates, see Grotz,
    "Die Stellung der römischen Kirche," 48–52.
[110] Cf. *Adv. haer.* 1,10,2 (*PG* 7,552,B1).
[111] Cf., e.g., *HE* 5,23,1 (Schwartz 488,13–14), where the emphasis is on the ... ἀνὰ
    τὴν λοιπὴν ἅπασα οἰκουμένην ..., and *HE* 5,23,4 (Schwartz 490,4) where the
    stress is on the many other unnamed bishops who shared the same opinion.

The reaction of Victor was his well-known excommunication of "the communities of all Asia, together with the neighboring Churches," or rather, as Eusebius reminds us, his *attempt* to cut them off from the common unity.[112] Both the vast scale of the excommunication and its formal nature[113] are underlined, yet Eusebius never once denies (or reports anyone who did) the competence of the Bishop of Rome to take this action however exaggerated it may have appeared to many observers then and since.

And to Eusebius, the excommunication of whole communities of Asia did appear exaggerated, though fundamentally justifiable. What is important to note here, and what is generally overlooked, is the justification Eusebius offers for the action of Victor. Victor of Rome excommunicated those in Asia, as though the Asian practice were heretical: ὡς ἂν ἑτροδοξούσας.[114] It would be false to conclude from this that Eusebius himself considered heretical, the custom he allowed Polycrates a few lines previously to defend so eloquently as Apostolic.[115] Eusebius rather suggests this as an excuse for Victor's over-zealous reaction, one which is understandable considering the close association between the Quartodeciman practice and the Montanist heresy.[116] Far from being anti-Roman,[117] the presentation by Eusebius is, at this stage, very much pro-Roman. The full import of this passage can only be judged within the context of Eusebius' positive appreciation of the preeminent authority of Rome in matters relating to the Apostolic Teaching.

The relationship of the Bishop of Rome to heretics, according to Eusebius' view, reflected the prototypical relationship between St. Peter and Simon Magus. Thus, in the present Book 5, the dismissal of Blastus (the Quartodeciman) and Florinus from the presbyterate of the Church of Rome on account of their confession of the Montanist heresy[118] was one instance of Rome's legitimate exercise of her Petrine authority. Immediately after the account of the Paschal Controversy, Eusebius quotes from a text which recalls how Victor, "the thirteenth bishop in Rome *after Peter*,"[119] excommunicated

---

[112] *HE* 5,24,9 (Schwartz 494,1–3).
[113] καὶ στηλιτεύει γε διὰ γραμμάτων ἀκοινωνήτους πάντας ἄρδην τοὺς ἐκεῖσε ἀνακηρύττων ἀδελφούς (*HE* 5,24,9 = Schwartz 494,3–5).
[114] *HE* 5,24,9 (Schwartz 494,3).
[115] Thus, Lohse, *Das Passafest*, 135.
[116] See above, pp. 97–98.
[117] Thus, Schwartz, *Einleitung*, 30.
[118] *HE* 5,15,1 (Schwartz 458,22–25).
[119] *HE* 5,28,3 (Schwartz 500,15–16). It is of note that Eusebius here explicitly refers to the Petrine Succession of Victor.

the heresiarch Theodotus the Cobbler,[120] and goes on to round off Book 5 with the story of the typical severity towards heretics expected from the Bishops of Rome, as illustrated in the case of Zephyrinus, Victor's successor, who hesitated to allow even a *repentant* heretic back into communion with the Church.[121] What Eusebius wishes to bring home to his readers in his account of the Paschal Controversy is that, in principle, Victor had every right to excommunicate, since Rome is expected to be severe with the heretics, *if in fact* it were a heresy.[122]

Those bishops who were displeased with the action of Victor, Eusebius' narration continues, in turn exhorted the Bishop of Rome to be considerate of "peace, unity and love towards one's neighbours;"[123] but discourses of theirs have been preserved where they assail Victor more quarrelsomely. Among these bishops was Irenaeus, who, though he *recommended* that the Mystery of the Lord's Resurrection ought to be held only on the Lord's Day,[124] counselled

---

[120] *HE* 5,28,6 (Schwartz 502,2–7).

[121] *HE* 5,28,12 (Schwartz 504,2–8).

[122] So also Socrates, *HE* 5,22,15: ἕως ὁ τῆς Ῥώμης ἐπίσκοπος Βίκτωρ ἄμετρα θερμανθεὶς, ἀκοινωνησίαν τοῖς ἐν τῇ Ἀσίᾳ τεσσαρεσκαιδεκατίταις ἀπέστειλεν (Hussey II, 626).

[123] *HE* 5,24,10 (Schwartz 494,5–8). McCue, "The Roman Primacy in the Second Century," 184, interprets this text to mean "that Rome has acted unwisely and unjustly by cutting itself off from the Asian Churches, and should now undo this wrong." Apart from the difficulties caused by the very logic of this thesis, McCue offers no independent evidence to support such an interpretation apart from the vague generalization that "it fits in much better with what we know of the second and third centuries," a contention McCue fails to substantiate. What the paraphrase of Eusebius does convey is that the action of Victor alarmed many bishops who, although they were prepared to opt for the "Roman practice" (cf. *HE* 5,23,2), were, it seems, not prepared to cut off from their communion those who, for good reasons, observed a different custom. However, as Hess points out, "The evidentiary value of Eusebius' report is somewhat clouded by the double agenda which he served by the telling" (Hess, *The Early Development*, 9).

[124] *HE* 5,24,11 (Schwartz 494,9–11), "La formule employée par Eusèbe est assez intéressante, parce qu'elle reflète clairement, non pas l'usage de IIe siècle, mais la conception de Pâque de temps d'Eusèbe. . . ." Mohrmann, "Le conflit pascal au IIe siècle," 158–159. As already mentioned, Mohrmann gives no evidence in support of her affirmation. According to Brox, "Tendenzen und Parteilichkeiten im Osterfeststreit," this paraphrase of Eusebius is highly tendentious, when seen in the light of his reconstruction of the original attitude of Irenaeus (p. 299). However, until such time as the objections to this thesis (e.g., von Campenhausen, "Ostertermin oder Osterfasten," 124–125 and 138) have been answered, the opinion of Huber, *Passa und Ostern*, 30, still deserves our attention: "Doch muß man es zumindest für möglich halten, daß Euseb hier nicht die Formulierungen seiner eigenen Zeit gebraucht, sondern diejenigen, die er in den ihm vorliegenden Synodalakten vorfand. Man hat den Eindruck, daß er den Synodalbeschluß wörtlich

Victor not to excommunicate whole Churches for observing an ancient custom,[125] and not to treat the matter of the fast as though it were one of Faith, but rather as one of legitimate diversity of custom, which claimed the sanction of an Apostolic Tradition.[126] Further, Irenaeus pointed out, previous generations had tolerated such diversity and goes on to list Victor's predecessors who, in spite of a similar variation in the observance of the Feast, lived in Peace.[127] The most renowned of Victor's predecessors was Anicetus, who, even though he differed with Polycarp about some other matters, remained in communion with him.[128] It is within this context that Irenaeus enunciates his dictum: "the discord concerning the fast confirms [our] concord in the Faith."[129] The main point of Irenaeus is that the Quartodeciman custom is not a matter that touches on the question of orthodoxy so that divergence from it would entail excommunication from the Church. The unanimity in the *Faith*, which Irenaeus held as a first principle, and which was a necessary consequence of the unanimity of the Apostles and the existence of *one Apostolic Tradition*, did not necessarily extend to matters of liturgical and pastoral *custom*. According to his dictum, diversity in such matters could strengthen the more fundamental unity in the one Faith.[130]

Since Eusebius explicitly commends this irenic intervention of Irenaeus,[131] we are permitted to conclude that, circa 303, the author of the *original History* shared the earlier attitude of the Bishop of Lyons towards those who followed a different custom to that observed by his own Church at Caesarea, which custom he was

zitieren will und daß er dessen knappe Formulierung für das Referat über den Brief des Irenäus übernimmt."

[125] *HE* 5,24,11 (Schwartz 494,12–14).

[126] *HE* 5,24,12–13 (Schwartz 494,15–25); *HE* 5,24,16 (Schwartz 496,11–13).

[127] *HE* 5,24,14–17 (Schwartz 494,28–496,19).

[128] *HE* 5,24,16 (Schwartz 496,7–15). See von Campenhausen, "Ostertermin oder Osterfasten," 114–138, who defends the thesis originally proposed by Theodore Zahn in 1891, namely that the discussion between Polycarp and Anicet did not concern the date of Easter but rather the fast which proceeded the celebration of the Feast.

[129] . . . ἡ διαφωνία τῆς νηστείας τὴν ὁμόνοιαν τῆς πίστεως συνίστησιν. (*HE* 5,24,13 = Schwartz 494,24–25).

[130] Both Socrates and Sozomen contend that the Paschal Controversy was resolved on the basis of this principle: . . . καὶ γὰρ οἱ τῆς αὐτῆς πίστεως ὄντες διαφωνοῦσι περὶ τὰ ἔθη πρὸς ἑαυτούς, Socrates, *HE* 5,22,31 (Hussey II, 630); see also Sozomen, *HE* 7,19,1 (Bidez-Hansen 330,3–11). See also von Campenhausen, "Ostertermin oder Osterfasten," 119–122, who recently drew attention to this point which has tended to be underplayed in the literature about the Paschal Controversy.

[131] *HE* 5,24,18 (Schwartz 496,20–24).

convinced was sanctioned by "the Apostolic Succession."[132] It is Irenaeus'
distinction between the Faith (Apostolic Teaching) and legitimate liturgical customs which enables Eusebius to present the overzealous reaction of
Victor as justified in principle, since Victor considered the Quartodeciman
custom to be heterodox, but not in fact, since he, like Irenaeus before
him, holds that the Asians observed an ancient *practice* with roots in the
O.T., which enjoyed the sanction of the Apostolic Succession at Ephesus.
The only specifically Eusebian emphasis is on the close association of this
custom with the Montanist heresy as well as on the *limited, local nature* of
the Asian custom in contrast with the universal practice followed by the
rest of the world and defended—not wisely but too well—by the Bishop
of Rome, acting presumably on the basis of his Petrine Succession and with
the consciousness of his unique responsibility for the universal Church.

With regard to the first appearance of a synod of bishops as a means
of establishing the unanimity which manifested the unity of the Church
Universal and guaranteed participation in that unity, we gather the following information from the account of the Paschal Controversy by Eusebius.
The "synods"—if we may be permitted to call them such—would not
appear to have been institutionalized but were rather *ad hoc* gatherings of
neighboring bishops who assembled together in the various provinces—
Palestine, Rome, Pontus, Gaul, Osrhoene, etc.,[133]—in order to consult one
another on a disputed topic and establish their common mind or unanimity. They met under the presidency of a bishop who either enjoyed personal
prestige among his peers (like Palmas in Pontus, who as the oldest bishop
presided) or occupied the most eminent see in the area (like Irenaeus of
Lyons). Due to the honor accorded to the Church of Jerusalem, the bishop
of that Church shared the presidency of the Palestinian gathering with the
bishop of the major see of the region, Caesarea.[134] We cannot definitely

---

[132] *HE* 5,25,1 (Schwartz 496,25–30). It should be noted that Eusebius inserts his
paraphrase and quotation from the *Letter of the Synod of Palestinian bishops*
immediately after his recommendation of Irenaeus' solution. The proper place
for this information in the narrative ought to have been that following *HE*
5,23,3, but to make his point Eusebius inserts it here. Situated after the solution
proposed by Irenaeus, this witness to the custom followed by the Palestinian
Churches, and, according to the quotation from the letter quoted by Eusebius,
by the Alexandrian Church, helps to remind the reader that, whatever one might
think of the overreaction of the Bishop of Rome, what he stood for was in fact
the general practice.

[133] *HE* 5,23,3–4 (Schwartz 488,22–490,6).

[134] *HE* 5,23,3 (Schwartz 488,22–25).

ascertain from Eusebius who, if anyone, took the initiative to call the various "synods." Only in the case of Asia Minor do we have clear evidence that the Bishop of Rome was responsible for the "synod" there. Polycrates of Ephesus asserts: "I could mention those bishops who are present with me, whom you (= Victor and the Church of Rome) deemed worthy to be summoned by me and whom I assembled."[135] It is most likely that, as Lietzmann suggests,[136] Victor also called on the other Churches to end the controversy. What is striking is not simply the initiative of the Bishop of Rome, which may itself have been prompted by difficulties with Asian communities in Rome who held the Quartodeciman custom,[137] but the compliance of the Asian (and other) bishops with this initiative.

The main point of their "synods," however, was to establish their unanimity on the disputed issues, as Eusebius tirelessly points out: ". . . with one mind (μιᾷ γνώμῃ) they prescribed in the form of letters for those in every (Church) an ecclesiastical decree (ἐκκλησιαστικὸν δόγμα) to the effect that the mystery of the Lord's Resurrection from the dead be celebrated on no other but the Lord's Day. . . ."[138] However, the *uniformity* of the bishops, rather than their unanimity, is stressed by Eusebius as we gather from this text and from his repeated references to "the one and the same opinion and judgment of the bishops"[139] and to the "single definition" issued by them.[140] This slightly exaggerated emphasis of Eusebius is most likely due to his own sympathy with the majority view—which, as already noted, coincided with that of his own Church. But by doing so he unintentionally tended to deny, by implication, that which he explicitly affirmed: he insisted explicitly on the unanimity of the bishops but in fact was only talking about the vote of the *majority* of the bishops, thus giving the impression that their authority was

---

[135] *HE* 5,24,8 (Schwartz 492,20).
[136] Lietzmann, *Geschichte*, bd. II, 247. See also von Campenhausen, "Ostertermin oder Osterfasten," 117.
[137] This was first suggested by G. La Piana, "The Roman Church at the End of the Second Century," in *HThR* 18 (1925), 201–277, whose historical reconstruction on the whole goes beyond the actual evidence, in particular his basic contention that Victor's motivation in the controversy was to secure the triumph of the monarchical episcopal system; La Piana also concludes that Victor thus laid the foundation of a new system of inter-Church relations in which the function of the Roman hierarchy, in the whole Church, secured for itself a higher value. Zernov and Jalland, to mention but two scholars, took up and developed the ideas of La Piana.
[138] *HE* 5,23,2 (Schwartz 488,18–21).
[139] *HE* 5,23,4 (Schwartz 490,4–5).
[140] *HE* 5,23,4 (Schwartz 490,6).

quantitatively ascertainable and thus quantitatively constituted.[141] Polycrates displays a different attitude. Although he too calls on the authority of the Apostolic Succession at Ephesus and the "many multitudes" of bishops who agreed with him, he takes his ultimate stand on the basis of his most personal conviction.[142] There the agreement with his fellow-bishops, which the courageous Bishop of Ephesus talks about, is the oneness of heart and soul of Irenaeus.[143] This concord or unanimity is rooted in the union of man with God—for which reason Polycrates can repeat the words of Peter: one must obey God rather than man. It, as Irenaeus suggested, can distinguish between the internal consent to the truth and its expression in "institutions," such as diversity of custom. It is manifested in "spatial unanimity," which can in effect produce uniformity—but uniformity itself cannot engender it. Such concord is likewise the "force of Tradition" which, though expressed in different languages, "is one and the same."[144] Later, St. Athanasius will develop this concept of unity based on internal consent, in which the emphasis is given to the σκοπός of Tradition rather than superficial uniformity.

Eusebius' superficial concept of unanimity, as the agreement of the majority, may also have been influenced in this particular instance by his underlying apologetic motive to present the Church as the perfect harmonious society, the acme of civilization. It can hardly be doubted that the Paschal Controversy and the overzealous action of Victor, even if it could be justified on the grounds of Rome's traditional severity towards heretics, presented certain difficulties for the apologist Eusebius. Here was an instance where the center of the Church's unity, by being true to its principles, seemed to create disunity and disharmony. Eusebius overcomes his difficulty by emphasizing that the majority were on the side of Victor, and by having recourse to the irenic formula proposed by Irenaeus. It is likely that he would have preferred the later solution of the Nicene Synod as supported by Constantine, whereby the Quartodecimans were made conform to the more universal custom—but that decision was over twenty years away when he wrote his original *History*. For the moment, he plasters over the cracks in his rigid theory caused by the tension between his ideal, or rather

---

[141] The fact that the letter of an individual bishop could be of equal moment with that of a "gathering" of bishops argues against any mere quantitative concept of what constitutes synodal authority.

[142] *HE* 5,24,6–7 (Schwartz 492,8–16).

[143] See *Adv. haer.* 1,10,2 (PG 7,552,B1).

[144] Irenaeus, *Adv. haer.* 1,10,2 (PG 7,552,B4–5).

idealized Church, and the historical reality, using the solution (*sic*) of
Irenaeus to do so.

Finally, we must note how the Paschal Controversy throws light on
the role of the Bishop of Rome within the universal Church. Each bishop
is not only responsible for his own local Church—but for the universal
Church, whose inner unity finds expression in that mutual agreement
which arises from assent to the one Apostolic Teaching. In case of dispute,
recourse should be made to those Churches which by virtue of their origins
could claim direct Apostolic Succession, and which consequently carry
even greater responsibility for the Church's unity. Among these Churches
claiming direct Apostolic Succession, the Church of Rome as represented
by her bishop, the successor of St. Peter, Leader of the Apostles, enjoyed
a preeminent authority, due to her "superior origins," and was thus preeminently *responsible* for the unity of the Church. Her preeminence was
largely passive, as the recognized touchstone of orthodoxy or apostolicity. Her action in the Paschal Controversy was on the other hand one of
direct involvement. If we accept that Victor took the initiative to "call" the
"synods" throughout the Church, then his action was but a development
of the Bishop of Rome's traditional responsibility. His motives in calling
the bishops to assemble together were in the first place the same as those
which prompted Irenaeus to advise disputants in doctrinal issues to have
recourse to Rome: i.e., to establish unanimity in an issue he considered to
be a matter of the Faith. The responsibility for the Churches which the
Bishop of Rome held was, materially considered, like that of any bishop—
universal in extent. But its formal character was such, due to its Petrine
Succession (hinted at by Polycrates of Ephesus), that Victor's initiative in
assembling the "synods" of bishops in various regions in the East and West
was accepted without the slightest hesitation by the rest of the Church.
Only this formal, Petrine character of Victor's responsibility could account
for the apparently immediate response of the universal episcopate to his
call, implicitly recognizing the right of the Bishop of Rome to so act.
Eusebius, writing over a century later, agrees with this initiative; he could
and did on other occasions point to the Letters of Clement and his successor Soter to the Church of Corinth as instances of such "intervention"
and direct action.

As already mentioned, Eusebius concludes Book 5 with a copious
quotation from a work *Against the Heresy of Artemon*,[145] which

---

[145] *HE* 5,28,1–19 (Schwartz 500,3–506,18). See Connolly, "Eusebius H.E. v.
28," 73–79, who upheld the opinions of Lightfoot, Harnack, and others, that
the author was in all probability Hippolytus. Comparing *HE* 5,28,12 with

illustrates how Victor of Rome exercised the responsibility due to his "office" as successor to St. Peter with regard to an issue which, unlike the Paschal Controversy, was unquestionably heretical. The followers of the heresy tried to call on the support of Victor in order to defend themselves against their rejection by his successor Zephyrinus.[146] They apparently refer to his "passive" authority, i.e., a number of them could possibly claim that they lived in Rome during his reign yet he did not excommunicate them. The writer of the document retorts with the evidence that Victor had in fact excommunicated Theodotus, "the founder and father of this God-denying revolt."[147] The picture of Victor's successor Zephyrinus, found in the second excerpt from this work, *Against Artemon,* is one which portrays the almost typical severity with heretics[148] which, from the time of its foundation by Peter down to the exaggerated reaction of Victor to the Easter question, Eusebius would have us believe marked the Church of Rome: it is the working out of the prototypical confrontation between Peter, the founder of the Church, and Simon Magus, the founder and father of all heresies.

§3 Book 6: Rome and Alexandria—the St. Peter/St. Mark Prototype

If it is true that the events in Book 5 concerning the Bishop of Rome and his role in condemning any aberrations from the Apostolic Teaching were "typical" instances of the Peter-Simon Magus "prototype," then one could say that Books 6 and 7 illustrate the Peter-Mark "prototype" and the way it stamped the relationship between Rome and Alexandria. Even when describing the origins of the famous catechetical school at Alexandria in Book 5, Eusebius could not resist an oblique reference to the Church of Rome. There we find that Eusebius introduces Clement of Alexandria into the narrative as a "namesake of the man who once ruled the Church of the Romans and was a disciple of the Apostles."[149] This

---

Philosophumena 9,2, long accepted as a composition of Hippolytus, one's confidence in such an assertion is gravely weakened.

[146] These followers were probably Asclepiodotus and the "second" Theodotus mentioned in *HE* 5,28,8–9 (Schwartz 502,16–21).

[147] *HE* 5,28,6 (Schwartz 502,2–5).

[148] Cf. *HE* 5,28,7–12 (Schwartz 502,11–504,8). Zephyrinus is shown as being so hostile to heresy that he is prepared to readmit an evidently sincerely repentant heretic to communion with the Church only with the greatest reluctance.

[149] *HE* 5,11,1 (Schwartz 452,7–8).

may have been due to the generous use made of Clemens Romanus by his namesake in Alexandria.[150] But more likely it was prompted by the desire of Eusebius to allude to the traditional association of Alexandria and Rome, whose prototype was the relationship between Peter and Mark as interpreted by Eusebius.[151] Book 6 deals with the greatest names associated with that School, whose fame helped to increase the influence of the Alexandrian Church until, at the time of Eusebius, she was second only to Rome in eminence. Up to Books 6 and 7, which deal with the third century, Alexandria and its Church played little or no role in the *History:* in Book 4 there was a passing reference to Basilides who founded a school of heresy there,[152] and in Book 5 the brief but compact reference to Pantaenus the Philosopher, the first known head of the Alexandrian School just mentioned.[153] The third reference—and the only one which refers specifically to the actual *Church* of Alexandria—was found in the Letter of the Palestinian bishops who gathered together to discuss the Easter question.[154] Book 6, however, is dominated by the towering figure of Origen, while Book 7 is largely seen through the eyes of his one-time pupil, and later Bishop of Alexandria, Dionysius.

As Schwartz observed, Books 6 and 7 are primarily distinguished from the foregoing books by their almost exclusive attention to two single personalities, Origen and Dionysius.[155] The two final books of the original *History* are, then, more biographical in content than Books 2–5. Although Eusebius helped his master Pamphilius compose an *Apology for Origen* during the imprisonment of the latter (308–309),[156] the biographical sketch found in Book 6, which of course was written as part of the original *History* before 303,[157] shows no overt preoccupation with such a defense of

---

[150]   See Lightfoot, *Clement of Rome*, 158–160.

[151]   See also *HE* 5,11,5 (Schwartz 452,22–25), where Eusebius quotes Clement, *Stromata*, 1,1, to the effect that the true tradition concerning the blessed, salvific Teaching had come down to him through his teachers, directly from Peter, James, John, and Paul (*PG* 8,700,A9–15).

[152]   Cf. *HE* 4,7,3 (Schwartz 310,2). Mention could also be made of *HE* 4,2,1–5, which describes the insurrection of the Jews at Alexandria, although the text tells us nothing about the Church there.

[153]   *HE* 5,10,1f. (Schwartz 450,12f.).

[154]   *HE* 5,25,1 (Schwartz 498,1–6).

[155]   Schwartz, *Einleitung*, 31; these views, however, need some modification, as will be seen below.

[156]   Schwartz, "Eusebios," *PWK* VI, col. 1384–1385.

[157]   The reference to the *Apology for Origen* in *HE* 6,33,4 (Schwartz 588,21–24) seems to confirm the opinion of Schwartz that the original *History* was

Origen's orthodoxy.[158] Particularly noteworthy is the restraint Eusebius shows in his presentation of Origen's strained relations with bishop Demetrius of Alexandria. And yet this biographical sketch in Book 6 was not totally free from an underlying interest: he presents the story of his hero in such a way as to gain the maximum sympathy of the reader for the cause of Origen. Thus, we find Eusebius devoting an unusual amount of space to the succession at Jerusalem[159] which culminated in the succession of Alexander. The latter succession was, to speak anachronistically, marked by two "canonical irregularities," (i) the translation of Alexander from his former see in Cappadocia to Jerusalem and (ii) the dual episcopacy of Alexander together with Narcissus.[160] The episcopacy of Alexander at Jerusalem is ultimately justified by Eusebius due to a unique revelation and Divine "Dispensation" (οἰκονομία), using the latter term in the sense of an exceptional intervention of God. The reason for relating this narrative is, of course, the fact that Alexander was one of the bishops who ordained Origen to the presbyterate[161] and so any hint of irregularity in his claims to the bishopric of Jerusalem had to be excluded. Likewise, we find other incidents in the life of Origen, which are apparently related in order to portray the great writer as one who abhorred, fought against, and overcame heresy.[162]

written during the Great Persecution and was first circulated after 311. But this text is evidently part of a later interpolation (*HE* 6,33,1–4), as is shown by the contradiction between the account of Beryllus of Bostra given in *HE* 6,33,1–3, where the bishop is described as a *heretic* of monarchist tendencies, and the account given earlier in *HE* 6,20,2, where Beryllus is included in the synchronism of *orthodox writers* under Zephyrnus of Rome! So, too, *HE* 6,23,4b, which contains a reference to the *Apology*, must be considered a later interpolation. Lawlor and Oulton, *The Ecclesiastical History*, vol. II, 218–220, had commented earlier on the chronological confusion at this stage of the narrative, attributing it to the careless method of Eusebius; their proposed solution gains credibility when one considers *HE* 6,23,4b as an interpolation by Eusebius during a later Revision.

[158] See Schwartz, *Einleitung*, 31.

[159] *HE* 6,8,7–6,11,3 (Schwartz 536,6–542,12).

[160] *HE* 6,11,1–3 (Schwartz 540,21–542,12).

[161] *HE* 6,8,4–5 (Schwartz 536,6–19). It is possible that this text is also a later interpolation and that the original reference to Origen's ordination was in *HE* 6,23,4a (Schwartz 570,10–13), where he omitted any reference to the consecrating bishops.

[162] See, for example,: Origen's refusal, while still a youth, to join a heretic in prayer (*HE* 6,2,14 = Schwartz 522,24–524,1); his visit to Rome (*HE* 6,14,10 = Schwartz 552,9–12), to which we will return; his conversion of the heretical Ambrose the Valentinian (*HE* 6,18,1 = Schwartz 556,9–12); his attack on the Gnostic heresy of the Helkesaites (*HE* 6,38,1 = Schwartz 592,13–594,2).

In spite of its biographical character, Book 6 retains the basic form of the previous *History* up to this point, according to which the events related and the literature described by Eusebius are presented in each book within a basic chronological framework marked primarily by the successive "reigns" of the Roman bishops. Thus Eusebius' "Life of Origen" in Book 6 is presented as though it encompassed the reigns of those Roman bishops who ruled from Zephrynus (198–217) up to and including Fabian (236–250). While it is true that the biography of Origen occupies the greater part of the book, yet it by no means exhausts its content, since even the "Life" is interspersed with such information as the account of the literary testaments of Clement of Alexandria and Serapion of Antioch; likewise, after the death of Origen, Book 6 devotes considerable space to the Decian Persecution and the resultant Novatian Schism. Thus, although the Life of Origen is the main subject of Book 6, it is subsumed into the general *History* of the Apostolic Successions.

The reign of Zephrynus was introduced in Book 5, where the Bishop of Rome was, as will be remembered, described as one who was renowned for his severity towards heretics, even repentant ones. The successions at Alexandria, Antioch, and Jerusalem are not, as is usual, grouped under the notice of the Roman bishop's succession, but are spaced out within the period of his reign,[163] since each of these bishops was deserving of some special comment, mostly due to their connection with Origen. The rest of the notices concerning the successions, however, revert to the more familiar pattern of grouping the bishops of Alexandria, Antioch, or Jerusalem together under the succession at Rome, the Bishop of which, enjoys the primacy in each case.[164]

---

[163] *HE* 6,2,2 (Schwartz 520,2–3) = the successions at Alexandria; *HE* 6,8,7–6,11,3 (Schwartz 536,24–542,12) = at Jerusalem; *HE* 6,11,4 (Schwartz 542,13–15) = at Antioch.

[164] Cf. *HE* 6,21,1–2 (Schwartz 566,22–568,4) = Rome and Antioch; *HE* 6,23,3 (Schwartz 570,7–10) = Rome and Antioch, followed by Alexandria (*HE* 6,26,1 = Schwartz 580,10–15); *HE* 6,29,1 (Schwartz 582,2–13) together with *HE* 6,29,4 (Schwartz 584,6–10) = Rome, Antioch, and Alexandria, to which *HE* 6,35,1 (Schwartz 590,10–12) ought to be added; *HE* 6,39,1–4 (Schwartz 549,3–15) = Rome, Jerusalem, and Antioch.

[165] *HE* 6,14,10 (Schwartz 552,9–12). Commenting on this passage, Oritz de Urbina, "Patres graeci," 106–107 remarks: "Epitheton τὴν ἀρχαιότατην ex ἀρχὴ derivatum, vel habet sensum originis vel auctoritatis. Hic vero sensus 'antiquissimae' Ecclesia romanae non aptatur, ut patet. Ergo praeferendus sensus auctoritatis. Cum vero adeat articulus et gradus superlativus, vertenda esset expressio per 'maximae inter omnes auctoritatis' (v. gr. italice 'la più autorevole')." See also Grotz, "Die Stellung der römischen Kirche," 37–38.

The following entry deserves special attention. "Admantius (since this also was Origen's name) himself writes somewhere that he dwelt at Rome when Zephrynus was at that time ruling the Church of the Romans, saying: 'Desiring to behold the most ancient Church of the Romans.'"[165] This incident immediately recalls the many "visitors" to Rome recorded by Eusebius, especially that of Hegesippus, the goal of whose journey was to establish the Apostolic Tradition as handed down through the Apostolic Succession. The text of Origen quoted by Eusebius reechoes the famous dictum of St. Irenaeus, that one should have recourse to the most ancient Churches[166] in order to receive a clear and definitive ruling on the Faith— the "greatest and most ancient" being the Church of Rome.[167] Thus, like his presentation of Irenaeus at the beginning of his ecclesiastical career, Eusebius also portrays Origen as a great orthodox writer who, from the start of his life in the service of the Apostolic Teaching, enjoyed communion with the principal authority in the Church's Apostolic Succession. To sojourn in Rome, and not to incur excommunication, implied communion with that Church.

The reign of Zephyrnus comes to an end with a typical Eusebian synchronism of orthodox writers under the Bishop of Rome: Beryllus of Bostra,[168] Hippolytus,[169] and Gaius[170] are mentioned, to whom could possibly be added the earlier mention of Serapion of Antioch[171] and Clement of Alexandria.[171a]

At the end of his life, Origen is again associated with the Bishop of Rome, who at the time was Fabian. Origen's torture and imprisonment during the Decian Persecution is described in terms of a martyrdom—even though Origen did not die at the time—and receives the singular honor of a mention after the notice of the martyrdoms endured by bishops Fabian of Rome, Alexander of Jerusalem, and Babylas of Antioch.[172] The intention of the author is to put

---

[166] Irenaeus, *Adv. haer.* 3,4,1 (Rousseau-Doutreleau 46).

[167] Irenaeus, *Adv. haer.* 3,3,2 (Rousseau-Doutreleau 32).

[168] *HE* 6,20,2 (Schwartz 566,10–13). See comment above, footnote 157: on the way, Eusebius' attitude to Beryllus evidently underwent a radical revision.

[169] *HE* 6,20,2 (Schwartz 566,13–14). Hippolytus is, rather significantly, described as "presiding over another Church somewhere"—thus avoiding any treatment of the reputed controversy between Hippolytus and the Bishop of Rome, Zephyrnus, and his successors, during which it is claimed that Hippolytus was set up as an antipope, until his reconciliation with bishop Pontianus of Rome during their exile. See Jalland, *Church and Papacy*, 128–136.

[170] *HE* 6,20,3 (Schwartz 566,14–21).

[171] *HE* 6,11,4–6,12,6 (Schwartz 542,13–546,8).

[171a] *HE* 6,13,1–6,14,9 (Schwartz 546,9–552,8).

[172] *HE* 6,39,5 (Schwartz 594,15–596,4).

his hero on a par with these martyr-saints and Successors of the Apostles. But this is not the only association of Origen with Fabian of Rome. Eusebius informs his readers, that, towards the end of Origen's life, the great teacher wrote to Fabian, the Bishop of Rome, and to many other rulers of the Church concerning his orthodoxy.[173] The acceptance of such letters would mean the recognition by these bishops of Origen's orthodoxy. The fact that Eusebius singles out the Bishop of Rome for explicit mention reminds the reader of the Peter-Mark relationship developed in Book 2— and twice referred to in Book 6, where Eusebius quotes the versions of Clement of Alexandria and Origen about the origins of Mark's Gospel.[174] This association of bishop Fabian with Origen most likely accounts for the inclusion by Eusebius of the unusual story of Fabian's election to the episcopal throne of the Roman Church in a similar way as the special association of Origen with Alexander of Jerusalem prompted Eusebius to include the rather extraordinary story of the latter's election to the See of Jerusalem. The election of Fabian is described as follows.

After the death of Anteros, the brethren in Rome assembled to choose a successor from among the many noble and distinguished *episcopabili*: no one even considered Fabian, a man just up from the country (ἐξ ἀγροῦ), until suddenly a dove flew down and lighted on his head—"a manifest imitation of the Holy Spirit who descended on the Savior in the form of a dove"—whereupon the whole people, moved as though by a divine spirit, cried out with one voice "ἄξιος" and placed him on the θρόνος τῆς ἐπισκοπῆς.

Why did Eusebius include this story in his *History*? He was not particularly fascinated by the miraculous;[175] neither can he quote

---

[173]   *HE* 6,36,4 (Schwartz 590,27–592,2). The final clause (Schwartz 592,2–3) is a later interpolation, as can be gathered from the reference to the *Apology for Origen*. Ruhbach, *Apologetik und Geschichte*, 9, suggests that Fabian of Rome was a student of Origen, but the only evidence he offers to support this contention is a reference to this text, which does not inform us that Fabian was a student of Origen but that Origen had written to him, as well as to other bishops, about his orthodox teaching.

[174]   *HE* 6,14,6 (Schwartz 550,19–25); *HE* 6,25,5 (Schwartz 576,11–15).

[175]   Foakes-Jackson, *Eusebius Pamphili*, 83, singles out *HE* 5,5,1–3 as an example of the few miraculous events recorded by Eusebius. The story of Narcissus of Jerusalem in *HE* 6,9,1–3 (Schwartz 538,2–15) and that of the springs at Caesarea Philippi (*HE* 7,17,1 = Schwartz 670,17–672,2) are further examples. On the whole, the *History* is remarkably free of the "wondrous" element that marked and marred such works as the Pseudo-Clementine writings. See also Milburn, *Christian Interpretations of History*, 68. However, one cannot conclude from this that Eusebius was disinterested in the miraculous, but only that his interest was, in comparison with other writers such as those of the

any written source for his information about this incident, but prefaces the story with the familiar φασίν, "it is said," which generally indicates an oral tradition. This martyr-bishop is one of the few early Roman bishops about whom information can be gathered from reliable sources,[176] but to the best of my knowledge this story is only found in Eusebius. Considering the story itself, one cannot help but observe certain characteristics which recall the Eusebian portrayal of St. Peter: the choice of Fabian as Bishop of Rome was a divine election, the result of a divine intervention, as the language used conveys. The man himself, though later renowned for his administrative ability[177] and virtuous character, which enabled him to suffer martyrdom under Decius,[178] is here portrayed as one who had just arrived from the land, insignificant in comparison with the many distinguished members of the Church who, humanly speaking, would have been more suitable for the episcopacy. And yet it is to the humanly considered, insignificant Fabian, as Eusebius tells us, that the great writer Origen in his old age wrote concerning his orthodoxy.[179] It is possible that the inclusion of the story of St. Fabian's divine election in the *History* had its raison d'être in Eusebius' intention to highlight the divine guidance which directs the authority of the Bishop of Rome.

The narrative of the remaining part of Book 6 moves from the Decian Persecution to its aftermath, the *Novatian Schism*. As far as Eusebius could judge from the evidence available to him, the issues at stake were (a) the treatment of the *lapsi* after the Decian Persecution, and (b) the question as to the legitimate Bishop of Rome. Eusebius, a moderate by nature and learning, rejected the extreme puritanical position taken by Novatian, with regard to the impossibility of the repentant *lapsi* being reconciled and received back into communion with the Church. The leniency of Dionysius and his understanding of those who had proved weak in time of persecution[180] found a sympathetic ear in the writer of the original

apocryphal literature in particular, moderate and restrained. The author of the
original *History* and its later Revisions was primarily interested in the general
miracle of the Church's triumphant march through the ages, of her victory over
all her enemies, be they heretics or persecutors.

[176] The most important source is St. Cyprian, Ep. 9 (Hartel 488–489).

[177] *Le Liber Pontificalis* (Duchesne 148–149).

[178] *HE* 6,39,1 (Schwartz 594,3–6). See also Cyprian, Ep. 9 (Hartel 488–489).

[179] *HE* 6,36,4 (Schwartz 590,27–592,2). Eusebius' extensive treatment of the election of Alexander to the See of Jerusalem was, as we saw above, also prompted
by that bishop's special association with Origen.

[180] The attitude of Dionysius of Alexandria to the *lapsi* is illustrated in his Letter to
Fabius of Antioch, who tended to favor the more severe stand of the *Katharoi*,
cf. *HE* 6,42,5–6 (Schwartz 610,26–612,11).

History. So too the recognition of Cornelius as Bishop of Rome and the rejection of his rival, Novatian, by Dionysius of Alexandria seemed a clear-cut, obvious judgement to the later historian. But Fabius, the Bishop of Antioch, did not seem to think that either of these two questions were so easily answered.[181] The Letters of Dionysius to Fabius, as preserved by Eusebius, are primarily concerned with convincing the Bishop of Antioch of the need for leniency,[182] while the Letter of Cornelius quoted by Eusebius is primarily preoccupied with demonstrating the legitimacy of his claim to the See of Rome, mostly by attacking the person of the rival claimant.[183] Dionysius, who recognized Cornelius, wrote an irenic letter to Novatian, appealing to him not to divide the Church.[184]

From this controversy, a compact picture of the institutional structure of the universal Church around the middle of the third century can be formed. We observe first how the three bishops of the major sees, Rome, Alexandria, and Antioch, are beginning to manifest clear signs of the later "patriarchal" system. Recognition by the universal episcopate, i.e., reciprocal communion, which was essential for each bishop, was now established in two ways: first of all, through communion with one's fellow-bishops within the "sphere of influence"[185] of one major see, whose bishop was in turn in communion with the bishops of the other two major sees. In the schism of Novatian, Cornelius had to demonstrate that he, and not his rival claimant, was in communion with his fellow-bishops in Italy, Africa, and the surrounding regions in order in turn to establish communion with his fellow-bishops in Antioch and Alexandria. From the presentation of Eusebius, one is left with the impression that the "synod," as an institution, is also becoming more developed, but now as a body operating in a more formal way *within* the sphere of influence of the major sees. Unanimity, with regard to the treatment of the *lapsi* and the consequent excommunication of Novatian, was first established by synods within the immediate "sphere of influence" of Rome and then communicated to the other two major sees. The main assembly, we are told, was the synod of sixty bishops, and even more presbyters, which gathered at Rome under Cornelius the bishop, while the rest of the bishops

---

[181] *HE* 6,44,1 (Schwartz 624,6).
[182] Cf. *HE* 6,42,5–6 (Schwartz 610,26–612,11); *HE* 6,44,1–6 (Schwartz 624,6–626,7).
[183] Cf. *HE* 6,43,1–22 (Schwartz 612,13–624,5).
[184] Cf. *HE* 6,45,1 (Schwartz 626,9–23).
[185] The exact nature of this influence is difficult to determine. It would be anachronistic to speak in terms of the later, more refined concept of jurisdiction.

privately considered what action should be taken.[186] What may be considered a typical Eusebian tendency in this narrative is the insistence by the author of the *History* on the uniformity of the synodal decision.[187]

Eusebius tells us that he was in possession of letters from Cornelius to the Bishop of Antioch, Fabius, which communicated this unanimity. What is of particular interest first of all is the composition of these letters; they appear to consist of one covering letter, describing the unanimous agreement on the issues in question as arrived at by the bishops in the West (Rome, Italy, Africa, and the surrounding areas) with four appendices, comprising of (i) a set of letters in Latin from Cyprian and the bishops of Africa, (ii) the minutes of the Synod of Rome, (iii) a letter from Cornelius, probably demonstrating the legitimacy of his election as Bishop of Rome, and (iv) a letter from Cornelius on the person of Novatian, his history, etc.[188] What is so interesting is Eusebius' comparative silence on the controversies in Africa which preceded and accompanied the Novatian schism in Rome. The letters he refers to as coming from Cyprian most probably refer to the Synod of Carthage, around May 251, which preceded the Roman synod. Most historians who see the history of this period through the eyes of Cyprian[189] interpret the Synod of Rome as merely supporting the resolutions of the Synod of Carthage.[190]

Eusebius rather emphasizes the Synod of Rome as the more important of the two and adds the information, which is not to be gleaned from Cyprian's writings, to the effect that the Bishop of Rome communicated the unanimous agreement of both these synods and of the rest of the bishops in the West to the major sees in the East and in Egypt.[191] This "communication" was not simply of an

---

[186] *HE* 6,43,2 (Schwartz 612,18–22).

[187] Cf. *HE* 6,43,2 (Schwartz 612,22).

[188] Cf. *HE* 6,43,3–4 (Schwartz 614,3–15) and *HE* 6,43,5–20 (Schwartz 614,18–622,23).

[189] See, e.g., Lietzmann, *Geschichte*, bd. II, 235–236.

[190] See St. Cyprian, *Letter to Antonianus*, Ep. 55,6 (Hartel 627–628).

[191] Cf. *HE* 6,43,3 (Schwartz 614,6) = Cornelius informs Antioch; *HE* 6,46,3 (Schwartz 628,9–10) = Dionysius of Alexandria received a letter from Cornelius. Roethe, *Synoden*, 39f., rightly observed that the letters of the respective Synods of Carthage and Rome reflect the different procedures according to which the respective synods operated. In the letter from the Africans, the opinion of the actual writer (Cyprian) was clearly distinguished from the authoritative judgement of the assembled bishops, who are the real senders of the letter. On the other hand, the Letters of Cornelius of Rome to Fabius of Antioch were evidently letters from the Bishop of Rome, the last of which mentioned the names of the participants in the Roman synod in order to demonstrate the greater support enjoyed by Cornelius in comparison with the

informative character but carried the authority of the one who communicated and, once accepted by the other major sees, signified universal
unanimity; it thus became a final authoritative witness to the Faith of
the Church, recognition of which being a condition for admittance to
communion. The latter is illustrated by the list of bishops attached to the
Letter of Cornelius of Rome to Fabius of Antioch, which both signified
their assent to the decision and their communion with the Bishop of
Rome.[192] In the presentation of these events by Eusebius, we note again the
emphasis on the numerical strength of the bishops who gave their assent
to the judgement of the Synod of Rome.[193] Only the Letter of Dionysius of
Alexandria to Novatian[194] gives some inkling of the nature of that assent:
it must be one of personal conviction.

Fabius of Antioch, however, was inclined to accept neither the
Letter of Cornelius nor the arguments of Dionysius;[195] he seems to
have favored a stricter line with regard to the *lapsi*, and so was sympathetic to Novatian. A synod was called at Antioch, by whom we do not
know for certain,[196] to discuss the issue, but already opponents of the
rigorists were organizing opposition and, since Fabius died before the
synod took place, carried the day.[197] For the first time, it would appear,
a synod rejected the authority of the Apostolic Successor at Antioch,
even if the man who held that authority was dead and his successor on
the throne. Twenty years later the Synod of Antioch will depose and
excommunicate one who was not dead, Paul of Samosata. From the
beginning of Antioch's rise to prominence in the history of the Church,
as told by Eusebius, the relationship of the bishop of that Church to
the neighboring bishops who formed the synod would seem to have

rival claimant to the Roman See. Roethe, however, did not consider the incipient
"patriarchal" system of the mid-third century Church, which helps to explain
both the different procedures of the African and Roman synods as well as their
intrinsic relationship; neither did Roethe pay attention to the unique authority
attributed to the See of Rome within the universal Church due to her "superior
origins."

[192] Cf. *HE* 6,43,21–22 (Schwartz 622,24–624,5).
[193] This is also reflected in Cyprian, Ep. 55,6 (Hartel 628).
[194] *HE* 6,45,1 (Schwartz 626,13–23).
[195] Cf. *HE* 6,44,1 (Schwartz 624,6).
[196] Cf. *HE* 6,46,3 (Schwartz 628,8–15). According to Lietzmann, *Geschichte*, bd. II,
266, it was Fabius of Antioch who actually called the synod. Downey, *History of Antioch*, 308–309, suggests Helenus of Tarsus, as indicated by *HE* 6,46,3.
[197] Cf. *Letter of Dionysius of Alexandria to Stephen of Rome*, in *HE* 7,4,1–7,5,2
(Schwartz 638,10–640,2).

been one of tension and disagreement, which is in sharp contrast to the unanimity in Rome and, presumably, in Alexandria. In the ecclesiological debate which was sparked off by the controversies that surrounded Athanasius' claim to the See of Alexandria in the second quarter of the fourth century, this event caused by the Novatian Schism will play a major role in the Eusebian attack on the primacy of the Bishop of Rome.

At this stage, Eusebius simply reports the incident without seeing its implications for that discussion. Our author is still involved, in Book 6, in a presentation of the Church's history where Rome's primacy is undisputed (though not explicitly defined). This he indicated in Book 6 by his allocation of the first place to the successions at Rome in relationship to the other successions, by the way he presented the claim of Cornelius to the See of Rome and his attitude to the question of the *lapsi* as correct, by his synchronism of orthodox writers in the reign of Zephrynus, who was renowned for his strictness towards heretics, and by his semi-biographical sketch of Origen, who was portrayed as one who enjoyed communion with the Bishop of Rome both at the opening and conclusion of his career, and so reflected the Peter-Mark prototype found in Book 2. This prototype is even more pronounced in Book 7, where Eusebius introduces us to the person and writings of Dionysius the Great of Alexandria.

§4 Book 7: The Final Period of the Apostolic Successions

With Book 7, Eusebius' original *History* of the Apostolic Successions comes to a close. The present text of Book 7, however, contains material which does not belong to the original version but was either adjusted or totally rewritten during the 1st Revision after 311. According to my analysis of the text—which analysis will be outlined in Chapter Four—the original text ends with *HE* 7,80,21 while *HE* 7,30,22–7,32,32 properly belongs to the 1st Revision.

In the original form of Book 7, to which we now turn our attention, Eusebius' early attitude to the Bishop of Rome as Successor to St. Peter and his unique position within the universal Church is still discernible, even though one begins to notice a certain strain between the ideal concept of the Bishop of Rome's function (originally articulated in terms of the Peter-Simon Magus and the Peter-Mark "prototypes") and the actual role he played in the major issues which occupied the attention of the Church in the second half of the third century. But even the very attempts by Eusebius to reconcile his ideal with the evidence of his historical research—mostly by way of suppressing information which could not be harmonized with the ideal—betray his original attitude to the Bishop of Rome. The major issues in the second half of the third century included the Baptismal Controversy, Sabellianism, and the controversy which surrounded Paul of Samosata. As in the previous books, the events of this period are arranged within the framework provided by the successive reigns of the Roman bishops, whose succession at Rome provides the occasion for notices concerning the successions to the other major sees.[198]

As Irenaeus was the dominant personality in the Church at the end of the second century, Dionysius of Alexandria was the most prominent at the end of the third—earning for himself the title "the Great."[199] Eusebius holds him in the highest esteem, since he combined the peacemaking temperament of Irenaeus with the theological sympathies of Origen, whose most illustrious pupil he in fact was.[200] He was a man who, above all, was renowned for his gentle ability to settle disputes, using one weapon only—that of theological persuasion leading to personal conviction.[201] For this reason he became involved in most of the major controversies of the day, adding greatly to the influence and renown of the Church of Alexandria over which he presided.

Eusebius presents the events of Book 7 very much through the pen of Dionysius, whose writings he tells us in the Prœmium to Book 7 will supply his primary sources. Half of his letters, quoted in this book or simply mentioned in passing by Eusebius, were written to one Bishop of Rome or other, or to some of the Roman presbyters.[202] As in the case of the Paschal Controversy under Victor, where

---

[198]   *HE* 7,2,1 (Schwartz 636,18–636,1); *HE* 7,14,1 (Schwartz 668,1–10); *HE* 7,27,1 (Schwartz 702, 1–4) together with *HE* 7,28,3 (Schwartz 704,2–4).

[199]   Cf. Proem to Book 7 (Schwartz 636,1).

[200]   Cf. *HE* 6,29,4 (Schwartz 584,10).

[201]   This trait of Dionysius' character is best illustrated in his treatment of the heresy of one Nepos (an Egyptian bishop), as seen in his own account of how he spent three successive days of continuous discussion, proving the errors of the heresy and reconciling to the Church its many followers in the district of Arsinoë (cf. *HE* 7,24,6–9 = Schwartz 688,9–690,8).

[202]   To Stephen of Rome: *HE* 7,5,1–2 (Schwartz 638,15–640,2); to his successor, Sixtus II: *HE* 7,5,4–7,6,1 = Schwartz 640,8–642,11); to the Roman presbyter, Philemon: *HE* 7,7,1–5 (Schwartz 642,15–644,22); to Dionysius of Rome, when the latter was still a presbyter: *HE* 7,8,1 (Schwartz 646,5–12); to Sixtus of Rome (a second letter): *HE* 7,9,1–5 (Schwartz 646,15–648,13);

Eusebius followed the line taken by Irenaeus; the author of the *History* likewise adopts the attitude of Dionysius to the similar type of controversy about the rebaptism of heretics which raged while Stephen was Bishop of Rome.

a) The Baptismal Controversy

The return of followers of Novatian to the Church raised the question of the rebaptism of heretics—though in actual fact the followers of Novatian were initially schismatics and not heretics in the strict sense of the term.[203] Cyprian of Carthage, however, would not recognize the baptism either of heretics or schismatics,[204] due to his rigorous application of the principle, outside the Church there is no salvation. Dionysius of Alexandria who, as we remember, supported the stand of Cornelius of Rome in the Novatian Controversy, also agreed with the Roman tradition, as defended by Cornelius' successor Stephen, to the effect that schismatics or heretics ought not receive a "second Baptism" on their return to the Church; this was the rule and the prescribed form (τὸν κανόνα καὶ τὸν τύπον) of the Church of Alexandria, as handed on to them by his predecessor "Pope Heraclas."[205] But Cyprian and his fellow-bishops in Africa, supported by two synods in Asia Minor,[206] considered that baptism was necessary. Eusebius does not inform us of the reasons given for their opposition to the views of Stephen. He simply quotes from a letter of Dionysius to Stephen where the Alexandrian bishop appeals to the Bishop of Rome to consider the newly won peace of the Church where, after both the persecution and the threat of the Novatian schism, peace, concord, and unanimity had been established among the bishops.[207] Later, in a letter to the Roman presbyter Philemon, Dionysius is more explicit in his support for the

two other letters are mentioned, but not quoted from, which Dionysius of Alexandria wrote to Sixtus and Dionysius of Rome: *HE* 7,9,6 (Schwartz 648,14–19); later Eusebius refers to the four treatises written by Dionysius on the subject of Sabellianism, and which he sent to his namesake at Rome: *HE* 7,26,1 (Schwartz 700,16–18).

[203] Dionysius of Alexandria, however, comes close to accusing Novatian of heresy, when, in his Letter to Dionysius of Rome (who at the time was still a presbyter), he demonstrates that the rigorism of Novatian was based on a "most profane teaching about God" (*HE* 7,8,1 = Schwartz 646,8), i.e., one which denied the mercy of God.

[204] Cf. Cyprian, Ep. 69,1 (Hartel 749f.); also Ep. 74,7 (Hartel 804–805). See article on "Ketzertaufe" by J. Finkenzeller, in *LThK*² VI, col. 131–133.

[205] *HE* 7,7,4 (Schwartz 644,6–7); cf. also *HE* 7,9,1–5 (646,16–648,13).

[206] Cf. *HE* 7,7,5 (Schwartz 644,19).

[207] Cf. *HE* 7,5,1–2 (Schwartz 638,15–640,2).

Asian and the African Churches: there the practice of rebaptizing "heretics" was a local tradition of long standing, a custom which must be respected.[208] His position in the dispute parallels that of Irenaeus in the Paschal Controversy. Like Irenaeus, Dionysius supports the ruling of the Church of Rome, but in the interest of peace and harmony appeals to the Church of Rome (through Philemon) to tolerate what is a (local) custom and not a matter of Faith, pointing out that this custom was adopted by two synods at Iconium and Synnada.[209] The Alexandrian bishop stresses the authority of the decisions of these synods: "Do not move your neighbour's boundary stone, which your fathers placed . . ." (Deut 19,14) is the scriptural text he calls on to support his argument.[210] This statement is of tremendous importance since it witnesses to the consciousness of the synodal authority at the time and, even more so, since it is the first appearance of a new principle, that of the relative autonomy of the different provinces which tended to deny the right of intervention by another authority. The principle as enunciated by Dionysius is based on the difference between necessary universal *agreement* in matters of *Faith* and legitimate diversity with regard to *customs*. Considering the intrinsic relationship between Faith and its expression in custom and practices, this solution of Dionysius—however intellectually attractive it may be—stood little chance of translation into practical policy, since, as the Letters of Cyprian and Firmilian of Caesarea in Cappadocia clearly demonstrate,[211] the opponents or supporters of a particular practice inevitably stress the theological basis of their custom, and so ultimately raise the question of custom on to the level of Faith. Even if the proviso of Dionysius, with regard to the due application of the principle (namely the autonomy of various regions to determine matters of *custom*), proved impractical and so forgotten, the feeling of a certain autonomy engendered by the Paschal and the Baptismal Controversies lasted and played a major role in determining the development of the synodal structure, particularly in large tracts of the East during the Arian Crisis—and long after.

The low-profile presentation of the part played by Cyprian and the African Church in the Novatian Controversy is matched by the

---

[208] Cf. *HE* 7,7,5 (Schwartz 644,16–22).

[209] *HE* 7,7,5 (Schwartz 644,19).

[210] *HE* 7,7,5 (644,21–22).

[211] See Cyprian, Ep. 74 and 75 (Hartel 799f. and 810f.). As is well known, at Nicaea the Roman and Alexandrian customs, with regard to both the Paschal and the Baptismal questions, were adopted by the bishops who were predominantly of an eastern provenance.

even lower-keyed portrayal of the major roles taken by Cyprian and Firmilian of Caesarea in the actual Baptismal Controversy. The lack of attention to Cyprian could be attributed to either lack of sufficient documents concerning the African contribution to the debate or to Eusebius' reputed lack of mastery of the Latin tongue.[212] But it could also be due, as I suggest, to Eusebius' embarrassment at the extent of Cyprian's opposition to Stephen. Eusebius, it would seem, favoured the views of Stephen, yet must recognize that the opposition to the opinion of the Bishop of Rome was led, not by a heretic, but by a great bishop and renowned Martyr. Of even greater embarrassment to the author of the *History* was the part played by Firmilian of Cappadocia whom he apparently revered.[213]

It is easy to appreciate how much Eusebius was attracted to the solution of Dionysius, which respected both the custom defended by Stephen and that upheld by Cyprian and Firmilian. However, the irenic intervention of Dionysius occurred *after* that action by Stephen of Rome which marks the Baptismal Controversy with its special significance for the understanding of the authority of the Church of Rome: his excommunication of all those who did not hold to the Apostolic Tradition as handed on in the Church of Rome. Eusebius only refers to this indirectly—through a quotation from Dionysius' letter to Stephan's *successor* Sixtus II[214]—and passes over in complete silence the impassioned reaction of Firmilian.[215]

---

[212] See McGiffert, *Eusebius*, LNPF², 106, footnote 9.

[213] Cf. *HE* 6,27,1 (Schwartz 580,16–21), where Firmilian's admiration for Origen is described. See also *HE* 7,28,1 (Schwartz 702,13–14). On Firmilian, see the article by E. W. Benson, in *DCB*, vol. II, 521–522.

[214] *HE* 7,5,4 (Schwartz 640,8–12).

[215] The letter is only preserved in the Latin translation of Cyprian and found in the collection of letters attributed to the Bishop of Carthage as Ep. 75 (Hartel 810–827). (Re. the genuineness of the letter, see J. Ernst, *ZkTh* 20 (1896) 364–367; also, Quasten, *Patrology* I, 128–129.) In the course of this letter, Firmilian turned rhetorically on Stephen, who had reminded the Eastern bishops of his Petrine Succession (Ep. 75,17 = Hartel 821) and had based his stand in the Baptismal Controversy on the authoritative, Apostolic Tradition of Saints Peter and Paul (Ep. 75,6 = Hartel 813–814), and accused the Roman bishop of stirring up strife and contention throughout the Churches of the whole world: "Moreover, how great a sin have you heaped up for yourself, when you cut yourself off from so many flocks! For it is yourself that you have cut off. Do not deceive yourself, since he is really the schismatic who has made himself an apostate from the communion of ecclesiastical unity. For while you think that all may be excommunicated by you, you have excommunicated yourself alone from all . . ." (Ep. 75,24 = Hartel 825; transl., *ANL*, 396). Firmilian did recognize Rome's obligations to be severe with

Less than forty years after Firmilian's death (268), Eusebius must have recognized not only that the position taken by both the African and the Asian Churches was not the generally accepted tradition as handed down by the Apostles and as witnessed to by the Churches of Rome and Alexandria, but also how incorrect Firmilian was in his interpretation of Stephen's excommunication as an action which only resulted in Stephen cutting himself off from the communion of ecclesiastical unity. As in the case of the Paschal Controversy and the excommunicatory action of Victor, so too here in the Baptismal Controversy, Eusebius finds himself in agreement with the reasons which moved the Bishop of Rome to excommunicate large areas of the East (and Africa), but considered the action as imprudent since the issue was one of custom not of Faith and the result as not very conductive to "peace and harmony." Nevertheless, he cannot have failed to appreciate how this action of Stephen's was consistent with the traditional severity with heretics which, according to Eusebius' own witness, characterized the Church of Rome, whose bishops were the successors to St. Peter, the detector and destroyer of the father and founder of all heresies. For this reason, the indirect reference to Stephen's excommunication of the African and Asian Churches occurs only *after* the death of Stephen in a letter of Dionysius of Alexandria to Sixtus II of Rome.[216] There is no hint that Sixtus might have reversed the decision of his predecessor; on the contrary there is a clear indication that he continued the policy of Stephen, if we are to judge from another letter from Dionysius of Alexandria to Sixtus, asking the Bishop of Rome for his counsel on a complicated case involving the application of the Roman tradition, the principle of not demanding the baptism of repentant heretics.[217]

> heretics, which obligation arose from being the Cathedra Petri (cf. Ep. 75,17 = Hartel 821), but he evidently considered that the authority of an Apostolic Throne was conditioned by communion with the universal episcopate. It is of note that he was one of the leading bishops who participated at the Synod of Antioch that opposed the Novatian tendencies of Fabius of Antioch (cf. *HE* 6,46,3 = Schwartz 628,12). Later, he will take part in the important synod of that same Church which will depose another successor to St. Peter in the See of Antioch, Paul of Samosata (cf. *HE* 7,28,1 = Schwartz 702,13f. and *HE* 7,30, 3–4 = Schwartz 706,11–24). This is mentioned in passing since it evidently played an important role in the formation of the mentality of the Church in the east, as we will see when we come to examine the so-called Arian crisis of the later fourth century (see below, Part Two). What really concerns us at this juncture is the embarrassment of Eusebius in the face of this very attitude of Firmilian, as is suggested by his silence on the matter.

[216]   *HE* 7,5,4 (Schwartz 640,8–12).
[217]   Cf. *HE* 7,9,1–5 (Schwartz 646,16–648,13).

However undesirable the excommunication by Stephan may have been, its motive was becoming more and more appreciated as being correct—the Synod of Arles (314) and the Great Synod of Nicaea (325) would later testify to that. The contention of Firmilian that Stephen had cut himself off from the communion of the universal Church only demonstrated how more and more difficult it was to ascertain that unanimous agreement which ought to manifest this communion: Firmilian considered that the agreement of the Asian bishops plus that of the African bishops was sufficient to prove unanimity—but Eusebius could see how provincial his judgement was. Dionysius, we have seen, tried to cut the Gordian knot by recognizing both the correctness of the Roman tradition and the ability of the Bishop of Rome to take the action he did, and at the same time by appealing to Rome for the recognition of relative ("provincial" or local) autonomy in matters of *custom* as determined by the local synod of bishops. Apart from the other weaknesses of Dionysius' proposition already discussed, his solution would unintentionally but inevitably lead to authority being determined not by real unanimity but merely by majority vote, since the support of a sufficient number of bishops could sanction a custom.[218]

b) Sabellianism

When we come to consider the marked reticence of Eusebius in his treatment of the subject most obnoxious to him and his fellow Origenists— Sabellianism—we are faced with another remarkable attempt by the author of the *History* to evade unpleasant but serious issues. His selective treatment of the Baptismal Controversy, and in particular the part played in it by Firmilian of Caesarea, is a clear incidence of such an evasion. Another evasion was his description of the most celebrated writer in third century Rome, Hippolytus, as one who "presided over another Church somewhere,"[219] although the man who was later to be revered as a martyr and saint apparently functioned for some time as a rival claimant to the See of Rome. His scanty treatment of the Sabellian heresy reveals another evasion by Eusebius, this time concerning the highly respected Dionysius of Alexandria; in common with the other two, this incident also involves the Bishop of Rome and Eusebius' concept of his authority.

---

[218] Dionysius explicitly stresses the numerical or quantitative element in *HE* 7,7,5 (Schwartz 644,16–22), when he talks about the opinion being adopted by "the most populous Churches," and by brethren at synods in many other places.
[219] *HE* 6,20,2 (Schwartz 566,13–14).

Of Sabellius himself nothing definite is known apart from his heresy, which was a version of modalist Monarchianism, claiming that the one Godhead differed only in his modes or operations.[220] Such views were particularly detested by the followers of Origen, who due to his philosophical presuppositions emphasized the distinctness between Father and Son and the autonomy of each ὑπόστασις. Since the teaching of Sabellius was disturbing the Church in Lybia Pentapolis (Cyrenaica), Dionysius of Alexandria, the most distinguished pupil of Origen, was brought into a debate on the heresy, expressing his views in a number of letters to the bishops of that region.[221] Whether he took this initiative of himself in the consciousness of his "patriarchal" responsibility or not we cannot judge definitively from the available evidence, but it is generally assumed that he did. On the basis of his reputation as a theologian—and as a pupil of such a famous master—his views would have been sought for in any event,[222] as they were in the Baptismal Controversy and will be in the controversy over the teachings of Paul of Samosata. But in his defense of the distinction between the Father and Son, Dionysius left himself open to the charge of subordinationism. Some fellow ecclesiastics had recourse to Rome, as Athanasius tells us,[223] where they accused him before the Roman bishop, who at the time was his namesake, Dionysius of Rome. The Bishop of Rome assembled a synod there and communicated their unanimous judgement to bishop Dionysius of Alexandria,[224] insisting on the unity of substance (ὁμοούσιος) between Father and Son. In reply, Dionysius of Alexandria composed four books, entitled *"Refutation and Defence,"*[225] which he sent to the Bishop of Rome.

Eusebius refers to the views of Dionysius of Alexandria on Sabellianism twice. His first reference is to an excerpt of a letter by the

---

[220] See Harnack, *Lehrbuch der Dogmengeschichte*, vol. I, 760f.

[221] Ammon, Bishop of Bernice, Telesophorus, Euphranor, and Euporus are given as his correspondents by Eusebius, *HE* 7,26,1 (Schwartz 700,13–16). Athanasius refers to Dionysius' Letter to Euphranor and Ammonius, which the Arians called on as an authority in support of their views (cf. *De sent. Dion.* 12,13, and 26 = Opitz 55,12, and 17).

[222] This would seem to be implied by his own description of the rise of the heresy in the Pentapolis, as found in his Letter to Sixtus of Rome and quoted in *HE* 7,6,1 (Schwartz 642,3–11).

[223] Athanasius, *De sent. Dion.* 13,1 (Opitz 55,10–15). See also *De syn.* 43,4 (Opitz 268,29–269,2).

[224] Athanasius, *De sent. Dion.* 13,2 (Opitz 55,15–19); *De syn.* 43,4 (Opitz 269,2–3).

[225] Athanasius, *De sent. Dion.* 13,3 (Opitz 55,20); *De syn.* 43,4 (Opitz 269,4), where excerpts from this letter are to be found.

Bishop of Alexandria to Sixtus II, the successor of Dionysius of Rome, in which the incursion of the heresy in the Pentapolis is described, as well as a brief note as to the nature of the heresy itself and his own involvement in the discussions; according to this excerpt, the reader is informed that Dionysius of Alexandria also sent copies of his letters on the subject to Sixtus.[226] The second reference to the Sabellian heresy simply mentions that the Letters of Dionysius to the bishops in the Pentapolis were still extant, adding quite casually that the Alexandrian bishop had composed four other treatises on the same subject which he addressed to his namesake at Rome, omitting any reference to either the circumstances or even the title as given by Athanasius.[227] The impression the reader is left with would lead him to conclude that the letters, which in fact, caused Dionysius of Alexandria to be cited before Dionysius of Rome had been read and approved by his successor Sixtus. Since there is no mention of the synod at Rome nor of the letter of Dionysius of Rome which spurned the Alexandrian Dionysius to refute the charges, Eusebius gives no hint of Dionysius' need to defend his orthodoxy before the Bishop of Rome.

Schwartz suggests that Eusebius found this yielding of the Alexandrian bishop to his namesake at Rome "ärgerlich."[228] It is clear that Eusebius was embarrassed by the event. Why? It is not because he denied Rome's right to authoritatively interfere—a right which Dionysius' accusers from the Church of Alexandria also recognized, as indeed the reaction of Dionysius himself implicitly confirmed. On an earlier occasion, Eusebius drew the reader's attention to a letter Dionysius of Alexandria had written to Dionysius of Rome, when the latter was still a presbyter and not yet bishop, which testifies to the high regard the Alexandrian bishop held towards his namesake's learning and person.[229] We have seen how appreciative Eusebius is of Rome's traditional strictness with regard to orthodoxy, even though he would have preferred a somewhat more tolerant attitude when it came to questions of customs claiming the support of a legitimate Apostolic Tradition or a large number of bishops. But in the Sabellian Controversy, the issue was not one of custom but of the *Faith*.

We may well suspect that Eusebius would have been more sympathetic to the original Letters of Dionysius of Alexandria to the bishops of the Pentapolis, which he had in his possession as he told us, than to the "Sabellian" tendencies he found in the *Refutation and*

---

[226] *HE* 7,6,1 (Schwartz 642,3–11).
[227] *HE* 7,26,1 (Schwartz 700,13–18).
[228] Schwartz, *Einleitung*, 39.
[229] *HE* 7,7,6 (Schwartz 644,23–646,3).

Defence written in reply to the objections of Dionysius of Rome.[230] To put it in another way, Eusebius would have been less than sympathetic to the doctrines advocated by the Bishop of Rome and accepted by Dionysius the Great—which fact alone would have been enough for him to quietly pass over the whole subject and so evade the very awkward crisis of conscience for himself due to his own Origenist convictions and their apparent clash with the Church of Rome, whose authority in matters of Faith he so highly respected. Here he had no Solomonian solution for the crisis between two apparently opposing beliefs, as had been provided by Irenaeus and Dionysius of Alexandria in the other controversies where similar clashes occurred. How long could he continue to evade the issue itself? At the Synod of Antioch held immediately before Nicaea, his own theological beliefs on the relationship between the Father and Son would be condemned and at Nicaea he was on trial for his suspect theological opinions. He escaped excommunication at Nicaea by accepting with serious mental reservations the Creed which was adopted there,[231] but his acceptance of the doctrine originally proposed by Dionysius of Rome resulted, as we will see, in Eusebius' abandonment of the Apostolic Authority on which Dionysius of Rome's proposal ultimately rested.

Even though the strain on Eusebius' original attitude to the great Church of Rome and the divine guidance which marked both its Founder and his successors is beginning to show, his presentation of the final incident in his history of the Church, which relates to the Bishop of Rome, shows how consistent his basic attitude has remained. This incident concerns the heretical Bishop of Antioch, Paul of Samosata, who was deposed by a synod of bishops meeting at Antioch in 268 on account of his teaching which was a form of Dynamic Monarchianism.[232]

c) Paul of Samosata

When the heretical views of Paul became known, a synod was called at Antioch. The neighboring bishops gathered together to

---

[230] See the informative article by Opitz, "Dionys von Alexandrien und die Libyer," 41–53. Athanasius insists that Eusebius knew of the fact that the controversial term ὁμοούσιος had been used by both Dionysii (cf. *Ad Afros* 6 = *PG* 26,1040, C1–9), as indeed is confirmed by the reference Eusebius makes in his *Letter to the Church of Caesarea* after Nicaea (325), where he talks about "some learned and illustrious bishops" who had used the term ὁμοούσιος (*Urkunde* 22,13 = Opitz 46,4–6).

[231] *Urkunde* 22 (Opitz 42f.).

[232] Concerning the case of Paul of Samosata, see Batiffol, *La paix constantinienne*, 100–109.

discuss the issue and examine Paul's life and teaching at several meetings.[233] Firmilian of Cappadocia was the leading prelate at the synod.[234] Presumably on account of his renown as a theologian and peacemaker, Dionysius of Alexandria was also invited to attend,[235] but he excused himself on account of old age and bodily weakness, and in fact died before the deliberations were concluded.[236] After several attempts to win over Paul,[237] a final synod was eventually held, which by common assent (ἐκ κοινῆς γνώμης) drew up an epistle or encyclical addressed "To Dionysius [of Rome] and Maximus [of Alexandria] and to all our fellow-ministers throughout the world, bishops, presbyters, deacons and to the whole Catholic Church under heaven,"[238] informing the Church Universal of its decision to remove Paul of Samosata from the bishopric and excommunicate him for teaching false doctrine. Paul, however, refused to relinquish possession of the Church property. The emperor was eventually petitioned to remove Paul. His judgement, which Eusebius praises, was that the building ought to be assigned to those "with whom the bishops of the (Christian) teaching in Italy and the city of the Romans should communicate" (οἷς ἂν οἱ κατὰ Ἰταλίαν καὶ τὴν Ῥωμαίων πόλιν ἐπίσκοποι τοῦ δόγματος ἐπιστέλλοιεν).[239] Doubt has been cast on the credibility of the latter half of this report[240] and indeed it is, at first glance, remarkable that an emperor of the pre-Constantinian era should display such a knowledge of internal Church procedure as is presumed in this notice, or should be moved to act on motives which were determined by such knowledge. The suggestion of Loofs, that the notice of Eusebius was based on an oral tradition preserved in Antioch,[241] is rather arbitrary. On the contrary, one can say that when Eusebius has recourse to an oral tradition, he is generally careful to distinguish such from the more reliable documentary evidence by prefacing the oral report with φασί, the absence of which in this case favors the existence of documents at Eusebius' disposal.

233 *HE* 7,28,2 (Schwartz 702,22–704,2).
234 Cf. *HE* 7,28,1 (Schwartz 702,13f.); *HE* 7,30,4 (Schwartz 706,17f.). See Burke, "Eusebius on Paul of Samosata," 13.
235 *HE* 7,27,2 (Schwartz 702,7–10).
236 *HE* 7,28,3 (Schwartz 704,2–4).
237 *HE* 7,30,4 (Schwartz 706,17–24).
238 *HE* 7,30,2 (Schwartz 706,1–3).
239 *HE* 7,30,19 (Schwartz 714,3–7). Regarding the translation, see Caspar, *Geschichte des Papsttums* I, 579–580.
240 Loofs, *Paulus von Samosata*, 58–59; Lietzmann, *Geschichte* III, 87. See also Instinsky, *Bischofsstuhl und Kaiserthron*, 107, footnote 34.
241 Loofs, *Paulus von Samosata*, 58.

Roethe tentatively suggested[242] that the emperor could have had before him the report of the Synod of Rome's deliberations, which synod, it is argued, must have taken place in order to examine the deposition of Paul and the claims of Domnus to the See of Antioch. This would explain the unusual sequence in the phrase: "the bishops of Italy and the city of the Romans" as found in the Eusebian text, since fragments of another report (from the Synod of Rome, 313, regarding the Donatists)[243] demonstrated how the Bishop of Rome (Miltiades) likewise delivered his judgement as the last of all the participants.[244] Eusebius' source, then, could have been a document containing the judgement of the emperor, the basis of which judgement was the Roman synodal report. Confirmation of this hypothesis might be found in the use of the term τοῦ δόγματος in the Eusebian text to describe the Church, which, it has been suggested,[245] is probably a translation of the actual words used by the Aurelian. Accepting the basic trustworthiness of the text as reporting an actual judgement of the emperor, attempts have been made to explain the stated motive of the Aurelian's decision in terms which are primarily political.[246] The emperor, it is claimed, decided to allot the Church buildings to those who evidentially distanced themselves from the Palmyrian party, with whom Paul was intrinsically bound, by demonstrating their "Roman" sympathies, proof of which was provided in the written communication with the Bishops of Rome and Italy. But the text provides not a shred of positive evidence that the orthodox party, in its endeavors to regain possession of the Church building, utilized the new political constellation in Antioch where the Palmyrian dynasty was ousted and Roman dominance reasserted. Indeed the apolitical attitude of the orthodox party can be seen in their failure, so far as we can judge, to capitalize on an action of Paul's, which in itself could have been sufficient to have Paul removed from the city, if not from this world: namely the erection of a high throne for himself (in the Church), which in civil terms meant the usurpation of privileges exclusively reserved to the emperor, as the perceptive study of Instinsky brought to light.[247] There is not the slightest hint that this

---

[242] Roethe, *Synoden*, 50–51.

[243] Optatus, I, 24 (*PL* 11,933,A5).

[244] See Roethe, *Synoden*, 51 and 75f.

[245] Oulton, *The Ecclesiastical History*, vol. II, 224.

[246] Caspar, *Geschichte des Papsttums* I, 94–95, who basically repeats the suggestion made by Loofs, *Paulus von Samosata*, 59; also, Roethe, *Synoden*, 50–51; Instinsky, *Bischofsstuhl und Kaiserthron*, 24–25; Girardet, *Kaisergericht und Bischofsgericht*, 15f.

[247] Instinsky, *Bischofsstuhl und Kaiserthron*, 11–24.

possible *lèse majesté* was ever proposed by the Synodal Fathers at Antioch as a reason for Paul's deposition.[248] Though such an action was criticized by the Fathers in their Letter to Rome and Alexandria as unbecoming for a disciple of Christ,[249] it was not that or any such misbehavior but his *heretical teaching* which, according to the Synodal Fathers, necessitated his deposition. A possible indication that the Aurelian judged the case in accordance with these terms, i.e., as a contestation between two rival claimants to legitimately represent a religious or philosophic sect (as he would have seen it), may be found in his description of the Church implied in the terms: τοῦ δόγματος found in the Eusebian text and which, as already mentioned, may well have been taken from a document containing the actual decision of the emperor.

While it cannot be denied that Aurelian's judgement could have been influenced by his own aversion to Paul on account of the Antiochene bishop's previous associations with the House of Palmyra or by his sympathy for anything that displayed "Roman" centralizing tendencies, the text itself provides no support for such a theory. In the first place, the terms of reference are non-political. Rome is considered here, as has been aptly remarked by Bardy, as the capital of Christianity and not as the capital of the empire: the emperor can hardly have been totally ignorant of the position among Christians held by the Bishop and Synod of Rome, even if the theoretical basis of this preeminence was, as is likely, unknown to him.[250] Secondly, the "written communication" mentioned in the Eusebian notice refers to a wholly different subject matter than that presupposed by an interpretation of the text in political terms: it refers to the establishment of the universal "communion" (κοινωνία) by means of *Letters of Communion*. Although it is likely that the emperor had before him the report of a Synod of Rome ratifying the election of Domnus to succeed Paul as Bishop of Antioch, the Aurelian's judgement does not directly refer to the actual *literary connection* between the orthodox party in Antioch and (ecclesiastical) Rome but, using the optative case, enunciates what is in fact *a principle* according to which the case ought to be settled: the party in communion with the Bishop and Synod of Rome should be recognized as the legitimate claimant. It is inconceivable that the emperor invented this principle; he simply gave recognition to the internal procedures of a corporate body regarding the determination of its legitimate local representatives in a

---

[248] This is proposed by Instinsky.
[249] *HE* 7,30,9 (Schwartz 708,24–25).
[250] Bardy, *Paul de Samosate*, 363.

dispute between two claimants to this title concerning property owned by the corporate body.[251]

From the above it is not unreasonable to conclude that the orthodox party petitioned the emperor to restore the Church building to the legitimate representative of the Christian Religion in Antioch, that is to say, to the claimant and his supporters who fulfilled the necessary conditions imposed by the said corporate body to determine its local leader in Antioch, the final condition being proof of communion with the Bishop and Synod of Rome. Producing the report of the Synod of Rome's deliberations where the deposition of Paul was confirmed and the election of Domnus ratified, the orthodox party alone could confidentially approach the civil authority and request the emperor to have Paul removed from the building to which he no longer had any legal claim.

What is of specific interest to our study is the attitude of Eusebius. He found the judgement of the emperor "most fitting." That is, the principle adopted by the civil authority to decide the dispute coincided with his own (and his contemporaries') understanding of the role of the Bishop of Rome within the universal Church as the final arbiter of Orthodoxy, whose authority was based on the Petrine source of his Apostolic See. In other words, the imperial decision gave recognition to the basic principle of that ecclesiology of which the original *History* was but a demonstration. This was in turn the highest recognition of the Christian Religion which Eusebius, in his pre-Constantinian days, could possibly conceive. With this incident, Eusebius aptly brings his original *History* to a close.

In itself, this historic event would have repercussions beyond the destiny of Paul of Samosata and his heretical teachings which were condemned at this synod. We noticed how the incipient "patriarchal system" with its internal structure of provincial synods began to take definite shape in the Novatian Controversy. This "system" manifests itself again in the way the Church attempted to deal with the person and teaching of Paul of Samosata—with one substantial difference, which would greatly influence the subsequent development of ecclesiastical structures.

The synod communicated their unanimous decisions (which apart from the excommunication of Paul also included the election of his successor Domnus) to the two other principal sees,[252] which

---

[251] See Bardy, *Paul de Samosate*, 362.

[252] See also Bardy, *Paul de Samosate*, 308–315 (especially p. 311), where the French scholar argues convincingly that the letter was addressed to Rome and Alexandria—in that order—on account of Rome's authority *propter potentiorem principalitatem* and Alexandria's special authority which she enjoyed in the East—and not on account of the political importance of the two cities.

ipso facto meant a communication to the rest of the Catholic world, as the address of the encyclical made clear. The acceptance of this letter by the Bishops of Rome and Alexandria involved the recognition at the universal level of the synod's judgements regarding both the heresy and the legitimate Bishop of Antioch. However, the synod's initial action in deposing the previous incumbent of this major Apostolic See affirmed the authority of the provincial synod to be in some sense *superior* to that of the Bishop of the Major Petrine See of Antioch.

Previous to this, the individual bishops would have refused to remain in communion with one of their brethren holding heretical views; now they take action as a corporate body and excommunicate him. Further, the bishop in question was not simply a bishop but the Successor to one of the three most distinguished Apostolic Sees, to which one ought to have recourse when in doubt as to the Apostolic Teaching. Yet here the Successor was plainly heretical; the unanimity of his fellow-bishops on the unacceptability of his teaching resulted in his excommunication and replacement by an orthodox bishop. Had Fabius of Antioch not died before an earlier synod of bishops assembled to condemn the Novatianist sympathies he showed, then he too would most probably have received similar treatment from his fellow-bishops. In any event the net result of these two cases was to undermine the authority of the incipient "patriarch" of Antioch. No future holder of that see would ever command the authority which the occupants of Rome and Alexandria did and would continue to exercise. And when the authority of Alexandria commenced to suffer under the various crises spawned by Arius and his followers, the ground was prepared for the rise to prominence of the new city on the Bosporus and its subsequent development into a Patriarchate. Further, due to the breakdown of the complementary relationship between the occupants of the major sees and the provincial synods within their sphere of responsibility, which occurred in the Synods of Antioch, it was no accident that the final development of the incipient "patriarchal" system (with its recognized preeminence of Rome) into the incipient "papal" system during the fourth century found its opposition centered around Antioch, where a body of bishops under the influence of a small faction with the backing of the empire pitted the *corporate* power of the synod (now the *provincial* synod) against the individual bishop and claimed more and more autonomy from the universal episcopate.

As the first known appeal to the imperial authority since St. Paul's famous appeal to Caesar (Acts 25, 10–12) this aspect of the event at Antioch deserves some attention.[253] Up to then the Church-Empire relationship was determined by the double-principle to be found, for example, in the writings of Dionysius which describe his confrontation with the Deputy-prefect of Egypt, Aemilianus, during the Valerian persecution.[254] According to this double-principle, the attitude of the Christian to the imperial authority ought to be one of loyalty and submission, even to the extent of offering prayerful intercession for the well-being of the emperor and his empire;[255] should, however, the civil authority attempt to interfere with the deepest personal convictions of the individual, then the Christian must reply in the words of Peter to the High Priest: "One must obey God rather than men" (Acts 5,29).[256] The Synod of Antioch, after excommunicating Paul of Samosata, now goes one step further and in effect invites the imperial authority to recognize the civil consequences of its decisions, although one must add that the issue involved the possession of a building and so came within the civil law's terms of reference.

Within four decades, Constantine was invited to intervene in a similar controversy connected with the incipient Donatist Schism in Africa and reacted as the Aurelian did, that is by referring the case to the judgement of the Bishop of Rome and his synod. When the schismatic Africans demanded a larger synod to review the judgement of Rome, Constantine acquiesced, though somewhat reluctantly, and arranged for a *larger* synod to meet at Arles (314). By calling for a revision of the Bishop of Rome's synodal judgement, Constantine not only transgressed traditional ecclesiastical norms which considered the decision of the Bishop of Rome as definitive, but he also reversed what seems—towards the end of the third century—to have been the more

---

[253] Burke, "Eusebius on Paul of Samosata," 17, suggests that the appeal of the Synod of Antioch to the emperor was not entirely unprecedented and refers to Gallienus' Letter to Egypt, which resulted from the appeal of the bishops there for the restoration of previously confiscated property; but such an appeal was of an entirely different nature to that which resulted from the deposition of Paul by the Antiochene synod. Girardet, *Kaisergericht und Bischofsgericht*, 12–14, points to the attempts by certain "heretics" (the followers of Thebutis?) to denounce the relatives of the Lord before Domitian (*HE* 3,19,1–3,20,6 = Schwartz 232,12–234,18) and again before Atticus, the Consul at the time of Trajan (*HE* 3,32,1–6 = Schwartz 266,19–270,6), as examples of appeals by those who probably considered themselves "orthodox" for the intervention of the State. The relevance of these two incidents for the question of the Church's attitude to the empire is questionable.

[254] *HE* 7,11,1f. (Schwartz 654,2f.). See Andresen, "Der Erlaß des Gallienus," 385–398.

[255] *HE* 7,11,8 (Schwartz 656,13–18). See also *HE* 7,1,1 (Schwartz 636,14) regarding prayers of the Church for the Emperor Gallus.

[256] *HE* 7,11,5 (Schwartz 654,19–656,1). This scriptural text had been earlier used by Polycrates of Ephesus against Victor of Rome (*HE* 5,24,7 = Schwartz 492,16).

positive relationship between the Church and the "civil" authority, which permitted a certain initiative on the part of the Church to request the civil authority to give effect to her decisions, though it would not tolerate an intervention by that civil authority in the process of ecclesiastical judgement itself. The history of the so-called Arian crisis in the fourth century, in particular the history of Athanasius, will show how hard the orthodox elements in the Church had to fight in order to restore the former balance between the Church's independence of judgement on the one side and on the other a legitimate though limited dependence on the civil authority to put the Church's judgement regarding civil matters into effect. The need for a realignment arose from the destructive influence of the principle which Eusebius would develop, namely, that in the new historico-salvific situation of the Constantinian Church, the final authority in the Church would no longer be vested in the Bishop of Rome or the Apostolic Succession but in the Sacral Emperor who had embraced Christianity. The evolution of Eusebius' thought in this direction, and the gradual abandonment of his earlier attitude to the Apostolic Successions and to the Bishop of Rome as enjoying the preeminent authority within the Church, will be traced in the following chapter.

§5 Summary

The history of the Church of the Apostolic Successions made up the content of Books 4–7. The form of the *History* was determined by the two models which Eusebius adopted and smelted into one to suit his purpose. The first and the most predominant model was based on the imperial history of a people, where, however, the bishops took over the function previously occupied by the imperial rulers so that the historical events were ordered and presented according to their successive reigns. The second model was taken from the history of the philosophical schools, where the orthodox writers appropriated the position of the philosophers. In Books 4–7, we saw how in fact the dynastic line of the Petrine Succession of the Roman bishops was primarily singled out to establish the framework of the *History*: the events and personalities that make up the history of the second and third centuries were presented within the reigns of the successive Bishops of Rome. Alexandria's successions shared this function with Rome in Book 4, but in the later books they were less consistently associated with those of Rome in determining the chronology of the *History*, while the bishops of Antioch were rarely mentioned in this connection. The successions at Jerusalem played no part in this function.

Although the main subject of Books 4–7 was to portray the succession of "Christian philosophers" (the orthodox writers and teachers) and their battle against the heretics, the successors of Simon Magus, yet Eusebius' discussion of this topic was nonetheless presented within the overall framework of the Apostolic "dynastic" successions. Thus, for example, the various periods in the "Life of Origen" were described as the major events in the reigns of the Bishops of Rome from Zephyrinus to Fabian. This too accounts for the typical Eusebian synchronisms of orthodox writers under Soter and Zephrynus (as earlier, under Clement of Rome), where Eusebius' understanding of the relationship between the Apostolic Authority (preeminently but not exclusively present in the successors of St. Peter) and the Apostolic Teaching is mirrored. This relationship is the historical embodiment of the prototypical relationship between St. Peter and St. Mark. His care to record the "visits" of such orthodox writers as Polycarp, Hegesippus, Irenaeus, and Origen to the Church of Rome likewise reflected the same Eusebian preoccupation with the close association between these Teachers and the center of the Apostolic Authority which "guaranteed" their orthodoxy. However, it is the relationship between the Church of Rome and the Church of Alexandria that primarily embodies the prototypical relationship between Peter and Mark, their respective founders, as can be seen in the way the greatest literary figures of the Alexandrian School— Clement, Origen, and Dionysius—are all shown to have been associated with Rome, however tenuously, as in the case of Clement, or tendentiously as in the case of Origen. The close connection between the Churches of Rome and Alexandria was brought home to the reader by the way Dionysius of Alexandria was shown to follow both the official Roman ruling with regard to Novatian and the Roman custom in the Baptismal Controversy, as well as reminding his readers that Dionysius wrote to the Bishop of Rome for guidance on complex questions.

In his presentation of the main controversies which engaged the Church in the second and third centuries, Eusebius is consistently on the side of the Bishops of Rome, depicting the various issues so as to present the position taken by Rome in the most favorable light. In the *Paschal Controversy* (Book 5), the stand of Victor of Rome is defended as that which is based on Apostolic Tradition and is at one with the universally accepted practice, whereas the Asian custom, though "more ancient," as it was rooted in the Jewish practice, and though it could claim Apostolic sanction, is shown to be but a local one. He agrees with the irenic attitude of Irenaeus towards the Asian Church, but never once questions the right of the Bishop of Rome to intervene and act as he did. Indeed, one is left with the impression that Eusebius considered Victor's action in excommunicating whole communities in Asia Minor to be a typical, though exaggerated, instance of Rome's traditional severity towards heretics in the tradition of Peter's relationship to Simon Magus, the father of all heresies. Eusebius' presentation of the *Novatian Schism* (Book 6) is remarkable for its concentration on the activities of Cornelius and the Synod of Rome, to the detriment of the part played by St. Cyprian and the Synod of Carthage. This, however, may be due to lack of information regarding the African Church. The attitude of Eusebius to the *Baptismal Controversy* under Stephen of Rome (Book 7) is basically the same as his view of the Paschal Controversy, recognizing the correctness of the general practice regarding the rebaptism of heretics defended by Stephen, but sympathetic to the suggestion of Dionysius of Alexandria that a certain diversity in matters of local customs be tolerated. Again, he never doubts the *right* of Stephen to intervene and excommunicate, were the matter an issue of *Faith*. The reaction of Firmilian of Cappadocia to Stephan's excommunication is ignored, though this too could be accounted for on the basis of lack of documentary evidence. When the Synod of Antioch appealed to the emperor regarding *Paul of Samosata* (Book 7) and Aurelian based his judgment on the principle that in the case of a dispute between rival claimants to a particular see, he who could prove communion with the Bishop of Rome ought to be considered the legitimate claimant, Eusebius found this judgment "most fitting" since it accorded with his (and his contemporaries') understanding of Rome's preeminent authority within the Church Universal.

In the *Sabellian Controversy* (Book 7), however, Eusebius came up against the unexpected. The Bishop of Rome who, as Successor to St. Peter, was expected to provide the Apostolic Teaching with the final sanction of his Apostolic Authority, as well as to detect and to repudiate error, appeared to lend his authority to a teaching which, to all intents and purposes, approximated to the dreaded heresy of Sabellianism. Further, when Rome succeeded in compelling Dionysius, the successor to St. Mark in the See of Alexandria and the great exponent of Origenist orthodoxy, to adopt the dreaded term ὁμμοούσιος, Eusebius must have found himself in a serious predicament. He had no doubt as to the orthodoxy of his own Origenist Christology, and, at this stage at least, could not question the correctness of the ecclesiology he had defended in his "Apology for the Apostolic Church" which constituted the original *History*. But now his Ecclesiology collided with his Christology. How could the final Apostolic Authority in the Church, guided by Divine Providence from its inception by St. Peter, err in matters of Faith? Since Eusebius, it would seem from the above, accepted that, *a priori*, the Bishop of Rome could not err in matters of the Apostolic Faith, then he simply suppresses the details of the controversy between the two Dionysii and instead intimates that the earlier views of Dionysius (which resulted in the Alexandrian bishop's theology being censured by the Bishop and Synod of Rome) had been accepted by Sixtus II (the predecessor of Dionysius of Rome) and that there was nothing essentially different in the later opinions of the Alexandrian Dionysius which he expressed in the "four other treatises" he sent to his namesake in Rome. But, as we will see in the following chapter, the issue could not be suppressed for long. It would eventually erupt and play a decisive part in the transformation of Eusebius' original Ecclesiology, which began with the trauma of the Great Persecution.

CHAPTER FOUR
Dawn of a New "Dispensation"
(Books 8–10)

When Eusebius first conceived the *History* we have just been considering, that is in the golden days which followed the Peace of Gallienus, the martyrs like the Apostles were figures of the past. Thus, when the Great Persecution, as it came to be known, broke out in the year 303, it was totally unexpected and its effects on the mind of Eusebius were traumatic—the vestiges of which trauma we will endeavor to trace in this chapter.[1] After eight years of terror,

---

[1]   In this connection, see Eger, "Kaiser und Kirche in der Geschichtstheologie Eusebs von Cäsarea," 97–115; Farina, *L'impero*, 165. Eger describes the attitude of Eusebius to the empire as undergoing three different stages of development: "In der ersten Periode (before 313) schreibt er die von Gott gesetzte Aufgabe, die Königsherrschaft Christi auf Erden durchzusetzen, allein der Kirche zu; in der zweiten (between 313 and 324) erkennt er dem Imperium neben der Kirche eine gewisse äußere providentielle Haltung bei dieser Aufgabe zu; in der dritten (after 324) überträgt er in den Konstantinschriften die spezifische Aufgabe der Kirche zugleich auch dem Kaiser" (p. 115). Wallace-Hadrill, *Eusebius*, 175, questions the rigid categorization of Eger and draws attention to the earlier theological presuppositions which enabled his later development to take place. Though Eger's study ignores the chronological problems regarding the *History's* composition and so suffers accordingly, yet his basic perception

Eusebius again took up his pen to add an appendix to the original *History*, describing briefly the unforgettable epoch he had himself witnessed. This was the original form of Book 8 as reconstructed by Laqueur. But before tacking this appendix on to the previous work, Eusebius was naturally compelled to round off the original *History*—the extent of which we will shortly examine. These two literary activities make up the 1st Revision of the *History*.

Six months later, in October 311, persecution again broke out in the East, which Eusebius understood to be a continuation of the earlier one and behind which the Emperor Maximian stood. Eusebius' information was scant—a possible indication that the persecution which lasted until 313 was not too intense[2]—and so in his 2nd Revision, after the end of this period of the persecution, most of his attention is given to the *mortes persecutorum* theme, describing the grisly deaths of the "tyrants" in a further addition to the original form of Book 8. Another feature of this Revision is his adjustment of the original form of Book 8, made necessary by the new information he had received—the text of the palinode of Galerius among others. With the peace of 313, Eusebius was able to put his hands on more documents and gather material from various sources other than mere notices of local historical interest, and so he prepared for a major revision of his history of the persecution. The general history of the persecutions was thus conceived, while the local martyrs he had himself witnessed were removed from Book 8 and formed the basis of a second work "On the Martyrs of Caesarea." Working now on two separate manuscripts, he tackled the latter on a chronological basis and later broadened its scope to cover the martyrs of Palestine,[3] while into the text of the *History* he inserted a list of martyrs arranged not chronologically but according to locality.

The 3rd Revision, one which was much more radical than any of the foregoing, was taken in hand probably around 317, the generally

retains its validity: a development did take place, one admittedly rooted in his earlier presuppositions. The course of Eusebius' gradual, yet ultimately radical, change of attitude to the empire and in particular to the emperor can be traced in the various Revisions of the original *History* between 311 and 325.

[2]   This second period of the persecution began with the new restrictions imposed by the emperor on the freedom of worship but soon the blood of the martyrs flowed again: Peter of Alexandria was killed on November 24, 311, followed by the presbyter Lucian of Antioch on January 7, 312, at Nicomedia.

[3]   Here, Laqueur added his own support to the views of Preschen, which Violet, *Die Palästinischen Märtyrer des Eusebius von Cäsarea*, Leipzig, 1896, defended against Lightfoot, *DCB*, vol. II, 319–320. Lawlor and Oulton, *The Ecclesiastical History*, vol. II, 48, footnote 48, found the arguments of Violet unconvincing.

accepted date of the Dedication of the Church at Tyre at which Eusebius—now a bishop—delivered the great Panegyric (= the contents of the original book). Around the same time, he came into the possession of two sets of documents, one of which aimed at justifying the Licinian-Constantinian double-monarchy from the point of view of Roman nationalism, and the other a collection of imperial documents establishing, among other things, the new recognition of the Church in juridical terms.[4] It is difficult to say exactly when, after 317, Eusebius undertook to revise his previous work in accordance with the new information available to him. The result of this revision was that the now overcrowded Book 8 was expanded into two books, 8 and 9, while the Panegyric at Tyre made up the original form of Book 10.

Before the *History* was finally "published," a final Revision, the 4th, took place as occasioned by the breakup of the Licinius-Constantine double-monarchy, the retreat of the former from Christianity, his defeat at the hands of Constantine (the Battle of Chrysopolis, 324), and the reunification of the empire under one emperor, one manifestly sympathetic to the Christian Religion. Accepting the above outline of the *History's* final evolution—for the greater part the result of Laqueur's painstaking analysis—it is the object of this chapter to trace the developments in the thought of Eusebius during the various stages of revision which resulted in the final three books in their present shape. It should, however, be stressed that Laqueur's nuanced reconstruction gives the impression—probably the correct one—that the various stages of the Revisions flowed one into the other. However, for the sake of clarity in presentation, we have grouped the various Revisions into four more or less clearly discernible stages.

§1 The 1st Revision: After the Edict of Galerius, 311
According to Laqueur's reconstruction, this revision resulted in the "Urform" of Book 8 and was made up of three sections: (i) a description

---

[4]   Laqueur, *Eusebius als Historiker*, 217, goes beyond the evidence in suggesting that this set of documents was part of the official imperial propaganda aimed at winning over the Christian community. As bishop of one of the main metropolitan sees, Eusebius would have automatically received a copy of these documents which were so pertinent to ecclesiastical affairs. Their presentation as a set of documents in the *History* is more than likely due to Eusebius' own propaganda purposes (see below, pp. 158–159).

of the martyrs Eusebius had himself witnessed;[5] (ii) the history of the empire in its relationship to the Church, recalling the sufferings inflicted on the empire for the persecution it inaugurated;[6] (iii) the end of the first stage of the persecution.[7]

Though it is beyond the scope of this study to go into the many textual and literary problems related to these final three books, nonetheless there is one text which needs to be discussed, however briefly and inadequately, since it is a key text for a proper understanding of the radical development which took place in the thought of Eusebius as a result of the persecution. The text is *HE* 8,1,1–8,2,3[8] and the problem is whether this text in its present form and in its present position belongs to the Urform of Book 8 as Laqueur unquestionably assumes;[9] in other words, does it belong to the 1st Revision or, as I am inclined to think, to the 4th.

The 1st Revision, which produced the Urform of Book 8, now no longer extant except through some delicate and hypothetical reconstruction, also includes the present conclusion to Book 7. To our great loss this part of the Revision was not treated in any detail by Laqueur. Before examining the problem as to whether the text of *HE* 8,1,1–8,2,3 belongs to the 1st Revision, we must therefore first of all try to establish the precise extent of the initial part of that Revision and, having established that, see whether the mind of Eusebius reflected there matches the attitude of Eusebius to be found in the problem text.

The brief description of the reigns of Probus, Carus, and Diocletian serves to round off the subject matter of the first seven books—the "Successions of the Apostles." The persecution is only mentioned *en passant*,[10] its coverage is reserved for the newly planned Book 8.

---

[5]   *HE* 8,1,1–8,2,3 (Schwartz 736,1–742,7); original form of *De mart. Pal.* 1,1–4 (Schwartz 907,3–908,23); *HE* 8,3,4 (Schwartz 744,15); *HE* 8,13,7 (Schwartz 774,2–7, in the form as found in MS: Σ). See Laqueur, *Eusebius als Historiker*, 33–39; 65f.; 85.

[6]   *HE* 8,13,9a (Schwartz 774,11–14); *HE* 8,13,10a (Schwartz 774,17–20); *HE* 8,13,11b (Schwartz 776,1–3, parallel text 911,8f.); *HE* 8,15,1b (Schwartz 786,23–788,5); *De mart. Pal.* 3, 6b–7 (Schwartz 911,11–19). See Laqueur, *Eusebius als Historiker*, 49–58.

[7]   *HE* 8,15,2a (Schwartz 788,1–2), which text is not mentioned by Laqueur but which is probably part of the following text which he does discuss: *HE* 8,15,2b–8,16,1 (Schwartz 778,8–788,16); *HE* 9,1,2–6 (Schwartz 802,13f.); *HE* 9,1,7a (Schwartz 807,1–2 = MS ATER); *HE* 9,1,8 (Schwartz 804,8–806,2); *HE* 9,11,8b (Schwartz 825,2–6). See Laqueur, *Eusebius als Historiker*, 65–76.

[8]   Schwartz 736,1–742,7.

[9]   See Laqueur, *Eusebius als Historiker*, 39.

[10] E.g., HE 7,32,1 (Schwartz 716,20); HE 7,32,4 (Schwartz 718,5–6); HE 7,32,28 (Schwartz 728,24–26); the mention of Peter of Alexandria's martyrdom (HE 7,32,31 = Schwartz 730,13–15) is most likely a later interpolation, as is indicated by the self-contradiction in the text (see Lawlor and Oulton, *The Ecclesiastical History*, vol. II, 264), This

Working back from the references to the persecution in the final chapter of Book 7, which could only have been written after 311, one observes first of all that HE 7,30,22–7,32,32 constitutes, from the point of view of the subject matter, an integral subsection. The foregoing subsection deals with the deposition of Paul of Samosata by the Synod of Antioch, 268, and shows no signs of being written during the persecution; but it concludes with a short description of the Emperor Aurelian's change of attitude to the Christians, the subject matter of which does touch on the persecution.[11] The smoothness with which the continuing narrative moves from the description of Aurelian's reign to the reigns of his successors and the first mention of the persecution under Diocletian would seem to argue against positing HE 7,30,22 as the beginning of 1st Revision. Where a breakdown occurs—not very roughly but nonetheless distinctly—is between HE 7,30,19, which brings the deposition of Paul of Samosata to an end, and HE 7,30,20, the beginning of the description of the Aurelian reign: in HE 7,30,19 the mention of the emperor is in a sense secondary to the main topic, the deposition of Paul, whereas in HE 7,30,20–21 the attitude of the emperor to the Church, as illustrated by his "intervention" in the case of Paul, is presumed to have been the main topic itself.

It seems, then, that the description of the changing attitude of Aurelian towards the Church—a description which, as we will see, is tendentious and of great import to gauge the mind of Eusebius—was the point where Eusebius took up the threads of the earlier work (the "Successions"), quickly knotted them together in the subsection HE 7,30,22—7,32,32, and then went on to write the first draft of Book 8. This, as will be immediately made clear, will have important implications both for establishing the mind of Eusebius immediately after the trauma of the persecution as well as for establishing the date when the problem text of HE 8,1,1–8,2,3 was, as it seems to me, interpolated into its present position in the text.

The 1st Revision then, opened with a description of the change of attitude by the Emperor Aurelian towards the Church. In contrast with his former disposition as manifested in his "most fitting"

was probably inserted during the 2nd Revision, when the second reference to the same martyrdom was included in the list of martyrs that Eusebius inserted into the original form of Book 8 (HE 8,13,7 = Schwartz 772,24–29). Schwartz, Nachrichten, 1904, 529, footnote 3, calculated the date of the martyrdom as November 24, 311. See, however, Lawlor and Oulton, The Ecclesiastical History, vol. II, 264 and 293, who argue in support of the year 312.

[11] HE 7,30,20–21 (Schwartz 714,9–19).

intervention at the request of the Church in the case of Paul of Samosata, towards the end of his reign he was counselled to stir up persecution against the Church.[12] However, according to Eusebius, he was prevented from doing so by the Divine Justice. Interpreting this, Eusebius maintains that the frustration of Aurelian's plans was a clear demonstration to all that the rulers of this life could not proceed against the Church of Christ unless the Hand which champions us were to consent as a divine and heavenly judgment, whose object was correction and change (of heart) whenever it saw fit.[13] These two short statements betray significant changes in the mind of Eusebius himself: the persecuting emperor is no longer seen as simply *the enemy of God* and of His Church, as Nero and his successors were originally regarded by Eusebius,[14] but is now considered more as an *instrument in the hand of Providence* to be used by Him according to His plans. Consequently, the concept of persecution begins to change from being the enemy's contribution to the battle waged by the adversaries and demons against piety and true religion[15] to becoming more the divine means of discipline, leading to deeper inner conversion, used by Providence when He saw the need.[16] The implications of the first change are obvious. Should the emperor become a Christian, then his providential instrumentality could take on a more positive coloring—as indeed it would by the time Eusebius undertook his 4th and final Revision. It is easy to anticipate how the traditional, two-dimensional attitude of the Christian to the State[17] would naturally tend to disappear so that the double-principle of obeying God first and

---

[12] *HE* 7,30,20 (Schwartz 714,9–12).

[13] *HE* 7,30,21 (Schwartz 714,13–19).

[14] For example, Domitian (cf. *HE* 3,17,1 = Schwartz 230,8–15). Re. Eusebius' understanding of the emperors as persecutors, see Farina, *L'impero*, 156–157.

[15] Cf. *HE* 5, "Proem," 3–4 (Schwartz 400,13–402,2) as also *HE* 5,2,6–7 (Schwartz 430,10–22), which, though it does not stem from the pen of Eusebius, yet it articulates the same sentiments as are to be found in the Proem.

[16] It could be objected that a similar concept of "persecution" (understood in terms of the Church's chastisement) is to be found at the very beginning of Eusebius' narration of the final aim of the original *History* (Aim F). But there (*HE* 2,25,4 = Schwartz 176,12–13) the concept appears within a quotation from Tertullian (*Apol.* 5)—in itself, of no great moment, since Eusebius' quotations generally reflect his own ideas, were it not for the fact that it is clearly out of tune with its immediate context where Nero is described as a fighter against God" and not as the instrument of God "the author of our Chastisement," as the quotation from Tertullian puts it. What is of greater import, is the concept of "chastisement" used by Tertullian: it conveys the idea of the purification of gold (= the life of faith) through the fire of persecution, a concept quite different from that of Eusebius, who saw persecution as the means used by God to bring back those who had strayed from the life of faith to their former purity.

secondly submitting to the civil authority becomes fused into the one principle: obey the emperor.

But it is the second change in the mind of Eusebius which deserves closer attention at this stage since its implications are not so clear. No longer the result of the Enemy's machinations against the Church of Christ, persecution is now understood as the means used by God to chastise and lead his erring people back to their original service of Him. In other words, persecution of the Church is beginning to be seen in terms of God's treatment of His People in the Old Testament. Further, we note how the prevention of Aurelian's plans to persecute the Church by the intervention of the Divine Justice was explained so as to imply that the Church at the time was not in need of chastisement. When Eusebius mentions that the persecution was accomplished under Diocletian and his successors, the reader is left to draw his own *implication* that consequently the Church must have been in need of discipline and chastisement.[18] But, true to his apologetic purpose, which tended to underplay anything derogatory with regard to the Church, Eusebius makes no explicit reference to the actual evils within the Church which so "caused" the persecution.

The presentation of the causes of the persecution as found in the problem text of *HE* 8,1,1–8,2,3 is, by contrast, blatantly explicit: the Church is displayed as having grown lax and slothful on the freedom afforded them by the Peace of Gallienus and the golden age which followed it; this led to envy and faction fighting, Eusebius loudly maintains, among both the rulers and the members of the Church—bringing down the Divine Wrath on them in the form of persecution and the great humiliations suffered by the rulers. We notice, first of all, that the passage no longer shows signs of any apologetic reticence concerning the weakness of the members of the Church; indeed, as *HE* 8,2,3[19] makes clear, Eusebius is writing no longer for those outside the Church, the reading public of his original *History*, but for "ourselves," namely the Church.[20]

---

[17] E.g., *HE* 7,1,1 (Schwartz 636,13–14) and *HE* 7,11,8 (Schwartz 656,14–18), which stress the loyalty and submission of the Christian to the state, and *HE* 7,11,5 (Schwartz 654, 19–656,1) where the limits of this loyalty are determined according to the principle enunciated by St. Peter in his speech to the High Priest: one must obey God rather than men (Acts 5,29).

[18] Cf. *HE* 7,30,22 (Schwartz 714,19–25).

[19] Schwartz 742,5–7.

[20] In his Proem to Book 8, Eusebius informs his readers that he considers it an obligation to hand on an account of the persecution for the knowledge τῶν μεθ᾽ ἡμᾶς (Schwartz 736,4), whereas at the conclusion of the passage in question, he informs us that he will add to the general history those things which

This alone would suffice to indicate that the passage did not belong to the 1st Revision, since, as will be shown, the rest of that Revision is strongly apologetic,[21] as indeed is the 2nd Revision.[22] Secondly we notice that the theme of chastisement by Divine Justice has given way to the concept of persecution as punishment by the Divine Wrath: the time of chastisement is over, since inflamed to anger by the wicked misconduct of the Church—and its rulers in particular—the Deity (τὸ θεῖον) not only punished His People but, using a quote from Ps 88,40 (*LXX*), Eusebius now maintains that He has overturned "the covenant with His servant." This displays a much later development of the ideas of Eusebius, first found seminally in the opening of the 1st Revision as discussed immediately above. Further, it should be observed that the "envy" and faction-fighting among the rulers and people of the Church, so vividly described in the passage in question, contrasts strikingly with the picture painted in the *History* up to, and after, the reign of Aurelian, where the bishops were seen to act in exemplary fashion "with one mind."[23] The impression the reader gains from the post-Aurelian situation, as depicted in the final chapter of Book 7 that formed part of the 1st Revision, is that the litany of praise for the successors of the Apostles, both bishops and teachers, which characterized the original *History* of seven books, is continued there in the way Anatolius, Pamphilus, Pierus, Melitius, and Peter of Alexandria are treated.[24] There is but one flaw in the picture— the simple mention of Marcellinus, Bishop of Rome, whom, we are told, "the persecution overtook"[25] and with whom the successions at Rome abruptly come to an end. Marcellinus, as we will see, was later accused of having compromised himself during the persecution, and the ambiguous statement of Eusebius would seem to indicate that something was

will be of profit πρώτοις μὲν ἡμῖν αὐτοῖς, ἔπειτα δὲ καὶ τοῖς μεθ᾽ ἡμᾶς (*HE* 8,2,3 = Schwartz 742,5–6). The unnecessary repetition indicates the probable presence of an interpolation. What is of particular interest is the new emphasis in the second passage: πρώτοις μὲν ἡμῖν αὐτοῖς. This signifies a radically different audience as that intended by the original *History*. Originally Eusebius, the Apologist, set out, ostensibly, to write for a non-Christian audience, but now he has dropped the apologetic form and speaks directly to the Church and her members. But even in the course of the 3rd Revision, Eusebius still retains the basic form of the Apology and presumes a non-Christian addressee (cf. *HE* 8,13,8 = Schwartz 774,10). See Laqueur, *Eusebius als Historiker*, 48–49; 93f.

[21] See Laqueur, *Eusebius als Historiker*, 12f.
[22] See below, pp. 154–156.
[23] *HE* 7,30,1 (Schwartz 704,18).
[24] Cf. *HE* 7,32,1–32 (Schwartz 716,16f.).
[25] *HE* 7,32,1 (Schwartz 716,19–20).

amiss, which Eusebius, true to his slightly suspect apologetic concern, tries to whitewash.

In sharp contrast with this reticence (as displayed in the 1st Revision) is the blanket condemnation in the problem text *HE* 8,1,1–8,2,3 which attacks all those who were tried by the persecution and, having failed, made a shipwreck of their salvation.[26] Finally, we note how in the passage in question, the Golden Age of the pre-persecution era was said to have been marked in particular by the honor and freedom accorded to the Church by the imperial rulers, in particular the esteem shown by these rulers to the Christians.[27] However, the examples of this greatly desired "recognition" by the imperial rulers—the raison d'être of his whole apologetic endeavor—do not include the very obvious one of Aurelian's implicit recognition of the Church, as manifested in his intervention in the case of Paul of Samosata, although one would expect such a mention if the passage in question truly belonged to the 1st Revision, which began at precisely this point.[28] The examples he does use—the honor enjoyed at the imperial court by the servants Dorotheus and Gorgonius[29]—can in fact help us date the passage in question, which, as the above four observations together indicate, must be a later interpolation.

To the above four observations, it may be added that the interpolated passage *HE* 8,1,1–8,2,3 destroys the customary style of Eusebius as found in the previous books of the *History*, which generally begin with brief chronological orientation points, usually details of the successions of the emperor, as can be seen in the specifically "historical" Books 3 to 7; when a book also includes a Proem, such as Books 3 and 7, then this Proem is brief, consisting of not more than 4 or 5 lines to be immediately followed by the chronological information. If we remove the interpolated passage *HE* 8,1,1–8,2,3 from the Urform of Book 8, then we find the same pattern as in Books 3 and 7: a short Proem consititing of a few lines and concluding with the words: . . . καὶ ἄρξεταί γε ὁ λόγος ἡμῖν ἐντεῦθεν[30] which is almost identical with the end of the Proem to Book 7: ἐμοὶ δ᾽ ὁ λόγος ἐντεῦθεν ποιήσεται τὴν ἀρχήν.[31] Both of these conclusions thus refer to the chronological data which is expected

---

[26] *HE* 8,2,3 (Schwartz 742,2–3); cf. also *De mart. Pal.* 12 (Schwartz 942,21—946,12), which Laqueur, *Eusebius als Historiker*, 7, observes is related to *HE* 8,2,1–2.

[27] *HE* 8,1,1–2 (Schwartz 736,6–13).

[28] Namely with *HE* 7,30,20–21.

[29] *HE* 8,1,4 (Schwartz 736,18–22).

[30] Schwartz 736,4–5.

[31] Schwartz 636,4–5.

to follow. Like Book 7 which opens, as expected, with the chronological information regarding the succession of the Emperor Gallus, so too our newly constructed Book 8—i.e., minus the interpolated passage—moves from the Proem into the chronological information regarding the date of the persecution: "The 19th year of the reign of Diocletian. . . ."[32]

The question now arises as to which Revision does the interpolation of *HE* 8,1,1–8,2,3 (which we will now call *Interp C*) belong. The references to the imperial servants Dorotheus and Gorgonius in *HE* 8,1,4 help provide an answer. Reference to these two imperial servants occurs again later in the text (in *HE* 8,6,1) where they are mentioned as examples of the glorious martyrs of the Nicomedian Church. As noted above, Dorotheus and Gorgonius were held up in *HE* 8,1,4 as examples of the recognition accorded to Christians by imperial rulers, which characterized the golden days of the pre-persecution Church. Apart from the different usages to which these two men were put by Eusebius in the two passages, two further observations may be made on comparing the two texts: (i) the second text, when it mentions the two imperial servants adds a qualifying descriptive clause about the honor and love shown to them by their masters which presupposes that the reader is unfamiliar with the former history of these men; (ii) *Interp C* is clearly a development of the second, since the honor shown to the two servants by their masters, which according to the second text was not less than that given to their own *children,* is now described as being greater than that shown by "the rulers" to the provincial *rulers* and governors. Now the second text makes up part of the 2nd Revision and can thus be dated between 312–317, which means that *Interp C* was inserted into its present position after that date, i.e., during the 3rd or 4th Revision. To judge from the extent of the exaggeration between the first mention of the imperial servants in *HE* 8,6,1 and that found in the interpolated text, *HE* 8,1,1–8,2,3, it is more than likely that the interpolation took place during the 4th Revision, a conclusion which is confirmed by the discovery of the motive for such an interpolation, as will be seen when we examine the 4th Revision.

Meanwhile let us return to the 1st Revision, putting *HE* 8,1,1–8,2,3 aside until we come to examine the 4th Revision, and examine the mind of Eusebius during the peace which resulted from the Edict of Galerius, making use of Laqueur's reconstruction and our amendment just discussed.

---

[32] *De mart. Pal.* 1,1f. (Schwartz 907,3f.); see Laqueur, *Eusebius als Historiker*, 65–76.

As already mentioned, the *apologetic character* of the original *History* is carried over into the 1st Revision. This particular characteristic is nowhere more evident than in the way Eusebius interprets and presents the split in the empire, something unheard-of up to then,[33] as the punishment meted out to the pagans for their persecution of the Christians. This is conveyed by contrasting the peace, harmony, and prosperity enjoyed by the empire during the pre-persecution period,[34] attributable to the friendly disposition of the civil authority towards the Church, with the disastrous consequences for the empire once she had embarked on a policy of hostility towards the Church: added to the civil war just mentioned, the empire also suffered pestilence and famine.[35] Thus, the "peace" of Galerius in 311 was interpreted by Eusebius as due to a change of mind in the rulers brought about by their recognition of how the Divine and heavenly Grace thus watched over His People.[36] It should be noted how the effect of the Peace is described as a light shining forth out of the night of persecution.[37] The metaphorical usage of the image of light is a favorite one of Eusebius. We saw it in connection with St. Peter's divinely determined journey to Rome and to the West to destroy the darkness of error and evil. It will again be taken up by Eusebius when he comes to deal with the emperor, who achieves a Peace more impressive than Galerius and who is seen to occupy the position within the Church previously occupied by the Successors of St. Peter: Constantine. But that is to anticipate the eventual development of Eusebius' thought.

We have already touched on the new concept of the persecuting emperor, no longer seen simply as the *instrument of the Devil* and the successor of Nero but as an *instrument in the hands of Divine Justice* to chasten His People when He saw fit, and we have seen how this change in his attitude to the emperor effected another change in his understanding of the causes of persecution. As is to be expected, this shift of emphasis was bound to have repercussions in Eusebius' understanding of martyrdom, its nature and place in the Church: if now the cause of persecution is to discipline a lax Christian people and not, as formerly, the reaction of the forces of evil to the presence of Christ in the Church and in the virtuous life of His

---

[33] *HE* 8,13,11 fin. (Schwartz 776,1–3) = parallel text in *De mart. Pal.* 3,6f. (Schwartz 911,9–13).

[34] *HE* 8,13,9 (Schwartz 774,11–14); cf. also *De mart. Pal.* 3,6.

[35] *HE* 8,15,1–2 (Schwartz 786,23–788,7).

[36] *HE* 8,16,1 (Schwartz 788,8–16); cf. parallel text in *De mart. Pal.* 13,14 (Schwartz 950,1–7). The reference to the 10th year in *HE* 8,16,1 (Schwartz 788,8) is a later interpolation.

[37] *HE* 9,1,8 (Schwartz 804,8–806,2); cf. *De mart. Pal.* 3,7 (Schwartz 911,14–19).

People, then martyrdom can no longer be conceived as the crowning of the perfect Christian life. But before we look at the new understanding of martyrdom as reflected in the fragments, which apparently make up that part of the *Urform* of Book 8 which describes the persecution as witnessed personally by Eusebius, it will be necessary to examine briefly the earlier concept of martyrdom as found in the original *History*.

Martyrdom was originally conceived in traditional terms as the crowning of the Christian life of virtue, as in the case of St. Stephen the Protomartyr, where the traditional understanding in terms of the imitation of Christ and His Passion is still discernible.[38] Reechoing Tertullian's understanding of martyrdom as the seed of Christians, Eusebius presented, as the climax of St. Peter's mission to found the Church, his martyrdom in Rome (with St. Paul) at the hands of Nero.[39] A similar understanding may be presumed to underlie the lists of martyrs in Book 3[40] and Book 4.[41] Up to this, one can observe the influence of Eusebius' sources—sometimes copiously quoted—and the traditional concept of martyrdom they contain.[42]

But in Book 5, Eusebius begins to reveal the nature of his own estimation of martyrdom. There we find another example of Eusebius' method, according to which he receives a traditional concept but reinterprets it in the light of his own more fundamental concepts of Redemption and Christology. He assumes that he is interpreting the traditional concept authentically but in fact does it quite inadequately—the cause of the inadequacy being, as will become clear, the radical divergence between the genuine roots of the traditional understanding and the false source of the new interpretation, i.e., Eusebius' own inadequate theology. The traditional perception just outlined is, for example, to be found in the text of the letter written by the Churches of Gaul to those in Asia and Phrygia concerning the martyrs who suffered in Lyons and Vienne during the seventeenth year of Marcus Aurelius' reign, in imitation of the one and original martyrdom of Christ, "the faithful and true martyr." It is a share in His Witness through the confession of one's Faith.[43]

---

[38] *HE* 2,1,1 (Schwartz 102,15–19), where Eusebius also notes the play of words suggested by the name of the Protomartyr.

[39] *HE* 2,25,5–8 (Schwartz 176,16–178,14).

[40] For example, *HE* 3,5,2 (Schwartz 196,1–13).

[41] For example, *HE* 4,16,7–4,17,13 (Schwartz 358,1f.).

[42] See, for example, the "Martyrdom of Polycarp," quoted in *HE* 4,15,3f. (Schwartz 336,4f.).

[43] *HE* 5,2,2–4 (Schwartz 428,7–430,2).

How superficially Eusebius grasped this appreciation of martyrdom is revealed in the opening of Book 5, where he previews the narrative concerning the martyrs of Gaul: without even mentioning the name of Our Lord or using the concepts of "witness" or "confession," martyrdom is compared to the triumphs of soldiers in wars and bloodstained battles,[44] the only difference being the type of war, now waged by the Christian for truth and piety, for the "very peace of the soul."[45] This is a stoic concept rather than a Christian one. The stoical type of interpretation meant that the nature of the instrument which achieved the required "peace of soul"—namely here persecution—has at this stage in the evolution of Eusebius' thought been neutralized, since the demons, the original cause of the persecution, are now considered to be simply unseen adversaries who contend with the "athletes of religion" (= the martyrs) in the "most peaceful battles" for "truth and religion."[46] This is a far cry from the concept of martyrdom found in the Letter of the Churches of Gaul where martyrdom was understood in terms of the perfect imitation of Christ. So too the trophies, victories, and crowns won by the athletes of religion are conceived by Eusebius in terms of everlasting memorials, like those of the epic heroes of old,[47] and no longer in terms of the crown of martyrdom worn by St. Stephen, even though the text might well allude to the same. Written in the golden age of the Peace of Gallienus, Eusebius was evidently talking about the *distant* heroes of the past, little aware of the impending persecution and the horrific scenes he would himself witness.[47a] The truth is that Eusebius' basic understanding of Christianity, as primarily a civilizing, refining process,[48] already faintly discernible among the presuppositions to be found in his Introduction to the original *History* (Book 1), was incapable of penetrating and grasping in any satisfactory way the traditional concept of martyrdom. Martyrdom ought not to be, as it was for the early Eusebius, an

---

[44]   *HE* 5,1,3–4 (Schwartz 400,13f.); also, *HE* 9,1,9–10 (Schwartz 806,2–12). However, in *HE* 8,4,3 (Schwartz 746,10) the term ὁμολογία is indeed used—though it seems to convey the meaning of loyalty rather than confession as understood in its original sense—much in the same vein as the term ἔνστασις is used in *HE* 8,4,4 (Schwartz 746,13).

[45]   *HE* 5,1,4 (Schwartz 400,17–402,2).

[46]   *HE* 5, "Proem," 4 (Schwartz 400,19–20).

[47]   Cf. *HE* 5, "Proem," 4 (Schwartz 400,23–402,1).

[47a] Kraft, *Einleitung*, 37, aptly comments: "Denn in dem ganzen Werk war eine Katastrophe wie die diokletianische Verfolgung eigentlich nicht vorgesehen. Für eine wirkliche Gefahr, die die Kirche an den Rand ihrer Existenz brachte, war im Grunde kein Platz in dem Werk."

[48]   This concept is developed by Eusebius in his *Demonstratio evangelica* (cf. *DE* 8, "Proem," 11 = Heikel 351,3–18) and more fully in the 4th Revision of the *History* (see below, pp. 170–173 = *Interp A*).

extrinsic luxury for the epic figures of history who afterwards could function as exemplars in our struggle to achieve peace of soul. Neither is it sufficient to conceive martyrdom as consisting primarily in some heroic feats of endurance, as Eusebius would have us believe. Martyrdom is intrinsic to the Christian life considered as the imitation of Christ who died and rose on the third day, into whose death we are born in Baptism, and from whose crucified side we are nourished in the Sacraments. Whatever concrete form it may take, the Christian life, whose source is the Cross, must find its ultimate expression in martyrdom, finally dying to self so that we may rise to God. But for Eusebius, the Cross was not intrinsic to his theology,[49] and thus martyrdom was similarly but a foreign body in his basic thought patterns.

By the time Eusebius once again sat down to revise his original *History* in the wake of the unexpected and bloody persecution, when the weakness of many was laid bare and the strength of others stood out in sharp contrast, his understanding of martyrdom had undergone a further development: persecution is now seen as the instrument of God to chastise and discipline a lax Church, whose weakness of faith is seen in terms of moral cowardice, while the martyrs are pictured as brave heroes.[50]

In this connection, let us look more closely at the strange description of the last Bishop of Rome listed by Eusebius, and who brings the list of the successions at Rome to such an abrupt end: Marcellinus.[51]

According to the *Catalogus Liberianus* (354), Marcellinus was Bishop of Rome from 296–304. Theodoret, apparently interpreting Eusebius more favorably than is warranted, talks about Marcellinus having *distinguished* himself during the Diocletian

---

[49] Eusebius could not and did not deny the historical event of the Passion, death, and Resurrection of Our Lord. But those passages which deal explicitly with the subject, sometimes at considerable length (e.g., *Theoph* 3,3,41f. = Gressmann 148,1—160,8), illustrate his awkwardness in the face of this Mystery. His treatment concentrates primarily on finding "reasons" why the Body, which the Divine Logos assumed as His earthly Instrument to interpret His Divinity, suffered death. Even though many of his arguments are culled from tradition, yet they are extrinsic to his theology of the Divine Logos. For a summary of Eusebius' thought on this subject, see Berkhof, *Theologie*, 132–139, where further references to Eusebius' treatment of the death of Christ are to be found.

[50] Cf. Eusebius, *De mart. Pal.* 1,3 (Schwartz 908,5–12).

[51] On Marcellinus, cf. the article by Barmby, in *DCB*, vol. III, 804–806, and that by Enßlin in *PWK* XIV, col. 1448–1449; Caspar, "Kleine Beiträge zur älteren Papstgeschichte," 321f.; Seppelt, *Geschichte der Päpste*, bd. I, 65–66.

Persecution.[52] The Donatists on the other hand preserved a less flattering memory of the Bishop of Rome, accusing him (with little impartiality) of being a *traditor* and a *thurificatus* both of which accusations St. Augustine dismisses as calumny.[53] Yet the memory persisted and in the *Catalogus Felicianus* (530) he is indeed represented as both a *traditor* and a *thurificatus*—but as one who repented, was later beheaded for his Faith and so received the crown of martyrdom.[54] His name is missing from several of the Roman bishops' lists, due, according to Caspar, to an attempt at a *damnatio memoriae* by his rigorous successor Marcellus, which could, at the very least, suggest some type of lapse by Marcellinus. Whatever the historical truth of that incident, no direct light is shone on it by Eusebius. He simply reports that the persecution "had overtaken" Marcellinus[55]—an ambiguous statement which would indicate that something was amiss. Even stranger is the silence of Eusebius on the continuation of the history of the Roman Church and the succession of its bishops down to his own day. The successions in Antioch, Jerusalem, and Alexandria are given up to the time of writing this, his 1st Revision, ca. 311,[56] but the succession of the Bishops of Rome ends with Marcellinus, who died on October 25, 304.[57]

A glance at that turbulent period in the history of the Roman Church[58] displays the following picture. After the death of Marcellinus there was an unusually long period of 2 years and 7 (or 8) months, during which the See at Rome was vacant, until Marcellus became bishop in 307 (May 27 or June 26).[59] From the inscription set up on his burial place by Pope Damasus, it appears that after the initial persecution in Rome, Marcellus tended to be severe if not actually rigoristic in his attitude to the *lapsi* and the question of their readmission. This resulted in such disturbances within the Church in Rome that riots and bloodshed ensued as the warring factions worked out their party differences. The bishop, Marcellus,

---

[52] Theodoret, *HE* 1,3,1 (Parmentier-Scheidweiler 7,14).

[53] Augustine, *Contra litteras Petiliani* II, 92,202 (CSEL 52, Petschenig 125,22); *De unico baptism* VII 16,27 (CSEL 53, Petschenig 28,12f.).

[54] Mommsen, *Monumenta,* vol. I, 242.

[55] *HE* 7,32,1 (Schwartz 716,20).

[56] *HE* 7,32,2–4 (Schwartz 716,20–22; 718,5–6); *HE* 7,32,29 (Schwartz 728,26–29); *HE* 7,32,30–31 (Schwartz 730,2–15).

[57] See Schwartz, *Zur Geschichte des Athanasius* (*Nachrichten*, 1904), 530, note 1.

[58] Cf. Duchesne, *Histoire II*, 92–97.

[59] On Marcellus, see Duchesne, *Le liber Pontificalis,* xcix–c; Caspar, "Kleine Beiträge zur älteren Papstgeschichte," 321–333; also the article by Enßlin in *PWK* XIV, col. 1494. According to Seppelt, *Geschichte der Päpste*, bd. I, 66, almost four years elapsed between the death of Marcellinus and the election of Marcellus.

was exiled by Maxentius as the author of this discord—suffering unjustly, according to the inscription of Damasus, for the crimes of another (= the leader of the opposition). He died on January 16, 308, possibly after his return to Rome, having completed but 6 (or 7) months and 20 days in office and was succeeded by one Eusebius[60] (April 18, 308), who apparently favoured a slightly milder policy towards the readmission of the *lapsi* or at least was more successful than his predecessor in the enforcement of his policy. But Eusebius too was exiled, together with the leader of the laxist opposition, Heraclius, who may well have been elected antipope by his own party. Again, the exile was by order of the tyrant Maxentius. Eusebius died in exile after a short pontificate of 4 months and 16 days.[61] Due in part to the divided state of the Church, the see was again vacant for another long period of 1 (or 2) years, 2 months, and 14 days until Miltiades was elected.[62] Miltiades reigned from the July 2, 310 (311?) to January 10 or 11, 314 and was Bishop of Rome when Eusebius of Caesarea undertook his 1st Revision.

Why is Eusebius silent on the history of the Roman Church after Marcellinus and why did the successions there end with him? It is possible but highly unlikely that Eusebius was ignorant of what was happening in the Church of Rome. Even if his information was scant in the year 311, yet why did he still remain silent during the second Revision (after 312) when more information was at his disposal, and when he added the information about Peter of Alexandria's martyrdom to the text of his 1st Revision?[63] The most plausible answer is Eusebius' own dismay at the disarray and discord rampant in the principal Church, which ought to be the source and center of peace and concord within the Church Universal. The situation at Rome, during and after the persecution, revealed a picture very much at variance with the idealized concept of Eusebius as to the office of the Bishop of Rome. At a distance (and possibly due to tendentious information), Eusebius could well have mistakenly considered the hard policy of the successors of Marcellinus, Marcellus, and Eusebius of Rome, as Novatianist and so "discovered"

---

[60] See the entry in the "*Catalogus Liberianus*," ed. by Duchesne, in *Le Liber Pontificalis*, vol. I, 6–7. On Eusebius of Rome, see the article by J. Bryce, *DCB*, vol. II, 303–305; Schwartz, *Nachrichten*, 1904, 531–533; Caspar, "Kleine Beiträge zur älteren Papstgeschichte," 331–333.

[61] See entry in the "*Catalogus Liberianus*," ed. by Duchesne, in *Le Liber Pontificalis*, vol. I, 8–9.

[62] On Miltiades, see article by J. Barmby, *DCB*, vol. III, 917–919; Enßlin, *PKW* XV, col. 1706–1707.

[63] *HE* 7,32,31 (Schwartz 730,13–15).

heresy, as he would have considered it, in the successors of St. Peter. Further, instead of working for the unity, peace, and concord of the Church, both these successors were exiled by the pagan authority for disrupting the peace and being the authors of discord. From what, to Eusebius, must have seemed like the lapse of Marcellinus down to the accession of Miltiades, his contemporary at the time of writing the 1st Revision, the most distinguished see in the entire Church appeared to have been in a state of dissolution as characterized by the two relatively long vacancies. This then was the state of the Church after the Successor of St. Peter (Marcellinus) had offered incense to the successor of Nero. In this 1st Revision, the silence of Eusebius with regard to the state of the Church in Rome is in line with his general apologetic approach, according to which he painted the best picture possible of the Church, ignoring the flaws of her members, in particular her rulers, the bishops. Once the need for such propaganda was over, then Eusebius could and would paint another picture.

§2 The 2nd Revision: After 312

The peace which resulted from the Edict of Galerius in 311 was short-lived in the East. Persecution soon broke out again, especially around Antioch, where, apparently, the Emperor Maximian was behind it and which Eusebius saw as a continuation of the earlier one. His information was not very extensive and so his amendments to the 1st Revision were not too radical.[64] Only one development in his thought, as reflected in this Revision, is of significance to our study; that which concerns his concentration on the *emperors* as those primarily responsible for the persecutions and not simply the vague concept of the *enmity of the empire,* which was used in the 1st Revision. It may be added that the author's attitude to martyrdom, to be gleaned from the list of bishop-Martyrs he inserted into

---

[64]   *HE* 8,12,11 fin.–8,13,7a (Schwartz 770,27–774,2); *HE* 8,13,9b (Schwartz 774,14–17); *HE* 8,13,10b–11a (Schwartz 774,20–776,1); *HE* 8,13,15b (Schwartz 778,7–11); *HE* 8,14,18b (Schwartz 786,17–23); regarding the previous references, see Laqueur, *Eusebius als Historiker*, 47–65. *HE* 9,1,2–6 (Schwartz 802,13f.) was removed and replaced by *HE* 8,16,2–8,17,11 (Schwartz 788,16–794,24). This Revision also included Appendix to Book 8, verses 1a & 4b (Schwartz 796,2–3 and 796,19–797,1,4) as well as the present form of *HE* 9,1,1–9,1,11 (Schwartz 802,1–806,18). See Laqueur, *Eusebius als Historiker*, 65–92. The rest of the Revision was made up of: *HE* 9,2,1a–1b (Schwartz 806,19–808,2); *HE* 9,4,2a (Schwartz 808,20–22); *HE* 9,7,1a (Schwartz 812,19–21); *HE* 9,7,15–9,8,3 (Schwartz 820,10–822,12); *HE* 9,10,14–15 (Schwartz 846,12–848,8); *HE* 9,11,1b–3a (Schwartz 848,12–25); *HE* 9,11,7–8 (Schwartz 850,22–852,6); see Laqueur, *Eusebius als Historiker*, 96–191.

the text, reveals the same emphasis as found in the 1st Revision, i.e., the heroic feats of endurance displayed by these men are underlined[65] as well as their singular bravery.[66]

This Revision, then, is primarily marked by Eusebius' focus on what Laqueur calls the *mortes persecutorum* theme: Diocletian is afflicted with madness and is thus forced to abdicate;[67] since the emperors denied freedom to the Christians, they themselves became embroiled in warfare against each other;[68] Galerius' change of heart is now attributed to Divine Providence, since, as we are told, Providence, after being reconciled with His People, inflicted the emperor with a foul disease as a punishment for his persecution of the Christians so that Galerius was moved to confess God and order the cessation of the persecution.[69] The relatively friendly attitude of Constantius (and his son) in the West is noted; in his rewriting of the history of the persecution, Eusebius is careful to point out how Constantius was rewarded by God for his friendly attitude to the Church. But Maximian, who plotted against Constantine, the son of Constantius, died a shameful death,[70] while the Emperor Galerius, now the "chief author of the entire persecution,"[71] is depicted as reaping the whirlwind of the Divine wrath for his previous hostility to the Church.[72]

Even at this stage, Eusebius merely tacitly acknowledges that the persecution was ultimately caused by the failures of the Christian People and so could be considered a "divine judgment,"[73] which lasted until Providence became reconciled to His People.[74] But what these failures were is not mentioned; the author is more concerned to display how the persecutors suffered for doing violence to Christ.[75]

Such then is the *leitmotiv* of the text which made up the 2nd Revision and which in Laqueur's reconstruction was originally included in the *History* as a type of appendix to the *Urform* of Book 8: God is still the "Champion of His own Church"[76] who stops the

---

[65] Cf. *HE* 8,13,4 (Schwartz 772,13).
[66] Cf. *HE* 8,13,6 (Schwartz 772,23).
[67] Cf. *HE* 8,13,11a (Schwartz 774,22f.).
[68] Cf. *HE* 8,14,18fin.—8,15,1 init. (Schwartz 786,17–23).
[69] Cf. *HE* 8,16,2f. (Schwartz 788,16f.).
[70] Cf. *HE* 8,13,15 (Schwartz 778,7–9).
[71] Cf. *HE* 8,16,3 (Schwartz 788,25).
[72] Cf. *HE* 8,16,4–5 (Schwartz 790,1–11).
[73] *HE* 8,16,3 (Schwartz 788,26).
[74] Cf. *HE* 8,16,2 (Schwartz 788,21).
[75] See also *HE* 9,10,5 (Schwartz 848,8).
[76] *HE* 9,7,16 (Schwartz 820,15–16).

proud boasting of the tyrant and metes out punishment on the empire and the tyrannical emperors for their enmity towards His People.[77] For Eusebius, at this stage of his development, God, if one may say so, is still seen as "independent" in the use of the various instruments at His disposal: the persecutions are His instruments which serve to purify and reconcile the Church to Himself, while the natural catastrophes are seen as God's punishment on the hostile empire for its persecution of the Christian People; finally the mortal sickness which afflicts the emperors is God's instrument to bring the persecuting emperors to their senses.

§3 The 3rd Revision: After 317[78]

Proceeding in two fairly distinct stages, this Revision produced such a radical overhaul of the *Urform* of Book 8 (and its original appendix) that two books were formed out of the original one, comprising in substance the present Book 8 and Book 9. While yet another book was added, Book 10, which at this stage contained only the Panegyric at Tyre. The Revision was necessitated by two developments: first by the new knowledge accumulated by Eusebius after the so-called Edict of Milan, 313, when the new peace created more suitable conditions for the distribution and collection of source material from all parts of the Church and the empire, and secondly by the new significance which Eusebius began to read into this "Peace."

Having access to a more complete picture of the persecution, Eusebius removed the original account of the martyrs he had witnessed himself, replaced it with an ἐπιτομή which sketched in very general terms the beginning of the persecution and the behavior of the rulers of the Church,[79] and then went on to include a fairly lengthy text which described in greater detail various martyrdoms, arranged not chronologically but according to locality.[80] With the text he removed, he began to compose a new work, "On the

---

77   Cf. *HE* 9,8,1–3 (Schwartz 820,18–822,12).

78   See Schwartz, *Einleitung*, liv–lv; Laqueur, *Eusebius als Historiker*, 216. The date of this Revision is determined by the date of the Dedication Sermon delivered at Tyre. Bardy, "La theologie d'Eusèbe de Césarée," 9, suggests that it occurred around the year 318, whereas Schwartz and Laqueur opt for 316–317. The sermon was delivered by Eusebius sometime after his own elevation to the See of Caesarea (see Kraft, *Einleitung*, 44–45).

79   *HE* 8,2,3fin.–8,3,4 (Schwartz 742,8–744,14). See Laqueur, *Eusebius als Historiker*, 34–39.

80   *HE* 8,4,1–8,12,10 (Schwartz 744,16–770,13).

Martyrs of Caesarea," which he eventually broadened to cover Palestine. This new presentation of the martyrs marks the first phase of the 3rd Revision.

An examination of his new treatment of the martyrs found in this Revision reveals, first of all, a new change of emphasis: it is no longer the rulers of the Church who share the limelight but individual Christians, such as the imperial servants Dorotheus, Gorgonius, and Peter.[81] In fact, among the many martyrs whose deeds are cited, only two bishops are mentioned, Anthimus of Nicomedia[82] and Phileas of Thmuis.[83] Commenting on this, it would seem, Eusebius informs us that when the persecution first broke out, many rulers of the Churches indeed showed courage and endurance under terrible torments but countless others (μυρίοι δ' ἄλλοι) proved weak and cowardly.[84] Of the latter category no further details are given, and yet such a frank statement is no longer quite as fettered by the previous apologetic concern of the writer. It would seem that Eusebius is moving towards a more spiritualized concept of the Church and is less concerned than earlier with the institutional type of Church: accordingly, he never again takes up the "Successions." So too in the Panegyric at Tyre, which was added to the *History* as Book 10, the author unambiguously refers to the cause of the persecutions as the moral rot of the Church: this led to her fall, so that, deprived of virtue, she lay dead on the ground and no longer thought uprightly about God.[85]

In contrast with the many (bishops) whose souls were numbed with cowardice, the martyrs are now presented very much as figures of heroic bravery and endurance, "soldiers of Christ's Kingdom."[86] They are described as those "who display marvelous zeal for the sake of piety (εὐσεβείας) towards the God of the Universe;"[87] the term εὐσέβεια here conveying more the idea of *loyalty* than lived-faith. Nonetheless, there are still many vestiges of the traditional concept of martyrdom scattered throughout the text, such as the attribution of the strength which sustained the martyrs

---

[81] *HE* 8,6,4–5 (Schwartz 748,25–750,5).
[82] *HE* 8,6,6 (Schwartz 750,6). It should be noted that attention is mainly devoted to the two imperial servants Dorotheus and Gorgonius in Eusebius' description of the martyrs at Nicomedia.
[83] *HE* 8,9,7f. (Schwartz 758,16).
[84] *HE* 8,3,1 (Schwartz 742,20).
[85] *HE* 10,4,57–58 (Schwartz 878,28f.); see also *HE* 9,8,15 (Schwartz 826,13–19).
[86] *HE* 8,4,3 (Schwartz 746,9).
[87] *HE* 8,4,1 (Schwartz 744,17).

to Our Savior, Jesus Christ, who was the object of their witness[88]—although the term μαρτυρέω, here used in the passive, is probably to be interpreted here as "to show loyalty."[89] There is also a very interesting reminder of the martyrdom of St. Peter as, in some sense, prototypical, since the name "Peter" is understood by Eusebius to be synonymous with martyrdom.[90] But the main thrust of Eusebius' thought is revealed in the inclusion of stories about self-inflicted deaths as martyrdoms, such as the suicides committed by a certain woman and her daughters who drowned themselves rather than be subjected to the indecent assaults of the soldiers who had captured them.[91] Eusebius likewise betrays his inadequate understanding of martyrdom by his apparent obsession with the horrific tortures suffered by the martyrs.[92] Once the immediate cause of these tortures was removed—namely the persecuting emperor—then not only would the tortures cease but martyrdom would be no more in the Church.

The second phase of the Revision was occasioned by two sets of documents which came into Eusebius' hands. According to Laqueur, the first was a collection of documents which set out the foundation of the Licinius-Constantine double-monarchy from the point of view of purely nationalistic Roman interest,[93] while the other set comprised of documents which were illustrative of the changed attitude of the emperors to the Church, and which were published as a collection by the emperors as part of their propaganda to win over the Church.[94] It is possible that Laqueur is correct with regard to the first set of documents, a matter that is not too relevant to our study and so can be left aside, but with regard to the second set of documents, another more likely explanation as to their origin as a *collection* is to be preferred: since these documents all deal with the new legal status of the Church, they would have been automatically available to Eusebius, now bishop of the important metropolitan see of Caesarea, and thus were most probably collected *by him* in

88 *HE* 8,7,2 (Schwartz 752,19–21); see also *HE* 8,8,1 (Schwartz 754,27); *HE* 8,9,5
     (Schwartz 756,31). See especially the text inserted into *HE* 8,10,2f. (Schwartz
     760,1f.) and attributed to Phileas of Thmuis.
89 See above, footnote 44.
90 *HE* 8,6,4 (Schwartz 748,27–750,1).
91 *HE* 8,12,3–4 (Schwartz 766,23f.). See also the similar story of the noble Roman
     lady, who plunged a sword into herself rather than be subjected to a similar
     indecency (*HE* 8,14,17 = Schwartz 786,5–15). In this connection, see *HE* 8,6,6
     (Schwartz 750,13–14).
92 See, e.g., *HE* 8,6,3 (Schwartz 748,16–25); *HE* 8,7,1f. (Schwartz 752,11f.).
93 See Laqueur, *Eusebius als Historiker*, 216.
94 See Laqueur, *Eusebius als Historiker*, 217.

the course of time. As a collection these documents were, as Laqueur suggests, appended to the end of the text of the 3rd Revision, the original Book 10;[95] this, it seems to me, was done for Eusebius' *own* propaganda purposes—to demonstrate the new status enjoyed, according to God's providence, by a Church now purified and cleansed by the persecution; the new status of the Church is glowingly portrayed in the Panegyric which Eusebius delivered at Tyre, at the dedication of a newly rebuilt Church. What interests us at the moment is the *significance* of this new status of the Church for the development of Eusebius' thought as reflected in the Panegyric.[96]

The very occasion of the Panegyric at Tyre—the dedication of a newly rebuilt Church—was sufficient to suggest to Eusebius a richly symbolic parallel to the new status enjoyed by Christians in the wake of the persecution: a new Church[97] had arisen, built on the ruins of the old.[98] Here for the first time we encounter quite explicitly the consciousness of Eusebius—that he and his contemporaries were living through a new epoch in the life of the Church and the history of the world, and so he praises God in the following way: "Great is He who alters the seasons and the time, removing kings and establishing them[99] (Dan 2,21). . . . He has put down princes from their thrones and has raised the lowly (Lk 1,52) from the earth."[100] In the previous Revision, we noticed how the detachment of the historian, a relative matter at the best of times and even more relative with regard to the apologist Eusebius, gives way more and more to the subjective tendencies of the chronicler who is recording world-shattering events; but in this particular case, Eusebius gives way to the even more dangerous tendencies of the orator who was not uninclined to be carried away by his own rhetoric. What humanly speaking was impossible had become a reality—almost overnight. The Emperors (Licinius and Constantine) had not only put an end to the State's intermittent yet at times ruthless persecution of the Church, but, going beyond any hoped-for toleration, they were actively at work establishing Christianity as the state-religion in fact if not in name,[101] and intervening directly in the Church's internal affairs in order to heal its divisions.[102] Considering the

---

[95] These documents are only preserved in the MS group ATER (Schwartz 883,20f.).
[96] See also the commentary of Berkhof, *Kirche und Kaiser*, 85–87.
[97] Cf. *HE* 10,4,3 (Schwartz 862,25); *HE* 10,4,7 (Schwartz 864,18); also, *HE* 10,4,2 (Schwartz 862,22).
[98] Cf. *HE* 10,4,26 (Schwartz 870,10–19).
[99] *HE* 10,4,8 (Schwartz 865,8–9).
[100] *HE* 10,4,8 (Schwartz 865,10–11).
[101] Cf. *HE* 10,5,15f. (Schwartz 887,5f.).

rather primitive causal concept of Divine Providence which underlies
Eusebius' thought, it is only to be expected that he would eventually consider the individual most responsible for this unexpected turn of events as
being in a special way an instrument of God.[103] However, that development
only occurred seven years after the 3rd Revision.

At this present stage in the evolution of his thought, Eusebius attributes
the new era to the work of Christ, "the second cause of good deeds on our
behalf"[104]—the Father being the first cause—whose activity is described in
terms of His work of Redemption.[105] The allusions to Christ's Redemption
are so thick that it is difficult to distinguish which event is here the subject
of the discourse—whether the original redemptive work of Christ or the
new era introduced by the "Edict" of Milan. A closer inspection of the
text reveals that Eusebius is in fact portraying the new era in terms of that
Redemption: "... and when we were, I will not say, half-dead, but even by
this time altogether foul and stinking in tombs and graves, He raised us
up and saveth us *now as in the days of old*. ..."[106] Significantly, he also uses
the familiar concepts of light and darkness to describe the appearance of
the Savior in a world controlled by evil spirits.[107] Further, in this new era
Eusebius tells us that which was foretold long ago has now come to pass.[108]

The subordinationist understanding of Christ (= the second cause
of our Redemption) enables Eusebius to conceive Him as the "angel of
great counsel" and "the great commander of God"[109] while the martyrs
are seen to be his soldiers. The result of their victory over the tyrants and
the impious rulers, the puppets of "the demon who loves evil,"[110] is the
unheard-of rejection by the emperors of the ancient idols, which rejection followed their recognition of Christ as the "child of God" and their
confession of Him as the "supreme Emperor of the Universe,[111] as can be
gathered from the inscriptions set up to record His victory where He is proclaimed as Savior; these inscriptions they set up "in the midst of that city

---

102   Cf. *HE* 10,6,1f. (Schwartz 890,3f.); *HE* 10,7,1f. (Schwartz 891,1f.).
103   See Eusebius, *VC* 3,66 (Winkelmann 119,30–31) and *VC* 4,45 (Winkelmann
      139,17–18), where Constantine is described as *the* instrument of God.
104   *HE* 10,4,10 (Schwartz 865,23).
105   Cf. *HE* 10,4,10f. (Schwartz 865,22f.).
106   *HE* 10,4,12 (Schwartz 866,16–17). Translation, Oulton.
107   Cf. *HE* 10,4,13 (Schwartz 866,21–24).
108   Cf. *HE* 10,4,33 (Schwartz 872,18f.); *HE* 10,4,29 (Schwartz 871,18–19).
109   *HE* 10,4,5 (Schwartz 867,16): see Is 9,6 and Jos 5,14.
110   Cf. *HE* 10,4,14 (Schwartz 867,1).
111   *HE* 10,4,16 (Schwartz 868,1).

which rules all those on earth" (= Rome).[112] In this new era, it may be observed, Rome also has its significance—but one in accordance with that which characterizes the new era: the recognition of Christianity by the emperors, itself the fulfilment of the deepest desires of the Apologist Eusebius. The political significance of Rome, once of a *negative* theological nature as "Babylon," the center of the unredeemed world and so the center of the mission of the Church, now begins to take on a *positive* theological significance in the mind of Eusebius as he moves towards his new ecclesiology of the Imperial Church built on the "(Apostolic) foundations," now understood in a mere chronological sense of a past event which has meanwhile been surpassed.[113]

In the highly spiritualized ecclesiology of this middle stage of Eusebius' development, the bishop is presented as a type of the prototypical High Priest, Jesus Christ.[114] Drawing a parallel between the relationship of the Son to the Father expressed in Jo 5,19, Eusebius maintains that the bishop looks to Christ as to a teacher, with the pure eyes of the mind and perceives the actions of Christ as patterns or archetypes.[115] Alluding later to the scene of Pentecost, the presbyters and deacons would seem to be compared with the Apostles and those with them who were filled with the Holy Spirit,[116] "while in the ruler of all (= the bishop), as is right, the entire Christ hath taken his seat."[117] The sacramental concept of the bishop as successor to the Apostles has given way to the idealized concept of him as a type of Christ, while the earlier understanding of the local Church as the local realization of the Church Universal has given way to the concept of the local Church, as itself, the perfect image of the ideal, spiritualized Church, a concept which naturally tended to give greater emphasis to the autonomy of the local Church. Consequently, there is no reference in the Panegyric to the bishop's relationship to his fellow-bishops. The significance of this development is that the way is left open for an alternative organ, other than the bishops, which would embody and symbolize the universal dimension of the Church. For the later Eusebius, Constantine, as sole emperor, would ideally fit this role. And so the

[112] *HE* 10,4,16 (Schwartz 868,4).
[113] Cf. *HE* 10,4,21 (Schwartz 869,6f.).
[114] Cf. *HE* 10,4,23f. (Schwartz 869,22f.).
[115] Cf. *HE* 10,4,25 (Schwartz 870,10–19). Here Eusebius seems to refer in the first place to the design of the Church building, but also, allegorically, to the building up of the living Church (the faithful). In this speech, Eusebius continually moves from the concrete to the allegorical.
[116] Cf. *HE* 10,4,66 (Schwartz 881,18–22).
[117] *HE* 10,4,67 (Schwartz 881,22–23).

Vita Constantini will go on to compare the emperor with "some general bishop constituted by God," when he "convened synods of the ministers of God" in order to remove the differences which existed between them.[118] Likewise, Constantine's own claim to be a bishop "ordained by God to oversee what is external to the Church"[119] would later be seen by Eusebius to be quite fitting.[120] However, at this stage in the development of his thought, which could be termed the "middle stage" of his ecclesiology that is characterized by a more spiritualistic attitude to the Church's nature, Eusebius recognizes but one general bishop over the Church—God Himself.[121]

There are frequent references in the Panegyric to God, the Father of the Universe as the παμβασιλεύς,[122] a term also used with respect to Christ[123] and possibly understood in accordance with Eusebius' subordinationism[124] in a derived or secondary sense. What is of note, however, is that the bishop, even though considered to be the ruler of all,[125] is never described as participating in the Kingship but only in the Priesthood of Christ. One could say that a vacuum already exists in Eusebius' theology which would one day be filled by the emperor as the earthly type of the divine prototype in a similar way as the bishop is the type of Christ—the High Priest. This, however, as we will see, is a later development, whose final

---

[118] *VC* 1,44,2 (Winkelmann 38,27–28). See Straub, "Constantine as ΚΟΙΝΟΣ ΕΠΙΣΚΟΠΟΣ," especially pp. 50–55. Straub is of the opinion that "Eusebius was in fact a very competent interpreter and an effective inspirer of the emperor's own political intentions and of the concept of his special mission" (p. 50). It seems to me that Eusebius' influence on Constantine may have been greater than Straub suggests, as will be pointed out below. Straub may be criticized for taking the attitude of the later Eusebius as though it were the general view of the Church at the time. The conflicts which disturbed the Church in the second quarter of the fourth century should remind us not to treat Eusebius as though he were the adequate representative of the general fourth-century Christian attitude to the emperor.

[119] *VC* 4,24 (Winkelmann 128,21–22). See Straub, "Kaiser Konstantin als ἐπίσκοπος τῶν ἐκτός," in *Stud. Pat.* I, 678–695.

[120] *VC* 4,24 (Winkelmann 128,19).

[121] *HE* 9,8,15 (Schwartz 826,15). Notice also the recurrence of the themes of light and darkness, which marked the decisive arrival of St. Peter in Rome. They will later characterize the equally decisive "arrival" of Constantine as the head of the Imperial Church. See above, p. 54f., re. Peter, and p. 187f. below, re. Constantine.

[122] *HE* 10,4,6 (Schwartz 864,12); *HE* 10,4,65 (Schwartz 881,8); also, *HE* 10,4,47 (Schwartz 876,24).

[123] *HE* 10,4,16f. (Schwartz 867,23f.).

[124] Cf. *HE* 10,4,65 (Schwartz 881,7f.), where this subordinationism is explicit. See also *HE* 1,2,7–9.

[125] *HE* 10,4,67 (Schwartz 881,22).

expression is to be found in the Tricennial Speech of Eusebius, Constantine's panegyrist in Constantinople, 335, where he describes the emperor as εἰκὼν ἑνὸς τοῦ πανβασιλέως.[126] Here in the Panegyric of Tyre, after describing the cause of the persecutions in O.T. terms, as the punishment wrought by the Deity on a Church that had chosen what is evil and sensual,[127] Eusebius has arrived at the stage where he considers the souls of the emperors, both *Licinius* and Constantine, to be chosen instruments of the Word to cleanse the whole world of all destructive men and the God-hating tyrants.[128]

Another feature of the 3rd Revision is the fact that Eusebius is primarily, but not exclusively, interested in the *Eastern situation*,[129] so that the famous victory of Constantine over Maxentius "at Rome" is only summarily mentioned[130] whereas the story of Licinius' war against, and eventual victory over, Maximian is painted in greater detail.[131] But what both victorious emperors have in common is the way God used them to restore peace to His People so that the light of this peace "shone down on us from Him, manifesting to all that God had established Himself as bishop (ἐπίσκοπος) through all that had happened to us, on the one hand scourging and in due season correcting His people by means of misfortunes, while on the other showing mercy and kindness to those who place their hope in Him after sufficient discipline."[132] Here again we notice the explicit reference to the persecution as God's way of disciplining his wayward people.

Since Eusebius in this new presentation of the persecution used, according to Laqueur, a set of documents similar to those at the disposal of Lactantius for his composition of *De mortibus persecutorum,* characterized by their Roman-nationalistic standpoint, it is important to see how Eusebius has taken them and reinterpreted them in accordance with his own deterministic ideas of providence and history.[133] Far from observing any change in Eusebius' own

---

[126] Eusebius, *LC* 7,12 (Heikel 215,21–22).

[127] *HE* 10,4,57 (Schwartz 878,28f.).

[128] *HE* 10,4,60 (Schwartz 879,19f.).

[129] See Laqueur, *Eusebius als Historiker*, 149.

[130] *HE* 9,9,1 (Schwartz 828,1). In the 4th Revision, Eusebius inserts a fuller description of the Battle at the Milvian Bridge (*HE* 9,9,2–12, see p. 185, re. *Interp E*).

[131] *HE* 9,10,1f. (Schwartz 838,16f.).

[132] *HE* 9,8,15 (Schwartz 826,13–19). Regarding the theme of light, see footnote 121 above.

[133] Laqueur uses the term "metaphysical" in a way which is unacceptable, indeed unwarranted, in order to describe Eusebius' view of history which is

Geschichtsauffassung from such a deterministically-providential concept to a politically-orientated one, i.e., his abandoning the idea of God as the ultimate mover in historical events and in its place recognizing for the first time the place played by human motives in history,[134] we observe a growing accent on the way God "manipulates" history—a simplification and exaggeration of the profound Christian concept of Providence, one which Eusebius understood too mechanically and imperfectly. The tragedy is that Eusebius was too ready to identify in a simplistic way, the instruments of God—a readiness which is strikingly evident in the radical developments in his thought as will be seen in his final Revision of the *History*.

§4 The 4th and Final Revision: Between 325 and 326

If only because it gave the *History* its final definitive form,[135] this Revision is by far the most important. Before considering the various details of the Revision, it will be necessary to call to mind the *Sitz im Leben* of Eusebius at the time of its composition. The *terminus a quo* is the defeat of Licinius by Constantine at Chrysopolis on September 18 or 20, 324. Since the text contains references to Constantine's son, Crispus, as though he were alive and still enjoying the favors of both Constantine and God,[136] then the *terminus ad quem* is determined by the execution of Crispus on the charge of treason in the year 326. The period thus defined by the internal evidence of the text coincides with events, both in the

---

based on a concept of providence that implies a type of determinism and ignores the realms of human freedom.

[134] According to Laqueur, Eusebius first of all defended the theory that the empire suffered the consequences of its persecution of the Christians when it was divided in two; then he saw that the emperors suffered personally for their part in the persecution (see Laqueur, *Eusebius als Historiker*, 49–58); after the persecution, Eusebius heard about the peaceful attitudes of Constantius I and his son Constantine and this destroyed his concept of the emperors as basically hostile to the Church—even in Licinius nothing was found to be held against him—and so he came to the conclusion that the catastrophic condition of the empire was due to the *political* fact that it was split, as a result of the different attitudes of the emperors to the Christians which rendered the imperial authorities incapable of pursuing any common policy (see Laqueur, 58–64). Laqueur, p. 65, maintains that the first two theories presupposed the hand of God, but that the third one merely reflected profane political thought.

[135] This form has come down to us in the MS group BDMΣΛ.

[136] *HE* 10,9,6 (Schwartz 902,1).

history of the Church and in the personal life of Eusebius, which had profound effects on our author's ecclesiology.

At the level of the Church's history, the period during which the 4th Revision was undertaken was dominated by the unprecedented sole rule of an emperor manifestly sympathetic to the Christian Religion. The heady optimism of the post-persecution Church, which found its eloquent expression in Eusebius' Panegyric at Tyre, had been temporarily dampened by the oppressive regulations of Licinius in the East.[137] Though hardly constituting a full scale "persecution," as Eusebius would now have us believe, they certainly brought home to the Church how fragile was her "peace" and how dependent her "security" was on the whim of the emperor. The victory of Constantine over Licinius restored that "peace." Here was an emperor whose very father had displayed tolerance towards Christians in the dark days of Diocletian,[138] and whose own record of interest and actual involvement in the life of the Church was, as Constantine himself pointed out,[139] consistently constructive and sympathetic. The victorious emperor soon granted to the Churches in the East those privileges he had previously bestowed on the western Churches.[140] The whole Church could now breathe freely, happily enjoying a position within the empire that, only two decades previously, would have been unthinkable. Christians in the East, who had suffered most during the persecutions, had even more cause to rejoice than their western brethren and so gave thanks to God for their newfound liberation and the unaccustomed recognition by the State. That Eusebius shared their euphoric sentiments is evident.[141]

However, the situation *within* the Church presented a less encouraging picture to Eusebius' eyes as he glanced around him. The debris of the persecutions could still be observed in the disorder which plagued the post-persecution Church. Apart from the Donatist Controversy in Africa, which the Bishop of Rome and his synod "failed" to settle, the Church in Rome itself was only recovering from the dissension and schisms, which resulted from the recurrent post-persecution problem as to the right attitude of the Church towards the *lapsi*. In Alexandria, the Church there was

---

[137] *HE* 10,8,10f. (Schwartz 894,18f.).
[138] Cf. *HE* 9,9,1 (Schwartz 826,20–21), which text belongs to this, the 4th Revision (see Laqueur, *Eusebius als Historiker*, 149–150).
[139] See the *Letter of Constantine to Alexander and Arius* (*Urkunde* 17,2 = Opitz 32, 11–16).
[140] Eusebius, *VC* 2,24–42 (Winkelmann 58,8–66,11).
[141] See Eusebius, *VC* 2,19 (Winkelmann 55,22–56,17), which text recalls the spirit of those heady days.

likewise rent by the Meletian Schism and that which centered around Coluthus, while Antioch was disturbed by the Paschal Controversy as well as doctrinal disputes and violations of Church order.[142] In a word, the principal sees, which ought to have been the centers of the universal *Pax* and *Koinōnia* had become the epicenters of discord. Added to all of this, a new controversy had arisen in the East, emanating from Alexandria and threatening to embroil the eastern Churches in sharp disputes and bitter dissensions: the Arian Controversy.

Soon after the 3rd Revision of the *History* had been completed, Eusebius became personally involved in the doctrinal dispute between the Bishop of Alexandria and his rebellious presbyter, Arius. His support for Arius drew Eusebius out of his library, where he had viewed both the history of the Church and contemporary events with some (admittedly relative) detachment, into the fray of ecclesiastical politics and the making of history itself. The details of his well-documented advocacy of Arius' cause need not occupy our attention here.[143] Instead we will concentrate on those developments which took place after September 324, and which led to Eusebius' personal encounter with the emperor.

Constantine first heard of the Arian Controversy at Nicomedia, whither he had moved his court after the battle of Chrysopolis.[144] It is likely that his informant was the bishop of that city, the friend and namesake of Eusebius of Caesarea.[145] Eusebius of Nicomedia, it seems to me, was most probably responsible for Constantine's initial intervention in the Alexandrian dispute. Within a month of his victory over Licinius, Constantine, recalling his intervention in the Donatist dispute in Africa[146] but forgetting the ineffectual outcome of his endeavors, once again intervened in the internal affairs of the Church by writing a letter addressed to Alexander and Arius, requesting them to refrain from useless philosophical hair-splitting and come to an agreement with each other. He entrusted the letter to his advisor and delegate, Ossius of Cordova. At Alexandria, Ossius perceived the radical nature of the theological

---

[142] See the *Letter of the Synod of Antioch*, 324/5 (*Urkunde* 18 = Opitz 36,1f.). Regarding the date of this document, see below, footnote 148.

[143] See, e.g., the *Letter of Eusebius of Caesarea to Euphration of Balanea* (*Urkunde* 3 = Opitz 4,1f.) and his *Letter to Alexander of Alexandria* (*Urkunde* 7 = Opitz 14,1f.), dated around 318 and 320 respectively. See also the *Letter of Arius to Eusebius of Nicomedia* (*Urkunde* 1,3. = Opitz 2,4). See Berkhof, *Theologie*, 163–186, for an outline of Eusebius' involvement in the dispute.

[144] Cf. *Urkunde* 17,4 (Opitz 32,24–27).

[145] See de Clercq, *Ossius of Cordova*, 198.

[146] *Urkunde* 17,2 (Opitz 32,11f.).

conflict and took the side of Bishop Alexander. In all probability, he sent word to the emperor informing him of the gravity of the matter and suggested that a synod be held to settle the issue.[147] The synod was arranged for Ancyra. Ossius then journeyed to Antioch, where he presided over a synod[148] called to elect a successor to Philogonius. Eustathius, an opponent of Arius, was elected and the controversy concerning Arius' teaching was discussed. This resulted in the temporary excommunication of Eusebius of Caesarea together with Theodotus of Laodicea and Narcissus of Neronias, all three of whom were given until the "great and sacerdotal Synod of Ancyra" to reconsider and repent.[149]

The effect on Eusebius, the great Church apologist and avowed defender of the orthodox Faith, of this humiliating excommunication must have been shattering. Since it is unlikely that Eusebius would have returned to his Church, Berkhof's suggestion is indeed plausible, namely that Eusebius departed for the pro-Arian Bithynia where he embarked on a tour of the Churches there, pleading his cause and enlisting support.[150] When Constantine decided to change the venue of the Synod to Nicaea, in the heart of Bithynia and within the sphere of influence of the Metropolitan See of Nicomedia, occupied by his colleague and namesake, the Bishop of Caesarea's hopes must have been raised somewhat.[151] But Eusebius went to Nicaea with mixed feelings. On the one hand, he could be expected to share the novel excitement and anticipation of his fellow-bishops, who from all corners of the οἰκουμένη (and beyond) were being transported to Nicaea by the imperial post in

---

[147] See de Clercq, *Ossius of Cordova*, 225–226.

[148] See Chadwick, "Ossius of Cordova and the Presidency of the Council of Antioch, 325," 292–298. For a summary of the discussion concerning the authenticity of this document (as well as a bibliography), see de Clercq, *Ossius of Cordova*, 207f. See also Nyman, "The Synod of Antioch (324–325) and the Council of Nicaea," 483–489. There have been recent objections to the general consensus of opinion, which attributes the synodal letter to the Synod of Antioch, 324–325; in particular, the objections raised by D. L. Holland, in *ZKG* 81 (1970), 163–181, have been answered by L. Abramowski, *ZKG* 86 (1975), 356–366.

[149] *Urkunde* 18,15 (Opitz 40,17).

[150] See Berkhof, *Theologie*, 177–178. According to Berkhof, the fragments of sermons preserved in Eusebius, *CM* 1,4 (Klostermann 26,27–31,24) are to be attributed to this period. There is a possible allusion to his own excommunication and enforced absence from Caesarea in Eusebius, *VC* 3,66,3 (Winkelmann 119,22–31).

[151] Stead, "Eusebius and the Council of Nicaea," 85–100, argues that the intentions of Ossius and Alexandria to "discredit" Eusebius were only partially successful.

order to participate in a synod that would, for the first time in history, visibly manifest to the world the universal representative character implicit in the constitution of every synod, and to join with the emperor in celebrating the twentieth anniversary of his reign. The contrast with the situation of the Church during the persecutions, reminders of which were present in the mutilated bodies of some of the bishops, could not have been more vivid. That universal recognition of the Christian Religion which had been the goal of Eusebius' life and work as an apologist had at last become a reality. Eusebius was, to judge from his own account, clearly overawed by the emperor's presence.[152] On the other hand, the zealous upholder of orthodoxy and bishop of the important metropolitan see of Caesarea entered the palace at Nicaea, burdened with the disgrace of excommunication and the taunt of heresy, a man on trial for the orthodoxy of his beliefs and his right to preside over the Church of Caesarea. In the course of the synod, Eusebius managed to clear his name, at the cost of his convictions. He publicly accepted the obnoxious ὁμοούσιος and subscribed to the condemnation of Arius. The letter Eusebius wrote to his Church at Caesarea justifying his *volte-face* is remarkable for two reasons; firstly, it reveals the bad conscience of the bishop due to his *sacrificium intellectus,*[153] and secondly it gives, as the final justification for his action, the authority, not of the synod, but of the emperor.[154] His excommunication

[152] See, for example, Eusebius' own account of the emperor's arrival at the Synod of Nicaea (Eusebius, *VC* 3,10,3 = Winkelmann 85,8–12).

[153] "E. (= Eusebius) ist von dem Vorwurf, dem gottgeliebten und gottliebenden Kaiser ein schweres Sacrificium intellectus gebracht zu haben, nicht freizusprechen, aber gemeine Motive haben den Gelehrten, dem die Herrschsucht seines Namensvetters und des Athanasius fremd war, nicht geleitet" (Schwartz, "Eusebios," in *PWK* VI, col. 1414). With regard to the attitude of Schwartz to St. Athanasius, see below, p. 235f.

[154] See the *Letter of Eusebius of Caesarea to the Church of Caesarea* (*Urkunde* 22 = Opitz 42–47). According to this document, it was the emperor who approved the statement of Faith made by Eusebius (v. 2), who suggested the adoption of these same doctrines with one change only—the insertion of the term ὁμοούσιος (v. 7)—explained how this term ought to be interpreted (v. 7) and even offered an interpretation of one of the most dreaded anathemas (v. 16). The text of the letter refers explicitly to the *Synod* as such on one occasion only (v. 1). It never refers to the participants as "bishops" but merely talks of them in the impersonal form of the third person plural (vv. 9, 11,14,15). The general impression to be gathered from the letter is that the emperor, and not the bishops, dominated the synod, and that his authority was final. See the similar observations made by Higgins, "Two Notes," 240–241, who comments: "Though Eusebius does not say explicitly that he signed the creed at the wish of Constantine, he undoubtedly implies it. For him, the emperor was

was lifted, he retained possession of his see, but his allegiance was no longer to the Church of the Apostolic Successions: Eusebius' conversion to Constantine was complete.

The fact that the Synod of Nicaea was not referred to by Eusebius in the course of the 4th Revision could be interpreted to mean that the final Revision preceded that event. If so, then it must have taken place between September 324, the victory of Constantine over Licinius, and the assembly of the Synod of Antioch, around the end of 324 and the beginning of 325, where Eusebius was excommunicated, since in all probability Eusebius did not return to Caesarea, or his books, until after Nicaea. But it is unlikely that Eusebius undertook such a radical Revision during those three months, since the time was too short in view of the working pace of Eusebius, and more importantly considering the lack of a sufficient motive to account for one of the two more important elements in the final Revision.

The absence of any reference to Nicaea can be otherwise accounted for: Eusebius, due to his own personal humiliation at Antioch and the effective "support" given to the hated Sabellian heresy by the universal Synod of Nicaea, including his own *placet,* had every reason *not* to mention Nicaea. It will be seen that the two themes which dominate the final version, are: (1) the definitive end of the old order in the Church and (2) the beginning of the new order in the Church as centered around Constantine, the new instrument of God in Salvation History. While it is possible that the second theme could have been written after the victory of Constantine over Licinius and before the Synod of Antioch, yet the first theme, as presented particularly in *Interp C,* presupposes the Synod of Antioch and the Great Synod of Nicaea. It will be seen that the 4th Revision is but a continuation of Eusebius' own self-defense for his acceptance of the Synod of Nicaea, which apology began with his Letter to the Church of Caesarea. In that letter he attributes his acceptance of the synodal judgments to the authority of the

everything and the Fathers of the Council nothing . . . Constantine undertook to win them (= the small group of bishops at Nicaea, who supported Arius) over personally, as Eusebius makes clear in his own case in the letter. Constantine's gracious condescension in pleading with him as one friend to another must have left an indelible impression on him." With regard to the role supposedly played by the Caesarean Creed at the Synod of Nicaea, see Kelly, *Early Christian Creeds,* 220–226; Berkhof, *Theologie,* 180. Considering the markedly tendentious tone of the letter, the information it imparts about the course of events at Nicaea must be considered of little historical value—certainly not sufficient to justify such a reconstruction of the synod as that, e.g., attempted by Lietzmann, *Geschichte* III, 106.

emperor, while in the 4th Revision we will see how he attempts to formulate, for the first time, the *theoretical basis* of that authority, the mature expression of which is to be found in the *Oration* delivered before the emperor on the thirtieth anniversary of his reign and in the *Vita Constantini.*

This Revision consists in (i) the two interpolations into the original Introduction to the *History* (Book I), *Interp A* and *Interp B*;[155] (ii) the interpolation in the 1st Revision, *Interp C*;[156] (iii) the removal of a passage from Book 8, now known as the Appendix to Book 8, and its replacement, a reedited version of the same, *Interp D*,[157] (iv) the interpolations into the text of the 3rd Revision, *Interp E*;[158] and (v) the removal of the collection of documents previously attached to the end of Book 10, which illustrated Constantine's support for and intervention in Church affairs, and their replacement with the first *Hymn to Constantine*.[159] The different parts of the Revision are arranged in the sequence now found in the present text.

Because of the importance of this 4th Revision, we will examine each part of the Revision in somewhat more detail than we have been able to do up to this.

a) The two interpolations, Interp A and B, now found in Book 1.
Interp A (*HE* 1,2,17–27 = Schwartz 20,14–28,10) deals with the Birth of Christ and its providential or historico-salvific coincidence with another historical event: the beginning of the Roman Empire.[160]

The providential coincidence of the *Pax Romana* with the Coming of Christ within God's Plan of Salvation was a topic touched on by the earlier apologists, such as Melito of Sardis,[161] and was later taken up by Origen,[162] though not in any great detail.[163] It was Eusebius who took up these seminal ideas and developed them to the full.[164]

---

[155] See below, Note I, pp. 192–200.
[156] See above, pp. 141–147.
[157] See Laqueur, *Eusebius als Historiker*, 76–84.
[158] See Laqueur, *Eusebius als Historiker*, 149–150.
[159] See Laqueur, *Eusebius als Historiker*, 193–209.
[160] Cf. *HE* 1,2,23 (Schwartz 24,21–23).
[161] *HE* 4,26,7–11 (Schwartz 384,19–386,15).
[162] Origen, *Ca. Cel.,* 2,30 (Koetschau 157,18–158,20).
[163] See Grillmeier, *Christ in Christian Tradition*, 250–251, for a short account of the early history of this topic as well as bibliographical information.
[164] See Peterson, *Der Monotheismus*, 81–93, whose findings have since come under criticism (see below, Chapter Five, footnote 41). Although the substance of Peterson's analysis has not, in my opinion, been affected by the recent criticism, yet it should be clear that his readiness to see in the ideas found in the *Demonstratio,* a clear allusion to the contemporary scene does not find

In the original History of the Apostolic Successions, the under-standing of the Pax Romana as the providential arrangement of peaceful conditions for the successful fulfilment of the Church's mission to evan-gelize the Nations was described as the penultimate condition for the foundation of the Church by St. Peter.[165] But it was only after the persecu-tions that Eusebius developed these ideas, which he inherited from Melito and Origen in his own individual way.

Eusebius' growing interest in the Pax Romana and its coincidence with the Birth of Our Savior can be seen in the *Praeparatio*,[166] where the unification of the empire under Augustus is seen as the fulfilment of the prophecy contained in Ps 71,7 (*LXX*), regarding the abundance of Peace, and that in Is 2,4, concerning the promise that "they shall beat their swords into plough-shares . . . etc." According to the context, Eusebius is intent on demonstrating the benefits to the human race which ensued from the Coming of Christ. The Pax Romana is related to Christ's Coming as effect is related to its cause. Eusebius maintains that the barbarous customs of the Nations had been tamed due to the refining influence of His utter-ances now spread throughout the world. In the *Demonstratio,* Eusebius understands the coincidence somewhat differently. There he sees the sig-nificance of the synchronism of Christ's Coming and the unification of the greater part of the world under the one rule of the Romans primarily in the favorable conditions it created for the speedy and unhindered spread of the Christian teaching.[167] In his exegesis of Is 7,11f., he interprets the rule of the Roman Empire over all nations as the literal fulfilment of the prophecy contained therein. In the course of that extraordinary discourse, he again refers to the instrumentality of the unified empire in enabling the teaching of Christ to shine on all men.[168] Within the same work, Eusebius once more remarks on the unexampled peace which has filled all nations from the time of His coming,[169] i.e., the Peace of Augustus and the sole rule of the Romans,[170] a view which betrays vestiges of the concept as found in the *Praeparatio,* according to which the Advent of Christ was considered to be the metaphysical cause of the Pax Romana.

support in the light of our analysis, since the *Demonstratio* was written before the sole rule of Constantine, 324, and, what is more significant, before Eusebius' conversion to Constantine, 325.

[165] Cf. *HE* 2,2,6 (Schwartz 112,11–13). See above, p. 48.
[166] Eusebius, *PE* 1,4,3–5 (Mras, vol. I, 15,3–16,7); see Farina, *L'impero,* 141–143, 150–154, 150–163.
[167] Eusebius, *DE* 3,7,30f. (Heikel 145,21 f.).
[168] Eusebius, *DE* 7,1,71 (Heikel 310,26–37).
[169] Eusebius, *DE* 9,17,13–14 (Heikel 441,19–25).
[170] Eusebius, *DE* 9,17,18 (Heikel 442,8–15).

Thus, while in the *Praeparatio,* Eusebius emphasized the salvific-historical significance of the Pax Romana as proof of the beneficial effects of Christ's Coming on the human race, the *Demonstratio* on the whole sees the significance primarily in terms of the provision, arranged by Providence, of the most favorable conditions possible for the dissemination of Christ's teaching throughout the world, a theme originally mentioned in the original *History*.[171] But in this interpolated text a new significance or rather a new emphasis is given to the beginning of the Roman Empire: it is seen as the *climax* of those civilizing effects of the Mosaic Law which had spread throughout the world, subduing the savage unbridled brutality of fallen man and creating in its place peace and mutual intercourse.[172] Here Eusebius meets the objection as to why the proclamation of the Divine Logos to all men only occurred recently and not previously. His reply is that previously men were not ready to receive that Knowledge of the Father (ἡ τοῦ πατρὸς γνῶσις).[173] But when they were ready, when the ground had been prepared, then the Divine Logos appeared and that was at the beginning of the Roman Empire.[174] Eusebius has now moved beyond his earlier view of seeing the empire as the *physical* condition arranged by Providence for the universal proclamation of the Christian Teaching to the point where he considers the Roman Empire as the expression of the necessary *spiritual* condition of mankind to receive Knowledge of the Father. Neither does Eusebius regard the sole rule of Rome as the first fruits, so to say, of the Coming of Christ, as he did in the earlier *Praeparatio;* such an attitude presupposed a view of pre-Christian man as corrupt and in need of a physician.[175]

In one of the passages in the *Demonstratio,* which evidently provided the source of inspiration for the ideas found in *Interp A*,[176] and which answered the related question as to why Christ only appeared in recent times, Eusebius developed the idea that man was not ready to receive Christ until such time as the ground had been properly prepared through the civilizing effects of the Mosaic Law.[177] There, no mention was made of the Roman Empire in connection with this concept. At that time Eusebius saw the significance

---

[171] Cf. *HE* 2,2,6 (Schwartz 112,11–13).   [172] *HE* 1,2,18–23 (Schwartz 20,17–24,23).
[173] *HE* 1,2,23 (Schwartz 24,17–19).   [174] *HE* 1,2,23 (Schwartz 24,22–23).
[175] This theme Eusebius developed in the *Demonstratio* (*DE* 4,10,9f. = Heikel 166,7f.) but primarily with regard to the Hebrew Nation, though the other nations are included by way of inference.
[176] See below, p. 193f.
[177] Eusebius, *DE* 8, "Proem," 11 (Heikel 351,3–18). The main preoccupation of Eusebius in *DE* 8 is the coincidence between the end of the Jewish successions and the Advent of Christ.

of the Pax Romana primarily in terms of creating the necessary (physical) conditions for the spread of the Gospel. But in the interpolated text *A,* Eusebius has united these two ideas, so that the Pax Romana is now seen as the final fruits of that civilizing process inaugurated by the Mosaic Law and according to which mankind was prepared to receive the Knowledge of the Father when the Divine Logos definitively appeared in the form of man. Our clue as to what moved Eusebius to take this step is to be found most probably within the general context of the 4th Revision, specifically in the Hymn of Praise to Constantine. Anticipating that text, we can here single out one verse of it where the hymn reaches its climax with a description of the reunification of the empire under the sole rule of Constantine "as in the days of old,"[178] an obvious reference to the Pax Romana. It would seem then that the *Interp A* was inserted into the text of the original *History* so as to enable Eusebius to draw attention to the parallel between the Coming of Christ and the Advent of Constantine. In such a parallel there would be little significance in any emphasis on the physical conditions for the spread of the Christian Teaching created by the unification of the empire. On the other hand, there was much to be gained from presenting the Pax Romana as the final fruits of the way God prepared the human race for the Coming of Christ, creating the necessary *spiritual* conditions within mankind through the refining influence of the Mosaic Law: parallel to the original Pax Romana, the reunification of the empire secured by Constantine's victory over Licinius could then be seen as the climax of those preparations begun by Providence with the chastisement of His People during the unexpected winter of the persecution; such preparations blossomed into the spring marked by the legal recognition of the Church in the Edict of Milan and other positive legislation, and matured in the summer of massive Church-building and restoration; the autumnal harvest then produced the reunification of the empire under the "Christian" Emperor as the first-fruits of this preparation.

The new epoch Eusebius had already proclaimed in his sermon at Tyre, when he spoke of a new Church rising from the ruins of the old, has taken on its definitive shape; the empire, united under one "Christian" Emperor is now the spiritual condition for true Knowledge and not the Apostolic Church.[178a]

Interp B (*HE* 1,6,1–11 = Schwartz 42,8–52,20): This passage, it will be remembered, was also interpolated into the Introduction to

---

[178] *HE* 10,9,6 (Schwartz 902,1–6).
[178a] Re. Eusebius' theological reasoning at work here, see Farina, *L'impero*, 154–165.

the original *History*. It is in essence a summary of arguments Eusebius had first discussed in the *Eclogues* (sometime after 309) and then in greater detail in the *Demonstratio* (ca. 320). In both instances, the context was a discussion on Christ the Ruler as the fulfilment of the prophecies contained in Gn 49,10 and Dan 9,20–27, where the arguments were based in part on information Eusebius had gathered from *Africanus* and quoted in the original draft of the *History* (1,7,11–12) to the effect that Herod was not of Hebrew stock, and in part on Josephan sources where Herod's treatment of the High-Priests and their στολή of Office was related. The thrust of the discussions, both in the *Eclogues* and in the *Demonstratio,* was the same: The accession of Herod, the first foreigner to be called King of the Jews,[179] marked the cessation of the Jewish Succession of High Priests and Rulers at the time of Christ's appearance and *so fulfilled the said prophecies.* But in this interpolation, which is composed primarily of a summary of the above arguments, the main topic is no longer the demonstration of how the prophecies were fulfilled, even though there are fleeting references to Gn 49,10 and Dan 9,24–27, but rather the coincidence between the end of the Mosaic Succession and the Coming of Christ *as seen in itself.*

Interp B is not merely a summary of the arguments previously presented in the *Eclogues* and the *Demonstratio.* The way Eusebius edits his original sources and presents them here displays a specific nuance not previously emphasized. The editorial amendments, such as the phrases ἐκ προγόνων διαδοχῆς εἰς ἐκεῖνο τοῦ καιροῦ διαρκέσαντα βασιλέα τε ὁμοῦ καὶ ἀρχιερέα[180] and εἰς ὅν ὕστατον τὰ τῆς τῶν ἀρχιερέων περιέστη διαδοχῆς,[181] which were inserted into the original text of *Eclogae Propheticae* 3,46 (*PG* 22,1184,B11–C4), reveal the specific intention of Eusebius: he wishes to draw attention to the end of the High Priestly Successions, not as the proof of earlier prophecies, though these are mentioned in passing, but as a fact of Salvation-History itself.

Perhaps the most telling betrayal of Eusebius' tendentious purpose is his statement in *HE* 1,6,10 to the effect that Herod was the first to lay hold of the στολή of the High Priest and to lock it up under his own seal, which practice, we are told, was followed by his son Archeleus and the Romans. The actual text of Josephus[182] (the

---

[179]   Cf. Eusebius, *Ecl,* 3,46 (*PG* 22,1184, D4); also, Eusebius, *DE* 8,1,45 (Heikel 360, 11–12).
[180]   *HE* 1,6,6 (Schwartz 50,14–15).
[181]   *HE* 1,6,7 (Schwartz 50,19–20).
[182]   Josephus, *Antiq.* 18,4,3 (Niese, vol. IV, 157,16).

source of this information) was quoted by Eusebius both in the *Eclogues*[183] and the *Demonstratio*.[184] Josephus informs us that it was not Herod but the Romans who had placed the High Priestly Vestment under a seal—the seal of the High Priests! In the *Eclogues* and the *Demonstratio,* Eusebius so edited the Josephan text as to cut out the reference to the fact that the Romans had placed the στολή under the seal of the Priests and so avoid any suggestion that the High Priestly Succession continued after Herod. But in the paraphrase of the same Josephan passage found in *Interp B*, Eusebius would have us believe that Herod had taken the στολή and locked it up under *his own seal*.[185] In this way, Eusebius wishes to underline the definitive termination of the High Priestly Succession and authority at the time of Christ's Coming: at that time, the στολή of the High Priest (the symbol of his office and authority) passed into the hands of Herod (the first foreigner to rule the Jews), who locked it away under his own seal (that is, under the seal of his own illegitimate authority).

Interp B was inserted into that section of the original Introduction (Book I) which deals with the chronology of Our Lord's appearance in the flesh. In its new context, *Interp B* suggests to the reader that the providential coincidence of the termination of the High Priestly Succession with the Coming of Christ was more than just a coincidence or even the fulfilment of an earlier prophecy. Here it now suggests that there was a type of causal relationship between them: when the High Priestly Succession ended, *then* Christ the Ruler appeared and with him a new "dynasty" (the Apostolic Succession) emerged in Salvation History.

The question remains to be answered as to why Eusebius was suddenly moved to insert this particular text *(Interp B)* into his original *History*. We must first examine the rest of the 4th Revision in order to discover the main preoccupation which dominated the mind of Eusebius at the time, and then perhaps we might be in a better position to suggest his precise motive for the inclusion of this particular text about the end of the Jewish Successions. At this stage we can but point to a certain revealing anomaly. In the 1st Revision, undertaken after the first persecution, Eusebius brought his original *History* to an end by rounding off the "Apostolic Successions"

---

[183] Eusebius, *Ecl,* 3,46 (*PG* 22,1185,D10–1188,A9).

[184] Eusebius, DE 8,2,95 (Heikel 385,6–13).

[185] In an unpublished article entitled "Eusebius' Handling of his Josephan Sources," Dr. D. S. Wallace-Hadrill, who was kind enough to let me read his manuscript, defends the honesty and reliability of Eusebius. And yet he has to admit that *HE* 1,6,10 is an inaccurate amalgam in *oratio obliqua* of three passages in Josephus' *Antiquities*.

and the lists of the bishops of the major sees. He never returned to this theme again, even though it was the main object of his originally conceived work. Then suddenly in the final Revision he gathers together the information he had been working on in the intervening period in other treatises about the end of the Jewish Succession and its providential coincidence with the Birth of Christ, and inserts a summary of this into his Introduction to the original *History*. Is he thereby warning his readers to watch out for the possible end of another succession—perhaps even the Apostolic Succession? The rest of the 4th Revision would suggest an affirmative answer to that question, as we will see.

b) Interp C (HE 8,1,1–8,2,3 = Schwartz 736,6–742,7).

The primary significance of this text is the way its inclusion radically alters the original purpose of the entire *History*. As already pointed out, the *History* was originally the product of apologetic literature and was thus composed for those outside the Church. This apologetic concern was paramount right up to the 3rd Revision, ca. 317,[186] where we consistently found Eusebius showing how God is on the side of the Church, which was by implication perfect, even though the persecution in his own day forced him to concede to his readers that the Church was in need of some purification. The apologetic motive in Eusebius is most marked, for example, in the 2nd Revision, where God is depicted as punishing the empire and the hostile emperors for their attacks on the Church. Similarly, even though the fact that the Christians were in need of chastisement is acknowledged, yet no details as such were given about their failures or about the faults which brought down the Divine Justice on the Church in the form of the persecutions. Writing for those outside the Church, the *History* in general tended to gloss over the flaws of her members. But this interpolated passage, now inserted into the opening of Eusebius' treatment of contemporary affairs in the Church's history, unrestrainedly condemns the situation of the pre-persecution Church as though it were corrupt through and through, and announces that the purpose of the final three books, at least, would be to recall the recent events of the persecution and deliverance, not for the sake of those outside the Church but "in the first place *for ourselves* and then for those who come after us."[187]

---

[186] See, for example, *HE* 9,8,4–11 (Schwartz 822,12–824,20) and *HE* 9,8,15–9,9,1 (Schwartz 826,9–828,1 = ATER MS group), which texts are part of the 3rd Revision. See Laqueur, *Eusebius als Historiker*, 190.

[187] *HE* 8,2,3 (Schwartz 742,5–6).

In sharp contrast with the mild rationalization found in the earlier Revisions, to the effect that the persecutions were needed to punish and cleanse the Christian people, but without giving any details as to what their defects in fact were, we find in this text a violent castigation of the faction-fighting between the rulers of the Church (and the laity), which, Eusebius would have us now believe, arose from the abuse of that freedom which the Church enjoyed in the golden era of the pre-persecution days.[188]

In the original version of the pre-persecution situation in the Church, as found for example in the 1st Revision, we found no trace of this wholesale denunciation of Church rulers (and people) said to be entangled in bitter rivalries, but rather a litany of praise for bishops in all parts of the Church[189]—the silence about Rome being the most notable negative feature of that version. The original *History* of seven books which ended with the "Golden Age," introduced by the "Peace of Gallienus," mentions but one controversy of note in the pre-persecution situation of the Church: the case of Paul of Samosata.[190] But even there the bishops are described as behaving with one mind[191] when they gathered at Antioch to condemn the heretic. But now in this interpolated passage we find Eusebius speaking globally of a break-up of unanimity and the formation of rival factions within the Church at that time. The rivalry is no longer caused by heresy or schism. In the place of heresy, Eusebius introduces a new concept to describe the cause of division in the Church: φθόνος, *personal envy* on the part of the bishops.[192] As will be presently seen, this new concept of *envy* is Eusebius' own escape hatch.

What caused Eusebius to alter the basic purpose of the *History* so radically that the original apologetic purpose gave way to the new exhortative one aimed at the Church herself? It seems to me that it was primarily due to the humiliation suffered by Eusebius at Antioch, where he was excommunicated for heresy.

When one compares Eusebius' presentation of the events previous to the persecution of Diocletian, as found in the interpolated passage under consideration with that found either at the end of the original *History* or in the 1st Revision, two new *motifs* are to be observed. The first *motif* is summed up in the contention that the State's toleration of the Church in the pre-Diocletian period was in

---

[188] Cf. *HE* 8,1,7 (Schwartz 738,11f.).
[189] Cf. *HE* 7,32,1–31 (Schwartz 716,16–730,15).
[190] *HE* 7,27,1f. (Schwartz 702,1f.).
[191] *HE* 7,30,1 (Schwartz 704,18).
[192] *HE* 8,1,6–8 (Schwartz 738,6–26).

fact a type of recognition of the Church's teaching (δόγμα)[193] as well as a condition for her expansion, the fulfilment of her universal mission.[194] This *motif* clearly reflects more the situation of the Constantinian era than the pre-Diocletian period. This anachronism is used by Eusebius in order to draw his reader's attention to what he now wishes to consider was a situation parallel to the contemporary peace of Constantine. One possible reason for the parallel may be found in the second *motif*: the insistence that the rivalries between the rulers of the Church were caused by the spirit of "envy" and were in turn the cause of God's wrath and judgment which befell the Church in the form of the traumatic persecutions.[195] Again it could be said that Eusebius apparently wishes to draw a parallel, this time in the form of a warning: he wishes to condemn the then current contentions which centered around the person and teachings of Arius by pointing to the disastrous effects of discord within the Church—it calls down on the Church the Wrath of God. But in fact, Eusebius goes beyond this parallelism and arrives at a fundamentally new interpretation of the Great Persecution, one already adumbrated in the rhetoric of the Panegyric at Tyre, namely that the Wrath of God had obliterated the pre-persecution Church,[196] the Church of the Apostolic Successions. We will return to this topic again; for the moment let us examine the significance of the new understanding of the origins of discord in the Church, *the spirit of envy*.

Viewing past history, Eusebius found it relatively simple to conceive the Church as one homogeneous body which effectively excluded heresy from its midst and so preserved unanimity and unity. When he came to discuss those disquieting controversies about the rebaptism of heretics and the celebration of Easter, he found refuge in Irenaeus' dictum that "Discord in custom could more clearly manifest concord in Faith," a solution moreover which later enjoyed the authority of Dionysius of Alexandria. But faced with disunity within the Church in his own lifetime, when the apologist found himself accused of heresy by a synod of fellow-bishops, Eusebius discards the categories of heresy and divergent traditions as causes of unrest and exclusively attributes their origin to "envy." When, towards the end of his life, Eusebius once again comes to write about the issues raised at the Synod of Nicaea, he repeats his contention that the Arian controversy in Alexandria is

---

[193] *HE* 8,1,1–2 (Schwartz 736,6–13).
[194] *HE* 8,1,5–6 (Schwartz 736,22–738,10).
[195] *HE* 8,1,6–9 (Schwartz 738,6–740,16).
[196] *HE* 8,1,8–9 (Schwartz 738,20–740,16).

to be attributed to the "envy" which disturbed the peace of the Church there.[197] The usefulness of the concept, which attributed the ultimate cause of heresy to personal envy, thus removing it from the objective level of Faith to the subjective jealousy of men, is evident.[198] For Eusebius, the great opponent of heresy, the possibility that he himself had fallen into error was inconceivable. The authority of those who in his eyes were responsible for the crisis at Alexandria,[199] succeeded in having him excommunicated at Antioch and procured the triumph of "heresy" at Nicaea, could more easily be dismissed once it was established that they were motivated by a spirit of envy.[200] But Eusebius would not appear to have been content to stop there. He goes on to question the very nature of their (Apostolic) authority.

It is the disillusionment of Eusebius in the Church he once set out to defend and, ostensibly, prove to the non-believing world to have been perfect from its inception down to the present, but which turned around and excommunicated him unjustly, as he would maintain; it is this disillusionment which is so clearly discernible in the interpolated passage, *Interp C.* There is more than a little skepticism in this rather sweeping account of the Church's inability to maintain of herself that concord, unanimity, and peace essential to her nature and mission. This new critical attitude is most pronounced in his castigation of the cowardly and ignominious conduct

---

[197] Eusebius, *VC* 3,4 (Winkelmann 82,20). See also *VC* 3,59 (Winkelmann 111,26) regarding Eustathius of Antioch.

[198] See, for example, the use made of this concept in the *Letter of the Synod of Jerusalem*, 335 (preserved by Athanasius, *De syn.* 21,2–7 = Opitz 247,22–248,17). The letter announced the "rehabilitation" of Arius and his admittance to Communion. It bears the imprint of Eusebius' thought and style.

[199] See Eusebius, *VC* 3,4 (Winkelmann 82,20–83,1).

[200] Thus, in his description of the deposition of Eustathius, one of his most trenchant opponents at Antioch and Nicaea, Eusebius stressed the presence of the "spirit of envy" as the source of the controversy that led to the deposition of the Bishop of Antioch (cf. Eusebius, *VC* 3,59,1–5 = Winkelmann 111,24–112,2). It is commonly held that this usage of the term "envy" by Eusebius was due to the exasperation felt by an irenic moderate in the face of the intransigence of the pro-Nicaea supporters. Such an interpretation is to be found for example in Berkhof, *Theologie*, 169. However, Berkhof does recognize in the attitude of Eusebius a remarkable duplicity, due on the one side to his apparent attempt to distance himself from the controversy, and on the other due to his actual intervention on behalf of Arius. Eusebius was really a hawk in dove's plumage, as his ecclesiastical politics after Nicaea abundantly testify (see Kraft, *Einleitung*, 64f.). As Berkhof put it, "Auch bei Eusebius haben also nicht nur Lehrfragen, sondern auch Machtfragen eine Rolle gespielt" (*Theologie*, 172).

of so many during the persecutions[201]—which reaction is all the more surprising when one considers his former "laxist" attitude to the Novatian controversy.[202] In the 3rd Revision, Eusebius was frank enough to admit that "countless others" in the Church displayed timidity in the face of the persecution. That comment was only made in passing.[203] The main emphasis was on the "very many (bishops)" who had behaved courageously. On the other hand, the emphasis in *Interp C* is on the shameful conduct of the bishops during the persecutions on whom, in the prophetic words of Ps 106,40 (*LXX*), "the Lord poured contempt."[204]

The only bishop mentioned by name in the *History,* whose actions might possibly be described as being less than honorable during the persecution, was Marcellinus, Bishop of Rome, "whom the persecution overtook."[205] Otherwise no names are mentioned. That was in the 1st Revision. Likewise, in the final Revision now being considered, no names are recorded despite the scathing attack on what Eusebius considered to be the disgraceful behavior of so many of the rulers in the Church. The reason seems to be his wish to discredit the episcopal authority in general.[206] Nonetheless, the picture he paints of the ignominies suffered by some rulers of the Church in retribution for their earlier crimes, particularly in *De mart. Pal.* 12, which is evidently out of place in its present context, and which is generally held to be textually related to the interpolation we are now studying, does betray possible clues as to the identity of some of these bishops.

In the latter text, Eusebius talks about "presidents of Churches" who were condemned to look after camels and feed the imperial horses.[207] Is it possible that Eusebius here refers to Marcellus, Bishop of Rome (307–308), who, according to a tradition preserved in *Le Liber Pontificalis,* was condemned by Maxentius to tend the

---

[201] *HE* 8,2,1–3 (Schwartz 740,16–742,7).

[202] See above, p. 121f.

[203] Cf. *HE* 8,3,1 (Schwartz 742,20).

[204] Cf. *HE* 8,2,1 (Schwartz 740,22–23).

[205] *HE* 7,32,1 (Schwartz 716,20).

[206] The objection could be raised that such an intention could hardly be presumed in one who was himself a bishop. But, as will be seen, Eusebius here attacks the "old fashioned," independent, episcopal authority, based on the Apostolic Succession. His new understanding of ecclesiastical authority is an authority derived from the imperial power. As a bishop of the post-persecution Church, he would have considered himself part of the new "dispensation."

[207] Eusebius, *De mart. Pal.* 12 (Schwartz 946,21–27).

imperial horses.[208] The plausibility of this assumption is heightened by the fact that, as already mentioned above, Marcellus was known to have taken a fairly rigorous stand on the question of the readmission of *lapsi,* a stand which resulted in such schism within the Church of Rome that the tyrant Maxentius banished him to exile as the author of discord; thus it can be reasonably presumed that when Eusebius refers to "schism among the confessors"[209] it is likely that he is referring to this notorious controversy, which was in turn carried on by the eventual successor of Marcellus, Eusebius of Rome. Both Marcellus and Eusebius were also exiled—again it is possible that our Eusebius refers to these three exiles when he talks about the fulfilment of the prophetic word (*LXX*, Ps, 106,40) to the effect that the Lord poured contempt on princes and caused them to wander in a land untrodden and pathless.[210]

We have already noted the irregular silence of Eusebius on the subject of the successions at Rome, which in the 1st Revision came to an abrupt end with the ambiguous reference to Marcellinus in contrast with the other sees of Antioch, Alexandria, and Jerusalem, whose successions were carried down to the date of the 1st Revision (and in the case of Alexandria, to the 2nd Revision). That silence would now appear to have been partially broken in the interpolated passage (and its related text in *De mart. Pal.*), where Eusebius seems to castigate the behavior of the Bishops of Rome during the persecution. The fact that again no names are given is possibly due, as has been mentioned, to the further disillusionment of Eusebius with his fellow-bishops who condemned him at Antioch in 324, so that his skepticism regarding Rome was extended to cover them also. Those bishops were led by Eustathius, Bishop of *Antioch*, defending the cause of Alexander of *Alexandria,* and were in all probability presided over by Ossius of Cordoba, who though not officially representing the Bishop of Rome, could have been taken to be such. In other words, it was not simply his fellow-bishops who condemned Eusebius at Antioch, but the Bishops of Rome, Antioch, and Alexandria, the three principal sees he had once understood to constitute in their various ways the highest Apostolic Authority.

If we understand this to be the mentality of Eusebius, as determined by his *Sitz im Leben* at the time of the 4th Revision when he inserted this interpolation, then we can better interpret the significance of so much of this text which is otherwise merely enigmatic.

---

208 See Duchesne, *Le Liber Pontificalis,* 164; see also pp. xcix–ca. However, the legend is not very reliable in its other details.

209 Eusebius, *De mart. Pal.* 12 (Schwartz 947,1–2).

210 *HE* 8,2,1 (Schwartz 740,23–24).

As already mentioned, the interpolated passage radically altered the purpose of the *History* (or rather the final three books) by directing its message to those *inside* the Church. The message of the final three books is now to proclaim how the persecutions, which were caused by the "faction-fighting" among those rulers of the Church, who were motivated by the "spirit of envy,"[211] were the expression of God's Wrath. We are immediately reminded of the way Eusebius previously interpreted the punishment meted out to the Jewish Nation by God for their rejection of His final offer of salvation. There it marked the definitive end of the old dispensation and the spiritual significance of Jerusalem. Here, Eusebius interprets the fury of the Divine Justice experienced by the Church during the persecutions as marking the end of the Apostolic era or "dispensation." This he expressed in the words of Ps 88,40 (*LXX*), seeing the prophetic utterance as having been fulfilled in his own day: "'He (God) has overturned the covenant with His servant and cast his sanctuary to the ground' through the demolition of the Churches."[212] This text can best be appreciated through reference to the *Demonstratio* 8,2,117f.,[213] where, within the context of the discussion previously mentioned about the end of the Jewish or Mosaic Succession coinciding with the Coming of Christ, Eusebius judges the end of the succession to mean the end of the Old Covenant and the beginning of the New, while the destruction of the Temple is likewise explicitly referred to.[214] The "covenant" here[214a] is understood to mean the previous "dispensation" of the Apostolic Successions, while the demolition of the Churches during the persecutions recalls the destruction of the Temple at Jerusalem. The quotation from Ps 88 continues up to v. 46, so as to enable Eusebius to demonstrate how the persecution was the fulfilment of the prophecies contained in the psalm, where the ignominies suffered by the Church in her human and material fabric are no longer seen as means of participation in the Cross of Christ but merely as shameful indignities. When Eusebius quotes Ps 88,45 (*LXX*) about how the Lord cast His servant's *throne* to the ground, the allusion

---

[211]   *HE* 8,1,6–8 (Schwartz 738,6–26). Since he apparently considers that this entire passage (*Interp* C) is part of the 1st Revision, Kraft (*Einleitung*, 37–39) is forced to postulate a struggle for power in an unnamed city which enveloped the people of the city and the bishops of the surrounding country, and which occurred in the final decade of the third century. Kraft claims that this "incident" was seen by Eusebius as the cause of the persecution.

[212]   *HE* 8,1,9 (Schwartz 740,5–7).

[213]   Heikel 389,3f.

[214]   Eusebius, *DE* 8,2,124 (Heikel 390,8–15).

[214a] That is, in the text of the *History* (*HE* 8,1,9).

is probably to the end of the authority (= throne) previously enjoyed by the Church, namely the Apostolic Authority. The rhetoric of the Panegyric of Tyre, where Eusebius spoke of the new Church rising from the ruins of the old, had become for him a reality of Salvation History.

In the light of the above, the previous interpolation (*Interp B*) concerning the end of the Jewish Succession receives a new meaning. It would indeed seem to have been inserted during this revision with the purpose of forewarning his readers of the possible end to another succession, the Apostolic Succession. Or, if this was not Eusebius' explicit or exclusive purpose, then at least we can say that *Interp B* and *Interp C* manifest Eusebius' own mind and show part of the rational basis he was creating so as to enable him to justify the radical changes in his ecclesiology. In spite of the vested interest due to his own personal predicament, it must not be imagined that Eusebius would take up a new concept of the Church unless he could at least rationalize the change, just as he had previously attempted to justify in his Letter to the Church of Caesarea his own acceptance of the *Symbolon* of Nicaea, which acceptance saved him from definitive excommunication, deposition from his see, ignominious exile, and personal disgrace.

c) The Appendix to Book 8 and its replacement—HE 8,13,12–14.
Whatever truth there may be in the contention that the Bishop of Rome stepped into the political vacuum left in the West by the emperor when he moved his capital and court to Byzantium, it is as true to say, if not more so, that the emperor in the East stepped into the ecclesiological vacuum in Eusebius' thought, which resulted from the inadequacy of his theology, his disillusionment with the Petrine and Apostolic Succession, and the effect on his person from the Synods of Antioch and Nicaea. This will be seen when we now take up the rest of the final Revision.

The new era ushered in by the Great Persecution was characterized, as we saw in the previous Revisions, by a new understanding of the emperors as instruments of God, first to punish his wayward people and eventually to rescue them.

Already in the 2nd Revision, Eusebius had noticed the relatively friendly attitude of Constantine's father, Constantius I, towards the Christians, and had begun to distinguish between him (together with his son Constantine) and those other emperors who were hostile to Christians and so met with dreadful ends. In the 3rd Revision, Constantine *and* Licinius had increased their stature in the eyes of

Eusebius and were described as the chosen instruments of the Word to cleanse the whole world (of evil). By the time Eusebius came to make this, his 4th Revision, the amiable relations between the two emperors had deteriorated: Licinius, having oppressed his subjects, eventually found himself in open war with Constantine. He was defeated by Constantine, aided at sea by his son Crispus, and finally submitted at Chrysopolis on the September 18, 324.

The final Revision of the *History* is characterized by the *damnatio memoriae Licinii,* as Schwartz originally expressed it,[215] according to which, earlier references to Licinius of a favorable nature are now qualified by such phrases as "(he) . . . who had not yet become mad."[216] On the other hand, Constantius and his son are painted in ever brighter colors as always being friendly to the Christians and receiving the favor of God. The text that makes up the present Appendix to Book 8 was removed from its original position and in its place was inserted that section of it which dealt exclusively with Constantius and Constantine, but now rewritten to give greater glory to both.[217] Of particular significance is the new dignity conferred on Constantine, as the comparison between the original text and the revised text reveals:

Original Text	Revised Text
ὅς εὐθὺς	τούτου παῖς Κωνσταντῖνος εὐθὺς
ἀρχόμενος βασιλεὺς τελεώτατος	ἀρχόμενος βασιλεὺς τελεώτατος
καὶ Σεβαστὸς πρὸς τῶν στρατο-	καὶ Σεβαστὸς πρὸς τῶν στρατο-
πέδων	πέδων καὶ ἔτι πολὺ τούτων
	πρότερον πρὸς αὐτοῦ τοῦ
ἀναγορευθείς, ζηλωτὴν	παμβασιλέως
ἑαυτὸν τῆς πατρικῆς περὶ τὸν	θεοῦ ἀναγορευθείς, ζηλωτὴν
ἡμέτερον λόγον εὐσεβείας κατ-	ἑαυτὸν τῆς πατρικῆς περὶ τὸν
εστήσατο.[218]	ἡμέτερον λόγον εὐσεβείας κατ-
	εστήσατο.[219]

Thus, according to the revised text (*Interp D*), it is God Himself who had preordained that Constantine be emperor. Constantine has become the Elect One of God.[220]

---

215 Schwartz, *Einleitung,* xlvii–li.
216 *HE* 9,9,1 (Schwartz 828,2–3).
217 Cf. *HE* 8,13,12–14 (Schwartz 776,3–778,2).
218 See Appendix 5 (Schwartz 797,6–8).
219 Cf. *HE* 8,13,14 (Schwartz 776,18–778,2).
220 This is the first mention of a theme which Eusebius will later develop more fully; see Berkhof, *Theologie,* 55–59.

d) Interpolation in the text of the 3rd Revision, Interp E: HE 9,9,1–12.
Eusebius' narration of the Italian campaign of Constantine found in this
interpolation is of much interest. In the previous Revisions, Eusebius had
paid little attention to the history of Constantine as such, perhaps due to
lack of information. That he did not mention the Italian campaign, the
news of which must have reached the ears of Eusebius before this, is most
surprising.[221] At any event, *Interp E* makes up for his former negligence;
here Eusebius describes Constantine's magnificent campaign in Italy (312)
which culminated in his defeat of Maxentius and his triumphal entry
into Rome. The Battle at the Milvian Bridge is depicted in terms of the
Crossing of the Red Sea, "reenacted" as it were in contemporary history.[222]
Now seen as the "type" of Moses, Constantine and his army sing, if not in
words yet in deeds, a new canticle of triumph to God, the Ruler of all and
Author of his victory, before entering Rome to the joyful acclamations of
the Romans, who hailed him as their Redeemer, Savior, and Benefactor.[223]
The emperor, mindful of his Divine Helper, ordered that a τρόπαιον of
the Savior be placed in the hand of his own image that was set up in the
center of Rome.[224] The memorial of Constantine, the Elect One of God
and Redeemer of the Roman people, Eusebius informs us, now bore in its
right hand the τρόπαιον of the Savior, an allusion, possibly, to the earlier
notice about the tombs of Peter and Paul in Rome, which were decorated
with the τρόπαια commemorating their participation in Christ's Passion
and his triumph over death.[225]

*e) The Hymn to Constantine (*HE *10,8,1–10,9,9).*
Removing the collection of documents illustrating the new positive attitude of the imperial authority to the Church that he had appended to the
end of the 3rd Revision, Eusebius replaces them with his first hymn in
praise of Constantine. It clearly reveals the radically transformed ecclesiology of Eusebius.

The actual causes of the war between Constantine and Licinius
are obscure, but now Eusebius interprets them in historico-salvific
terms. The reputed intrigues of Licinius against Constantine and
their eventual war are seen to result from nothing other than Licinius'

---

[221] *HE* 9,9,1 (Schwartz 826,24–828,1) simply mentioned the *fact* of Constantine's
   victory over Maxentius, without further comment.
[222] *HE* 9,9,4–6 (Schwartz 828,16–830,8).
[223] *HE* 9,9,8–9 (Schwartz 830,13–832,3).
[224] *HE* 9,9,10–11 (Schwartz 832,3–14).
[225] Cf. *HE* 2,25,7 (Schwartz 178,3–6).

decision to do battle against the God of the Universe,[226] who is now assumed to be exclusively on the side of Constantine, as his Friend, Protector, and Guardian.[227] The expulsion of Christians from the court and some laws of Licinius, regarding the harsher treatment of prisoners, are blown up into the dimensions of a persecution against Christians.[228] Other innovations of Licinius concerning marriage, funeral customs, and taxes are also listed,[229] none of which would appear to be specifically directed against Christians but are here presented as though they formed part of a persecution. Some Christians may well have been exiled[230] and Churches desecrated,[231] although Licinius' reputed execution of bishops described in *HE* 10,8,14–17 betrays no ostensible anti-Christian motive since they were executed on criminal charges and not for being Christians.[232]

In contrast with Licinius, "God the champion of souls that are his own . . . , leading forth his servant Constantine with a lofty arm, caused a great luminary and savior towards all to shine out suddenly, as it were, in profound darkness and gloomy night."[233] What is most fascinating about this rhetorical fanfare, which definitively ushers Constantine on to the stage of ecclesiology, is how closely this description parallels the previous portrayal of St. Peter and his confrontation with the instruments of evil—both Nero and Simon Magus—in Book 2. But here it is Constantine who has God as his Friend, Protector, and Guardian[234] and Licinius who "affected the evil manners and wickedness of the impious tyrants,"[235] and who—like the first fighter against God, Nero—waged an impious and terrible war against Constantine,[236] which Eusebius equates with doing war against "the God of the Universe" whom Constantine worshiped.[237] Parallel to Eusebius' earlier account of Nero's depravity, the author is now even more loquacious in his

---

[226] *HE* 10,8,8 (Schwartz 894,8–12).
[227] *HE* 10,8,6 (Schwartz 892,25f.); *HE* 10,8,9 (Schwartz 894,17).
[228] See Baynes, *Constantine the Great and the Christian Church*, 16.
[229] *HE* 10,8,10–12 (Schwartz 894,18f.).
[230] *HE* 10,8,13 (Schwartz 896,18f.).
[231] *HE* 10,8,15 (Schwartz 898,1–6).
[232] See Lawlor and Oulton, *The Ecclesiastical History*, vol. II, 320.
[233] *HE* 10,8,19 (Schwartz 898,22–26).
[234] *HE* 10,8,6 (Schwartz 892,26).
[235] *HE* 10,8,2 (Schwartz 892,1–4).
[236] *HE* 10,8,3 (Schwartz 892,10–13).
[237] *HE* 10,8,8 (Schwartz 894,9). This is repeated in *HE* 10,8,9 (Schwartz 894,13f.), where the allusion to Nero and the other persecutors who followed him is clearer. Cf. *HE* 2,25,5 (Schwartz 176,16–17).

description of the many "depravities" of Licinius,[238] which like those of his predecessor, Nero, culminated in a persecution of the Church.[239] On the other hand, like Simon Magus, Licinius at first concealed his evil intentions,[240] but Constantine's Protector, "who brought to light the plots that were devised secretly and in darkness," preserved the emperor from the plots of the wicked[241]—as he had once protected Peter from the conspiracies of the Jews to kill him.[242]

The description of the persecution under Licinius reaches its climax when Eusebius informs us that ". . . there was nothing to prevent him [= Licinius] from putting [his purpose] into effect, had not God, the champion of the souls that are His own who immediately foresees what is to take place, leading forth his servant Constantine with a lofty arm, caused a great luminary and saviour towards all to shine out suddenly, as it were, in profound darkness and gloomy night."[243] We notice in particular the allusions to the rhetorical description of Peter's coming to Rome: "shielded in divine armor for such matters, like some noble General of God," who "brought the precious merchandise of spiritual light from the East to those in the West, proclaiming the Kingdom of Heaven, Light itself and the Saving Word for souls."[244] The recurrence of the themes of "light" and "darkness" is very striking,[245] as is the inversion of images used to describe the two personalities: Peter,

---

[238] *HE* 10,8,10–13 (Schwartz 894,18f.).

[239] *HE* 10,8,14–18 (Schwartz 896,25f.).

[240] *HE* 10,8,5 (Schwartz 892,23).

[241] *HE* 10,8,6 (Schwartz 892,25–27).

[242] Cf. *HE* 2,9,4 (Schwartz 126,2–6). See above, p. 49.

[243] *HE* 10,8,19 (Schwartz 898,21–26).

[244] *HE* 2,14,6 (Schwartz 138,20–28).

[245] The peace which resulted from Galerius' Edict of Toleration was described in the 1st Revision in terms of a light shining forth out of the night of persecution (*HE* 9,1,8 = Schwartz 804,8–806,2).In the 3rd Revision, the same imagery is used to depict the new era of peace which was introduced by the "Edict" of Milan but attributed to Our Savior (*HE* 10,4,13 = Schwartz 866,21–24), who, as the general ἐπίσκοπος of His Church, shone down on his people the light of His peace (*HE* 9,8,15 = Schwartz 826,13–19). But in the 4th Revision here, it is Constantine, the instrument of God *par excellence* who overcame the last of the persecutors, who is presented as the luminary (φωστήρ) who now illuminates the Church that was once overshadowed by the night of Licinius' persecution—thus, recalling how Peter was previously compared to the greatest of all physical luminaries, the Sun, when Eusebius described Peter's journey to Rome in terms of bringing the spiritual light of the Gospel from the East to the center of the unredeemed world in the West, which was languishing in the darkness of error and threatened by the father of all heresies, Simon Magus.

who could truly be called the servant of God, was previously described
as a general of God, while here the actual general Constantine is called
the servant of God. But Eusebius surpasses himself when he describes the
emperor as: "the savior towards all" (σωτήρ τοῖς πάσιν), "all" here referring
to the *bishops*, as the context shows. The emperor has become the savior
of the bishops, a return to the concept of the Sacral Emperor as σωτήρ.
The total inversion of perspective is finally manifested in the nature of the
victory of the new "Peter" over the new "Nero." For St. Peter, that victory
cost him his life; the new "Peter" gained the world.

In the 1st Revision, Eusebius brought his original *History* to an end
before going on to relate the contemporary events he had himself witnessed. In effect, he rounded off the "Apostolic Succession," as indeed he
tells us explicitly.[246] This may have been originally intended merely as a literary device so as to enable him to present the contemporary events simply
as an Appendix and not as part of the *History* strictly speaking. However,
as we saw, the Appendix was enlarged in the 2nd Revision and eventually
became part of the *History* in the 3rd, forming three new books which
were not merely appendices. But the theme of the successions, the theme
of the original *History*, was not taken up again. The 4th and final Revision
records Eusebius' definitive conversion to Constantine and the birth of
the Imperial Church as distinct from the Apostolic Church he originally
set out to defend. He never again takes up the threads of the Apostolic
Succession, since that period or dispensation is over, God having overturned the covenant with that Church by means of the Great Persecution;
meanwhile the Apostolic Church has given way to the Imperial Church.
What had once been merely a literary device has become a historical fact.

The particular nuance Eusebius gave to the traditional concept of
Apostolic Succession was, as our analysis in Chapter One showed us,
determined by his stress on chronological sequence as understood in terms
of the period of a dynasty. After completing the original *History,* Eusebius
became more and more preoccupied with the significance he saw in the
termination of the High Priestly Succession (= Dynasty) on the accession
of Herod, the first foreigner to rule the Jews; this he understood as the
fulfilment of the prophecies of Gen 49,10 and Dan 9,20–27, when Christ
the Ruler appeared. In *Interp B,* Eusebius introduced a new note into this
theme by seeming to imply that there was a causal relationship between the

---

[246] *HE* 7,32,32 (Schwartz 730,16–21); *HE* 8, "Proem" (Schwartz 736,1–5). Compare
with *HE* 1,1,1 (Schwartz 6,1–2) and *HE* 1,1,4 (Schwartz 8,9–17).

end of the Jewish Succession and the Coming of Christ, as though one dynasty gave way to another (that of Christ which issued in the Apostolic Succession). Since, as his presuppositions showed,[247] Eusebius tended to emphasize the continuity between the old and the new dispensations and ignore the discontinuity, there was no reason for him to doubt the possibility of yet another dynasty replacing the Apostolic one and so ushering in a new era in the history of Salvation. As we know from *Interp C,* Eusebius, motivated partly from righteous anger at the discordant state of the three main seats of the Apostolic "Dynasty" (in particular the "apostasy" of the Bishop of Rome, the principal see), partly from his own personal humiliation at Antioch, and partly from his genuine shock that the greatest and most representative synod ever held up to then, Nicaea, could officially declare heretical tenets he himself held to be orthodox, newly interpreted the persecutions as the Wrath of God that effectively obliterated the Church of the Apostolic Succession as it had once obliterated the Jewish Nation, the Temple, and the religious significance of Jerusalem.

Interp A contained the developed reflections of Eusebius on another providential coincidence connected with the Coming of Christ: the Pax Romana. Again, a new note was introduced into his previous reflections, which also began after the persecutions in the causal connection between the establishment of Augustus' sole rule over a united empire, now seen as the culmination of God's activity in civilizing unredeemed, brutalized men, and the Coming of Christ—the Pax Romana becoming the spiritual condition of mankind for the reception of Christ. In the first Hymn to Constantine, Eusebius explicitly draws attention to the parallel between the Pax Augustana and the reunification of the empire under Constantine. Once again, the reunification of the empire and the establishment of universal peace after decades of turbulence enabled Constantine, the new instrument of God, depicted as the Elect One of God in *Interp D,* and in *Interp E* as the new Moses, to finally emerge as the new Peter engaged in battle with the leader of the forces of darkness, Licinius, whose prototypes were Nero and Simon Magus. Like some great luminary, Constantine comes to the East as "the savior towards all," namely the bishops. The authority of the Apostolic Succession, which through Christ had replaced the authority of the High Priests, is now being supplanted by the authority of the emperor. Eusebius has, through his interpretation of history and

---

[247] See above, pp. 20–21.

contemporary events, worked out a plausible theoretical basis for his infamous acceptance of the emperor's authority at Nicaea.[248] For Eusebius then, the dawn of a new era in the History of Salvation had finally broken: the Apostolic Church founded by St. Peter, which was obliterated in the dark night of the persecutions, has been replaced by the Imperial Church as founded by Constantine, the instrument par excellence of God, the Universal Emperor.

§5 Summary

Eusebius originally set out to write a history of the Apostolic Successions. He conceived the Church as a universal "nation," the origins of which were divine (metaphysically, due to the preexistent Logos, and, historically, due to the divine foundation through the instrumentality of St. Peter and the Apostles) and the destiny of which was guided by Providence (through the instrumentality of the Apostles' successors, in particular those who shared the Petrine Succession). The Apostolic Succession was two-fold—a succession of Apostolic Authority in matters of Faith to be found primarily in the Petrine Succession of the Bishop of Rome, though not exclusively, and one of Apostolic Teaching defended and handed on by orthodox teachers and writers. The *History* of this People should, according to the original aims, demonstrate how God, working through these instruments, overcame their enemies, the persecutors, and the heretics. In the course of the original *History,* some tensions were already apparent between the ideal presupposed by Eusebius and the evidence of the historical documents, which tensions he was able to accommodate either through the more profound insights of St. Irenaeus and St. Dionysius of Alexandria or by simple omission.

[248] Ruhbach, "Die politische Theologie Eusebs von Caesarea," 255, singles out, as the real merit of Eusebius, the fact that he recognized the significance of the change that occurred in the year 313 and interpreted it theologically. The German scholar attempts to repair the damage done to Eusebius' character and theological abilities by authors such as Overbeck and Burckhardt, but could possibly be accused of going a little too far in the opposite direction. It is surprising that Ruhbach, though he rightly insists on the methodological necessity of examining the works of Eusebius with regard to their chronological sequence, neglects to examine the various Revisions of the *History* and the development of Eusebius' thought therein, the composition of which covered almost a quarter of a century. He also ignores the significance of Eusebius' activity at Nicaea, and underplays the role played by the Bishop of Caesarea in the imperial and Church politics, which led up to and resulted from the Great Synod of Nicaea.

The brutal facts of the contemporary events he himself witnessed and lived through eventually shattered his former ideology of the Church. Before the first draft of the original *History* was completed, the false security of the Church built on the Peace of Gallienus was undermined by the horrors of the unexpected persecution. What Eusebius had considered to be a phenomenon of past history had become part of his personal experience: martyrdom. His own inadequate concept of martyrdom's place in the life of the Church failed to prepare him to interpret these events correctly. After the persecution, Eusebius hastily completed the original *History* of the Apostolic Successions and never took it up again (= 1st Revision). In its place a new, more spiritualized understanding of the Church began to take its place. The Church, as an institution, was no longer defended as the perfect society, though his apologetic purpose prevented him from openly admitting this. Instead, he implicitly admits that the Church was in need of chastisement, for which God used the emperors, although they too suffered for attacking what was, nonetheless His Church (= 1st and 2nd Revisions). With the end of the persecutions and the unhoped-for recognition of the Church by the Emperors, Licinius and Constantine, Eusebius sees a new Church arising phoenix-like out of the ashes of the old. He now expands the Appendices and additions he made during the 1st and 2nd Revisions into three separate Books (8–10) thus continuing the original *History,* though no longer the History of our Apostolic Succession properly so-called (= 3rd Revision). In this "middle period" of his ecclesiological development, Eusebius, in line with his spiritualizing tendencies as prompted by his disappointment with the failures of so many bishops during the persecution, especially the Bishop of Rome, and by the general disorder of the institutional Church in the wake of the persecution, particularly at Rome, Alexandria, and Antioch, sees God Himself as the general ἐπίσκοπος who oversees the whole Church.

The euphoria of the Panegyric delivered at Tyre was momentarily dampened by the threat of another persecution in the East, at the instigation of Licinius. This threat was finally removed by Constantine's victory over the Eastern emperor, Licinius, who was once celebrated by Eusebius as an instrument of God but now is recognized as the enemy both of God's people and of God's Friend, the Elect One. Eusebius' disillusionment with the pre-persecution Church of the Apostolic Successions was complete when the representatives of this Church secured his excommunication at Antioch and succeeded in promulgating what he personally believed to be heterodox doctrines at the Great Synod of Nicaea. He reluctantly—and only formally—accepted the decisions of that synod, for which he has long been accused of prevarication. His Letter to the Church of Caesarea clearly shows that he submitted not on account of the Apostolic Authority of the Synod but because of the emperor's authority, which he now recognizes as constituting the supreme authority in the new Church of the post-persecution Dispensation. In the 4th and Final Revision, written as a justification for his submission to the emperor's authority, Eusebius alters the basic purpose of the *History* so that it is no longer even ostensibly aimed at those outside the Church, but at the members of the Church. He summarizes his post-persecution reflections on how one previous succession gave way to another at the time of Christ's coming and how at the time of that event, Providence arranged that it coincide with the Pax Romana, thus drawing the attention of his readers to the true significance of the new era introduced by God's Elect One, Constantine who, having overcome all his enemies, reunited both empire and Church. A new dynasty (= succession) inaugurated by the new Peter has appeared to achieve what the old one failed to do, unite empire and Church as the One People under the one God of Christianity.

Note I
INTERPOLATIONS IN THE ORIGINAL HISTORY
(BOOK 1)

Apart from the interpolation of the short passage in Chapter One of Book 1, which described Aim G in the list of aims,[1] Laqueur also demonstrated that the two separate sections[2] dealing with the forgeries, known as the *Acts of Pilate,* are likewise later interpolations.[3] It seems, however, that there are at least two other passages which deserve consideration as later interpolations: *HE* 1,2,17–27 and *HE* 1,6,1–11.

§1 HE 1,2,17–27 (Schwartz 20,14–28,9) = *Interp A*
This text, which I will call for the sake of convenience *Interp A,* deals with the question as to why the Christian kerygma was not

---

[1]   *HE* 1,1,2 (Schwartz 6,14–15).
[2]   *HE* 1,9,2–4 (Schwartz 72,3–78,18); *HE* 1,11,1–9 (Schwartz 76,9–80,14).
[3]   Laqueur, *Eusebius als Historiker,* 121f.

proclaimed long ago to all men and nations, as it is now; Eusebius answers that only when men were sufficiently ready to receive this knowledge of the Father, did Christ appear. His reply deals with the Fall of man, instances the various appearances of the preexistent Logos to chosen men in the O.T., through whom the seeds of true religion were scattered throughout the world to prepare man for the reception of knowledge of the Father, and draws attention to the coincidence between the appearance of the Logos in human form and the beginning of the Roman Empire as though the former preparation climaxed in the formation of the Roman Empire; even though the life, death, and Resurrection of the Incarnate Word are mentioned, the passage stresses above all His divine restoration in Heaven, which is described in terms of the fulfilment of the prophecies contained in Dan 7. The text ends with a reference to the *Prophetic Eclogues* and to "other works" where, Eusebius tells us, he had more convincingly considered the prophetic utterances and collected proofs concerning Our Lord.[4] Since Book 1 was written before the year 303 and the *Prophetic Eclogues* between 303 and 312,[5] then this text clearly seems to be an interpolation.

On the other hand, Wallace-Hadrill suggests[6] that the text refers not to the *Eclogues* but to the earlier *General Elementary Introduction* from whose final books, the *Eclogues* were extracted.[7] This alternative is not very convincing for two reasons: (i) the plural of ἐν οἰκείοις ὑπομνήμασιν ... συναγαγόντες would seem to indicate that Eusebius is referring to more than one work and thus was more likely specifying both the *General Elementary Introduction* and the *Eclogues*;[8] moreover, (ii) no account is taken of the ἐν ἑτέροις, i.e., other works where Eusebius had treated similar proofs concerning Our Lord. The "other works" immediately suggest the *Praeparatio* and the *Demonstratio Evangelica,* as a closer examination will confirm.

We can limit our observations mainly to the *Demonstratio Evangelica* since it seems to be a development of the earlier *Praeparatio's* presupposing its arguments. The Proem to the 6th book of the

---

4   *HE* 1,2,27 (Schwartz 28,7–10).

5   Schwartz favors the date 310: cf. *PWK* VI, col. 1387.

6   Wallace-Hadrill, *Eusebius,* 49–50.

7   Cf. Eusebius, *Ecl.* 3, "Proem" (*PG* 22,1120,D5f.). See also *Ecl* 4,35 (*PG* 22,1261,B13–C3).

8   According to Wallace-Hadrill, the four books of the *Eclogues* together with the *Commentary on Luke* (*PG* 24,529–605) comprise the lost work: *Demonstratio Ecclesiastica* (cf. *HThR* 67, 1974, 55–63). If this is so, then it is possible that Eusebius refers here to this work and its companion, the *Praeparatio Ecclesiastica.*

Demonstratio exhibits many striking parallels with *Interp A*. At times the similarities are almost verbal.[9] The subject of both is basically the same, namely, to give reasons why "the complete wisdom and all-perfect teaching of Christ"[10] did not appear long ago but only in our times (i.e., the Christian era).

What is the relationship between our interpolated passage *HE* 1,2,17–27 (= *Interp A*) and the *Proem* to *DE* 8? That the text of the *Demonstratio* develops ideas originally found in *Interp A*, is a possibility which cannot be completely ruled out, since some concepts found in the latter are indeed given fuller treatment in the *Proem* to Book 8 of the *Demonstratio*. Further, the *Proem* describes itself as a summary of an earlier coverage.[11] But when we compare the *Proem* with *Interp A*, three observations can be made which militate against such a proposition: (i) *Interp A* covers three subjects, the preparation for Christ, His Coming, and His Divine Restoration (or Second Coming), whereas the *Proem* only treats of one, the first and admittedly biggest subject (the Preparation);[12] the second topic, the Coming or—to be more specific—the coincidence between the First Coming of Christ and the beginning of the Roman Empire[13] is not found in the *Proem* but in the earlier Books 3 and 7, as well as Book 9,[14] while the third topic, His Divine Restoration as the fulfilment of Dan 7,[15] is likewise only to be found in Book 9 of the *Demonstratio*;[16] (ii) in *Interp A*, however, each of these three topics, found scattered throughout the *Demonstratio*, are integrated into a single coherent unit in the form of a summary presentation that shows greater precision of thought and indicates a more developed treatment of the three main topics than is to be

9   Compare, for example, *HE* 1,2,19a (Schwartz 22,5–8) with Eusebius, *DE* 8, "Proem," 6b (Heikel 350,4–8). Compare also *HE* 1,2,20 (Schwartz 22,15–21) with *DE* 8, "Proem," 9b (Heikel 350,27–34).

10 τὴν τοῦ Χριστοῦ πάνσοφον καὶ πανάρετον διδασκαλίαν ... (*HE* 1,2,17b = Schwartz 20,16–17). Cf. Eusebius, *DE* 8, "Proem," 9a (Heikel 350,24–25): τὸν πάνσοφον καὶ τὸν πανάρετον τοῦ Χριστοῦ λόγον.

11 Cf. *DE* 8, "Proem," 5 (Heikel 349,27–30).

12 Compare *HE* 1,2,18–23a (Schwartz 20,17–24,16) with *DE* 8, "Proem," 6–11 (Heikel 350,1–351,18).

13 *HE* 1,2,23b (Schwartz 24,17–23).

14 Cf. *DE* 3,7,30–40 (Heikel 145,21f.); *DE* 7,1,49f. (Heikel 307,4f.); *DE* 9,17,18 (Heikel 442, 8–15).

15 *HE* 1,2,24–26 (Schwartz 26,6–28,7).

16 The text of Dan 7,9 is mentioned in Eusebius, *PE* 11,38,1 (Mras, vol. II, 78,14–16), while Dan 7,10 occurs in *PE* 7,15,3 (Mras, vol. I, 393,11f.). Neither of these could be considered as parallel passages to *HE* 1,2,24–26. On the other hand, Eusebius uses Dan 7,9a,10,13,14 within a similar context and interpretation in *DE* 9,17,4–8 (Heikel 440,3–32) as is to be found in *Interp A*.

found in the *Demonstratio*;[17] (iii) the reference in *DE* 8, "Proem," 5 to an
earlier treatment of the subject discussed therein does not in all probability
refer to *Interp A* since, in spite of the similarity of content, the stated subjects of both are different: the subject of the *Proem* is the explanation as to
why Christ appeared in recent times and not long ago, whereas the subject
of *Interp A* is formulated by Eusebius as an explanation of the reasons why
He was not proclaimed to all men and nations long ago as He is today.[18]
To summarize: Eusebius has condensed into the short passage now found
in Book 1 of the *History* (= *Interp A*) arguments which were previously
scattered through the *Demonstratio* (and the *Praeparatio*), a number of
which he had previously summarized in the course of the *Demonstratio*
itself in the *Proem* to Book 8.

The unsuitability of the passage in its present context confirms the
hypothesis that the passage in the *History* is a later interpolation. The main
argument of the disputed passage is not directly related to the proper
subject matter of Chapter Two, which, according to the stated Contents
of Book 1, should give us a summary description of the preexistence of Our
Savior and Lord Jesus Christ, and of His Divinity.[19] In contrast with this
main topic, *Interp A,* as has already been mentioned, attempts to answer
the question as to why He only appeared in recent times to all men.

When was the passage interpolated into its present position? The
terminus a quo is 320, i.e., after the composition of the *Demonstratio*.
This means that the interpolation belongs to the 4th Revision. This suggestion is confirmed by the internal evidence. The coincidence between
the coming of Christ and the beginning of the Roman Empire, one of
the main topics of the interpolated passage, is likewise treated in the
4th Revision,[20] where the parallel is drawn between the coming of
Christ and the coming of Constantine, both of which events, in the
eyes of Eusebius, were marked by the unification of the empire. It seems
most likely, then, that Eusebius inserted this passage, which contains a
summary of his earlier treatment in the *Praeparatio* and the *Demonstratio*
on the coincidence between the coming of Christ and the beginning of
the Roman Empire into its present position in Book 1, so as to enable

---

[17] With regard to the development of Eusebius' thought between the *Demonstratio*
and the text we are discussing (*Interp A*), see our discussion of the 4th Revision
above pp. 172–173.

[18] Cf. *HE* 1,2,17 (Schwartz 20,14–16) and compare with *DE* 8, "Proem," 5 (Heikel
349,27–30).

[19] Schwartz 2,6–7.

[20] Cf. *HE* 10,9,6 (Schwartz 902,2–6).

him to make the parallel between the Coming of Christ and the coming of Constantine at the climax of his Hymn to Constantine composed as part of the 4th Revision.

§2 HE 1,6,1–11 (Schwartz 42,8–52,20)

This passage, which we will refer to as *Interp B,* contains many features also found in the previous one. It is concerned with the birth of Christ, as was *Interp A,* but this time the providential coincidence is not the beginning of the Roman Empire but the end of the Jewish "successions." Again, this passage (like *Interp A*) refers to an exegesis of Daniel—this time the text is Dan 9—which, the author informs us, he had previously treated in detail in other works. Lawlor considers[21] that the other works here referred to are the *Prophetic Eclogues* 3,45[22] where this text (Dan 9,22–27) is quoted, though the actual discussion, which indeed bears many resemblances to that in *Interp B,* is properly speaking to be found in *Ecl* 3,46.[23] Lawlor also mentions the much more detailed commentary on the Daniel text, which forms the subject of a Chapter in the *Demonstratio* (*DE* 8,2).[24] However, he rules out any reference to the latter here since, even according to Lawlor's own dating system, the 1st "Edition" containing Books 1–8 of the *History* (i.e., including *Interp B* since the possibility of an interpolation was not considered) was published in 311, while the *Demonstratio,* according to Lightfoot's dating, was written circa 313.[25] But again it must be noted that Eusebius refers not just to one work where he has previously interpreted Dan 9 but to several. Since it is most likely that 303 is the latest date for the composition of the original *History* of seven books, then even if Eusebius only refers to the *Prophetic Eclogues,* which could not have been composed before 309 but sometime later, this would be sufficient to indicate that *HE* 1,6,1–11 is an interpolated passage. The internal evidence confirms this and can help us to date the interpolation.

In *Interp B,* Eusebius paraphrases a text of *Africanus* regarding the ancestry of Herod (*HE* 1,6,2–3). The actual text of *Africanus* is in fact given in the following chapter (*HE* 1,7,11–14). This type of repetition does not necessarily indicate the presence of an

---

[21] Lawlor and Oulton, *The Ecclesiastical History*, vol. I, 19, footnote 4, and vol. II, 53.

[22] *PG* 22,1176,A11–D8.

[23] *PG* 22,1176,D9f.

[24] *DE* 8,2,1f. (Heikel 361,1f.).

[25] Lawlor and Oulton, *The Ecclesiastical History*, vol. II, 53.

interpolation since, as we have seen, Eusebius often uses the *information* gathered from his sources in one passage and later in a different context quotes the actual *source* itself, but nonetheless this particular repetition arouses one's suspicions due to the unusual proximity both of extracted information and actual source. A more serious objection to the hypothesis that *HE* 1,6,1–11 is a later interpolation is the statement of Eusebius in *HE* 1,7,1 to the effect that the author, from whose writings he was about to quote, had been previously mentioned—a reference to *HE* 1,6,2–3. This objection is likewise ambiguous since it too could conceivably have been an editorial amendment whenever *Interp B* was placed into its present position. Our first concern, then, must be to clarify the relationship between the text of *Africanus* and the paraphrased information gleaned from that text which is to be found in *Interp B*, and then go on to examine the relationship between *Interp B* and both the *Eclogues* and the *Demonstratio*.

In the *Africanus* text, the subject of the non-Jewish ancestry of Herod is mentioned in order to illustrate the concern of the Hebrew families to preserve the memory of their good birth; it is part of Eusebius' prime witness in his defense of the genuineness of Our Savior's genealogy. On the other hand, the *Africanus* text, or more specifically, that part of *Africanus* that provides information about Herod, is here used in *Interp B* to prove how the Jewish succession of High Priests and rulers (the Succession of Moses) came to an end with Herod since that ruler of the Jews had no Hebrew blood in him.[26] A similar usage of the same information gleaned from *Africanus* is to be found in the *Prophetic Eclogues*[27] where it forms part of an exegesis of Gn 49,10, demonstrating the fulfilment of that particular prophecy but within the general context of a discussion on the fulfilment of Dan 9,22–27. It is remarkable that in *Interp B*, the paraphrase of *Africanus* is likewise loosely linked with the prophecies of Gn 49,10 and Dan 9,24–27. Apart from the similarity of usage, the two passages betray remarkable verbal affinity, as can be seen in the following comparison:

Ecl 3,46[28]	*HE* 1,6,2[29]
ὡς μὲν ὁ Ἰώσηπος παραδίδ-	ὡς μὲν Ἰώσηπος παραδίδ-
ωσιν, Ἰδουμαῖος κατὰ πατέρα	ωσιν, Ἰδουμαῖος ὢν κατὰ πατέρα

[26] Cf. *HE* 1,6,2–3 (Schwartz 48,12–50,1) and compare with *HE* 1,7,11–12 (Schwartz 58,17–60,5).
[27] *Ecl* 3,46 (*PG* 22,1183,C7f.).
[28] *PG* 22, 1184,C4–10.
[29] Schwartz 48,11–16.

τὸ γένος ὢν Ἀράβιος δὲ κατὰ
μητέρα, ὡς δ᾽ ὁ Ἀφρικανὸς
οὐ μικρῷ πρόσθεν ἐμνήσθημεν·

                   Φασὶν
οἱ τὰ κατ᾽ αὐτὸν ἀκριβοῦντες
Ἀντίπατρον (τοῦτον δ᾽εἶναι
αὐτῷ πατέρα) Ἡρώδου τινὸς
Ἀσκαλωνίτου τῶν περὶ τὸν
νεὼν τοῦ Ἀπόλλωνος ἱερο
δούλων   γεγον-
έναι.

τὸ γένος Ἀράβιος δὲ κατὰ
μητέρα, ὡς δ᾽ Ἀφρικανὸς

(οὐκ ὁ τυχὼν δὲ καὶ οὗτος
γέγονε συγγραφεύς), φασὶν
οἱ τὰ κατ᾽ αὐτὸν ἀκριβοῦντες
Ἀντίπατρον (τοῦτον δ᾽εἶναι
αὐτῷ πατέρα) Ἡρώδου τινὸς
Ἀσκαλωνίτου τῶν περὶ τὸν
νεὼν τοῦ Ἀπόλλωνος ἱερο-
δούλων καλουμένων γεγον-
έναι·

From the above it seems quite evident that Eusebius had the text of the
Eclogues open in front of him when he was writing *Interp B*. But apparently
the paraphrase reminded him of the actual *Africanus* text he had previously
incorporated into the original because the very next sentence[30] could only
have been directly taken from that source, since the information it imparts
is not to be found in the *Eclogues*. Yet the four sentences immediately following,[31] where a substantial section of *Ecl* 3,46 is concisely summarized,[32]
indicate once again Eusebius' dependence on the *Eclogues* in the composition of this section, although there is also clear evidence of dependency
on the *Demonstratio*.[33] The final three sentences or verses of *Interp B*[34]
complicate the picture since they are clearly paraphrases of a passage in
the *Demonstratio* 8,2,88–98,[35] which is itself most probably a development
of *Ecl* 3,46. Whereas the two Josephan sources referred to by Eusebius in
Interp B (*HE* 1,6,9–10) are actually quoted in the passages from the *Eclogues*
and the *Demonstratio* just mentioned,[36] it is those arguments deduced
from the Josephan sources in the *Demonstratio* which are summarized in

---

[30]   *HE* 1,6,3 (Schwartz 48,16–50,1). Cf. *HE* 1,7,11 (58,15–22).
[31]   *HE* 1,6,4–7 (Schwartz 50,1–22).
[32]   Cf. *Ecl* 3,46 (*PG* 22,1175,D11–1183,C4). Note in particular the striking similarity
       between *HE* 1,6,6–7 (Schwartz 50,11–22) and *Ecl* 3,46 (*PG* 22,1183,B11–C4).
[33]   Compare *DE* 8,2,75–78 (Heikel 381,10–22) with *HE* 1,6,6–7.
[34]   *HE* 1,6,8–10 (Schwartz 50,22–52,11).
[35]   Heikel 383,24–385,27.
[36]   Josephus, *Antiq.* 20,247–249 (Niese, vol. IV, 317): quoted in *Ecl* 3,46 (*PG*
       22,1185,C4–D5) and in *DE* 8,2,93–94 (Heikel 384,27–385,6).
       Josephus, *Antiq.* 18,92–93 (Niese, vol. IV, 157): quoted in *Ecl* 3,46 (*PG*
       22,1185,D9–1188,A9) and *DE* 8,2,95 (Heikel 385,6–16).

Interp B.[37] In this case, however, it would appear that Eusebius is paraphrasing from memory, to judge from the mistake he makes when he informs us that Herod was the first to lock up the sacred stole of the High Priest and place it under his own seal,[38] even though the actual passage in Josephus[39] informs its readers that Herod, and his son after him, indeed took possession of the sacred vestment, but the Romans returned it to the High Priests, placing it in a stone chamber under *the seal of the priests* and keepers of the temple. In the *Eclogues,*[40] Eusebius so edited the quotation that the reader is left with the impression that the stole ended up in a chamber under *a seal of the Romans.* The same edited quotation, with minor variations, is used by the author again in the *Demonstratio.*[41] The reasons for these editions and for the very singular lapse of memory—if such it can be called—according to which, in the *Interp B,* Herod is reported on the authority of Josephus to have placed the sacred stole (symbol of the High Priestly authority) under *his own seal* (symbol of Herod's civil authority), has been dealt with in Chapter Four above.

To summarize: we saw how the first mention of Herod's ancestry in the *Africanus* text, quoted by Eusebius in the original *History (HE* 1,7,11), was used by him for a different purpose in the *Eclogues (Ecl* 3,46), namely, to demonstrate the fulfilment of the prophecies contained in Gn 49,10 and Dan 9,22–27, which topic was later developed in greater detail in the *Demonstratio (DE* 8,1–8,2). The interpolated passage summarizes the thought of Eusebius as found in both the *Eclogues* and the *Demonstratio,* most probably with the former work open before him and paraphrasing the latter from memory. Prompted by the mention of Herod's ancestry in the *Eclogues,* Eusebius again consulted the original text of *Africanus* and added some more details to the paraphrase from the Eclogues. To conclude—since *Interp B* paraphrases certain sections of the *Demonstratio* (which was written ca. 320), then this *Interp B* must, like the former interpolation, belong to the 4th Revision.

In confirmation of the above, it should be noted that four chapters later in *HE* 1,10,3–4 (74,2–7) there is a passing reference to the end of the Jewish successions in the course of a discussion about the time of Our Lord's death, when Annas and Caiphas held the office

---

[37] Compare *HE* 1,6,8 (Schwartz 50,27–52,1) with *DE* 8,2,92 (Heikel 384,19–23) and *DE* 8,2,98 (385,20–27).

[38] *HE* 1,9,10 (Schwartz 52,7–11).

[39] *Antiq.* 18,93 (Niese, vol. IV, 157).

[40] *Ecl* 3,46 *(PG* 22,1185,D10–1188,9).

[41] *DE* 8,2,95 (Heikel 385,6–13).

of High Priest. The reference is in the form of a parenthesis, which is
inserted to explain the mention of the two High Priests (Lk 3,2). It betrays
no knowledge of the discussion in *Interp B* and in fact sees no significance
at all in the breakdown of the traditional regulations governing the succession of High Priests, which significance first engaged Eusebius' attention in
the *Prophetic Eclogues,* then later in the *Demonstratio*, and which is found
in its most developed form in *Interp B.*

CHAPTER FIVE
Final Analysis

Although, as the research of Schwartz and Laqueur originally brought to
the surface, the *History,* as we know it in its present form, is the product
of a lengthy redaction of an original draft, yet F. Ch. Baur's impression
of Eusebius' monumental composition as a unified work[1] still retains a
certain validity. As Wallace-Hadrill aptly remarks, "the *History,* despite
its chronological disorder, reads like a plain straightforward narrative.
Its simplicity is akin to that of the Gospel's, a simplicity which conceals
certain dogmatic presuppositions of which the story itself is the narrative
expression."[2] This English scholar rightly draws attention to the importance of such presuppositions in any estimate of Eusebius' position as an
historian. Our analysis of the original *History,* book by book, and then the
various Revisions in their chronological sequence, has revealed two sets
of suppositions on which the work rests: (i) Eusebius' more fundamental
or axiomatic assumptions, which did not change, and (ii) the secondary
presuppositions, more limited in extent than the former, which were
subject to change. It will be our task in this chapter to summarize these,
giving the greater part of our attention, however, to the implications for
both of Eusebius' attitude to the Bishop of Rome.

Underlying the "unity" of the ten books, and the Revisions
they contain, is a certain consistency of thought, which, despite variations of emphasis, enabled Eusebius to gradually move from his
original apology for the Apostolic Church to his later incipient theology of the Imperial Church, and so to see Constantine, the sole

---

[1]   Baur, *Die Epochen der kirchlichen Geschichtsschreibung*, 24.
[2]   Wallace-Hadrill, *Eusebius*, 168.

ruler of the empire and the Church, as the "logical" climax of the Church's triumphant march through the history he first set out to narrate. The inner cohesion of the *History* is due to a set of fundamental "constant" suppositions, which are partly of a formal nature and partly of a material nature. The formal presuppositions include Eusebius' overriding apologetic purpose, as well as his approach to theology, which made him an ideologist rather than a genuine theologian, and his static attitude to history, which understood history "prototypically," i.e., as the reembodiment of certain prototypes within a predetermined program of divine direction in human affairs. The most basic material presuppositions include, first and foremost Eusebius' primitive, causal concept of Providence, as well as his concept of salvation primarily as a form of civilization and enlightenment, and, most importantly, his triumphalist understanding of the Church as a "perfect society" both in its inception and in its march through the ages.[3] A fourth presupposition of great importance was Eusebius' emphasis on the continuity between the Old and the New Testaments.

These suppositions on which the *History* rested, both formal and material, all have one thing in common: they display Eusebius' basic failure to appreciate the centrality of the Cross of Christ. Thus, his basic apologetic concern, in itself good, missed the mark, since it tended more and more to avoid the scandal of the Cross, the stumbling-block to the Jews, and folly to the Greeks. Without the Cross to help him shatter the fetters of rational thought, Eusebius turned his ecclesiology into an ideology, that is, into a closed rational system in contrast with a genuine theology which ought to be a systematic penetration of the event and mystery of Salvation. As a consequence of his inability to grasp the final significance of Christ's death, he failed to understand history as the arena of man's choice and God's irreversible decision. Eusebius' concept of Providence did not allow for the activity of God in weakness, humiliation, and even human failure. In other words, he failed to take cognizance of man's free will in Salvation History. His idea of salvation concentrated on the effects rather than the cause (and so misunderstood the effects as well), while his triumphalism ensured that he was quite unable to penetrate either the mystery of Christ's triumph on the Cross, or the place of suffering and martyrdom in the Church—or the brutal fact (so unpleasant for an apologist of Eusebius' bent) that the Church was founded not on any epic figure

3   An even more basic, theological, presupposition was his monotheism, which cannot be considered here: see Peterson, *Der Monotheismus*, 92f.

of heroic virtues but on one of those who are "low and contemptible" (cf. 1 Cor 1,25–31), such as Peter the fisherman who denied his Lord. Finally, had Eusebius allowed his thought to be molded by the Cross, then he would have avoided the easy mistake of overemphasizing the actual continuity between the Old and the New Testaments, since it is precisely the Cross which creates the even more radical discontinuity between them.

On the other hand, these basic assumptions, or rather their inadequacies, give the *History* a certain logic and unity. His apologetic concern to present the Church as anything but a stumbling-block or, humanly considered, a mere folly, led him to certain accommodations regarding the unpleasant side of the Church's history, small at first, but later more serious when it came to his account of the persecution he himself experienced. Such compromises eventually prepared him for a radical change of sides, as it were, once the need for "accommodation" was clearly removed. As an ideologist, he had recourse to history to illustrate his preconceived ideas—instead of entering a genuine dialogue with history which clarifies and perfects theological propositions—so that when he altered his ideology, he could with equanimity turn to history for the desired confirmation. In this he was aided by a basically static concept of history as the working-out in time of eternal prototypes and predetermined events. The most important material presupposition which gives the *History* its internal cohesion, is, of course, his primitive concept of Providence, which enabled the author of the *History* to determine the workings of God with the greatest ease and security, aided, as he was, by an early Old Testament concept of God as one who manifestly rewards the good and punishes the evil here on earth. His triumphalist concept of the Church naturally led him to extend to Constantine a sincere but much too uncritical welcome, while on the other hand it blinded him to the real significance of the Church's ignominious experience during the persecution. The new era inaugurated by Constantine promised to realize to the full all the possibilities of salvation, since civilization had reached its acme in the Christian Empire, and through the instrument of Constantine, God had secured the final triumph over the enemies of the Church and so ushered in a new dispensation in the history of Salvation.

Among the "variable" and less basic presuppositions, we have, in the above examination, noted: the ambiguous understanding of the relationship between the Church and the imperial powers, the concept of persecution, and his closely related idea of martyrdom. In all of these, Eusebius started out with the more traditional understanding he had absorbed none too deeply from his predecessors and his sources, but in the course of the *History's* composition, each underwent a definite transformation in accordance with the more fundamental, axiomatic assumptions just outlined. We saw at the very beginning how Eusebius took another such "secondary concept," that of the Apostolic Successions, and gave it his own nuance, one which eventually led to his abandonment of the original sacramental idea. By introducing two distinct types of succession, Eusebius had prepared the conceptual groundwork for his later ecclesiology. That aspect of the original Apostolic Succession, which was concerned with authority, was separated from that relating to the content of the Apostolic Teaching so that two "offices" resulted, one of the rulers of the Church (the bishops) and the other of the teachers (who need not necessarily be bishops). When the holders of the office of authority in the Church disqualified themselves, first through their disgraceful behavior during the persecutions and then through their adoption of "hetero-dox" tenets—as Eusebius would have seen it—at Antioch and possibly Nicaea, he was conditioned to look for a new office-holder, and he found Constantine. The Apostolic Teaching was, of course, preserved by him and his fellow Origenists. As the Apostolic Succession replaced the Jewish High Priestly succession, so Constantine and his successors would replace the Apostolic one. Now absorbed into the imperial system, the bishops derived their authority no longer from their Apostolic constitution, but from the emperor. Thus, the Bishop of Rome, once the central authority in the Church as the successor of St. Peter, will be described by the later Eusebius as the Bishop of "the Imperial City."[4]

When Eusebius at first conceived his *History*, the possibility that the Church could undertake such a far-reaching evolution in her con-stitution as that reflected in the various strata of the finished work could not have been entertained by the author. Quite the opposite: he understood the Church to have been always so constituted as he and his contemporaries experienced it, and to remain such until the whole world recognized the truth it contained and worshiped the one God, the God of the Christian Religion. Our interest in the actual evolution of Eusebius' thought is primarily determined by the light it throws on his original "ecclesiology," in particular those defects in it which in fact led to his effective abandonment of it later. This is important, if we are to evaluate Eusebius concept of the Church as truly representative of the traditional

---

[4]   Cf. Eusebius, *VC* 3,7 (Winkelmann 84,18). See Eusebius, *DE* 3,7,22 (Heikel 144,10f.), where this development was anticipated.

ecclesiology he set out to defend. Our analysis has shown that Eusebius' teaching on the Church, insofar as it can be gathered from the imprint it has left on the face of the original *History,* belonged to that set of presuppositions in Eusebius which we have called secondary and variable—not that they are variable in themselves, but only in the actual evolution of Eusebius' thought. The filter through which Eusebius received and transmitted the more authentic Tradition of the Church was made up of those fine threads we have described as his axiomatic and more basic assumptions of both a formal and a material nature. Thus, for example, Eusebius tended to interpret the consciousness of the Church regarding her nature in terms of an ideology. In this he was in large part determined by the concern he inherited from the Apologists who, defending themselves from the ridicule of the pagans over the youth of Christianity, were intent on demonstrating the antiquity of the Christian Religion[5] and its concomitant, the immutability of its dogma or teaching.[6] It is against this background that Eusebius started out on his historical investigations, with the purpose of proving effectively that the Church of his experience and that of his contemporaries was identical with that founded originally by the Apostles.

He did not, to the best of my knowledge, invent any of the multiple pieces of information[7] which he used to build up the *collage* we know as the *History*. What he did was to place the evidence of the various oral and written sources at his disposal in the service of his *apologia* for the Church. In the original *History,* Eusebius was generally faithful to this evidence, which indicates how closely his "ecclesiology" of that period matched the traditional understanding. What was peculiarly Eusebian was determined by his axiomatic presuppositions such as: (a) a rigid and over-idealized concept of the Church, as derived from his apologetic and ideological frame of mind, and (b) the over-simplification which resulted from his naive concept of Providence, his superficial triumphalism, and his understanding of the Church as a perfect society founded on men who, as God's instruments, were thus presumed to be paragons of virtue rather than simple human beings. The most important *a priori* of Eusebius was his prototypical approach to history and the motivating force behind it: his aetiological interest.

---

5   Nigg, *Die Kirchengeschichtsschreibung,* 5–6.
6   Baur, *Die Epochen der kirchlichen Geschichtsschreibung,* 15–16.
7   The most famous calumny made against Eusebius blamed him for the alteration of the Josephan text known as the *Testimonium Flavianum* (Josephus, *Antiq.* XVIII, 63f.), and quoted by Eusebius on three occasions including *HE* 1,11, 7–8. This was refuted by Wallace-Hadrill, "Eusebius of Caesarea," in *JEH* 25 (1974), 353–362.

Just as he prefaced his *History* with a short defense of the divinity of the preexistent Logos in whom the Christian Religion has its ultimate origin and thus its claim to divine truth, Eusebius pays particular attention to the traditions relating to the origins of those Churches, and the successions of their bishops, which enjoyed a unique authority in the Church of Eusebius' own day. Again, it must be emphasized that Eusebius does not invent these traditions but selects and arranges the historical evidence for them in such a way so as to illustrate their contemporary significance. In this he may be accused of exaggeration and overemphasis. But in his basic affirmations, Eusebius was as much the mouthpiece of the pre-persecution Church as he was of the new Constantinian era.[8] Eusebius' description of the origins of the principal Churches within the *ecclesia universalis* was, therefore, not primarily concerned with conveying purely historical information but rather in delineating the prototypes of these main Churches with the purpose of explaining the origin of the authority or special honor enjoyed by them at the turn of the century. In this he was merely articulating the commonly accepted belief of his contemporaries; this in turn makes Eusebius a very important witness for the history of the Church's self-understanding. We will now summarize our findings relevant to this and "test" these findings against some independent contemporary witnesses before we review the causes which led Eusebius to confine his earlier ecclesiology to the realms of past history and to mold a new one to suit the new "dispensation" in which he found himself.

Contrary to the commonly accepted opinion of scholars that Eusebius considered Rome to be just one of the main Churches, no different from Alexandria, Antioch, or Jerusalem,[9] our analysis of the original *History* first of all established a recognized preeminence of the Church and Bishop of Rome on the part of the early Eusebius. Secondly, our study has revealed how each main See is not only in some way, directly or indirectly, related in its origins to St. Peter, but how the nature of this relationship in turn determines the nature of the authority enjoyed by these Churches at the opening of the fourth century—in particular, the preeminent authority of the Church of Rome and its bishop. Thirdly, we have seen how, for

---

[8] Defending Eusebius' enthusiastic assent to the new Constantinian era, Kartaschow, "Die Entstehung der kaiserlichen Synodalgewalt," 138, rejects the accusation that Eusebius was a mere court flatterer and prefers to describe him as the "Wortträger der kollektiven Stimme der Kirche."

[9] E.g., Hertling, "Communio und Primat," 117.

Eusebius, St. Peter is, as Spokesman/Leader of the Apostles, considered to be the principal Founder of the Church, after Christ.

The nature of the preeminent authority enjoyed by the bishop and Church of Rome at the end of the third and the opening of the fourth centuries is unfolded within the highly idealized—indeed one could almost say mythological[10]—presentation of the related destinies of St. Peter and Rome as portrayed in Books 2 and 3. The theological significance of Rome and Jerusalem is primarily depicted in terms of the contrasting destinies of the two divinely-chosen instruments of God, St. Peter and St. James. The aetiological tendency of Eusebius goes beyond his stated aim to present the Apostolic Successions of the major Churches and seeks to explain how the nature of the authority invested in these Successors to the Apostles is determined by the different origins of these sees.

Jerusalem deserves the *honor* she enjoys[11]—so Eusebius will tell us in so many words—because of her unique association with Our Lord Jesus Christ; His relatives, according to the flesh, constitute the beginning of its succession list. However, the Church as such does not enjoy Apostolic Succession in the strict sense of the term—and consequently no greater authority than that of any other Church—since (i) it traces its origins back to James, who was not an apostle but was appointed to the bishopric of Jerusalem by the three Apostles, Peter, James, and John,[12] and (ii) the original divine purpose of this Church was thwarted by the Jews who refused the last offer of Grace incorporated in the person of James.

The authority of *Alexandria* is similar to that of Jerusalem in so far as it is a derived authority—derived that is from Peter. But here the link is closer and the authority correspondingly greater. The figure of Mark—the interpreter of Peter but no apostle in the strict sense—characterizes the authority enjoyed by the Church of Alexandria as the great center of Christian learning and piety. Perhaps it would be more accurate to describe her authority as being originally a *moral* authority, one ultimately subject to the

---

[10]   Nigg, *Die Kirchengeschichtsschreibung*, 15f., argues that the *History* is rooted in a mythological conception of history.

[11]   This "honor" is illustrated in *HE* 5,23,3, which mentions the unique instance of a dual presidency of a synod. There it is reported that the Synod of Palestine was presided over by the Bishop of Caesarea (who was the actual Metropolitan bishop) and the Bishop of Jerusalem (who probably presided due to the special respect shown to that city, although it cannot be completely ruled out that the moral stature of the actual Bishop of Jerusalem at the time—Narcissus—may have had some influence).

[12]   *HE* 2,1,2–4 (Schwartz 102,19–104,14).

Apostolic Authority of Peter, be it found in Antioch or Rome.[13] The Apostolic Teaching, for which Alexandria was renowned, traces its origin back, through St. Mark, to the original Proclamation of St. Peter on which the Church was founded. Further, one of the philosophers who most influenced her interpretation of that teaching—Philo—is also described by Eusebius as having had direct recourse to St. Peter in Rome.

Antioch, however, ought to have enjoyed real authority. Her privileged position as the center of unity for the East is derived from the fact that the Church there was "founded" by St. Peter and its bishops are considered to be his successors. But even at the time of writing, the theoretical authority of its bishop had been greatly undermined by the presence of at least one heretical "successor" (Paul of Samosata) and the possibility of an earlier one (Fabius). This is reflected in the low and colorless profile cut by this Church in the early books of the *History,* being mentioned but once in Book 2 (in a loose association with the initial "foundation" of the Church Universal by Peter[14]) and twice in Book 3 (two passing references to St. Ignatius of Antioch and his predecessor). The first explicit mention of Peter's association with the Church and her succession occurs at the end of Book 3.[15]

In vivid contrast with the other three "distinguished" Churches, the *Church of Rome* is seen as endowed with a predominant authority superior to that of all other Churches and, based on her unique association with St. Peter and on her place within the Divine Plan, both as the alternative to Jerusalem and as the center of the universal mission of the Church. St. Peter, as we have seen, is for Eusebius the Spokesman of the Apostles, whose office it is to found the Church Universal through their preaching, and, as their Leader, may be considered to be the Founder of the Church par excellence. Alone of the Apostles, he is considered by Eusebius to have been the subject of a particular Divine Dispensation. Moved by Divine Inspiration, he inaugurated the Universal Mission to the Gentiles. His own mission field was not a limited one but spanned the world from East to West, until at Rome, the center of the unredeemed world (Babylon), he brings his mission to its climax with the final witness of his martyrdom there. At Rome, his divinely guided activities

---

[13]   This could possibly explain the reference to Alexandria and the Church there in the *Letter of the Synod of Palestine* (*HE* 5,25,1), implying that Alexandria, like the Churches of Palestine came within the Eastern "sphere of influence," whose center was Antioch.

[14]   *HE* 2,3,3–4 (Schwartz 112,29–114,12).

[15]   *HE* 3,36,2 (Schwartz 274,18).

stamp that Church—and in particular the authority and function of his successors—with that character for which it was renowned to Eusebius and his contemporaries at the end of the third century. The confrontation, first in Samaria but decisively in Rome, of Peter and Simon Magus between the Leader of the Apostles and so the Founder of the Church par excellence on the one hand, and the Father and Founder of all heresies on the other is the prototype of the confrontations between the Successors of St. Peter, the Bishops of Rome, and the successors of Simon Magus, the heresiarchs. As we would formulate it, the Petrine function of the Bishop of Rome is to detect and condemn heresy—a function not attributed to the personal ability or perception of the occupant but rather the charism attached to the office, as the emphasis on the divine activity in that episode clearly suggests.[16] The corollary to this is the function of Peter (and consequently of his Successors) to approve and sanction the work of orthodox writers, as is figuratively portrayed in the prototypical relationship between St. Peter and St. Mark, his interpreter. Again, this function is exercised according to Eusebius on the basis of Divine Inspiration and is not due to the natural ability of the office holder.[17]

But the significance of Rome is not as such exhausted in this highly idealized concept of the unique authority attributed to its Church. The relationship between Peter and Mark also typifies the relationship between the great Church of Rome and the renowned Church of Alexandria, and illustrates how the moral Authority of Alexandria, which as the center of Christian learning and asceticism, and thus embodied the tradition of Mark, was finally subject to the Apostolic Authority of the Successor of St. Peter. Finally, it was in Rome that St. Peter—together with "The Apostle" who, however, plays a secondary role in the *History*—gave final witness to the Faith with his blood, a witness which itself is testified by the tombs of the Apostles in Rome, in the first of the many confrontations between the civil authority and the Church, between the successors of Nero and those of Peter.[18] As Turner aptly put it, "the earliest primacy of the Roman Church was a primacy of suffering."[19]

---

[16] Cf. *HE* 2,14,4–6 (Schwartz 138,11–28).

[17] Cf. *HE* 2,15,1–2 (Schwartz 138,28–140,13).

[18] The roots of the tradition concerning St. Peter and Rome, which tradition Eusebius draws on for his presentation of Book 2, can be traced back to around the year 100, if we are to accept the findings of E. Peterson in his article, "Das Martyrium des Hl. Petrus nach der Petrus-Apokalypse," published in his collected works entitled: *Frühkirche, Judentum und Gnosis*, Rome-Freiburg-Vienna, 1959, 88–91. There he opposes the thesis of O. Cullmann, who claimed: "Bis in die zweite Hälfte des zweiten Jahrhunderts behauptet kein

What we have outlined above is the *theory* of Eusebius with regard to some of the various authorities enjoyed by the main Churches at the end of the third century and the opening of the fourth century. In trying to explicate what is but implicit in the narrative presentation of the Foundation of the Church by Eusebius, the impression may have been given to the reader that the author of the *History* was equally explicit. That this is not so may be gathered from the silence among commentators and students of Eusebius with regard

Dokument explizit den Aufenthalt und das Martyrium des Petrus in Rom" (see Cullmann, *Petrus: Jünger, Apostel, Märtyrer*, 123). Peterson argues firstly that the text of the *Ascensio Isaiae* 4,2f., dated circa 100 by Charles and Tisserant, but rejected as evidence by Cullmann, does indeed refer to Peter's martyrdom at Rome by the matricide Nero in the veiled language characteristic of the style used at the time for such prophetic utterances as contained in the *Ascensio*. Peterson goes on to draw our attention to a second text, which is most revealing with respect to the findings of our analysis given above. This text is the third/fourth centuries papyrus-fragment of *Peter-Apocalypse,* first published by C. Wessely, *PO* XVIII/3, Paris, 1924, 482f., and newly edited by M. R. James in *JThS* 32 (1931), 270–279. According to Peterson, a certain literary relationship exists between the *Apocalypse* and the *Ascensio.* In the *Apocalypse,* however, Peter is explicitly mentioned and his martyrdom at Rome is clearly alluded to. The relevant text is as follows. Our Lord speaks: "ἰδοὺ ἐδήλωσά σοι Πέτρε καὶ ἐξεθέμην πάντα καὶ πορεύου εἰς πόλιν ὀπύσεως καὶ πίε τὸ ποτήριον, ὃ ἐπηγγειλάμην σοι, ἐν χειροῖν τοῦ Υἱοῦ τοῦ ἐν Ἅιδου, ἵνα ἀρχὴν λάβῃ αὐτοῦ ἡ ἀφάνεια καὶ σὺ δεκτὸς τῆς ἐπαγγελίας." ("Behold I have clarified and expounded all to you, Peter. Let you therefore go to the capital of fornication and drink the cup [of martyrdom], which I have promised you, at the hands of the son of him who is in Hades, so that the beginning of his annihilation may come to pass and you are found worthy of the promise." The reading of the text is that proposed by Peterson.) The German scholar drew attention to the remarkable fact that both in the *Ascensio* and in the *Apocalypse,* the martyrdom of Peter is related without any reference to that of Paul. Further, both texts describe the martyrdom of Peter in terms of the eschatological concept of history held by Christians at the turn of the second century, which also provided the background out of which developed the *Acts of Peter* and the Simon Magus legend (p. 90). Peterson emphasizes that it is not without significance that in this context Rome is called "the capital of fornication." Of even greater significance, he maintains, is the way the martyrdom of St. Peter is seen as the beginning of the annihilation of the Antichrist (p. 91). It is precisely these three points—or rather nuances—which are present in the implicit ecclesiology of Eusebius, and which demonstrate the faithfulness of the author of the *History* to the traditions of the Church with regard to her origins.

[19] Turner, *Studies in Early Church History*, 226. Turner continues: "So again two hundred years later the signal for the persecution of Decius was given by the martyrdom of pope Fabian, and that for the Valerian persecution by the martyrdom of pope Xystus. 'You in Rome,' wrote a Carthaginian to a Roman confessor under Decius, 'have the greater struggle, and therefore greater glory than we, for you have faced the great dragon, the precursor of Antichrist himself' (Cyprian, Ep. 22,1)."

to what is here summarized in a comparatively black and white fashion. It appears to this writer that, up to now, students of the Papacy may have given too much attention to the rich material to be found in the *Ecclesiastical History* for the study of the early understanding of the position of the Church of Rome and too little study as to how Eusebius himself uses and understands this documentary evidence. Neither have the full implications of the research of Schwartz and Laqueur been taken into consideration. And while it must be admitted that Eusebius' own views on the authority of the Bishop of Rome are not to be gathered *prima vista* from the text but are arrived at only at the end of a process of interpretation of his writing, and so subject to the limitations of every interpretation, yet the verifiable results of such a study are of all the greater interest to the historian of dogma insofar as their implicit nature itself bears witness to the ideas shared and unquestioningly accepted by its author and audience alike; and this in fact is the object of our inclusion of this study previous to our analysis of what seems to us to constitute a very significant stage of further reflection on these commonly accepted ideas. Students of Eusebius on the other hand have been so preoccupied with the myriad other problems raised by this monumental work—in particular, the chronological problems caused by the succession lists—that the broader issues implied by the presence of these lists have apparently been overlooked. Again, these broader issues are not unambiguous, a fact which must be underlined in the face of the apparent clarity to be found in the summary of findings just given with regard to what we have categorized as the "theory" of Eusebius on the authority of the bishop and Church of Rome and of the other main Churches. The two major points to be gathered from the above analysis of the *History* are: (i) the general acceptance in the practice of the Church at the opening of the fourth century of three major centers of *authority* within the Church Universal, apart from the *honor* paid to Jerusalem, within which the bishop and Church of Rome enjoyed a preeminence indeed a "primacy," and (ii) Eusebius' theory or theology with regard to the origins, nature, and function of these different types of authority. An independent check on the validity of this interpretation of the *History* may be found in the Synod of Nicaea for the first, and the first Synod of Constantinople for the second.

Due to the limited scope of this study, one must leave aside any detailed examination of the great event at Nicaea, 325. Here we simply wish to refer to the famous Canons VI and VII issued by the synod. As Ratzinger pointed out,[20] Canon VI marks the formation of definitive Primacies, later called Patriarchates, which exercised extensive *administrative* functions within their respective regions. This is a development of the earlier structure of the Church, which we saw was both "synodal" and "primatial,"[21] whereby the three main sees of Rome, Antioch, and Alexandria exercised a certain ill-defined primacy within their sphere of influence, communicating the decisions of the local or "provincial" synods to each other and so to the Church Universal. Canon VI clarifies this "sphere of influence" and speaks about ἐξουσία, thus introducing the idea of jurisdiction, more specifically, metropolitan jurisdiction.[22] It says nothing about the relationship of the sees to each other, but concerns itself solely with the internal structure of what later became to be known as the Patriarchates. Yet the canon does betray these relationships in a way consistent with our findings in the above analysis of the original *History*. The main point of the canon is to grant jurisdictional authority to the Bishop of Alexandria.[23] Our study of Eusebius indicated that initially the influence of the Church of Alexandria was mainly due to her being the center of Christian learning within the Church; it was more a moral than a jurisdictional authority—one which extended beyond Egypt, Libya, and the Pentapolis. The canon now informs us that within the latter area, the custom had arisen which the synod now recognizes as constituting that which we would call the beginnings of jurisdictional authority. The model for such authority, the canon tells us, is the similar authority exercised by the Bishop of Rome. What is of note is that, whereas the position of Alexandria called for clarification, such was not needed for Rome. Even the ambiguity which surrounds the See of Antioch, as was seen in the original *History,* is reechoed in Canon VI. There is, significantly, no mention of the *Bishop of* Antioch, but only the vague statement that "similarly with regard to Antioch and in the other provinces, let the *Churches* retain their privileges," which

[20]   Ratzinger, "Primat und Episkopat," in Ratzinger, *Volk Gottes*, 132.
[21]   Ratzinger, "Primat und Episkopat," 130–131.
[22]   See Jalland, *Church and Papacy*, 203–204. Dvornik, *The Idea of Apostolicity*, 6–18, argues that "The Nicene Fathers went even further and provided, consciously or unconsciously, a basis for the formation of a supra-metropolitan body in the Church" (p. 8). Dvornik, however, overemphasizes the influence of the imperial administrative structures in the formation of this incipient "supra-metropolitan" system and has been criticized by E. Lanne for doing so; see below, footnote 24.
[23]   See the comments of various scholars collected by Percival, *The Seven Ecumenical Councils*, LNPF², 15–16.

would seem to reflect the dubious nature of the authority exercised by the actual *bishop* there.[24] Finally, the position of *honor*[25] accorded to the Church of Jerusalem and its bishop, the Successor of St. James, is definitively and canonically recognized as such, "saving the right due to the Metropolitan" (= Caesarea), as Canon VII puts it.

The Synod of Constantinople, 381, now recognized as the Second

[24] The contrast between the clearly defined *extent* of Alexandria's jurisdiction and the vagueness concerning that exercised by Antioch has been variously interpreted. Many, like Bardy, "Alexandrie, Antioche, Constantinople (325–451)," in *L'Église et Églises*, Chevetogne, 1954, 186–187, interpret this as an indication of a "victory" for the See of Alexandria in her reputed competition for prestige in opposition to her "rival," the See of Antioch. Such an interpretation fails to convince on the simple grounds that the bishops of these two sees, Alexander of Alexandria and Eustathius of Antioch, apparently cooperated closely at the Synod of Nicaea. See Sellers, *Eustathius of Antioch*, 26f. That such a rivalry could have played a role in the subsequent controversies, which involved both Alexandria and Antioch (as well as Rome), is a matter for debate. But at the time of Nicaea, the shadow of Paul of Samosata (and in particular his deposition) hung over the See of Peter at Antioch and darkened its renown. It is, however, quite probable that the Synod of Nicaea was prompted to define the extent of Alexandria's jurisdiction by the threat to the same, as posed by the Meletian bishops in Egypt itself, who, at the time of Nicaea, numbered at least 29 and were in control of almost the whole Nile Delta and valley (cf. Norberg, *Athanasius and the Emperor*, 10–13). Commenting on the Canons of Nicaea, Dvornik, *The Idea of Apostolicity*, 11f., claims on the other hand that Antioch had lost its leading position during the second century but, thanks to the political importance of the city in the administrative structure of the empire, especially after the reforms of Diocletian, had at the time of Nicaea "already occupied a privileged position in Church organization similar to that of Alexandria" (p. 12). Considering the influence of St. Ignatius of Antioch alone, it is difficult to imagine that Antioch's influence could have declined so rapidly in the second century, as Dvornik's theory would presume. And as far as one could judge from the original *History,* the prestige of Antioch was in the decline at the turn of the fourth century—despite the reforms of Diocletian—and, as the history of the rest of the fourth century shows, its influence continued to decline. Regarding the decline of Antioch's eminence, see Kreilkamp, *The Origin of the Patriarchate of Constantinople*, 25–27.

[25] Lanne, "Partikularkirchen und Patriarchate," 466, is apparently unaware of the ambiguous role played by Eusebius at the Synod of Nicaea. It is doubtful if the Bishop of Caesarea played "a significant role" at Nicaea in any positive sense, as Lanne claims, but it is almost certain that he was in no way responsible for the "Ehrenvorrechte" granted by Nicaea to Jerusalem. I am not convinced by the arguments of Kreilkamp, *The Origin of the Patriarchate of Constantinople*, 50f., in support of his thesis that the concept of τιμή involved at least the "right" to convene synods.

Oecumenical Council, is best known for its Creed. But it is also known for the much-disputed Canon 3, which, for the first time, claimed a primacy of honor for Constantinople as the New Rome. What is of interest here is the response of the Church of Rome to that claim. It is to be found in an unofficial collection known as the *Decretum Gelasianum*.[26] But first, a brief word about the historical context, without going into too much detail.

The Eastern bishops had reassembled in Constantinople in 382 and had written to Rome to excuse themselves for attending a synod summoned by Damasus of Rome. In their letter they mentioned what they called the distinguished sees of the East: Constantinople ("the new city"), the Apostolic Church of Antioch ("where the venerable name of Christian was first given"), and Jerusalem ("the mother of all Churches") in that order.[26a]

According to the text preserved in the *Decretum Gelasianum* 3, the Synod of Rome responded by pointing to the Petrine foundation of the three sees of Rome, Alexandria, and Antioch. No satisfactory account has been given for this attribution of a Petrine authority to these sees. The scholarly consensus claims that it was an invention of Damasus, perhaps influenced by Ambrose of Milan, who played an important role at the Synod of Rome. For example, A. Michel speculates that, once Nicaea had established these three sees, reasons had to be found to justify this preference, initially on the basis of the mystical number "three," before Damasus took up and developed the Cyprian idea of the Cathedra Petri.[27]

---

[26] See Schwartz, "Zum Decretum Gelasianum," 161–168; T. G. Jalland, *Church and Papacy*, 255–257; Ritter, *Das Konzil von Konstantinopel*, 96–97. See also K. Baus and E. Ewig, *Die Reichskirche nach Konstantin*, 260–262. The claim that *Decretum Gelasianum* 3 is the response of Damasus to the Synod of Constantinople has more recently been disputed; see L'Huillier, *The Church of the Ancient Councils*, 121–122, mainly following F. Dvornik, *Byzanz*, 69–74, who was of the opinion that Damasus was not troubled by the fact that the Bishop of Constantinople was honored by giving him a preeminence second only to Rome. For a more complete account of the Synod of Rome's response to Constantinople, 371, see my article, "Eusebius's Original Ecclesiology," in Sotiris Mitralexis and Andrew Kaethler (eds.), *Mapping the Una Sancta: Eastern and Western Ecclesiology in the 21st Century* (Winchester, 2022).

[26a] Cf. Alberigo, *Conciliorum Oecumenicorum*, 62–63.

[27] Michel, A., "Der Kampf um das politische oder Petrinische Prinzip der Kirchenführung," in Grillmeier-Bacht, *Konzil von Chalkedon*, 491–562.

But the simple answer is to be found in the original ecclesiology of Eusebius, which has been ignored up to now. First of all, *Decretum* 3 stresses that the Roman primacy was not based on any synodal decision but rather thanks to the promise of the Lord to Peter, namely the "Tu es Petrus" (Mt 16:18–19, which is quoted in full). In other words, the primacy is of divine origin. After mentioning Paul's martyrdom in Rome on the same day as St. Peter, the text continues:

> The first see of Peter the Apostle belongs to the Roman church, "having no spot or wrinkle or any such thing" [Eph. 5:27]. And the second see was consecrated at Alexandria in the name of blessed Peter by Mark his disciple and evangelist, and he, after being sent forth by Peter the Apostle to Egypt, preached the word of truth, and accomplished a glorious martyrdom. Moreover, the third see of the most blessed Apostle Peter at Antioch is held in honour because he dwelt there before he came to Rome, and there first of all the name of the new-born race of Christians had its origin.[28]

This is a precise summary of the Apostolic ecclesiology which shaped the original version of Eusebius' *Church History* composed before the outbreak of the Great Persecution, 303.

The extent to which Eusebius was faithful to the traditional ecclesiology inherited from *previous* generations is strikingly illustrated in the way our reconstruction of his ecclesiological presuppositions generally matches the findings of K. Hofstetter: "In the first two centuries, the Petrine office in the Church comes to light as an episcopal continuation in the role of the Bishop of the Mother-Church of the position of Peter within the school of Apostles. Until 62/63 (= the Martyrdom of James) Jerusalem is the Mother-Church, from then on Rome."[31] Should Hofstetter's findings on the whole be acceptable,[32] then we have a further independent check on the general reliability of Eusebius' early "ecclesiology." And indeed, despite certain divergences from the evidence of the earliest witnesses, such as the omission of any reference by Eusebius to Peter's

---

[28] Jalland, *Church and Papacy*, 256–257; footnotes 29 and 30 have been deleted after revision.

[31] Hofstetter, "Petrusamt," 387.

[32] See Ratzinger, *Volk Gottes*, 128–129.

presidency of the (universal) Church at Jerusalem,[33] the basic affirmations of Eusebius' narrative, especially in Books 2–3, closely resemble the oldest evidence, as, for example, the two ideas which, according to Hofstetter, can be traced from the New Testament up to the third century: (i) Before the destruction of Jerusalem, during the Apostolic times, the official Judaism was granted a further opportunity for repentance; the definitive turning point in the matter and the expulsion of Israel out of the Holy Land (gûlûth) first commenced with the persecution of the Apostles. (ii) The present gûlûth of Israel is identified with the Babylonian Captivity.[34] Although it would be useful and illuminating to compare the details of Eusebius' understanding of the Church with that found in the earlier tradition, such an exercise is beyond the scope of this particular study.

It is now time to review briefly the causes for the change which took place in Eusebius' understanding of the Church's constitution. As an apologist, Eusebius' originality consists in his use of the witnesses of tradition to create a history of the Church. He is indebted to previous writers such as Irenaeus, Origen, and Dionysius of Alexandria. He was true to his sources, generally speaking, but only in the superficial way of an ideologist—that is, he failed to see either their limitations or even their deeper implications. One example was his inability to grasp the full meaning of such a major, generally recognized concept as that of *unanimitas*, which when applied to the universally held teaching of the Church signified the *manifestation* of the Church's unity based on the one Apostolic Tradition, but which for Eusebius tended to become the conformity of the majority and so the *cause* of unity within the Church. In general, it can be said that when it suited his apologetic purpose, Eusebius did not hesitate to omit or reinterpret his sources, but only on what seemed to be minor issues. However, the basic inconsistency between his fundamental "axiomatic assumptions" of a material nature as to the working of Providence, and the nature of salvation, to mention but two, and on the other hand his inherited "secondary concepts" of the Apostolic Successions, martyrdom, and the attitude of the Church to the State ultimately conditioned him for a radical reinterpretation of his ecclesiology given the historical and personal situation in which he found himself during and after the Great Persecution.

It seems to me that the transformation of Eusebius' ecclesiology from that of the Apostolic Successions to that of the Imperial

---

[33] See Cullmann, *Petrus: Jünger, Apostel, Märtyrer*, 30f.; Hofstetter, "Petrusamt," 373.
[34] Hofstetter, "Petrusamt," 378.

Church went through four main stages: (i) the preparatory stage marked by the tensions between his ideal Church and that found in the actual documentary evidence (= the original *History*, Books 1–7); (ii) the trauma of the persecutions which shattered his triumphalist concept of the Apostolic Church and which revealed the human weakness of her rulers, especially the Successors of St. Peter (= 1st and 2nd Revisions); (iii) the epoch-making recognition of the Church by the emperors (= 3rd Revision); and finally, (iv) Eusebius' personal humiliation at Antioch, and the spectacle at Nicaea, 325, which moved him to abandon definitively the "Apostolic" Church and, at the same time, converted him to the Emperor Constantine, now recognized by Eusebius as the new Peter, founder of the Imperial Church and source of her authority.

In the development of his thought from the traditional ecclesiology of the Apostolic Successions to the new ecclesiology of the Imperial Church, which took place in the course of the four Revisions, the above analysis confirmed the correctness of Laqueur's observation regarding Eusebius' methodology, namely, that the author of the *History* did not shy away from grafting a new theory onto the old text, and that in doing so he did not always remove the old pieces of the text but rather at times he gave them a new meaning by placing them in a new context, while at other times he simply left them as they were so that occasionally distorted pictures were produced.[35] Eusebius left the original *History* stand, but placed it within a new context and gave it a new orientation, as indicated by the insertion of Aim G.[36]

Eusebius was not an original thinker in the only sense acceptable to the theologian, namely in the sense of one who had the depth of perception needed to penetrate the truths of the Faith and the nature of the Church, handed down from one generation to the next in such a way as to perceive the original teaching of the Apostles, distinguish it from the misunderstandings that arise both from external influences and the limited comprehension of the popular mind, and articulate it in such a clear, systematic, and attractive way that his enquiring readers could rediscover for themselves the original vision of Faith, taste truths which had either been half-forgotten or inadequately articulated up to his day, and uncover new implications for man's understanding of reality, which had not previously been fully grasped. The originality of Eusebius lay primarily in his literary achievement that earned for him the title of Father of Church History and in the apologetic methodology

---

[35]   Laqueur, *Eusebius als Historiker*, 55. See also Lawlor, Eusebiana, 245.
[36]   See above, pp. 14–15.

which inspired that and all his other works, i.e., his use of history in its totality in the service of traditional apologetics. However, it must be added that since one cannot separate form from content, Eusebius' achievement was not simply to have forged a new genre in theological literature but also to have introduced a new understanding of that which he at first set out to defend. But this understanding was original, not in the sense of being true to the original reality, but in the sense of what is known to the Church as a *novum*: the introduction of an idea foreign to the original nature of the Church and the truth she incorporates.

By turning to history to demonstrate the truth of what the Church is and teaches, Eusebius was beating an original path in the wellexplored terrain of apologetics. But he used a faulty compass to direct him—an oversimplified concept of God's intervention in history. His idea of Providence was more suitable to a *deus ex machina*, while his understanding of history was in the last analysis deterministic since he ignored the element of human freedom and its concomitant, human failure.[37] His attempt was doomed to end in failure since he had overreached his own limits: it is the saint alone who can recognize God's action in history and not the philologist or academic historian. Ruhbach maintains that Eusebius' true merit was to recognize, at once, the change that occurred in the years 311 and 313 (the new attitude of the empire to the Church, according to Ruhbach), and to have interpreted them theologically so that the "konstantinische Wende" was seen as a salvific act of God.[38] Apart from our contention that Eusebius' conversion to Constantine only occurred in the year 325, though it had been prepared by his reflections on the persecution and its aftermath, we find it difficult to be able to assent to such a positive assessment of Eusebius' achievement.

Turning to the scattered memoirs of history, Eusebius found it relatively easy to demonstrate how the Church of his day—i.e., at the end of the third century and the beginning of the fourth century—was identical with the Church founded by St. Peter and the Apostles. If necessary, he could select, edit, and omit as it suited his purpose. However, it should not be forgotten that his editing was, considering the enormous quantity of material used by him, relatively small and insignificant, which itself would point to the general trustworthiness of his account of the Church's first three centuries (Books

[37] Ruhbach, *Apologetik und Geschichte*, 138, defends the Eusebian concept of Salvation History as though it were an affirmation of God's sovereignty and freedom in opposition to all human opinion.

[38] See Ruhbach, *Apologetik und Geschichte*, 186.

1–7), even if we had no external means to control it, as well as to his general faithfulness to the Church's understanding of herself at the time he originally sat down to compose the *History*. But his understanding of the Church's Apostolic nature was too rigid—and thus superficial—to cope with the reality of the historical Church he himself experienced (Books 8–10 together with the later interpolations). When his ideas were not confirmed by his personal experience, he slowly but effectively abandoned his original ideas and forged new ones.

But he only abandoned his secondary ideas, i.e., those on the surface of this thought process, not his more fundamental, axiomatic assumptions, which in fact provided him with the intellectual justification for his "development." His formal apologetic aim, to demonstrate God's action in history, made him susceptible to adopt the role of the prophet and attempt to interpret the contemporary events he himself had witnessed all too readily and uncritically. He was a man who not only recognized the spirit of the times, but one who was caught up and swept away by the same spirit, which is not necessarily, if at all, the Spirit of God. His axiomatic assumption of a material character relating to Providence and its direction of the historic process, however, helped to cloud his critical sense, while his deterministic view of history prepared him to conceive the new era, begun by the persecutions and brought to its completion by the sole rule of an emperor who recognized the Christian religion in terms of a new epoch in Salvation History, a new dispensation parallel to the coming of Our Lord. Perhaps the most influential supposition of Eusebius that made him incapable of perceiving the true nature of the Church, and eventually enabled him to become a convert to Constantine and the idea of the Imperial Church, was his understanding of Salvation primarily as enlightenment and civilization, where the Cross of Christ was extrinsic to its nature, as were suffering and martyrdom.

The persecution was a shock to him and the human weakness it uncovered a scandal. Due to his personal experience, he began to interpret the persecution in terms of chastisement and finally as an expression of God's wrath instead of a participation in the Cross and in those sufferings which, according to Col 1,24, complete what is lacking in the sufferings of Christ. The highly spiritualized ecclesiology, which marked his middle period, especially in the 3rd Revision, easily gave way to the Imperial Church that Eusebius finally adopted—once Constantine came to the East, removed the last persecutor of the Church (Licinius), became sole ruler of the empire, and was at work helping to heal the divisions within the Church.

Eusebius, not unmoved either by his own personal humiliation which resulted from his temporary excommunication at Antioch in 324/325, due to his Arian sympathies, or by the condescension of the emperor, who presumably spoke to him at Nicaea, 325, and persuaded him to go along with the rest of the Synodal Fathers against his deepest convictions, saw in the person of Constantine, the ultimate union of civilization, culture, and Christianity.[39] It is difficult to determine to what extent he was mouthpiece of the popular mind—one of the sources of practical or material heresy once it is carried away by the enthusiasm of the day or fossilized in the customs of yesterday—and to what extent he helped to mold that amorphous but very real (and politically relevant) entity. It seems to me that in the original *History*, he articulated commonly accepted traditional ideas, even though he gave them a slightly new emphasis. In the 1st, 2nd, and 3rd Revisions, his own interpretation became more pronounced, and yet he most probably still reflected in general the reaction of the Church, particularly in the Eastern part of the empire, towards the Great Persecution and, after the persecution, the growing recognition by the imperial authority, as was seen in his Panegyric at Tyre, 317. But after Nicaea, 325, he becomes more and more the molder both of public opinion, especially in the East, and, it seems to me, of Constantine's self-consciousness of his role as the Christian Emperor within the new Imperial Church.[40]

While a detailed presentation of the final form of his new ecclesiology, as found primarily in the *Laus* and *Vita Constantini,* would take us beyond the scope of this study,[41] we will in Part Two trace the

[39]   See Opitz, "Euseb von Caesarea als Theologe," 13.

[40]   Straub, "Constantine as ΚΟΙΝΟΣ ΕΠΙΣΚΟΠΟΣ," 50, is of the opinion that "Eusebius was in fact a very competent interpreter, and an effective inspirer, of the emperor's own political intentions and of the concept of his special mission." For a comprehensive account of Eusebius' imperial ecclesiology, see Farina, *L'impero,* 187–255; 269–270, who claims that Eusebius was more influenced by Constantine than the other way around. See my comments in the new Introduction.

[41]   Peterson's *Der Monotheismus* and Berkhof's *Kirche und Kaiser* still remain the classic works, although they have come in for much criticism. Peterson, among others, was sharply criticized by C. Schmitt, "Eusebius als der Prototyp Politischer Theologie," (1970). A more balanced stand is taken by Ruhbach, "Die politische Theologie Eusebs von Caesarea" (1976), and, before him, by Schneemelcher, "Kirche und Staat im 4. Jahrhundert" (1967), who also criticizes Berkhof. The one-sided interpretation of Berkhof is well complemented by the critiques of Aland, "Kaiser und Kirche von Konstantin bis Byzanz" (1960), and Kartaschow, "Die Entstehung der kaiserlichen Synodalgewalt," (1950). See Ruhbach, *Die Kirche angesichts der konstantinischen Wende,* 407–411, for a useful bibliography which, however, must be supplemented by that given by Grillmeier, *Christ in Christian Tradition* (1975), 249–250, footnote 2. Of

effects of his thought on the history of the post-Nicene period, when we
come to analyze the documents of St. Athanasius. There we will see how
the Church, aided by the perception of the great Bishop of Alexandria,
endeavored to come to terms with the effects of Eusebius' *novum* through
its rediscovery of the Apostolic Church within the changed external circumstances of the new general attitude of the empire to the Church.

particular importance is the recently published dissertation by J.-M. Sansterre,
"Eusèbe de Césarée et la naissance de la théorie 'Césaropapiste,'" *Byzantion*
42 (1972), 131–195, 532–594, where the more important works, such as those
of Peterson and Berkhof, are discussed. In the light of the findings above, the
contention of Sansterre that Eusebius only developed his political theology after
the Synod of Jerusalem, September 335, needs to be modified, since the later
ideas, found in their developed form in the oration of Eusebius known as the
Laus Constantini, were already present in the 4th Revision of the *History.* The
decisive date for the birth of the Eusebian "political theology" was the Synod of
Nicaea, 325. However, the Synod of Jerusalem, 335, was of special significance,
since, as we will see, it manifested the implicit recognition, by the bishops there,
of the Eusebian ecclesiology. Sansterre, unfortunately, worked on the theory of
Schwartz, with regard to the date of composition of the *History* and its various
Revisions. Nevertheless, the general result of his study complements the findings
outlined above. He agrees that the author of the *History* was the theoretician
for the Eusebians, not only with regard to their Trinitarian doctrine (against
Eustathius and Marcellus of Ancyra) but also with regard to their ecclesiology. Sansterre argues above all that Eusebius was not so much the precursor of
Caesaropapism (which, he maintains, presupposes a "dualism" between Church
and State) but was rather the author of a theory which *identified* the Church with
the Christian Empire and in which the emperor enjoyed the ultimate authority,
superior even to that of an ecumenical synod. This theory found its fullest expression in the *Triakontaetērikos,* which was delivered by Eusebius before the emperor
at Constantinople after the fateful Synod of Tyre/Jerusalem in 335. With regard
to the later "reception" of Eusebius' so-called political theology (more correctly
termed his imperial ecclesiology), see in particular the critical article by M.
Azkoul, "Sacerdotium et Imperium: The Constantinian Renovatio According
to the Greek Fathers," in *ThSt* 32 (1971), 431–464. Azkoul criticizes such studies
as those of Peterson, Setton, Berkhof, and Dvornik when they conclude that the
Constantinian *renovatio* perpetuated Hellenistic kingship and its link between
monarchy and monotheism, and that the task of translating such kingship into
Christian terms was accomplished by Eusebius of Caesarea, while the Greek
Fathers, as his "disciples," merely extended his thinking. According to Azkoul,
the Greek Fathers in fact fought against the Eusebian (Hellenistic) synthesis of
empire and Church when they articulated their own understanding of the relationship between both entities on the basis of the Chalcedonian confession and
the model of Hebrew kingship. The Greek Fathers, Azkoul maintains, related
sacerdotium and imperium to each other according to the analogy of the two
Natures of Our Lord Jesus Christ, the priesthood being superior to the imperial
authority by virtue of its spiritual function within the empire, as illustrated by
Justinian's *Symphonia,* quoted by Azkoul, pp. 432–433.

Note II
MT 16,18 IN THE WRITINGS OF EUSEBIUS[1]

§1 Eusebius' Original Ecclesiology

In the original *History,* only two references to the Matthean text concerning the Confession of Peter at Caesarea Philippi are to be found. Neither of these stems from the pen of Eusebius, but from the works of his two most revered authorities, Origen and Dionysius of Alexandria. In the course of a series of extracts, which have, as their common theme, Origen's views on the canon of Scripture, Eusebius quotes from the great Alexandrian's fifth *Exposition on the Gospel according to St. John,* where Origen discusses the Epistles of the Apostles. There he says of Peter: "Peter, on whom the Church of Christ is built, against which the gates of Hell will not prevail, has left only one letter that is generally recognized."[2]

Though it is true that in his *Commentary on Matthew*, Origen interprets this text in such a way as to make Peter representative of all "gnostics,"[3] here he interprets the text literally and not allegorically or mystically, and so refers to the historical personality on whom the Church of Christ is built.[4] It is this same literal interpretation

[1] See Ludwig, *Primatworte*, 45–48; Rimoldi, *L'Apostolo san Pietro*, 201–204.

[2] *HE* 6,25,8 (Schwartz 578,1–3).

[3] Cf. *Comm. in Matt.* 12,10 (Klostermann 84,17–86,12). See Ludwig, *Primatworte*, 40–41.

[4] When Origen poses the rhetorical question: "If you consider that the Church as a whole is built by God only on that one Πέτρος alone, what do you say about John, Son of Thunder, or any of the [other] Apostles?" (*Comm. in Matt.* 12,11 = Klostermann 86,15f.), he is not necessarily engaging in a polemical attack on the "Roman doctrine of the Primacy," as Ludwig, *Primatworte*, 41, asserts. See also Eno, "Origen and the Church of Rome," 41–50. It is clear that Origen (and his readers) presupposed the primacy of Peter in the foundation of the Church—otherwise the text makes no sense—and it is possible that he may have wished to criticize the *Alexandrian* claims based on the Petrine Succession there, but it should be remembered that the primary intention behind the passage has nothing to do with the literary sense of the Matthean text that is here alluded to. This passage must rather be understood according to the mystical or spiritual interpretation of Mt 16,18 that Origen uses here. Accordingly, Mt 16,18 is applied to all the "perfect," and not only to Peter, who are likewise to be considered as "rocks" (cf. Klostermann 86,24 and 87,23f.; also, *Comm. in Matt.* 12,10 = Klostermann 86,4–12, where Origen's mystical concept of the Church comes to the fore). That Origen attributed some kind of primacy to the historical Peter can also be gathered from *Comm. in Matt.* 13,14 and 13,31, concerning which Giles, *Documents*, 48, aptly

of Mt 16,18 which is presupposed by Eusebius in his presentation of the foundation of the Church by Peter and the Apostles in Book 2 of the *History,* since the basic thrust of that book tends in the same direction. There Eusebius affirms and illustrates how the foundation of the Church—a mission entrusted to the Apostles—was inaugurated by Peter, their Leader and Spokesman, whose special Divine Dispensation led him to proclaim the Gospel of Light from the East to the West and to definitively establish the Church in the center of the unredeemed world, Rome. Through the agency of Peter, the gates of hell—error and persecution, as represented by Simon Magus and Nero respectively—could not prevail against the Church.

The second reference to Peter's Confession is to be found in a quotation from the work of Dionysius of Alexandria, Περὶ ἐπαγγελιῶν, in which the Bishop of Alexandria attacks the Chiliastic teaching of the Egyptian bishop Nepos.[5] There Mt 16,17 is quoted, according to which Peter is called blessed because of the revelation he received.[6] It is possible that Eusebius alludes to Mt 16,17 in his account of the composition of Mark's Gospel, where he again refers to a revelation Peter received on that occasion,[7] though in fact the nature of the revelation was not the same. Also relevant, is the description of Peter's primary role as προηγορος (Spokesman) of the Twelve.

§2 Eusebius' Ecclesiology in the Middle or Transitional Stage

When Eusebius actually quotes the text of Mt 16,18 himself, his ecclesiology is in its transitional stage. In the *Demonstratio,* composed between 312–320, he quotes Mt 16,15–19 in full. A discussion of the integrity of the authors of Scripture forms the context in which the text is used. As proof of Peter's personal integrity, Eusebius points out how the record of Peter's teaching, the Gospel of Mark, does not contain the full story of the confession at Caesarea, which would enhance Peter's own reputation, whereas the account of Peter's denial and fall is related in all honesty, even though it does not redound to his glory.[8] There we learn nothing more about

comments: "Here Origen definitely believes that Peter held some sort of primacy. His conclusion from the tribute money incident is reasonable, but, though his ideas in §31 are unscriptural and absurd, they show that he is determined to establish a Petrine Primacy somehow or other. . . ."

5 Cf. *HE* 7,24,1f. (Schwartz 684,21f.).
6 *HE* 7,25,10 (Schwartz 694,12–14).
7 See above, p. 43.
8 Eusebius, *DE* 3,5,88f. (Heikel 127,4f.).

how Eusebius further interpreted the text and can but presume that he understood it primarily in the literal sense.

A little later, the reader comes across a passage which is almost a brief summary of Book 2 of the original *History*, and which, like Book 2, seems to allude to the Matthean text. In a rhetorical flourish, Eusebius declares his own astonishment at the Power of the Word, which manifested itself in the multitudes it won for Itself and the multitudinous Churches founded by the unlettered and lowly disciples of Jesus, not in any obscure and unknown place, but in the most noble cities of imperial Rome, Alexandria, and Antioch, and throughout Egypt, Europe, and Asia.[9] It will be first of all observed how Peter is no longer singled out as the founder *par excellence,* as in the *History,* but is assumed into the generic description of the unlettered and lowly disciples of the Lord. And yet the mention of Rome, Alexandria, and Antioch, the three Petrine Churches, indicates that Peter's role in the foundation of the Church, which arose from the promise of Christ in Mt 16,18, is specifically alluded to. However, it is no longer the semilegendary figure of Peter, who "due to his virtues was the Spokesman of all the other (Apostles),"[10] that is here referred to, but the unlettered and lowly fisherman (who needed Mark as his interpreter). The accent is, further, on the *Power of the Word,* who used these poor instruments to achieve his purpose. Eusebius has also abandoned the traditional understanding of Rome as the center of the unredeemed world and now sees it as the imperial city, and the seat of a quantitatively great or large Church. The attention to the Power of the Word and the quantitative or political importance of the main Churches reflect the change of emphasis in Eusebius' thought, due both to his disillusionment with the earlier aetiological interpretation of the importance generally attributed to these Churches, a disillusionment which resulted from the shattering experience of the persecutions, and the new relationship between Church and the Roman Empire which began with the "Edict" of Milan, 313.

In the *Praeparatio,* also written between 312 and 320, Eusebius again gives expression to his wonder at the *Power of God,* this time at work in contemporary history—the manifestation of which was in Eusebius' eyes even greater than that displayed in the historical foundation of the Church. Here the shift of emphasis in Eusebius' interpretation of Mt 16,18, as noted above in the *Demonstratio,* is more clearly discernible:

---

[9]   Eusebius, *DE* 3,7,22 (Heikel 144,9–12).
[10]   *HE* 2,14,6 (Schwartz 138,23).

The Church also which he foretold by name stands strongly rooted, and lifted up on high as the vaults of heaven by the prayers of holy men beloved of God, and day by day is glorified, flashing forth unto all men the intellectual and divine light of the religion announced by Him, and is in no way vanquished or subjected by His enemies, nay, yields not even to the gates of death, because of that one speech uttered by himself, saying: Upon the rock will I build my Church, and the gates of hell shall not prevail against it.[11]

This is a description of the triumph of the post-persecution Church, now basking in the unhoped-for recognition by the highest authorities, as expressed in the "Edict" of Milan. The passage is strongly reminiscent of the sentiments of Eusebius expressed in the Panegyric at Tyre and reflects the spiritualized ecclesiology at this transitional stage. Thus, the Rock on which the Church is built is not Peter but the Power of God, as can be gathered from his interpretation of Mt 16,18 in an earlier passage:

... when He prophesized that His doctrine should be preached throughout the whole world inhabited by man for a testimony to all nations, and by divine foreknowledge declared that the Church, which was afterwards gathered by His own power out of all nations, though not yet seen or established in the times when He was living as a man among men, should be invincible and undismayed, and should never be conquered by death, but stands and abides unshaken, settled, and *rooted upon His own power as upon a rock that cannot he shaken or broken*—the fulfilment of the prophecy must in reason be more powerful than any word to stop every gaping mouth of those who are prepared to exhibit a shameless affrontery.[12]

From this text we gather that the foundation of the Church as a universal Religion is now understood by Eusebius to have been completed by the universal recognition of the Christian Religion by the Emperors (Licinius and Constantine) and thus the prophecies of Mt 28,19 and Mt 16,18 have been fulfilled. The gates of Hell which cannot prevail against the Church are no longer understood to refer primarily to the attacks on the Church by the enemy under the guise of error and heresy but to the sheer brutality of the persecutions which threatened to exterminate the Church physically.

[11] Eusebius, *PE* 1,3,11 (Mras, vol. I, 12,14–13,2). Transl., Gifford, *Eusebii Pamphili*, 9.
[12] Eusebius, *PE* 1,3,8 (Mras, vol. I, 11,21–12,7). Transl., Gifford, *Eusebii Pamphili*, 8–9.

In his *exegesis* of Ps 17,16, the date of which is uncertain but is probably to be counted among his later writings,[13] Eusebius interprets τὰ θεμέλια τῆς οἰκουμένης as referring to the powers of the Divine Wisdom, through whom creation was founded and the world set firm. He immediately goes on to say that if one considers the οἰκουμένη to be the Church of God, then it is Christ who in the first place is the foundation, while the prophetic and Apostolic words are foundations only in a secondary sense.[14] With regard to Christ, he calls on Mt 16,18 to prove his point and interprets the text with the aid of 1 Cor 10,4 and 1 Cor 3,11: Christ is the one and only Rock on which the Church is built, even though the prophetic and Apostolic utterances are, following Eph 2,20, also known as foundations of the Church. It should be noted that Eusebius does not say that the Apostles and prophets are themselves the foundation of the Church (cf. Eph 2,20) but only their *utterances* or teaching, and that only in a secondary sense.[15] The reason for this is most probably his wish to avoid any suggestion of his earlier concept of the Apostolic Successions.

§3 The Later Ecclesiology of Eusebius

How radically Eusebius rejected his earlier dual Apostolic Succession, which was made up of both Apostolic Authority and teaching, in favor of one which consisted in teaching only—ignoring any historico-sacramental link of the contemporary Church with the primitive Apostolic Church—is to be seen in the next text from his writings which deals with Mt 16,18: *Theophany* 4,11,[16] composed around 333. This text records the one occasion when Eusebius explicitly engages in an exegesis of the Matthean text, rather than either alluding to it or drawing on it to help explain either historical events or other scriptural texts. After quoting Mt 16,17–18, he continues:

Dies Wissen (des Simon), daß er Christus sei, der Sohn des lebendigen Gottes, nahm er an und nannte dies ganze Begreifen mit Recht πέτρος, weil es weder zerrissen noch erschüttert wird. Deswegen nannte er auch jenen Mann, eben seinen Jünger, den

---

[13] See Quasten, *Patrology* III, 338.
[14] *Comm. in Ps.* 17,15–16 (*PG* 23,173,C8–176,A13).
[15] Ludwig, *Primatworte*, 44–45, rightly points to the way Eusebius places Eph 2,20 into the background.
[16] Gressmann, 181,15f.

früher (so) genannten Simon: „Petrus" wegen des Wissens, über das
er hinterher prophezeite und sagte: „auf diesen Felsen will ich meine
Kirche bauen, und die Riegel der Scheol sollen sie nicht überwältigen."
Er weissagte zugleich die Zukunft und versprach, sie selber zu bauen
und das Werk zur Vollendung zu bringen dadurch, daß seine Kirche
auf das über ihn verliehene Wissen wie auf einen festen Grundstein
gegründet und gebaut werde allein durch seine Macht in Ewigkeit und
daß die Pforten des Todes sie niemals besiegen würden. Die Erfüllung
zeigte er besser als alle Worte (es darstellen können). Denn Myriaden
Verfolgungen und viele Arten des Todes ergingen über seine Kirche,
vermöchten aber nichts wider sie. . . .[17]

The very awkwardness of the argumentation reveals how Eusebius is
here forcing an interpretation on the text of Mt 16,17–18 which does
not fit. He has rejected the earlier literal interpretation of Origen, which
simply stated that the Church of Christ was built "on Peter"—which
interpretation formed the backbone of his original *History*. As his treatment of Mt 16,18 in the *Praeparatio* and the *Commentary* on Psalm 17
showed, there is but one Rock or foundation on which the Church is built:
Christ, or rather, the Power of God. This idea is also the most important
one in this passage. A little later Eusebius states unambiguously "Denn
nicht durch die Kraft der Menschen und nicht durch die Vorzüglichkeit
der Lehrer wurde seine Kirche gegründet, sondern er, der verhieß und
durch die Tat seiner Verheißung bis jetzt erfüllt hat, er hat in der ganzen
Menschenwelt durch göttliche Kraft den *Bau und das Wachstum* seiner
Kirche befördert."[18] It is the Power of God which is the foundation on
which the Church is built. But Eusebius had to find a way of reconciling this truth with the statement of Mt 16,18. His difficulty is shown in
the way he affirms in the one line how Christ named the *knowledge* of
Peter, πέτρος, while in the next he says that He gave the name of Peter
to Simon, adding that this was because of his knowledge. What is clear
is that the prophecy of our Lord, according to Eusebius, does not refer
to the person or mission of Peter as such: this is the point of the whole
passage. Eusebius' original ecclesiology was based on the literal interpretation of Mt 16,18, but that ecclesiology disappeared in the night of the
persecutions and in its place stands the Church of the "new dispensation," in which the prophecies of Christ have been fulfilled through the
manifestation of His Power in overcoming His enemies (the persecutors)

[17] Gressmann, 181,25–182,5.
[18] Eusebius, *Theoph* 4,11 (Gressmann 182,20–24).

and in securing the establishment of His Church as the one recognized religion of the οἰκουμένη.

Earlier in the *Theophany*,[19] Eusebius comments on Mt 4,18–22, the call of Peter, Andrew, James, and John to become fishers of men, in a way that reechoes a passage in the *Demonstratio* discussed above.[20] Eusebius is again intent on illustrating the way God manifested his Power in those unlettered fishermen:

> Ein Beweis aber für das damals von Simon Vollbrachte sind die bis jetzt leuchtenden Kirchen, die viel voller sind an geistigen Fischen als jene Fahrzeuge, wie es die ist zu Caesarea in Palästina, wie die zu Antiochien in Syrien, wie die in der Stadt der Römer. Denn man berichtet, daß Simon selber diese Kirchen und alle in der Nachbarschaft gründete, und diejenigen in Ägypten, eben in Alexandrien, stellte er ferner selber (freilich nicht durch sich, sondern durch den zum Jünger gewonnenen Markus) für sich auf. Während er nämlich selber in Italien und unter den Nachbarvölkern weilte, machte er seinen Jünger Markus zum Lehrer und Fischer für die in Agypten.[21]

We note that Peter is no longer the Spokesman-Leader of the Apostles, but simply one among others.[22] Neither is he considered to be the founder of the Church par excellence but the founder of individual Churches (Caesarea, Antioch, Rome, and Alexandria), i.e., merely a historical personage who was used as an instrument by the Power of God, the effects of whose works were to be seen not in any special authority to be attributed to them or their bishops, but simply in the large number of "geistige Fischen" (= Christians) who still populated those Churches. There is no allusion to Peter's reputed confrontation with Simon Magus at Rome or to his martyrdom in the city he once understood to be the capital of the unredeemed world.

The final text is from the *Laus Constantini*—a work which is closely related to the *Theophany* just quoted.[23] More specifically, the text is taken from the second half of the *Laus,* which is a treatise composed by Eusebius for presentation to the emperor on the occasion of the Dedication of the Church of the Holy Sepulcher at Jerusalem (335).

The treatise opens with the declared intention of Eusebius "to stand as interpreter of thy (= Constantine's) designs, to explain the

---

[19] Eusebius, *Theoph* 4,6 (Gressmann 170,21–174,16).
[20] Eusebius, *DE* 3,7,22 (Heikel 144,9–12).
[21] Gressmann 173,30–174,5.
[22] See also Gressmann 174,6–16.
[23] See Gressmann xiv–xx.

counsels of a soul devoted to the love of God." He continues: "I propose to teach all men, what all should know who care to understand the principles on which our Savior employs his power,"[24] i.e., the reason for the Incarnation of the preexistent Logos. In other words, he wishes to show Constantine's place in the design of God for the salvation of the world. Thus, the work reaches its climax when Eusebius, having described the coincidence of the Pax Romana with the Advent of Christ, when "two roots of blessing, the Roman Empire, and the doctrine of Christian piety, spring up together for the benefit of man,"[25] jumps to the contemporary history of the Church (when these two roots were absorbed into one under Constantine). There the situation of the post-persecution Church is depicted as the final proof of God's Power at work in the world. The destruction of the Temple and the Jewish Race, which Eusebius contrasted with the foundation of the Apostolic Church at Rome in the original *History,* is here contrasted with the attempted destruction of the Church by the persecutors which failed and in fact ushered in the new era in the history of the Church and of the world:

> Respecting the temple of these wicked men, our Savior said: "Your house is left unto you desolate" (Mt 23,38): and, "There shall not be left one stone upon another in this place, that shall not be thrown down" (Mt 24,2 paraphrased). And again, of his church he says: "I will build my church upon a rock, and the gates of hell shall not prevail against it" (Mt 16,18).[26]

The latter text reminds Eusebius of the promise to Peter and thus he continues:

> How wondrous, too, must that power be deemed which summoned obscure and unlettered men from their fisher's trade, and made them the legislators and instructors of the human race![27]

He then goes on to couple the promise to Peter (Mt 16,18), just mentioned, with the prophecy of Our Lord in Mt 10,18: that his disciples would be brought before kings and rulers for their confession of His name[28] and to show their fulfilment in the recent martyrs, who are now considered the (real) *successors of the Apostles.*[29] Then from the triumph of the martyrs Eusebius makes the sudden transition to Constantine, who, by implication, is the successor *par excellence* of

---

[24] Eusebius, *LC* 11,7 (Heikel 225,16–20). Transl., McGiffert, *Eusebius*, LNPF², 596.

[25] Eusebius, *LC* 16,4 (Heikel 249,17–18). Transl., McGiffert, *Eusebius*, 606.

[26] Eusebius, *LC* 17,8 (Heikel 256,19–23). Transl., McGiffert, *Eusebius*, 609.

[27] Eusebius, *LC* 17,9 (Heikel 256,24–26). Transl., McGiffert, *Eusebius*, 609.

[28] Eusebius, *LC* 17,10 (Heikel 257,1–3).

[29] Cf. Eusebius, *LC* 17,11 (Heikel 257,7–12).

the Apostles, since he has triumphed over every enemy.[30] Finally, Eusebius reaches the climax of his exposition with a rhetorical reference to the *Pax Romana* as the final manifestation of God's Power working in history[31]— not the Pax Augustana but the Pax Constantiniana.[32]

In this passage, then, the Rock on which the Church is built is first and foremost the Power of God, and in a secondary or derivative sense, the instruments He uses to achieve His purpose: Peter and the Apostles who first proclaimed his Law, then the heroic martyrs who endured the attacks of the adversaries through His Power and thus triumphed over them, and finally Constantine, who conquered every enemy through the Power of God and definitively established the universal Peace foretold by the prophets.

---

[30] Cf. Eusebius, *LC* 17,11 (Heikel 257,13–17). He does not mention Constantine by name, but refers to his reign as a manifestation of God's Power: ἀλλὰ βασιλέων εἰς τοσοῦτον αἰῶνα τίς πώποτε κρατῶν διετέλεσεν; τίς δι᾽ οὕτω στρατηγεῖ μετὰ θάνατον καὶ τρόπαια κατ᾽ ἐχθρῶν ἵστηοι, καὶ πάντα τόπον καὶ χώραν καὶ πόλιν, Ἑλλάδα τε καὶ βάρβαρον, ὑπὸ τάττει ἀοράτῳ καὶ ἀφανεῖ δεξιᾷ τοὺς ἀντιπάλους χειρούμενος.

[31] Cf. Eusebius, *LC* 17,11 (Heikel 257,17f.).

[32] See, especially, Eusebius, *LC* 17,14 (Heikel 256,16–20).

PART TWO

The Historico-Apologetic Writings of
St. Athanasius of Alexandria

CHAPTER SIX
Methodological Preliminaries

§1 Basic Approach

There are two ways of attempting to uncover St. Athanasius' understanding of the position occupied by the Bishop of Rome within the universal Church: that of the historian and that of the theologian. Since the turbulent history of this Successor of St. Mark in his battles *contra mundum* brought him into direct contact with three consecutive Successors of St. Peter—Julius I, Liberius, and, to a lesser extent, Damasus—then it is clear that an historical examination of these contacts and their related events should reveal Athanasius' view of Rome's significance. The alternative (theological) approach is based on a systematic examination of the Athanasian texts relating to the Successors of Peter in Rome with the purpose of discovering the theological motives expressed or implied in those references. These two approaches are not mutually exclusive when one considers that the greater majority of the references to the Bishop of Rome in the works of Athanasius are made in connection with historical events in his own life, so that these texts are themselves part of the evidence at the disposal of the historian, while the theologian must interpret the same statements within the historical context that produced them.

The historian, therefore, is constrained to examine texts which, since they stem from the pen of a prominent bishop and theologian, are couched in terms derived from ecclesiastical and theological principles, and thus he is forced to come to grips with the theological issues involved. On the other hand, when evaluating the theological content of such documents, the theologian is forced to enter, however reluctantly, into the hazardous terrain of history in order to clarify the *Sitz im Leben* of what are in the case of Athanasius in particular, occasional writings. This is absolutely necessary in order to help the theologian disentangle the nuances which color and shape Athanasius' understanding and presentation of controversies he was personally engaged in. As a student of theology, my approach must of necessity be the literary/theological one, and it will be the object of this study to bring to light precisely those theological nuances which, for the most part, have been ignored up to now.

But the justification of the approach to Athanasius' ecclesiology adopted here is not only based on the limits imposed on the writer by his own particular discipline. Although the historical events, which form the subject matter of the documents we will attempt to analyze, enjoy a chronological priority before the texts themselves, and the interpretation of those events by Athanasius to be found in them, yet the *Zugang* to these events is only possible to us today by means of these texts, i.e., through the interpretation of Athanasius. The historian has, of course, at his disposal other sources and texts with which he can to a certain extent "measure" the subjective element in the writings of Athanasius. Nonetheless, not only the fact that many of his other sources, such as the fifth-century ecclesiastical historians, Sozomen and Socrates, were greatly influenced by the Athanasian interpretation of the events that surrounded his person in the fourth century, but also the fact that the writings of Athanasius constitute the main primary source for almost half the fourth century, demand that before the historian attempts his reconstruction of the history of the period immediately following the Great Synod of Nicaea with the aid of Athanasius, a thorough examination of the literary and theological character of these documents must be undertaken.

Aware of the subjective element in the writings of Athanasius, most modern historians are content to assume that this is sufficiently taken into account once one posits that these documents were all more or less motivated by self-interest on the part of the powerful Bishop of Alexandria.[1] Even if this were true—and it

---

[1]   See, for example, O. Seeck, "Untersuchungen zur *Geschichte* des Nicänischen Konzils," *ZKG* 17 (1896) 1–71; 319–362. See Rogala, *Anfänge*, 114, who summarizes Seeck's argument as follows: "Der große Vorkämpfer der Orthodoxie erscheint dort als ein Mann, der im Interesse seiner Partei vor keiner Lüge zurückschreckt, selbst nicht vor der offenen Fälschung und der verleumderischen Beschimpfung seines toten Gegners." Seeck was conditioned in his judgement of Athanasius by his basic attitude to Christianity, according to which love of truth was a virtue which Christianity held in poor esteem (cf. Seeck, *Geschichte des Untergangs der antiken Welt*, band. III., 208f. and 442; see also Seeck, "Untersuchungen," 33–34). The attitude of E. Schwartz to Athanasius, which has had—and continues to have—such an enormous influence on Athanasian studies, is well summarized by Baynes, *Byzantine Studies*, 367: "To Schwartz Athanasius was always and in all circumstances the unbending hierarch; ambition, a ruthless will, and a passion for power are his constant characteristics." See also Caspar, *Geschichte des Papsttums* I, 186–187. For a critical analysis of the influence of Schwartz and Seeck, see Arnold, *The Early Episcopal Career*, 11–23.

will become evident that it is, at the very best, only partially true—it will be
obvious that the historian's own subjective attitude to the person and policy
of Athanasius will determine the nature and extent of the "self-interest,"
which it is assumed, colored his presentation of the many epoch-making
events in which he played a major role, or which had such an impact on
his own life and times. For example, E. Schwartz, whose contribution
to Athanasian studies[2] can hardly be judged of less importance than his
major contribution to the study of Eusebius, already acknowledged above,
approached Athanasius with "unverhohlener Abneigung,"[3] which, according
to the editors of his *Gesammelte Schriften*, was not so much directed against
the greatness of his person as against the halo around his head. Deprived
of this halo, Athanasius thus appeared to him as a writer of hate-filled
polemical pamphlets,[4] a power-hungry oriental potentate, unscrupulous in
the means he chose to achieve his supposed ends—the domination of the
Church in Egypt if not the entire East.[5] O. Seeck, previous to Schwartz,

[2]   F. L. Cross in his Inaugural Lecture published as "The Study of St. Athanasius,"
      Oxford, 1945 paid due tribute to the importance of the contribution of Schwartz
      to Athanasian studies despite the fact that the German scholar has since been
      proved wrong on many points (p. 10).

[3]   W. Eltester and H.-D. Altendorf in their preface to the *Gesammelte Schriften* of
      Schwartz, bd. III, vi. See also Schwartz's own comment, *Nachrichten*, 1911, 384
      (= *Gesammelte Schriften*, bd. III, 209).

[4]   "Man darf nicht übersehen, daß die sog. hist. Ar. ein von Haß sprühendes
      Pamphlet ist" (Schwartz, "Zur Kirchengeschichte," 140, footnote = *GS* IV, 15,
      footnote 2). Schwartz dismissed the historico-apologetical works of Athanasius as
      mere "Publizistik" (cf. *Nachrichten*, 1911, 367 = *GS* III, 188), a judgement which
      appears to have been adopted by most scholars since: see Caspar, *Geschichte des
      Papsttums* I, 182; Setton, *Christian Attitude Towards the Emperor*, 78. Szymusiak,
      Apologie a l'empereur Constance. Apologie pour sa fuite, 36, note 1, is slightly less
      derogatory in his judgement when he points out that, "L'évêque d'Alexandrie est
      un publiciste de talent et un polémiste de grande envergure, non sans défauts
      certes, mais d'une éloquence irrésistible."

[5]   Schwartz, *Nachrichten*, 1911, 370 (= *GS* III, 192). See also Caspar, *Geschichte
      des Papsttums* I, 138; Lietzmann, *Geschichte* III, 220f. According to Baynes,
      Constantine the Great and the Christian Church, 6 (and 36), the master key to
      Schwartz's analysis of the personalities of both Athanasius and Constantine was
      provided by the idea of "Der Wille zur Macht," which resulted in a view of both
      men that is essentially inhuman. H. Opitz, the student of Schwartz who provided
      us with the critical edition of most of Athanasius' historico-apologetic writings,
      also saw the Bishop of Alexandria as "eine durch und durch machthungrige
      Persönlichkeit." Even the successor to Opitz in the preparation of the critical
      edition of Athanasius, W. Schneemelcher, who gently censured the approach of
      his predecessor, nonetheless states: "Die Urkunden wie auch die Apologien geben
      ein eindeutiges Bild von dem Treiben des Athanasius, von seinen Intrigen und von
      seinem Machtstreben" (Schneemelcher, "Athanasius von Alexandrien als Theologe

went even so far as to see in Athanasius the arch-forger who in pursuit of his thirst for power and dominance did not refrain from concocting documents to support his claims.[6] The "forgeries" of Seeck have long been recognized as genuine,[7] the judgment of Schwartz has since been modified, and Athanasius' character, as well as his theology, has been partially rehabilitated,[8] but the research on Athanasius and his writings still bears the mark of his most recent defamations.[9] Historians sympathetic to Athanasius and his cause[10] have on their part tended to give perhaps a little too much credence to the literal presentation of the events which marked the life of the Alexandrian bishop, as he himself depicted them, and have likewise given too little attention to the theological significance of his writings.

und als Kirchenpolitiker," 251). However, he attributes it not so much to the reputed thirst for power on the part of Athanasius but to his "non-Pauline" concept of the Church as a "Heilsanstalt, die die Erlösung verwaltet..." (p. 253). This is simply false. Tetz, "Athanasius und die Einheit der Kirche," uncovers the spiritual ecclesiology of Athanasius rooted in oneness with Christ; Tetz also demonstrates how seriously Schwarz erred in his opinion of Athanasius. See also, Larentzakis, "Einige Aspekte," 242–259.

[6]   See above, footnote 1.

[7]   See Rogala, *Die Anfänge des arianischen Streites*; Seiler, *Athanasius' Apologia contra Arianos*, 39–40; Baynes, "Athanasiana," 61–65.

[8]   Regarding the character of Athanasius, see Baynes, "Athanasius," in *Byzantine Studies*, 367–370; Schneemelcher, "Athanasius von Alexandrien als Theologe und als Kirchenpolitiker;" Peeters, "Comment S. Athanase s'enfuit de Tyr en 335," 131–177 (= "L'épilogue de Synode de Tyr en 335," 131–144); von Campenhausen, "Athanasius," 72–85. The renewed interest in the rich theology of Athanasius is witnessed to by several works such as, L. Bouyer, *L'Incarnation et l'Église-Corps du Christ dans la théologie de saint Athanase*, Paris, 1943; G. Florovsky, "The Concept of Creation in Saint Athanasius," in *Stud. Pat.* IV (TU 81), 1962, 36–57; J. Pelikan, *The Light of the World*, New York, 1962; D. Ritschl, *Athanasius: Versuch einer Interpretation*, Zurich, 1964; T. F. Torrance, "Spiritus Creator: A Consideration of the Teaching of St. Athanasius and St. Basil," in Torrance, *Theology in Reconstruction*, London, 1965, 209–228; Ch. Kannengiesser, "Athanasius of Alexandria and the Foundations of Traditional Christology," *ThSt* 34 (1973), 103–113; and, above all, the remarkable work of P. Merendino, *Paschale Sacramentum*, Münster/Westf., 1964. This list is not intended to be exhaustive.

[9]   See, for example, J. Češka, "Die politischen Hintergründe der Homousios-Lehre des Athanasius," especially pp. 305–310.

[10]   Such as Bardy, "La crise Arienne," 144, who, though he warns us not to take the reportage of Athanasius too literally, quotes *Hist. Arian.* 36,1f. as an actual speech of Liberius, although it is in all probability a literary device used by Athanasius. See also Marot, "Les conciles romains," 451–452, and Seppelt, *Geschichte der Päpste*, bd. I, 97, who quotes a "speech" of the Arians, though it is in fact a literary composition from the pen of Athanasius.

Thus, before the documents of Athanasius are used by historians to reconstruct the historical events reported therein, as well as their significance for the history of the Church in the fourth century, they must necessarily be examined by the theologian in order to determine both their precise literary genre and their theological significance. Further, it may be added, the secular historian, if he enters the sphere of ecclesiastical history, must himself grasp the significance of the issues around which the events of the fourth century revolved. To consider these events in purely secular terms of the "power game," and to try to ignore that Power which enables sinful men to transcend their sinful condition and devote their lives in selfless dedication to the revealed truth must, of necessity, lead to a reconstruction that is ultimately based on fiction, i.e., on the projections of the twentieth-century empirical historian armed with his own scale of secular values.

It is then the task of the theologian to draw attention to the importance—at least for the participants—of the actual issues involved in the controversies of the fourth century, and to distinguish, as precisely as possible, between the ideals which motivated the participants in the events[11] and the behavior, at times the ambiguous behavior, of the men who professed such ideals. It is not sufficient to be aware that *aliter dicunt homines ac faciunt.*[12] The student of Church history must consider, with sympathy, the complexity of the human situation where both the pressures of a given political situation—always unique—and/or the more or less inadequate performance of the individual can at times darken or hide the ideal he espouses. This means, effectively, that a purely historical examination or reconstruction of certain events—such as Athanasius' flight to the emperor in the wake of the Synod of Tyre, 335, or his recourse to the Bishop of Rome four years later—can provide, at the most, rather weak indications of the Alexandrian bishop's attitude, either to the emperor or to the pope, and thus must be treated with great reserve when an attempt is made to reconstruct his ecclesiology.

Before we turn to analyze the historico-apologetic writings of Athanasius, we must, therefore, first of all attempt to outline the motivating force or forces in the life and person of the Bishop of Alexandria.

[11] See also Schneemelcher, "Athanasius von Alexandrien als Theologe und als Kirchenpolitiker," 247, who recognizes the need to take the theology of Athanasius as one's starting point.

[12] Setton, *Christian Attitude Towards the Emperor*, 12.

This will take up the greater part of the rest of this chapter. We will then examine the particular hermeneutical principles necessary for an accurate interpretation of these documents according to the mind of their author. We must also take a brief look at the question of the relationship between the writings of Eusebius and those of Athanasius before we actually move on to the analysis of the texts themselves. In the main body of this study, we will concentrate on an examination of the documents with the purpose of discovering Athanasius' understanding of the Church—in particular, his attitude to the Bishop of Rome—as it is reflected in them. An interpretation of the historical events will only be attempted where it is clearly demanded by the interpretation of the text, such as the need to establish the *Sitz im Leben* or to measure Athanasius' interpretation of certain events by comparing it with the events themselves. Otherwise, no effort will be made to trace the history of Athanasius in any detail or in any systematic way. But first let us take a look at the contemporary situation of scholarship with regard to Athanasius' attitude to the Bishop of Rome.

§2 *Status quaestionis*
Apart from passing references to Athanasius' attitude to the Bishop of Rome, to be found in the various histories of the Papacy[13] or in biographies of Athanasius,[14] there are but two studies which treat the question in any detail and both approach it from the standpoint

---

[13] According to Caspar, *Geschichte des Papsttums* I, 138, Athanasius turned to the Bishop of Rome (Julius I) for support, without clarifying the nature of the Alexandrian bishop's motives; but the context indicates that Caspar wished to convey the impression that the recourse of Athanasius to Rome was merely part of his battles, not always waged with the cleanest weapons, to secure his position as the Alexandrian "Pope." It should be noted that Caspar is mainly concerned with the significance which the Athanasius-affair assumed, under the astute direction of Julius in its (to his mind, self-motivated) development towards the later Papacy. Similarly, Jalland, *Church and Papacy*, 212, simply states that, after Gregory of Cappadocia "was solemnly 'provided' by an imperial edict," Athanasius "found it expedient to leave his city and seek allies in the West." Haller, *Das Papsttum*, 66f., goes one step further and depicts Athanasius as the strong man who conducted affairs much to his own advantage in Rome, where Julius fell under his influence. Seppelt, *Geschichte der Päpste*, bd. I, 86f., gives no indication of what the motives of Athanasius might have been.

[14] Möhler, *Athanasius der Große*, 355–356, follows the ancient historians Socrates and Sozomen, and thus gives the impression that the persecuted orthodox bishops, including Athanasius, who laid their cases before Julius of

of the historian; there are no comprehensive studies from the point of view of the theologian.[15] Of the two historical studies, the first forms part of a dissertation presented at Tübingen in 1933 by K. F. Hagel, entitled: *Kirche und Kaisertum in Lehre und Leben des Athanasius.* There, Athanasius' association with the Bishop of Rome is considered within the larger canvas of the Alexandrian bishop's fight to assert the Church's autonomy. According to Hagel, whose work is generally recognized as inadequate though not without value,[16] Athanasius had to do battle against two fronts: the imperial despotism and the papalist aspirations of the Roman bishop.[17] Hagel maintains that only once did Athanasius clearly claim sanctuary at Rome, namely, during the second exile when he turned to Julius I, a move which was prepared by his years in Trier during the first exile and which was brought about by the desperate situation he found himself in at the time—when he was constrained to

Rome, were attracted to Rome by the special dignity of that see (cf. Sozomen *HE* 3,8,3 = Bidez-Hansen 110,27) which the Synod of Sardica clarified as due to its being the See of Peter the Apostle. Apart from noting Athanasius' magnanimous restraint and lack of bitterness in his presentation of the fall of Liberius, Möhler, *Athanasius der Große*, 486, makes no comment on the relevance of this incident in relationship to the attitude of Athanasius towards the position occupied by the Bishop of Rome within the universal Church. Lauchert, *Leben des heiligen Athanasius*, 52–53, simply informs his readers that the Bishop of Alexandria took refuge in Rome in compliance with Julius' invitation to attend a synod there. Regrettably, Lauchert passes over the fall of Liberius in silence—a fact that does not speak well for the quality of his biography. Bardy, *Saint Athanase*, 68f. gives no indication of Athanasius' motives for his journey to Rome.

[15] The treatment of Batiffol, *Cathedra Petri*, 215–229, is exceptional. It was recently reexamined and defended in all but minor points by Winter, "Recourse to Rome," 477–509. Batiffol limited his examination to the appeal of Athanasius to Rome at the time of Julius. See also the references to Athanasius in the study of Monachino, "Communio E Primato Nella Controversia Ariana," 43–78.

[16] Whereas Setton, *Christian Attitude Towards the Emperor*, 54, 72, 74, accepts the findings of Hagel without criticism. Schneemelcher, "Athanasius von Alexandrien als Theologe und als Kirchenpolitiker," 252, footnote 25, describes Hagel's dissertation as "unzureichend und mit schweren Mängeln behaftet." Norberg, *Athanasius and the Emperor*, 7, recognizes that Hagel's work has its merits, but criticizes it for not taking sufficient account of the political events of the time, and for ignoring the decidedly controversial character of Athanasius' writings. Ruhbach justifies the inclusion of an extract from the study of Hagel in his collection: *Die Kirche angesichts der konstantinischen Wende* (Darmstadt, 1976), 257–278, merely on the grounds that it represents the earlier state of research and has its contribution towards the formation of opinion even though it may add little to the knowledge of history.

[17] Hagel, *Kirche und Kaisertum*, iii and 83.

grasp any helping hand. Athanasius, Hagel continues, could not and would not pay the price that was demanded of him by Julius (namely, to recognize the papalist aspirations of the Roman bishop) and therefore he deserted the pope after the Synod of Sardica.[18] Hagel further claims that it was clear to his contemporaries, that such a hero of the Faith could not subordinate himself to Liberius, who displayed such weakness in the decisive hours of Athanasius' battle for a free Church, and that, consequently, the Bishop of Alexandria gave no consideration at that stage to a supremacy of Rome.[19] Neither did the successor of Liberius—Damasus—dare to advocate papalist tendencies in the face of Athanasius.[20]

Of positive merit in the study of Hagel is the attempt to determine at the outset of his investigation Athanasius' understanding of the nature of the Church, her external organization and internal unity.[21] That his evaluation of Athanasius' ecclesiology is gravely deficient will become clear in the course of this study, when we turn our attention to the analysis of the documents themselves. Here it is sufficient to note that his conception of Athanasius' ecclesiology is marred by his failure to take into consideration the understanding of the Church's nature held by previous generations and by his contemporaries, or even the external structure of the Church at the opening of the fourth century.[22] Further, it may well be added that Hagel's own dualistic ecclesiology of external organization and internal unity reflects a post-Reformation dichotomy between matter and spirit, according to which the external organization of the Church is something purely functional, and thus extrinsic to the essential nature of the Church conceived in terms of the inner life of grace. Such a concept has no place in the thought of Athanasius, whose sacramental concept of the Church excludes any such superimposition of two non-related levels.

Also of positive note is Hagel's endeavor to interpret the primary sources at his disposal—the works of Athanasius himself—

---

[18]   Hagel, *Kirche und Kaisertum*, 82–83.
[19]   Hagel, *Kirche und Kaisertum*, 76–77; 82.
[20]   Hagel, *Kirche und Kaisertum*, 77; 82.
[21]   Hagel, *Kirche und Kaisertum*, 1–14.
[22]   The action of the Eusebians in requesting Rome to sanction their nomination of Pistos as the successor to the "vacant" See of Alexandria, as well as the precedents they invoke to justify their actions (the cases of Novatian and Paul of Samosata), reflect this understanding; even, as we will see below, this particular incident involved a new departure from the traditional procedure. Hagel, *Kirche und Kaisertum*, 6–7 incorrectly interprets the incipient patriarchal system, which is clearly discernible in the writings of Athanasius, as an innovation on the part of the Alexandrian bishop.

according to their *Sitz im Leben* and the intention of their author. But unfortunately Hagel based much of his analysis on the thesis proposed by R. Seiler,[23] that one of the major documents, previously known as the *Apologia contra Arianos*, was not composed as a unit at a particular point in time but is the result of several rewritings over an extended period of time,[24] a proposal that has failed, justifiably as we will see, to find recognition.[25] Hagel also took little notice of the literary form employed by Athanasius, either in this or in another major source: the *Historia Arianorum*.[26]

More recently, Ch. Piétri reexamined "La question d'Athanase vue de Rome (338–360)" in a paper presented to the *Colloque de Chantilly* (September 23–25, 1973), which was organized to mark the occasion of the 16th centenary of Athanasius' death.[27] Like Hagel, Piétri's approach is basically that of the historian. His conclusions are also remarkably similar to those of the German scholar, though they differ in the details. Putting aside the related question of Athanasius' relationship to the empire, Piétri reconstructs and analyses the two major incidents in the life of Athanasius which involved the Bishop of Rome. These were: (i) Athanasius' recourse to Rome during the second exile that resulted in the Synod of Rome, 340–341, and its aftermath, the Synod of Sardica, 343; (ii) the so-called Lapse of Liberius. Piétri bases his study on the stated assumption that, since little information about Rome or its bishop is to be found in the writings of the Bishop of Alexandria, Athanasius did not journey to Rome on account of any ecclesiological theory but simply because it was convenient for him at the time in order to establish his rights in the face of stiff opposition. Deprived from the outset of any ecclesiological dimension, Piétri reconstructs the events leading up to the Synod of Rome, and the later developments that climaxed in the Synod of Sardica, primarily in political terms. He claims that due to the reciprocal advantage, both to the Bishop of Alexandria and the Bishop of Rome—the former seeking the only support available to him at the time, while the latter saw in his support for Athanasius

---

[23] R. Seiler, *Athanasius' Apologia contra Arianos (ihre entstehung und datierung)* (Dissertation: Tübingen), Düsseldorf, 1932.

[24] Hagel, *Kirche und Kaisertum*, 18.

[25] Since Opitz, *Untersuchungen*, 158–160, footnote 3, sharply rejected the daring hypothesis of Seiler, the thesis has been abandoned (see Quasten, *Patrology* III, 34–36). See below, p. 292f.

[26] See Hagel, *Kirche und Kaisertum*, 61–62.

[27] The papers were published by Ch. Kannengiesser, *Politique et Théologie chez Athanase d'Alexandrie*, Paris, 1974, 73–126.

an opportunity to extend his ecclesiastical, political influence within the Christian Empire to include the East—an intimate alliance between Athanasius and Julius was entered into, one that climaxed in the Synod of Rome and Julius' gentle but clear assertion of the papal prerogatives. However, at Sardica, Athanasius found other means of engaging the support of the West and thus Julius ceased to be a privileged spokesman for Athanasius. From this point on, Piétri claims, the alliance between the two Apostolic Sees lost much of its warmth. The fall of Liberius finally produced a grave rupture in the relations between Rome and Alexandria.

The weakness of Piétri's reconstruction is to be found primarily in his expressed presupposition that, when he turned to Rome, Athanasius was motivated not by any ecclesiological principle but simply by the exigencies of the political situation he found himself in at the time. Here he displays the influence of Schwartz's prejudgment on Athanasius. He also shares the German philologist's characterization of Athanasius' historico-apologetic writings as inflamed with polemics. His justification for the basic assumption on which his paper rests, namely, the lack of any understanding on the part of the Bishop of Alexandria of Rome's specific theological significance, is as follows. Within the vast opus produced by Athanasius, one can discover, with great difficulty, but one allusion to Mt 16,18. Further, only on one occasion is the city of Rome accorded the title of metropolis, and that in an incidental clause which has nothing to do with its pope.[28] With regard to the allusion to Mt 16,18, Piétri follows J. Ludwig, who in his account of the exegesis of the Matthean text in the early Church mentions only this one allusion,[29] thus giving the (wrong) impression that this is the only allusion or reference to be found in Athanasius. We have already seen how deficient Ludwig's treatment of Mt 16,18 was in the writings of Eusebius. His inadequate treatment of Athanasius will be seen when we examine the position occupied by Peter and his Confession at Caesarea Philippi within the corpus of Athanasius' writings in Chapter Seven. The second text, concerning Rome's status as a metropolitan see, is most probably *Hist. Arian.* 35,2, though Piétri does not give any details of the reference. This text does refer to

[28] Piétri, "La question d'Athanase vue de Rome," 94. He adds: "l'ecclésiologie fondamental ne l'intéresse vraiment que larsqu'il lui convient de fonder en droit sa querelle contre une meute d'adversaire." But surely it is the latter which the researcher must uncover if he is to understand Athanasius' concept of the Church.

[29] Athanasius, *Serap. I*, 28. See Ludwig, *Primatworte*, 47. Piétri also refers to the rather meagre findings of Rimoldi, *L'Apostolo san Pietro*, 204–205.

the Bishop of Rome.[30] It is in fact part of the key-text which will help us discover Athanasius' theological understanding of the position held in the Church Universal by the Bishop of Rome.

§3 The Driving Force of Athanasius' Life: The Final Thrust of His Writings

If we are to examine the historico-apologetic writings of Athanasius in order to determine the intention of the author behind the various statements he makes with regard to the Bishop of Rome, then we must first of all ascertain the general purpose of each writing as a whole, as well as the literary form he chose as his medium to express it. But before attempting any such exercise, we must endeavor to appreciate the driving force of Athanasius' career and the basic aim that underlies all his literary *engagements*. Whereas Eusebius' youth and early concept of the Church were both conditioned by the deceptive Peace of Gallienus, it is not untrue to say that both the character of Athanasius,[31] who was born ca. 295, and his understanding of the nature of the Church and the Faith were molded by the experience of the Great Persecution that raged with all its fury in Egypt during the most impressionable years of his youth. He was never tempted to equate Salvation with civilization, unlike Eusebius, who tended to reduce the meaning of the Cross to an empty emblem. Thus, in the opening chapter of Athanasius' earliest known work, *Contra Gentes*,[32] the Cross is mentioned, not as something additional or

[30] See Ortiz de Urbina, "Patres graeci," 113.

[31] von Campenhausen, *Griechische Kirchenväter*, 72. Bright, "Athanasius," 181, col. A, observes: ". . . his career is best appreciated when we recognize in him the confessor's spirit."

[32] The controversy about the date of the double treatise, *Contra Gentes—De Incarnatione,* which now spans almost three centuries, shows no sign of abatement. The defenders of the early dating, circa 318, first proposed by Montfaucon in his introduction to the first edition of Athanasius, 1698, such as Stülcken, *Athanasiana,* 23 (± 323) and Hoss, *Studien über das Schrifttum*, 85–90 (circa 320), have of late been losing ground to the followers of Tillemont, who in 1702 proposed the years 337 or 346 as the possible date of composition, mainly on the supposition that the author was a writer of experience. For reasons other than those proposed by Tillemont, Schwartz, "Der s.g. Sermo major," 41, footnote 1, together with Thomson in his 1971 Oxford edition of the text (p. xxiii) and, especially, Kannengiesser, "La date de l'Apologie," argue strongly for the period of Athanasius' first exile at Trier as the date and place of composition. (An attempt was made by Nordberg to date the composition around 362, but this has been refuted by Kannengiesser.) For a useful outline of the discussion, see Rondeau, "Une nouvelle prevue de l'influence littéraire," 424–427. The date of the first exile was

peripheral but as the cause or source of Salvation. In the companion volume, as it were, to that work, *De incarnatione*, he introduces a comprehensive discussion of the mystery of Christ's death by describing it as τὸ κεφάλιον τῆς πίστεως.[33] Consequently, suffering and persecution can be expected by the true follower of Christ, not external peace and riches.[34]

A few months before his fifth exile, Athanasius in his 37th *Festal Letter* for the year 365 (preserved in a Coptic fragment) puts into the mouth of the Arians words which could well have flowed from the pen of Eusebius: "If your faith were upright, then why do they persecute you, why is the Church repeatedly disturbed? We, however, we live in peace and think as it pleases us to think. And we have become rich, without opposition from anyone."[35] On the other hand, Athanasius reveals his own attitude in his 29th *Festal Letter* (for the year 357 and also only preserved in a Coptic fragment). Written during his third and most severe exile, Athanasius assures the faithful that God does not abandon His people when they suffer unjustly, but that He consoles them in His own way: "He speaks to those, who for the sake of the faith suffer violence;

rejected by van Winden, "On the Date of Athanasius' Apologetical Treatises," *VigChr* 29 (1975), 291–295 on the basis of *C. Gentes* 6 and *De incarn.* 2, where Athanasius refers to "the heretics" but evidently does not mean the Arians. Thus, maintains van Winden, at the time of writing, Athanasius did not think of Arianism as a heresy; the double treatise must therefore be dated early in the career of the writer. This argument of van Winden is not too convincing. The text reads: οἱ ἀπὸ τῶν αἱρέσεων = some heretics, namely those who had erred on the doctrine of creation (such as the Marcionites). In my opinion, the arguments of Hoss, *Studien über das Schrifttum*, 85–90 in favor of a date around the year 320 have not been overruled by the proponents of a later date. Hoss argues that the term ὁμοούσιος is not used where one would expect it (e.g., *C. Gentes* 46 fin.), were the double tract composed after Nicaea. He also points to the evident unanimity of Christians assumed by Athanasius (*De incarn.* 46 and 49), which could only describe the situation in the Church prior to 320 (or between 325 and 330). The light polemics against the Arians, which Hoss detects (*De incarn.* 32; 47; 55), indicate an early phase in the controversy before Nicaea, as does the apparently fresh memory of the Great Persecution (cf. *De incarn.* 28 in particular), to which could be added the equally fresh remembrance of the apotheosis of Diocletian (*C. Gentes* 9). An early date is also suggested, according to Hoss, by the impression left with the reader that the author's study of Plato was of recent vintage and that his theology is in its infancy. Hoss finally points to the absence of any reference to monasticism. Egypt seems to be the place of composition. See also Meijering, *Orthodoxy and Platonism*, 104–113.

[33] *De incarn.* 19,4 (Kannengiesser 336). See also *Vita Ant.* 74–75 (*PG* 26,945, B2–949,A8).

[34] Cf. *Vita Ant.* 79 (*PG* 26,952–953).

[35] Merendino, *Osterfestbriefe*, 86; cf. *Vita Ant.* 79.

for all that he allows us to fight, so that we can prove ourselves as having been tested."[36] Here there is no trace of Eusebius' angry God who punishes a wayward Church in order to purify it, but rather the mystery of redemptive suffering where the innocent suffer: "... for, having tested them as 'gold in the furnace,' as Wisdom affirmed, God found them worthy of Himself."[37]

"When one experiences the need for help in the form of affection or in the form of recognition by one's acquaintances, it is that then God—since He is good and that which He does, He does for our salvation—puts His servants to the test, and He does so frequently."[38] This text was written at the time when Athanasius, excommunicated by major synods in the East and in the West, was divested of all official recognition apart from that accorded to him by the Bishop of Rome and a relatively insignificant number of fellow-bishops who had accepted exile rather than subscribe to his condemnation. At the time he wrote this (357), he could hardly have realized to what extent he was to be put to the test. Approximately a year later, news arrived in Egypt that the Bishop of Rome had apparently abandoned both Athanasius and the Nicene cause. That incident belongs to a later chapter. Let us for the moment return to the two texts from the 29th *Festal Letter,* just quoted, since they provide us with pointers which can help us detect the driving force of Athanasius' life.

"He speaks to those, who for the sake of the faith suffer violence." This firm assurance of God's presence in the midst of persecution is developed more fully in what must be the most attractive and profoundly spiritual works of Athanasius, his *Apologia de fuga sua*, which was composed a few months after the 29th *Festal Letter* in the year 357. Basing his defense for his flight before his persecutors on the axiom that a certain time has been allotted to each man,[39] a time to live and a time to die (Eccl 3,2), which is hidden from the mind of man but revealed by the Spirit,[40] Athanasius argues that before their appointed death or martyrdom, the saints, following the example of the Lord, had a duty to flee their enemies,[41] not on the pretext of cowardice, since in fact they were subject to severe sufferings, but so that, thus purified and found worthy of God,[42] they

---

[36]   Merendino, *Osterfestbriefe*, 76; see also the beautiful text from the 28th *Festal Letter* (356) in Merendino, *Osterfestbriefe,* 69–71.

[37]   *Serap.* 3,5–6, as quoted in *De fuga* 19,3 (Opitz 81,16–17).

[38]   Merendino, *Osterfestbriefe,* 76–77.

[39]   Cf. *De fuga* 14,1–15,5 (Opitz 78,1–79,12).

[40]   Cf. *De fuga* 17,1 (Opitz 79,30).

[41]   *De fuga* 16,1–18,5 (Opitz 79,13–81,9).

[42]   *De fuga* 19,1–3 (Opitz 81,10–22).

might the more effectively teach the people.[43] Such a flight, then, is part of God's (οἰκονομία),[44] according to which the saints of old were graced with unique personal revelations by God before they returned to their people in order to do God's mighty deeds: like Jacob, who when fleeing was favored with divine visions, or like Moses, who during his exile saw the great sight in the burning bush, or David, who was consoled by God.[45] For the N.T., Athanasius instances St. Paul, who being persecuted and fleeing before his persecutors, was caught up into the third heaven in order to enable him to fully preach the Gospel from Jerusalem to Illyricum."[46] There are three points worth nothing here: (a) external suffering and persecution effect a purification in God's servants; (b) but this is complemented by interior graces from God, who reveals himself to the persecuted and infuses them with new power; (c) suffering and divine consolation have the same end, which is the proclamation of the Gospel and the actualization of God's saving deeds. These three points can be considered as a type of self-confession on the part of Athanasius. They can provide us with the key to his character and the fundamental motives of his writings.

a) Athanasius the Man

Athanasius was first and foremost a saint.[47] This self-evident fact needs to be asserted in the face of the doubts cast on his character which have been so generally, if only tacitly, accepted in recent times.[48] Having said this, one must add an explanatory word about

[43] *De fuga* 20,1–21,5 (Opitz 81,23–83,11).

[44] *De fuga* 19,3 (Opitz 81,20–21).

[45] *De fuga* 20,1–4 (Opitz 81,23–82,10). Cf. the parallel passage in *De fuga* 18, 1–4 (Opitz 80,23–81,4). This parallelism illustrates the methodology of Athanasius, who in his "repetitions" treats the same subject from two different sides, the one complementing the other in such a way that the second statement uncovers the deeper meaning of the first, while the second statement receives its full significance only in the light of the former.

[46] *De fuga* 20,5 (Opitz 82,11–16). Cf. the parallel text *De fuga* 18,5 (Opitz 81, 5–9).

[47] See bishop Gregorius, "The Significance of Saint Athanasius for the Coptic Orthodox Church," in Kannengiesser (ed.), *Politique et Théologie*, 21–27. See also Lauchert, *Leben*, 137.

[48] To appreciate the change of attitude towards Athanasius, compare the description of the saint's character by Robertson, "Prolegomena," lxvi–lxviii, who in 1891 affirmed that "In the whole of our minute knowledge of his life there is a total lack of self-interest," with the portrait of Češka, where Athanasius is described as placing his personal advantage above fundamental questions ("Die politischen Hintergründe der Homousios-Lehre des Athanasius," 307–308). Češka is aware of the lack of credibility which ought to be attached to malicious rumors (p. 307), but justifies his acceptance of such slanderous

sanctity, since it is a concept that almost invites distortion and misunderstanding. It does not imply that a man was and is, at all times, perfect, but that he, a sinner like all men, became holy in the course of his life and grew into that perfection which is Christ. That Athanasius knew himself to be a sinner and in need of perfection, and consequently in need of purification, is precisely the first of the three points to be gathered from his "self-confession" outlined above. The importance of this observation lies in its implications for the study of his life and actions. It means that the student has no need to gloss over any imperfections which the documentary evidence might seem to indicate, and indeed that he should have the courage to paint a picture of the saint that includes "the warts and all,"[49] once he is convinced that such exist.

Although extremely able and talented, Athanasius was still a young and inexperienced man when he mounted the throne of St. Mark on June 8, 328. Despite his training and preparation in the chancellery of Alexandria as secretary and deacon to his predecessor, St. Alexander, he had few ready-made answers to the host of problems that confronted him in the bewildered state of an Egyptian Church in the process of recovery after years of persecution where a major heresy had its home, and where after an uneasy peace the rigorist Meletians (the "Church of the Martyrs") again lapsed into schism.[50] Apart from these major questions, and the plethora of pastoral and administrative problems which the Great Persecution threw up, Athanasius had to face an entirely new situation that the Church, as a whole, was unprepared for—namely, the new status of a Church which enjoyed the ambiguous protection and recognition of the imperial authority.

He was by nature a strong personality who commanded a penetrating intellect, coupled with a superb memory that had been cultivated by a broad education in philosophy and theology,[51] and who

gossip with the hollow, and historically groundless, generalization to the effect that we would possess even more such rumors if the works of the Arians had been preserved, as though the quantity of malicious rumors made them more credible! However, it would be false to conclude that all modern scholars shared the same opinion. Pelikan, *The Light of the World*, 77, for example, underlines the moral character of Athanasius, though he is a little too optimistic when he claims that even historians and theologians unsympathetic to orthodox beliefs are obliged to concede the same.

[49] Baynes, "Athanasius," in *Byzantine Studies*, 370.
[50] See Norberg, *Athanasius and the Emperor*, 10–13; Bardy, "La politique religieuse de Constantin," 526–527.
[51] Gwatkin, *Studies*, 72–73, footnote 2; Bardy, "Athanase d'Alexandrie," in *DHGE* IV, 1316–1317.

was not unskilled in the art of rhetoric and legal debate.[52] As a deacon, he evidently left his mark at Nicaea though probably not in the actual assembly,[53] and like every great man instilled either admiration or revulsion in those he encountered, but never indifference.

A scholar generally sympathetic to the greatness of Athanasius accused him of being "a persecutor and a man of violence who was always complaining of the violence of others."[54] And yet the evidence for this is slight and mostly *ex parte*. Apart from the rather generalized accusations of his enemies, the only substantial evidence seems to be that offered by a Greek papyrus preserved in the British Museum, recently dated May-June 335, which is a letter from one Callistus, a Meletian monk, who wrote to a fellow schismatic and blamed bishop Athanasius for an attack made on one of the schismatic gatherings by the local police.[55] The apparent

[52] "Both Gwatkin, *Studies*, 71, and Bardy, "Athanase d'Alexandrie," *DHGE* IV, 1316, remind us of the claim of Sulpicius Severus—that Athanasius cultivated the study of law. Whatever the historical truth of this, it is clear that the historico-apologetic writings of Athanasius bear all the marks of a mind well skilled in legal debate (whether due to natural ability or training is relatively unimportant). This observation was also made by Baynes, "Athanasius," in *Byzantine Studies*, 368. See also Bright, "Athanasius," 180, col. B.

[53] See the *Letter of the Synod of Alexandria, 338,* preserved by Athanasius, *Apol.* 6,2 (Opitz 92,6–7). See also Socrates, *HE* 1,8,13 (Hussey 39–40); *HE* 1,23,2 (Hussey 130); Sozomen, *HE* 1,17,7 (Bidez-Hansen 38,13–14); Theodoret, *HE* 1,26,2 (Parmentier-Scheidweiler 81,1–4). The ancient historians apparently based their accounts, at least in part, on the reference found in the *Letter of the Synod of Alexandria*, the historical credibility of which cannot be doubted considering the fact that so many of the participants at the Synod of Nicaea were still alive. See Lauchert, *Leben*, 25–26; Bardy, "Athanase d'Alexandrie," in *DHGE* IV, 1318, stresses the limited influence which could have been exercised by the young deacon. See also de Clercq, *Ossius of Cordova*, 232, footnote 61 for literature.

[54] Baynes, "Athanasius," in *Byzantine Studies*, 368; also, Williams, *Arius*, 239.

[55] See Bell, *Jews and Christians*, 53–71. Authors who find in Bell their justification for giving more attention to what were previously considered mere calumnies than would normally be warranted, and thus use them as historical evidence, tend to forget the very limited conclusion of the English scholar: "We must conclude that there was a germ of truth in the picture given of Athanasius by his enemies as a self-willed, unruly man, apt to treat even the imperial authority with contempt" (p. 57). It may be added that Bell here betrays his own criteria for judging the person of Athanasius: it seems that the final extent of Athanasius' self-will was his apparent contempt for the "imperial authority." That authority was in Athanasius' eyes legitimate, indeed even sacred, but it was limited and secondary to the dictates of conscience and to the divine authority entrusted to the Church. To the emperor and to the Eusebian party, Athanasius must indeed have appeared self-willed and "unruly," as he did to Bell. For a full examination of Bell's

silence of Athanasius in the face of such charges has been interpreted by a number of modern historians as an implicit admittance of guilt. This silence, however, could and perhaps should be otherwise interpreted: the absurdity of such accusations did not call for a refutation. It is of note that this is basically the reply of the Synod of Alexandria, 338 (and thus the reply of Athanasius himself), when the Synodal Fathers categorically rejected the various accusations.[56]

The caricature of Athanasius as a man of violence is contradicted by his own words, written while in exile in Trier, to the Church of Alexandria in his 10th *Festal Letter* (for Easter, 338), where he encourages his flock to look on their persecutors as friends, to imitate the forgiveness of David, the meekness of Jacob, and the pity of Joseph towards those who had inflicted evil on them, and above all to follow the example of Our Savior, who grieved for those who do such things.[57] Attention should also be drawn to the later Athanasius, who, when he had been restored to his see after his third exile and enjoyed what his enemies had misused against him up to then, namely, the sympathy of the emperor instructed his devoted followers not to mock or ridicule their former enemies since God alone has the right to judge, but to adopt a noble demeanor towards those who had caused him and his followers so much suffering.[58] Perhaps the most revealing action which betrays his fundamental generosity and true greatness, that is, his greatness of heart, is his magnanimous gesture of friendship to those who had formally condemned him, once he was convinced of their sincere motives and fundamentally orthodox intention—this gesture was first made in his work *De synodis*.

Sanctity is not some kind of vague goodwill to all men that, under the guise of toleration, appears to transcend the principles and

---

generally fair evaluation of the British Museum Papyrus, 1914, see the balanced comments of Peeters, "Comment S. Athanase s'enfuit de Tyr en 335," 141–143. Simonetti, *La Crisi Ariana*, 115, places the evidence of the document in its historical context in such a way as to make the charge quite plausible. For a detailed and balanced analysis of Bell's findings, see Arnold, *The Early Episcopal Career*, 62–89.

[56] Cf. Athanasius, *Apol.* 5,1–5 (Opitz 90,41–91,32). See the sober judgement of Gwatkin, *Studies*, 74: "As for the charges of perfection, we must in fairness set against the Meletians who speak through Epiphanius (*Haer.* 68,7) the explicit denial of the Egyptian bishops (*Apologia contra Arianos* 5). And if we are to take into account his own pleas for toleration and the comprehensive charity of *De synodis* and of the Council of Alexandria, we must pronounce the charges disproved.

[57] Robertson, *Athanasius*, LNPF[2], 529–530.

[58] Cf. the 36th *Festal Letter,* in Merendino, *Osterfestbriefe*, 82–83.

convictions for which other men give their lives but which is itself often intolerant of such men. Sanctity, considered solely as a human phenomenon involves precisely such a tenacious perseverance in the living out in the deepest recesses of the soul that truth whose authority is God alone, and in the courageous public witness to the truths revealed in Christ.[59] Such perseverance and courage Athanasius displayed in his life-long turbulent confession of that Faith he knew to be handed down to him from Christ through the Apostles and the Fathers.[60]

When it was clear what was expected of him, then he pursued his goal with an iron determination. This singularity of purpose is perhaps his most striking characteristic as a man. But early on in his career as a bishop, Athanasius had to come to grips with a situation, for which there were no precedents to guide his actions. He was commanded by the emperor to appear before, what was in effect, an Imperial Commission, though it was primarily composed of bishops: the so-called Synod of Tyre.[61] When we come to examine that event in some detail later on, the ambivalent nature of that assembly will become more evident, where the bishops who controlled the meeting, the Eusebians, "put forward the name of a synod [yet] ground its proceedings upon [the authority of] an Emperor."[62] There Athanasius found himself face to face with the Imperial Church of Eusebius, who may possibly have been president of the assembly.[63] The actions of Athanasius before, during,

---

[59] See Lauchert, *Leben*, 134.

[60] Athanasius, *Ep. encycl.* 1,8 (Opitz 170,14–18); *Ad epp. Aeg. et Lib.* 20 (*PG* 25,585,B14–15); *Ad Adelph.* 6 (*PG* 26,1080,A11–B1). See also 2nd *Festal Letter*, 330 (Robertson, *Athanasius*, LNPF², 510–512 = Larsow, *Fest-Briefe*, 64–70).

[61] This is clear not only from the objections to Tyre made by the Synod of Alexandria, 338 (cf. *Apol.* 8,3–4 = Opitz 94,10–17), but also from the *Letter of Constantine* summoning the Synod of Tyre and preserved by Theodoret, *HE* 1,29,1–6 (Parmentier-Scheidweiler 83,10–85,4), where the emperor, although warning the bishops to act impartially and in accordance with ecclesiastical and Apostolic norms, makes it clear on whose authority the synod was summoned, and who was finally responsible for order at the assembly—the Consular Dionysius. Compare *Apol.* 71,2 (Opitz 149,1–4). For a full discussion, see below, p. 355f.

[62] Athanasius, *Apol.* 10,1 (Opitz 95,26). Translation, with slight adaptation, from Atkinson, LNPF², 106.

[63] See Robertson, "Prolegomena," xxxix; Gwatkin, *Studies*, 90, footnote, follows Lightfoot, who cast doubt on the presidency of Eusebius of Caesarea at Tyre, and suggests that Flacillus of Antioch presided. But Flacillus is not mentioned in this connection by any primary source. Lightfoot probably used *Apol.* 81,1 (Opitz 161,1) to justify his suggestion. There, a letter from Count Dionysius to the Synod of Tyre is quoted; the name of the Antiochene bishop is quoted

and after that event, as well as the legal debates which it generated, will form the subject matter for a substantial part of the following chapters. Due to the general currency of Schwartz's theory that the driving force of Athanasius' life was political ambition, we must therefore take a brief look at the more general question of his attitude to the State, or rather to the imperial authority.

It is only partially true to maintain that Athanasius was born into the Imperial Church order which he accepted as a given fact and to which he adhered for the rest of his life.[64] Though it can be presumed that he shared the general euphoria within the Church that accompanied the end of the persecutions and the recognition of the Church by the State,[65] yet it is surprising that his double apologetic work, *Contra Gentes—De Incarnatione,* which may have been written as early as ca. 320, displays no sign of such unbridled enthusiasm for the new state of affairs as can be found in Eusebius' Panegyric delivered at Tyre around the year 317. On the contrary, Athanasius is solely preoccupied with the recent powerful witness to the Faith in Christ borne by the martyrs during the persecutions.[67] How little Athanasius in comparison with Eusebius evaluated the recognition by the empire as a *conditio sine qua non* for the spread of the Christian religion can be gathered from a passage in the *Vita Antonii,* which was presumably written around 358,[68] i.e., around the time

there at the opening. This reference is of little significance since the text, as we have it, is but a fragment, probably not from the opening of the letter, and contains what appears to be an "aside"—a passing reference to a conversation Dionysius had with Flacillus. Apart from the text normally used to prove the presidency of Eusebius (*Apol.* 8), attention may be drawn to the *Letter of the Synod of Tyre to Constantine* (Socrates, *HE* 1,33), which betrays the hand of Eusebius.

64   von Campenhausen, *Griechische Kirchenväter,* 72.

65   However, I find no evidence to support the contention of Barnard, "The Date of S. Athanasius' Vita Antonii," 173, who is of the opinion that in the early part of his career Athanasius "held substantially Eusebius of Caesarea's view of the Emperor." The evidence provided by Barnard is not convincing. So also, the importance attributed by Hagel (*Kirche und Kaisertum,* 11–14) and Setton (*Christian Attitude Towards the Emperor,* 72f.) to the comparison Athanasius makes between God's relationship to Creation and the emperor's presence in a city is greatly exaggerated; this analogy used by Athanasius must be taken for what it is—an analogy—and not as evidence of the young writer's attitude to the emperor. Footnote 66 has been deleted after revision.

67   For example, *De incarn.* 28,1–5 (Kannengiesser 366–367). See Hoss, *Studien über das Schrifttum,* 87–88, who refers to this text as one of the indications that the apologetic work is a product of the young Athanasius.

68   This is the date given by Quasten, *Patrology* III, 39. Barnard, "The Date of S. Athanasius' Vita Antonii," *VigChr* 23 (1974), 169–175, attempted to define the date of composition more precisely and suggested late 357 or early 358. Barnard worked on the assumption that the *Vita* was written for private

when the persecution of the orthodox by the Arians, backed by the Emperor Constantius both in the East and in the West, had reached its climax. There he asks: "When has the knowledge of God shone so brightly [as now]?"[69]

At Nicaea (325) he witnessed the great spectacle of a synod that aimed to be universal both in intent and in its external form. Up to then, synods of necessity were regional in their composition. The universal claim made by synodal judgments was only implicit and so required their "reception" by the rest of the Church, usually by means of *Letters of Communion*. For the first time in the Church's history, the universal claims of synodal judgements were explicitly manifest in the physical assembly itself, due solely to the patrimony of the emperor, who alone could make such a meeting physically possible. But one will search in vain among the writings of Athanasius for even the slightest indication that the presence of the emperor, which so overawed the learned Bishop of Caesarea, had in any way influenced that unique assembly of bishops. If Athanasius were our only source for the history of that synod, then we would have to conclude that Constantine was not even present at the momentous event.[70] At Nicaea, the intentions of the bishops and the emperor coincided.

Elected to the See of St. Mark three years later, Athanasius was soon to experience the danger inherent in the imperial patronage. When the emperor began to interfere directly in the affairs of the Church by demanding the admittance of Arius, or at least those ostensibly sympathetic to his cause, to communion at Alexandria,[71] the young Bishop of Alexandria refused. His refusal to obey the

circulation and claims that the attitude of Athanasius to the emperor—cool and reserved—reechoes that found in *De fuga* and contrasts strikingly with the attitude found in *Hist. Arian*. The basic assumption of Barnard was rejected by Brennan, "Dating Athanasius' Vita Antonii," *VigChr* 30 (1976) 52–54, who insists that the work was composed for public circulation and could have been written before, during, or after *Hist. Arian*.

[69] *Vita Ant.* 79 (*PG* 26,953,A13).

[70] See Higgins, "Two Notes," 238f.; de Clercq, *Ossius of Cordova*, 237. In my opinion, the implications of this insight for the history of the Synod of Nicaea have yet to be worked out.

[71] *Apol.* 59,5 (Opitz 140,1–4); Socrates, *HE* 1,27,1–6 (Hussey 142–144). The theory of Norberg, *Athanasius and the Emperor*, 19–21, deserves serious consideration. According to the Finnish scholar, Constantine instructed Athanasius not to prevent the reintegration of the Meletians into the Church, which Athanasius refused to do on the basis that the Meletians and Arians were in contact with one another. However, as our analysis will show (see below, p. 346f.), it appears that Athanasius only became aware of the alliance between the Meletians and Eusebians (= Arians) at a later date, while its full implications first manifested themselves at Tyre, 335. Barnard, "Some Notes on the Meletian Schism," 399–400, points out that the alliance between both

emperor demonstrates Athanasius' courage of conviction. It also contradicts the assumption that he accepted the imperial order, into which he
was born, simply as a given fact.

The increasing interference of the emperor in the affairs of the Church
after Nicaea,[72] motivated by what seems to have been a genuine desire on
the part of Constantine to establish peace within the Church, not only
for political considerations but due to his religious convictions,[73] was
greeted with enthusiasm by Eusebius of Caesarea and his namesake of
Nicomedia.[74] As we will see, the theory of the Imperial Church, worked
out by Eusebius during the final revision of his *History*, was in fact being
translated into terms of practical politics. For example, Eusebius in his
account of the deposition of Eustathius of Antioch (the principal defender
of Nicene orthodoxy in the East)[75] attributes the authority of the synod,
which deposed the Bishop of the Apostolic See of Antioch and over which
he probably presided,[76] to the emperor.[77] In fact, the actual intervention of
the emperor only occurred sometime after the deposition in connection
with the election of a successor. That intervention, it is claimed, was the
first indication of the emperor's new policy of direct intervention in the
affairs of the Church.[78] At least seven other bishops of the Nicene conviction were likewise removed from their sees by imperial rescripts,[79] one

parties was originally of a political nature; only later did the Meletians, at least
some of them, adopt Arian tenets.

[72] See Bardy, "La politique religieuse de Constantin," 516–551, especially 532–537;
also, Rahner, *Kirche und Staat*, 78–84.

[73] See, e.g., Baynes, *Constantine the Great and the Christian Church*; Straub,
"Constantine as ΚΟΙΝΟΣ ΕΠΙΣΚΟΠΟΣ," both of whom drew attention to
this quality of the emperor; see, especially, Girardet, *Der Kaiser und sein Gott*.

[74] It is my conviction that Constantine was in turn greatly influenced by the
theoretician of the *Reichskirche*, Eusebius of Caesarea, whom the emperor
evidently respected.

[75] See Sellers, *Eustathius of Antioch*, 39f. See also Schwartz, "Zur Kirchengeschichte,"
159–160 (*GS* IV, 39–40), who draws attention both to the connection of
Eustathius with the "Samosatene" community in Antioch, the παυλιανίσαντες,
and to his apparent success in helping the See of Antioch acquire impressive
political power. Is it possible that Eustathius attempted to restore the prestige of
Antioch, or rather its primacy in the East, due to its Petrine Succession? See also
Bardy, "La politique religieuse de Constantin," 528–533. With regard to the date
of the Synod of Antioch, which deposed Eustathius, see Hess, *Canons of Sardica*,
148–150, where he argues convincingly for the latter half of the year 328.

[76] Sellers, *Eustathius of Antioch*, 44.

[77] See Eusebius, *VC* 3,59,1–5 (Winkelmann 111,24–112,21).

[78] Batiffol, *La paix constantinienne*, 372; Bardy, "La politique religieuse
de Constantin," 532.

[79] βασιλικοῖς γράμμασι; cf. *Hist. Arian.* 5,2 (Opitz 185,14–19).

of whom, at least, Asclepas of Gaza, was deposed at a synod that was again presided over by Eusebius of Caesarea.[80] When Athanasius was summoned before the Synod of Caesarea (334), he refused. Theodoret maintained that the refusal was based on Athanasius' fear of his judges.[81] He had reason to fear them.[82] In any case, the repeated insubordination of the young Bishop of Alexandria irked Constantine, as can be gathered from the letter of the emperor summoning the bishops to Tyre, threatening anyone who might dare to disobey—meaning Athanasius—and appointing the Consul Dionysius to keep order at the meeting.[83]

Against his will, Athanasius set out for Tyre.[84] When he realized how justified his fears were regarding the composition of the assembly, made up of those who were at enmity with him and the Nicene Creed,[85] he then made the mistake of going to the source of that synod's authority, the emperor—a decision apparently taken with little reflection and forced upon him by desperate circumstances, where, as Sozomen informs us, his life was in danger.[86] Due to the ambiguous nature of the Synod of Tyre, his enemies could (and did) later claim that he had flaunted ecclesiastical authority by appealing to the emperor. It appears that he went to Constantine to procure a genuine ecclesiastical synod or, failing that, to seek at least a hearing from the emperor for his defense with regard to charges which included indictments of a civil nature.[87] Since he had unwillingly travelled to Tyre only at the behest of the

---

[80]   See Bardy, "La politique religieuse de Constantin," 533.

[81]   Theodoret, *HE* 1,28,3 (Parmentier-Scheidweiler 82,22–83,3).

[82]   See Lauchert, *Leben*, 41–43; Norberg, *Athanasius and the Emperor*, 21–27, for an account of the intrigues of the Eusebians against Athanasius.

[83]   The text of the letter is preserved by Eusebius, *VC* 4,42,1–5 (Winkelmann 136,20–138,9); Theodoret, *HE* 1,29,1–6 (Parmentier-Scheidweiler 83,10–85,4). See also Socrates, *HE* 1,28,1–4 (Hussey 149–150). "Cette lettre expose très clairement l'attitude de l'empereur: malgré les déclarations que nous avons pu noter ici où la, Constantin ne se reconnaît pas la droit de juger un évêque: il confie ce soin au council, mais il est persuadé que tout se passersa selon ses désires" (Bardy, "La politique religieuse de Constantin," 542). See also Baynes, "Athanasiana," 60.

[84]   *Apol.* 71,2 (Opitz 149,3–4). Cf. *Letter of Constantine* convoking Tyre (Theodoret, *HE* 1,29,1–6 = Parmentier-Scheidweiler 83,10–85,4, and par.). See also the *Letter of the Egyptian Bishops at Tyre* to the other bishops assembled there = *Apol.* 77,2 (Opitz 156,26).

[85]   See *Letter of the Egyptian Bishops at Tyre* = *Apol.* 77,2f. (Opitz 156,24f.).

[86]   Cf. Sozomen, *HE* 2,25,14 (Bidez-Hansen 86,12–14). See Peeters, "Comment S. Athanase s'enfuit de Tyr en 335," 166. See also *Letter of the Synod of Alexandria*, 338 = *Apol.* 3,3 (Opitz 89,12–13).

[87]   *Letter of the Synod of Alexandria*, 338 = *Apol.* 9,2 (Opitz 95,3–8).

emperor, then he was forced, by the logic of the circumstances, to place his defense in the hands of same emperor once a just hearing at Tyre turned out to be an impossibility.[88] Whatever the emperor thought of the charges brought against Athanasius by the Eusebians, the only way Constantine could deal with this independent spirit was to subject him to temporary exile.[90]

His exile at Trier provided Athanasius with time to reflect on the "Synod" of Tyre and its implications. As we will later see, from this time on the Bishop of Alexandria, thus purified by his exile, began to grasp anew, and to formulate more explicitly, the necessary distinction between the imperial and the ecclesiastical or Apostolic Authority. I am not convinced by the claim that, at the outset of his career, Athanasius shared the same attitude to the emperor as Eusebius of Caesarea. It would be more correct, it seems to me, to recognize that the attitude of the young Bishop of Alexandria was akin to that of the early Church articulated, for example in the writings of St. Irenaeus and Tertullian.[91] Those writers, following Rom 13,1–7,[92] affirmed that all political authority has its ultimate source in God and so deserves the obedience of all men, including Christians, insofar as the wishes of the prince do not conflict with the conscience of the Christian. The implications of the new situation of the Church, due to her recognition by the emperor—characterized on the one hand by the ambivalent attitude of Constantine due to his admixture of benevolence and totalitarianism, and on the other due to the creation of an essentially new ecclesiological understanding of the Church's nature by Eusebius and the utilization of same by his namesake, Eusebius of Nicomedia—only became clear to Athanasius with the debacle at Tyre and its aftermath.

---

[88] This is the argument of the Egyptian bishops at Tyre in the *Letter to Count Dionysius* = *Apol.* 79,2 (Opitz 160,5–9) and repeated by Athanasius, circa 20 years later (*Apol.* 86,1 = Opitz 164,12–14). Lietzmann, "Die Anfänge des Problems Kirche und Staat," 11, gravely misrepresents this action, when he claims: "It was precisely Athanasius, who refused to recognize the legal power of this ecclesiastical judgement and demanded a direct imperial decision. The same Athanasius, who in later times appears as champion of ecclesiastical freedom in opposition to the browbeating of the State, had in person introduced into the Eastern Church the appellation from the ecclesiastical to the civil court." Footnote 89 has been deleted after revision.

[90] See Rogala, *Anfänge*, 93–94; also, Batiffol, *La paix constantinienne*, 387. "L'ambition de l'empereur était de montrer son authorité et de la faire réguer sur l'Église aussi bien sur l'Etat" (Bardy, "La politique religieuse de Constantin," 545).

[91] See Batiffol, *La paix constantinienne*, 7–26.

[92] See Schlier, *Römerbrief*, 386–393.

Suffering and persecution were, for Athanasius, the occasion of a purification and deeper penetration of the truth he professed and defended, not
only in the sphere of the Christological and Trinitarian dogmas, but also in
his ecclesiology. The context of his reflections on the relationship between
Church and empire was the institution of the synod. The synod, then, was
the arena where Athanasius, armed only with the traditional understanding
of the Apostolic Church and his unshakable faith in Christ,[93] grappled
with the totalitarianism of the empire on the one side and on the other,
with the temptation on the part of the Church to compromise her message
and her freedom for the sake of the peace of this world that the emperor
seemed to offer.[94]

b) Athanasius the Saint

The driving force of Athanasius' life and writings can only be fully understood when one goes beyond the personal characteristics of the man to the
core of his being—his life in union with God. His model here was the great
mystic, St. Antony the Great, whose *Vita* he wrote not only from hearsay
but evidently from personal experience of that great saint.

In the opening pages of his early work, *contra Gentes,* he describes the
end for which man was created and to which he was restored by Christ:
the contemplation of God face to face.[95] This Antony had, to an eminent
degree, achieved and so Athanasius later held him up as an example to be
imitated.[96] The Synodal Fathers of Alexandria (338) described Athanasius
as "one of the ascetics."[97] This need not imply that he had spent a type of
novitiate in the desert prior to his service in the Church of Alexandria, as
was once assumed from a textual variant in the introduction to the *Vita*

---

[93]   Cf. *Vita Ant.* 65 (*PG* 26,936,B5–15).

[94]   Caspar astutely observed: "In the course of the fourth century, the institution
       of the synod became the ground, on which, for the first time the powers of State
       and Church competed with each other . . ." (Caspar, *Geschichte des Papsttums* I,
       136).

[95]   *C. Gentes* 2 (Thompson 6–8). See Roldanus, *Le Christ et l'homme*, 25f.

[96]   See, for example, *Vita Ant.* 14 (*PG* 26,864,B9–C4) and compare this text with
       Vita Ant. 20 (*PG* 26,873,A6–B12), where the thought of *C. Gentes* 2 is reechoed
       (see Ritschl, *Athanasius*, 41–42, who however fails to appreciate the meaning of
       the "natural" or pure soul and its virtues, i.e., the soul in its original, grace-filled
       condition). See also *Vita Ant.* 7 (*PG* 26,853,B11); *Vita Ant.* 34 (*PG* 26,893,B1–7);
       Vita Ant. 39 (*PG* 26,900,B1–2); *Vita Ant.* 60 (*PG* 26,932,A9); *Vita Ant.* 65
       (*PG* 26,933, C2–936,B15); *Vita Ant.* 66 (*PG* 26,936,C5); *Vita Ant.* 67 (*PG*
       26,937,C1–940, B9); *Vita Ant.* 73 (*PG* 26,945,A8–9). See Steidle, "Homo Dei
       Antonius," 154.

[97]   *Apol.* 6,5 (Opitz 92,26). See commentary of Opitz on this text.

Antonii,[98] but it does bear witness to his early renown as one obviously devoted to the spiritual life.[99] Both his later association with Antony[100] and his evident insight into the inner life of the "man of God" *par excellence*[101] cannot be explained in mere political terms. They reveal a basic sympathy of mind and heart between two truly great men, whose greatness had its source in God. However, it is not only Athanasius' reputation as an ascetic, nor his association with St. Antony which allows us to catch a glimpse of his soul. It is his insistence in the *Apologia de fuga sua* on the mystical graces received by the saints of the O.T. and the N.T. who suffered persecution that reveals the intimacy of Athanasius with Him, for whose truth he suffered and fought so tenaciously and courageously.

In the desert during the third exile, where he was stripped of all human support and encouragement, Athanasius wrote to his severely persecuted faithful not to despair but to trust absolutely in God: "For the love of God surpasses that of men: the works of men have an end, the goodness of God, however, never ceases."[102] He can quote the words of St. Paul with confidence: "But in all these things we are more than conquerors, for nothing shall separate us from the love of God" (Rom 8,35–37).[103] In his darkest hour—after the Synods of Arles and Milan, under the pressure of the State-backed Arian party, had abandoned his cause, and after Liberius of Rome and Ossius of Cordova had finally weakened under the combined pressure of the Arian party and the imperial power,

---

[98] "Probably," according to Lauchert, *Leben*, 5–6; 35–36; 137. On chronological grounds, Gwatkin, *Studies*, 106 (following Tillemont) rejects the possibility of an early association of Athanasius with Antony. See also Bardy, "Athanase d'Alexandrie," in *DHGE* IV, col. 1317. Much more convincing is the textual argument of Hertling, *Antonius der Einsiedler*, 7–9 (footnote 1), where he demonstrates how the probable reading of the Proem to the *Vita Ant.* (*PG* 26,840,A5–9) argues against such a possibility: διὰ τοῦτο ἄπερ αὐτός τε γινώσκω (πολλάκις γὰρ αὐτὸν ἑώρακα), καὶ ἃ μαθεῖν ἠδυνήθην παρὰ τοῦ ἀκολουθήσαντος (*al.* παρ᾽ αὐτοῦ ἀκολουθήσας) αὐτῷ χρόνον οὐκ ὀλίγον, καὶ ἐπιχέοντας (*al.* ἐπιχέων) ὕδωρ κατὰ χεῖρας αὐτοῦ κτλ. See also Quasten, *Patrology* III, 40.

[99] Commenting on ἕνα τῶν ἀσκητῶν, Loofs, Athanasius von Alexandria, 197, observed: "What of course this only means is that he belonged to the band of those who devoted themselves in very dissimilar ways to the crowd of ascetics in the community."

[100] Cf. *Vita Ant.* 69–71 (*PG* 26,941,A4f.). See Hertling, Athanasius als Einsiedler, 9–10; Tetz, "Athanasius und die Vita Antonii;" Tetz, "Athanasius und die Einheit der Kirche," 214f.

[101] According to Tetz, "Athanasius und die Einheit der Kirche," 216–217, *Vita Ant.* 91 is a precis of Athanasius' spirituality.

[102] Merendino, *Osterfestbriefe*, 78.

[103] Cf. *De fuga* 20,5 (Opitz 82,12–13).

and so subscribed to his excommunication and deposition—Athanasius could write: "Our Savior, who was also left alone and exposed to the plots of his enemies, has also given us an example, so that if we, while persecuted, should be abandoned by men, we might not become fainthearted, but place our hope in Him and betray not the truth. For although at first the truth may appear to suffer affliction, yet those who persecute it will later recognize it."[104]

The source of such extraordinary conviction and confidence can only be the Truth, Christ Himself, whom he had encountered in a unique way, known as mystical, and in whose Body, the Church, he knew himself to be a participant. For Athanasius, the truth he defends, i.e., the divinity of Christ, was not simply the tradition he had received from "the Fathers," who in turn had received it from the Apostles and whose source was the historical Christ,[105] but also the experience of his personal faith, his *fides qua creditor,* which had been tried in the crucible of suffering.

Athanasius reports that St. Antony "said in private that in the life of the great Elijah the ascetic ought always to see his own as in a mirror,"[106] since Elijah was a man who lived daily in the presence of God, obedient only to His Will, and who preserved that purity of heart,[107] which is the final condition required "to see God."[108] Athanasius was true to his spiritual father. Later, he himself held up the Prophet Elijah as an example to Dracontius[109] and, when he was called upon to justify his own flight, he again pointed to the example of "the great Elijah" among others.[110] Indeed the comparison he makes between Lucifer of Cagliari and Elijah could more aptly be made with reference to himself.[111] Thus it is not surprising to see him turning to the life of the great O.T. man of God in order to find solace and encouragement at that moment in his life when the forces of evil seemed to have triumphed, that is, when the Bishop of Rome was forced to sign his condemnation and the one-time president of the Great Synod of Nicaea was compelled to subscribe to a *credal formula repugnant* to the Nicene Faith. Athanasius,

---

104 *Hist. Arian.* 47,3 (Opitz 210,27–30).

105 Cf. *Ep. encycl.* 1,8 (Opitz 170,14–15).

106 Cf. *Vita Ant.* 7 (*PG* 26,853,B13–C1).

107 Cf. *Vita Ant.* 7 (*PG* 26,853,B6–B13).

108 Mt 5,8. See *C. Gentes* 2 (cf. above, footnote 96).

109 Cf. *Ad Dracont.* 7 (*PG* 25,532,A13–14); *Ad Dracont.* 8 (*PG* 25,532,C8).

110 Cf. *De fuga* 10,6 (Opitz 75,18–20); *De fuga* 17,1 (Opitz 79,31–80,1); *De fuga* 18,4 (Opitz 81,3–4); *De fuga* 20,4 (Opitz 82,6–10).

111 See *Ad Lucif. II* (*PG* 26,1184,C14–1185,A7). Footnote 112 has been deleted after revision.

speaking in the third person singular, assures his readers, the Egyptian monks, that the enemies of Christ in their foolishness did not perceive that, by using force on Liberius and Ossius, "they were exhibiting not the deliberate choice of the bishops but the violence they themselves had applied, and that, should the brethren abandon (Athanasius), should friends and acquaintances stand afar off, and no one be found to console and comfort (him), yet far above all these, a refuge with God is all sufficient. For Elijah, while persecuted, was alone and God was to the holy man all in all."[113]

The driving force in Athanasius' life is not, therefore, der Wille zur Macht, as Schwartz believed, but the Power of God present in and to his soul. This, the Spirit of God, is also the source of his theology. In a discussion between Antony and certain "philosophers," Athanasius puts into the mouth of the great man of God the rhetorical question: how can one arrive at knowledge of God? ". . . through rational argument or the operation of faith? and which is better, the Faith that arises from the divine operation or the argument worked out by reason?"[114] When the philosophers opt for the former, Antony praises them: "You have spoken well, since Faith arises from the proper disposition of the soul, while dialectic merely rests on the skill of its inventors."[115] Echoing St. Paul, he affirms: "We Christians preserve the Mystery not in the wisdom of Greek logic but in the power of faith bestowed on us by God through Jesus Christ."[116] The proper disposition of the soul is that purity of heart by which we see God.

That Athanasius achieved this intimacy with God—the summit of contemplation, as the hymn of the Greek Church for his feast day claims[117]—is best documented by his dogmatic writings, most of which were composed either during or after his third exile,[118] when he was tested to the limits of human endurance and God was to him all in all. How else can one explain the acute awareness of God's transcendence that permeates his dogmatic writings[119] and the equally vibrant consciousness of His Spirit's immanence in the

---

[113] *Hist. Arian.* 47,2–3 (Opitz 210,22–26); cf. *Or. C. Ar. III,* 47 (*PG* 26,421, C1–424,C2).

[114] *Vita Ant.* 77 (*PG* 26,952,A1–3).

[115] *Vita Ant.* 77 (*PG* 26,952,A6–8).

[116] *Vita Ant.* 78 (*PG* 26,952,B1–4); cf. 1 Cor 1,17.

[117] Quoted by Lauchert, *Leben,* 145.

[118] See Quasten, *Patrology* III, 26–27; Shapland, *The Letters of Saint Athanasius concerning the Holy Spirit,* 16–18. See below, Chapter Eight, footnote 100.

[119] See, e.g., Bouyer, *L'Incarnation et l'Église,* 37–38; 47–48; 61–62; Florovsky, "The Concept of Creation," 36–57.

Church, in her members who are infused with His life,[120] and in her Scriptures which He inspired.[121] Likewise, it is not merely some theory which made Athanasius so sharply aware of the role played by the Holy Spirit in the enlightenment of the faithful,[122] so that he can describe eternal life itself (salvation) in terms of divine illumination.[123]

Athanasius, however, was by the same token sensitive to the inadequacy of man's own apprehension of the mysteries God has revealed to us, an inadequacy he tells us that is due to the weakness of the flesh.[124] In his *Letter to the Monks*, Athanasius comments on some of the epistemological problems which arise from reflection on the truths of the Faith. He writes: "Since the more I desired to write, and forced myself to think about the Divinity of the Logos, so much the more did the knowledge [of it] recede from me; the more I seemed to have grasped it, all the more I knew myself to be deprived of it. And that which I seemed to understand, I was unable to write; but also, what I wrote was less than the weak shadow of the Truth which was in my mind."[125] If his union with God is the final source of Athanasius' theology, then it can be said with equal truth that this passage holds the secret of its depth, its certainty and its capacity to develop, as indeed happened with regard to his Trinitarian theology after the third exile, and as happened with his ecclesiology, as will be seen.

But Athanasius did not devote his life and risk death for his own private vision, his subjective version of the truth. What he defended was, in the first place, the Apostolic Teaching which was originally proclaimed in the Scriptures, handed on from one generation

---

[120] Cf. *Serap. I,* 22–24 (*PG* 26,581,C3–588,A3). See Laminski, *Der Heilige Geist,* 72–78; Shapland, *The Letters of Saint Athanasius concerning the Holy Spirit,* 122, footnote 9; 125, footnote 1. Cf. also *Serap. I,* 31 (*PG* 26,601,A7–605,A6); Laminski, *Der Heilige Geist,* 84. Even more impressive are the references to the activity of the Holy Spirit in the soul, as found in the *Festal Letters* and the *Commentaries on the Psalms* (see Laminski, *Der Heilige Geist,* 111–113 and 117–119 for references to the texts). See also Merendino, *Paschale Sacramentum,* especially 73–81.

[121] See Laminski, *Der Heilige Geist,* 106–110.

[122] Cf. *Serap. I,* 19 (*PG* 26,573,C8–D3); *Exp. in Ps. 75,5* (*PG* 27,341,D1–3). See Laminski, *Der Heilige Geist,* 67 and 119.

[123] See Pelikan, *The Light of the World,* 57–91; 98f.

[124] *Ad monach.* 2,2 (Opitz 181,22–23).

[125] ὅσον γὰρ ἐβουλόμην γράφειν καὶ νοεῖν ἐβιαζόμην ἐμαυτὸν περὶ τῆς θεότητος τοῦ λόγου, τοσοῦτον ἡ γνῶσις ἐξανεχώρει μακρὰν ἀπ᾽ ἐμοῦ καὶ ἐγίνωσκον ἐμαυτὸν τοσοῦτον ἀπολιμπανόμενον, ὅσον ἐδόκουν καταλαμβάνειν. καὶ γὰρ οὐδὲ ὃ ἐδόκουν νοεῖν ἠδυνάμην γράφειν, ἀλλὰ καὶ ὃ ἔγραφον ἔλαττον ἐγίνετο τῆς ἐν τῇ διανοίᾳ γενομένης κἂν βραχείας τῆς ἀληθείας σκιᾶς (*Ad monach.* 1,2 = Opitz 181,10–14).

to the next by the "Fathers," the successors of the Apostles, and in his own
day authoritatively defined by the universal episcopate represented at
Nicaea, 325.[126] The theology of his youth found in the double apologetic
work, *Contra Gentes—De Incarnatione,* was sharpened and deepened
by the Confession of Faith defined by Nicaea, as can be observed in his
Orationes contra Arianos, where his object was to demonstrate how the definition of Nicaea articulated the fundamental thrust (σκοπός) or meaning
of Scripture, or in *De decretis* and *De synodis,* where he demonstrates the
identity of intention between the "Fathers" and Nicaea. In the writings of
Athanasius which we will examine, it should become clear that the immediate aim of Athanasius is to help his readers to discern where exactly this
objective authority is to be found. His own personal conviction is insufficient, of itself, to justify the stand he took in the Arian conflict. What
the subjective condition of his soul enabled him to do was to enlighten
the mind so as to truly penetrate and articulate clearly those mysteries of
the Faith which are revealed in Christ and which were entrusted to the
Apostles and their successors.[127] Here, then, is the cause of Athanasius'
originality as a theologian: he could remain faithful to, and penetrate even
more deeply, the original Apostolic Teaching because he himself was one
with the source of that tradition, Christ Jesus Our Lord.

It is here also that we will discover the moving power behind
his "Kirchenpolitik," namely, his consciousness of his responsibility before God as a bishop. To him, as to all bishops, the heritage
of God (τὸν κλῆρον τοῦ θεοῦ) had been entrusted and not wealth or
political prestige due to the greatness of the city where his Church
sojourned.[128] This trust was both the Apostolic constitution of the
Church and the Apostolic Faith, which the bishops as "stewards
of the mysteries of God" (1 Cor 4,1) are duty-bound to preserve and

---

[126] Cf. *De decr. Nic.* 27,4–5 (Opitz 24,4–15); see also *Ep. encycl.* 1,8 (Opitz 170,14–
15); *Ad epp. Aeg. et Lib.* 20 (*PG* 25,585,B14–15).

[127] Cf. *De incarn.* 56–57 (Kannengiesser 464–469), where Athanasius stresses the
absolute necessity of having the right subjective dispositions in order to apprehend the objective truth of Scripture. See Möhler, *Athanasius der Große*, 109–110.

[128] Cf. *Letter of the Synod of Alexandria,* 338—*Apol.* 6, 7 (Opitz 93,5–7). Here
the bishops criticize the ambitions of Eusebius of Nicomedia, who had been
transferred from the comparatively insignificant See of Berytus to the Church of
Nicomedia, the imperial residence in Bithynia. See the earlier criticism of Bishop
Alexander of Alexandria, who mentioned this irregularity in his *Encyclical to All
Bishops* (*Urkunde* 4b,4 = Opitz 7,4–6), circa 319.

defend.[129] His relationship to his own Church of Alexandria can be deduced from the *Letter of the Synod of Alexandria* (338), where the ties which bind a bishop to his Church are said to be closer than that of a man to his wife.[130] This responsibility for the flock entrusted to him,[131] and for the Church Universal of which they were part, is the driving force of his life and of his involvement in what could be called, inadequately, Church politics. By way of comparison, attention could be given to missionary bishops of our own day who have to contend with the fluctuating political situation if they are to remain true to their responsibilities towards their faithful.

Athanasius never once refers to himself as the Successor of St. Mark, or indeed to any association between Alexandria and Mark (or Peter), although, as we have seen in our analysis of Eusebius' *History*, such a tradition must have been widespread in Egypt and in the East at the beginning of the fourth century. Yet it cannot be denied that vestiges of such a primatial consciousness, which found its theological justification in the Marcan tradition regarding its foundation, are to be discerned in the history of Athanasius.[132] If the young deacon's elevation to the See of Mark was accompanied by the very human weakness of ambition, the difficulties and sufferings which accompanied his episcopate from the very beginning of its forty-five years up to the final decade, including five exiles, must have refined it into non-existence, as they would have purified any intemperate zeal that may have marked the early stages of his awesome responsibilities.

The contention that the bishop's ambitions were not so much of a personal nature but were rather invested in asserting the primacy

---

[129]   Cf. *Ep. encycl.* 1,8 (Opitz 170,12–18). See also *Apol.* 17,4 (Opitz 100,8–10); *Ad Dracont.* 3 (*PG* 25,525,C12–D5).

[130]   *Apol.* 6,7 (Opitz 93,9–13).

[131]   See, for example, Athanasius' instructions to Dracontius: "It is therefore necessary that you know and be in no doubt that, whereas before your election [to the episcopacy], you could live for yourself, but once elected, you must live for those who elected you. Before you received the grace of the episcopate, no one knew you, but, after becoming (a bishop), the people expect you to bring them nourishment, namely the teaching of the Scriptures" (*Ad Dracont.* 2 = *PG* 25,525,A14–B4).

[132]   See, for example, the action of Athanasius in ordaining the Apostle to the Ethiopians, St. Frumentius, and sending him to evangelize Ethiopia (cf. Duchesne, *Histoire III*, 576–578). The *Letter of Constantius II to the Ethiopians*, preserved by Athanasius in *Ad Const.* 31, gives some insight into the primatial (or incipient patriarchal) authority exercised by the Bishop of Alexandria. Cf. *Ep. encycl.* 1.8 (Opitz 170,12–18). See also *Apol.* 17,4 (Opitz 100,8–10); *Ad Dracont.* 3 (*PG* 25,525,C12–D5).

of the See of Alexandria in Egypt if not in the entire Orient, as it will be remembered Schwartz held, has no foundation whatsoever. As we saw in our analysis of Eusebius' *History,* Alexandria's eminence was second only to Rome and was recognized as such in the East long before Athanasius was elected bishop, as was reflected in the Canons of Nicaea. Athanasius had no need to try to promote something that was already an accepted fact. It would be more correct to say that Eusebius of Nicomedia, as we will see, attempted to neutralize the primacy of Alexandria in the East in order to establish a new primacy based on the *political* importance of a city. That Athanasius opposed him and his ambitions, as his predecessor did, is natural; it cannot be interpreted as though it arose from any inordinate ambition. When Athanasius, and the Nicene cause he championed, eventually won general recognition, we find not the slightest trace of any attempt on his part to use this so as to further the influence of Alexandria. He simply appears to have recognized the traditional hierarchy of Rome, Alexandria, and Antioch.

c) *Athanasius the Pastor*

We have now arrived at the third point of Athanasius' "self-confession" as I have called it: the suffering which purifies and the consolation that God alone gives to his beloved are not ends in themselves but are means to promote the fuller proclamation and actualization of God's saving deeds.[133] This is Athanasius' overriding pastoral concern[134] and it is the final intention behind almost all of his writings. The *Festal Letters* most obviously manifest the deep pastoral concern of the Bishop of Alexandria; whether in season or out of season, in Egypt or in exile, he ceaselessly continued to instruct, exhort, warn, and console, right up to the end of his life,[135] the flock entrusted to his care. The *Vita Antonii* was not written as a rhetorical exercise in the adaption of Greek literary forms to Christian hagiography, though it was also that; it is aimed at the spiritual well-being of its readers, who are ceaselessly encouraged "to imitate" the saint[136] and who are, at the same time, instructed on how to distinguish between the Apostolic Faith and its heretical

---

[133] Cf. *De fuga* 20–21, in particular 21,2 (Opitz 82,21–25); also *Ad Dracont.* 8 (*PG* 25,532,B12–C12).

[134] Cf. Möhler, *Athanasius der Große*, 109; Duchesne, *Histoire II*, 168; Kannengiesser, "Athanasius von Alexandrien. Seine Beziehungen zu Trier," 145–147.

[135] Fragments of most of his letters up to 371 have been preserved in either Syriac or Coptic, as well as a few in Greek.

[136] Cf. *Vita Ant.,* "Proem" (*PG* 26,837,A8f.).

misinterpretation in a way that the more popular mind could easily grasp.

His early incursions into the literary and theological fields—long before he became a bishop—had an apologetic purpose, similar to that of the early Eusebius, which was: to lead his (Christian) reader to a deeper grasp of his Faith by means of an extensive discussion of the objections raised by pagans and Jews. The difference between Eusebius and Athanasius could be said to be similar to the difference between the propagandist and the philosopher; the former tries to bolster his reader's convictions with a mass of evidence, while the latter tries to lead his reader to a deeper understanding of the writer's own convictions. The great dogmatic works of Athanasius, such as the three *Orations against the Arians* and the *Letters to Serapion on the Holy Spirit*, are not polemical pamphlets but rather superb attempts to uncover the shallowness and unacceptability of the Christological or Pneumatological opinions of his opponents, and at the same time to open up the richness of the Apostolic Faith. He takes, as his starting point, the objections of his opponents and tries to argue from their point of view so as to lead them from there into the depth of the Nicene Faith. *De synodis* is characterized by his endeavor to work out criteria that would help his readers to distinguish between the genuine, authoritative synod and those that carry no weight of authority. To provide his persecuted and confused followers with guidance that would enable them to recognize where the genuine, authoritative witness to the Faith was to be found in the turmoil created by the State's violent intervention in the internal affairs of the Church, he wrote his so-called *History of the Arians,* as we will see in Chapter Ten. The pastoral aim in all Athanasius' works could be summed up as his concern to help his readers to exercise their "discernment of spirits,"[137] that is, to enable the readers to test the spirits of the times with regard to the events which took place in the Church and to distinguish the Apostolic Teaching from the errors of the age in which he lived.[138]

Athanasius' awareness of the profound mystery that he, by virtue of his office as Successor to St. Mark, was called upon to expound and to defend, together with the tremendous pastoral responsibility that this entailed, had a marked effect on his style and method of writing. In the letter to his friend and fellow-bishop, Serapion,

---

[137] Cf. *Vita Ant.* 22 (*PG* 26,876,B5–C2); *Vita Ant.* 38 (*PG* 26,900,A9–12).
[138] Cf. *Ad epp. Aeg. et Lib.* 4 (PG 25,548,A4–B2). Here he also instructs his readers to pray for the gift of discernment of spirits.

concerning the death of Arius, Athanasius points out what pains it cost him to write about the Divine Mystery and our Salvation, and how anxious he was lest he might, through his weak and inadequate exposition or through his obscurity of language, "cause damage to his readers,"[139] i.e., have a detrimental effect on their eternal salvation. Thus, we may conclude that he wrote with great determination and care. His object was not rhetorical excellence but clarity of thought, expressed in the most precise and simple terms possible and, as will be seen, presented according to a carefully worked-out plan that corresponds to an inner logic and definite thought structure.

In conclusion, attention may be drawn to the first known writing of Athanasius as a young bishop, not yet one year ordained: his 1st *Festal Letter*. There, the youthful Successor of Mark reveals his heart purely and simply. The battles that will mark most of the next forty-four years of his life have not yet begun. Here the Pastor speaks to his flock, encourages them to enter into the Fast wholeheartedly, so that they, like the saints of old, Moses, Elijah, and Daniel, might converse more purely with God. His concern is simply this: that the faithful might enter into the contemplation of God.[140] This, the contemplation of God, is the source and goal of Athanasius' life, his teaching and his battles against the world. The *Letter* concludes: "Let us remember the poor, and not forget kindness to strangers; above all let us love God with all our soul, our might and our strength, and our neighbors as ourselves. So may we receive those things which the eye hath not seen, nor the ear heard, and which hath not entered into the heart of man, which God hath prepared for those that love Him, through His only Son, our Lord and Savior, Jesus Christ; through whom, to the Father alone, by the Holy Ghost, be glory and dominion for ever and ever. Amen."[141]

§4 Method of Interpreting the Individual Writings of Athanasius

As in the case of Eusebius' *History*, our chief concern is to discover, first of all, the main purpose behind each of Athanasius' writings. Through an examination of both the *Sitz im Leben* of each writing and its literary genre, we will attempt to determine as precisely as

[139] *De morte Arii* 5 (*PG* 25,689,C2–9).
[140] Cf. *Festal Letter* I, 5–6 (Robertson, *Athanasius*, 508).
[141] *Festal Letter* I, 11 (transl. by Miss Payne-Smith in Robertson, *Athanasius*, 510).

possible the general aim of the author in each particular case. Having ascertained the principal aim, then we must work our way from the general context to the individual statement, from the basic thought structure to the various references to the Bishop of Rome, synods of bishops, imperial authority, etc. By placing the emphasis of our study on a search to discover the aim (σκοπός) of the author, we are in fact simply following the method employed by Athanasius himself in his interpretation of Scripture and Tradition, one which he, moreover, instructs his readers to apply in their attempt to understand his own writings.[142]

D. Ritschl made an important discovery with regard to the method of argumentation adopted by Athanasius in *De incarnatione,* but also to a lesser extent, he maintains, in the other works of the Alexandrian bishop. For Athanasius it evidently belongs to the very essence of theological reflection, that one must at the same time consider a statement from two sides, as it were, i.e., from the speculative-theological (or ontological) viewpoint and from the didactic-soteriological (or economic) viewpoint.[143] According to Ritschl, the *De incarnatione* is in comparison with the other works of Athanasius his most systematically worked-out composition. The other works—and presumably he has the dogmatic works chiefly in mind—are described as less structured and over-burdened with repetitions. It is not possible to contest this affirmation here, except to say that on closer inspection, these repetitions reveal precisely the systematic method of Athanasius, so well described by Ritschl, according to which he presents his arguments in a series of interrelated, double statements, taking-up a particular question and examining it from the two different points of view before moving on to develop its consequences in the next double argument. When we examine the place of St. Peter and his Confession of Faith at Caesarea Philippi in the next chapter, we will see how important is such an understanding of this double approach.

The double approach, arising from the essence of theological reflection concerning God as seen in Himself and God as seen in relationship to His creation, results in a certain pattern of thought, which characterizes Athanasius' writings. An idea is systematically worked out in pairs of arguments, one of which considers the subject matter from one point of view, while the second reflects on the same subject matter from the other point of view in such a way that one complements the other so that neither is fully comprehensible

---

[142] *De morte Arii* 5 (PG 25,689,C9–13).
[143] See Ritschl, *Athanasius,* 24–27.

without the other. It is our contention that what Ritschl affirms about the dogmatic works can also be applied to the basic thought structure of his historico-apologetic writings, though they do not deal directly with theological subjects: "The lines of thought (Gedankenführungen) are so interweaved in one another, that the first statement only becomes clear by means of the second. Each idea is, however, in itself developed to the very end. Then it also becomes evident how the second statement becomes intelligible in the light of the first."[144]

As mentioned above, the historico-apologetic writings of Athanasius have been dismissed as hate-filled, polemical pamphlets.[145] But the eminent British historian, N. H. Baynes, who has contributed so much to a more balanced view of the fourth century, came closest to a true estimate of these works. Warning future commentators not to do Athanasius the injustice of treating his apologies as though they were intended to be works of history, he observes: "They are, of course, the briefs of one who might have been an ornament of the Roman bar, and in common fairness to their author they must be treated as such. And then we can make allowance for the ecclesiastical Billingsgate, the bitter vituperation which it might otherwise be difficult to excuse."[146] That the *Apologia ad Constantium* can be described as a "brief," will be doubted by no one. It is devoid of all vituperation and has been aptly described as the most finished work of Athanasius.[147] It is our contention also that the work previously known as *Apologia contra Arianos* is most accurately called a legal brief, though not for the Roman bar. It was intended for an ecclesiastical court. There one will search in vain for traces of an ecclesiastical Billingsgate. The *Historia Arianorum,* which has been almost universally criticized for its abusive language, and which Schwartz called "ein von Haß sprühendes Pamphlet," is not indeed a legal document. It comes closer to a genuine "historical" presentation of events than Eusebius ever achieved, despite the subjective engagement of the author, since it attempts to uncover the human motives and the profound significance of the events he records. It is these events which occasion the blunt language that has offended so many academics of a more detached nature. There we will also discover a most carefully thought-out and systematic

---

[144] Ritschl, *Athanasius*, 25.
[145] See above, p. 235.
[146] Baynes, "Athanasius," in *Byzantine Studies*, 368.
[147] See Setton, *Christian Attitude Towards the Emperor*, 74. According to Gwatkin, *Studies*, 72–73, Athanasius modeled his *Apology to Constantius* on Demosthenes. See also Fialon, *Saint Athanase*, 285–287.

presentation of the said events, using a type of double-approach outlined above, which presentation is intended to clarify the significance of those events. Accordingly, in order to rediscover Athanasius interpretation of those historic occurrences, we must begin by trying to determine the inner structure of that document, as of the others. Apart from the thought structure, particular attention must also be paid to the *allusions* used by Athanasius. Since most of his works could be described as controversial writings, then it is obvious that the author will be dependent on commonly accepted ideas and concepts familiar to his audience. For this reason, allusions can often provide the interpreter with the necessary means to understand a text. To us today, such passing references may seem vague and unimportant, but they do reflect commonly accepted ideas and attitudes. And since we are intent on discovering the commonly accepted understanding of the Church in the fourth century, as well as Athanasius' own understanding of same, then these allusions, though often slight, can be of the greatest significance.

§5 The Question of Athanasius' Dependence on Eusebius

With regard to Eusebius, it was our contention that the ecclesiology he presupposed in order to compile his *History* is of importance to the theologian, first and foremost, due to the fact that it reflects the generally accepted understanding of the Church at the opening of the fourth century. It is this same common background which, in my opinion, is the source of Athanasius' understanding of the Church. Armed, however, with superior theological abilities, Athanasius is capable of penetrating this ecclesiology in a more profound way, one that is more faithful to the original. The abyss that separates the theological competence of Eusebius and Athanasius is commonly accepted.[148] And yet the opinion is gaining ground that a certain *literary* dependence between these two writers can be established.[149] An examination of this question is not called for here,[150] since it is

---

[148] See especially Möhler, *Athanasius der Große*, 331–341; also, Opitz, "Euseb von Caesarea als Theologe," 18; von Campenhausen, *Griechische Kirchenväter*, 74; Rondeau, "Une nouvelle prevue de l'influence littéraire," 427–433.

[149] Kehrhahn, *De sancti Athanasii quae fertur Contra Gentes oration*, Berlin, 1913, first drew attention to certain parallels between *C. Gentes* and the *Theophania* of Eusebius. More recently Rondeau, "Une nouvelle prevue de l'influence littéraire" (1968), demonstrated the existence of remarkable parallels in the *Commentaries on the Psalms*, which were composed by Athanasius and Eusebius.

[150] Regarding the discussion, see Grillmeier, *Christ in Christian Tradition*, 186–190.

obvious that, with regard to the original ecclesiological presuppositions common to both, neither is directly dependent on literary sources. And what is characteristic in the later theological reflection of both is so basically divergent that any direct literary dependence is to be ruled out, though in fact we will find Athanasius trying to counteract ideas with regard to the Imperial Church for whose general circulation Eusebius was primarily responsible.

Apart from their common cultural and theological background, certain other parallels can be found between Eusebius and Athanasius, not in their writing but in their lives, which affected their respective reflections. Both experienced the Great Persecution and reacted characteristically. With Eusebius it produced disillusionment with the early, traditional ecclesiology and so enabled him to move in the direction of the Imperial Church. But the persecution prepared Athanasius to understand the centrality of suffering and the Cross in the life of the Christian and the Church, and so helped him to rediscover the Church's Apostolic nature. Both bishops were excommunicated by synods of fellow-bishops. For Eusebius, this humiliation apparently sealed his disillusion with the Church of the Apostolic Successions, marked the final abandonment of his earlier ecclesiology and resulted in his definitive conversion to the Imperial Church of the new dispensation. On the other hand, Athanasius, who was excommunicated by several synods in the East and West, and not only one as in the case of Eusebius, was not tempted to abandon his faith in the divine authority of the synod; instead, he attempted to sort out the criteria by which a genuinely constituted synod could be distinguished from the multiplicity of synods which claimed authority but had no right to it. His most developed reflections are to be found in *De synodis,* which unfortunately cannot be examined below, since it would take us beyond the limits of this study. Finally, both Eusebius and Athanasius were confronted with the disappointing performance of weak Bishops of Rome, who apparently failed to live up to the ideal Successor of St. Peter as understood by the popular mind at the beginning of the fourth century. This failure effectively annulled the Bishop of Rome's claim to the Petrine Succession as far as Eusebius was concerned, but it enabled Athanasius to penetrate to the real significance of the office entrusted to the Successor of St. Peter at Rome.

CHAPTER SEVEN
St. Peter and His Confession of Faith
(Mt 16,16–18)

As Rome is the only Church to be qualified as great by Athanasius, so also St. Peter is the only apostle to receive the same description as μέγας, and that on five occasions.[1] When used by Athanasius,[2] this *epithet honoris* conveys the nuances of "holiness," "orthodoxy," "leadership in the witness of the Faith," and "authority." St. Peter, then, is singled out by Athanasius as participating in some special way in these attributes. It is our object here to clarify the reasons why the Bishop of Alexandria considered the Apostle Peter to be worthy of such a title though, as it has been pointed out,[3] the actual amount of information about St. Peter to be found in his writings is scant. Because of the importance of the classical text associated with the Petrine Office of the Bishop of Rome, namely, Matthew's account of Peter's Confession at Caesarea Philippi which climaxed in the Lord's promise to build His Church upon the Rock (Mt 16,16–18), we will begin our investigation with an examination of the part played by this text in the writings of Athanasius.

According to J. Ludwig,[4] there is but one allusion to Mt 16,18 in Athanasius; its value or relevance is questionable. But the one *allusion* of real importance—it is to be found in *Historia Arianorum* in connection with the lapse of Liberius—was ignored by Ludwig. We will also ignore it in this chapter and leave it to our analysis of the *Historia Arianorum* where Athanasius uses it in association with the Bishop of Rome; instead, we will examine the way the *text* of Matthew is used in the other writings. Our examination will not limit itself to Mt 16,18, but will include all references to the entire text, Mt 16,16–18, i.e., to the entire event that occurred at Caesarea Philippi and not simply its climax which has been sundered from its context by controversial theology. As we will see, the emphasis of Athanasius is on the Confession of Peter and not so much on the Promise of the Lord, though that is implied.

---

[1]   *De fuga* 25,2 (Opitz 85,9); *Hist. Arian.* 36,1 (Opitz 203,15); *Vita Ant.* 60 (*PG* 26,952,A1); *Or. c. Ar. II,* 9 (*PG* 26,165,C1); also, *De sent. Dion.* 7,1 (Opitz 50,15), where he is described as one of the great and blessed Apostles.
[2]   See below, pp. 513–514.
[3]   See Rimoldi, *L'Apostolo san Pietro,* 204–205.
[4]   See Ludwig, *Primatworte,* 47, who refers to *Serap. I,* 28. See below, footnote 60.

§1 The Confession of Peter and the *Regula Fidei*

The fundamental axiom which determined the exegesis of Athanasius was the acceptance of two ways of talking about the Logos: to speak of Him *ontologically* in terms of His Divinity, and to speak of Him *economically*, i.e., with regard to His relationship to created reality, specifically his activity in Creation and above all in Redemption as God made man. Each statement in Scripture must consequently be examined in order to establish which of these two aspects were intended by the Sacred Writer before an interpretation of the text could be undertaken. Put rather simply, the Arian heresy could be described in Athanasian terms as a failure to distinguish between these two interrelated understandings of the Faith, with the result that the ontological aspect was denied and attention was exclusively devoted to the economic aspect.

In opposition to this, Athanasius bases his whole defense of the orthodox position on the establishment and maintenance of the basic distinction between economic and ontological statements,[5] as well as clarifying the relationship between both. Consequently, in his exegesis of the scriptural texts, which the Arians call on to support their heresy, Athanasius tirelessly insists on examining each text to see which of the two categories the author of the text had in mind: in other words, he insists on the need to discover the intention of the Sacred Writer.[6] This very attempt to distinguish between economic and ontological statements is, according to Athanasius, to think correctly or in an orthodox way.[7] In his defense of the orthodox Faith—as worked out superbly in his major dogmatic work, the three *Orations against the Arians*—this distinction forms his basic hermeneutical principle: "Now the aim and formal principle (σκοπός … καὶ χαρακτήρ) of Scripture, we have often said, is this: the double profession in it concerning the Savior, that He was always God and is Son, being the Word, Radiance and Wisdom of the Father; and that afterwards He became [Son], for our sake

---

5   τὰ τοιαῦτα γὰρ πάντα ῥητὰ τὴν αὐτὴν ἔχει δύναμιν καὶ διάνοιαν βλέπουσαν εἰς εὐσέβειαν, καὶ δεικνύουσαν τὴν θεότητα τοῦ Λόγου, καὶ τὰ ἀνθρωπίνως λεγόμενα περὶ αὐτοῦ, διὰ τὸ γεγενῆσθαι αὐτὸν καὶ υἱὸν ἀνθρώπου. Καὶ εἰ καὶ αὐτάρκη ταῦτα (= this distinction) πρὸς ἀπόδειξιν κατ᾿ αὐτῶν, ὅμως ἐπειδὴ μὴ νοοῦντες τὸ παρὰ τοῦ Ἀποστόλου λεγόμενον, ἵνα τούτου πρῶτον μνησθῶ, νομίζουσιν ἐν τῶν ποιημάτων εἶναι τὸν τοῦ Θεοῦ Λόγον, διὰ τὸ γεγράφθαι, Πιστὸν ὄντα τῷ ποιήσαντι αὐτὸν … (*Or. c. Ar. II,* 1 = *PG* 26,149,A5–14).

6   Cf. *Or. c. Ar. I,* 54 (*PG* 26,124,B9–15) and *Or. c. Ar. II,* 44 (*PG* 26,240,C14f.), where Athanasius outlines his method of interpretation of the Scriptures. *Or. c. Ar. I,* 52 (*PG* 26,121,A12f.) scathingly criticizes the Arian method.

7   E.g., *Or. c. Ar. II,* 9 (*PG* 26,164,C12f.) and *Or. c. Ar. II,* 45 (*PG* 26,241,C3f.).

taking flesh from the Virgin Mary, Bearer of God."[8] This formal principle, corresponding to the aim of Scripture, is the κανών according to which individual statements were to be understood.[9] It is the "ecclesiastical aim" (τόν τε σκοπὸν τὸν ἐκκλησιαστικόν), which is, as it were, the "anchor of the Faith,"[10] and which, according to Newman, is the *Regula Fidei.*[11]

According to Athanasius, the Arians, by not adhering to this basic hermeneutical principle, tore the texts from their intended context and used them to suit their own preconceived ideas.[12] In the *Orations,* it is the immediate aim of Athanasius to refute the Arians by taking the texts they used to cloak their heresy in,[13] and to demonstrate the true meaning of the scriptural quotations through an examination of their immediate and general contexts. In so doing, Athanasius worked towards his ultimate aim in the *Orations:* to persuade his readers to accept the Nicene Faith, insofar as his analysis of the individual texts enabled him to enumerate the "formal principle" of Scripture which found its authoritative though abbreviated expression in the Nicene Creed. Consequently, the double profession of Faith (the ontological and economic theologies of Scripture) canonized by the Synod of Nicaea emerges from Athanasius' analysis of Holy Writ as Scripture's aim and formal principle.

In *De sententia Dionysii,* Athanasius endeavors to defend the use of the term "creature" by his predecessor, Dionysius of Alexandria, which usage the Arians were trying to turn to their advantage by calling on the authority of the great bishop to support their heretical teaching. Athanasius contends that similar ways of talking about the Son of God are to be found in the mouths of the Apostles,

---

8   *Or. c. Ar. III,* 29 (*PG* 26,385,A8–14). Cf. also *Or. c. Ar. II, 6* (*PG* 26,160,A5f.).

9   Cf. *Or. c. Ar. III,* 28 (*PG* 26,385,A2).

10   *Or. c. Ar. III,* 58 (*PG* 26,445,A13–14). Cf. also *C. Gentes 6.*

11   Commenting on the last reference, *Or. c. Ar. III,* 58, Newman says: "It is remarkable that he ends as he began, with reference to the ecclesiastical scope, or *Regula Fidei,* which has so often come under our notice, vid. Or. ii, 35 . . . , as if distinctly to tell us, that Scripture did not so force its meaning on the individual as to dispense with an interpreter, and as if his own deductions were not to be viewed merely in their own logical power, great as that power often is, but as under the authority of the Catholic doctrines which they subserve" (In Robertson, *Athanasius,* LNPF[2], 425, footnote 12.) See also the excellent article on "The Rule of Faith" as understood and applied by Athanasius in his exposition of Holy Scripture in Newman, *Select Treatises of St. Athanasius in Controversy with the Arians,* 250–253. For a similar attitude see Tertullian, *De praescriptione haereticorum,* 8–15.

12   Cf. *Or. c. Ar. I,* 52 (*PG* 26,121,A12f.).

13   Cf. *Or. c. Ar. I, 1* (*PG* 26,13,A14).

but that they all specifically refer to the Son in His Incarnate Nature. Peter is mentioned as the first witness to the Apostolic Teaching with regard to the redemptive activity of the Son of God, and reference is made to his Pentecostal speech (Acts 2,22–23).[14] Both St. Paul[15] and St. Stephen, "the Great Martyr,"[16] are also quoted. Such a way of talking about the Son of God, as a man or as a creature, is legitimate and necessary, according to Athanasius, insofar as the Apostles, when thus speaking about him, were engaged in the task of persuading the Jews to acknowledge the Divinity of the Son by leading them step by step from His Humanity to His Divinity, from the visible, historical facts and miracles to his (invisible) Godhead.[17] Thus admitting a certain epistemological priority for the historical Jesus, Athanasius emphasizes the ultimate, theological or ontological priority of the Divinity of the Son.

Returning to the New Testament, he calls on several quotations attributable to St. Peter and to St. Paul in order to demonstrate the final thrust of the Apostolic Teaching, the Divinity of the Son,[18] one of which is the Confession of Peter at Caesarea Philippi: "You are the Christ, the Son of the Living God." Mt 16,16 is but one of five texts attributed to St. Peter; there are three Pauline texts.[19] Here in *De sententia Dionysii*, the witness of Peter to demonstrate both the economic and ontological aspects of the Apostolic Teaching is not essentially different from that of the other witnesses, except that in both cases Peter's statements enjoy a certain priority. But in the *Orationes contra Arianos* the singular importance of St. Peter's witness to both aspects of the original teaching is explicitly underlined.

The aim of Athanasius in *Oratio II* is to demonstrate that the texts used by the Arians to prove the validity of their assertions about the Logos can and must be interpreted in an orthodox way.[20] To do this he reverts repeatedly to the double profession concerning the οἰκονομία and the οὐσία of the Word in order to prove it.[21] At the same time, Athanasius clarifies for his readers the full implications of this fundamental distinction, which for him constitutes the

---

[14] *De sent. Dion.* 7,1 (Opitz 50,14–16).

[15] *De sent. Dion.* 7,2–3 (Opitz 50,21–28). The references are to Acts 13,22–23; 17,30–31.

[16] *De sent. Dion.* 7,3 (Opitz 50,28–51,1). Reference to Acts 7,56.

[17] Cf. *De sent. Dion.* 8,2 (Opitz 50,9–17).

[18] *De sent. Dion.* 8,3–4 (Opitz 51,16–23).

[19] The other texts are Acts 3,15; 1 Pet 1,3; 2,25; 3,22; Rom 1,3; Heb 1,3; Phil 2,6.

[20] Cf. *Or. c. Ar. II*, 1 (*PG* 26,149,A5–B2).

[21] Cf., e.g., *Or. c. Ar. II*, 9 (*PG* 26,164,C12f.); *Or. c. Ar. II*, 45 (*PG* 26,241,C3f.); *Or. c. Ar. II*, 50 (*PG* 26,252,B15f.); *Or. c. Ar. II*, 53–54 (*PG* 26,275,C13f.).

Regula Fidei. In this way, the first "Arian text"—Heb 3,2—is dispensed with; the argumentation of Athanasius draws freely from the O.T. and the N.T., including a reference to the epistle of "the Great Peter."[22] To help him interpret the second controverted text—Acts 2,36—Athanasius replaces that text within its original context, which is Peter's speech at Pentecost. There he refers to the content of that address of Peter as the *doctrina principalis* regarding the οἰχονομία of God that was intended to lead his hearers to belief in the Son of God (that is his οὐσία as God), and calls Peter the ἀρχόμενος τῆς τοιαύτης ἀρχιδιδασκαλίας,[23] that is, the originator of this primary teaching concerning the "economy" of the Son. To prove that Peter acknowledged Him as God's Son in the absolute, ontological sense, Athanasius finally quotes Mt 16,16, the Confession at Caesarea.[24] Peter is therefore considered as the source of the Apostolic Teaching about Christ. Here, there is a faint echo of the appreciation of Peter as found in the original *History* of Eusebius, where the foundation of the Church was conceived primarily in terms of his proclamation of the Gospel.

The Confession of Peter is referred to twice in the main section of *Oratio II,* where Athanasius deals with the third disputed text of the Arians, the famous Prov 8,22. The first reference occurs at the conclusion of a list of five scriptural quotations, cited in order to demonstrate that the title "First-born of creation" (Col 1,15) referred to the Son's "condescension" and not to His Being.[25] At the opening of the final subsection which brings his exegesis of Prov 8,22 to a close, Athanasius again refers to Mt 16,16: "It is necessary to seek above all, whether He is the Son, and on this point especially to search the Scriptures. When the Apostles were questioned, this then Peter answered, saying *"You are the Christ, the Son of the living God."*[26] According to Athanasius, the affirmation by Peter of the Divine Sonship is "the sovereign principle of our Faith" (τὸ χύριον τῆς πίστεως ἡμῶν).[27] It is of note that Peter is here depicted as the spokesman or representative of the Apostles, and his confession is seen as representative of the Scriptures.

---

[22] *Or. c. Ar. II,* 9 (*PG* 26,165,C1).

[23] *Or. c. Ar. II,* 12 (*PG* 26,172,B5). See also *Exp. in Ps.* 73,20 (*PG* 27,337,C10–14), which singles out the tremendous efficacy of Peter's first speech at Pentecost in contrast with that of the rest of the Apostles.

[24] *Or. c. Ar. II,* 18 (*PG* 26,185,B3).

[25] *Or. c. Ar. II,* 62 (*PG* 26,280,A4–5).

[26] *Or. c. Ar. II,* 73 (*PG* 26,301,B14f.).

[27] *Or. c. Ar. II,* 13 (*PG* 26,301,C4–5). Newman's translation, see Robertson, *Athanasius,* LNPF², 388.

The first mention of the Confession in *Oratio III* emphasizes the revelation by the Father through Christ to Peter, and yet even here the apostle is also seen as the spokesman for the rest of the disciples.[28] The significance of the relatively detailed discussion of the scene at Caesarea, without one actual quotation from any of the Synoptic accounts, is entirely related to the context, which is a lengthy discussion on the difficult question about the knowledge of Christ. When the author comes to refer again to Peter's Confession as such, i.e., without actually quoting the text, the representative role is likewise implied. This is the final reference in the *Orationes*, where Peter is singled out as the "first" to confess the Lord as the Son of God, followed later by "all."[29] Since the confession of "all" the Apostles (Mt 14,33) occurred before the scene at Caesarea Philippi, according to the Matthean chronology,[30] then we must conclude that, as the immediate context in Athanasius suggests, the term πρῶτον used here refers to the primacy of Peter's Confession within the Plan of Salvation, which Plan is etched out here as a commentary on the text of Lk 2,52. "Παρὰ πάντων" refers, in the first place, to the Apostles as a body, but it also probably implies the Church Universal which they established.

The same combination of Mt 16,16 and Mt 14,33 is again found in Athanasius' *Expositiones in Psalmos* 88,8, where the representative character of Peter is most explicit: "... Peter, as from the mouth of all, cried out: '*You are the Christ, Son of the living God*' and again all (cried): '*Truly you are the Son of God*,' when He warned the sea and the winds."[31]

Let us summarize our findings so far. When, in *De sent. Dion.*, the formal principle of Scripture, based on the distinction between ontological and economic statements concerning the Son of God, was but faintly outlined, St. Peter's authority was called upon to illustrate both sides of the principle, but only as one witness among other scriptural authorities, who included above all St. Paul. However, in the course of the *Orationes*, Peter is presented as the originator of the economic aspect of the principle, while the ontological aspect—which is the raison d'être of the economic aspect, being that its ground or presupposition and its final goal—is

---

[28] Cf. *Or. c. Ar. III*, 46 (*PG* 26,421,A10f.).
[29] Cf. *Or. c. Ar. III*, 52 (*PG* 26,433,A14–B1).
[30] This is based on the supposition that Mt 14,33 is the second text, to which Ath2anasius refers in *Or. c. Ar. III*, 52. Newman suggests Mt 27,54 (the exclamation of the Centurion at the foot of the Cross) as the text in question—but this is most unlikely. Cf. also *Exp. in Ps.* 88,8 in the following footnote where the same combination of Mt 16,16 and Mt 14,33 is to be found.
[31] *Exp. in Ps.* 88,8 (*PG* 27,385,B8–12).

said to have had its origin in Peter's Confession at Caesarea Philippi. Because of the subordination of the economic to the ontological aspect, Athanasius can simply describe the Confession of Peter itself as "*the sovereign principle of our faith.*"

That this Confession was the effect of a direct revelation by the Father through the Son to Peter was the subject of part of a lengthy discussion on the knowledge of Christ. Of greater importance to our topic is the emphasis on the *representative character* of Peter's Confession, which emerged in the course of the above analysis: he confesses on behalf of all the Apostles, and this Confession alone may be referred to as representative of the thrust (σκοπός) of Scripture—a direct consequence of its identification with the sovereign principle of our Faith, the *Regula Fidei.* When in *Ad Serap. II,* 7–8, Athanasius summarizes his answer to the Arian interpretation of Prov 8,22, which answer he had previously worked out in detail in the *Orationes* (*Or. c. Ar. II*) on the basis of the *Regula Fidei,* he finally calls on Mt 16,16 in order to prove the ontological thrust of Scripture.[32]

The representative role of Peter and his Confession which emerged in the course of the *Orationes,* was, as we have seen, most explicitly formulated in the commentary on Ps 88,8. (In another commentary attributed to Athanasius, Peter is called ὁ κορυφαῖος[33]—a term also used by Eusebius of Caesarea[34] and his own contemporary, St. Cyril of Jerusalem.)[35] As mentioned above in Eusebius' original *History,* it was the representative character of Peter as the Spokesman/Leader of the Apostles that was emphasized. It is clear that the common tradition in the East and in Egypt, which both Eusebius and Athanasius feed on, recognized St. Peter as being representative of all the Apostles and thus their leader. For Eusebius, this meant that the sees which could claim a Petrine origin, either directly through his own proclamation or indirectly through his disciple Mark, enjoyed preeminent authority in witnessing

---

[32] *Serap. II,* 8 (*PG* 26,621,B2f.). The other texts are Jn 1,3; Ps 33,6; Ps 107,20; Prov 3,19; Ps 104,24; Ps 45,6–7; Is 61,11, in that order.

[33] *Exp. in Ps.* 15,9 (*PG* 27,105,A10). According to H. J. Sieben (*Theologie und Philosophie* 17, 1983, 260), the authenticity of this is doubtful, since it not found in the most dependable MS: Vat. Graec. 754.

[34] Cf. *Chron. ad ann.* 44. According to Maccarrone, "'Cathedra Petri' und die Idee der Entwicklung des päpstlichen Primates," 281, the use of the term κορυφαῖος to describe St. Peter first appears in the writings of the Neo-platonist, Porphyry: "Sie ist sehr wichtig für die Auffassung des petrinischen Primats, insofern sie die innige Verbindung zwischen *Petrus* und den Apostelkollegium ausdrückt."

[35] *Catech. II,* 3, according to Lampe, *Lexicon,* 769.

to the Apostolic Tradition. For Athanasius, Peter represented all the other Apostles insofar as that which he confessed under divine revelation was *ipso facto* the Confession of the Faith of all, while Peter was leader due to the origin of the Apostolic Teaching in his speech at Pentecost which marked the beginning of the Church's mission.

Before leaving the *Orationes,* it may be mentioned that on one occasion, Athanasius makes a passing reference to the rebuke of Peter (Mt 16,23). This text is, however, not introduced to highlight any aspect of Peter's character but to contrast these words of our Savior indicating His divine resolve with those of Mt 26,39, which depict His human dread in the face of death.[36] Another reference to Peter—the only remaining one in the *Orationes*—is more indicative of Athanasius' appreciation of Peter's authority. This text admonishes its readers to be attentive to the Blessed Peter ἀξιόπιστος γὰρ οὗτος γένοιτ' ἂν μάρτυς περὶ τοῦ Σωτῆρος,[37] before he goes on to introduce an exegesis of 1 Pet 4,1, which in pellucid terms articulates the economic theology of Scripture. This economic theology, we saw, was the content of the *doctrina principalis,* Peter's speech on the first Pentecost. The adjective ἀξιόπιστος is used sparingly by Athanasius in his writings. In negative contexts, i.e., where this quality is being denied, the term can mean simply "credible,"[38] or it can convey the idea of "ability to know God"—being used rather technically in this sense on two occasions to deny fallen man's innate ability to know God[39] or to be united with His Spirit.[40] When the term is used in its full positive sense to qualify certain "persons," it is once used in an explicitly technical sense to distinguish God's faithfulness (ἀξιόπιστος) from man's unfaithfulness, where it denotes the sense of God being the objective ground of man's subjective faith,[41] and on another occasion when this sense is implied it is extended to qualify the "saints," i.e., the writers of Scripture.[42] Qualifying the noun "witness"—as in the above reference to Peter—the adjective is used both in the simple sense of the force of authority due to documentary evidence that permitted

---

[36] *Or. c. Ar. III*, 57 (*PG* 26,441,B12f.). See also the reference to Peter's tears in *De virgin.* 17 (*PG* 28,272,B4f.).

[37] *Or. c. Ar. III*, 34 (*PG* 26,396,A13–14).

[38] *De decr. Nic.* 5,4 (Opitz 5,4); *De sent. Dion.* 6,2 (Opitz 50,4); *Ad epp. Aeg. et Lib.* 3 (*PG* 25,541,A4); cf. also *Apol.* 85,5 (Opitz 163,33).

[39] *De incarn.* 14,3 (Kannengiesser 315–316).

[40] *Or. c. Ar. I*, 49 (*PG* 26,113,B11).

[41] *Or. c. Ar. II*, 6 (*PG* 26,160,A8 and A13).

[42] *Or. c. Ar. I*, 36 (*PG* 26,85,C7).

no contradiction[43] or in the more limited sense of ecclesiastical authority.[44] St. Peter is the only individual described as a "credible witness concerning the Savior," and the implications to be gathered from the other uses of the term just outlined, particularly the overtly technical use of the term, indicate that the authority of that witness concerning the Faith was assumed by Athanasius to be particularly compelling since the source of that authority was ultimately divine: Athanasius most likely has at the back of his mind the revelation of the Father to Peter at Caesarea. The explicit emphasis on the value of Peter's witness is all the more striking considering the relatively few Petrine "sources" at his disposal in comparison with the copious works of other witnesses, in particular John and Paul, both of whom he naturally quotes more often than Peter.

§2 The Confession of Peter as the "Rock" on which the Church Is Built

Writing to his fellow-bishop Adelphius, Athanasius had occasion to elaborate a little on the economic theology. To support his contention that his exposition on the coming of the Lord in the flesh is "correct (orthodox) and anchored in the Apostolic Teaching" he calls on Peter (1 Pet 4,1) and Paul (Tit 2,13).[45] It is interesting that both here and earlier in *De sententia Dionysii,* where Athanasius' sketches his arguments with broad strokes, Peter and Paul are called upon in a representative fashion to witness to the Apostolic Tradition. In both of these cases, the predominant concern was the economic theology of the Son.

When, however, on another occasion the core of the Apostolic Tradition, the ontological theology of the Son, is the subject of his discourse, Athanasius refers to Peter's Confession alone as representative of the Apostolic Faith. This text is contained in the second of two fragments from a letter of Athanasius to "his sons," presumably the presbyters and deacons of Alexandria, preserved only in Latin.[46] Due to the importance of this text, a longer quotation than usual is called for:

---

[43] *Hist. Arian.* 8,2 (Opitz 88,4).
[44] *Apol.* 90,3 (Opitz 168,10).
[45] *Ad Adelph.* 6 (*PG* 26,1080,A10f.).
[46] *PG* 26,1189–1190. As Montfaucon suggested, this letter was probably written in the year 356, the date of the events recorded in the fragments. It is, however, possible that it was composed some considerable time after the events had

Deus quidem vos consoletur, novi autem quia non hoc solum vos contristat, sed contristat et illud, quia ecclesias quidem alii per violentiam tenuerunt, vos autem interim foris estis a locis; illi enim loca, vos vero habetis apostolicam fidem. . . .

Vos autem beati, qui fide in Ecclesia estis, in fidei fundamentis habitatis, et sufficientem satisfactionem habetis, fidei summitatem, quae in vobis permanet inconcussa; ex apostolica enim traditione pervenit ad vos, et frequenter eam exsecranda invidia voluit commovere, nec valuit: magis autem per ea quae commoverunt sunt abscissi. Hoc est enim quod scriptum est: *Tu es Filius Dei vivi,* Petro per revelationem Patris confesso et audiente: *Beatus es, Simon Barjona, quia caro et sanguis non revelavit tibi, sed Pater meus qui in coelis est,* et cetera. Nemo igitur unquam vestrae fidei praevalebit, dilectissimi fratres: si enim aliquando ecclesias reddiderit Deus, credimus enim hoc; verumtamen ne tanta ecclesiarum redditionem sufficit nobis fides. . . .

The Greek original most probably contained the full text of Mt 16,16–18, as is suggested by the abbreviation "et cetera," which may be attributed to the translator or copyist. Such an abbreviation is uncharacteristic of Athanasius, who in spite of copious references to the O.T. and N.T. is generally punctilious in his quotations, as befits his profound respect for Sacred Scripture. Further, the first sentence of Athanasius after the quotation clearly presupposes Mt 16,18c, while the "in fidei fundamentis habitatis," most probably refers to Mt 16,18b.

The Church, Athanasius tells his "sons," is not a physical place, but rather: wherever the Apostolic Faith is preached, and held by the faithful, there is the Church. He is not speaking primarily of the subjective faith but the objective Confession of that Faith which, as he expressly affirms, had been handed down through the Apostolic Tradition to them. What this Faith is, is nothing other than that which the Father had revealed to Peter and which Peter confessed, only to hear in turn that the Church would be built *on his Confession.* Athanasius assures his readers that, against this Confession of Faith, which was handed down to them from the Apostles (a possible

taken place, possibly in 357, to judge from the relatively calm, spiritual interpretation of the terrible events, which indicates a certain emotional detachment, the product of time and reflection. (Compare, by way of contrast, the impassioned reaction of Athanasius to the similar events which occurred in the year 339 and which were recorded in his *encyclical* of that year.) Montfaucon also suggested that the fragments were part of a *Festal Letter,* but this seems unlikely (see Robertson, *Athanasius,* LMPF², 550, footnote 7).

allusion to the Petrine tradition at Alexandria) and which the Orthodox profess, no one will prevail. The enemies of the Faith can have the Churches, he affirms, but for us, the Faith is sufficient.

There are three points to be made about the use of Mt 16,16–18 in the second fragment: (i) the exegesis of Mt 16,18, which is here implied, understands the promise of Our Lord—"upon this rock I will build my Church"—in terms of the "rock" being the Confession of Faith by Peter; (ii) the Confession of Faith by Peter is in turn identified with the Apostolic Faith which was handed on to the present generation through the Apostolic Tradition—implying the Apostolic Succession of the "Fathers"—and which, as the historical context of the letter would indicate, is itself to be identified with the Faith confessed by the Fathers at Nicaea, i.e., the most recent, authoritative witness to that Tradition according to the mind of Athanasius; (iii) the principal reason why Athanasius quotes the text is in line with the purpose of the letter, to assure his readers that, because the Apostolic Faith they held was divinely revealed and because of the explicit assurance of Christ that the gates of hell would not prevail against it, they should bear the present loss of the Churches, confident that no one could take away from them that which constituted the Church as such, namely, the Faith confessed by the Apostles and their successors.

The last point will be of particular relevance when we come to examine the use of Mt 16,16–18 in *Historia Arianorum,* but before that we must turn our attention briefly to consider to what extent the other two points are otherwise reflected in the writings of Athanasius. To do his we will examine the usage of the terms πέτρα and οἰκοδομέω (from Mt 16,18), as well as θεμελιόω and θεμέλιος, which is presumably the Greek term behind: "in fidei fundamentis."

Ἡ πέτρα is interpreted allegorically by Athanasius in his *Commentaries on the Psalms* to mean Christ. There he calls on 1 Cor 10,4 to aid his exegesis: ἡ πέτρα ἦν ὁ Χριστός. Christ is called the Rock in the sense of being the source of the individual's salvation,[47] while His θεία λογία are said to be the honey from the Rock which nourishes His People,[48] namely, His teaching which builds up the Church. On another occasion, he uses Mt 16,18b as a N.T. parallel to Ps 57,9: "God established her (= the City of God which Athanasius

---

[47]   *Exp. in Ps.* 26,5 (*PG* 27,149, A9–12); *Exp. in Ps.* 60,3 (*PG* 27,273,A8–14).
[48]   *Exp. in Ps.* 80,17 (*PG* 27,364,D7–9); cf. also *Exp. in Ps.* 39,3 (*PG* 27,192,A8–13).

identifies with the Church) forever."[49] This text offers us no more precise details as to what πέτρα might refer to.

The term, however, is used in a somewhat different sense in the *Letter of Athanasius to the Bishops of Egypt and Libya* (356), where he tells them that "the faithful disciple of the Gospel, having the gift of discernment in things spiritual, and having built his house of faith upon [this] rock, has secured himself firm and steadfast from all their deceits."[50] The "rock" referred to here is the "discernment of spirits"—a reference most probably to the ability to interpret Scripture according to what is the *Regula Fidei*. The N.T. text which Athanasius alludes to is Mt 7,24b and not, in the first place at least, Mt 16,18. It is worth recalling that in Mt 7,24b, the "rock" in the parable stands for the words of Our Lord, i.e., His Teaching. Athanasius applies it here to the teaching of the Church, the *Regula Fidei*. The only other apparent allusion to Mt 7,24b is that found in the *Historia Arianorum,* where Ossius is described as "having built his house of faith upon the rock."[51] The "rock" here most probably refers to the Nicene Faith,[52] which as we saw is identical with the *Regula Fidei*.

The term οἰκοδομέω, common to both Mt 7,24b and Mt 16,18b, is otherwise used by Athanasius, usually in analogies, to depict God's activity in Creation,[53] i.e., when not used merely *sensu proprio*.[54] Speaking directly of God's creative activity, he prefers the term θεμελιόω, a preference determined to a great extent by his exegesis of Prov 8,23.[55] This term is also found where Athanasius describes the new life of grace as *founded* in Christ,[56] again within the context of his exegesis of Prov 8,23, the key to which exegesis Athanasius informs his readers is the Confession of Peter, "the sovereign principle of our Faith."[57] Within this same context the term θεμέλιος is most frequently used, following 1 Cor 3,10–11, with reference to the incarnate Son of God as the foundation on which the Church is built: "Therefore according to His Humanity he is

---

[49] *Exp. in Ps.* 47,9 (*PG* 27,221,A1–4).

[50] *Ad epp. Aeg. et Lib.* 4 (*PG* 25,548,A5–9).

[51] *Hist. Arian.* 43,3 (Opitz 207,12).

[52] See *Hist. Arian.* 42,3 (Opitz 206,31–32).

[53] *Or. c. Ar. I, 23* (*PG* 26,60,A11); *Or. c. Ar. II, 77* (*PG* 26,309,B11); *C. Gentes* 43 (Thompson 118) and *C. Gentes* 47 (Thompson 132).

[54] E.g., *Ad Const.* 15–18 (Szymusiak 103f.).

[55] *Or. c. Ar. II,* 41 (*PG* 26,233,C10); cf. also *Or. c. Ar. I,* 57 (*PG* 26,132,B12); *Serap. II,* 1 (*PG* 26,609,A14); *Serap. II,* 4 (*PG* 26,613,B7).

[56] *Or. c. Ar. II, 73* (*PG* 26,301,B8); cf. also *Or. c. Ar. II,* 74 (*PG* 26,304–305 passim) and *Or. c. Ar. II,* 75 (*PG* 26,308–309 passim).

[57] *Or. c. Ar. II, 73* (*PG* 26,301,C1–5).

founded (θεμελιοῦται), so that we like precious stones could be built upon Him (ἐποικοδομεῖσθαι) and become a temple of the Holy Spirit who dwells in us. As He is the foundation (θεμέλιος) and we the stones built (ἐποικοδομούμενοι) upon Him, so also He is the vine and we are like branches joined on (to Him), not according to the Essence (κατὰ τὴν οὐσίαν) of His Divinity—since that would be impossible—but rather according to His Humanity. . . ."[58] Christ, then, is the foundation on which the Church is built.

On the other hand, when Athanasius writes to Serapion to defend the orthodox teaching with regard to the Holy Spirit, whose denial by the Tropici he saw as a logical conclusion from their error concerning the Son,[59] he affirms that the Church was founded (τεθεμελίωται) on the Trinitarian Faith, which the Lord gave, the Apostles proclaimed, and the Fathers defended.[60] "And that they may know this to be the faith of the Church, let them learn how the Lord, when sending forth the Apostles, ordered them to lay this foundation (θεμέλιον) for the Church, saying: 'Go and make disciples of all nations, baptizing them in the name of the Father and of the Son and of the Holy Spirit' (Mt 28,19). The Apostles went and thus they taught; and this is the preaching that extends to the whole Church which is under heaven."[61] Echoing the Eusebian concept of the foundation of the Church as the effect of the Apostles' preaching, Athanasius sees this foundation not only in historical terms (though these are clearly included) but in metaphysical, ever-contemporary terms. He has a more refined concept of the foundation of the Church as resulting from the preaching of the Apostles than that which we saw in Eusebius of Caesarea, since he stresses both the content of the preaching and the act of proclamation.

The content of the Apostolic Teaching, which for Athanasius is no mere abstraction but the objective Faith given by Christ and preserved from one generation to the next by the "Fathers,"[62] is thus understood by Athanasius to be the foundation of the Church in every age: "ille enim loca, vos vero habetis apostolicam fidem. . . ." Athanasius could therefore write to his "sons" in Alexandria,

---

58   *Or. c. Ar. II*, 74 (*PG* 26,304,B8–15). Cf. also *Or. c. Ar. II, 73* (*PG* 26,301,B9); *Or. c. Ar. II, 74* (*PG* 26,304,B2–C5).

59   *Serap. I, 2* (*PG* 26,532,B10f.).

60   *Serap. I, 28* (*PG* 26,594,C14–596,A1), cf. also *Serap. III, 6* (*PG* 26,633,C7). *Serap. I, 28* is the only text referred to by Ludwig, *Primatworte*, 47, in his study of the exegesis of Mt 16,18 in the Early Church. According to Ludwig, the text probably alludes to Mt 16,18. This is not directly evident from the immediate context.

61   *Serap. I, 28* (*PG* 26,596,B10f.). Transl., Shapland, p. 136.

62   Cf. *Serap. I, 28* (*PG* 26,594,D2). See also *Exp. in Ps.* 118,90 (*PG* 27,496,D3f.).

meaning that wherever the Apostolic Faith was preserved, there was the Church. In this sense, he exhorts his readers in another context to remain ἐπὶ τὸν θεμέλιον τῶν ἀποστόλων (cf. Eph 2,20) and to hold fast to τὰς παραδόσεις τῶς πατέρων,[63] as he had previously dismissed the Arians for having strayed from the foundation of the Apostles.[64] It is not without reason that on at least two occasions Athanasius explicitly links the objective Faith proclaimed by the Apostles with the traditions of the Fathers who preserved and handed on this truth,[65] indicating that for him Apostolic Teaching and Apostolic Succession together constituted Apostolic Tradition in the full sense of the term.

From the foregoing it follows that Athanasius understood that the "rock" or "foundation" on which the Church was built was in one sense Christ and in another sense the Apostolic Teaching. Considered ontologically, and in the strict theological sense, Christ is the rock or foundation,[66] but considered in terms of the economy of salvation, and in a relative theological sense, the Apostolic Teaching is said to be the rock or foundation of the Church.[67] Just as Christ is only known through the Apostolic preaching, so in turn the Apostolic Teaching is such insofar as its content is Christ.

Athanasius is no nominalist, as can be otherwise gathered from his attack on the extreme Arians who, according to him, use language not as they ought to, namely to signify reality and relate us to that which is signified, but only to convey opinions *about* what they think exists.[68] For Athanasius, the Apostolic Teaching signifies that which is: it is the means by which we know Christ, as Christ is the means by which we know the Father. Consequently, the Apostolic Teaching and Christ, though distinct, are one and the same, Christ being the metaphysical content of the Apostolic Teaching, while the Apostolic Teaching is the historical intellectual articulation of Christ preserved and handed on from one generation to the next by the Apostles and their successors, the "Fathers." This is reflected in a reference found in a short letter to two presbyters in Jerusalem, John and Antiochus, written near the end of his life (ca. 371–372), where after admonishing them to avoid discussion on disputed

---

[63] *De syn.* 54,3 (Opitz 277,16). It is possible that ἐπὶ τὸν θεμέλιον τῶν ἀποστόλων is a reference to 1 Cor 1,10.

[64] *De sent. Dion.* 27,3 (Opitz 66,25–27).

[65] *Serap. I, 28 (PG* 26,594,D2); *De syn.* 54,3 (Opitz 277,16).

[66] Cf., especially, *Or. c. Ar. II,* 74 (*PG* 26,304,B8–15); *Exp. in Ps.* 26,5 (*PG* 27,149,A9–12).

[67] Cf., especially, *Serap. I,* 28 (*PG* 26,596,B10f.); *Ad epp. Aeg. et Lib.* 4 (*PG* 25,548,A7).

[68] See *De syn.* 34,4–35,3 (Opitz 261,33–262,16).

points which were disturbing the faithful, he says: But let you, having your foundation (θεμέλιος) secure, which is Jesus Christ our Lord, and the confession of the Fathers concerning the Truth, avoid those who wish to say more or less than that. . . ."[69] Here it may be added, "the confession of the Fathers concerning the Truth" refers specifically to the Apostolic Teaching in its *contemporary* form: the Faith confessed by the Fathers at Nicaea.

When we return to the Latin fragments above, we note how consistent with the mind of Athanasius, as just outlined, is the identification there of the Confession of Peter with the rock on which the Church is found: (1) In that letter, the "rock" refers, in the first place, to the subject matter of the Confession—that which is confessed. (2) But when Athanasius identifies the (Nicene) Faith for which the Alexandrians are now suffering with the Confession of Peter, he does not intend merely to limit this to an identification of the subject matter in both, even though this is a prime concern of his, but he also points to a formal identification. The formal element is made explicit by the use of the phrase which introduces the quotation of Mt 16,16–18: *ex apostolica enim traditione pervenit ad vos,* et frequenter eam exsecranda invidia voluit commovere, nec valuit: magis autem per ea quae commoverunt sunt abscisse. Hoc est enim quod scriptum est: *Tu es Filius Dei vivi. . . .*

The scene at Caesarea, which, as we saw earlier, was understood by Athanasius to constitute the salvific-historical origin of the Apostolic Faith, is here viewed from another, broader perspective—namely in terms of the Apostolic Tradition which it thereby characterizes and of which it is the origin. The two formal elements of Peter's Confession—in the earlier analysis they merely appeared in the background—are: (a) God revealing, and (b) the specific human agency chosen by God to communicate His truth —namely Peter (the representative or spokesman of the Apostles) in his act of confessing. These two elements are understood by Athanasius to characterize the "Apostolic Tradition" as they characterized its salvific-historical origins. In other words, Athanasius tells his "sons" that the contemporary Church which confesses the Faith that Peter confessed does so because the Faith or Teaching has been preserved and handed down by the successors of Peter and the Apostles—whom Athanasius otherwise calls the "Fathers"— *through whom the Father continues to reveal His Son.*[70] (3) Since in

---

69 *Ad Joan. et Ant. (PG* 26,1168,A2–6).

70 This formal identification of the Confession of Peter and the Faith confessed by the Fathers at Nicaea has very important implications for Athanasius' theology of synodal authority.

the Apostolic Tradition, God continues to reveal the Son through His divinely-appointed agents from one generation to the next, evil[71] has been unable, up to the present, to corrupt the truth and will not prevail either in the present or future. The latter deduction is the *pointe* of the specific mention of Mt 16,16–18.

In summary, we can say that Athanasius conceived the Rock or Foundation on which the Church is built as, in the first place (i.e., metaphysically), Christ Himself. Considered historically or functionally, the Rock is the objective Faith handed down by means of the Apostolic Tradition. Thus, the *Regula Fidei*, which is the double confession regarding Our Lord, whose salvific-historical origins are to be traced back to Peter's Confession at Caesarea Philippi and his speech at Pentecost, can itself be called the Rock. Athanasius seems to interpret Christ's promise to Peter: "You are Peter and upon this rock I will build my Church" (Mt 16,18) as though the term "rock" referred to Peter's act of confession. But it is by means of the Apostolic Tradition, according to which God continues to reveal the nature of the Son through the human agency of the Fathers, that the Confession of Peter is actualized from generation to generation—the most recent for Athanasius being the Synod of Nicaea—and thus the Church that is built upon this foundation will prevail against all evil.

§3 The Confession of Peter and His Martyrdom in Rome

Before this third exile (ca. 354–355), Athanasius wrote a very moving letter to the abbot Dracontius, pressing him urgently to accept the responsibilities of the bishopric to which he had been recently elected. Dracontius wished to remain a monk and devote his life to the search for perfection rather than accept high office in public. Well aware of the danger for life and limb—which an orthodox bishop, and in particular one who sympathized with Athanasius, could expect in those turbulent times when Constantius was forcing the universal episcopate to subscribe to Athanasius' condemnation—the Bishop of Alexandria encourages Dracontius to accept the episcopacy as an opportunity for even greater perfection, namely the possibility of suffering for his Faith, even to the extent of martyrdom.

---

[71] "Invidia" here most probably means the source of envy (= the devil) and not the φθόνος of Eusebius (cf. *HE* 8,1,6–7) which describes the personal ill will among bishops.

Dracontius is exhorted to imitate Paul and the saints, who, after they had become stewards of the mysteries (1 Cor 4,1) pressed on to the ultimate end (σκοπός) of their calling. He continues: Πότε Παῦλος ἐμαρτύρησε, καὶ τὸν στέφανον λαβεῖν προσεδόκησεν, εἰ μὴ ὅτε ἀπεστάλη διδάσκειν; Πότε Πέτρος ὡμολόγησεν, εἰ μὴ ὅτε εὐηγγελίζετο, καὶ ἁλιεὺς ἀνθρώπων γέγονε.[72] We note first how the ὡμολόγησεν of Peter is paralleled to the ἐμαρτύρησε of Paul. This indicates, as confirmed by the context, that the Confession of Peter alluded to here is not that of Caesarea Philippi but Peter's final witness to that Faith which was revealed to him there. The substitution of the verb ὁμολογέω to describe Peter's act of martyrdom instead of the term μαρτυρέω used for Paul may be of no greater significance than that of a rhetorical flourish. But the central role played by Peter's Confession at Caesarea in the thought of Athanasius makes it more likely that Athanasius intentionally used the term to allude to the original confession at Caesarea with the very clear purpose of impressing on Dracontius that the martyrdom of Peter was the consequence of that original unique revelation to Peter, a consequence which Dracontius himself would recognize as being of even greater significance than the cause. The monk Dracontius could perhaps enjoy the intimacies of God's self-revelation in the solitude of the desert, argues Athanasius, but the bishop and fisher-of-men, to which vocation he is now being called, could mean for Dracontius (and for the Church) an even greater grace—martyrdom.

As our study of Eusebius' original *History* brought out, the martyrdom of Peter was understood to form the climax of Peter's vocation to found the Church.[73] The allusion in the Letter to Dracontius—to Peter's final confession, his martyrdom—reechoes the same early fourth-century belief.[74] This casual allusion is all the more revealing of the mind of Athanasius and his contemporaries, such as Dracontius, since its very casualness indicates the unquestioned assumption of the singular import attached to Peter's martyrdom—here linked intrinsically to his Confession at Caesarea as effect is related to cause, linked therefore implicitly with the promise of the Lord to Peter to found his Church on Peter's Confession.

---

[72] *Ad Dracont.* 8 (*PG* 25,532,C4–7).

[73] Paul's martyrdom on the other hand was acknowledged to have occurred historically at the same time as Peter's but possibly with a different salvific-historic purpose: his death with Peter marks the beginning of the end of the Apostolic era.

[74] No direct literary dependence is here suggested, but rather two different reflections of one common tradition.

That this final Confession of Peter was made in Rome, not accidentally or merely historically, but according to God's dispensation, is inferred from another passing reference to Peter and Paul to be found in the *Apologia de fuga sua*, written in the year 357, shortly before the "lapse" of Liberius. Two years or so after admonishing Dracontius for not accepting the responsibilities of the episcopacy, Athanasius himself was charged by his enemies with cowardice because he fled before them (his persecutors). The core of his defense is based on the example of Our Lord and the saints of the O.T. and N.T.: "when persecuted they fled, after escaping they remained steadfast, and when discovered they submitted to martyrdom."[75] To justify their action, Athanasius develops the concept of the "hour" of one's death which is determined by the providence and Dispensation of God.

Although he uses the terms καιρός and χρόνος in an interchangeable way, he recognizes very clearly what modern N.T. exegetes technically express with the term καιρός: The Word of God, creator of opportunities (καιρῶν), has revealed to us "that there is a time (χρόνον) measured out to each man, a time not based on chance, as some of the Greek thinkers mythologize, but one which He, the Creator, determined for each one according as the Father wishes."[76] The saints, like Our Lord, knew that there was a time for them to die and a time to flee, so that when the time determined by Providence for their death approached they did not "resist His dispensation (οἰκονομία).[77] To exemplify this, Athanasius points to the actions of Jacob, Moses, David, and Elijah before he mentions Peter and Paul: "Peter, who hid himself for fear of the Jews, and Paul the Apostle, who was let down in a basket and fled, when they heard '*you* (plural) *must bear witness at Rome*' (Acts 23,11) did not delay their departure, rather they departed rejoicing. And the one as though hastening to his friends exulted in his immolation, while the other did not shrink from his hour (καιρός) when it came but boasted saying, 'I for my part am poured out as a libation and the hour of my departure is at hand (2 Tim 4,6).'"[78]

The quotation of Acts 23,11 is of singular importance, since it is a key text determining the Jerusalem-Rome axis of the Acts of the Apostles, which Eusebius took over and brought into the closest possible association with the mission of Peter to found the Church.

---

[75] *De fuga* 22,2 (Opitz 83,19–20).
[76] *De fuga* 14,1 (Opitz 78,2–5).
[77] *De fuga* 17,6 (Opitz 80,19–20).
[78] *De fuga* 18,5 (Opitz 81,5–9).

In Acts, it is specifically addressed to Paul alone. Yet Athanasius with one change in the text—substituting the second person singular σε for the plural ὑμᾶς—includes Peter in the Divine Commission to bear witness to Him in Rome, thus displaying a similar tendency as found in Eusebius (without going as far as the latter who practically erased Paul). Again, Athanasius and Eusebius seem to reflect a common assumption in the East. As underlined by the divine δεῖ qualifying μαρτυῆσαι in the Acts 23,11 text, Peter's martyrdom, and that of Paul, were seen to be clearly part of the Divine Plan. What this dispensation demanded of Paul is elaborated on by Athanasius since it could be taken as a model for the Bishop of Alexandria's own "dispensation." Paul was preserved "so that from Jerusalem unto Illyricum the preaching of the Gospel might be completed" (Rom 15,19).[79] In a conscious parallel to his own activity, and that of his fellow-confessors in hiding, he states: "Behold therefore, when they (the Apostles) were engaged in the fight (for the truth)[80] they did not waste the time of their flight, nor when persecuted did they forget the needs of others; rather, being ministers of the Good Word, they did not begrudge sharing it with others, but, when they fled, they proclaimed the Gospel, warned of the wickedness of those who conspired (against them), and confirmed the faithful with their counsels."[81] It is tantalizing, however, that Athanasius gives us no precise indication at this stage as to what the Divine Dispensation of Peter involved and how his martyrdom at Rome was included in it. The subject matter of the letter did not call for it. All Athanasius wished to get across to his readers was the fact that the Divine Dispensation for Peter and Paul, which everyone knew climaxed in their death at the hands of Nero at Rome, *also* included a time of flight from their persecutors during which they had to fulfil their unique vocations.[82] This makes the casual reference to the δεῖ of Peter's final witness in Rome even more significant. Should we assume that his readers most probably shared Eusebius' earlier understanding of the divinely ordained mission of Peter to found the Church, which mission culminated at Rome with his martyrdom, then we can understand why Athanasius, apparently

---

79 Rom 15,19 as quoted in *De fuga* 20,5 (Opitz 82,15).
80 This is an allusion presumably to Sir 4,28. Cf. *De fuga* 22,1 (Opitz 83,18) for a clearer allusion to the same text.
81 *De fuga* 21,2 (Opitz 82,21–25).
82 In *De fuga* 25,2–3 (Opitz 85,8–13) there is another reference to the flight of "the great Apostle Peter" and that of "the Apostle Paul." There, the Arians are rhetorically warned not to presume to censure such men for their flight.

gratuitously, introduced Peter into the original quote from Acts 23,11, since otherwise his text would have been none the poorer for its omission. Our analysis above indicated that it was the conviction of Athanasius that the Church was founded on the *Confession of Peter*, and that having proclaimed the Gospel and become a Fisher-of-Men, Peter's original Confession was, as it were, consummated in his martyrdom. The present text adds the information that this martyrdom took place in Rome according to the Divine Dispensation—a conviction likewise shared by the earlier Eusebius. The strength of such a rhetorical allusion lies in the assumption that its readers will grasp its import without too much elaboration. The stronger the assumption, the more casual is the allusion.

§4 Summary

In his defense of the Apostolic Teaching as the *Regula Fidei*, i.e., the double confession of the ontological and economic understanding of the Son of God made flesh, Athanasius pointed to St. Peter as his chief witness, but by no means his only one. Though the references to him and his writings are, in comparison with the works of St. Paul or St. John, numerically smaller, yet for Athanasius the testimony of Peter to the Apostolic Teaching was paramount. He traced the origins of both aspects of the double confession back to Peter, whose value as an authority was enhanced by the status accorded to him as the spokesman for the Apostles in general, and as the originator of the Apostolic Teaching. The most outstanding characteristic of Peter that emerged from the writings of Athanasius was his representative function, and this was determined by his Confession of Faith at Caesarea Philippi. This function was further delineated insofar as, when he spoke on behalf of "all," he did so solely on account of the Divine Revelation that was given to him. His Confession of "the sovereign principle" of our Faith enjoyed a very clearly defined primacy within the Divine Plan as the origin and end of the Apostolic Teaching. The Apostolic Teaching, in turn, which leads men by way of consideration of the "condescension" of the Logos, with regard to His very Being as Son of God, has its historical and material source in Peter's speech at the first Pentecost, which enables Athanasius to describe him as the originator of the *doctrina principalis*.

Thus, although in the final absolute sense, Our Lord Jesus Christ is the Rock or Foundation on which the Church is built, and we are like precious stones built upon Him, the objective Faith of the

Church in Christ is also called the Rock, namely the double confession of the Logos as He is in Himself and as He is in relationship to us, His creatures whom He has redeemed. Consequently, in the one text where Athanasius apparently quotes the full text of Mt 16,16–18, he seems to understand the term "rock" in Christ's promise to Peter at Caesarea Philippi as though it referred to the actual Confession of Peter, i.e., Peter confessing. Thus, the Rock on which the Church is founded so that evil will not prevail against it (cf. Mt 16,18) is the contemporary confession of the Church's Faith by those who guarantee the preservation of the Apostolic Tradition from generation to generation, i.e., the Fathers at Nicaea, since through them God continues to reveal His Son.

Peter, who alone enjoys the epithet *honoris*, "great," received a divine commission, according to Athanasius, to bear witness to Christ in Rome, where his original testimony at Caesarea was brought to its completion with his martyrdom. His martyrdom at Rome was part of the Divine Dispensation regarding Peter. Quantitatively speaking, St. Athanasius imparts little information in his occasional writings with regard either to St. Peter, or the classical text Mt 16,16–18, or indeed Peter's connection with Rome. But the few passing references scattered throughout his works clearly indicate the central importance that both St. Peter and his Confession occupy in the mind of Athanasius; they also betray the general consciousness in the East with regard to Peter's martyrdom in Rome, i.e., it was part of the Divine Plan.

The points of contact with Eusebius are remarkable: Peter is depicted by both as the representative and Leader of the Apostles and their Teaching; the foundation of the Church and her Teaching was seen by each of the two writers, in his own way, as based on the proclamation of Peter, though Eusebius situated its historical beginning in Palestinian Caesarea, while Athanasius conceived it in terms of Peter's speech at Pentecost; both agree with regard to the primacy of Peter's witness to the Faith; both affirmed the Divine Dispensation concerning Peter's martyrdom in Rome and saw it as the climax of his life's mission. Eusebius provided us with more information because he was expressly concerned with the historical origins of the Church, whereas Athanasius simply alludes to what seem to be generally accepted ideas which no one contested. Only in his later imperial ecclesiology did Eusebius begin to question implicitly the traditional understanding of Peter and attempt to reinterpret it. It was during the controversies which surrounded the person of Athanasius that the ecclesiological implications of

St. Peter's unique function within Salvation History, and its association
with Rome, began to be contested openly due to the support given to
Athanasius by the Bishop of Rome.

CHAPTER EIGHT
The *Apologia*: Julius of Rome and the Ecclesiastical Authority of the Catholic and Apostolic Church

According to the MS evidence, the text which forms the subject of our
analysis in this chapter is known solely under the title *Apologia secunda*.[1]
Opitz, who recovered this title, correctly insisted that the caption given
to the text by Montfaucon: *Apologia contra Arianos* must be abandoned.
The superscription *Apologia contra Arianos* has influenced—one could
say prejudiced more accurately—the interpretation of the text up to the
present time. This work of Athanasius is generally accepted as a collection
of documents prepared for the simple purpose of vindicating his personal
innocence in the face of Arian accusations,[2] an assumption shared by
Opitz.[3] The consequences of this prejudgment—a judgement which, it
may be added, seems justified by the content of the work examined prima
vista—leave their mark both in the historian's quest to establish the precise
nature of Athanasius' one-sidedness (usually seen as motivated merely by
self-interest) in order to determine the credibility of his presentation of
the events here recorded, and in the theologian's attempt to interpret the
work as a whole, with a view to its theological presuppositions, which is
the proper object of this study.

But the same prejudgment has also played a not unimportant
part in the various attempts to fix the date of this particular work of
St. Athanasius. Before we examine the question of the date of the
Apologia secunda, attention must be drawn to the vague nature of
the title, most likely given to the work by those (or by him) who,
probably in Constantinople at the beginning of the fifth century,

[1]   Opitz, *Untersuchungen*, 104.
[2]   So, for example, Quasten, *Patrology* III, 34; see also See Bardenhewer, *Geschichte
der altkirchlichen Literatur* III, 61; Fialon, *Saint Athanase*, 148–150.
[3]   See the commentary of Opitz 138,30f.

made that original collection of Athanasian works, which formed the
origin of the MS tradition at our disposal.[4] This indicates that the exact
nature or purpose of the document was, at the very least, unclear. In contrast, the *Apologia de fuga sua* and the *Apologia ad Constantinum* were
easily so designated due to their obvious content. That the work we are
about to examine could not be so clearly described, forced the collector in
Constantinople to call it simply "the second defense," the precise nature
of which could not be determined. The vague title simply suggests that
the work contained a defense of the author; to whom it was addressed
or the exact reason for its origin were, however, not recognized by the
fifth-century compiler. That it was described as the "second" may be due
simply to its position in the collection, placed as it is after the *Apologia de
fuga sua* (and, with one exception, before the *Epistola encyclica*) in all MSS
of the "Apologienkorpus."[5]

§1 Date of Composition

Any attempt to establish the date of composition of the *Apologia secunda*
must first deal with its actual composition: its internal unity and the possibility of later interpolations or Revisions. This problem in turn raises the
question concerning the reason why Athanasius wrote the work in the first
place, and what prompted him to revise his work, should one find clear
evidence of later interpolations.

According to Bardenhewer,[6] Athanasius collected all the pertinent
synodal proceedings and judgements concerning his person, arranged
the official documents from the fifth decade of the fourth century in the
first part of his work (Ch. 3–58), and in order to expose the origins of the
intrigues against him, also included documents from previous decades in
the second part (Ch. 59–88). Apparently relying on the *terminus a quo*
as determined by the fact that the text evidently presupposes his return
to Alexandria on October 21, 346, and apparently shows no knowledge
of the relapse of Valens and Ursacius, Bardenhewer maintained that the
body of the work was written around 348, but not later than the relapse of

---

[4]   See Opitz, *Untersuchungen*, especially 157.
[5]   Opitz, *Untersuchungen*, 147.
[6]   See Bardenhewer, *Geschichte der altkirchlichen Literatur* III, 61. Similar arguments
      had been proposed by Robertson, *Athanasius*, LNPF², 97, in his introduction to
      the translation of the text, who, however, dated the composition 351.

Valens and Ursacius (ca. 350?), while the final two chapters (Ch. 89–90) were added later and cannot be dated before 357.[7] This solution was rejected by R. Seiler in his Inaugural Dissertation for the University of Tübingen, 1932. Following the example of his teacher, R. Laqueur, he challenged the basis of Bardenhewer's attempt to date the *Apologia*. Seiler found the method of dating by means of determining the *terminus ante* and *post quem* as inadequate, as indeed the attempt to determine the structure of the text by a simple description of the contents. He held that not only were the final two chapters added to the text at a later date, but that the main text, as we now have it, was not written at one particular period of time, but is the end product of over two decades of continual expansion and reworking on a rough draft originally made by Athanasius for use in his appeal before the emperor after his deposition at Tyre (335).[8]

This theory of Seiler's was flatly rejected by Opitz,[9] who, basing his opinion on his critical edition of the text, firmly affirmed the unity of the present text[10]—i.e., including the final two chapters, 89–90 and so argued for 357/358 as the date of composition.[11] Whatever criticism Opitz may deserve for his trojan work on the edition of the Athanasian texts,[12] it cannot be denied that he knew the actual texts and the history of their transmission inside out. Fully unjustified, therefore, is the criticism of Peeters, otherwise so penetrating, who in turn spurned the date as proposed by Opitz because the latter did not publish his reasons for coming to such a conclusion, and reverted to the theory of Bardenhewer.[13]

---

[7]   A modified version of the theory of Bardenhewer was recently proposed by Orlandi, "Sull'Apologia secunda," 54–56, who based his suggestion on the work of Opitz, which we will consider shortly, and on a more perceptive assessment of the *Sitz im Leben* of the author. According to Orlandi, the documents which Athanasius began to collect after his return from exile, 346, were incorporated into a full-scale work between 352 and 353, i.e., after the battle of Mursa, 351, when Constantius' attitude to Athanasius took a turn for the worst, and was completed between 355–356, when Chapter 90 was added.

[8]   Seiler, *Athanasius' Apologia contra Arianos*, 1–32. Hagel, *Kirche und Kaisertum*, 18 (and passim) uncritically accepted the findings of Seiler and based much of his reconstruction of the development of Athanasius' attitude towards the State on the various drafts suggested by Seiler.

[9]   Opitz, *Untersuchungen*, 158, footnote 3.

[10]   See the commentary of Opitz 87,1f.

[11]   See the commentary of Opitz 167,19f. See also Quasten, *Patrology* III, 34.

[12]   See, for example, Scheidweiler, "Zur neuen Ausgabe des Athanasius," 73–94. See also Schneemelcher, "Athanasius von Alexandrien als Theologe und als Kirchenpolitiker," 242–256.

Rather than scorn Opitz's option for a unified text by contrasting this with the German scholar's reputed preference for discovering interpolations, one should be all the more impressed by Opitz's conviction, born out of his life-long work on the Texts and the MS tradition, that the *Apologia* is a unified work. This in itself is, of course, insufficient to persuade us to accept the solution of Opitz, but it should warn us to be reluctant to diverge from his judgements regarding textual questions unless strong arguments to the contrary can be provided.

The theory of Bardenhewer, adopted by Peeters,[13] is, like that of Seiler, based on the assumption that Chapters 89–90 were later added to the main body of the work. The only justification for such an assumption given by Bardenhewer (no reasons are given by Seiler who simply accepts this as self-evident) is not the obvious divergence between the events recorded in the main section, covering the years up to ca. 347, and the final two chapters which refer to the events that occurred during the years 357–358 (as Peeters supposes); it is the absence of any mention in the main body of the work of the relapse of Valens and Ursacius into Arianism, which presumably occurred after the death of Constans early in 350[14] and not later than the Synod of Arles, 353. More than most arguments *ex silentio,* this one is very unstable indeed. When we look at it more closely, however, we will see that it does indeed hold one of the keys to the interpretation of the *Apologia.* [15] But first let us glance at the actual text which Opitz so positively affirmed to be a unified whole.

If Chapters 89–90 were indeed added at a later date to the text as Bardenhewer, Seiler, and Peeters maintain, then there ought to be a clear fissure between the end of Chapter 88 and the opening of Chapter 89. But instead of a break in the sequence, *Apologia* 88,3 ends with a rhetorical question: 3 (a) τίς τὰ τοιαῦτα καὶ τοσαῦτα θεωρήσας οὐκ ἄν εἴποι (b) ὅτι καὶ Οὐάλης καὶ Οὐρσάκιος εἰκότως κατέγνωσαν ἑαυτῶν (c) καὶ μεταγινώσκοντες τοιαῦτα καθ᾿ ἑαυτῶν ἔγραφαν, (d) μᾶλλον ἑλόμενοι πρὸς ὀλίγον αἰσχυνθῆμαι ἢ αἰωνίως τὴν τῶν συκοφαντῶν ὑπομεῖναι τιμωρίαν;[16] and *Apologia* 89,1 begins with

---

[13]   Peeters, "Comment S. Athanase s'enfuit de Tyr en 335," 174, footnote 2. It should be noted that Peeters ignores the debate of Opitz and Seiler.

[14]   See Seeck, *Regesten,* 197.

[15]   Opitz, in his commentary 87,2f., had already perceived that the Apologia presupposed the relapse of Valens and Ursacius.

[16]   Commenting on this text, Opitz 167,8 refers his reader to Chapter 58 and adds: "Hier ist der beste Beweis, daß der bisher fälschlich abgetrennte Teil II (ca. 59ff.) zu c. 58 gehört."

a subordinate clause: Διὰ τοῦτο γὰρ δικαίως καὶ ἐκκλησιαστικῶς ποιοῦντες καὶ οἱ μακάριοι ουλλειτουργοὶ ἡμῶν, neither of which indicates a fissure, since (i) the question, though rhetorical, begs an answer and (ii) the phrase Διὰ τοῦτο, which refers in the first place to *Apologia* 88,1–2 (as also to *Apologia* 88,3a), and thus to the purpose of the whole work (the ecclesiastical sentence of innocence on Athanasius), and in the second place to *Apologia* 88,3b–d, very naturally introduces the final summary of the entire work, linking Chapters 89–90 both to Chapter 88 *and* to the opening of the entire composition, Chapter One. The significance of the rhetorical question is to be found in *Apologia* 89,1, which continues: ἐπειδή τινες ἀμφίβολα τὰ καθ᾽ ἡμᾶς ἔλεγον καὶ ἀκυροῦν ἐβιάζοντο τὸ ὑπὲρ ἡμῶν κριθέντα, πάντα παθεῖν ὑπέμειναν νῦν καὶ ἐξορισθῆναι εἵλοντο ἢ λυομένας ἰδεῖν τὰς τῶν τοσούτων ἐπισκόπων κρίσεις. Here Athanasius refers to attempts (at Arles, 353, and Milan, 355) made by the Neo-Arian party led by Valens and Ursacius to force the bishops of the West, who at Rome and Sardica had pronounced Athanasius innocent, to reverse that judgement, but who instead preferred to endure suffering and exile.[17] The relapse of Valens and Ursacius into Arianism is thus, at least in this text, presupposed by the author of the *Apologia*.[18]

When we examine the function occupied by the two Western prelates in the *Apologia*, and compare it with the role they play in the other writings of Athanasius, we will see in the first place how far off the mark Seiler was in his thesis concerning the gradual evolution of the text over two decades, and so complement Opitz and his arguments regarding the unity of the composition,[19] and at the same

---

[17] Athanasius does not mention or reproach the many bishops in the West who bowed to the imperial will and acquiesced to the unjust demands of Valens and Ursacius.

[18] Orlandi, "Sull'Apologia secunda," 55, suggests that only Ch. 90 was added around 355–356, though he gives no argument in support of such a proposal apart from a possible motive on the part of Athanasius. But Chapters 89–90 evidently make up a literary unit, as indicated by the type of parallelism found in the two chapters which is typical of the style of Athanasius.

[19] These arguments are concisely outlined by Opitz, *Untersuchungen*, 158, footnote 3. They are, in my opinion, convincing. One need only comment that Seiler, unlike his master Laqueur, did not base his study on any textual evidence (such as divergences in the transmission of the text) but only on the generalization that: "Die meisten der historischen Werke des Athanasius sind uns nicht vollständig oder in Überarbeitung überliefert" (Seiler, *Athanasius' Apologia contra Arianos*, 35). This statement is based on (i) the incomplete *Commentary on Matthew 11,27* (*PG* 25,208–220), which is probably not an unfinished work of Athanasius, but rather the only surviving fragment of a larger work (cf. Quasten, *Patrology* III, 39), and which was probably not

time we will be able to take an important step towards fixing the date of composition more precisely than Opitz.

Apart from the passing references to Valens and Ursacius in the documents incorporated into this *Defense*—such as their membership of the commission sent to the Mareotis by the Synod of Tyre, 335, to hold an inquiry into the case of Ischyras,[20] and their deposition, together with other Arian bishops, by the Synod of Sardica, 343,[21]— the observer cannot but be impressed at the empirical fact that these two political ecclesiastics are singled out for special attention and are explicitly named by Athanasius in all the three major narratives

historical in character (see also Hugger, "Des hl. Athanasius Traktat in Mt. 11,27," 441); (ii) the apparent development that may be detected in *Ad Const.*, which, however, can be more easily explained as due to a sudden change of circumstances in the course of writing the defense since the work preserves its homogenous style; (iii) a dubious interpretation of *Ad monach.* 3; and (iv) a reference to *Or. c. Ar. IV*, which is not a genuine work of Athanasius. The only text which could offer some support to such a theory of revisions possibly undertaken by Athanasius is *De morte Arii* 5 (*PG* 25,689,B13–C2), where the author requests his friend, Bishop Serapion, not to allow the text he sent to him to be copied, but to return the text to him with the additions of anything he considered to be missing from the original. The instruction seems to imply that Athanasius was prepared to make any alterations which might seem necessary. This text warns us of the possibility of later *interpolations* but it does not justify either the generalization of Seiler just mentioned or the hypothesis of a continual reworking of the text over the period of two decades. Athanasius, whom Seiler himself describes as a "temperamentvoller Autor" (p. 7), was not an academic like Eusebius, who enjoyed the exercise of revising and recasting an original draft. The Bishop of Alexandria was a man of deep conviction and exceptional intellectual qualities, who wrote not for the joy of writing (if we prescind from the youthful double-apologetic treatise *C. Gentes—De Incarnatione*), but rather in order to defend and clarify his convictions. As can be gathered from the subsequent text of *De morte Arii* 5 (*PG* 25,689,C4), and as was pointed out at the end of the Chapter Six above, he took great pains to write accurately and clearly, and once he had confined his thought to papyrus—or whatever material he used—then he never undertook a revision of such a radical nature as that undertaken by Eusebius, to the best of our knowledge, but at the most could be expected to clarify one or other point with the addition of a line or two. As will be seen below, such minor adjustments can indeed be detected in the *Apologia*.

[20] *Letter of the Presbyters of Alexandria to the Mareotis Commission*, 335 = *Apol.* 73,2 (Opitz 152,10); *Letter of the Clergy of the Mareotis to Philagrius and Paladins*, 335 = *Apol.* 76,2 (Opitz 156,1); *Letter of the Synod of Alexandria*, 338 = *Apol.* 13,2 (Opitz 97,28);*Letter of Julius of Rome*, 341 = *Apol.* 28,1 (Opitz 107,29);*Letter of the Synod of Sardica*, 343 = *Apol.* 37,7 (Opitz 116,11–13), which contains the information that "certain wicked and abandoned youths" (= Valens and Ursacius) actually wrote the report of the said commission.

[21] *Letter of the Synod of Sardica*, 343 = *Apol.* 47,3 (Opitz 123,8).

which in the *Apologia secunda* connect the documents found in Part I (Ch. 1–58): namely, in the Preface to the entire work (Ch. 1–2),[22] in the connecting narrative between the *Letter of the Synod of Alexandria* and the *Letter of Julius*,[23] and in the introduction to the section covering the Synod of Sardica and its aftermath,[24] where they are simply listed with the other Arians. But that section reaches its climax when Athanasius produces his Greek translation of the Latin letter addressed by Ursacius and Valens to Pope Julius, in which they confess the falsity of their accusations against Athanasius, openly anathematize the Arian tenets, and then request that Julius once again receive them into communion. This letter is followed by a type of "Kommunionbrief" (again a Greek translation of the Latin original) addressed to Athanasius himself, in which the Pannonian bishops announce to Athanasius their return to communion with the Catholic Church. Both letters are quoted in full.[25]

A reference to the two bishops follows these documents almost immediately, which text can be identified as the primary *pivotal text* of the entire work, for it forms both a summary of Part I[26] and serves at the same time as an introduction to Part II, announcing the aim of the latter.[27] Soon after the opening of Part II, Valens and Ursacius are again mentioned as members of the Mareotis commission[28]—occupying the last two places in the list, as in the lists found in the earlier documents themselves. In like fashion, they are listed among the "commission," which went up to Constantinople after the Synods of Tyre and Jerusalem and there stage-managed the exile of Athanasius.[29] But before he proceeds to sum up the entire book in Chapters 89–90, Athanasius once again indirectly refers back to the pivotal text by asserting how the aim of Part II has been reached: there again Valens and Ursacius, alone of the Arian bishops, are explicitly mentioned.[30] We will later examine these references in somewhat greater detail.

The origins of Valens, Bishop of Mursa, and Ursacius, Bishop of Singidunum (Pannonia), are as obscure, as are the reasons for the

---

[22] *Apol.* 1,3 (Opitz 88,1–2); *Apol.*2,2 (Opitz 88,18); see also *Apol.* 2,3 (Opitz 88,24–26).
[23] *Apol.* 20,2 (Opitz 102,6–7).
[24] *Apol.* 36,2 (Opitz 115,9).
[25] *Apol.* 58,1–5 (Opitz 137,21–138,29).
[26] See the commentary of Opitz 138,30f.
[27] *Apol.* 58,6 (Opitz 138,30–139,3).
[28] *Apol.* 72,4 (Opitz 151,26).
[29] *Apol.* 87,1 (Opitz 166,1).
[30] *Apol.* 88,3 (Opitz 167,8). See the comment of Opitz quoted in footnote 16 above.

sudden appearance among the Easterners at Tyre, 335, of these two young bishops of Western provinces. There, they make their first appearance in history as members of the infamous Mareotis Commission, which Athanasius consistently condemned as *ex parte* through and through; they actually drew up the report of the said commission.[31] They were inseparable: in every move they made, they acted together. In the Mareotis Commission, in the commission which went up to Constantinople after Tyre and achieved the exile of Athanasius, in their common recantation to Julius and Athanasius once their careers were in jeopardy after their deposition at Sardica, and in their subsequent relapse into Arianism, they acted jointly. When they returned to power at the head of the Arian party, they received the full backing of the Emperor Constantius and, with his help, for a short period almost effectively dominated the entire Church East and West, from the Synod of Milan (355) until the Dual-Synod of Ariminum and Seleucia (359). The chill caused by the sinister shadow they cast over the Church during these four years at the height of their power—a height which their mentor, Eusebius of Nicomedia, whom they succeeded as leaders of the Arians, never attained—can be almost felt in the major texts we examine in this study, the present *Apologia* and the *Historia Arianorum*.

If we ignore the reference to the *Letter of the Synod of Alexandria*, 338, where they occur as members of the Mareotis Commission, the first records of Valens and Ursacius to be found in the other writings of Athanasius date from the year 343 and occur in two letters sent by Athanasius to the clergy and people of the Mareotis[32] and those of Alexandria,[33] informing them of the results of the Sardican Synod: the deposition and excommunication of the Arian party. In both references, Valens and Ursacius are mentioned but second to Theodore (of Heraclea) and Narcissus (of Neronias). Almost thirteen years later we find the next recorded reference in Athanasius' *Encyclical to his Fellow-Bishops in Egypt and Libya,* written soon after his expulsion from his Church by the imperial troops under the command of the Dux Syrianus,[34] on February 9, 356, and after he had received news of the "appointment" of his Arian successor, George of Cappadocia.[35] Again listed among the Arian

---

[31] See above, footnote 20.
[32] Cf. *PG* 26,1333,C12.
[33] *PG* 26,1336,B10.
[34] *Ad Const.* 25 (Szymusiak 116).
[35] *Ad epp. Aeg. et Lib.* 7 (*PG* 25,553,C34).

bishops, they are, however, given special attention in comparison with the others in the list, by a relatively detailed description of their discipleship of Arius in their youth and their previous suspension from the office of presbyter.[36] And yet they only occupy the sixth and seventh place in a list containing eighteen names of bishops who were either deposed at Nicaea or Sardica, or clearly received their office due to the influence of the Arian party. What is most conspicuous is the absence of any hint of their recantation to either Julius or Athanasius.

But when we look at the next reference to Valens and Ursacius, we observe (a) that they are now mentioned alone and (b) their recantation alone is the sole subject of this reference. In the *Defense* Athanasius addressed to the Emperor Constantius and composed between the February 9, 356, and the February 24, 357,[37] the Alexandrian bishop opens with the following statement: "Now with regard to ecclesiastical matters and the conspiracy mounted against me, it is sufficient to refer Your Piety to the witness of those things decreed by so many bishops, as is the repentance of Ursacius and Valens sufficient proof to all mankind that none of the charges which they raised against us possesses a shred of truth."[38]

In contrast with this sole reference, the *Historia Arianorum* (probably composed in October 357, as we will see) refers to them on at least eleven different occasions. Athanasius vents his rage on the episcopal pair, now at the height of their power. The texts, apart from one reference to their deposition by Sardica,[39] concentrate above all on their apparent repentance and recantation[40] as contrasted with their relapse into Arianism[41] (mentioned explicitly for the first time), their part at the Synods of Arles (353) and

---

[36] *Ad epp. Aeg. et Lib.* 7 (*PG* 25,553,A13–B2). This is the only information we have of their previous history; what historical credibility can be attached to these statements needs to be critically examined.

[37] Quasten, *Patrology* III, 57.

[38] *Ad Const.* 1,1–2 (Opitz 279,5–9).

[39] *Hist. Arian.* 17,3 (Opitz 191,32–33).

[40] *Hist. Arian.* 26,1–5 (Opitz 197,5–23), which text originally included full quotations of the letters to Julius and Athanasius (or rather their Greek translations), the titles of which, and the opening words, are now preserved. See also *Hist. Arian.* 29,2 (Opitz 198,21–28), which contains a relatively detailed description of the circumstances which surrounded their recantation, as well as *Hist. Arian.* 76,3 (Opitz 225,20–21); *Hist. Arian.* 79,3 (Opitz 227,32); *Hist. Arian.* 36,5 (Opitz 202,17–18).

[41] *Hist. Arian.* 29,1 (Opitz 198,17–21), where a comparatively detailed account is given; see also *Hist. Arian.* 34,3 (Opitz 202,17) and *Hist. Arian.* 36,5 (Opitz 203,30–31).

Milan (355),[42] and the persecution of the orthodox, which reached its climax with the lapse of both Liberius of Rome and Ossius of Cordova,[43] the final responsibility for which Athanasius puts at the feet of Valens and Ursacius.

In *De synodis* (dated ca. 361–362), they again feature as leaders of the Arian party, though their importance seems to have suffered somewhat since the composition of *Historia Arianorum*.[44] Their authorship of the "Blasphemy of Sirmium" and their attempt to top their previous success with the imposition of the "dated Creed" on the Synodal Fathers at Ariminum (359) are both noted.[45] We are also informed that their temporary success backfired and earned their deposition by the Synodal Fathers,[46] which marked the decline of their influence in ecclesiastical circles, though not at the court, at least while Constantius lived (i.e., up to 361). Finally in *Ad Afros* (369), their influence seems to be on the wane: they now take second place to Auxentius of Milan.[47] In neither of the last two works is their recantation mentioned.

This chronological outline of the appearance and growing importance of Valens and Ursacius within the other historico-apologetic writings of Athanasius can evidently help us date the *Apologia*. As we saw in our empirical analysis, Valens and Ursacius played a central role in the *Apologia*, unifying the various documents. If we take a closer look at the relevant texts, we will observe that, apart from some passing references to their participation in the *ex parte*

---

[42] Cf. *Hist. Arian.* 31,1 (Opitz 199,21–23) and *Hist. Arian.* 31,4 (Opitz 200,11–12).

[43] *Hist. Arian.* 41,1 (Opitz 206,4), where Athanasius places the blame for the scourging of Hilary the Deacon, one of the two delegates of Liberius at Milan, on the shoulders of "Ursacius, Valens, and the eunuchs, their accomplices," and thus points to them as the persons ultimately responsible for the persecution of Liberius; in *Hist. Arian.* 45,5 (Opitz 209,24–26), Athanasius portrays the lapse of Ossius as the Bishop of Cordova's forced communion with Valens and Ursacius.

[44] They are mentioned as the sole representatives of the Arian party in *De syn.* 1,3 (Opitz 231,13) and *De syn.* 9,1 (Opitz 236,18). But in *De syn.* 2,4 (Opitz 232,17) and 3,1 (Opitz 232,25), they are joined by Germinius of Sirmium (cf. *De syn.* 28,2), while according to *De syn.* 8,1 (Opitz 235,15–16), their place at the top of the Arian hierarchy is taken by Germinius and Auxentius.

[45] Cf. *De syn.* 28,2 (Opitz 256,26); *De syn.* 8,1 (235,15–16).

[46] *De syn.* 9,1 (Opitz 236,16–19).

[47] *Ad Afros* 1 (PG 26,1029,B8–9); see also *Ad Afros* 10 (PG 26,1045,D6), which reports their excommunication by Damasus of Rome. However, in *Ad Afros* 3 (PG 26,1053,10) the two Pannonian bishops still head the list.

Mareotis Commission[48] and in the delegation from Tyre/Jerusalem to
Constantine,[49] as well as their deposition by Sardica,[50] all the other references are situated in key positions in the text and have, as their subject
matter, the *recantation* of Valens and Ursacius. In his Preface to the
Apologia (Ch. 1–2), their former calumny and later change of mind is
used to stigmatize the earlier Eusebian party (which, it seems, had effectively conspired to secure the deposition of Athanasius at Tyre and his
banishment to Trier); there alone Athanasius refers to their recantation
on three occasions within the short narrative.[51] Linking the document
issued by the Synod of Alexandria (338) with the *Letter of Julius* of Rome,
the author of the *Apologia* gives, as the main cause of the Eusebian party's
refusal to accept the summons of Pope Julius to a Roman synod, the fear
of the Eusebians that those things *which Valens and Ursacius later confessed*
would be proved against them.[52] In the primary *pivotal text,*[53] Athanasius,
after summarizing Part I (Ch. 3–58), announces the double purpose of
Part II. Ignoring the first of this pair of objectives for the moment, the
second purpose reads: "I wish, with your permission, to describe the affair
in detail, beginning with its origin, so that you might perceive . . . that
Ursacius and Valens, though somewhat late in the day, did confess the
truth." Finally, the writer of this evidently well-planned and carefully
thought-out text, rounds off his tightly organized exposition[54] with another

---

[48] *Apol.* 72,4 (Opitz 151,26). See also the many references to the same fact in the
documents incorporated into the *Apologia,* as listed above in footnote 20.

[49] *Apol.* 87,1 (Opitz 166,1).

[50] *Apol.* 36,6 (Opitz 115,9).

[51] *Apol.* 1,3 (Opitz 88,1–6); *Apol.* 2,2 (Opitz 88,17–20); *Apol.* 2,3 (Opitz 88,24–26).

[52] *Apol.* 20,2 (Opitz 102,6–7).

[53] *Apol.* 58,6 (Opitz 138,30–139,3).

[54] As with the *Historia Arianorum,* so also in the *Apologia,* the main body of the text
is divided into two major parts. Each part is again subdivided into sections, which
complement each other. In Part I, the two sections are: Ch. 3–35 and Ch. 36–58,
the first dealing with the Synods of Alexandria and Rome and the second with
that of Sardica. Part II is divided into (i) Ch. 59–70, which deals with the first
stage in the conspiracy against Athanasius, beginning with the alliance between
the Eusebians and the Meletians and ending with the recantation of John Acarph,
the leader of the Meletians after Meletius, and (ii) Ch. 71–88, which deals with
the second stage of the conspiracy, the Synod of Tyre, giving particular attention
to the Mareotis Commission, where Ursacius and Valens were so prominent, and
ending with the recantation of those two Pannonian bishops, the present leaders
of the Arians (or, more precisely, the Eusebians). In the course of our analysis,
the compact quality of Athanasius' writing, particularly in Part II, will become
evident. Here it will suffice to draw attention to the way Section 1 of Part II is
rounded off with the pivotal text (*Apol.* 71,1 = Opitz 148,25–28): Athanasius

reference to the recantation of Valens and Ursacius:[55] "Who, observing such proceedings, will not declare that Valens and Ursacius were right to condemn themselves and, having recanted, wrote thus against themselves, preferring rather to suffer shame for a short time than to endure forever the retribution due to slanderers."

It is evident that the recantation of Valens and Ursacius is of the greatest importance to the author of the *Apologia*. If it can be accepted that this dramatic, though short-lived, change of heart on the part of these political Arians took place ca. 347,[56] then it is strange that Athanasius did not mention it in any other text (if we ignore the *Apologia* for the moment) until *Ad Constantium*, which may be dated end of 356, beginning of 357. It is further quite remarkable that Julius of Rome apparently did not send Athanasius a copy of Valens' and Ursacius' *Letter of Recantation* addressed to the Bishop of Rome. Athanasius tells us that Paulinus of Trier sent him a copy. But what is most remarkable is that Athanasius, when he quotes the Letter of Valens and Ursacius addressed to himself, in which the Pannonian bishops announce their readmittance to the Church's communion and request Athanasius to *answer* this letter, likewise quotes from the *copy* sent to him by Paulinus of Trier,[57] and not from the original which it might be presumed he had received.

Since the letter addressed to Athanasius does not contain the important information regarding the recantation of their conspiracy against him and their rejection of the Arian teaching but simply announces their return to communion, it is indeed possible that Athanasius did receive the original, but not knowing the reason for the readmittance (and possibly at first considering it a forgery),

---

informs us that the story of the first conspiracy so ended and introduces the theme of the following section, which will demonstrate how the earlier conspiracy drew its driving force not from genuine grievances arising from the behavior of Athanasius, but rather from the Eusebian involvement in the cause of Arius, which drove them to their second conspiracy that ended in the apparent victory at Tyre when Athanasius was deposed and Arius readmitted to communion. This pivotal text refers back to the opening of Section 1 (*Apol.* 59,4f. = Athanasius' refusal to admit Arius into communion at the demand of the emperor) and to the end of Section 2 (*Apol.* 84,1f. = the admittance of Arius to communion at Jerusalem and the deposition and exile of Athanasius).

[55] *Apol.* 88,3 (Opitz 167,7–10).
[56] See Seiler, *Athanasius' Apologia contra Arianos*, 44–47.
[57] τὰ μέντοι ἀντίγραφα ἀπεστάλη μοι παρὰ Παυλίνου τοῦ ἐπισκόπου Τριβέρων (*Apol.* 51,8 = Opitz 137,24–25). This clearly refers to both documents. Copies of the original Latin texts are preserved by Hilary, *Frag. hist.*, series B, II, 6 and 8 (Feder 143–145).

ignored the letter. It is equally possible that he never received the original. It appears that the only sign of a change of heart on the side of Valens and Ursacius that reached Athanasius was the fact that they had signed letters of peace (τοῖς εἰρηνικοῖς) presented to them by two presbyters and a layman who happened at the time to be travelling in that area—but it also seems clear that Athanasius did not enter into communion with them.[58] But when did, he received the *copies* from Paulinus of Trier?

Comparing the mention of Valens and Ursacius in the *Encyclical to his Fellow-Bishops in Egypt and Libya*, written probably in the first half of 356 (where they receive special attention from Athanasius but only occupy the 6th or 7th places respectively in the list of Arian bishops) and their mention in Athanasius' *Defense addressed to the Emperor Constantius*, written around the end of 356 and the beginning of 357 (where Valens and Ursacius alone of all Arian bishops are mentioned and the *Letter of Recantation* paraphrased in a text, which Opitz observed,[59] is a reference to the *Apologia*), then it is clear that between the composition of these two works, the copies of the two documents first came into Athanasius' hands.

To explain how this came about, I can only suggest the following. St. Paulinus of Trier, who possibly knew Athanasius from the days of the latter's first exile, first became aware of the threat to Athanasius posed by the two Pannonian bishops, when they, firmly in control of the Arian party and acting on behalf of the Emperor Constantius, attempted to secure the condemnation of Athanasius at the Synod of Arles at the end of the year 353. All present, including the Papal Delegates, succumbed to the imperial demand with the single exception of Paulinus. Again, at Milan (355), he refused to subscribe to the condemnation of Athanasius. He was exiled to Phrygia where he later died. Is it not likely that, after Milan (355), Paulinus sent an emissary to Trier to make copies of the two letters of Valens and Ursacius and, once in possession of these documents, sent them to Athanasius from his exile in Phrygia?

In the course of the year 356, probably in the early summer, the copies must have reached Athanasius in hiding on the out-skirts of Alexandria. That at least is certain, since Athanasius had no knowledge of them in February 356 (at the time he wrote his encyclical) and yet clearly knew of their existence by the time he composed *Ad Constantium* at the end of 356, or at the latest at the

[58] Cf. *Hist. Arian.* 26,5 (Opitz 197,21–23).
[59] *Ad Const.* 1,2 (Opitz 279,7–10).

beginning of 357. Athanasius at once realized the significance of these documents—the genuineness of which he never doubted and made the fullest possible use of them in his *Apologia*.

Thus, we can affirm with reasonable certainty that the *Apologia* was composed during the summer or early autumn of 356. The unity of its composition is confirmed by the way Athanasius uses these letters and their content to unify the disparate documents he incorporated into the work and to help him clarify the significance of the events covered by these documents by castigating the conspiracies of the Arians, which Valens and Ursacius later openly acknowledged in their letters to Julius and Athanasius.

Finally, a word about later interpolations. There is no evidence that Athanasius undertook any radical revision of his text. On the other hand, there are some indications that at least one minor alteration of the text (by Athanasius?) was undertaken (possibly between 367 and 370).[60] It seems to me that another such alteration was the inclusion of two parentheses in Chapter 89.[61] The failure to recognize these as later interpolations has bedeviled the question of dating the *Apologia* and resulted in the hypothesis of Bardenhewer that the whole of Chapter 89 (together with Chapter 90) was later added to the main body of the work. We have already shown how Chapters 89–90 are intrinsically related to the main body of the work and were part of the original composition. They make up a parallelism: both chapters refer to the witness of Liberius of Rome and Ossius of Cordova and their fellow bishops who in 355 suffered exile rather than condemn Athanasius.

Chapter 89 however contains two parentheses, which are clearly later interpolations. The first refers to Liberius and reads: εἰ γὰρ καὶ εἰς τέλος οὐχ ὑπέμεινε τοῦ ἐξορισμοῦ τὴν θλῖψιν, ὅμως διετίαν ἔμεινεν ἐν τῇ μετοικίᾳ γιγνώσκων τὴν καθ' ἡμῶν συσκευήν. The second paraphrase refers to Ossius: εἰ γὰρ καὶ πρὸς ὀλίγον φοβηθεὶς τὰς . . . πρὸς καιρὸν εἶξεν αὐτοῖς. The presence of these two interpolations is indicated (i) by the unusual length of the sentence where they are now incorporated (taking up 15 lines of Opitz's critical edition), which is uncharacteristic of the style of Athanasius; (ii) by the evident break in the narrative caused by these two parentheses, in particular that referring to Ossius, which, if the parentheses were part of the original draft, ought to have followed immediately after

---

[60] Jones, "The Date of the *Apologia contra Arianos*," 224–227, claims that *Apol.* 83,4 (Opitz 162,20–21) was inserted by Athanasius at that time.

[61] *Apol.* 89,3 (Opitz 167,19–20); *Apol.* 89,4 (Opitz 167,22–24). See the alterations in the text proposed by Scheidweiler, "Zur neuen Ausgabe," 82–83.

the mention of the Bishop of Cordova; but between the name of Ossius and the parenthesis is a fairly lengthy reference to the other bishops of Italy, Gaul, Spain, Egypt, Libya, and the Pentapolis, who also suffered the fate of banishment, which made it impossible for Athanasius to insert his interpolation at the appropriate point;[62] (iii) the two parentheses are in fact paraphrases of Athanasius' lengthy treatment of Liberius and Ossius in the *Historia Arianorum* and presupposes the latter, which was written in October 357, as we will see; (iv) the fact that the parallel reference to Liberius and Ossius in Chapter 90 betrays no knowledge of the two parentheses or their content (the lapse of the Bishops of Rome and Cordova). Thus, when Athanasius sat down to write the *Apologia* during the summer or early autumn of 356, Liberius, Ossius, and the other bishops of the West, such as Paulinus of Trier, were in exile, having been banished in 355 after the Synod of Milan; they were joined by other bishops of Egypt, Libya, and the Pentapolis, who had been removed from their sees in 356, probably by the Dux Syrianus.[63]

§2 *Sitz im Leben*

Julius of Rome died on the April 12, 352. The following year, Constantius, who in 350 became sole ruler, established his dominion in fact after the suicide of the Western "usurper" Magnentius on the August 10, 353. Sometime between the death of Julius and the end of Magnentius on the August 10, 353, a synod assembled at Antioch, if we can accept the testimony of Sozomen, and sent an encyclical to all bishops in which they claimed that Athanasius: ὡς παρὰ τοὺς νόμους τῆς ἐκκλησίας ἐπανῆλθεν εἰς Ἀλεξάνδριαν, οὐκ ἀναίτιος φανεὶς ἐπὶ συνόδου, ἀλλὰ φιλονικίᾳ τῶν τὰ αὐτὰ φρονούντων. . . .[64]

---

[62] Scheidweiler, "Zur neuen Ausgabe," 82–83, suggested that this reference to the bishops of Italy and the other provinces ought to be removed, since he considered it to be one of the two "störende Einschübe" in the present text of *Apol.* 89,2f.

[63] Cf. *Hist. Arian.* 31,3–6 (Opitz 200,5–22); see also the *Festal Index* and the *Historia acephala* for the years 355 and 356 (Larsow, *Fest-Briefe*, 35).

[64] Sozomen, *HE* 4,8,4 (Bidez-Hansen 147,25–27). Regarding the date, this is deduced from the position occupied by the account of this synod between Sozomen's report of the death of Julius (together with Liberius' election) in *HE* 4,8,2 and his mention of the death of Magnentius in *HE* 4,8,5. It is possible that Sozomen took his information from Sabinus. With regard to the objections raised by the Neo-Arians, compare these with the similar objections raised by the Eusebians to the recall of Athanasius from the first exile (cf. Sozomen, *HE* 3,2,8 = Bidez-Hansen 103,14–18; see also Sozomen, *HE* 3,5,3 = Bidez-Hansen 106,1–4). Footnote 65 has been deleted after revision.

The synod called on their fellow bishops not to hold communion with him but to enter into communion with George, who had been ordained by them to the See of Alexandria.

The reason given by the Synod of Antioch needs to be clearly understood. It was not the guilt of Athanasius with respect to the previous charges but the same accusation as raised by the Eusebians after Athanasius' return to Alexandria in 337, having completed his first exile: the return of Athanasius to Alexandria, they claimed, was *in violation of the rules of the Church.* They refer here to his deposition by the Synod of Tyre and insinuate that he was not restored to his see by the competent authority. It seems to me that this encyclical must be identified with the letter mentioned by Liberius in his letter to Constantius: *Obsecro, tranquillissime.*[66] As with the case of the earlier attempt in the reign of Julius to enforce the deposition of Athanasius at Tyre by means of an attempt to find recognition at Rome for a successor whom they elected, the Oriental prelates utilized the inexperience of the newly elected Bishop of Rome, Liberius, to secure his recognition of George of Cappadocia as the legitimate Bishop of Alexandria.[67] Around the same time a synod, apparently held in Alexandria, sent an embassy to Rome with a synodal letter from the 80 Egyptian bishops who had assembled there, defending Athanasius and requesting Liberius to respect the authority of Sardica and enter into communion with him, following the practice of his predecessor Julius.[68] However, it is possible that both the Synod of Antioch and that of Alexandria occurred at the same time—i.e., on receiving

---

[66] See Intervention, No. 31 (Joannou, *Die Ostkirche und die Cathedra Petri*, 106–108). Since Joannou makes no reference to the Synod of Antioch (which he seems not to have noticed), he is constrained to remain satisfied with a rather general reason to explain the origin of this letter, namely that the enemies of Athanasius made use of the opportunity afforded by the election of Liberius, without specifying further how this actually came to pass. Our findings confirm the basic insight of Joannou. On the other hand, I am unable to accept the interpretation of Joannou, when he contends that the contents of the letter referred to the charge of High Treason (brought against Athanasius for his alleged conspiracy with the usurper Magnentius, cf. *Ad Const.* 6–9). As we will see below, the documentary evidence seems to point fairly conclusively to the fact that charges of a civil nature were first brought against Athanasius after the Synod of Milan (355) had confirmed the judgement of Tyre with regard to the deposition of Athanasius. The "crime," which formed the content of the Antiochene Letter, was that Athanasius had transgressed *the laws of the Church.*

[67] See Sozomen, *HE* 4,8,2–4 (Bidez-Hansen 147,12–20).

[68] See: Intervention, No. 32 (Joannou, *Die Ostkirche und die Cathedra Petri*, 109–110). As the motive for this letter, Joannou suggests that Athanasius had heard of the new moves on the part of his enemies to reject him from the

the official report of Liberius' election to the See of Rome—each with the object of securing his communion for their respective claimants to the Throne of St. Mark, since the Letter of Liberius says that, at the same time as the Letter of the Oriental bishops, the Letter of the 80 bishops of Egypt arrived in Rome. Though it cannot be ruled out that Athanasius received word of the new Antiochene maneuver, yet here the traditional exchange of *Letters of Communion* is most likely the raison d'être of the Synod of Alexandria, as it was probably the immediate cause of the Synod of Antioch, and their respective letters to Rome.

Towards the end of the year 352, Liberius assembled a synod in Rome to examine the situation. He rejected the claims of the Oriental bishops and decided in favor of Athanasius—basing his decision on the "greater number of bishops," referring thereby to the Synods of Rome (340–341), Sardica (343), and Jerusalem (346).[69] After the judgement of Liberius and the Synod of Rome had been officially communicated, an objection was raised by the Neo-Arian party to the way the Bishop of Rome handled the Oriental letter at the Roman synod; it appears that this objection was made to the emperor.[70] Probably following the guidelines set by Sardica,[71] Liberius then requested the emperor to arrange the convocation of a synod at Aquileia to review the question[72] and, for this purpose, sent a delegation to the emperor led by Vincent of Capua.[73] A little later, Athanasius likewise sent a delegation headed by Serapion of Thmuis to the emperor:[74] they departed from Alexandria on May 19, 353.[75]

Alexandrian See. This seems a little inadequate. It is probable that Socrates, *HE* 2,26,4 (Hussey 266) makes a reference to this Synod of Alexandria. There he simply tells us that the synod confirmed the judgements of Sardica (343) and Jerusalem (346).

[69] See: Intervention, No. 33 and 34 (Joannou, *Die Ostkirche und die Cathedra Petri*, 111–113). It is unlikely that, as Joannou suggests, Liberius based his decision on the greater number of *Egyptian* bishops who supported Athanasius in comparison with the smaller number of Orientals. In all probability, Liberius refers to the previous, almost universal unanimity after Sardica, to which the Synod of Alexandria referred in their letter (see footnote 68).

[70] See Joannou, *Die Ostkirche und die Cathedra Petri*, 114.

[71] See Hess, *Canons of Sardica*, 119f.

[72] See: Intervention, No. 36 (Joannou, *Die Ostkirche und die Cathedra Petri*, 115–117). It seems that the question as to why Athanasius was not summoned before a civil court (Joannou 116) is not relevant, since, as far as one can judge, the initial charges brought against the bishop were of an ecclesiastical nature.

[73] See Intervention, No. 36 (Joannou, *Die Ostkirche und die Cathedra Petri*, 115).

[74] See Sozomen, *HE* 4,9,6 (Bidez-Hansen 149,4–11).

[75] Cf. *Festal Index* and *Historia acephala* for the year 353 (Larsow, *Fest-Briefe*).

No satisfactory reason for this Alexandrian delegation has been given.[76] The most likely immediate cause was, it seems to me, the decision of Liberius to request Constantius to assemble a synod at Aquileia. Athanasius sent his trusted friend, Serapion, together with four other bishops and three presbyters, to represent him. Four days after their departure, Montanus the Silentiarius, a court official, arrived in Alexandria with letters from the emperor,[77] which Athanasius later claimed he considered at the time to be forgeries, since they purported to be the emperor's reply to a request he never made, namely for permission to travel to Italy "so as to be able to make complete those things he considered deficient in ecclesiastical

---

[76] According to Sozomen, *HE* 4,9,4 (Bidez-Hansen 149,4–11), the immediate cause of the Alexandrian delegation was the news Athanasius received about plots which had been formed against him at the court, while the final aim of their mission was threefold: to reconcile the emperor with Athanasius, to reply, if necessary to the slanders of his enemies, and to take such measures as they considered best with regard to the Church and himself. The source of Sozomen's account appears to be the *Historia acephala* for the year 353, which simply reports the fact and the date of the departure of Serapion and his fellow-delegates. On the assumption that Sozomen had no other source material at his disposal (although such a possibility cannot be completely ruled out), then his account must be considered an interpretation of the bare facts reported in the *Historia acephala*. The unacceptability of his interpretation is suggested by the fact that, up to the time that Athanasius heard of the civil charges brought against him at Milan in 355, i.e., up to the time of writing *Ad epp. Aeg. et Lib.* in the year 356, Athanasius seems to have been ignorant of any reasons why the emperor should have been at enmity with him (cf. *Ad epp. Aeg. et Lib.* 5 = *PG* 25,549,A4–7) or why he should send a delegation to clear him of calumnies relating to his attitude towards the imperial authority. As we will see, the initial attempts to remove Athanasius were based exclusively it seems on the formal grounds of his reputedly illegal possession of the Alexandrian See. The third aspect of the delegation's aim as reported by Sozomen seems to be a faulty interpretation of *Ad Const.* 19 (see below, footnote 78). The cause of this misunderstanding can be traced to his faulty chronology at this point. He places the departure of Athanasius' delegation to the emperor *after* the Synod of Milan (355); cf. *HE* 4,9,1–5 (Bidez-Hansen 148,11–149,3). This error was due most probably to the mention of the emperor's presence at Milan in the *Historia acephala* for 353, which Sozomen understood as a reference to the emperor's presence at the Synod of Milan (355). The suggestion of Sozomen, that the Alexandrian delegation was occasioned by rumors which had reached Athanasius and which reported new conspiracies against the Alexandrian bishop being hatched at the imperial court, must be rejected as unlikely. Schwartz, among others, follows Sozomen (see below, footnote 78). Joannou, *Die Ostkirche und die Cathedra Petri*, 115, unaccountably reverses the chronological order given in the *Festal Index* and in the *Historia acephala*: he proposes that the Alexandrian delegation departed for the court *after* Athanasius had been summoned there by the emperor through his delegate Montanus.

[77] Cf. *Festal Index* and *Historia acephala* for 353 (Larsow. *Fest-Briefe*, 34).

matters."[78] This was an attempt to lure Athanasius away from Alexandria on the pretext of giving him an opportunity to straighten out the legal objections to his claim to the See of Mark. The letters of the emperor implied that Athanasius' claim was being questioned; they were evidently couched in terms of an order from the emperor, since one of the civil charges listed in *Ad Constantium* is that of disobedience to this imperial command. According to the evidence of the *Historia acephala*,[79] this letter greatly depressed the bishop—his claim to his see was in greater danger than he had imagined—and greatly troubled the people, causing such a tumult that Montanus had to depart Alexandria, having achieved nothing.[80]

Constantius set up his winter quarters at Arles, where, as the sole autocrat of the empire, he celebrated his Vicennalia of his reign (October 10, 353). He acceded to Liberius' request to assemble a synod, though not at Aquileia, as the Roman bishop had requested,

---

[78] *Ad Const.* 19 (Szymusiak 110); see also *Ad Const.* 21. It ought to be noted that this invitation betrays no hint of the later charges of high treason and lèse majesté brought against Athanasius, which he refuted in *Ad Const.* Contrary to the claims of Schwartz ("Zur Kirchengeschichte," 151 = *GS* IV, 129) and Joannou (*Die Ostkirche und die Cathedra Petri*, 116), it must be emphasized that there are no traces of such civil charges at this stage of the controversy. See the following note.

[79] According to Larsow, *Fest-Briefe*, 34, the entry in the *Historia acephala* reads as follows: Post quorum navigationem de Alexandria CC Constantio VI. Aug. et Constantio (falsch im T. Constante) Caesare II., Pachom XXIV die (May 19, 353), mox post IV dies *Montanus Palatinus* ingressus Alexandriam Pachom XXVIII, ejusdem Augusti litteras Constantii dedit episcopo Athanasio, per quas vetabat eos occurrere ad comitatum; ex qua re nimis vastatus est episcopus, et omnis populus fatigatus est valde, ita Montanus nihil agens profectus est, relinquens episcopum Alexandriae. The text is evidently corrupt, as Larsow pointed out, with regard to the actual textual reading of "Constante." It is clear that the passage as it stands makes little sense. If the imperial letters contained instructions that the Alexandrian delegation would not be admitted to the court, then why did Montanus depart from Alexandria, leaving the bishop behind him, as though his mission had failed? The imperial delegate most probably brought orders from the emperor to the effect that Athanasius should proceed to the court with Montanus. This is suggested by the paraphrase of the above text (*Historia acephala*) given by Sozomen (*HE* 4,9,7 = Bidez-Hansen 149,12–13), and receives confirmation from *Ad Const.* 19–21, where the Bishop of Alexandria defends himself against the charge of disobeying the imperial order to repair to the imperial court, which order Montanus had delivered to him in Alexandria. The text of the *Historia acephala* should probably read: per quas invitabat eum occurrere ad comitatum. See Seeck, *Regesten*, 199.

[80] Cf. *Festal Index XXV* (Robertson, *Athanasius*, LNPF², 504; Larsow, *Fest-Briefe*, 34). See Sozomen, *HE* 4,9,7 (Bidez-Hansen 149,13–16).

but at Arles with those bishops who had gathered there for the Vicennalian festivities, including Valens and Ursacius, who now enjoy the favor of the emperor and emerge here for the first time as leaders of the Neo-Arian party.[81] The bishops at Arles, including the Papal delegation, approve of the deposition of Athanasius, with the sole exception of Paulinus of Trier. The Alexandrian delegation waited in vain in Italy (where the synod called by Liberius ought to have taken place) until, probably after hearing of the fait accompli at Arles,[82] they returned to Egypt.

The emperor evidently was not pleased by the authoritative way in which Liberius had insisted to his legates that they adhere to the judgement of the Roman synod, 352.[83] The Bishop of Rome for his part did not apparently consider the synod he proposed as empowered to revise his judgement. Liberius was clearly displeased by the reversal of his judgement by the Synod of Arles and so requested that another synod be allowed to assemble.[84] The emperor conceded to his demand—but once again only partially—and assembled a synod at Milan (355). There, contrary to the design of Liberius, the Neo-Arian party succeeded in getting the emperor to compel the assembled bishops "to assent to the deposition which those unjust judges at Tyre decreed, and, once Athanasius was excluded from communion, to formulate a new creed."[85] Here the Roman Delegates, Eusebius of Vercelli, Lucifer of Cagliari, the priest Pancratius, and the Deacon Hilarius, together with Paulinus of Trier, Dionysius of Milan, Dionysius of Alba, and Phodanus of Toulouse refused to subscribe, and, with the exception of Deacon Hilarius, they were banished into exile. Paulinus, who was apparently appalled by the sinister power of Valens and Ursacius, now ensconced within the Court of Constantius and forgetful of their previous recantation, arranged to have copies of their Letters of Recantation sent to Athanasius.

Now Constantius was free to subject Athanasius to the civil consequences of the synod's judgement. Not satisfied with his mere

---

[81]   Their return to influence at the court was occasioned by the strange coincidence, according to which, the decisive battle of Constantius against the usurper Magnentius took place at Mursa (Sept. 28, 351), where Valens was bishop. Valens provided the emperor with moral support on the eve of the battle, cf. Sulpicius Severus, *Chron.* II, 38 (Halm 91,20f.).

[82]   Cf. *Festal Index XXV* (Robertson, *Athanasius*, LNPF², 504; Larsow, *Fest-Briefe*, 34).

[83]   See Joannou, *Die Ostkirche und die Cathedra Petri*, 118 (Erläuterung 2).

[84]   Intervention, No. 37 (= Joannou, *Die Ostkirche und die Cathedra Petri*, 118–119).

[85]   Theodoret, *HE* 2,15,1 (Parmentier-Scheidweiler 128,15–18).

ecclesiastical deposition, which at the most would have sent Athanasius into exile from his see, Constantius now produces his own charges of a civil nature against the "deposed" bishop: lèse majesté and high treason which carried the death penalty.[86] In August of that year (355), the Imperial Notary Diogenes arrived at Alexandria with the object of imprisoning Athanasius.[87] This he failed to achieve and so the following year the emperor sent the Dux Syrianus to remove the troublesome bishop; he arrived in Alexandria on January 6, 356.[88] From the evidence of our scanty sources, it appears that this mandate, like that of Diogenes, was based on the illegality of Athanasius' claim to Alexandria: the Dux was commissioned to execute the civil consequences of his deposition by Tyre. At this stage, it seems that Athanasius knew nothing of the Synod of Milan or his own condemnation on civil matters. Later Athanasius claimed that he could not believe that the emperor would reverse his earlier civil approval of Athanasius' right to the See of Mark.[89] Attempts by Athanasius to question the legal basis of Syrianus' mission[90] helped to stall his removal until the eve of February 9, when, after previously assuring the bishop that he would do nothing until he had received the necessary documents from the emperor and thus giving the bishop and his faithful a false security, Syrianus and his troops suddenly besieged the Church of Theonas, where Athanasius was holding a Vigil Service.[91] Both the violence done to the surprised faithful and the dramatic escape of their bishop have become almost legendary and need not be repeated here. They mark the beginning of Athanasius' third exile.

Athanasius was, at the time, over sixty years old. Nonetheless, he decided to face the rigors of the long journey to the West in order to plead his case in person before the emperor—as he had previously attempted to do at Constantinople in the wake of the Synod of Tyre.[92] Soon after he had set out on his journey, as he tells us himself, he heard reports ("it was rumored everywhere") that

---

[86] See footnote 72 above.

[87] *Festal Letter* and *Historia acephala* for 355 (Larsow, *Fest-Briefe*, 35). See *Ad Const.* 22 (Szymusiak 113) and *Hist. Arian.* 48,1 (Opitz 211,1–5).

[88] *Festal Letter* and *Historia acephala* for 356 (Larsow, *Fest-Briefe*, 35–36). Regarding the entrance of Syrianus and his violent activity in Alexandria, see *Ad Const.* 22–24 (Szymusiak 113–115); *De fuga* 24,2–6 (Opitz 84,10–85,4); *Hist. Arian.* 48,2–3 (Opitz 211,5–15); *Hist. Arian.* 81,6–10 (Opitz 229,13–230,8).

[89] Cf. *Ad Const.* 23–24 (Szymusiak 113–115).

[90] Cf. *Ad Const.* 22–24 (Szymusiak 113–115).

[91] Cf. *Ad Const.* 25 (Szymusiak 115–116).

[92] Cf. *Ad Const.* 27 (Szymusiak 118).

Liberius of Rome and Ossius of Cordova had been banished together
with the bishops who refused to subscribe at Milan (355), and that at
Arles, the Roman Delegates had been violently compelled to excommunicate him; while he was still at the same place in the (Libyan) Desert, the
news reached him that almost 90 bishops of Egypt and Libya had been
persecuted and their places given up to those who held Arian tenets.[93]
Undaunted, Athanasius decided to continue his journey to Constantius,
when a third report reached him to the effect that (i) Frumentius, the
Apostle of Ethiopia, whom Athanasius had ordained and sent into that
country to establish the Church there, was ordered to report to George,
whom the Arians had appointed successor at Alexandria (to recognize
the election of the latter and to accept his Arian tenets),[94] and that (ii)
he himself, Athanasius, had been found guilty of high treason and lèse
majesté, whose penalty was death.[95] This sentence had apparently been
passed by the remaining bishops at Milan, who (under the direction of
Valens and Ursacius) were completely subservient to the emperor.[96] It
should be noted here that this is the first time that Athanasius heard about
the grave charges of a civil nature that the emperor brought against him.[97]
On hearing this, Athanasius abandoned his plans to go to Constantius and
went into hiding in the desert.[98]

It is characteristic of Athanasius that the first known work of work of
consequence which he wrote in hiding was not a work of self-defense but
his lengthy *Encyclical to his Fellow-Bishops in Egypt and Libya* (ca. first half
of 356). This is an attack on the Neo-Arians, or more precisely the tenets
they profess, and its purpose is to uncover the nature of the Arian heresy,
and so encourage and console those fellow-bishops who suffered persecution and the loss of their sees due to their adherence to the Nicene Faith. It
is a remarkable little work—but one almost ignored by scholars. (There is,
as yet, no modem critical edition of the text.) It is Athanasius' first attempt[99]

---

[93]   Cf. *Ad Const.* 27 (Szymusiak 118–119).
[94]   Cf. *Ad Const.* 29 (Szymusiak 121); also, *Ad Const.* 31 (Szymusiak 125–126).
[95]   Cf. *Ad Const.* 29 (Szymusiak 121); also, *Ad Const.* 30 (Szymusiak 124).
[96]   Cf. *Hist. Arian.* 52,1–6 (Opitz 212,29–213,21).
[97]   See above, footnote 78.
[98]   Cf. *Ad Const.* 32 (Szymusiak 126–127). The chronology given above is based
       on the witness of Athanasius. I see no reason to doubt the credibility of his
       testimony—in particular, when one takes into consideration the nature of the
       document as a brief for the defense, composed with an eye to its examination in
       a Court of Justice where the statements could be verified or proved false.
[99]   This may also be deduced from *Ad epp. Aeg. et Lib.* 11 (*PG* 25,564,A9–13).

to refute the Arian heresy systematically and, at the same time, to present the theological basis of the Nicene Faith—based on (though not limited to) Scripture.

The *encyclical* announces the beginning of a new development in his life: his recourse to writing to expose and defend the Apostolic Faith for which he, as successor to St. Mark, the interpreter of Peter, had a special responsibility.[100] It contains, in germ, the major

[100] It is unfortunate that the scope of this study prevents us from developing in any great detail the consequences of this assertion that, it must be admitted, offends the present scholarly consensus. The following brief remarks must suffice and a fuller treatment to be postponed to a later study. In consequence of the opinion that the *encyclical* was the first attempt by Athanasius to tackle the theological issues raised by the post-Nicene "Arian" opposition party, several important questions regarding the date of composition of the other major works of his—e.g., the three *Orationes contra Arianos, De decretis Nicaenae synodi,* and *De sententia Dionysii*—as well as their relationship to each other and the other major works of Athanasius are automatically raised. Stülcken, *Athanasiana,* 44, hesitatingly suggested that *Ad epp. Aeg. et Lib.* presupposes the existence of *Or. c. Ar. II* and refers us in particular to a comparison of *Ad epp. Aeg. et Lib.* 15–16 (*PG* 25,573,Af.) with *Or. c. Ar. II,* 39 (*PG* 26,229Bf.). Stülcken was right to be hesitant (see also *Athanasiana,* 48), since it can be argued that the relationship is more probably the reverse: *Or. c. Ar. II,* 39 shows all the signs of a later date, since it is more tightly written and the ideas are more fully worked out than in the *encyclical.* With regard to the interdependence of *De decr. Nic.* and the *Orationes,* Stülcken, *Athanasiana,* 48–50, maintains that *De decr. Nic.* 28–31 is a slightly summarized version of *Or. c. Ar. I,* 30–34, thus indicating the priority of the *Orationes.* On the other hand, Hoss, *Studien über das Schrifttum,* 48f., demonstrated that the reverse is most likely the case. Further indications of the posteriority of the *Orationes* were suggested by Lippl, "Athanasius der Große," in *BVK* 2, 8. Gummerus, *Die Homöusianische Partei,* 186f., argued in favor of Stülcken against Hoss; although the detailed analysis of Gummerus shows that some of the details of Hoss' arguments need to be refined, yet Gummerus admits that not only can many of the parallels between the two documents be interpreted to suit either theory, but that, when one compares the two parallel texts in their entirety, *Or. c. Ar.* was written with greater care, with well-rounded transitions and well-founded argumentation, whereas *De decr. Nic.* is shorter, more hastily written, and lacks much of the stylistic finish of the former work. However, Gummerus further claims that the arguments of the *De decr. Nic.* are, for all that, more forceful: what is gradually developed in the *Or. c. Ar.* is sharply formulated at the first glance in *De decr. Nic.* Since the arguments for or against the priority or posteriority of each work, based on divergences in the parallel passages, are not conclusive, then we must seek another criterion to help us decide the issue. Here, it seems to me, that we must look to the other writings of Athanasius to see how he worked as a writer. We are fortunate to possess two texts, which can be dated relatively accurately, and which contain parallel arguments, the one shorter (and thus either a sketch of seminal ideas or the summary of earlier arguments) and the other longer (and thus either the development of earlier ideas or the first draft of ideas

ideas which he will later develop more completely, precisely, and with greater polish, e.g., in the three *Orationes, De synodis,* the *Vita Antonii,* and the *Historia Arianorum.* As yet the term ὁμοούσιος is not the center of the controversy, but simply the denial of the

which could be later summarized). Due to the respective dates of composition, there is, however, no difficulty in establishing that the ideas found in shorthand fashion in *Ad Const.* 32 (356), concerning the question of fleeing before one's enemies, were in *De fuga* (357) developed with greater care and attention to the line of argumentation. The short statement in *Ad Const.* is indeed more forcible in its very brevity and directness than *De fuga,* but this alone only indicates the basic consistency of Athanasius' thought. The picture of Athanasius as a writer, which can be gleaned from his *Letter to the Monks* (see above, p. 260; also p. 265), is that of a man who immediately grasped the basic concept, whose insight into the Mystery of our Faith was at once profound and immediate, and who afterwards tried carefully to express his crystal-clear perception as well as possible. Considering this, then it seems more likely that the *De decr. Nic.* was composed before the *Orationes.* It may be added that the earlier work Athanasius refers to in *De decr. Nic.* 5 was most likely a letter and not a treatise, such as the *Orationes;* it could have been *De syn.,* as indeed is suggested by the subject matter. (Gummerus, *Die Homöusianische Partei,* 192–193, uses this reference in support of his theory of the priority of the *Orationes.*)

With regard to the relationship of *De sent. Dion* to the *Orationes,* a similar situation occurs. Stülcken pointed to the connection which obviously exists between *De sent. Dion.* 10,1, where four central scriptural texts are quoted relating to the Logos in his incarnate condition, and *Or. c. Ar. I,* 53–*Or. c. Ar. II, 83,* where these texts are extensively examined (the examination being previously announced in *Or. c. Ar. I,* 53 and later summarized in *Or. c. Ar. III,* 1). Without further ado, Stülcken, ruled out the possibility of a later development of ideas first found in *De sent. Dion.,* though he fails to give any reason. (Gummerus 193, gives his full support to Stülcken.) But again, it appears that in all probability, Athanasius saw the relevance of these scriptural texts, jotted them down in *De sent. Dion.* in passing, and then used them as a type of program for the *Or. c. Ar.* where he introduced the texts in Book I, developed them in Book II, and summarized his treatment at the opening of Book III.

If then the *Orationes* are to be dated later than *De decr. Nic.* and *De sent. Dion.,* as indeed Montfaucon had earlier proposed (and Newman presupposed), our next problem is to attempt to date the two latter works (since only they are recognized as being able to provide us with clues to the time when they were written; the *Orationes* contain no indications). Though it is by no means conclusively proved, yet it is widely acknowledged that *De decr. Nic.* and *De sent. Dion* are so closely related to each other in aim and content that they were probably composed around the same time (cf. Stülcken, *Athanasiana,* 42–43; Robertson, *Athanasius,* LNPF[2], 173; Bardy, *Saint Athanase,* 113–114). Of the two, the *De decr. Nic.* has provided researchers with some, rather slight, indications of their composition. The main evidence is the text: μετ' ὀλίγον γὰρ καὶ εἰς ὕβρεις ἐκτραπήσονται καὶ μετὰ ταῦτα τὴν σπεῖραν καὶ τὸν χιλίαρχον ἀπειλήσουσιν (*De decr. Nic.* 2,2 = Opitz 2,15–17). According to many commentators (Stülcken 41; Robertson 149; Opitz following Schwartz in his

Divinity of the Logos by the "Arians" (Homoeans), and thus the term is not even mentioned. Instead, "the Faith defended by the ecumenical Synod at Nicaea," it is stressed, is sufficient for the

commentary), this implies a period of peace, though it also expresses fear before the threat of an imminent persecution, namely that of Constantius. Thus, Opitz dates the work around 350/351. Opitz also makes use of other indications: the text supposes that the two Eusebii are dead and Acacius is the actual opponent of Athanasius. The involvement of Acacius in the cause initially championed by the Eusebian party can be traced before 350—so Opitz—while Constantius only turned his attention to ecclesiastical affairs after the Battle of Mursa, 351. Without questioning these facts, it is clear that to posit 350/351 as the date of composition for *De decr. Nic.* fails to take into consideration the time factor involved in enabling news of these events to penetrate to Egypt. However, that point is secondary. What is more vulnerable is the assumption that the text refers to an imminent persecution by Constantius. When we look at the context of this passage, we note that Athanasius here castigates the general behavior of the Arian party, the new "Jews," who, once they perceive that their heresy has no rational basis, invent excuses by questioning what has been defined. Then, he continues, "they will shortly turn to insolence and after that they will threaten the cohort and the commander." The context presupposes a stage in the controversy when the arguments of the extreme Arians had evidently lost their power to convince and so they were trying to shift the center of the controversy into an open attack on the (Nicene) definition. This suggests a date after their Blasphemy of Sirmium (357), when the Nicene terminology was explicitly attacked and openly rejected. Confirmation for this is to be found in the opening sentence of *De decr. Nic.* 1,1 (which has been ignored in the discussion): "You have done well to let me know of the investigations undertaken by you with regard to those who advocate the tenets of Arius, among whom were certain associates of Eusebius as well as a majority of those brethren who think according to the mind of the Church." This important text evidently wishes to distinguish between the extreme Arians (= the minority, led by Acacius in the East and Valens and Ursacius in the West) and those (who were in the majority and) who wished to affirm the teaching of the Church, but nonetheless are counted among the "Arians." This distinction was first made by Athanasius in *De syn.,* after the divisions in the Arian camp became evident at the Dual-Synod of Ariminum and Seleucia, 359. Therefore, the opening verse of *De decr. Nic.* just quoted must have been written later than 359 and, most probably, after the composition of *De syn.,* which could not have been penned earlier than the end of that year.

To return to the earlier passage (*De decr. Nic.* 2,2) and its reputed reference to an imminent persecution by Constantius, we can see how out of place such a suggestion is in view of the later date of composition. The outrages which the text mentions are probably meant to refer to the earlier violence committed during the second and third exiles. The reference to the future threat *to* the cohort and the commander can hardly refer to an imminent persecution; rather it most probably refers to Jn 18,2 (which reports the arrest of Our Lord by the Roman captain and cohort) and is intended to draw attention to the new Jews (the Arians) who depend on the imperial power and military

orthodox,[101] since, at Nicaea, the Fathers anathematized the statements of the Arians and vindicated the truth.[102] But the main object of the letter is "pastoral:" to *encourage* his severely tried fellow-bishops to hold fast to the Faith which the Fathers defended at Nicaea, and to champion it with much zeal and confidence in the Lord.[103] The Egyptian and Libyan bishops, persecuted on account of their attachment to "the Faith received from Our Savior through the Apostles,"[104] are exhorted to have recourse to the source of grace

strength to arrest and detain the orthodox. The possibility that the Arians could now threaten the imperial authority itself—as is here suggested—points to a completely new historical situation, other than the time of Constantius, when the imperial authority enjoyed the unbridled support, both theoretical and practical, of the Neo-Arians; it reflects the situation of the Church under the Emperor Jovian (June 27, 363–February 17, 364), who supported the orthodox and who thus left himself open to the hostility of the numerically small but politically very influential Arian party. The peace to which Athanasius appears to refer in the classical text for dating the *De decr. Nic.* (and with it, *De sent. Dion.*) was the peace which the Church enjoyed under Jovian, and which gave Athanasius an opportunity to compose his dogmatic writings with the purpose of winning over "the majority of those brethren who think according to the mind of the Church," but who were unable to accept the Nicene definition and terminology. This *terminology*, Athanasius defended in *De decr. Nic.* and *De sent. Dion.* before he went on to unfold the *doctrine* in the *Orationes*, within the context of a dispute with the main Neo-Arian arguments.

A confirmation of this late date (363–364) for the composition of these two works is to be found in the doxology at the end of the text of *De decr. Nic.*: ὅτι τῷ θεῷ καὶ πατρὶ πρέπει δόξα, τιμὴ καὶ προσκύνησις σὺν τῷ συνανάρχῳ αὐτοῦ υἱῷ καὶ λόγῳ ἅμα τῷ παναγίῳ καὶ ζωοποιῷ πνεύματι νῦν καὶ εἰς τοὺς ἀτελευτήτους αἰῶνας τῶν αἰώνων. ἀμήν. (*De decr. Nic* 32,5 = Opitz 28,25–27). This doxology reflects an advanced stage in the theological reflection of Athanasius (such as is to be found in his letters to Serapion concerning the Holy Spirit), with its emphasis on the equal glory and worship due to the three Divine Persons of the Holy Trinity (in comparison with *De fuga* 27,2 = Opitz 86,23–24—an early doxology—and *Vita Ant.* 93 = PG 26,975,B2, which reflects a "middle stage"). If a date after *De syn.* (360), possibly during the reign of Jovian 363–364, is accepted for *De decr. Nic.* and *De sent. Dion.*, then the generally recognized date of composition for the three *Orationes*—i.e., between 356 and 361—must be revised, since, as we have seen, this work of three books was most probably written after the former two works. A full discussion of this complex question must be postponed for a subsequent study. In any case, what is clear is that they must have been written after 356, the date of composition of *Ad epp. Aeg. et Lib.*

[101] *Ad epp. Aeg. et Lib.* 5 (*PG* 25,549,B1–3).
[102] *Ad epp. Aeg. et Lib.* 13 (*PG* 25,566,C10f.); *Ad epp. Aeg. et Lib.* 17 (*PG* 25,577,B11–15).
[103] *Ad epp. Aeg. et Lib.* 21 (*PG* 25,588,A1–4).
[104] *Ad epp. Aeg. et Lib.* 20 (*PG* 25,585,B14–15).

and knowledge within them,[105] to pray for the gift of discernment of spirits,[106] and to seek the guidance of the "Fathers" (in this case, the Synod of Nicaea) and Scripture. Finally, Athanasius makes it clear to them that their refusal to deny the Faith is as much a type of martyrdom as refusing to burn incense.[107] With this exhortation, he announces a theme, which he will fully develop in *Historia Arianorum,* when he comes to describe the Fall of Ossius and Liberius.

The expulsion of the Egyptian and Libyan bishops brought home to Athanasius the seriousness of the threat posed by the Neo-Arian party in the East. The four attempts by the Synod of the Dedication at Antioch (341) and the efforts of subsequent synods in the East to produce a credal formula had evidently not been taken seriously by Athanasius up to then; according to him, their lack of unity and their frustrated endeavors to formulate a creed only exposed them to ridicule and robbed their statements of any credibility.[108] But it appears that he had underestimated their significance, which he now recognized as their fundamental enmity towards Nicaea. As he now tells us, this hostility towards the ecumenical synod at Nicaea, they managed to conceal up to the time when, confronted with the Nicene Faith of the Egyptian and Libyan bishops, they were forced to reveal their hand. Then their enmity towards the Apostolic Faith was drawn forth from its concealment like a serpent from his hole[109]—an allusion to the inventor of wickedness, the devil, whose tactic is to conceal and deceive.[110]

At this stage Athanasius appears to be convinced that the Emperor Constantius is ignorant of what has been carried out in his name,[111] and indeed he goes so far as to affirm that, once the emperor had heard of the atrocities, he would put an end to them.[112] As we will see, this conviction of the emperor's basic goodwill was only abandoned by Athanasius with reluctance. He changed his opinion in the light of growing evidence to the contrary. When he heard of his own condemnation on civil charges and the sentence of death brought against him, he evidently knew that something was wrong. But he had no details of the accusations at the

---

[105] *Ad epp. Aeg. et Lib.* 1 (*PG* 25,540,A3–8).
[106] *Ad epp. Aeg. et Lib.* 4 (*PG* 25,548,A12–B2).
[107] *Ad epp. Aeg. et Lib.* 21 (*PG* 25,588,A7–10).
[108] *Ad epp. Aeg. et Lib.* 6 (*PG* 25,549,C10f.).
[109] *Ad epp. Aeg. et Lib.* 20 (*PG* 25,585,C7–12).
[110] *Ad epp. Aeg. et Lib.* 1 (*PG* 25,540,B8–C1). *Ad epp. Aeg. et Lib.* 2 (*PG* 25,541,C1–2).
[111] *Ad epp. Aeg. et Lib.* 5 (*PG* 25,549,A4–7).
[112] *Ad epp. Aeg. et Lib.* 23 (*PG* 25,592,A10–14).

time he wrote the *encyclical*. A few months afterwards (in the summer of 356), the emissary from Paulinus of Trier arrived in Egypt and found Athanasius in his hiding place. If Athanasius had not by then heard of the details of his trial at Milan, the emissary from Trier could have informed him. What Paulinus had to convey to Athanasius was the news of the relapse of Valens and Ursacius, as well as the *evidence* of their earlier repentance to Julius. He must have made it clear to the Alexandrian bishop that the final responsibility for his present dangerous position rested not with the emperor, who was a mere instrument, but with the two Pannonian bishops.[113] Armed with this information and these revealing documents, Athanasius most probably returned to Alexandria incognito.[114] There he undertook the task of composing the *Apologia* (and *Ad Constantium*), where he most probably had some form of access to the episcopal archives. But to whom did he write and what purpose did the *Apologia* serve?

§3 The Addressees of the *Apologia*

The title *Apologia secunda* arose, as we pointed out, most probably from its position in the *Apologienkorpus,* compiled in Constantinople in the fifth century, where it follows the *Apologia de fuga sua.* But the latter work was written after the *Ad Constantium*, i.e., in June-July 357, after the arrival of George in Alexandria (February 24) and the events which occurred the following May, but before the death of Leontius of Antioch around October 357.[115] The

---

[113] Even in the *Historia Arianorum*, where Athanasius most severely castigates the emperor, he still held that he was only the weak instrument in their hands.

[114] The *Festal Index* XXIX for 357 (Larsow, *Fest-Briefe*, 36) informs us that during that year, a search for Athanasius was undertaken in Alexandria (presumably) after George entered the city and took possession of the see (February 24, 357). This suggests that Athanasius was in the city before that date. Due to the strength of his following in Alexandria, Athanasius could have enjoyed comparative freedom of movement in the city, at least until such time as the imperial troops had eventually taken control of the city. The delay of George's entry until February 357 proves that this was no easy task; it must have taken almost a year to subdue the city sufficiently so as to enable the Arian bishop take up residence. But the imperial troops never succeeded in wiping out the resistance; in the following year, Athanasius is again able to hide himself in Alexandria (*Festal Index* XXX for 358 = Larsow 36).

[115] See Robertson, *Athanasius*, LNPF², 254. It should be observed that the theme of *De fuga* was already foreshadowed in *Ad Const.* 32.

Apologia de fuga sua is the only writing of Athanasius which could possibly be described as one written in defense of his own person and activities. On the other hand, to describe the *Apologia ad Constantium* as written merely in self-defense, while not inaccurate, is inadequate. It is, more precisely, the *legal defense* of a man condemned to death for crimes amounting to high treason—with the difference that the lawyer and client are one and the same. As already pointed out above, it was written shortly after the *Apologia* we are studying (as can be gathered from the second sentence of *Ad Constantium*, which refers to the *Apologia*) and indeed it presupposes that the reader, i.e., the emperor, has read the latter. Is it possible that the *Apologia* was written in the first place for the emperor?

The proposition that Athanasius composed the *Apologia* for the emperor is not as far-fetched as might be thought at first sight. It has been pointed out above that Athanasius was genuinely convinced of the basic goodwill of the emperor; indeed, the emperor himself had expressly assured Athanasius of his continued benevolence in a letter to the bishop, written soon after the death of Constans, Athanasius' "protector" in the West. The latter document is quoted in full in *Ad Const.* 23. As he tells us there, he produced this letter when the Dux Syrianus first attempted to remove him from Alexandria, approximately six months previously, in order to challenge the right of the general to so act. It was Athanasius' confidence in the emperor's basic benevolence, and his belief that Constantius had been naively deceived by Valens and Ursacius, that prompted him to address a *Defense* to the ruler of the empire concerning the civil charges amounting to high treason. In it, Athanasius does not deny the emperor a certain authority with regard to the bishop's right *to exercise* his duties and responsibilities.[116] But Setton goes too far, it seems to me, when he states that the work "gives full expression to his (= Athanasius') ideal of the relationship of Christian Church and Imperial State, inspired by the apparent benevolence of Constantine towards the Church."[117]

---

[116] See also *Ad Const.* 25 (*SC* 56, Szymusiak, 116); *Ad Const.* 26 (*SC* 56, Szymusiak, 118).

[117] Setton, *Christian Attitude Towards the Emperor*, 74. Setton, who incorrectly dates *Ad Const.* "about the middle of 357" (p. 73), overinterprets the significance of this work, as does Hagel, whom he quotes. Had he paid more attention to the *Sitz im Leben* and the precise purpose of this document, then he would have avoided the unfortunate comparison he makes with the panegyrist who, he informs us, addressed Constantine in 310 at Trier. The care with which Athanasius composed *Ad Const.* was not due to his awe before the "sacred presence:" it has been shown above that Athanasius shows extreme

The possibility that Constantius made up at least part of the intended audience for the *Apologia* cannot thus be ruled out and, indeed, as the reference in *Ad Const.* 1 indicates, must rather be accepted as most probable. But Athanasius does not address this defense to him or to any single person. He addresses it to a collective audience: ὑμῖν μὲν γὰρ τοῖς γνησίοις ἀπολογοῦμαι, πρὸς δὲ τοὺς φιλονεικοῦντας παρρησιάζομαι τοῖς κατ᾽ αὐτῶν ἐλέγχοις.[118] Opitz concluded from this that the *Apologia* was addressed to friends, probably to the Egyptian friends of Athanasius.[119] This opinion could only be held with difficulty, if, as Opitz also maintained, the work were part of the bishop's "propaganda," and thus nothing but a personal vindication of innocence. But Athanasius had no need to prove his innocence to his fellow-bishops in Egypt and Libya, many of whom had lost their sees on account of their adherence to the Nicene Faith and their loyalty to Athanasius, whose innocence they themselves had but four years previously affirmed at least implicitly in their synodal letter to Liberius. Yet the Egyptian bishops did have a vested interest and a very important one in Athanasius' claim to Alexandria: the legality of their own election (if not the validity of their ordination) would have been in question if it could be proved that Athanasius was not the legitimate Bishop of Alexandria, since the Bishop of Alexandria was directly or indirectly the source of all ministry in Egypt.[120]

But in the quotation from the *Apologia* given above, which describes the addressees, Athanasius makes an important distinction between two types of readers he expects to have as his audience and to whom he addresses his *Apologia*: the upright and the contentious. In the preceding sentence, he addresses those of upright minds with the express purpose of persuading them not to listen to those who were attempting to revise the earlier *judgement* of his innocence.[121] In the sentence following, he clarifies what that earlier

care in most of his writings; if his diligence is even more marked in this work, it is due both to the legal nature of his *Defense* and to the seriousness of the issues involved. The undeniable respect for Constantius, which permeates this document—due in no small way to the use of formal terminology required by court procedure when addressing an emperor—hardly earns the description (however, modulated by a double negative) of flattery (cf. Setton 77). To postulate that the writing "may be thought to contain" what Athanasius wished the emperor to believe was his attitude towards him" (Setton 77) betrays the bias of Schwartz and Seeck.

118 *Apol.* 1,1 (Opitz 87,8–9).
119 See Opitz's commentary to 87,8f.
120 See below, Note III, pp. 553–559.
121 *Apol.* 1,1 (Opitz 87,2–8).

judgement was, which the contentious are trying to reverse: the judgement of Rome and Sardica.[122] The identity of those contentious people is expressed in the next sentence, where Athanasius mentions Valens and Ursacius.[123] The addressees of the letter then, it would seem, are the upright *Western bishops*, whom the party of Valens and Ursacius, either by persuasion or by force, had compelled to recognize the deposition of Athanasius by the Synod of Tyre and so reverse the judgement of Rome and Sardica. Athanasius hopes to demonstrate how unjustified this recognition is. This is confirmed, not only by the other references in the *Apologia* where the decisions of Rome and Sardica are contrasted with the recantation of Valens and Ursacius, but also by the reference to the *Apologia* found in *Ad Constantium*, where the former work is paraphrased with the help of the two key phrases: *the judgement of so many bishops* and *the recantation of Valens and Ursacius*.[124]

An interesting confirmation of the hypothesis that Athanasius addressed this *Apologia* to the Western bishops may possibly be found in *Apol.* 59,1–3. There Athanasius describes in concise but comprehensive terms, the origins and history of the Meletian Schism, which began with the deposition of Meletius by Peter, Bishop of Alexandria (300–311). If the *Apologia* had been written for the emperor or the Eastern bishops, or (most unlikely of all) the Egyptian and Libyan bishops, then this "excursus" would have been almost superfluous. Athanasius evidently considers that, notwithstanding the knowledge about this local schism which a few Western delegates might have learned over 30 years previously at Nicaea, his readers were sufficiently ignorant of the facts and times to be informed (or reminded) of the precise nature of the Meletian Schism, its origins, and short history. Even more revealing of the fact that the intended readers of the *Apologia* were unfamiliar with the Egyptian landscape, are two brief snippets of geographical and historical information which Athanasius provides about the district of the Mareotis—information which was certainly not required by the Egyptian bishops, nor by the Orientals.[125]

The reader will recall how Athanasius, it seems with reasonable certainty, only received copies of the Letters of Recantation of Valens and Ursacius after he had composed his first major work attacking the new Arian party: the *Encyclical to his Fellow-Bishops*

---

[122] *Apol.* 1,2 (Opitz 87,9f.).
[123] *Apol.* 1,3 (Opitz 88,2f.).
[124] *Ad Const.* 1,1–2 (Opitz 279,5–9).
[125] *Apol.* 63,2 (Opitz 142,26–27); *Apol.* 85,3 (Opitz 163,21–24).

in Egypt and Libya (around the middle of the year 356). They were sent to him by Paulinus of Trier, the only bishop to resist the party of Valens and Ursacius at Arles, and who was banished with the other orthodox bishops at Milan. The emissary from Paulinus who brought the letters to Athanasius must have informed Athanasius in detail as to what had actually taken place at Arles and Milan, details which his own delegation to the emperor, headed by Serapion of Thmuis, did not bring back with them, if we are to judge from *Ad epp. Aeg. et Lib.* 7 where Athanasius lists the leaders of the Neo-Arian party: there Valens and Ursacius are indeed mentioned but only in passing. Their influence at Arles is, at the very most, but faintly hinted at. It will also be remembered that the recantation of Valens and Ursacius witnessed to by the letters played such a major role in the narrative section of the *Apologia* that one could affirm the intrinsic unity of the composition from an analysis of same. Further, the significance of their recantation was so great for Athanasius that it finds mention naturally in his *Apologia ad Constantium*, addressed to their imperial benefactor and the instrument of their malice, and in the *Historia Arianorum.* Here in the *Apologia,* the function of the famous recantation is to discredit the campaign of the relapsed Valens and Ursacius to reverse the judgement of Rome and Sardica. This Athanasius achieves, first by using their recantation to expose that which he and his fellow-bishops and priests of Egypt consistently maintained about the debacle at Tyre,[126] namely, that Athanasius' deposition there was the result of a carefully stage-managed conspiracy (to which Valens and Ursacius confessed in their letter to Julius, though not explicitly in their letter to Athanasius) and, secondly, by uncovering the characterless of the leaders of that party which compelled the bishops at Arles and Milan to reverse the judgement of Rome and Sardica and to ratify the deposition of Tyre.

§4 The Literary Genre and Aims of the *Apologia*

The *Apologia* was, it thus seems, in the first place addressed to the Western bishops, presumably though not exclusively those present at Milan. This does not rule out the fact that Athanasius expected

---

[126] See *Apol.* 74–75 (Opitz 153,27f.); see also *Apol.* 77 (Opitz 156,22f.); *Apol.* 78 (Opitz 158,1f.). It is interesting to note that Valens and Ursacius are only mentioned in the first document, the *Letter of the Clergy of the Mareotis to the Synod of Tyre*; the latter had seen the Commission to the Mareotis in action, and so observed the involvement of the two Pannonian bishops. The

the emperor to read this defense of his ecclesiastically constituted right to the See of Mark, since the emperor had the physical power to prevent or to permit him to exercise his ecclesiastical office. Neither can the possibility be ruled out that Athanasius circulated this work among the Egyptian and Libyan bishops in order to assure them that his claim to the See of Alexandria was indeed legitimate and, thus by implication, that George, whom the Orientals appointed at Antioch in the year 352, had no ecclesiastical right to it. Whatever purpose these secondary usages of the *Apologia* might serve, the immediate object was to defend his ecclesiastical rights before the "court" of the Western bishops, especially those who had assembled at Milan. Though the recantation of Ursacius and Valens performs an important function in its entire composition, the *Apologia* was not *primarily* an attack on the two Pannonian bishops. It was used by Athanasius for the specific purpose just outlined, but the main object of the *Defense* was of another nature.

The close relationship of the *Apologia* to Athanasius' *Ad Constantium* has been referred to above. The latter was written soon after the *Apologia*: it was a composition which complemented it. *Ad Constantium* belongs to the literary genre of a *legal brief*, written with the purpose of vindicating himself from the charges of high treason. But there were two very different types of crimes for which Athanasius was condemned at Milan: those of a purely ecclesiastical nature and those of a civil nature. Athanasius dealt with the civil suits in *Ad Constantium* and refers the intended reader (Constantius) to the *Apologia* for his defense relating to those matters of a purely ecclesiastical nature.[127] Thus we are in a position to describe the precise literary genre of the *Apologia*. The *Apologia* is a (canonical) *legal defense,* written with the object of vindicating himself from charges of having violated *ecclesiastical law*. At this stage, the first important observation can be made with regard to the main subject of this study. Athanasius is supremely conscious of the distinction that must be made between matters concerning civil law and those concerning ecclesiastical law. This clarity was absent at Tyre in 335.

Egyptian bishops at Tyre (and thus also by implication Athanasius) did not consider these two characters sufficiently important to mention them in their letters to the synod or to the Comes Dionysius.

[127] περὶ μὲν οὖν τῶν ἐκκλησιαστικῶν καὶ τῆς κατ' ἐμοῦ γενομένης συσκευῆς αὐτάρκη τὰ γραφέντα καρὰ τῶν τοσούτων ἐπισκόπων μαρτυρῆσαι τῇ σῇ εὐλαβείᾳ, ἱκανὰ δὲ καὶ τὰ τῆς μετανοίας Οὐρσακίου καὶ Οὐάλεντος δεῖξαι πᾶσιν ὅτι μηδὲν ὧν ἐπέστησαν καθ' ἡμῶν εἴχεν ἀληθὲς (*Ad Const.* 1,1–2 = Opitz 279,4–8).

Without referring to the text itself for the moment, a glance back to the earlier *Sitz im Leben* can help us to delineate more sharply the precise nature of the accusation brought against Athanasius at Milan, and which he addresses in the *Apologia*. The one charge which is consistently brought against Athanasius from the beginning of the new phase of the Neo-Arian attack—after the death of Pope Julius and the election of his successor Liberius of Rome on the May 17, 352[128] up to his expulsion from the Church by the Dux Syrianus in February 356—is his legal right to the See of Alexandria. The attack began with the Synod of Antioch (352). There the synod accused Athanasius of *violating the laws of the Church* by returning to Alexandria, purely on the strength of the contentiousness of likeminded persons, though he was not seen to be blameless before the synod.[129] The Antiochene assembly refers to Athanasius' return to Alexandria after his exile in Trier, which chronologically followed his deposition at Tyre, on the strength of the *Letter of Constantine II*, the eldest son of Constantine the Great, and his return from the second exile in Rome and the West with the help of Constans, the Western emperor; the Orientals objected that Athanasius could only be reinstated once *their own* synod had reversed its previous decision at Tyre. They refused to accept the judgement of Rome/Sardica on which Athanasius rested his ecclesiastical claim to the See of Alexandria, and to which (ecclesiastical) judgement Constantius eventually granted his imperial (= civil) sanction. Against the wishes of Pope Liberius, who recognized anew the Rome/Sardican judgement, the Synod of Milan (355) confirmed the deposition of Athanasius at Tyre (335).

The charge brought against Athanasius at Milan (355) was, therefore, that of the Antiochene synod of 352, namely, that Athanasius had *violated the ecclesiastical law* since he ignored the synodal deposition of Tyre (335) and returned to his see solely on the strength of his "friends." The judgement passed by the Synod of Milan, under the pressure both of the Arian party and the imperial pleasure, was in effect, as Theodoret put it, an assent to the deposition

---

[128] Seeck, *Regesten*, 199.

[129] See above, footnote 67. It is of note that this is also the substance of the argument proposed by the Eusebians as their justification for recognizing at first Pistos and then Gregory as the legitimate bishops of Alexandria; Gregory had died in the meanwhile, and so now they attempted to place George on the throne of Alexandria on the basis of this apparent legal flaw regarding Athanasius.

of Athanasius by the Synod of Tyre, 335.[130] It also effectively reversed the judgement of Rome/Sardica on which Athanasius based his claim to the See of Alexandria. When, in the opening verse of the *Apologia*, Athanasius protests his innocence, he does not in the first place refer to the charges relating to his personal behavior brought against him at Tyre, but to his innocence regarding the accusation made by the Synod of Antioch (352), and finally raised at the Synod of Milan (355), to the effect that he had violated the law of the Church by ignoring the decrees of the Synod (of Tyre) and returning to Alexandria purely on the powerful influence of his friends.[131]

The *primary aim* of Athanasius in this legal defense before the Synod of Milan, written at the beginning of his third exile, was therefore to demonstrate how he had not violated the ecclesiastical law with regard to his return to the See of Alexandria.[132] Expressed in contrary terms, he had to prove that his refusal to abide by the deposition of Tyre was not based on the authority of his imperial sympathizers. The *secondary aim* was to expose the nature of the deposition of Tyre. In other words, he must demonstrate that it was this deposition which in fact violated ecclesiastical (and as we will see divine) law, since the Synod of Tyre acted in the name of the imperial authority (and in violation of the principles of justice). These two aims, the primary and the secondary, are reflected in the arrangement of the documents and arguments of Athanasius, and they determine the very structure of the *Apologia* itself.

§5 The Internal Structure of the *Apologia*

On the false presupposition that the *Apologia* was composed by Athanasius as a public apology in the face of the various charges concerning his personal behavior as Bishop of Alexandria, which were brought against him at Tyre, commentators have consequently tended to misinterpret the text, such as eagerly pouncing an implicit

---

[130] See Theodoret, *HE* 2,15,2 (Parmentier-Scheidweiler, 128,15–17).
[131] The friends here referred to are most likely Constantine II, who authorized his return from the first exile at Trier in 337, and Constans, who helped arrange the Synod of Sardica and whose intervention on behalf of Athanasius with his brother Constantius II finally secured the latter's approval for Athanasius' return from his second exile in the West.
[132] This, the primary object of the *Apologia*, Bardy, *Saint Athanase*, 112, had correctly perceived, even though he incorrectly assumed that it was written early in "la decade d'or" (346–356).

"admission of guilt" where they could detect either silences, rough summaries, or generalizations. They have also been unable to solve the puzzle
created by the unusual chronological sequence of events and documents as
found in this *"canonical" defense*. Part I of the *Apologia* (Ch. 3–58) covers
events which occurred between 338 and 347. Part II (Ch. 59–88) deals
with those events which had their origins in the fateful Meletian-Eusebian
alliance of 328 and culminated with the Synod of Tyre, followed by his
first exile and his return to Alexandria in 337. What is the reason for the
violence thus done to the sequence of events?

Opitz maintained that this rearrangement of the chronological events
was made with a view to the greatest possible propaganda for Athanasius'
own cause.[133] But it is almost self-evident that Athanasius could have
composed a much more effective piece of "Publistik" for his own personal
cause had he maintained the normal chronological sequence. Such a work
would then have begun with the conspiratorial alliance of the Meletians
and Eusebius (328) and have ended with the universal recognition of
Athanasius' innocence and the dramatic exposé of the conspiracy: the
Letters of Valens and Ursacius (347), where they openly acknowledge
such a conspiracy. Instead, the recantation is described right in the middle,
where it completes Part I, while the original alliance between the Eusebians
and the Meletians opens Part II. As already noted, the recantation of Valens
and Ursacius is not the primary aim of Athanasius; it is a background
theme used with superb effect by Athanasius to highlight the unscrupulous
nature of the "prosecution" at his trial in Milan.

A closer look at the Preface (Ch. 1–2), the pivotal text (Ch. 58,6),
and the Conclusion (Chs. 89–90) provides us with confirmation of the
true aim of the *Apologia*. Rejecting the demand (namely by the Neo-Arian
party at Milan (355), led by Valens and Ursacius) for a reappraisal of the
whole affair,[134] Athanasius draws attention to the judgement of Rome/
Sardica;[135] such an evident *ecclesiastical* judgement[136] renders further discussion superfluous.[137] And once one considers the nature of the conspiracy
(to which the present leaders of the Neo-Arian party—the prosecutors
in the case—once openly confessed), then one can only agree that the

---

[133] See the commentary of Opitz 138,30f.
[134] *Apol.* 1,1 (Opitz 87,5).
[135] *Apol.* 1,2 (Opitz 87,9f.).
[136] ἡ τῶν τοσούτων ἐπισκόπων ψῆφος. *Apol.* 2,1 (Opitz 88,10); *Apol.* 58,6 (Opitz
138,30); *Apol.* 90,3 (Opitz 168,11).
[137] *Apol.* 1,4 (Opitz 88,6–9).

bishops, who passed such a judgement concerning the case of Athanasius, acted "justly and in accordance with ecclesiastical law."[138] Thus, Part I (Ch. 3–58) has, as its object, the primary aim of the *Apologia* outlined above: to demonstrate how he had not violated ecclesiastical law but rather returned to Alexandria to exercise his office as bishop of the Church there after he had been judged innocent by the *appropriate ecclesiastical authority*. On the other hand, Part II is concerned with the secondary aim, which is to show how just and in accordance with ecclesiastical law such a judgement in fact was *in contrast with* the conspiracy mounted by the Arians and their violation of ecclesiastical and divine law, which they effected with the illegitimate help of the imperial authority, which conspiracy and violation of ecclesiastical law found its climax with his deposition at Tyre. The different aims, of which the first enjoys an undoubted primacy, are consequently the cause of the "violence" done to the chronological sequence.

§6 Analysis

a) Part I: The Primary Aim

Athanasius had to prove not so much that he was innocent but that he had been proved innocent by the competent ecclesiastical authorities. The object of our study is to uncover as precisely as possible what, according to Athanasius, constituted this authority. In the above analysis, this authority was summarily described as the "judgement of Rome/Sardica." We will now attempt to delineate as clearly as possible what this meant for Athanasius. First of all, let us take a brief glance at the documents incorporated into this the first part of the *Apologia,* according to the order given by Athanasius, and then we will look more closely at the connecting narrative where he indicates the importance to be attached to these documents.

(A)   The first document is the *Encyclical Letter of the Synod of Alexandria* (338), addressed[139] to the universal episcopate (*Apol.* 3,1–19,5). In it, the charges brought against Athanasius are comprehensively refuted by the Egyptian bishops. These charges concern not only accusations regarding Athanasius' behavior as a bishop, but also those of a formal nature relating

---

[138] *Apol.* 89,1 (Opitz 167,11–12).

[139] ... τοῖς ἀπανταχοῦ τῆς καθολικῆς ἐκκλησίας ἐπισκόποις. ...

born to his election as bishop and to his apparent recourse to the imperial authority after Tyre, 335. The second charge of a formal nature will occupy our attention later on, when we take a look at this document in its historical context. For the moment, it may suffice to say that this letter is the answer of the Egyptian bishops—and that of Athanasius, whose hand it has long been recognized is clearly discernible in its composition—to the Letters of the Eusebian Synod of Constantinople to Julius the Bishop of Rome,[140] requesting the latter to give recognition to the judgement of Tyre and accept Pistos—an Arian presbyter of Alexandria, newly elected by the Eusebians—to succeed to the "vacant" See of Alexandria, by exchanging *Letters of Communion* with him.[141] Julius of Rome had sent Athanasius copies of these documents.[142]

(B)   The famous *Letter of Julius to the Oriental bishops* assembled at Antioch and led by Eusebius of Nicomedia (*Apol.* 21,1–35,8). In this document, Julius replies to a letter he had received from the Eusebian-controlled Synod of Antioch (early 341) and reiterates the decision of the Synod of Rome concerning Athanasius (and Marcellus of Ancyra). Because of its singular importance for the fourth-century understanding of the primacy of the Bishop of Rome, and for the history of Athanasius, this document will be analyzed in detail in the following chapter.

(C)   *The Letter of the Synod assembled at Sardica* (343) *to the Church of Alexandria* (*Apol.* 37,1–40,3), a copy of which was also sent to the bishops of Egypt and Libya (*Apol.* 41). This letter announces to the Alexandrian clergy and people (and to the Egyptian bishops) how the Sardican bishops had recognized the justice of Julius' judgement, had consequently entered into communion with Athanasius,[143] and that they had deposed the rival claimant in Alexandria, Gregory.[144]

(D)   Then follows the *Encyclical Letter of "The Holy Synod assembled by the Grace of God at Sardica"* to the Bishops of the Catholic Church everywhere (*Apol.* 42,1–47,6), which differs from the foregoing in so far as it presupposes the judgement of Julius and the Synod of Rome[145] and the official acceptance of

---

[140]   Cf. *Apol.* 19,3 (Opitz 101,18–19); *Apol.* 42,5 (Opitz 119,23–24).
[141]   Cf. Joannou, *Die Ostkirche und das Cathedra Petri*, 36f. (= Intervention, No. 3).
[142]   Cf. *Apol.* 83,4 (Opitz 162,21–23).
[143]   Cf. *Apol.* 37,5 (Opitz 115,32–116,5).
[144]   Cf. *Apol.* 39,3 (Opitz 117,31–118,2).
[145]   Cf. *Apol.* 42,6 (Opitz 119,29–30).

Athanasius, Marcellus, and Asclepas into communion which resulted thereform;[146] it devotes its attention primarily to an exposé of the
"Eusebian" behavior, as manifested in their attacks on Athanasius,
Marcellus, and Asclepas, which expose climaxes in the deposition
of the Arian claimants to the Sees of Alexandria, Ancyra, and Gaza,
and the excommunication of the present leaders of the "Eusebian"
party.[147] This letter was signed by the participants of the Sardican
Synod,[148] in which list Athanasius includes the names of the bishops
from various provinces (Gaul, Africa, Italy, Cyprus, and Palestine)
who later subscribed to the encyclical letter—283 in all.[149]

(E) Three *Letters from the Emperor Constantius* (344?) inviting
Athanasius to repair to the court and so from there proceed to
Alexandria (*Apol.* 51,1–8).

(F) A *Letter from Pope Julius to the Presbyters, Deacons, and People of
Alexandria* (345?) on the occasion of Athanasius' return to his
Church (*Apol.* 52,1–53,6).

(G) Two *Letters of Constantius* (346), one to the Presbyters and
Deacons (*Apol.* 54,1–5) and the other to the People (*Apol.*
54,4–55,7) of the Alexandrian Church. The former proclaims
the civil recognition given by the emperor to the decrees of
Sardica[150]—though without mentioning these explicitly—

---

[146] The bishops state: τούτου ἕνεκεν τοὺς μὲν ἀγαπητοὺς ἀδελφοὺς ἡμῶν καὶ
συλλειτουργοὺς Ἀθανάσιον καὶ Μάρκελλον καὶ Ἀσκληπᾶν καὶ τοὺς σὺν αὐτοῖς
συλλειτουργοῦντας τῷ κυρίῳ ἀθώους καὶ καθαροὺς εἶναι ἀπεφηνάμεθα . . . (*Apol.*
47,1 = Opitz 122,37–123,3). The Sardican Fathers wish to stress how the violence
used by the Eusebian party, as well as their other misdeeds (e.g., translations from
one see to another) convinced them of the innocence of those they accused:
Athanasius, Marcellus, and Asclepas. The verb ἀποφαίνω is not a legal term but
simply signifies "to show forth," or "declare" to be (cf. Lampe, *Lexicon*, 218) in
the general sense of making an affirmation. In contrast with this terminology
compare (i) the language of the Sardican bishops regarding both the judgement
of Julius (= ἡ κρίσις) and the way the Bishop of Rome determined (= ὥρισεν), that
the bishops should not have any doubts about communion with Athanasius (cf.
Apol. 37,5 = Opitz 115,32–34); and (ii) the language used by the same bishops
when they themselves deposed the Eusebian leaders (= τούτους παμψηφὶ καθεῖλεν
ἡ ἁγία σύνοδος ἀπὸ τῆς ἐπισκοπῆς [*Apol.* 47,3 = Opitz 123,12]) and declared them
to be excommunicated (= ἐκρίναμεν [*Apol.* 47,4 = Opitz 123,12]).

[147] Cf. *Apol.* 47,3–4 (Opitz 123,8–15).

[148] *Apol.* 48,2 (Opitz 123,29–127,3).

[149] *Apol.* 49,1–50,3 (Opitz 127,4–132,3).

[150] *Apol.* 54,2 (Opitz 135,5–6).

while the latter encourages the people to receive Athanasius and to preserve the peace.[151]

(H) *Letter of the Emperor to Nestorius* (346), *Prefect of Egypt* (*Apol.* 56,1–3) cancelling the previous orders against Athanasius and those in communion with him, and granting them instead the immunities due to them.

(I) *Letter of the Synod held at Jerusalem* (346) *to the Presbyters, Deacons, and People of Alexandria* (*Apol.* 57,2–7) which rejoices with the Alexandrian Church for the restoration of Athanasius and witnesses to their recognition of him as the legal Bishop of Alexandria.[152]

(J) The two *Letters of Recantation of Ursacius and Valens,* the first of which is, as we saw, addressed to Julius of Rome (*Apol.* 58, 1–4), and the second to Athanasius (*Apol.* 58,4–5).

Thus arranged, the documents speak for themselves. They witness to the general recognition of Athanasius by the universal episcopate as sought by the Synod of Alexandria, 338 (= A), granted by Julius and the Synod of Rome (= B) and confirmed by the Synod of Sardica (= C + D); the *2nd Letter of Julius* (= F), the Synod of Jerusalem (= I), and even the leaders of the Arian party, Ursacius and Valens (= J): they also witness to the civil recognition given by the emperor to the ecclesiastical judgement (= E, G, H). Further, the documents themselves reveal a picture, as yet not too sharply delineated, of the constitution of the universal episcopate and the way it operated in the case of Athanasius and his recognition.

First of all, it is clear that the imperial authority plays but a secondary role. Its function is to give civil effect to ecclesiastical judgements (= E, G, H). On the other hand, a unique position among the bishops and synods is held by the Bishop and Synod of Rome. It is remarkable how conspicuous Julius of Rome appears in the documents. The *Letter of the Synod of Alexandria* (= A) was prompted by the appeal of the Eusebians to Julius, requesting him to recognize their candidate for the See of St. Mark; the three letters of the Synod of Sardica (= C + D) accept the judgement of Julius and the Synod of Rome (= B), and go one step further by excommunicating the Eusebian leaders; the six letters of the emperor are interspersed with a second letter of Julius, this time

---

[151] Cf. *Apol.* 55,2 (Opitz 135,24–27); also, *Apol.* 55,7 (Opitz 136,3–7).
[152] Cf. *Apol.* 57,4 (Opitz 137,7–10).

addressed to the Alexandrian Church (= F)—a text which is really super-
fluous since it adds nothing to that already found in documents B, C,
and D; while the collection of documents ends with the recantation of
Ursacius and Valens to Julius of Rome (= J). As was intimated in our
brief descriptions of the various documents, the universal recognition of
Athanasius was based on the judgement of Julius, Bishop of Rome: the
Synod of Sardica simply manifests its agreement with this judgement.[153]
This we will see more clearly in the next chapter. That synod, however, went
a stage further than Julius since it deposed and excommunicated the Arian
claimants and the Eusebian leaders. Likewise, the Synod of Jerusalem (= I)
merely subscribes in a sense to the restoration of Athanasius, although it is
possible that they were moved to so act by the civil confirmation given by
the emperor.[154] Finally, Valens and Ursacius submit their recantation not
to any synod, but to Julius of Rome, whose letters, they maintain, were the
cause of their repentance.[155] We will now examine the Introduction (*Apol.*
1–2) and the relatively sparse narrative which Athanasius uses to link the
various documents into a homogenous whole.

   In his Introduction, Athanasius makes no reference at all to the six
short documents which carried the seal of the imperial authority. This is in
accord with his principal object: to demonstrate that his restoration to his
see was in accordance with ecclesiastical law. The imperial documents, as we
saw, bear witness to the civil consequences which resulted from the ecclesiastical judgement. Such an ecclesiastical judgement, he explicitly affirms
in the Introduction, was given not only once or twice but many times.[156]
Then, as a type of prelude to the main body of the text, he summarizes
these judgements, which he will later demonstrate by quoting the relevant
documentary evidence in full: the first was that given at Alexandria, the
second at Rome, and the third at Sardica. Then he lists the provinces, 33
in all, outside Egypt, Libya, and the Pentapolis, which subscribed to the
decision of Sardica, most probably after synods were held to discuss the
subject.[157] At the end he mentions the recantation of Ursacius and Valens.[158]

---

[153] Cf. *Apol.* 35,1 (Opitz 112,30–32) where Julius describes in a general
   fashion the terms of reference of a synod he proposes to summon to
   review the case of Athanasius *in the presence of all* (so that all may be convinced of the justice of the matter). This synod materialized in Sardica.
[154] Cf. *Apol.* 57,5 (Opitz 137,10–13).
[155] Cf. *Apol.* 58,2 (Opitz 138,5).
[156] Cf. *Apol.* 1,2 (Opitz 87,9–10).
[157] Cf. *Apol.* 1,2 (Opitz 87,10–88,1).
[158] Cf. *Apol.* 1,3 (Opitz 88,1–6).

Athanasius seems to be at pains to emphasize the numerical strength of those who subscribed to the various sentences regarding his innocence. He draws attention to the assembly of almost 100 bishops in Egypt, to the fact that more than 50 participated in the Roman synod, that over 300 subscribed to the Sardican judgement, and concludes: "Consequently, everyone will confess that it is superfluous to try again that case which has already been examined by *so many eminent bishops* and judged on the basis of such clear evidence. . . ."[159] In contrast with "the decision (ψῆφος) of so many bishops,"[160] "such a multitude of witnesses,"[161] Athanasius contrasts the Arian faction led by Valens and Ursacius, whose recantation is the best condemnation of their character and their intent.[162] This emphasis on the quantity of bishops who judged him innocent was not, in the first place, prompted by any desire to demonstrate how he had the majority on his side and so draw attention by contrast to the minority against him, since it is striking that Athanasius fails to describe the size or number of his opponents.[163] It reflects rather the later concept of universal unanimity as the final ecclesiastical authority which, as we saw in Eusebius, became more and more evident at the end of the third and the beginning of the fourth centuries.[164] Athanasius, however, draws attention to a dimension which Eusebius tended to ignore, namely, the representative function of the bishops. This the Bishop of Alexandria does by drawing explicit attention to the various *provinces* represented by these numerous bishops, which provinces covered the world. The ecclesiastical authority that passed judgement on Athanasius is the universal episcopate, which judgement was expressed in their universal unanimity. Thus, Athanasius answers his enemies who claimed that he was restored to his see on the basis of the imperial authority.

Like the early Eusebius, Athanasius recognizes that the universal episcopate is not a completely homogeneous body, but that a special function is to be attributed to the Bishop of Rome. In his description of the universal unanimity witnessed to by the universal episcopate, with respect to his innocence, Athanasius writes that he was tried "a second time at Rome, when in consequence of letters from Eusebius,

---

[159] *Apol.* 1,4 (Opitz 88,6–8).
[160] *Apol.* 2,1 (Opitz 88,10).
[161] *Apol.* 2,2 (Opitz 88,14).
[162] Cf. *Apol.* 2,1–4 (Opitz 88,11–32).
[163] In any event, Athanasius knew that the Arians could possibly "produce" an equally impressive number of supporters in the East.
[164] See above, pp. 106–107 and p. 125.

both they and we were summoned, and more than fifty bishops met; and a third time in the Great Synod assembled at Sardica by order of the most religious Emperors Constantius and Constans."[165] The correspondence referred to here was that relating to the attempt by the Eusebians to have Pistos recognized as Bishop of Alexandria through the traditional exchange of *Letters of Communion* with the Bishop of Rome—and thus, by implication, achieve Julius' recognition of the condemnation and deposition of Athanasius at Tyre. As a result of this correspondence, Athanasius tells us, the Eusebian bishops and he himself were "summoned" (κληθέντων) to Rome. The use of the term καλέω to describe the action of "Rome" is significant since this is the term employed by Athanasius *specialiter* to describe the act of summoning participants *ad conveniendum imperatorem*,[166] a usage which reflects the general understanding of the term when employed in the legal technical sense of "to cite before a court."[167] It is of note that in the Greek translation of the *Letter of Julius,* a translation which most probably is the work of Athanasius, the term is used in this technical sense to describe the action of Julius when he "summoned" Athanasius and the Eusebians to appear before the Synod of Rome.[168] Although in the *Apologia* text we are discussing (*Apol.* 1,2), the term is found in the passive sense and thus Julius of Rome is not mentioned by name, yet the use of this term alone betrays the unique relationship of the Roman bishop to the other bishops, his right to summon the disputing parties, which is here simply taken for granted by Athanasius. The evidence to support the contention that Julius did in fact "summon" Athanasius and the Eusebians will be discussed below in detail.[169] The full significance of the use of καλέω is only seen in contrast with the term chosen by Athanasius to describe the involvement of Constantius and Constans in the convocation of Sardica: the bishops assembled at Sardica, so Athanasius tells us, according to the order (πρόσταξις) of these two emperors.[169a] By avoiding the term καλέω here, Athanasius was able to avoid the impression that the emperors convoked Sardica. What they did was simply enable the assembly to take place.

---

[165] *Apol.* 1,2 (Opitz 87,12–15). The translation is by Newman (in Robertson, *Athanasius*, LNPF², 100); I have used the term "synod" rather than "council" as used by Newman in order to avoid the terminological precision of the latter term, which precision was absent in the fourth century.
[166] Müller, *Lexicon*, col. 710.
[167] Liddell-Scott, *Lexicon*, col. 866.
[168] *Apol.* 29,2 (Opitz 108,33); see also *Apol.* 22,5 (Opitz 104,14).
[169] See below, p. 374f.
[169a] Cf. *Apol.* 1,2 (Opitz 87,14).

In the narrative connecting the first two documents, the *Letter of the Alexandrian Synod* (338) and the *Letter of Julius* (341), Athanasius very briefly summarizes the events which led to the Synod of Rome. Here the special position of the Bishop of Rome within the universal episcopacy is even more evident. The narrative opens with a reference to the *Encyclical Letter of the Alexandrian Synod*, which letter was, as we saw, addressed to "the Bishops of the Catholic Church everywhere;" Athanasius here informs his readers: "While the Bishops of Egypt wrote thus to all and to Julius the Bishop of Rome, the Eusebian party also wrote to Julius and, thinking to frighten me, requested him to summon (καλέσαι) a synod, and, should he wish, that Julius himself be the judge."[170] The *Encyclical of the Egyptian Bishops* itself gives no indication that it was originally intended for the Bishop of Rome. It was indeed occasioned by letters from Julius, informing the Church there of the Eusebian attempt to have Pistos recognized as Bishop of Alexandria,[171] but it consistently addressed itself to the universal episcopacy. And yet, Athanasius tells us now that it was written "to all and to Julius, the Bishop of Rome," once again distinguishing between the Roman bishop and all others. The significance is clear: the universal episcopacy involves, a priori, the Bishop of Rome. When Athanasius goes on to relate the origins of the Synod of Rome as a result of the machinations of the Eusebians, he once again manifests his own understanding of that which constitutes the difference between the Bishop of Rome and all other bishops: his right to summon a synod and, if necessary, to bypass the usual procedure of the synod and judge the issue himself. In the text quoted above, Athanasius first reports how the Eusebians had requested Julius to summon a synod; this is in essence confirmed by the *Letter of Julius*, who likewise informs us in greater detail of this appeal.[172] But according to Julius, it was the Eusebian *delegates* sent to Rome (Macarius the presbyter together with Martyrius and Hesychius the deacons) who, after they were refuted by the Alexandrian delegates (presbyters) at Rome, requested Julius "to convene (συγκροτῆσαι) a synod and to write both to Athanasius and to the Eusebian Party so that in the presence of all a just judgement might be given." Athanasius' summary account underlines the Eusebian request almost to the point of exaggeration. Most commentators follow Caspar and maintain that it was most unlikely that the

---

[170] *Apol.* 20,1 (Opitz 101,34–102,2).
[171] *Apol.* 19,3 (Opitz 101,13–14).
[172] *Apol.* 22,3 (Opitz 103,31–104,7).

Eusebians originally intended to request such a synod,[173] but that the suggestion was made by the Eusebian delegates, who were forced into a tight comer by the Alexandrian delegates and in their embarrassment found in this a tactical escape-hatch, namely, to have the proceedings adjourned and so give them time to adjust their strategy. This seems to be a reasonable reconstruction of the events. But whatever the actual motives of the Eusebian delegation—indeed they cannot be reconstructed with any certainty from the evidence at our disposal—the fact is that they must have clearly requested Julius to arrange a synod. At least that much must be accepted as historically accurate since it is stated so clearly by Julius in his letter to the Eusebians themselves, a letter which is otherwise characterized by sober objectivity and aimed at winning over the Eusebian party.

But Athanasius in his summary description adds a detail that is otherwise not confirmed by our other sources: "and, should he so wish, that Julius himself be the judge." It is not surprising that ancient and modern commentators consequently interpreted the Eusebian delegates' request in terms of an appeal to the synodal court of the Roman bishop.[174] This impression is strengthened by the succeeding narrative which serves to introduce the *Letter of Julius*: after Athanasius went up to Rome, Julius wrote to the Eusebians and sent delegates to them, but they, surprised to hear that Athanasius was personally present in Rome, declined to attend the proposed synod, which synod finally assembled (at Rome) and, accepting the defense of Athanasius, granted him the κοινωνία. The Synodal Fathers were indignant with the Eusebians.[175] Athanasius adds that the synod requested Julius to write accordingly to the Eusebians.

---

[173] Caspar, *Geschichte des Papsttums* I, 143; see also Girardet, *Kaisergericht und Bischofsgericht*, 80, who surely goes too far when he refuses even to consider the possibility that Julius might have called the synod. On the other hand, Girardet correctly reminds us that Rome was not originally foreseen as the necessary location of the synod, although as Roethe, *Synoden*, 82, points out, the summons, or invitation, of Julius was at least intended to be understood as a summons to an early meeting in Rome, The interpretation of Joannou, *Die Ostkirche und die Cathedra Petri*, 43–44, which Girardet, 81, footnote 207, attacks rather sharply, exaggerates the significance of this request by the Eusebian delegates: this he does, however, on the authority of Athanasius, whose interpretation he makes his own. With regard to the related question regarding the content of Julius' invitation, see below, p. 373f.

[174] See Socrates, *HE* 2,11,5–7 (Hussey 201); Sozomen *HE* 3,7,3 (Bidez-Hansen 109,13–14).

[175] Cf. *Apol.* 20,1–3 (Opitz 102,2–9).

As we will see below, the trial and admittance of Athanasius to communion took place at one session of the synod, while the reaction of the bishops at Rome to the Eusebians occurred at what could be termed the second session of the synod, which met to discuss the reply of the Orientals that arrived in Rome after the originally proposed synod took place in the winter of 340.[176] Athanasius does not mention the *Letter of the Eusebians*, though the general impression left by his presentation is that the Synod of Rome had been requested by the Eusebians, which request could be interpreted, according to Athanasius, as an appeal to the synodal court of the Roman bishop.

In the *Letter of Julius,* the Bishop of Rome affirms that the opinions he expresses in the letter are not simply his own but those of the bishops who had assembled in Rome.[177] When Athanasius takes up the narrative at the end of the letter, he states: "After the Synod of Rome wrote thus διὰ Ἰουλίου τοῦ ἐπισκόπου Ῥώμης, the emperors commanded (ἐκέλευσαν) that bishops both from the East and the West should meet together in the city of Sardica, since the Eusebian party again behaved shamelessly, disturbed the Churches and laid plots for many."[178] The first observation to be made regarding this text is the way in which Athanasius accurately records the unique relationship between the synod and Bishop of Rome. Though the Bishop of Rome expresses the opinion of the synod held there, as they had requested him, yet this synodal opinion receives a very special weight due to its communication by the Bishop of Rome. The opinion receives the authority of the Bishop of Rome, so that the Synod of Sardica later simply refers to the "judgement of Julius" which the Bishop of Rome had pronounced after cautious deliberation.[179]

Concerning the text as a whole, it should be noted that according to Athanasius, the motive for the assembly of bishops from East and West at Sardica was the refusal of the Eusebians to accept the Roman judgement and the disturbances which thereby ensued in the various Churches. In order to deal with the troublesome Eusebians (note the use of the conjunction ἐπειδή to introduce

---

[176] See below, pp. 379–381, 398.
[177] *Apol.* 26,3 (Opitz 106,35–38). See the commentary of Roethe, *Synoden*, 83f.
[178] *Apol.* 36,1 (Opitz 113,26–114,3).
[179] *Apol.* 37,5 (Opitz 115,33–34); see Roethe, *Synoden*, 86.

the subordinate clause dealing with the Eusebian party), the emperors, Athanasius informs us, commanded that a synod take place at Sardica. Here Athanasius accurately records the change of emphasis in the controversy which came about as a result of the Synod of Rome. It is the behavior of the Eusebians that is now on trial and not so much Athanasius, so that Sardica, as mentioned above, simply manifests its recognition of Julius' judgement in his case, but goes on to condemn the behavior of the Eusebians, and to depose and excommunicate them. The disturbances caused by the Eusebians provided the immediate motive, according to Athanasius, for the imperial involvement in the assembly of Sardica. But Athanasius so phrases this text that the action of the emperors seems to be in a certain sense also the ultimate consequence of the *Letter of Julius*— which letter, in its final paragraph it may be added, explicitly held out the possibility of another synod so that the guilty could be condemned in the presence of all, and also to prevent anarchy breaking out in the Churches.[180] In the latter text, however, Julius offers to assemble the contesting parties at another synod, should the Eusebians feel confident that they could produce fresh evidence.[181] In the next chapter we will examine the historical question as to who actually took the initiative to summon Sardica; here it suffices to state that, as far as Athanasius is concerned, the emperors were moved to interfere, not by any partiality towards Athanasius but by the disturbances in the Churches caused by the Eusebians, who had refused to abide by the judgement of Julius.

As a final observation it must be pointed out how careful Athanasius is to avoid the impression that Sardica might have derived its authority from the emperors. This he indicates not only by the use of the general term κελεύω instead of the technical καλέω, but especially by his affirmation that the synod assembled without any counts or soldiers present,[182] in contrast with the Eusebian party who arrived with the Counts Musonianus and Hesychius, with the help of whose authority (τῇ ἐκείνων ἐξουσίᾳ) they had hoped to achieve their aims.[183]

Consequently Athanasius, describing the (legal) situation after Sardica, links the express intention of the Emperor Constantius to restore him to his see in Alexandria with the universal unanimity expressed at Rome/Sardica and the provincial synods which

---

[180] *Apol.* 35,1 (Opitz 112,30–32).
[181] Cf. *Apol.* 34,5 (Opitz 112,27–29).
[182] Cf. *Apol.* 36,3 (Opitz 114,9–11).
[183] Cf. *Apol.* 36,2 (Opitz 114,7–9).

subscribed to their manifestly ecclesiastical judgement. This he achieves by stating that the emperor's three invitations to him to come to court and be restored to Alexandria (= Document E), were the result of the emperor's learning about what had been previously decided by the ecclesiastical authority.[184] Athanasius has in recent times been accused of ignoring the most important and, for an understanding of the events after Sardica, the most decisive facts such as the death of the "antipope" Gregory in Alexandria (June 26, 345).[185] These details he describes in *Historia Arianorum* 17,1f. Here he is not interested in the historical process as such but wishes to show the legal relationship between his civil restoration by the emperor and his ecclesiastical restoration by the universal episcopate. The former was ultimately the effect of the latter. Considering the lack of interest on the part of Athanasius in relating details concerning the actual historical circumstances which attended his return to Alexandria, it is all the more surprising that he includes information about his visit to Rome on his journey to the imperial court at Antioch.[186] We have already mentioned that the *Letter of Julius to the Alexandrian Church* (Document F) is really superfluous since it adds nothing to the previous *Letter of Julius* or to the letters of the Sardican Synod. The connecting narrative reads: "While the Emperor wrote such (letters), I, having received them, went up to Rome to take my leave of the Church and its bishop, as I was in Aquileia when he wrote them."[187] One might well be tempted to see in this a simple report of a journey to Rome, that was suggested by the proximity of Aquileia and Rome, and thus of no particular significance. And indeed, at the time it occurred, it may well have had no further significance apart from witnessing to the good relations which existed between the respective Bishops of Rome and Alexandria.[188] But the inclusion of this notice here in a text, otherwise devoid of superfluous historical details, as well as the quotation of the *2nd Letter of Julius*, itself of no great importance, means that the notice and the letter were of some particular relevance to the object of the *Apologia,* namely to demonstrate that he was restored by the competent ecclesiastical authority.

---

[184] Cf. *Apol.* 51,1 (Opitz 132,8–10).
[185] See Opitz in his commentary.
[186] *Apol.* 52,1 (Opitz 133,14–18).
[187] *Apol.* 52,1 (Opitz 133,14–18).
[188] Schwartz, "Zur Kirchengeschichte," 141 (= *GS* IV, 16) comments that Athanasius did not bother too much about Julius after Sardica; see also Piétri, "La question d'Athanase vue de Rome," 116–117. Such an opinion is groundless.

The term συντάξασθαι, to take leave (of the Church and Bishop of Rome) contains the nuance of "making one's final arrangements" and could possibly be taken to mean "rounding off the procedure of Sardica." In any case, we will be not be too far off the mark if we see in the attention given to his journey to the Church and Bishop of Rome, the attempt by Athanasius to underline the one all-important fact—that he was restored to Alexandria by the ecclesiastical authority and not on the basis of an imperial order. For this reason, the *Letter of Julius to the Alexandrian Church* is inserted by Athanasius before the two letters of Constantius to the Alexandrian Church, just as Athanasius stresses that he took leave of the Bishop of Rome before he went to Antioch to see the emperor and to receive from him the necessary civil permission to return to his city.

After the second set of three letters (Documents G + H) from Constantius to the Alexandrian clergy, to the people, and to the prefect, Athanasius mentions another historical event, the Synod of Jerusalem (346), which acknowledged his restoration to his see. The notice had at least two purposes. It stresses once again the ecclesiastical dimension of his restoration after the quotation of the imperial documents. It also emphasizes that even the Palestinian bishops—who were presumably present at Tyre (335) and its aftermath, the Synod of the Dedication of the Church of the Holy Sepulcher at Jerusalem—received Athanasius into their communion. Part I ends with the *Letters of Recantation of Ursacius and Valens*, which, Athanasius tells us, were addressed to Julius, Bishop of the Elder Rome, and to himself.[189] This reference to the Elder Rome (τῆς πρεσβυτέρας Ῥώμης) may well be intended as a comparison with Constantinople, the New Rome, though the motive for such a comparison is missing from the text, unless one sees in it an indirect protest against the attempt to set up on the Bosporus, a new Christian capital of the empire. The adjective πρεσβύτερος (with its ecclesiastical undertones, cf. 1 Pet 5:1) highlights the superiority of the Roman Church—a tendency, which, as we saw, was clear in the Introduction and in the connecting narratives.

To summarize, we can say that in Part I of the *Apologia*, Athanasius demonstrates the legality of his possession of the Alexandrian See by proving that he was declared innocent by the competent ecclesiastical authority. This authority is first and foremost the universal episcopacy and was expressed by means of their universal

---

[189] *Apol.* 58,1 (Opitz 137,21–24).

unanimity. Just as in the documents themselves, the judgement of the Roman bishop is of decisive importance for establishing that unanimity (Sardica and the subsequent provincial synods manifest their recognition of Julius' sentence), so too in the Introduction and connecting narratives, the Bishop of Rome is singled out from all other bishops as one whose relationship to the universal episcopacy is essential and not accidental, so that an encyclical (like that of the Synod of Alexandria, 338) addressed to all bishops, was *of necessity* understood to have been addressed to the Roman bishop. Moreover, the Bishop of Rome is attributed by Athanasius with the right to convene a synod, whose participants included, or were intended to include, bishops of both East and West. According to Athanasius, the Roman bishop had the right to cite the disputing bishops to attend the synod which he convened. He likewise recognizes that the authority attributed to the decisions of that synod was not derived from the assembly as such but, as Sardica likewise affirmed, from the Bishop of Rome, who in communicating the decisions of the Synod of Rome gave them the weight of his own judgement. Athanasius apparently contrasts the Bishop of Rome, who could *convoke* the Synod of Rome, and the emperors, who could but *order* that the bishops assemble at Sardica, as a result of the disturbances caused by the Eusebians since that faction refused to accept the Roman decision, but who were not otherwise entitled to interfere in it. This contrast was repeated in the striking mention of the Alexandrian bishop's visit to Rome before he departed for the imperial court at Antioch, and in the otherwise superfluous inclusion of a *2nd Letter of Julius* (this time to the Alexandrian Church) before the quotation of the imperial letters to Alexandria announcing the return of the bishop whom the emperor had previously banished; these letters were to be understood as the civil consequences of the ecclesiastical judgement. And finally, Athanasius describes Rome as πρεσβύτερος, the Church which is in some way superior to other Churches.

b) Part II: The Secondary Aim

In contrast with the judgement on his innocence passed by "so many eminent bishops and judged on the basis of such clear evidence,"[190] i.e., by the competent ecclesiastical authority, whose judgement was well-founded, Athanasius uncovers in Part II, both the nature of the authority at Tyre that deposed him in 335 and the

---

[190] *Apol.* 1,4 (Opitz 88,6–8).

nature of the events which led to his deposition, namely, the conspiracy mounted by the Eusebians in association with the Meletians.

It is beyond the scope of this chapter to examine this secondary aim and how Athanasius executes it in any great detail. Since the circumstances leading up to Athanasius' deposition are not relevant to the main topic of this chapter, we can bypass them for the moment and devote some attention—brief though it may be—to the way Athanasius questions the authority of Trye, or rather its claim to be considered a synod in the traditional sense of the term.

In brief, Athanasius presents his historical outline (backed with full documentary evidence) of the conspiracy that ended with his deposition at Tyre in such a way as to highlight what he considers to be the hallmarks of the Eusebians: their irregular dependence on the imperial authority and their Arian sympathies. According to the Bishop of Alexandria, the immediate object of the Eusebian-Meletian conspiracy was to have him condemned by the emperor, using fair means or (more usually) foul. Tyre is thus depicted as the culmination of their questionable efforts; its authority was founded primarily on the imperial power; it was not an ecclesiastical synod in the traditional sense of the term. In other words, Athanasius wishes to demonstrate that it was not he who ignored the law of the Church and based his claim to Alexandria on the support of his "friends," the Western emperors, Constantine II and Constans, but the Eusebians, who violated both the laws of the Church and the divine law of justice, and who tried to manipulate the imperial authority to secure his deposition. At the same time, Athanasius is concerned to uncover the ultimate motive and driving force of the Eusebian conspiracy: their espousal of the Arian cause and their enmity against the orthodox. Let us take a glance at the text of Part II, to see how Athanasius executes his double aim.

The main object of the author in Part II is attained primarily by showing how, at each stage of the events which led up to Tyre, the Eusebian-Meletian conspiracy had as its one constant objective: to achieve the condemnation of Athanasius by the Emperor Constantine—an objective they failed to realize, according to Athanasius. He distinguishes between two main phases of the conspiracy.[191] The

---

[191] The two stages are clearly distinguished by Athanasius so that his legal defense might achieve the optimal effect on the ecclesiastical court. He opens the second stage with the words: Οὕτω μὲν οὖν τέλος ἔσχεν ἡ συσκευή . . . (*Apol.* 71,1 = Opitz 148,25), which refer back to the first stage just described, before he goes on to relate the events which surrounded Tyre, which he also describes as a conspiracy (cf. *Apol.* 72,5 = Opitz 151,19–20).

first stage (*Apol.* 59–70) ends with a *Letter of Constantine to Athanasius*, clearing him of the final and most serious charge brought against him by the Meletians,[192] to which he appended two documents which witnessed to the recantation of two of the main participants in the anti-Athanasian plot, the bishop Arsenius,[193] whom Athanasius was accused of having murdered, and John Arcaph,[194] who succeeded Meletius as leader of the schismatics. The second stage of the conspiracy (*Apol.* 71–88), is primarily concerned with the assembly at Tyre; it too ends with a letter of an emperor, Constantine II,[195] this time to the Church of Alexandria, announcing the return of Athanasius, to which is appended a reference to the later judgement of a multitude of bishops[196] (= Sardica and the other provincial synods), who condemned his enemies, and a reminder of the recantation of Valens and Ursacius.[197]

In his whole presentation, Athanasius is insistent on one thing: it was not he, but the Meletians and Eusebians who took the initiative and initially "troubled the ears of the Emperor"—a phrase to which we will return. The first stage of the conspiracy began soon after his ordination as Bishop of Alexandria, when, according to Athanasius,[198] Eusebius of Nicomedia entered into a conspiratorial alliance with the Meletians.[199] Then Athanasius describes four different attacks he had to endure at their hands, each of which is characterized by the way the conspirators endeavored to secure the condemnation of Athanasius on various charges, mostly of a

---

[192] *Apol.* 68,1–7 (Opitz 146,4–147,7).

[193] *Letter of Arsenius to Athanasius = Apol.* 69,2–4 (Opitz 147,11–148,8).

[194] *Letter of Constantine to John = Apol.* 70,2 (Opitz 148,13–24).

[195] *Apol.* 87,4–7 (Opitz 166,11–29).

[196] *Apol.* 88,2 (Opitz 167,5–7).

[197] *Apol.* 88,3 (Opitz 167,7–10).

[198] It is not necessary at this stage to discuss the historicity of the following assertions on the part of Athanasius, since it is not relevant to our interest in this section. Here we are primarily concerned with the way Athanasius wishes us to understand the historical chain of cause and effect. The historical events will be discussed in Chapter Nine.

[199] *Apol.* 59,4–60,1 (Opitz 139,18–140,15). Here Athanasius links the unsuccessful attempt of Eusebius (backed by the emperor) to force Athanasius to receive Arius into communion with the first Meletian calumny. In this way he stamps the succeeding attacks as ways and means used by Eusebius (and his fellow conspirators) to get revenge on Athanasius: the *origin* of the conspiracy (N. B. τὴν μὲν οὖν ἀρχὴν = Opitz 139,20) is to be found in the basic opposition of Eusebius and his associates to Nicaea and their advocacy of Arius (Compare *Apol.* 71,1 = Opitz 148,25–28). Thus, Athanasius achieves the second part of his aim in Part II.

civil but also one of an ecclesiastical nature, by appealing directly to the emperor (and thus bypassing the ecclesiastical authority). These latter accusations involved such varied charges as imposing a law on the Egyptians regarding Church vestments,[200] attempting to bribe Philumenus, the *magister officiorum*, into a treasonable conspiracy,[201] and murdering bishop Arsenius.[202] The accusation of an ecclesiastical nature concerned the breaking of Ischyras' chalice by Athanasius' presbyter Macarius, and is mentioned twice;[203] this charge will form the core of the case for the prosecution at Tyre. In Athanasius' presentation, the murder-charge occupies the greater part of his attention in the first phase of the Eusebian-Meletian conspiracy against him. But each attack is marked by a characteristic method of the conspirators: their immediate recourse to the Emperor Constantine.[204] But, Athanasius tells his readers, such action inevitably ended in the *acquittal* of Athanasius and, not unusually, the confession of guilt by one or other of the participants in the conspiracy.

The object of Athanasius in his portrayal of the Eusebian-Meletian machinations against him is not so much to inform his Western fellow-bishops of the details involved in the accusations brought against him, but rather to demonstrate *their pattern of behavior*, which pattern, the Bishop of Alexandria maintains, marked the assembly at Tyre in 335. Thus, he affirms at the opening of the second phase, which deals with the Synod of Tyre, that having failed to achieve their objectives in the first stage of the conspiracy, the Eusebians "again provoke the Meletians and persuade the emperor to give orders that a synod be held anew at Tyre. Comes Dionysius is dispatched to the synod while a military guard was given to the Eusebian party."[205] The role of Comes Dionysius and the imperial guard at Tyre is repeatedly emphasized by Athanasius: that Comes exercised compulsion;[206] he was the instrument of the Eusebians;[207] further, the Commission sent to the Mareotis to investigate

---

[200] *Apol.* 60,2 (Opitz 140,15–18).

[201] *Apol.* 60,4 (Opitz 141,1); see Girardet, *Kaisergericht und Bischofsgericht*, 59.

[202] *Apol.* 63,4f. (Opitz 143,7f.).

[203] *Apol.* 60,4 (Opitz 143,22–23); *Apol.* 63,1–65,1 (Opitz 142,24–144,6); see Simonetti, *La Crisi Ariana*, 112.

[204] Regarding the Church tax, cf. *Apol.* 60,2–3 (Opitz 146,15–21); regarding Philumenus, cf. *Apol.* 60,4 (Opitz 141,2–3); regarding Arsenius, cf. *Apol.* 65,1f. (Opitz 144,3f.); regarding the chalice of Ischyras, cf. *Apol.* 60,4 (Opitz 140,22–23 and *Apol.* 65,1 (Opitz 144,4–6).

[205] *Apol.* 71,2 (148,28–149,2). Compare the similar description of the Arian party's arrival at the proposed Synod of Sardica (*Apol.* 36,2 = Opitz 114,7–9).

[206] Cf. *Apol.* 72,1 (Opitz 151,13).

[207] Cf. *Apol.* 72,3 (Opitz 151,17f.).

the circumstances surrounding the reported breaking of the chalice, was provided with a military escort[208] and was accompanied in its "investigations" by the apostate Prefect of Egypt, Philagrius,[209] whose presence intimidated the witnesses.[210] When he describes his own reaction to the proposed Synod of Tyre, Athanasius clearly affirms that he was unwilling to take part in such an assembly and only went because the emperor wrote to him and laid a peremptory command on him to attend.[211] This express order of the emperor, together with the constitution of the synod, as an imperial authority, and the activities of the Mareotis Commission, as though it were a civil commission, are presented by Athanasius distinctly and unambiguously so as to enable him to explain the reason why he fled from the synod to Constantinople, where he had recourse to the emperor: "While they were thus brewing and concocting these conspiracies, we went up and set before the Emperor the unjust conduct of the Eusebian party, since it was he who ordered that the synod take place and his comes presided over it."[212]

Constantine reacted by summoning the bishops assembled at Tyre to report on the proceedings and to answer Athanasius' charge of ill treatment and impartiality.[213] Athanasius continues his narrative by informing his readers that a Eusebian delegation from Tyre—including Eusebius of Caesarea—repaired to the emperor, not to answer for their misconduct but in order to bring yet another calumnious charge against the Bishop of Alexandria: namely, that he had obstructed the shipment of corn from Alexandria to Constantinople.[214] In order to attest the fact of this charge, Athanasius mentions five bishops who were present and heard the charge,[215] and the anger of the emperor who reacted by sending Athanasius to Gaul without even granting him a hearing.[216] "But," he concludes, "this (= the exile of Athanasius to Trier) rather manifests their wickedness; for when Constantine the Younger, of blessed memory, sent us back to our own country, he remembered what his father had written and so wrote the following:"[217] and

---

208 Cf. *Apol.* 72,4 (Opitz 151,27).

209 Cf. *Apol.* 72,4 (Opitz 151,26–27); *Apol.* 72,6 (Opitz 152,4–5).

210 Cf. *Apol.* 75,2 (Opitz 154,25–27); *Apol.* 75,3 (Opitz 154,29–30).

211 Cf. *Apol.* 71,2 (Opitz 149,3–4).

212 *Apol.* 86,1 (Opitz 164,12–14).

213 Cf. *Letter of Constantine to the bishops assembled at Tyre* = *Apol.* 86,2–12 (Opitz 164,16–165,35).

214 Cf. *Apol.* 87,1 (Opitz 165,36–166,4).

215 Cf. *Apol.* 87,2 (Opitz 166,4–5).

216 Cf. *Apol.* 87,2 (Opitz 166,5–8).

217 *Apol.* 87,3 (Opitz 166,8–10).

then Athanasius quotes the letter of the said Constantine II, restoring him to Alexandria, in which the young emperor states that his father dispatched Athanasius to Trier in order to protect the bishop from his bloodthirsty enemies.[218]

In all of this, Athanasius is intent on proving: (i) that his return to Alexandria on the strength of the restoration granted by Constantine II—which, we remember, was one of the instances intimated by the Synod of Antioch (352), according to which Athanasius violated "ecclesiastical law"—was fully in accord with the nature of the former proceedings, which were of a civil nature; (ii) that the Synod of Tyre had no right to be considered as an ecclesiastical authority but was rather constituted as an imperial court, one which, moreover, was conducted in an impartial and unjust manner, and thus contrary to the divine law of justice.

To uncover the final motive of the Eusebian-Meletian conspiracy, Athanasius, at the opening of Part II, links the Meletian disturbances in Egypt with the attempt by Eusebius of Nicomedia to force him, who was but newly elected to the See of Mark, to receive Arius back into the communion of the Alexandrian Church.[219] And at the climax of his presentation of the Synod of Tyre, Athanasius again refers back to Eusebius' effort to force him to admit Arius and his associates into communion, and claims there that his refusal to do so was the ultimate cause of the conspiracy.[220]

The significance of the *Apologia* for Athanasius' understanding of the Bishop of Rome's primacy can only be appreciated against the background of the larger canvas of the ecclesiological developments that occurred within the span of time covered by the documents quoted and the events described by Athanasius in this work. An examination of the historical events and some of the more pertinent documents can help us, by way of comparison with the presentation of Athanasius, to determine more precisely the attitude of Athanasius himself to these. These questions must now be examined, beginning with the origins of the Eusebian-Meletian conspiracy.

[218] *Apol.* 87,4–7; in particular, *Apol.* 87,4 (Opitz 166,15).
[219] Cf. *Apol.* 59,1–4 (Opitz 139,4–21).
[220] Cf. *Apol.* 85,1 (Opitz 163,11–16).

CHAPTER NINE

The Defense of the Apostolic Church in the Face of the Imperial Church of the Two Eusebii

We have seen how already in the composition of two separate legal tracts—one (*Apologia*) addressed to the Western bishops with the object of demonstrating the fact that he had been proclaimed innocent and thus restored to his see by the competent ecclesiastical authority, and the other (*Ad Constantium*) addressed to the emperor in which he defended himself from criminal charges of a civil nature such as high treason—Athanasius would appear to distinguish clearly between the ecclesiastical and the imperial authority. In the *Apologia* itself he carries this distinction a step further by contrasting his own acquittal by the competent ecclesiastical authority acting in conformity with divine law,[1] with the infamous Synod of Tyre, which he proves was neither constituted in accordance with ecclesiastical principles (i.e., distinct from State interference) nor conducted in accordance with the divine law of justice (since it was part of a conspiracy and resorted to the use of force).[2] The necessity of this distinction was itself the first lesson Athanasius learned at Tyre, where he came face to face, not only with the conspiracy of the Eusebians and Meletians, but also with the threatening new reality of the Imperial Church of Eusebius—Bishop of Caesarea and author of the *Church History*.

§1 The Synod of Tyre, 335

It is most likely that Athanasius only gradually became aware of the conspiratorial alliance between the Eusebians and Meletians, and it was only at Tyre that he was finally convinced of same. The

---

[1] See the insistence of Julius that the case of Athanasius be tried "in the presence of all" *Apol.* 22,3 (Opitz 104,5–6); *Apol.* 35,1 (Opitz 112,30–32). See also the various references to the way Julius and the Synod of Rome acted in all respects according to ecclesiastical law (*Apol.* 25,1 = Opitz 105,32; *Apol.* 29,1 = Opitz 108,29; *Apol.* 32,4 = Opitz 111,4; *Apol.* 34,4 = Opitz 112,23) in comparison with the Eusebians who violated such laws (*Apol.* 21,5 = Opitz 103,11–12; *Apol.* 22,2 = Opitz 103,23–31; *Apol.* 30,1–3 = Opitz 109,9–23; *Apol.* 32,4 = Opitz 111,5–8; *Apol.* 34,3 = Opitz 112,16–18).

[2] See the important *excursus* of Athanasius on the divine law of justice, *Apol.* 82,2 (Opitz 161,20–25); see also *Letter of the Egyptian bishops to the Synod of Tyre* = *Apol.* 77,9 (Opitz 157,29–30).

events he causally connects in the *Apologia*—the frustrated attempt of Eusebius of Nicomedia to have Arius restored with the help of an imperial decree[3] on the one hand, and on the other the four Meletian charges made before the emperor regarding the tax on the Egyptians, the alleged attempted bribery of "a certain Philumenus," the breaking of the chalice, and the murder of Arsenius[4]—were originally probably not seen to have had any inner connection until the alliance became patently obvious at Tyre. But his suspicions had been aroused prior to that event. In the documents relating to Tyre (preserved in the *Apologia*), one can trace the growing awareness of the fact that a conspiracy was afoot, although the precise nature of the plot is unclear.[5]

When Athanasius refused (ca. 329–330) to admit Arius into communion, Eusebius, Bishop of Nicomedia, who had been restored to his see and to the favor of the emperor, consequent to the very brief exile inflicted on him for his association with those

---

[3] See above, Chapter Eight, footnote 199.

[4] See above, p. 313f.

[5] The presbyters and deacons of the Mareotis in their *Letter to the Mareotis Commission* = *Apol.* 73,1–5 (Opitz 152,10–153,24), accuse the commission of acting with obvious impartiality and conclude that this must be part of a conspiracy *against them* = *Apol.* 73,3 (Opitz 152,21–23). However, in their *Letter to the Synod of Tyre* (*Apol.* 74,1–75,6 = Opitz 153,28–155,31), they affirm that the conspiracy is directed against their bishop, Athanasius (*Apol.* 74,2 = Opitz 153,31). In their *Testimony to Philagrius, Prefect of Egypt* = *Apol.* 76,1–5 (Opitz 155,32–156,18), there is no mention of a conspiracy. The bishops of Egypt who accompanied Athanasius to Tyre came closer to the truth when they in their *Letter to the Bishops assembled at Tyre* = *Apol.* 77,1–10 (Opitz 156,22–157,35) protested that a conspiracy had been formed *against them* by those bishops who either played a leading role in the synod or who made up the Mareotis Commission; they were evidently at enmity with them and with all who hold orthodox opinions (*Apol.* 77,2–3 = Opitz 156,24–31). It is noteworthy that the Eusebians alone are said to be the authors of the conspiracy. This the bishops also affirm in their *1st Letter to the Comes Dionysius* = *Apol.* 78,1–7 (Opitz 158,1–24), repeating once again that the conspiracy is directed towards *all the orthodox* (*Apol.* 78,3 = Opitz 158,7–9). But in their *2nd Letter to the Comes Dionysius* = *Apol.* 79,1–4 (Opitz 159,25–160,18) they become aware that the Meletians *and* Eusebians are in some way together involved in a plot, one which they believe is directed *against the Catholic Church in Egypt* (*Apol.* 79,1 = Opitz 159,28–160,5), though the nature of the plot is vague. Finally, Bishop Alexander of Thessalonica in a *Letter to Dionysius* = *Apol.* 80,1–3 (Opitz 160,21–161,4) objects to the conspiracy, which he says has evidently been formed *against Athanasius,* since they packed the commission sent to the Mareotis with those to whom Athanasius had objected and without informing the rest of the bishops present; Alexander also warns the Comes that the Colluthians, Arians, and Meletians had joined in a confederacy with each other and were capable of effecting great damage (*Apol.* 80,3 = Opitz 160,27–29).

condemned at Nicaea, succeeded in persuading Constantine to order Athanasius to do so, and to threaten the Alexandrian bishop with deposition and exile should the latter disobey.[6] Athanasius did not obey the emperor but rather tried to convince him that such an actioan was impossible.[7] Here the young bishop on the throne of Mark acted firmly and courageously. But he had behind him the clear authority of the traditional practice of the Church regarding the non-admittance of those who had obviously diverged from the Apostolic Tradition.[8] This was not the case with regard to the various moves made by the Meletians to extirpate the Bishop of Alexandria.

The initial charges brought against Athanasius by the Meletians were primarily of a civil nature and carried the death penalty: usurping the local imperial authority by imposing a tax on the Egyptians (lèse majesté)[9] and entering into a conspiracy with Philumenus (high treason).[10] Thus, Athanasius was forced to defend himself before the imperial authorities[11] as would have been the case in pre-Constantinian times, and as it is the case today in most nations of the world. Due most probably both to the gravity of the indictments, which directly affected the imperial status, and to the new civil status accorded by Constantine to the bishops in general, the emperor personally heard the charges and gave the verdict. One cannot conclude from this, as is claimed, that Athanasius' defense before the emperor signifies an implicit recognition on the part of the Alexandrian Bishop of the Imperial Church as conceived by Eusebius of Caesarea.

The situation became more complex when the Meletians unexpectedly slipped in an accusation of an ecclesiastical nature (the breaking of the chalice) at the moment when Athanasius, who had been summoned to the imperial court at Psammatheia (ca. 331–332) to

---

[6] Cf. *Apol.* 59,4–5 (Opitz 139,20–140,10).

[7] Cf. *Apol.* 60,1 (Opitz 140,11–12).

[8] It is significant that Athanasius in his 2nd *Festal Letter* (for Easter, 330) devoted his attention mainly to the concept of *Apostolic Tradition* and the nature of heresy. His object is simple: to emphasize that "there is no fellowship whatever between the words of the saints (= Apostolic Tradition) and the fancies of human invention (= heresy)" (*Festal Letter* II, 7 = Robertson, *Athanasius*, 512).

[9] See Girardet, *Kaisergericht und Bischofsgericht*, 57–58 for details.

[10] See Girardet, *Kaisergericht und Bischofsgericht*, 58–60 for details.

[11] Girardet aptly comments (p. 60): "Der Stand des Angeklagten, die Tatsache, daß er ein kirchlicher Amtsträger ist, stellte offenbar noch kein Problem dar; Maßstäbe für die Gerichtsbarkeit über Bischofe bilden sich erst allmählich ... und sicher beeinflußt durch Präzedenzfälle wie diesen heraus."

discuss the charge concerning the imposition of the tax, found himself confronted with the second indictment: that he had given financial support to Philumenus, presumably with the alleged purpose of encouraging him to rebel.[12] The charge concerning the breaking of the chalice was apparently not taken seriously by the emperor.[13] Athanasius was able to prove his innocence on both charges of a civil nature and so was dismissed in peace by the emperor.[14]

Undaunted, the Meletians again take up the charge regarding the breaking of the chalice, which the emperor had ignored but which was of a purely ecclesiastical nature, and with it, engaged in an active campaign to calumniate Athanasius.[15] To this they add a new indictment, the alleged murder of Arsenius,[16] which again complicates the picture, since it involved both the State, as a crime of murder, and the institutional Church as a crime committed by a bishop against a bishop. But since it did not involve any treasonable matter, the emperor sent Dalmatius, his half-brother, to institute the judicial inquiry into the charge[17] (in the year 333) but cancelled it on receiving word from Athanasius that Arsenius had been discovered. In his communication to the emperor, Athanasius reminded the emperor of the explanation about the affair of the chalice that he had made to Constantine at Psammatheia over a year previously.[18]

It is at this stage that the Eusebian party make their first appearance on the Alexandrian horizon since the abortive attempt to force Athanasius to admit Arius to communion. Eusebius and his associates were on their way to Antioch to participate in some capacity in the proposed imperial inquiry, either to give evidence or, as has been proposed, to act as a *consilium* of the imperial judge.[19] In either case, the suspicions of Athanasius must have been

---

[12] Cf. *Apol.* 60,4 (Opitz 140,22–141,3).

[13] Cf. *Apol.* 65,1 (Opitz 144,3–6); *Apol.* 65,4 (144,18–19).

[14] Cf. *Letter of Constantine to the People of the Catholic Church at Alexandria* = *Apol.* 61,1–62,7 (Opitz 141,4–142,23): that Athanasius had at this stage no suspicion of a conspiratorial alliance between the Eusebians and the Meletians is indicated by his 4th *Festal Letter* in 332, written at the imperial court, where he mentions only the Meletians as his adversaries (cf. *Festal Letter* IV, 5 = Robertson, *Athanasius, LNPF*[2], 517).

[15] Cf. *Apol.* 63,1–65,1 (Opitz 142,24–144,4).

[16] Cf. *Apol.* 63,4 (Opitz 143,7–10).

[17] Cf. *Apol.* 65,1 (Opitz 144,6–7).

[18] Cf. *Apol.* 65,4 (Opitz 144,17–20).

[19] Cf. *Apol.* 65,4 (Opitz 144,20–21). According to Socrates, *HE* 1,27,21 (Hussey 148) the emperor sent Eusebius and Theognis so that the case might be tried *in*

roused. It is not surprising, therefore, that Athanasius associates the Arians and the Meletians together for the first time in his *Festal Letter* for Easter, 334.[20] In that letter, he speaks about the Jews who can no longer properly celebrate the Passover (since they cannot sacrifice the lamb) and then suddenly turns on the Arians and Meletians: "At this time the altogether wicked heretics and ignorant schismatics are in the same case; the one (= the Arians) in that they slay the Word, the other (= the Meletians) in that they rend the coat."[21] The coat referred to here is the seamless tunic of Our Lord, symbol of the unity of the Church—an allusion to Jo 19,23–24.[22] In this passage, the Arian party of the Eusebians and the Meletians are mentioned together in the same breath, but their alliance is not otherwise indicated.[23]

The Meletians failed to secure the condemnation of Athanasius on civil charges. Their attempt to have him tried by a civil court on charges which involved ecclesiastical discipline also backfired. They next questioned the legality of his episcopal election,[24] having

---

their presence. Girardet, *Kaisergericht und Bischofsgericht*, 63–65, argues from this that these and other bishops were summoned to act as the *consilium* of the *iudex delegatus*, who alone had the authority to pass judgement.

[20] Robertson, *Athanasius*, LNPF2, 521 (= Larsow, *Fest-Briefe*, 90); see also Schwartz, *NGG* (1911), 413 (= *GS* III, 246–247).

[21] Translation by Miss Payne-Smith. It should be noted that in his *Festal Letter* for the previous year (= Robertson, *Athanasius*, 518), Athanasius also referred to the heretics and schismatics in association with the Jews—but the reference is only in passing and apparently of no further significance than a general exhortation to his flock not to imitate such people. His attack is chiefly directed against the *schismatics* "who rend the coat of Christ." A parallel reference to that found in *Festal Letter VI*, 6, occurs in the *Festal Letter X*, written in Trier in 337 (for Easter, 338); see Robertson, *Athanasius*, 531.

[22] See Aubineau, *La tunique sans couture du Christ*, 100–127, especially 107–111.

[23] In the parallel text in the 10th *Festal Letter* (see above, footnote 21), the alliance is clearly underlined: "they are united together, as men of kindred feelings."

[24] Cf. *Letter of the Synod of Alexandria, 338* = *Apol.* 6,4–5 (Opitz 92,12–27). In his presentation of the Synod of Tyre in Part II of the *Apologia*, Athanasius does not deal with this topic in any detail; he simply refers us to the above-mentioned *Letter* and to the witness of the Egyptian bishops, presbyters, and people who found no fault with him (*Apol.* 71,3–4 = 149,4–9). The "silence" of Athanasius was not prompted by any desire to brush over this incident—and thus prove his "guilt" or the shakiness of his claim—but simply by the fact that (i) his election was not questioned by the Synod of Milan and had long since faded from the controversy surrounding his person (see below, Note III, pp. 553–559), and (ii) his presentation of Tyre was preoccupied with showing the partiality of the synod, its place in the plot laid against him, and the questionable basis of its authority; accordingly, he concentrated on the infamous Mareotis Commission.

apparently previously complained to the emperor about the youth of the bishop,[25] and intensified their public campaign against Athanasius, using in particular the calumny based on the reputed breaking of the chalice of one Ischyras by Macarius, a presbyter of Alexandria.[26] Since these accusations against the Alexandrian bishop were of a purely ecclesiastical nature, they could only be settled by a synod.

According to Theodoret, the Eusebians at the court persuaded Constantine to convene a synod at Caesarea in Palestine in order to try the case.[27] This occurred in the year 334.[28] But Athanasius refused to attend. We do not know the exact reason for his refusal. It could well have been due to his misgivings about the public sympathy with Arius and his cause that characterized Eusebius of Nicomedia and his party who had gathered there to judge him. In any case, he had good grounds to doubt the real possibility of a just examination by those same prelates[29] who had come to the Orient either to witness against him, or to assist in the judicial enquiry into the "murder" of Arsenius that the emperor had ordered to be held at Antioch; they had simply continued their journey to Caesarea and were now ready to judge him on ecclesiastical charges. Evidently his impression that a conspiracy against him was afoot was being confirmed.[29a] What was, however, unexpected in Alexandria was the prominent position Eusebius of Caesarea was expected to play at the proposed synod. As can be deduced from the *Letter of the Egyptian Bishops to the Bishops Assembled at Tyre,*[30] the participation of Eusebius of Caesarea in this proposed synod, where, as metropolitan, he evidently would have presided, marked the moment when the Egyptian bishops first became aware of his enmity towards them. Athanasius' refusal to come to Caesarea provided his enemies with yet another indictment which they used at Tyre: disobedience

---

[25] Cf. *Letter of Constantine to the People of the Catholic Church at Alexandria* = *Apol.* 62,3 (Opitz 142,5).

[26] Not only is this charge the one to which Athanasius gives most attention, but also Sozomen. *HE* 2,25,3 (Bidez-Hansen 84,13–15) lists it as the first of the many accusations which were finally brought against Athanasius at Tyre.

[27] Theodoret, *HE* 1,28,2 (Parmentier-Scheidweiler 82,15–21).

[28] *Festal Index* VI (334) = Larsow, *Fest-Briefe*, 28.

[29] Cf. Sozomen, *HE* 2,25,1 (Bidez-Hansen 84,8–9). Athanasius would also have been suspicious of Eusebius of Nicomedia, not least due his transfer from Berytus to the See of the Imperial Residence, in which position he now dared to sit in judgement on the Successor of St. Mark.

[29a] See *Festal Index* VI (= Robertson, *Athanasius*, LNPF2, 503; Larsow, *Fest-Briefe*, 28).

[30] Cf. *Apol.* 77,10 (Opitz 157,34).

to the emperor.[31] We will later examine the significance of this. For Athanasius himself, the convocation of the Synod of Caesarea provided him with a further indication that the Meletian disturbances in Egypt were not simply due to local rivalry but were part of a larger concerted action also involving those bishops who, before and after Nicaea, espoused the cause of Arius.[32] But it was only at Tyre, it seems, that the full extent of the conspiracy became evident.

The assembly at Tyre was originally intended as a type of prelude[33] to the huge gathering of bishops at Jerusalem (335), where they were to mark the Tricennalia of Constantine's reign by attending the dedication of the basilica, newly erected on the site of the Holy Sepulcher and financed by the emperor. The purpose of the synod at Tyre was to examine the disturbances in the Egyptian Church and to secure "peace and concord" for the Church,[34] which was the aim of Constantine's Church-policy and which *seemed* to coincide with the traditional concept of Church unity—at least as superficially conceived by Eusebius of Caesarea. Athanasius was reluctant to attend and only did so on the express order of the emperor,[35] who threatened to banish anyone who would dare disobey his command.[36]

When Athanasius and his fellow-bishops from Egypt arrived in Tyre, they discovered how justified was their original reluctance to attend the synod. The list of charges against Athanasius, originally two—the validity of his election and the breaking of the

---

[31]   Cf. Sozomen, *HE* 2,25,17 (Bidez-Hansen 86,22–27).

[32]   In his *Festal Letter* VII (for Easter, 335), written after his summons to Caesarea (and before the convocation at Tyre), Athanasius again mentions "all those who are aliens from the Catholic Church, heretics and schismatics" (Robertson, *Athanasius*, LNPF², 525), but in contrast with the previous letters, especially V and VI (see above, footnote 21), where he concentrates on the schismatics, here he gives his attention almost exclusively to the heretics (the sympathizers of Arius). His renewed interest in the heretics is shown by the repeated echoes of anti-Arian polemics, according to which he stresses that only those "who acknowledge the truth in Christ" (*Festal Letter VII*, 3 = Robertson 524) can participate in the Paschal Feast (cf. v. 4–8 = Robertson 524–526).

[33]   Cf. Eusebius, *VC* 4,41.

[34]   See the *Letter of Constantine to the Synod of Tyre,* in Eusebius, *VC* 4,42,1–5 (Winkelmann 136,20–138,9). "Die Synode zu Tyrus war wesentlich veranlaßt durch den Wunsch des Constantin, bei seiner Tricennalienfeier die gesamte Kirche in Frieden zu sehen und gedacht als eine Art Begleiterscheinung der prunkvollen Einweihung der Grabeskirche in Jerusalem" (Lietzmann, "Chronologie," 252). See also Socrates, *HE* 1,28,1 (Hussey 149).

[35]   Cf. *Apol.* 71,2 (Opitz 149,3–4); Sozomen, *HE* 2,25,2 (Bidez-Hansen 84,11); Socrates, *HE* 1,28,4 (Hussey 150).

[36]   Cf. *Letter of Constantine to the Synod of Tyre* (Eusebius *VC* 4,42,4 = Winkelmann, 137,24–138,1).

chalice—had been expanded to include a variety of indictments that were
no longer of a purely ecclesiastical nature but also included those of a civil
nature,[37] added to which was the charge of the murder of Arsenius.[38] But
what finally convinced Athanasius and his supporters that they were the
subjects of a conspiracy was the way the trial was conducted, above all its
blatant partiality.[39] The Egyptian bishops who accompanied Athanasius
to Tyre claimed that, at the root of this partiality, was the enmity of the
leading factions at the synod (the Eusebians and the Meletians) "to the
orthodox."[40] How right they were only became evident a short interval later when the same Oriental bishops gathered at Jerusalem for the
dedication of the Church of the Holy Sepulcher and received Arius
back into communion.

Consequently, Athanasius, writing in the *Apologia* over twenty years
after Tyre, causally connects his refusal to receive Arius into communion at
Alexandria, as requested by Eusebius of Nicomedia, with the first Meletian
attacks on his person: the ultimate cause of the Eusebian-Meletian conspiracy was the Arian heresy[41] just as the ultimate cause of the more recent
attacks, led by Valens and Ursacius on his right, to the See of Alexandria
is, he claims, also the Arian impiety.[42]

Ordered by the emperor to admit Arius into communion,
Athanasius dissented; the Alexandrian bishop refused to recognize the
imperial authority in matters pertaining to the Faith. But when the

[37] Cf. Sozomen, *HE* 2,25,3–6 (Bidez-Hansen 84,12–29). The charges, mostly
relating to the alleged violent behavior of Athanasius at Alexandria, were rejected
by the Synod of Alexandria, 338 (*Apol.* 5,1ff. = Opitz 90,41ff.); see also *Apol.*
71,3–4 (Opitz 149,4–11). It is also important to note that the sentence passed
by the Synod of Tyre apparently did not mention these charges (cf. Sozomen,
HE 2,25,15f. = Bidez-Hansen 86,14f.)—surely an indication in itself that the
accusations rested on shaky foundations.

[38] Cf. *Apol.* 72,2 (Opitz 151,15); Sozomen, *HE* 2,25,7ff. (Bidez-Hansen 85,1ff.) gives
what appears to be an accurate account of the actual trial at Tyre; he seems to have
had the minutes of the assembly at his disposal. According to Schwartz, *NGG*
(1911), 414 (= *GS* III, 248–249), this is an excerpt from the Meletian *libellus
accusationis* preserved by Sabinus in his collection of synodal documents. The
reappearance of the murder charge can only be explained on the grounds that
either Constantine neglected to inform Eusebius of Nicomedia and his party
of the exact reason why he cancelled the Antiochene inquiry into the alleged
murder, or the Meletians felt that Athanasius could not prove his innocence in
the matter.

[39] See above, footnote 5.

[40] Cf. *Apol.* 77,2–3 (Opitz 156,24–31); *Apol.* 78,3 (Opitz 158,7–9).

[41] See above, pp. 347–348.

[42] Cf. *Apol.* 89,4–90,3 (Opitz 167,25–168,10).

Meletians opened their offensive by bringing indictments relating to purely civil matters, Athanasius did not hesitate to defend himself before the imperial authority, even to the point of appearing personally at the Court of the Emperor. Likewise, over twenty years later, condemned again on charges mounting to lèse majesté, high treason, and civil disobedience, Athanasius had no scruples in composing a legal defense for presentation before the emperor (*Ad Constantium*).[43] The situation however became more complicated when accusations concerning ecclesiastical discipline were brought before the emperor by the Meletians.

When he composed the *Apologia* (356) Athanasius was clear as to the necessary procedure. He defends himself against such charges in a legal document addressed to his fellow-bishops in the West. They alone were competent to judge. But he never once denied that their judgement, the independent judgement of the competent ecclesiastical authority, had civil implications for the imperial authority: the emperor should recognize it and act accordingly. When the imperial troops led by Dux Silvanus tried to remove Athanasius from his see in February 356, Athanasius did not produce the documents relating to Rome/Sardica but the imperial decrees which gave that ecclesiastical judgement civil weight and permitted the bishop to return to his city after his second exile. Athanasius, while recognizing the distinct spheres of ecclesiastical and imperial authority, did not conceive them as totally separate from each other—but as intrinsically related to one another. Neither did he ever deny the emperor the obligation to assemble synods and give their decisions civil sanction, but he did deny his direct interference with regard to initiating and controlling the synod's procedure. This clarity was the end-product of his reflection on his experience at Tyre.

What Athanasius came face-to-face with in Tyre (335) was not simply the conspiracy of the Eusebians and Meletians, but the Imperial Church of Eusebius of Caesarea, who played a major part in the proceedings of the synod and may well, as Metropolitan, have acted as the episcopal president.[44] As to the emperor's own

---

[43] Athanasius was apparently ignorant of the fact that at Milan (357), the emperor had agreed to the principle that bishops could not be judged by imperial judges, irrespective of the nature of their crimes.

[44] According to Girardet, *Kaisergericht und Bischofsgericht*, 69, footnote 130, Eusebius was not even present at the synod. Both the *Letter of the Egyptian Bishops at Tyre* (*Apol.* 77,10 = Opitz 157,34) and the accusation made by bishop Potamon of Heraclea (who claimed that Eusebius had "sacrificed" during the persecution, cf. *Apol.* 8,3) imply his presence at least; they also suggest that he was a major participant. There is, further, some evidence (admittedly slight) that the

attitude toward the synod, it may be debated whether or not, as Girardet suggests, the *iudex* at the trial was Constantine, while the bishops were simply his *consiliarii*.[45] What is undeniable is the fact that the leading personalities at the synod, the Eusebians, did so think. The theory of the Imperial Church received its concrete form at the so-called Synod of Tyre.[46] As shown above, Eusebius of Caesarea had first articulated this ecclesiology in the final Revision of his *History; it found* its definite expression in *Laus Constantini* (originally intended for deliverance before the emperor at Jerusalem, consequent to the Synod of Tyre, but in fact held in the imperial palace at Constantinople, after the Eusebians had succeeded in banishing Athanasius to Trier). The synod is now conceived by the Eusebians in the wake of the new dispensation inaugurated by Constantine in terms of an ecclesiastical institution within the jurisdictional structure of the empire.

One obvious proof of the fact that the Eusebians considered the synod to be but an organ of (and so subordinate to) the State is its

Letter of the Synod of Jerusalem to the Emperor bears traces of his influence (see above, Chapter Four, footnote 198). Apart from the considerable prestige he enjoyed as an apologist and Church historian, Eusebius, as the Metropolitan, would have had the right to preside, at least nominally. (The factual direction of the assembly seems to have been in the hands of the Comes Dionysius, cf. *Apol.* 8,3 and 86,1.) For an account of the political machinations of Eusebius of Caesarea after Nicaea, 325 (generally underplayed), see Kraft, *Einleitung*, 64–70.

[45] Girardet, *Kaisergericht und Bischofsgericht*, 68. See following footnote.

[46] See the detailed and instructive account by Girardet, *Kaisergericht und Bischofsgericht*, 71, which unfortunately treats the testimony of Athanasius with unwarranted skepticism. Also, I find it difficult to accept Girardet's interpretation of ψηφίζονται as though it referred to an advisory *votum* of the imperial *consiliarii* (as distinct from the synodal judgement = καταδικάζουσι) and not to an actual judgement. It seems to me that the distinction made by Girardet is not valid on the grounds that (i) the emperor is simply informed of the proceedings; (ii) his confirmation was not sought for before the synod communicated its judgement to their fellow-bishops; (iii) the use of the related term ψῆφος (Sozomen *HE* 2,25,17 = Bidez-Hansen 86,23) does not refer to an advisory vote but an actual sentence or condemnation. That which characterizes Tyre is the consciousness of the bishops—or at least their leaders—to pass sentence on Athanasius, a sentence which they assumed had *automatically* the weight of a civil judgement and not simply an ecclesiastical one. Here, Tyre and Nicaea must be considered as essentially different, as the Synod of Alexandria (338) later affirmed; Caspar, *Geschichte des Papsttums* I, 141, held that this distinction was unjustified since both were *Reichskonzilien*. Such an opinion could only be defended if one were prepared to accept the picture of Nicaea as painted by Eusebius of Caesarea in the *Life of Constantine* (and if one compares it with his presentation of the Synod of Tyre), then indeed the distinction indeed has faded—blurred by Eusebius' later interpretation of the events as seen from the perspective of his ecclesiology of the Imperial Church.

sentence on Athanasius to the effect that, by refusing to attend the previous synod at Caesarea, the Bishop of Alexandria had thereby "scorned the
commands of the ruler."[47] But even more revealing is the reason given by
the same bishops at Jerusalem in their letter to the Alexandrian Church
justifying their admittance of Arius and his associates into communion:
"The most God-loving Emperor on the authority of his letter (διὰ τῆς
ἐπιστολῆς) witnessed to the correctness (ὀρθοτομίαν) of their Faith, which
he ascertained from them, and which having heard it himself by word
of mouth, he approved and expounded to us; in an appendix to his own
letters, he described (or decreed? = ἔγγραφον) the orthodoxy of those men;
this [Faith] all of us recognize to be sound and ecclesiastical."[48] Here the
final authority in the Church, even in matters of Faith, is the emperor, who
in the ideology of Eusebius had taken over and indeed gone beyond the role
traditionally assigned to the Bishop of Rome as successor to St. Peter, as
the young Church historian once held. Eusebius in his oration, which was
originally intended to be delivered on the same occasion, calls Constantine
"the Servant of God," "the Representative of the Almighty Sovereign,"[49] and
whom he, the bishop, does not "presume to instruct," since the emperor is
himself "taught by God."[50]

This new dimension of the Synod of Tyre, Athanasius only fully recognized after the event, most probably after his exile, when he received the
records and documents connected with the synod from Julius of Rome in
the year 338.[51] It is likely that, during his stay at Trier, he was made familiar with the Tricennial Oration delivered by Eusebius of Caesarea before
Constantine at the imperial court in Constantinople, a short time after his
banishment into Gaul. The speech pleased the emperor so much, it may
be said, that Constantine loaded the bishops who were present at the time
(= the Eusebians) with distinctions of every kind.[52] Even without a copy
of the oration, Athanasius had sufficient food for thought during his exile
on the periphery of the Roman Empire, when he reflected on the events
leading up to and during the Synod of Tyre.

[47]   Cf. Sozomen, *HE* 2,25,17 (Bidez-Hansen 86,22–27).
[48]   *De Syn.* 21,3 (Opitz 248,2–6).
[49]   Eusebius, *LC* 7,12 (Heikel 215,17 and 21–22).
[50]   Eusebius, *LC* 11,1 (Heikel 223,25–29). See, e.g., Setton, *Christian Attitude
        Towards the Emperor*, 49f.
[51]   Cf. *Apol.* 83,4 (Opitz 162,18–23). Julius had received the minutes of the pro-
        ceedings at Tyre from the Eusebians, who had previously sent them to Rome in
        their attempt to have Pistos recognized as the new Bishop of Alexandria.
[52]   Cf. Eusebius, *VC* 4,46 (Winkelmann 137,4–6).

He had been drawn into the spider's web of the *Reichskirche* by the way the Meletians slipped charges of an ecclesiastical nature in between the accusations of a civil nature and brought them before the imperial judge. Likewise, he had been continually driven into the defensive by the Meletians, who ceaselessly mounted one charge after another against him and presented them to Constantine. Even though he could clear himself, some of the mud flung by his enemies eventually left its mark and, like not a few scholars in recent times, Constantine became uneasy and probably began to wonder whether or not there might after all be some truth in the many accusations. By the year 334, the court's attitude towards Athanasius had turned decidedly cool, as could be detected in the appointment of Philagrius as Prefect of Egypt (at the latest after Easter of that year), a man of ruthless energy, ready to carry out any order of the emperor, irrespective of the party involved,[53] and whom Athanasius described as an apostate. It was clear from the peremptory command of the emperor that Athanasius could not have afforded to disobey the imperial order to attend Tyre, as he had done with regard to the proposed synod at Caesarea.

With remarkable verve and using dramatic gestures tinged with a certain bravado, the young bishop mounted his defense at Tyre, even with respect to those charges, such as murder and violence, which were of a civil nature. This he did despite the obtrusive way the imperial troops were employed in the running of the trial. It must have been obvious to him that the trial, held by order of the emperor and under the direction of the Comes Dionysius, was being conducted more like an imperial commission than a genuine synod.[54] Once he was convinced that he was the object of a more far-reaching conspiracy than he had imagined, and thus could not expect justice, he escaped from Tyre and in his desperation went up to appeal to Constantine, despite the lack of sympathy he knew he would encounter, just as his fellow-bishops from Egypt had appealed to Dionysius to refer the case to the emperor,

[53] See Schwartz, *NGG* (1911), 413 (= *GS* III, 246).
[54] Cf. *Apol.* 86,1 (Opitz 164,13–14). Girardet's opinion that Dionysius most probably did not actually participate in the synod itself (*Kaisergericht und Bischofsgericht,* 68) is difficult to defend in the face of the clear affirmation to the contrary by the Egyptian bishops—including Athanasius—in their synodal encyclical (*Apol.* 8,3 = Opitz 94,11), written in the year 338, but three years after the event, and composed with an eye on a future synod where the statement could be verified or disproved. The fact that bishops at Tyre (also) communicated with Dionysius does not indicate, as Girardet holds, that he did not take part in the synod itself. According to the *Letter of the Synod of Alexandria*, 338, Dionysius "presided" over the gathering. See above, footnote 44.

and just as he himself had previously defended himself on charges, such as high treason and murder, and would do so again twenty years later before Constantius II.

Considering the complexity of the situation, both personal and legal, it cannot be simply affirmed without reservation that, by appealing to the emperor, Athanasius recognized the *Reichskirche*. What in fact he had done was to transgress a canon, which but five years previously the Eusebians had formulated at a synod in Antioch, and which in its own way translated Eusebius' ideology of the Imperial Church into concrete institutional form. This is Canon XII of the Synod of Antioch, 330.[55] According to this canon, any bishop deposed by a synod who "might presume to trouble the ears of the emperor" ought to be turned over to a larger synod; should he, ignoring the latter, be troublesome to the emperor, then he is not worthy of pardon nor worthy to have the opportunity to otherwise defend himself.[56] On two separate occasions in the *Encyclical Letter of the Alexandrian Synod* (338), this canon is clearly alluded to in such a way as to leave no doubt in the reader's mind that such a charge was unfounded.[57]

The significance of Canon XII is its assumption that the Church is but a type of state department, with its own administration organized according to provincial units (the canon affirms the autonomy of the provincial synod as does Canon XV) but incorporated within, and thus ultimately subordinate to, the State. Here we do not have the differentiated concept of the autonomy of the Church vis-à-vis the empire found in the writings of Athanasius but the complete *identity* of Church and Empire, according to which the synod, as an institution of the Christian Empire, operates within it, albeit with a limited autonomy with regard to matters and persons within its sphere of influence, but whose authority is ultimately derived from, and so subject to, the emperor. One could say that the "principle of subsidiarity" within is being rigidly applied. The canon forbids an appeal to the emperor, not on grounds of a separation of ecclesiastical and imperial authority but because it considers the emperor to be *above* the Church, as one who should not be troubled with matters which could be dealt with at the "lower" level of the

---

[55] For a full discussion of the controversy surrounding the date of these canons, see Appendix II, "The Origin of the Canons of Antioch," in Hess, *Canons of Sardica*, 145–150. Joannou's reasons for opting for the date 341 (*Die Ostkirche und die Cathedra Petri*, 71–72) are not sufficiently convincing to alter the conclusions of Hess.

[56] Cf. Joannou, *Fonti*, 115. Joannou, *Die Ostkirche und die Cathedra Petri*, 71.

[57] *Apol.* 3,5–7 (Opitz 89,19–90,15); *Apol.* 4,4 (90,33–34).

"State Department of Ecclesiastical Affairs," as it might be called today.[58]

That the authority of these self-sufficient provincial synods was seen to be ultimately derived from the emperor, who could of course intervene at will, is demonstrated by the way Eusebius of Caesarea reports[59] on the deposition of Eustathius of Antioch by a synod there (ca. 327 according to Simonetti). Using intentionally vague language about the troubles caused in that city by "the spirit of envy,"[60] Eusebius solely attributes the restoration of "peace" (i.e., law and order in accordance with the Eusebian concept) to the emperor. No explicit mention is made of the synod that deposed Eustathius but only to the imperial embassy, an unnamed Comes, whom Constantine sent to "plead" with the Antiochene people, and to Eusebius himself "through whose intervention peace had been restored."[61] The intervention referred to here is the Synod of Antioch,[62] over which Eusebius presumably presided. The president of the synod is thus put on the same level as an imperial embassy and his intervention (and that of the synod) is seen as a means used by the emperor to achieve his goal of "peace" (law and order). This is also the way Eusebius wishes us to interpret the Synod of Nicaea.[63] Such too is his description of the Synod of Tyre: once the "spirit of envy" began to cast its shadow over the bright day of the emperor's

---

[58] See also Canon XI (Joannou, *Fonti*, 113). Cf. Farina, *La Crisi Ariana*, 244f.

[59] Cf. Eusebius, *VC* 3,59,1–5 (Winkelmann, 111,24–112,21).

[60] This is Eusebius' favorite euphemism to describe the origin of those tumults which were in fact caused by the controversies surrounding the Nicene Definition and first used by him in the final Revision of his *History*. See above, p. 177f. See the interesting observation of Socrates, *HE* 1,23,6 (Hussey 131).

[61] Eusebius, *VC* 3,59,5 (Winkelmann, 112,18).

[62] See Socrates, *HE* 1,23,8–1,24,7 (Hussey 132–135); Sozomen, *HE* 2,19,1f. (Bidez-Hansen 74,25f.). The most complete account of this synod is given by Theodoret, *HE* 1,21,1–9 (Parmentier-Scheidweiler 70,1–72,3), who apparently had the minutes of the synod at his disposal. The prime mover at the synod was, he tells us, Eusebius of Nicomedia. But in the list of Eusebius' associates, who he brought with him from Jerusalem (whence he had made a spectacular pilgrimage, transported by imperial horses and carriage), his namesake of Caesarea is given first place. (At Antioch, the latter was evidently used as a "front" for the Nicomedian bishop.) What is of particular interest is the information that the Eusebians encountered strong opposition to the unjust condemnation of Eustathius on trumped-up charges from many other bishops present at the synod "who were responsible for the Apostolic Teaching and knew nothing of the deceitful assaults." Thus, the Eusebians rushed to the emperor and convinced him of the justice of the condemnation. The implication here, as in the account of Eusebius of Caesarea, is that the final authority which removed Eustathius was the imperial authority.

[63] See his presentation in *VC* 3,6,1–2 (Winkelmann 83,18f.).

golden reign, Constantine ordered a synod at Tyre, set them, as it were, against this evil spirit, and ordered them to proceed thence to Jerusalem for the Tricennalia celebrations (and the dedication of the Church of the Savior), after they had settled the disputed matters.[64]

Apparently alluding to the accusations of the Eusebians, that Athanasius had, by appealing to the emperor after his escape from Tyre and his deposition by the bishops assembled there, "troubled the ears of the Emperor," the Synod of Alexandria (338) replies by protesting that it was his accusers who in fact "do not cease to agitate the imperial ears (with fresh reports) against us."[65] The agitation, the Egyptian bishops explain, concerned those charges (of a civil nature) such as violence and murder, with which his enemies attempted to secure the banishment of Athanasius.[66]

This rhetorical use of the Eusebian accusation regarding the transgression of the stipulations laid down by Canon XII does not signify an implicit recognition of the said canon and its ideological basis in the Imperial Church conceived by Eusebius of Caesarea. The synodal letter, which is otherwise not lacking in irony,[67] simply takes hold of the content of the charge and demonstrates how the Eusebians themselves are far more guilty of that which they now so piously fling at the feet of Athanasius. The letter itself, however, goes straight to the heart of the complex question regarding the legal status of Tyre when it unequivocally asserts that the Eusebians "put forward the name of a synod and ground its proceedings upon the authority of the Emperor."[68] A few lines later the letter states: "If they, as bishops, claimed for themselves alone [the right to pass] judgement, then what need [did they have] of Comes and soldiers?"[69] This sentence reveals how very different was the understanding of the synod shared by the

---

[64] Eusebius, *VC* 4,41,1–4 (Winkelmann 136,6–19).

[65] *Apol.* 3,5 (Opitz 89,19–20). *Apol.* 4,1 (Opitz 90,16–17) refers to the contrast between the supposed conduct of Athanasius and the actual behavior of his enemies.

[66] *Apol.* 3,5–7 (Opitz 89,21–90,15).

[67] Cf., e.g., *Apol.* 3,6 (Opitz 90,5–6).

[68] *Apol.* 10,1 (Opitz 95,27. Translation slightly adapted from that of Newman in Robertson, *Athanasius*, LNPF², 106. See also *Apol.* 10,2 (Opitz 95,33).

[69] *Apol.* 10,2 (Opitz 95,31–32). Commenting on this letter, Caspar (*Geschichte des Papsttums* I, 140–141) observes: "Damit erklang zum ersten Mal ein Protest, der nicht so bald verstummt, vielmehr bei verschiedenen Gelegenheiten in der nächsten Zeit wieder laut geworden ist. Christliches Gefühl und kirchliches Selbstbewußtsein sträuben sich heftig dagegen, daß die staatlichen Gerichte in die Austragung einer Bischofssache hineingezogen wurden. . . ."

Egyptian bishops in comparison with that held by the Eusebians. The Egyptians recognized the correctness of the claim that bishops alone should judge ecclesiastical matters; what they could not accept was the new imperial ecclesiology into which the traditional episcopal claim had been, as it were, subsumed.

Incorporated into the Christian Empire, the synodal authority of the Church was being transformed into a *corporate* institution (itself a new development) which enjoyed but a relative autonomy within its own terms of reference. And thus, the Egyptian bishops led by Athanasius reject in principle, for the first time explicitly it would seem, the attempt to transform the Church into a *Reichskirche*, by attacking the Eusebian axiom that the final authority in the Church—from which all other authority is derived, and in which it participated—is the emperor. Now Athanasius begins his battle against the Imperial Church of Eusebius of Caesarea. On the level of reflection this is marked by the rediscovery of the *Apostolic* nature of the Church behind the shadow cast over her by the Imperial Church, first conceived by Eusebius of Caesarea, then adopted by Constantine, and finally transformed into practical terms by Eusebius of Nicomedia.

§2 The 10th Festal Letter for Easter, 338

It is misleading to say that Athanasius' deposition at Tyre and his exile to Trier awakened the Alexandrian bishop to the magnitude of the danger which the Arians were capable of causing to the integrity of the Church's *Dogma,* as has been suggested by an eminent authority.[70] The events which led up to and culminated in the Synod of Tyre brought home to Athanasius the danger they posed for the continued existence of *the Church itself* and its ability to act according to the traditional norms of ecclesiastical behavior. At Tyre, Athanasius had become aware of the unscrupulous way the political Eusebians threatened to disrupt the life of the Church. He himself had experienced in his person the extent to which they, in conspiracy with the Meletians, were prepared to go in order to achieve their aims—to the extent of trying to get Athanasius condemned to death for several trumped-up charges which amounted to high treason or lesè majesté.[71]

---

[70] See Kannengiesser, "Athanasius von Alexandrien. Seine Beziehungen zu Trier," 149–150.

[71] The final charge brought before the emperor at Constantinople—about preventing the shipment of corn—would also have secured for Athanasius the

In the remarkably noble *Festal Letter* composed in the year 337, either at Trier or on his return journey to Alexandria, Athanasius' main concern was to assure his faithful that the attempts by the Eusebians and Meletians to disrupt the unity of the Church in Alexandria, by securing the exile of their bishop, had been frustrated first of all by the profound fact that the unity of the Church was mystical and not spatial: "For although we are spatially separated, yet the Lord, the Giver of the Feast Who is Himself our Feast, Who is also the bestower of the Spirit, brings us together in mind, in harmony and in the bond of peace."[72] Here we get a glimpse of an ecclesiology which Athanasius will develop over twenty years later in *De synodis.* He goes on to encourage the faithful not to let the previous distressing situation dampen the song of praise which should now well up all the more due to the foregoing affliction endured by the Church,[73] to exhort them to forgive their enemies after the example of the saints of the Old Testament and, above all, the example of Christ,[74] to remind them of God's consolation in distress,[75] and finally to warn them not to fear their enemies.[76]

But as the ultimate and absolutely essential means of preserving the unity of the Church, Athanasius instructs his flock to grow in Christ, Who united us to the Father and Who by His Incarnation became weak that we might be strong, so that we might be victorious over all things, even death.[77] It is this last instruction which sparks off Athanasius' derisive attack on the Arian teaching, not for the danger it contains but in order to ridicule the Arian blasphemy which, he says, is basically an ungrateful failure to recognize the reason why God became man.[78] But the point of the

death penalty. That the emperor "only" exiled him to Trier was certainly an act of mercy on the part of Constantine, as the Egyptian bishops affirmed in 338. It was not illogical that his son Constantine II should have interpreted the bishop's banishment to Gaul as a sign that his father wished to protect Athanasius from the danger to his life posed by his "bloodthirsty enemies." (See *Apol.* 87,4–7 = Opitz 166,11–29 and compare with the account of the proceedings at Constantinople given in the *Letter of the Synod of Alexandria,* 338 (*Apol.* 9,3–4 = 95,10–20.)

[72] *Festal Letter* X, 2. Translation by Payne-Smith in Robertson, *Athanasius,* LNPF[2], 528.

[73] *Festal Letter* X, 3 (Robertson 528).

[74] *Festal Letter* X, 4–5 (Robertson 529–530).

[75] *Festal Letter* X, 6 (Robertson 530).

[76] *Festal Letter* X, 7 (Robertson 530).

[77] *Festal Letter* X, 8 (Robertson 530–531).

[78] *Festal Letter* X, 9 (Robertson 531).

letter is reached when he triumphantly declares that the attempts of the Arians and Meletians to destroy the God-given unity of the Church have failed since Christ has rescued His Church,[79] a reference probably to the permission of Constantine II (dated June 17, 337) to allow Athanasius return to his see.[80] He exhorts the faithful "to thank Him with me and on my behalf, this being the Apostolic custom, which these opponents of Christ (the Eusebians), and the schismatics (the Meletians) wished to put an end to and to break off."[81] In other words, the Eusebian-Meletian conspiracy had failed since no temporal power or spatial distance could separate him, the legitimate bishop, from his flock in Alexandria, which unity is founded in Christ and finds its purest expression in the Eucharist, whose source is the Paschal mystery,[82] where bishop and faithful thank God together: this is the "Apostolic custom," Athanasius proclaims, which the opponents of Christ and the schismatics tried to destroy.

The danger to the Church as posed by the Arians was thus not seen by Athanasius on his return from Trier as though it referred to the integrity of her teaching, but rather to the Apostolic constitution of the Church. What is of note in the 10th *Festal Letter*, where, significantly, Athanasius mentions the Arians by name for the first time,[83] is the fact that Athanasius draws attention, again for the first time in his writings, to the Apostolic nature of the Church and her activities. It opens with a reference to Athanasius' previous letters to the presbyters in Alexandria who had come to fear their adversaries; in those letters, Athanasius now tells us, he had "exhorted them (= the presbyters) to be mindful of the Apostolic boldness of speech"[84] and how he himself had fulfilled the duty of announcing the date of the feast (which fell to him as Bishop of Alexandria), since he feared to be condemned by "the Apostolic counsel: 'render every man his due.'"[85] Here he points to the source of the Alexandrian presbyters' authority as preachers and that of their bishop's responsibilities; it is Apostolic and therefore

---

[79] *Festal Letter* X, 10–11 (Robertson 531–532).

[80] See Opitz 166,11 (Commentary).

[81] *Festal Letter* X, 11 (Robertson 532).

[82] Compare *Festal Letter* V, 3 (Robertson 518).

[83] This important fact was highligted by Kannengiesser, "Athanasius von Alexandrien. Seine Beziehungen zu Trier," 149. Though to be precise, one must point out that Athanasius probably did not mention Arius as such (as Kannengiesser maintains) but the "Ariomaniacs," falsely translated into Syriac as "Arius and Manetes" (see Robertson 531, note 11).

[84] *Festal Letter* X, 1 (Robertson 528).

[85] *Festal Letter* X, 1 (Robertson 528).

must be exercised accordingly. The letter concludes with the following words, already quoted above in part:

> For, if having brought us out of the deceitful and famous Egypt of the opponents of Christ, He hath caused us to pass through many trials and afflictions, as it were in the wilderness, to His holy Church, so that from hence, according to custom, we can send to you, as well as receive letters from you; on this account especially I both give thanks to God myself, and exhort you to thank Him with me and on my behalf, this being the *Apostolic custom*, which these opponents of Christ (the Eusebians), and the schismatics (the Meletians), wished to put an end to, and to break off. The Lord did not permit it, but both renewed and preserved *that which was ordained by Him through the Apostle[s],* so that we may keep the feast together, and together keep holy-day, *according to the traditions and commandments of the fathers.*[86]

This passage opens with a reference to "the deceitful and famous Egypt of the opponents of Christ," i.e., the land of bondage under the authority of the Pharaoh—an allusion to the Imperial Church of the Eusebians, whom Athanasius often describes as opponents of Christ.[87] The text continues by referring to the afflictions suffered by Athanasius and his flock, which sufferings are compared to the wilderness, while the "promised land" is the "free" Church, which allows Athanasius to communicate freely with his people "according to custom." This custom was mentioned at the opening of the letter, when he referred to his (Apostolic) duty as bishop to announce the Feast of Easter. Then follows the reference to the thanksgiving or Eucharist which bishop and people celebrate together. This union of pastor and flock in the Eucharist, whose source is the Paschal Mystery,[88] is the Apostolic custom, which "the opponents of Christ and the schismatics" attempted to destroy. Their attempt failed since the Lord prevented it. Instead, He renewed and preserved that apostolically established unity in His Church, "that which was ordained by Him

---

[86] *Festal Letter* X, 11 (Robertson 532). Translation by Miss Payne-Smith. Larsow's German translation (*Fest-Briefe*, 113) diverges substantially from the English (e.g., "vielmehr erneuerte und erhielt er ihn [= den apostolischen Brauch], der von den Aposteln als Vorbild aufgestellt war...). It speaks of "the Apostles" (plural) and not the singular given by Payne-Smith: the plural is, according to the context, probably more correct.

[87] See, e.g., *Festal Letter* X, 9 init. (Robertson 531).

[88] Compare *Festal Letter* V, 3 (Robertson 518).

through the Apostles." Here we will not go far off the mark if we see in this "Apostolic custom," a reference to the Apostolic constitution of the Church instituted by the Lord Himself, namely, the Apostolic Succession. The passage ends with a reference to the (more general concept of the) Apostolic Tradition of the Church, when Athanasius affirms that he and his Church would celebrate the Paschal Feast by keeping to "the traditions and commandments of the fathers."

As confirmation of the thesis that all that led up to and happened at Tyre, 335, opened the eyes of Athanasius to the grave danger, not only to himself personally nor in the first place to the *Church's teaching,* but to the *Apostolic constitution of the Church* posed by the Imperial Church as conceived by Eusebius of Caesarea and realized in practice by his namesake of Nicomedia, and that consequently in this *Festal Letter* for Easter (338), he reveals for the first time his newly acquired awareness of this threat; attention may be drawn by way of contrast to the reaction of Athanasius when the Arian teaching as such posed a danger to his Church. This occurred on two occasions, at the beginning of his pontificate as Bishop of Alexandria, around the years 329–330, and a second time in the year 356, when Athanasius discovered that Egyptian bishops were being deposed for the sole crime of being adherents to the Nicene Creed. On the first occasion, the reaction of Athanasius is reflected in his *Festal Letter* for Easter, 330: this letter, written after the attempt to restore Arius to communion in Alexandria, is devoted to a clarification of the Apostolic Tradition regarding the transmission of the Apostolic Teaching, its nature, source, and implications. On the second occasion, as we saw above, Athanasius responded to the fresh challenge offered by the Neo-Arian party, who were not satisfied with the political control of Church affairs but who also wished to alter the teaching of the Church, by writing his first work explicitly attacking the Arian tenets: his *Encyclical to his Fellow-Bishops in Egypt and Libya,* which contains in germ, the arguments he will later develop more thoroughly and systematically, especially in the three *Orationes.*

As demonstrated above,[89] all the works of Athanasius which deal exclusively with dogmatic questions are to be dated after the year 356. The significance of this assertion, which contradicts the scholarly consensus, does not have to be underlined. Athanasius' battles with the Arians from 330 to 356 did not take place on the Christological front. As we have already indicated (and will further demonstrate), the theological question

---

[89]   Cf. Chapter Eight, footnote 100.

which primarily occupied his attention in those years was the ecclesiological one. His major dogmatic tracts were not written for the extreme
Arians but were composed at a time when the tide had turned against the
latter in the East, and when the Neo-Nicene party began to emerge after
the Dual-Synod of Ariminum and Seleucia, 359. Then Athanasius had
a critical but basically open and receptive audience. To convince them
of the truth defended at Nicaea, Athanasius plumbed the depths of the
Christian Mystery and expounded it with clarity—and with confidence
that his hearers would understand and accept it. This understanding he
did not presume to exist in the years 329–330 when he stoutly maintained
"there is no fellowship between the words of saints and the fancies of
human invention."[90] This also was the stand he took up to the year 359;
he did not enter into debates on the Nicene Faith. But when he perceived
the radical change in the situation of the Church in the East (and in the
West) which manifested itself at the above mentioned Dual-Synod, then
he relaxed his stand and became flexible enough to be creative. The result
was: his major dogmatic compositions.

In contrast to the *Festal Letter* for Easter, 330—Athanasius' first
response to the danger of the Arian *heresy*, where he found refuge in the
concept of the Apostolic Tradition of Teaching—Athanasius reacted in
337 to the Imperial Church of the two Eusebii by drawing attention to
the *Apostolic constitution of the Church,* rooted as it is in the Apostolic
Succession. He points out that the source of the presbyters' preaching and
the bishop's duty is Apostolic; in contrast with the Imperial Church of the
Eusebians in bondage to the empire, he highlights both the freedom and
Apostolic nature of the Church, where bishop and people are united in
the celebration of the Paschal Mystery in accordance with the Apostolic
custom (= succession), and celebrate the Paschal Feast in accordance with
the dictates of the Apostolic Tradition (= teaching).[91]

§3 The Encyclical Letter of the Synod of Alexandria, 338

Athanasius' hymn of triumph due to the Lord's victory over "the
opponents of Christ and the schismatics" was soon drowned by the

---

[90] *Festal Letter III,* 7 (Robertson 512).
[91] It should be noted that in the previous *Festal Letters*—ignoring the second
      which deals with the Apostolic Tradition—the term "Apostolic" occurs but
      rarely, almost exclusively to describe a precept or utterance of St. Paul: see

hue and cry of the Eusebians, once again engaged on their crusade to remove him from the See of Alexandria. Nine months or so after Athanasius wrote the above *Festal Letter*, they attempted to have Pistos, an Arian, recognized by the Bishop of Rome as the successor to Athanasius, whom they held to have been legally deposed by the Synod of Tyre. From the ecclesiological point of view, the Eusebians at this stage display, both in their actions and in the remnants of their correspondence at our disposal, an interesting mixture of the early Apostolic (or Petrine) ecclesiology of Eusebius and his later imperial ecclesiology.

The endeavors of the Eusebians to promote their candidate for what they, after Tyre, considered to be the vacant See of Alexandria, illustrate the blend of two basically contradictory ecclesiologies. Though they considered Athanasius deposed by the new type of synod, which preserved the accidentals of the traditional episcopal assembly but in essence was no more than an imperial institution, nevertheless, they took up the traditional practice of finding recognition for the Successor of St. Mark by securing his communion with the Bishop of Rome.

As we saw in Part One, this practice had crystalized over the first three centuries and was based on the Apostolic constitution of the Church. The participation of a bishop in the Apostolic Succession was guaranteed by his communion with the universal episcopacy and was in practice achieved by his communion with other sees of direct Apostolic origin and, above all, those of Petrine origin. By the end of the third century (as reflected in the original draft of Eusebius' *History*), Rome, Alexandria, and Antioch, in that order of importance, had emerged as "primatial" sees (= incipient patriarchal system) whose communion with each other guaranteed communion with the universal episcopate for the bishops within their sphere of influence. Even there we noted the gradual breakdown of this system marked by the decline of prestige previously enjoyed by Antioch. The near-deposition of Fabius and the actual removal of Paul of Samosata from this Oriental See of Peter (on the grounds of heresy) by synods of neighboring bishops greatly weakened the authority of the succeeding bishops of Antioch, and increased the importance of the Oriental synod as an institution superior to the individual bishops, even a successor to St. Peter. It is of note that,

Festal Letter IV, 4 (Robertson 516); *Festal Letter V*, 5 (Robertson 519); *Festal Letter VI*, 1 (Robertson 520). The other references are to the "Apostolic company," from which Judas was estranged (*Festal Letter VI*, 11 = Robertson 523) and to the "Apostolic likeness" which the saints preserve (*Festal Letter VII*, 3 = Robertson 524).

after the deposition of yet another Bishop of Antioch in 328, Eustathius
(the original champion of Nicene orthodoxy), there is no trace in the
records at our disposal of any attempt to have his newly elected successor
recognized by Rome through the exchange of *Letters of Communion*. That
no trace has survived may, however, have been due to the simple fact that
Eustathius' two followers[92] died soon after their respective appointments.[93]
In the deposition of Eustathius and the attempts to find a successor, what is
striking is the role played by the emperor; it marked a new phase of direct
involvement in affairs of the Church by Constantine, one that was warmly
welcomed by the Eusebians.[94] Two years or so later, the Synod of Antioch
formulated the canon mentioned above, thus giving institutional form to
Eusebius' ecclesiology of the Imperial Church. It is not without significance that Canon XV of the same synod established as law, the principle
of (provincial) synodal autonomy—not the relative autonomy relating
to *liturgical practice* proposed by Dionysius of Alexandria over fifty years
previously,[95] but absolute autonomy with respect to *jurisdiction*. The canon
declares that once a bishop has been judged by the unanimous vote of the
bishops within a province, then he may no longer be judged by others.[96]
This canon will play a major role in the Eusebian justification of their
stand in the case of Athanasius' deposition by Tyre. It is indeed possible
that Canon XV (formulated by the Eusebians who evidently controlled
the synod) was—as, for example, Batiffol suggested—in particular, aimed
at excluding an appeal to Rome.[97]

When the Eusebians requested Julius to grant communion to
their candidate for the See of Alexandria, they only expected him to
give his stamp of approval and were evidently perturbed when he

---

92 Cf. Schneemelcher, "Zur Chronologie des Arianischen Streites," col. 398.

93 It is interesting that Socrates could report a tradition to the effect that the
    See of Antioch was vacant for eight consecutive years after the deposition of
    Eustathius (*HE* 1,24,8 = Hussey 135), thus perhaps indicating the questionable
    legitimacy of the bishops, who, according to Theodoret, were appointed to the
    see—Euphronius and Flacitus (*HE* 1,22,1 = Parmentier-Scheidweiler 72,7–10).

94 Eusebius, *VC* 3,59,1–3,62,3 (Winkelmann 111,24–117,6). It is not a little ironic,
    that in his letter to the Synod of Antioch depreciating the removal of Eusebius
    from Caesarea and recommending the faith of Euphronius (one of the other
    candidates for the see), the emperor should instruct the synod to act in a way
    which would be conformable to the tradition of the Apostles.

95 See above, p. 122.

96 Canon XV (Joannou, *Fonti*, 116).

97 Batiffol, *La paix constantinienne*, 446. Hess, *Canons of Sardica*, 112, objects to
    this interpretation, but on weak and unconvincing grounds.

insisted on the right to judge for himself the merits or demerits of the case. But their action in applying for the customary recognition from the Bishop of Rome was a relic of the pre-Constantinian Apostolic Church with its hierarchy of Petrine Sees. As with other actions of the Eusebians, they retained the traditional forms (as for example the synod) but invested them with a new content or, as in the case of the exchange of the *Letters of Communion* between the major sees of Rome, Alexandria, and Antioch, they retained the form and emptied it of its content.

From now on the prestige of the Bishop of Antioch, which had been in the decline for over half a century, is gradually assumed by the Bishop of Constantinople, capital city of the new Christian Empire (= the Imperial Church). In the year 338, Eusebius, who had previously been translated from the relatively unimportant Berytus (= Beruit) to the city of the imperial residence at Nicomedia, arranged his second translation to Constantinople. As Jalland pointed out, Eusebius who possibly owed his original appointment to Berytus and his translation to Nicomedia, then the imperial capital of the East, to the influence of Constantia, wife of Licinius, aimed at acquiring for his see a primacy over the whole "Diocese of the East" as it then existed.[98] With the foundation of Constantinople, he translated himself and his ambitions to that see,[99] which legally was but a suffragan see of the Metropolitan See of Heraclea. The rise of Constantinople and the fall of Antioch's primatial claims are dramatically illustrated by the translation of Eudoxius from Antioch, which see he had taken over in the year 358 (having previously functioned as Bishop of Germanica), to Constantinople in the year 360.[100] In time, the suffragan see of Constantinople would

---

[98] Jalland, *Church and Papacy*, 198, note 1. See also Kreilkamp, *The Origin of the Patriarchate of Constantinople*, 16–19.

[99] Cf. Jalland 216. The English historian, however, suggests that, at the beginning of the Arian controversy, Eusebius of Nicomedia who had admitted Arius and his associates to communion, though they had been excommunicated by Alexander of Alexandria, attempted to win the support from the provinces of Palestine "perhaps to counteract the growing influence of the See of Antioch, to which Canon 6, in securing the rights of other Churches, appears to allude" (*Church and Papacy*, 202, footnote 2). But Canon 6, as we saw above (Chapter Five, p. 211f.) records the decline of Antioch's influence: into the vacuum created by this decline, Eusebius entered, armed with the ecclesiology of the Imperial Church as created by his namesake of Caesarea, secure in his own connections with the imperial household, and his acquired position as Bishop of the New Rome.

[100] Cf. also Kreilkamp, *The Origin of the Patriarchate of Constantinople*, 25–27.

achieve a primacy over all other sees in the East including the Petrine See of Antioch.

The synod that elected the Alexandrian presbyter, Pistos (who, with Arius, had been deposed by Bishop Alexander and excommunicated by the Synod of Nicaea), to fill the "vacant" See of Alexandria, and had him ordained by Bishop Secundus, who was likewise deposed and excommunicated by the same authorities,[101] was held at Constantinople probably soon after Eusebius had secured possession of the new imperial capital in 338. But the debate which ensued after the synod had written to Julius and had sent delegates to Rome to arrange for the exchange of the *Letters of Communion* was carried out between Rome and Antioch, not with the bishop of the latter city but with the permanent synod which was set up there in 338, where Constantius had established his winter quarters.[102] Already in 330, a synod held at Antioch formulated and approved the famous Canons XII and XV mentioned above, which crowned the anomalous development at Antioch of the provincial synod's autonomy as an "institution" and its superiority above the individual bishop, completing a process which began with the attempted deposition of Fabius and the actual deposition of Paul of Samosata. As we will shortly see, the principles enshrined in these canons form the basis of the Antiochene rejection of Julius' intervention in support of Athanasius and the other Oriental bishops such as Marcellus of Ancyra, Cyrus of Beroea, Euphration of Balanea, Hellanicus of Tripolis, and Asclepas of Gaza.[103] But the presence of these Oriental bishops in Rome, whither they apparently spontaneously journeyed to complain about the injustices they claimed to have suffered at the hands of the Eusebians and to seek redress, points to the original consciousness in the East of Rome's preeminence that marked the first draft of Eusebius' *History,* and which was still alive in the East despite the apparent ascendancy of the Imperial Church.

We have already seen how Athanasius and his fellow-bishops in Egypt reacted to the new Eusebian initiative in Rome. In the *Letter of the Synod of Alexandria,* 338, they categorically reject the

---

[101] Regarding Pistos and Secundus, cf. *Letter of Julius (Apol.* 24,2 = Opitz 105,11–15).

[102] See Norberg, *Athanasius and the Emperor,* 35. "Um rasch und einheitlich vorzugehen und den Kaiser dauernd beherrschen zu können, kamen die Führer der eusebianischen Partei regelmäßig in Antiochien zusammen, wo Konstantin sein Winterquartier zu nehmen pflegte: ἐνδημοῦσα σύνοδος, die später in Konstantinopel zu tagen pflegte und schließlich, seit dem 9. Jahrhundert, das leitende Organ der orientalischen Kirche wurde, tritt hier zum ersten Male in Erscheinung" (Schwartz, *NGG,* 1911, 480 = *GS* III,279).

[103] See Opitz's commentary on *Apol.* 33,1 (Opitz 111,11).

claims of the Eusebians regarding the sentence of Tyre by asserting that the Eusebians "put forward the name of a synod and ground its proceedings on the authority of the Emperor."[104] The Egyptians attack the new ecclesiology of the Imperial Church. This is the corollary of Athanasius' rediscovery, as it were, of the true *Apostolic* nature of the Church, as revealed in the 10th *Festal Letter,* composed over a year before he returned to Alexandria after his first exile in Trier. It should be emphasized that the *Letter of the Alexandrian Synod* quite simply takes for granted that the Arian heresy, as such, is assumed to have been dealt with effectively and definitively by the "Ecumenical Synod" of Nicaea.[105] The *letter* attacks the Eusebians for evidently being in *communion* with those condemned and excommunicated, and it makes the telling point that the Eusebians (though they pay lip service to it) thus ignore such a great synod, while they usurp the title of synod for their own unlawful coterie that has no right to be so named.[106]

This contrast between Nicaea and Tyre is of great significance in comparison with the portrayal of Eusebius of Caesarea, who puts both on the same level, if not actually considering Tyre/Jerusalem to be greater than Nicaea.[107] Here the two ecclesiologies are sharply delineated from each other. In Eusebius' Imperial Church, Tyre/ Jerusalem was evidently superior to Nicaea, while for Athanasius, only Nicaea deserved to be called a synod (he never once in his writings even mentions the fact that the emperor was present there) because it was, as he will develop in *De synodis,* truly ecclesiastically constituted (though called and enabled by Constantine!), while Tyre derived its authority and constitution from the emperor.

The Egyptian bishops contend that the object of the conspirators' activities is, indeed, to uproot the orthodox;[108] but the crime they are accused of is that by doing so they annul the decrees of such a great synod.[109] Their support for the heresy is an affront to the Church which condemned it.[110] The main accusation made by Athanasius and his fellow-bishops in Egypt is not against the Arian heresy—since that had been rejected by Nicaea—but against the way the Eusebians blatantly repudiated clear ecclesiastical judgements through their evident support for Arius and his associates whom

---

[104] See above, p. 360.
[105] Cf. *Apol.* 7,2 (Opitz 93,18–21).
[106] Cf. *Apol.* 7,2 (Opitz 93,21–23).
[107] Cf. Eusebius, *VC* 4,41 and *VC* 4,47.
[108] Cf. *Apol.* 7,3 (Opitz 93,23–25).
[109] Cf. *Apol.* 7,3 (Opitz 93,25).
[110] Cf. *Apol.* 19,2–3 (Opitz 101,10–19).

they admitted to communion at Jerusalem after they had deposed Athanasius at Tyre. Since what the Eusebians are doing is contrary to the teaching of Christ, what is at stake is the very existence of the Church itself.[111]

One particular action of Eusebius of Nicomedia is singled out for special condemnation, namely his translations from Berytus to Nicomedia and thence to Constantinople.[112] These are condemned not only because they are contrary to the Church's law (Canon XV of Nicaea) but especially because such ambitions on the part of Eusebius display his understanding of what religion is: for him wealth and the greatness of cities are everything, while he thinks slightingly on "the heritage of God" to which he had been appointed. According to this, the heritage of God, a bishop is more indissolubly united to his Church than a man to his wife. Here a theme is touched on—in fact, Athanasius' predecessor almost two decades earlier had already perceived its implications[113]—which from then on would play a major role, even down to our own day, in the discussions concerning the Roman primacy: the significance of the political importance of a city for the Church or see established there. For Athanasius, as for Bishop Alexander and the early Eusebius before him, the size or political importance of a city was of no consequence for the see it contained. But in the new Imperial Church it was evident that the political importance of a city would indeed affect the prestige attributed to its bishop.

§4 The *Epistola Encyclica* of Athanasius, 339

Recognizing from the unexpected reaction of Julius of Rome that Pistos, due probably to his blatant Arian history, stood no chance of general recognition, the Eusebians held a synod in Antioch at the beginning of the year 339, appointed Gregory of Cappadocia to succeed Athanasius (after Eusebius of Emesa had refused),[114] and, without waiting for confirmation from Rome, sent him to Alexandria. There his unexpected appointment was announced by the Prefect Philagrius. According to the account of Athanasius, at a time when he was living in peace with his fellow-bishops and carrying

---

[111] Cf. *Apol.* 19,4 (Opitz 101,19–26).

[112] Cf. *Apol.* 6,6–7 (Opitz 92,27–93,13).

[113] *Urkunde* 4b,4. This document, known as the *Depositio Arii*, was, according to Newman, *Athanasius II*, 3–6, written by Deacon Athanasius, then secretary to Alexander.

[114] Cf. Sozomen, *HE* 3,6,1–4 (Bidez-Hansen 107,14–108,3); Socrates 2,10,1 (Hussey 193).

out his regular pastoral duties, "the Prefect of Egypt suddenly made public a rescript, bearing the form of an edict, to the effect that a certain Gregory of Cappadocia was coming from the (Imperial) Court."[115] The faithful protested vehemently, only to be met with the strong arm of the law. Philagrius ruthlessly attacked the Church, established order, and thus enabled Gregory to take possession of the See of Alexandria.[116] Athanasius fled and, before he departed for Rome, addressed a hastily composed *Encyclical Letter to his Fellow-Ministers Everywhere*, from which we have just quoted. In this letter, Athanasius calls on his fellow-bishops to make his cause their own, to rise in protest against the outrages committed against the "famous Church of the Alexandrians," such as the actual violence done to his people, especially the violent separation of the legitimate bishop from his faithful and the threat of a heretical usurper,[117] and above all to refuse to exchange *Letters of Communion* with Gregory.[118]

Again in this *encyclical* it is not the threat to the integrity of the faith of the Alexandrians posed by the Arian Gregory that chiefly occupies the attention of Athanasius, but the way the appointment of the Cappadocian contravenes the ecclesiastical canons, while his taking possession of the See of Alexandria with the aid of external force demolishes them.[119] Athanasius is not unaware of the danger to the Faith occasioned by Gregory's appointment, but his primary concern is for the integrity of the Church as such. Thus, he stresses at the outset that the ecclesiastical

> canons and forms were not given to the Churches at the present time, but were well and truly *transmitted from the Fathers to us.* Neither had the Faith its beginning in our day, but *was passed on to us from the Lord through his disciples.* So that those things *which have been preserved in the Churches from the beginning up to now* may not be destroyed in our own day and those things entrusted to us be sought from us, rouse yourselves, Brethren, as "stewards of the mysteries of God" when you see them plundered by others.[120]

The canons criticized here are possibly those of Antioch mentioned above, which formed the legal basis of the Eusebian case, as will be

---

[115] *Ep. encycl.* 2,1 (Opitz 170,27–29).
[116] *Ep. encycl.* 3,1 f. (Opitz 171,21f.).
[117] *Ep. encycl.* 7,3 (Opitz 176,21–25).
[118] *Ep. encycl.* 7,4 (Opitz 176,25–29).
[119] Cf. *Ep. encycl.* 2,3–4 (Opitz 171,4–20).
[120] *Ep. encycl.* 1,8 (Opitz 170,12–18).

seen. What is certain is that Athanasius here rejects the new "forms" now introduced to the Church: the form of an imperial edict as the authority which determines an episcopal appointment. In contrast with this innovation, Athanasius appeals to the canons and forms transmitted from the Fathers and which, like the Faith, were rooted in the beginning of the Church, i.e., in the Apostolic Church.

The previous year (338), the brethren at Rome, Athanasius reminds his fellow-bishops everywhere, had written (decreed?) that a synod take place to settle matters.[121] The Eusebian reaction, as we have seen, was to appoint a less irreputable character and have him installed on the orders of the emperor. After dispatching his *encyclical,* Athanasius, ousted from his see, departed for Rome. What moved the Bishop of Alexandria to flee to Rome? Whether he recognized in the Bishop of Rome a unique authority over and above that of the other bishops of the universal episcopate, to whom he had appealed in his encyclical, cannot be answered until we have further information about his understanding of the Bishop of Rome's office: this he himself provides as we will see in the *Historia Arianorum.* There he also describes the events covered here in a way which is itself enlightening. According to that presentation, Athanasius informs us that he sailed to Rome in order that the synod proposed by Julius might be held "as had been determined" by the Bishop of Rome.[122]

§5 The Synod of Rome, 340–341

What did Julius determine when he called a synod? His original letters to Athanasius and to the Eusebians have not been preserved and, since the evidence in Athanasius and the ancient historians is unclear, opinions differ as to whether he originally proposed Rome as the venue for the synod or not.[123] According to the *Letter of Julius to the Orientals* preserved in the *Apologia,* the Bishop of

---

[121] Cf. *Ep. encycl.* 7,2 (Opitz 176,16–17).

[122] *Hist. Arian.* 11,1 (Opitz 188,29–30).

[123] According to Jalland, *Church and Papacy,* 213, Julius proposed that the new synod be held at Rome; Joannou, *Die Ostkirche und die Cathedra Petri,* 43–44, claims that both parties were supposed to appear before the Roman synodal court. Schwartz, *NGG* (1911), 485 (= *GS* III, 285) maintains that the location of the synod was left open, and there was no talk about an actual summons. Girardet, *Kaisergericht und Bischofsgericht,* 80, denies that the synod, proposed by the Eusebian delegates after they found themselves in a tight corner, was intended to have been called by Julius or held in Rome. See Brennecke, *Hilarius von Poitier,* 5–15, for an alternative, though unconvincing, account.

Rome affirms that the Eusebian delegates requested him "to convene a synod (σύνοδον συγκροτῆσαι) and to write both to Athanasius, the Bishop of Alexandria, as well as to the associates of Eusebius in order that in the presence of all a just judgement might be executed; for they promised in that case to prove all the charges brought against Athanasius."[124] Athanasius informs us that the synod proposed by Julius could be held wherever the contending parties desired.[125] Thus, it seems that no set location for the synod was fixed by the Bishop of Rome. And yet the invitation to the synod was not only couched in terms which resembled a citation, so that Julius himself in the above-mentioned letter had to assure the enraged Orientals that Athanasius was also summoned (κληθείς) by a letter from him similar to that sent to the Eusebians,[126] but it also must have included the suggestion that Rome would be the most suitable location,[127] a suggestion that may possibly be deduced from a reference in the text of the above-mentioned *Letter of Julius to the Orientals.*[128] As we remember from our analysis of *Apologia* 20,[129] Athanasius also described this action of Julius as though it amounted to a citation before the Synodal Court of Rome. This impression must have also been made on the other Oriental bishops who, around the same time as Athanasius, went up to Rome to lay their case before Julius, as Socrates wrote.[130]

To the best of my knowledge, historians have shown little interest in the reason why these Eastern bishops (who had been deposed

---

[124] *Apol.* 22,3 (Opitz 104,4–6).

[125] *Hist. Arian.* 9,1 (Opitz 188,7).

[126] Cf. *Apol.* 29,2 (Opitz 108,33–34). This text can only refer to the original invitation of Julius (338) and not to the *2nd Letter of Julius* appointing the date for the synod; since Athanasius was in Rome when the latter was composed and thus did not have to travel to Rome as the text here referred to presupposes. See Batiffol, *La paix constantinienne*, 418, footnote 2. See also *Letter of Julius* = *Apol.* 22,5 (Opitz 104,14). For evidence that Athanasius understood the invitation of Julius in terms of a summons, see *Hist. Arian.* 11,1 (Opitz 188,29–30). See in this context, Socrates, *HE* 2,11,7 (Hussey 201) and Theodoret, *HE* 2,4,2 (Parmentier-Scheidweiler 97,24–98,2), who likewise interpret the *1st Letter of Julius* in 338 as a summons: ὁ δὲ τῷ τῆς ἐκκλησίας ἑπόμενος νόμῳ, καὶ αὐτοὺς καταλαβεῖν τὴν Ῥώμην ἐκέλευσε καὶ τὸν θεῖον Ἀθανάσιον εἰς τὴν δίκην ἐκάλεσε.

[127] See Roethe, Synoden, 82.

[128] Cf., e.g., Apol. 23,4 (Opitz 104,37–39): καὶ ὅμως τούτων ὄντων ἡμεῖς ὑπὲρ ἀκριβείας οὔτε ὑμῖν (= the Eusebians) οὔτε τοῖς ὑπὲρ αὐτῶν (= the Alexandrians) γράψασι πρόκριμα ποιοῦντες προετρεψάμεθα τοὺς γράψαντας ἐλθεῖν, ἵν' ἐπειδὴ κτλ.

[129] See above, pp. 334–335.

[130] Cf. Socrates, *HE* 2,15,2–3 (Hussey 206). See also Sozomen, *HE* 3,8,1–2 (Bidez-Hansen 110,17–27).

under Constantine during the rise of the Eusebian party after 330, returned to their sees after his death, and then once again were banished)[131] journeyed to Rome *around the same time*.[132] It is possible that the Eusebians mentioned at least two of them, Marcellus of Ancyra and Asclepas of Gaza, in their letter to Julius requesting his recognition of their candidate for the See of Alexandria, Pistos,[133] and thus Julius, in turn, likewise invited them to attend the proposed synod,[134] though there is no actual documentary evidence to support this suggestion.[135] Neither is there any concrete evidence to help us discover why the others, Lucius of Adrianople, Cyrus of Beroea, Euphration of Balanea, Hellanicus of Tripolis, and Paul of Constantinople all appear in Rome between 339 and 340. The most reasonable cause, seems to me, is the *1st Letter of Julius* convening the synod, whose likely venue was understood to be Rome, even though the question of location was in principle left open, and to which Athanasius and the Eusebian party as such[136] were together summoned to prove their reciprocal accusations and to answer for the charges each party brought against the other. Once the Oriental bishops received news of Julius' decision to call a synod,[137] and of the fact that their enemies had been summoned to

[131]   See Opitz's commentary to *Apol.* 33,1 (Opitz 111,11), who also gives a list of these bishops and the references to them in the sources. However, he fails to include Paul of Constantinople, cf. Sozomen, *HE* 3,8,1 (Bidez-Hansen 110,18).

[132]   An exception is Joannou, *Die Ostkirche und die Cathedra Petri*, 55–56, who suggests that it was Athanasius who occasioned the presence in Rome of so many famous bishops from the East, so as to give the proposed synod the character of a Catholic demonstration against the Arian heresy: but for Athanasius at this stage, it was not so much the heresy supported by the Eusebians which troubled him as the destruction of the Apostolic Church and his claim to the See of Mark.

[133]   Cf. *Letter of Synod of Sardica to the Bishops of the Catholic Church Everywhere* (*Apol.* 42,5 = Opitz 119,23–25).

[134]   Joannou, *Die Ostkirche und die Cathedra Petri*, 49–50, claims that Marcellus and Asclepas were summoned to appear before the court of the Roman bishop. The evidence at our disposal does not allow us to make such a categorical statement. Opitz, commenting on *Apol.* 32,1 (Opitz 110,19), asserts that before the Synod of Rome negotiations had already taken place between Antioch and Rome about Marcellus, who arrived in Rome around the same time as Athanasius.

[135]   The reference given above in note 133, which refers to correspondence between the Eusebians and Julius concerning Athanasius, Marcellinus, and Asclepas (the main text produced by Joannou, *Die Ostkirche und die Cathedra Petri*, 49), is vague and could refer to several letters written by the Eusebians to Julius between 338 and 341.

[136]   Julius reports how the Orientals were upset that he addressed his original letter to Eusebius and his associates only and not to them all; cf. *Apol.* 26,1 (Opitz 106,23).

[137]   Cf. *Ep. encycl.* 7,2 (Opitz 176,16–17), which presupposes that the letter of

prove their accusations against Athanasius, and to defend themselves in the face of the charges brought against them by Athanasius and the Egyptian bishops, they too decided to journey to Rome (possibly to give evidence for the prosecution) and likewise to seek redress for the wrongs they had suffered at the hands of the Eusebians. They also apparently assumed that the synod would take place in Rome.

In any case, with the arrival of Athanasius at the See of Peter (339, before winter), the question about the venue was no longer open: his presence there had decided the issue. The *2nd Letter of Julius* which he sent to the Eusebians did not mention the location—Rome is apparently assumed—but simply *appointed the day* for the synod to take place,[138] i.e., sometime in the autumn or winter of the year 340.[139] Though it is inaccurate to state that the *1st Letter of Julius*, calling for a synod to be held in the presence of all parties, concerned, must have clearly taken the side of Athanasius,[140] yet it is obvious that the letter indicated the grave doubts Julius had as to the credibility of the accusations of the Eusebians: their delegates in Rome were so obviously confounded by the Alexandrian delegation's refutation of their charges that one of their members, the presbyter Macarius, though ill, fled Rome by night.[141] The *2nd Letter* must have also indicated the displeasure of Julius that the Eusebians evidently jeopardized the effectiveness of the proposed synod by the clever maneuver of abandoning the obviously unacceptable (Arian) Pistos, and prejudiced its findings regarding Athanasius by appointing yet another successor Gregory,[142] having him installed in Alexandria by imperial edict; it was only after he had actually taken possession of Alexandria

Julius convening a synod was, though addressed to the contending parties, circulated among all the bishops. It is however possible that this encyclical of Athanasius was the means by which the Orientals received news of Julius' proposal.

[138] Cf. *Apol.* 25,3 (Opitz 106,9–10); *Hist. Arian.* 11,1 (188,30–32).

[139] Cf. Roethe, *Synoden*, 83, footnote 4; Opitz, however, dates the synod at the beginning of 341. As will be discussed below (see p. 379f.), the synod apparently assembled on two occasions, the first on the appointed day and the second after the arrival in Rome of the papal legates from Antioch at the beginning of 341. The decisive texts for the chronology of this period are: *Letter of Julius* = *Apol.* 25,3 (Opitz 106,12–13); *Apol.* 29,2 (Opitz 108,30–32). The chronology proposed by Joannou, *Die Ostkirche und die Cathedra Petri*, 57–70 is unacceptable. See the discussion below.

[140] See Caspar, *Geschichte des Papsttums* I, 145.

[141] Cf. *Letter of Julius* = *Apol.* 24,3 (Opitz 105,18–22).

[142] See *Letter of Julius* = *Apol.* 30,1 (Opitz 109,6–8).

that Gregory requested the traditional communion letters from Rome.[143]

On the other hand, the Eusebians must have been perplexed to find themselves summoned to defend themselves on various charges raised by the Alexandrians, the most serious being the contention that they had contravened the decisions of Nicaea in matters of Faith (= admitting Arius) and ecclesiastical practice (= episcopal translations). The *2nd Letter of Julius* composed after the arrival of Athanasius, which decided on the date for the synod, apparently left its readers in no doubt that it was intended as a citation to appear before the Synod of Rome and answer the charges brought against them,[144] and was so understood by Eusebius of Nicomedia.[145] It is likely that it expressed grave disappointment that, unlike Athanasius, the Eusebians failed to respond to the proposed synod and so aroused suspicion as to their sincerity.[146] And yet, as Julius himself repeatedly affirms, his letters summoning the Eusebians to Rome were written in charity.[147] Since, even after refusing to attend the Synod of Rome and then sending Julius a letter full of contentiousness and bitter irony, the Bishop of Rome did not close his heart to the Eusebians, but in his letter to the Eusebian-controlled Orientals, he tried once again to reason with them sincerely and objectively, then it can be *a fortiori* assumed that he, in his previous letters summoning them to the synod, tried to avoid any sign of bias. His sole object was to ensure that a "just judgement be given in the presence of all."[148] The *2nd Letter* was

---

[143] See *Letter of Julius = Apol.* 24,1 (Opitz 105,5–8).

[144] Cf. Sozomen, *HE* 3,8,3 (Bidez-Hansen 111,1–3). It should be noted that this reference to the *2nd Letter of Julius* has been incorrectly placed *after* the Synod of Rome (340) by Sozomen and included with the letters written by Julius after that event, in which the Bishop of Rome announces the admittance to communion of the Oriental bishops who came to Rome. See below, footnote 154.

[145] See Caspar, *Geschichte des Papsttums* I, 145. See also *Apol.* 33,4 (Opitz 111,30–31).

[146] Cf. *Hist. Arian.* 11,1 (Opitz 188,30–32). According to Schwartz, *NGG* (1911), 492 (= *GS* III, 295), "Athanasius' römische Reise *wurde so hingestellt*, als ob er der früheren Aufforderung des Julius, sich zu einer Synode einzufinden, Folge geleistet hatte" [my emphasis]. This statement reflects Schwartz's hostility to Athanasius, as does the following statement: "Das Schreiben, mit dem Julius und Athanasius die Verhandlungen mit Antiochien wieder aufnahmen, forderte nur dem Scheme nach zu einer Synode auf; es war so grob und hochmütig gehalten, daß es die Ablehnung provozieren mußte, die dann als Argument für das schlechte Gewissen der 'Arianer' benutzt werden sollte" (296).

[147] Cf *Letter of Julius = Apol.* 21,1 (Opitz 102,17); see also *Apol.* 21,3 (Opitz 102,21f.): Julius here refers to both his *2nd* and *3rd Letters;* see below, note 159.

[148] Cf. *Letter of Julius = Apol.* 22,3 (Opitz 104,5–6); *Apol.* 35,1 (Opitz 112,30–32). Girardet, *Kaisergericht und Bischofsgericht,* 85, observes that the roles have

brought to the East by the papal delegates, the presbyters Elpidius and Philoxenus.[149]

The appointed day for the synod (late 340) arrived but the Eusebians did not turn up. The synod took place, examined the cases of both Athanasius and Marcellus, heard the reports given by the other Oriental bishops, and, satisfied with their defense, admitted them to communion and restored each to his own see.[150] It is strange that in the contemporary literature which deals with these events the *Letter of Julius* communicating the results of the synod to the rest of the Church has been overlooked, or simply identified with Julius' reply to the Eusebians.

The main evidence for an earlier letter of Julius—the *3rd Letter* in his correspondence with the Eusebians—in which he communicated the result of the Synod of Rome to the East, is the *Letter to the Orientals* preserved in the Apologia, which we will from now on call the *4th Letter of Julius* in anticipation of our findings. This document, the *4th Letter of Julius,* is the reply of Julius to the letter from the Synod of Antioch which, after they had been detained in Antioch until January 340,[151] the papal delegates Elpidius and Philoxenus brought back with them from the East and handed to Julius in February or March of that year. In his reply, Julius of Rome states: "The bishops in any case now assembled on the appointed day and concurred with this judgement, which, *writing to you once again,* I signify to you. . . ."[152] The phrase ἥν πάλιν γράφων clearly implies that Julius had previously communicated the decisions of the Synod of Rome that took place in the latter part of the year 340. Both Socrates and Sozomen[153] inform us that, after Julius had examined the case of Athanasius and the other Oriental bishops and had admitted them to communion (i.e., after the Synod of Rome, 340), he restored them to their sees "fortifying them with commendatory letters,"[154] while Sozomen gives us

---

been reversed: the Eusebians now find themselves in the position of the accused. This seems to be an exaggeration since both Athanasius and the Eusebians were *both* the objects of various charges. Julius, it seems, did not act *ex parte,* as Girardet suggests, but endeavored to remain as impartial as possible.

[149] Cf. *Apol.* 20,1 (Opitz 102,2–3); *Hist. Arian.* 11,1 (188,30–32).

[150] See Socrates, *HE* 2,15,3 (Hussey 206). Sozomen, *HE* 3,8,2 (Bidez-Hansen 110, 24–26).

[151] Cf. *Letter of Julius = Apol.* 25,3 (Opitz 106,12–13).

[152] Cf. *Letter of Julius = Apol.* 26,3 (Opitz 106,35–37).

[153] See above, footnote 150.

[154] Socrates, *HE* 2,15,3 (Hussey 206). See also Sozomen, *HE* 3,8,3 (Bidez-Hansen 110,27–111,1) and *HE* 3,8,4 (Bidez-Hansen 111,4–6). As mentioned above in footnote 144, Sozomen incorrectly considered the *2nd Letter of Julius,*

a paraphrase of the *Letter of Julius to the Eastern Bishops*: "He wrote to the
bishops in the East, reproaching them for judging unjustly the cases of these
men (= Athanasius and the other Oriental bishops in Rome) and disturbing the Churches by not adhering to the doctrines [defined] at Nicaea."[155]
It was this letter—together with the letters written by Julius to the various
Churches in the East (restoring to their sees the deposed bishops who had
laid their individual cases before him—that prompted the Eusebians to call
a synod together at Antioch (under the presidency of Danius of Caesarea
in Cappadocia), and reply at last to the citation of Julius (= his *2nd Letter*).
This at least is the presentation of Socrates and Sozomen, who had a copy
of the Eusebian reply (now lost) before them, which they both quote, or
rather paraphrase.[156] Their picture of the events which succeeded the Synod
of Rome (340) also fits into the chronology of events.

Julius tells us that Athanasius waited (in Rome) in the hope that
the Eusebian delegation would turn up for one year and six months,[157]
that is, until around February 341, since he arrived in Rome, at the
very latest, around the autumn of 339. The Roman presbyters, Elpidius
and Philoxenus, presumably not long after the arrival of Athanasius in
Rome, travelled to the East with the *2nd Letter of Julius* summoning
the Eusebians to appear before the Synod of Rome on the appointed
day. They probably departed before the winter of 339–340 set in. They
were kept waiting in Antioch until January 341, as we saw above, i.e.,
until the *3rd Letter of Julius* communicating the judgement of the Synod
of Rome (ca. autumn 340) arrived in Antioch. This *3rd Letter,* which
announced the admittance of Athanasius and the others to communion,[158]
still refrained from taking the necessary consequence of excommunicating

---

(*HE* 3,8,3 = Bidez-Hansen 111,1–3), appointing the date [on which the Synod
of Rome should be held], as though it were written *after* that event. This was an
easy error to make, considering the fact that the reply of the Eusebians (January
341), which Sozomen had before him and was his main source, evidently referred
to in the *2nd Letter of Julius* (late 339), addressed to the Eusebian party as
such (ὀλίγους δὲ ἐκ πάντων εἰς ῥητὴν ἡμέραν παρεῖναι ἐκέλευσε [= *HE* 3,8,3 =
Bidez-Hansen 111,1]) as well as to the letter, or letters, to the Oriental bishops
as a whole, announcing the decisions of the Synod of Rome, 340 (καὶ τοῖς ἀνὰ
τὴν ἕω ἐπιοκόποις ἔγραψε [*HE* 3,8,3 = Bidez-Hansen 110,27–28]).

[155] Sozomen, *HE* 3,8,3 (Bidez-Hansen 110,27–111,1).
[156] Cf. Socrates, *HE* 2,15,4–5 (Hussey 206–207); Sozomen, *HE* 3,8,4–8
   (BidezHansen 111,4–26). See above, footnote 154.
[157] Cf. *Letter of Julius* = *Apol.* 29,2 (Opitz 108,30–32).
[158] Cf. *Letter of Julius* = *Apol.* 34,3 (Opitz 112,18–19); Sozomen, *HE* 3,8,6
   (Bidez-Hansen 111,14–15). Both texts are paraphrases of the Eusebian reply.

the Eusebians,[159] and apparently he once again invited them to defend themselves in the face of the charges brought against them by the Orientals in Rome.[160] The reaction of the Antiochene bishops to the news of what had happened in Rome, which probably reached them in January 341, was to assemble a synod there and compose their famous reply: "elegantly expressed and composed with great legal skill, though filled with much irony and not without its share of the most terrible threats," as Sozomen tells us.[161] Its author was probably Eusebius, now of Constantinople.[162] The emissaries of Julius were so appalled by the sharp reaction of the Eusebians in Antioch that, as Julius tells us, they returned to Rome with the reply of the Eusebians in the hand, distressed by what they had witnessed in Antioch.[163] Julius himself was so perplexed by the *Letter of the Orientals*,[164] which he repeatedly describes as full of contentiousness,[165] that after much deliberation he kept it to himself in the hope that some would after all turn up in Rome (to answer the charges brought against them) and "so as not to cause distress to many of those here, should the letter become public."[166] Since no one arrived, it became necessary to produce it: "I tell you openly brethren," wrote Julius to the Eastern bishops, "all were astonished and could hardly believe that such things were ever written by you: since the letter was full of contentiousness and not of love."[167]

§6 The Letter of the Synod of Antioch, January 341

After the return of Elpidius and Philoxenus from Antioch, Athanasius left for an unknown destination. He had good reason to

---

[159] This is the reason why Julius can affirm with confidence in his *4th Letter* that his previous letters were written "in charity" (see above, footnote 147); again in his *4th Letter*, he refuses to pass judgement on the Eusebians until they had an opportunity to defend themselves openly; cf. *Apol.* 35,1 (Opitz 112,30–32).

[160] Cf. *Apol.* 21,4 (Opitz 103,6).

[161] *HE* 3,8,4 (Bidez-Hansen 111,7–9); Schwartz, *NGG* (1911), 494–496 (*GS* III, 297–300) reproduces the comprehensive paraphrase of the *Letter of the Eusebians* made by Sozomen, into which he inserts the fragments found in Julius' *4th Letter*, with one exception, see below, footnote 185.

[162] Schwartz, *NGG* (1911), 494 (= *GS* III, 297).

[163] *Letter of Julius = Apol.* 21,4 (Opitz 103,4).

[164] Cf. *Apol.* 21,2–4 (Opitz 102,16–103,7).

[165] Cf. *Apol.* 21,2 (Opitz 102,18); *Apol.* 21,4 (Opitz 103,9); *Apol.* 34,3 (Opitz 112,19); see also *Apol.* 32,4 (Opitz 111,5).

[166] *Apol.* 21,4 (Opitz 103,5–7).

[167] *Apol.* 21,4 (Opitz 103,7–10).

hide himself. According to Socrates, Athanasius had meanwhile been
threatened with the death penalty by Constantius: the Eusebians had
accused him of appropriating to himself the proceeds of the sale of corn
granted to the poor of Alexandria by Constantine.[168] Julius, after he had
kept the contents of the Eusebians' letter to himself for a period, sent for
Athanasius to return to Rome.[169] Then what could be called the second
session of the Synod of Rome met to consider the *Letter of the Orientals*.
The Synodal Fathers were angry with the Eusebians, Athanasius tells us,
and requested Julius to write accordingly to the Eusebians,[170] the result of
which was the *4th Letter of Julius* preserved by Athanasius in his *Apologia*.

Julius and the other bishops who read the *Letter of the Eusebians*
were shocked to the core. Julius, above all, was so upset that he kept its
contents secret as long as possible (probably after Easter, 341). The *Letter
of the Eusebians* amounted to the threat of a schism—based not, in the
first place, on Christological differences (the Arian heresy is not directly
involved) but on a new understanding of the nature of the Church. If it
is true, as Schwartz held, that the most bitter polemics in the *Letter of the
Synod of Antioch* were directed "against the prerogatives which the Roman
See assumed for itself,"[171] then one could understand his reaction. But this
statement of Schwartz, though close to the matter, does not do justice to
the case of the Eusebians.

There is no denying the fact that the Eusebian-controlled Orientals
were enraged with the authoritative intervention of Julius in those
affairs which they considered to come under the sole responsibility of their (by now autonomous) provincial synod.[172] They maintain

---

[168] Cf. Socrates, *HE* 2,17,1–3 (Hussey 213). This charge was first raised by the
Eusebians in their letters to the three emperors and to Julius of Rome (338); cf.
Apol. 18,1–4 (Opitz 100,25–101,3). It appears that the Roman delegates brought
back news to the effect that the Emperor Constantius tended to give credence to
these charges; cf. Socrates, *HE* 2,17,4 (Hussey 213); Sozomen 3,9,1 (Bidez-Hansen
111,27–28); Sozomen 3,9,5 (Bidez-Hansen 112,24–28).

[169] Cf. Socrates, *HE* 2,17,4 (Hussey 213); Sozomen, *HE* 3,10,1 (Bidez-Hansen
112,30–31).

[170] Cf. *Apol.* 20,3 (Opitz 102,9–11). It is possible that this was the assembly of the
fifty bishops which took place in the Church of the Presbyter Vito, though as
pointed out above, that was more probably the original synod.

[171] Schwartz, *NGG* (1911), 496 (= GS III, 300). See also Girardet, *Kaisergericht und
Bischofsgericht*, 86–87, who is however more differentiated in his judgement than
Schwartz.

[172] This is the main point of the *Letter of the Eusebians* according to Socrates,
HE 2,15,5 (Hussey 206–207): it is also the first topic in the reply of
Julius—ἀσάλευτον ἔχει τὴν ἰσχὺν ἑκάστη σύνοδος καὶ ἀτιμάζεται ὁ κρίνας
ἐὰν παρ' ἑτέρων ἡ κρίσις ἐξετάζηται (*Apol.* 22,6 = Opitz 104,18–19; see also

that his reexamination of the judgement bypassed a synod—Tyre is intended—and so shows contempt for that synod, "since each synod possesses unshakable authority." As precedents, they refer to the cases of Novatian and Paul of Samosata[173] and accuse Julius of having actually transgressed the canons,[174] referring most probably to the Canons of Antioch, mentioned above, where the Imperial Church of Eusebius assimilated and radically brought to its completion the local tradition at Antioch concerning synodal authority, which was born in the controversies surrounding the persons of Novatian and Paul of Samosata.[175] The difficulty in interpreting this document lies in the letter's intentional ambiguity, which Sozomen described as full of threats, i.e., in its polished language laced with biting irony, which Julius unambiguously condemns.[176] Referring to their letter, the Bishop of Rome explains his motive for inviting them to the Synod of Rome and adds: "We are forced to conclude that in those [passages] where you appear to pay honor (τιμᾶν) to us, you have spoken in such a way so as to transform them with a certain irony."[177] The passages he refers to are those

---

Apol. 22,1 = Opitz 103,21)—a charge which he repeatedly returns to (cf. *Apol.* 23,2 = Opitz 104,30; *Apol.* 23,4 = Opitz 104,41–105,1; *Apol.* 24,4 = Opitz 105,23–24; *Apol.* 25,1 = Opitz 106,1). See also Sozomen, *HE* 3,8,6 (Bidez-Hansen 111,15–17).

[173] Cf. *Letter of Julius* (*Apol.* 25,1 = Opitz 105,26–27).

[174] Cf. *Letter of Julius* (*Apol.* 29,3 = Opitz 108,34).

[175] See above, pp. 115–119 and 128–135. Girardet, *Kaisergericht und Bischofsgericht*, 82–84, rightly calls attention to the legal background at the beginning of the fourth century, as reflected in the earlier canons in order to understand the argument of the Eusebians. However, the precedents he suggests are, with the one exception (the Canons of Antioch mentioned above), unacceptable: (i) Canons XVII (XVI) and LIII of Elvira, to which he refers (where the admittance to communion of an excommunicated cleric by another bishop is excluded), were in fact modified by Canon V of Nicaea so as to allow the reexamination of his case by the provincial synod—to which canon Julius appeals in order to support his intervention on behalf of Athanasius and the other Orientals, but which Girardet inexplicably ignores; (ii) the dispute between Cyprian and Stephan of Rome cannot be considered as a precedent, since the issue was not one of jurisdiction but liturgical custom; (iii) even if one were to accept Girardet's interpretation of the protest of the Donatists against the "Court of Miltiades in Rome" (313) (namely, that the basic principle regarding excommunicated clerics enunciated at Elvira was extended to cover the excommunication of a bishop by his fellow-bishops), it must again be pointed out that this principle was radically modified by Nicaea. Girardet's discussion of the Canons of Antioch ignores their ideological and historical background, as well as the fact that these canons were apparently of a local nature (Julius seems to have been ignorant of them).

[176] Cf. *Apol.* 21,2 (Opitz 102,16–20); *Apol.* 21,4 (Opitz 103,9–10); *Apol.* 21,5 (Opitz 103,10–12).

[177] *Apol.* 21,3 (Opitz 103,1–3).

paraphrased as follows by Sozomen:[178] φέρειν μὲν γὰρ πᾶσι φιλοτιμίαν τὴν
Ῥωμαίων ἐκκλησίαν ἐν τοῖς γράμμασιν ὡμολόγουν, ὡς ἀποστόλων φροντιστήριον
καὶ εὐσεβείας μητρόπολιν ἐξ ἀρχῆς γεγενημένην, εἰ καὶ ἐκ τῆς ἔω ἐνεδήμησαν
αὐτῇ οἱ τοῦ δόγματος εἰσηγηταί. οὐ παρὰ τοῦτο δὲ τὰ δευτερεῖα φέρειν ἠξίουν,
ὅτι μὴ μεγέθει ἢ πλήθει ἐκκλησίας πλεονεκτοῦσιν, ὡς ἀρετῇ καὶ προαιρέσει
νικῶντες.... ("They confessed in their letter that, according to the general
opinion, the Church of Rome held a position of honor—though one not
untinged with ambition—as it was the school of Apostles and capital of
orthodoxy from the beginning, even though those who introduced the
teaching came from the East to reside there. In comparison with this, they did

---

[178] Sozomen, *HE* 3,8,5 (Bidez-Hansen 111,9–14). See Caspar, *Geschichte des
Papsttums* I, 146–147. In his book, *Kaisergericht und Bischofsgericht*, 157–162,
Girardet has many important contributions to make to a fuller understanding
of the text, yet the general tendency of his interpretation is unacceptable, since
it is based on the (unproven) assumption that the Eusebians make reference to
a justification for his intervention in Oriental affairs given reputedly by *Julius,*
which in turn reflected the (ambition-fired) self-consciousness of the Roman
Church (pp. 158–159). But it would seem from the historical run of events,
that Julius simply *acted* in the awareness of his special responsibility as Bishop
of Rome: he did not consider it necessary to justify his action (after all it was
the Eusebian appeal for the recognition of Pistos that set the lawsuit in motion)
and thus was utterly dumbfounded when the Eusebian letter arrived, which
suddenly and inexplicably not only refused to accept the judgement of Rome
but for the first time actually questioned the right of the Bishop of Rome to so
act. Further as one will see, there is no need to posit a self-justification by Julius
(whose preeminence, it may be said, the Eusebians then presumably proceed
to half-recognize while at the same time robbing it of any real significance) as
the point of departure for the text of the Eusebian letter: as we have seen in the
History of Eusebius, the ideas contained in this paraphrase of Sozomen were
not strange to the Orient, but were common currency. Girardet, unaware of the
ecclesiological background to be unearthed in the early Eusebius, works on the
unfounded *a priori,* that the Roman Church developed a claim to a spiritual
preeminence out of her traditional renown for her *Fürsorglichkeit* (which he
proposes as the primary meaning of φιλοτιμία in the text) on the basis of, Julius
claimed, that Rome was the capital of orthodoxy from the beginning (p. 161).
(i) With regard to the translation of the text, Girardet rightly points to the
ambiguity attached to the term φιλοτιμία and briefly discusses three meanings:
honor, ambition, and generosity. He opts for the latter as the primary meaning
and bases his option on Cassiodorus' translation of Sozomen. This, however, is
not sufficient proof that either Sozomen in his paraphrase, or the Eusebians in
their original letter, ever intended this particular meaning. (The scale of meanings
attached to the term is much greater than Girardet states: see Lampe, *Lexicon,*
1484; see the illuminating discussion of this term by von Ivánka, *Rhomërreich
und Gottesvolk,* 45–48.) My option is based on the complementary text of Julius
(*Apol.* 21,3 = Opitz 103,1–3), where he gives his own description of the text paraphrased by Sozomen: there Julius affirms that on the one hand the Eusebians pay
honor (τιμᾶν) to the Church of Rome, while on the other hand they cloak this

not deign to occupy the second position, as evidence that in terms of the might and multitude of a Church they did not excel, as they [were] victorious in virtue and character.")

Though philological analyses of the various terms can help the interpreter, yet such alone are incapable of unravelling the original meaning of this puzzling text.[179] The task of the interpreter is complicated both by the fact that the text is a paraphrase, and that which is paraphrased is not a simple, straightforward statement, but an intricate series of statements, which themselves are shrouded in

honor with irony. At least Julius understood the text to refer primarily to the honor due to the Church of the Romans. And yet soon after Julius uses the term φιλοτιμία to describe the ambitious display of words, which characterize the *Letter of the Eusebians* (*Apol.* 21,5 = Opitz 103,10), which letter he otherwise describes as full of φιλονεικία and so bereft of charity (*Apol.* 21,4 = Opitz 103,9; *Apol.* 21,2 = Opitz 102,18), possibly with the intentional allusion, by means of contrast, to the former term. Thus, a proper translation of φιλοτιμία must take this second nuance also into account. In an attempt to do justice to both the primary and secondary meaning, I have translated the term as: "a position of honor—not untinged with ambition." (ii) The next term which is not easy to translate is ἀποστόλων φροντιστήριον. Here Girardet's observation (pp. 158–159) is important, namely, to the effect that the translations given by Montfaucon (*domicilium apostolorum*) and by Caspar (Gedächtnisstätte der Apostel) need to be supplemented with the meaning to be derived by the usage of the term otherwise found in Sozomen, namely, the meaning of a "... 'Mönchsklause,' was nicht nur die Wohnstätte der Mönche bezeichnet, sondern auch vor allem den Ort, an dem er betet und Schriftstudien treibt...." And thus in our text, "als den Ort, an dem er über die Lehren der Apostel (Petrus und Paulus), vielleicht auch über die apostolische Ordnung der Kirche, in besonderer—ökumenischer—Verantwortung 'nachgedacht' wird" (p. 159). However, Girardet attributes this to the "Selbstverständnis der römischen Kirche," whereas it, as well as the former nuances, reflect ideas which, as we saw, were used by Eusebius of Caesarea in his original *History*. The translation of this term adopted here is taken from Hartranft, *Socrates and Sozomen*, LNPF² II, 287; although it takes into consideration the point recently made by Girardet, yet it fails to render the other nuances and must remain inadequate. (See the comments of Möhler, *Athanasius der Große*, 356, note 68.) Its final justification, however, lies in the phrase following the particle ὡς, which pointedly reminds the Church of Rome that the actual teaching was brought there from the East, thus attempting to rob Rome's claim (to be the "school of Apostles") of its authority. (iii) The arguments of Girardet (p. 160) to the effect that the μέγεθος ἢ πλῆθος mentioned in the second part of the Sozomen text does not refer to concepts found in the previous *Letters of Julius* but are now introduced into the discussion by the Antiochene synod (and may in fact refer to the Church of Antioch), are convincing. (iv) On the other hand, his interpretation of ἀρετὴ καί προαίρεσις fails to convince, though he is right to point to a certain correspondence between the first and second part of the Sozomen text on which he bases his observations: as we will see the two clauses are indeed related to each other—but only by way of contrast.

[179] See comments in previous note.

irony. It is obvious that any translation, or any interpretation that attempts
to reconstruct the original content and intent of the Eusebian letter,
cannot claim to be definitive. And yet it is precisely the element of irony
that can provide us with the surest, though by no means easiest, key to an
understanding of the text. On the one hand, we have the reaction of Julius
of Rome to the irony directed at the authority on which he had spontaneously acted up to then; and, it may be added in parenthesis, that there
is no evidence to suggest that Julius acted in any other way but simply out
of the consciousness of his traditional responsibility, as Bishop of Rome,
when drawn into the Eastern controversy by the Eusebian exchange of
communion letters for their candidate for the Alexandrian See, and by the
claims of Athanasius to same.[180] What shocked Julius so profoundly was,
as we will see, the unexpected attack of Eusebius on what he had taken
for granted, an attack couched in ironic language. On the other hand,
the irony itself (in order to be effective) must have been based on ideas
which were, at least in part, common to East and West as well as a new
element, the *pointe* of the Eusebian attack, which was similarly based on
common knowledge, though not of a flattering nature. We will not go far
wrong if we have recourse to the ideas found in both the earlier and the
later Eusebius of Caesarea, his two "ecclesiologies" which, we have already
seen, played important roles in the actions of the Eusebian party up to now.
Indeed, as we will now see, it is these two ecclesiologies together with his
transitional "ecclesiology," which above all enable us to make sense of this
very important though strange text. Finally, to control our interpretation,
an eye must be kept on the other fragments of the Eusebian letter at our
disposal in order to see whether they confirm or contradict our findings.

The Eusebians "confessed in their letter that, according to the general
opinion, the Church of Rome held a position of honor [though one not
untinged with ambition]." The ambiguity of the term φιλοτιμία prompted
us to insert the phrase in brackets after what seems to have been the primary
meaning of the term.[181] Julius evidently perceived the negative nuance of the
term, since he himself describes the author of the letter of having written
it φιλοτιμίας λόγων ἕνεκεν—"with an ambition of exhibiting his power
of language," as Newman translated the phrase.[182] The Bishop of Rome

---

[180] Even in his reply to the Eusebians, the level of Julius' reflection on the nature
of the authority he so spontaneously exercised as Bishop of Rome is not very
developed.

[181] See footnote 178.

[182] *Apol.* 21,5 (Opitz 103,10); cf. Robertson, *Athanasius*, LNPF², 111.

affirms in the next breath that such language is not needed in ecclesiastical matters, but rather (respect for) the Apostolic canons.[183] It can be argued that Julius here refers to the Apostolic nature of the Church, according to which Rome occupied a position of real honor due to the recognized preeminence of her see. But in the ambiguous term φιλοτιμία, as used by the Eusebians, lurks the shadow cast over that Petrine preeminence by the two major controversies in the East—the Baptismal and Paschal disputes—when, for a time, an important group of bishops in the East, led by Polycrates of Ephesus and Firmilian of Cappadocia, opposed the stand taken by the respective Bishops of Rome, and when it appeared to them that Rome was usurping her position with undue ambition. As we saw in Eusebius' original *History*, this opposition was seen by the majority in the East as unjustified at least by the turn of the fourth century. But the action of Julius—not his summons of the Eusebians to the Synod of Rome, but his reversal of the decision of the Synod of Tyre and his admittance of Athanasius (and the other Orientals) to the communion—must have reawakened this latent stream of opposition to the apparent "ambitions" of Rome. Reechoing Polycrates and Firmilian, the Eusebians in their letter accuse the Bishop of Rome of "lighting up the flame of discord"[184] when "unanimity prevailed in the Churches" of the East[185] and affirm that "the honor due to [all] bishops is the same and equal."[186]

Here is enunciated once again an ecclesiological principle that is of major importance; later we will see how Julius and Athanasius understand it. For the moment, we should recall that the presence of so many other persecuted Oriental bishops in Rome witnesses, as was pointed out above, to the general consciousness of Rome's preeminence recorded by the earlier Eusebius, which saw no opposition between the equality of all bishops and the preeminence of the Bishop of Rome—or rather *his primacy*, which the Eusebians implicitly refer to when they affirm that they in Antioch are not prepared to occupy "the second position." In its own way, this "confession" of the Eusebians, "according to the general opinion the Church of Rome held a position of honor (= primacy)," is a most important witness to the general attitude of the East to the Church of Rome.

---

[183] Cf. Apol. 21,5 (Opitz 103,11–12).

[184] φλόγα διχονοίας ἀνάψαντες (*Letter of Julius* = *Apol.* 25,1 [Opitz 105,30]).

[185] ὁμόνοιαν γεγενῆθαι ἐν ταῖς ἐκκλησίαις (*Letter of Julius* = *Apol.* 34,1 [Opitz 112,8]). It should be noted that Schwartz overlooked this reference to the Eusebian letter in his compilation of such references (see note 161).

[186] ἴσην καὶ τὴν αὐτὴν ἡγεῖσθε τιμὴν τῶν ἐπισκόπων (*Letter of Julius* = *Apol.* 25,2 [Opitz 106,3–4]).

The fact that their terminology (assuming that Sozomen has reproduced it exactly, as indeed it would seem he does from Julius' reaction)
insinuates undue ambition to that primacy, only demonstrates their
irony and the clever way that they thus attempt to neutralize that
same "confession."

Having confessed that the Church of Rome was generally held to
occupy a position of honor, dubious though it appeared to them, the
Eusebians add a phrase giving the reason for this general opinion: "as [ὡς]
it was the school of Apostles and capital of orthodoxy from the beginning." This is a very compact summary of the ecclesiology that formed
the structure of the original *History* of Eusebius. The term ἀποστόλων
φροντιστήριον signifies in its primary sense, the school of Apostles, and
implies that there the Apostles lived and their teaching was preserved
and handed on down through the generations.[187] In the original draft of
his *History*, we saw how Eusebius framed his account on the traditional
understanding of the preeminent authority attributed to those sees which
claimed direct Apostolic Succession, so that (as Irenaeus maintained) in
cases of dispute, recourse could be made to them, since there one could
expect that in them, the Apostolic Tradition was more surely preserved.
In our analysis of the *History*, we also saw how Mark, the founder of
the See of Alexandria, sat at the feet of Peter and recorded his proclamation there in his Gospel. Both these ideas are alluded to in the term
ἀποστόλων φροντιστήριον. Eusebius, however, stressed the element of
Rome's *authority* in matters of orthodoxy—which authority was rooted
in the authority of St. Peter, according to the *History*, whose divinely
appointed journey to Rome, his mission and above all his martyrdom
there, climaxed his special commission to "found" the Church and thus
established Rome, the center of the unredeemed world. Rome had replaced
Jerusalem in the N.T. dispensation as "capital" of the new Christian
Nation; there, heresy is annihilated and heretics routed by the successors
of Peter, just as, prototypically, Simon Magus, the father of heresies, had
been overcome by Simon Peter, the founder of the Church there and
source of her Teaching. This element of authority in matters of teaching
is clearly alluded to by the Eusebians when they couple the term εὐσεβείας
μητρόπολις ἐξ ἀρχῆς with the foregoing term ἀποστόλων φροντιστήριον. But
then the Eusebians add a phrase which confirms the interpretation just

---

[187] See note 178 above. There reference is made to Caspar's translation as
"Gedächtnisstätte der Apostel," which I have here adopted and given a new
nuance—one that is demanded by the primary meaning: a "school" here alludes
to the way the teaching of a philosopher, for example, is preserved and handed on.

given while at the same time attempts to discredit its justification: "though those who introduced the teaching came from the East." This reference to the divinely-appointed mission of Peter and Paul to Rome, which Eusebius described with reference to Peter alone in terms of the light which rose in the East and settled in the West (in Rome), is now used to imply at least an equal claim on the part of the East to authority in matters of teaching, if not an actual priority due to the fact that the East could claim a temporal precedence. Thus, the Eusebians, by their ironically formulated inversion of the commonly accepted primacy of the Roman Church and its justification as understood in the East, claim that they are not prepared to "occupy the second position." They then go on to explicate more fully why they refuse to be thus treated: should they be satisfied with a subordinate position, then they would have to admit that in the East, no Church existed that "in greatness and numbers" did not excel the Roman Church. As has been pointed out by Girardet, following Harnack,[188] the most populous Churches at the time were not in the West but in the East, namely in Asia Minor, so that it is most likely that the Eusebians here refer to Antioch. The Eusebians, however, do not wish to measure the size of cities; they simply hint that in this respect they are not inferior to Rome. Why they do not make capital out of this is of note.

In another fragment of their letter, apparently in close connection with their affirmation of the important ecclesiological principle regarding the essential equality of all bishops, the Eusebians assert that they do not "estimate bishops according to the greatness of their cities."[189] Julius had no difficulty in uncovering this blatant lie: the action of their leader, and probable author of the Eusebian letter, belied this assertion in his own personal history, namely by his successive translations, first from the See of Berytus (at the time second in importance only to Antioch) to that of the imperial residence, Nicomedia, and from thence to the new capital of the Roman (and Christian) Empire, Constantinople.[190] In the spirit of conciliation, which characterizes Julius' letter, the Roman bishop only alludes to Eusebius of Nicomedia, but the allusion is clear, since this charge against Eusebius

---

[188] Girardet, *Kaisergericht und Bischofsgericht*, 160.

[189] εἰ οὖν ἀληθῶς ᾽Ἴσην καὶ τὴν αὐτὴν ἡγεῖσθε τιμὴν τῶν ἐπισκόπων καὶ μὴ ἐκ τοῦ μεγέθους τῶν πόλεων,᾽ ὡς γράφετε, ᾽κρίνετε τοὺς ἐπισκόπους᾽ (*Letter of Julius* = *Apol.* 25,2 [Opitz 106,3–4]).

[190] The text quoted in the previous note continues as follows: ἔδει τὸν πεπιστευμένον μικρὰν μένειν ἐν τῇ πιστευθείσῃ καὶ μὴ ἐξουθενεῖν μὲν τὸ πεπιστευμένον, μεταβαίνειν δὲ εἰς τὴν μὴ ἐγχειρισθεῖσαν, ἵνα τῆς μὲν παρὰ θεοῦ δοθείσης καταφρονῇ, τὴν δὲ τῶν ἀνθρώπων κενοδοξίαν ἀγαπήσῃ (*Apol.* 25,2 = Opitz 106,5–7).

of Nicomedia was raised by the Synod of Alexandria, 338,[191] and presumably formed part of the charges brought against the Eusebians which Julius summoned them to Rome to answer. It would seem that for this reason, the Eusebians did not insist on the importance of cities, both in practice and in theory. Almost in contradiction to their supposed profession regarding the equality of all bishops irrespective of their sees, they more truthfully reveal their own conviction about the preeminence of sees positioned in cities of central political importance, when in the text we are examining, placed as it was at the opening of the letter, they remind Julius that they in the East were not inferior in this regard. Here the influence of the later, imperial "ecclesiology" of Eusebius, though slight, is manifest.

But the Eusebians' trump-card is their daring rejection of any claim on the part of the Church of Rome to a primatial authority on the basis of her unique Apostolic origins or due to the traditional recognition she enjoyed as the capital of orthodoxy; this is found in their final statement. This is the second phrase introduced by the particle ὡς in Sozomen's paraphrase, parallel to the first ὡς-phrase where the traditional ecclesiology with its justification for Rome's special position of honor finds expression; it indicates the most convincing reason for the rejection by the Eusebian-controlled Synod of Antioch of Rome's authority: "as they (= the Orientals) [were] victorious in virtue and character." Here again it is Eusebius' *History* that provides us with the key to understanding this otherwise opaque text—not his earlier Apostolic ecclesiology, nor the later imperial ideology which replaced it, but the "middle phase," when he first began to distance himself clearly from his earlier, more traditional understanding of the Church's constitution. We may recall how the experience of the persecution shook his earlier, somewhat idealized concept of the Church that he had not too deeply grasped. What seems to have disillusioned Eusebius most was the reputed failure of the Bishop of Rome, Marcellinus, to resist the forces of evil, and the apparent chaos in the Roman Church in the wake of the persecution, where rigorists and laxists tore apart what was generally held to be the center of the Church's *communio*. In contrast with the reputed *thurificatus* and *traditor* who occupied the see founded on the blood of Peter, Eusebius himself witnessed the innumerable martyrs who resisted the onslaught of the forces of evil and crowned the Eastern Churches with glory. It is to this same contrast, it would seem, that the Eusebians allude, when they claim that they were victorious in virtue and

---

[191]   Cf. *Letter of the Synod of Alexandria*, 338 = *Apol.* 6,6–7 (Opitz 92,29–93,13).

character. Just as Eusebius began to abandon his former ecclesiology, or rather reduced it to a historic monument of bygone days now surpassed by a more spiritualized ecclesiology built on the virtue of the recent martyrs, so too his Eusebian sympathizers give lip-service to the traditional primacy accorded to the Church of Rome (and its bishop in particular) but empty it of any real authority or significance. This ironic reminder of the superiority of the Eastern Churches, which had suffered more grievously than their Western counterparts, most likely provided the sharpest edge to the irony which, as we saw, characterized the entire text.

What we have examined is but a paraphrase. The full extent of the highly sophisticated ridicule of the Eusebians, couched in polished language, as Sozomen observed,[192] and full of contention, as Julius complained, must of necessity have been muted in the process of being compactly summarized. The original text of the Eusebians, therefore, must have been more clearly vituperous so that, as Julius reports, it upset him to such an extent that he kept its contents secret as long as possible, and when eventually he made its contents known at the reconvened Synod of Rome, the other bishops—who included Athanasius, it may be remarked—"were all astonished and could hardly believe that such things were ever written by you (= the Eusebians).[193] The Bishop of Rome and the bishops who attended the synod, mostly Italians presumably, but also possibly counting among their number some Orientals, who like Athanasius had not yet returned to their sees, had reason to so react. The *Letter of the Eusebians,* was nothing less than an insidious attack on the Apostolic nature of the Church and its central authority based on the Petrine Succession.

As a historical document, the Eusebian letter is of the greatest importance. It marks the beginning of the rift between East and West in their respective conceptions of the nature of the Church. For this reason alone, it deserves the closest attention. But, as will become more evident, it also plays a central role in the development of Athanasius' ecclesiology: this will become apparent in the following chapter. It should be clear, however, that Schwartz's judgement of the letter is unacceptable: the most bitter polemics in the letter were not directed against the prerogatives which the Roman See *"assumed for itself,"* as he unjustifiably maintained, but those which were *generally* attributed to the bishop and Church of Rome both in the East and the West.

---

[192] Cf. Sozomen, *HE* 3,8,4 (Bidez-Hansen 111,8–9).
[193] *Letter of Julius = Apol.* 21,4 (Opitz 130,8–9).

Before we leave this important document, we must take a more detailed look at some of the legal arguments of the Eusebians, which they produced to justify their actions in the East, and which were so skillfully articulated, that Sozomen, who was himself trained in jurisprudence, could not refrain from commenting on this characteristic of the Eusebian letter.[194] The arguments have already been summarized above in our introductory remarks to the text we have just examined.[195] The Eusebians reject the intervention of Julius (and the Synod of Rome) in the affairs of the Eastern provinces and accuse him of having transgressed the canons. As already pointed out, the canons they refer to are most probably the Canons of Antioch, where the principle of the autonomy of provincial synods was given canonical expression in Canons XII and XV. These canons, as we saw, reflect the fossilization under the pressure of the Imperial Church of a local custom, which grew up in Antioch as a result of the attempted deposition of Fabius and the actual dethronement of Paul of Samosata. And indeed in their letter the Eusebian-controlled bishops in Antioch remind Julius of these precedents.

When they demand that Julius acknowledge both the deposition of the bishops they had removed and the appointment of their successors,[196] they give us their reason: "since those priests who had proceeded them in the East had offered no stiff opposition when Novatian was deposed by the Roman Church."[197] It will be remembered that Eusebius recorded in his *History* how the then Bishop of Antioch, Fabius, was in fact sympathetic to Novatian, and so did not wish to acknowledge Cornelius, and how the surrounding bishops assembled in synod to depose Fabius on that account, which deposition was prevented by the Bishop of Antioch's death.[198] The Synod of Antioch thus recognized the claims of Cornelius and rejected Novatian. The description given by the Eusebians in their *letter* is, however, only partially true: there was indeed opposition, that of Fabius, whom they do not mention. But what is more important is the way the Eusebians twist the historical facts to suit their own theory of synodal autonomy. In their letter to Julius, they make it clear to him that "his sanction was not necessary, should they wish to expel anyone from the Churches; for they themselves

---

[194] Cf. Sozomen, *HE* 3,8,4 (Bidez-Hansen 111,8).
[195] See above, pp. 382–383.
[196] Cf. Sozomen, *HE* 3,8,7 (Bidez-Hansen 111,17–20).
[197] Cf. Sozomen, *HE* 3,8,7 (Bidez-Hansen 111,21–23).
[198] Eusebius, *HE* 6,44,1 (Schwartz 624,6); *HE* 6,46,3–4 (Schwartz 628,8–17). See above, p. 118.

did not object when they (= the Bishop and Synod of Rome) threw Novatian out of the Church."[199] Thus they demand of Julius that, according to the precedence set by the earlier Synod of Antioch, which had recognized the Synod of Rome's decision with regard to Novatian, he too should simply accept their "decisions,"[200] i.e., without examining their judgement because such an examination would imply contempt for that synod.[201] That this is the core of the Eusebians' legal defense is proved by the fact that Julius alone makes five references to the latter point,[202] and that the case of Novatian is the only piece of information common to our three main sources for the Eusebian letter: Julius, Socrates, and Sozomen.[203] But the mere fact that the decision of Rome in electing Cornelius and ejecting Novatian caused such a controversy at Antioch, so that a synod assembled to decide the issue and even intended deposing one of their members, namely, the occupant of the prestigious Petrine See of Antioch, demonstrates that the Oriental predecessors of the Eusebian-controlled Synod of Antioch did not uncritically accept the judgement of the Roman synod that elected Cornelius, but rather examined the claims of Cornelius with great diligence before extending their communion to him and rejecting the claims of Novatian.

It is interesting to note that the historians in fifth-century Constantinople, Socrates and Sozomen, do not mention the other precedent given by the Eusebians: Paul of Samosata. It is Julius alone who informs us that the Eusebian-controlled Orientals pointed to the precedent of the case of Novatian *and that* of Paul of Samosata in order to support their contention that "the decrees (τὰ δόγματα) of [all] synods ought to be in force," i.e., have equal binding force and cannot be overruled by another synod.[204] According to our analysis

---

[199] καὶ σύνοδον ἐν τῇ Ἀντιοχείᾳ κηρύξαντες, συνελθόντες ἐν αὐτῇ, γνώμῃ κοινῇ σφοδρότερον δι' ἐπιστολῆς ἀντεγκαλοῦσαι τῷ Ἰουλίῳ δηλοῦντες μὴ δεῖν κανονίζεσθαι παρ' αὐτοῦ, εἰ βούλοιντο ἐξελαύνειν τινὰς τῶν ἐκκλησιῶν· μηδὲ γὰρ αὐτοὺς ἀντειπεῖν, ὅτε Ναύατον τῆς ἐκκλησίας ἤλαυνον (Socrates 2,15,5 [Hussey 207]). This is the only part of the letter mentioned in detail by Socrates, which indicates how central this point was to the case made by the Eusebians.

[200] *Letter of Julius = Apol.* 22,1 (Opitz 103,21).

[201] Cf. *Letter of Julius = Apol.* 22,6 (Opitz 104,18–19); See also *Apol.* 23,2 (Opitz 104,30); *Apol.* 23,4 (Opitz 104,41–105,1); *Apol.* 24,4 (Opitz 105,23–24); *Apol.* 25,1 (Opitz 106,1).

[202] See previous footnote.

[203] See *Letter of Julius = Apol.* 25,1 (Opitz 105,26–27); Socrates, *HE* 2,15,5 (Hussey 207); Sozomen, *HE* 3,8,7 (Bidez-Hansen 111,21–23).

[204] *Letter of Julius = Apol.* 25,1 (Opitz 105,26–27): ἐκ τοῦ κατὰ Νοβάτον καὶ τὸν Σαμοσατέα Παῦλον παραδείγματος τὰ τῶν συνόδων ἰσχύειν δόγματα χρή.

of the little evidence for the deposition of the Samosatene at our disposal, namely, the account preserved in Eusebius' original *History*,[205] it would appear that when the Antiochene synod appealed to the Emperor Aurelian to recognize the claim of the successor to Paul as Bishop of Antioch, they produced, as evidence for his claim to the see, the report of the Synod of Rome, which apparently examined the case, recognized the deposition of Paul, and granted communion to Domnus, his successor. The detailed description of the reasons which persuaded the Antiochene synod to so act with regard to Paul, and which were carefully presented in the *Letter of the Synod of Antioch to the Bishops of Rome and Alexandria*—Eusebius[206] quotes some excerpts and they are of considerable length—can only have had one purpose: to persuade the said bishops (and their synods) of the correctness of their judgement. Such a careful presentation of their case against Paul of Samosata thus implies that the case had been scrutinized and reexamined before the Roman and Alexandrian Churches were prepared to extend their communion (= recognition) to the proposed successor in the now vacant see. But again, as in the precedent of Novatian, the Eusebians contort the historical facts in order to provide a proof from tradition for their newly formed principle of absolute synodal authority, which could also be described as the principle of non-intervention. This principle they canonized in Canons XII and XV of Antioch, as already pointed out, and now they can accuse Julius of having "transgressed the canons."[207]

In our analysis of Eusebius' *History* in Part I, we proposed that the case of Fabius, the Antiochene sympathizer of Novatian, and the deposition of Paul of Samosata in particular were of prime importance (i) for the history of the decline not only of the authority previously enjoyed by the Bishop of Antioch but also for the ecclesiological basis of that preeminence, namely his Petrine Succession; and (ii) for the growth of a new authority of the synod as an institution in Antioch, as well as a new understanding of the nature of the synod as such, i.e., as an authority superior to that of individual bishops. Our present analysis of the Eusebian letter, with its explicit reference to these two cases, its attempt to discredit, by means of irony, the Petrine authority of Rome, and its endeavor to twist history to justify the new synodal institution, complements in its own way our previous analysis. It must be added that the Eusebians

---

[205] See above, pp. 129–133.
[206] Eusebius, *HE* 7,30,1–17 (Schwartz 706,1–712,24).
[207] *Letter of Julius* = *Apol.* 29,3 (Opitz 108,34).

radicalize the local tradition at Antioch. They are "traditionalists," in the strict or extreme sense of the word, insofar as they adopt a partially understood, limited or local tradition, and transform it into a rigid system, and in fact produce something entirely novel in the history of the Church.[208] As we have seen, the catalyst in this process was the appearance of the Imperial Church, conceptually prepared by Eusebius of Caesarea and translated into practice by Eusebius of Nicomedia, now of Constantinople. The synod has become an autonomous institution within the larger, all-embracing reality of the "Christian Empire."

However, in the fragments of the *Letter of the Eusebians* at our disposal, the latter element, the Imperial Church, makes only one very faint appearance, i.e., in the hint that as far as the claim to superiority on the basis of the size (= political importance) of a city was concerned, the East was equal if not in a better position than Rome. This very fact illustrates how difficult it must have been for Julius to grasp the intention of the Eusebians: their ideological

[208] Girardet, *Kaisergericht und Bischofsgericht*, 89–90, claims that the Eusebian-controlled Orientals here defend the theory of the "altkirchliche Idee," according to which, "Jene kirchliche Gerichtsversammlung gilt als eine Versammlung der ganzen Kirche." As we saw in Part I, it was each local Church that, in the first place, could be understood as representative of the entire Church—once its bishop was in communion with main Apostolic Churches. So also, those synods which assembled to discuss issues concerning the *teaching of the Church* and *liturgical customs* were evaluated as assemblies of the Church Universal, in so far as their decisions manifested the unanimity of the entire Church; this was usually confirmed by the reception of such decisions. To extend the description of such synods to cover "jene kirchliche Gerichtsversammlung" is, it seems to me, unjustified; by avoiding the more technical term "synod," and coining a new, more general, term "Gerichtsversammlung" (it does not appear in Der große Duden), the reader is given the impression that the new Eusebian synodal court (which passed judgement not on teaching or custom but on the misbehavior of fellow-bishops) could be identified with the traditional concept of a "synod" (see Marot, "Vornicäische und ökumenische Konzile," 23). It may be observed that even with regard to the precedent given by the Eusebians themselves—the case of Paul Samosata—the bishop was not judged and removed because of his *misbehavior* but because of his alleged *heresy*. Girardet attempted to elaborate on the "altkirchliche Idee" in his article "Appellatio: Ein Kapitel kirchlicher Rechtsgeschichte in den Kanones des vierten Jahrhunderts," *Historia*, vol. 23 (1974), 98–127. In that article, Girardet bases his hypothesis on what he says is the witness of Tertullian and Cyprian, according to which, when a bishop speaks, he does so for the whole Church since he judges in the name of Christ; there is no appeal against his judgement, since his colleagues all have the same "charismatic" rank as he. This thesis does not convince as it is built on two rather shaky assumptions:

background, so fundamentally different from his Apostolic ecclesiology, only once came to the surface, and even there it was camouflaged by the untruth that they, the Eusebians, did not measure the prestige of bishops according to the size of their cities. The corollary of the latter was the affirmation of the important principle, with regard to the equality of all bishops. It was this principle (quantitatively understood) that provided them with justification for their special understanding of the synod. Once they denied special authority to a bishop because of the claims of his see to direct Apostolic or Petrine origins—this was *in practice* denied by the action of the earlier Synod of Antioch in the case of Fabius and Paul of Samosata, and *in theory* by the imperial ideology of Eusebius who replaced the Apostolic nature of the Church's authority with the imperial order—then they could only interpret this principle in a pragmatic or quantitative way. The equality of all bishops is no longer based on the fact of their participation in the Apostolic Succession—which participation allowed both for an essential equality and, within this, a complementarity of offices with more or less sharply delineated roles assigned to them by the Apostolic constitution of the Church—but rather on the status or function of the "office-holders" within the basically static imperial order. The essential equality of all bishops due to their sacramental participation in the Apostolic Succession has been replaced by a purely legal concept of the bishop as the occupant of a clearly defined office

(i) a one-sided interpretation of the imperfectly worked-out "ecclesiology" of Tertullian or Cyprian, and (ii) the seemingly arbitrary distinction he makes "zwischen ideeller (geistlicher) Verbindlichkeit und der faktischen Unverbindlichkeit kirchlicher Urteile" ("Appellatio," 101). With regard to (i), attention may be drawn to the work of M. Bévenot, already quoted, "A Bishop is Responsible to God Alone (St. Cyprian)." Bévenot demonstrates that Cyprian's ecclesiology was more nuanced than Girardet's thesis outlined above; this even applies to the dictum of Cyprian which makes up the title and subject of Girardet's article, and which the Bishop of Carthage did *not* understand to mean: "No one has a right to interfere with *me*" (p. 414). What it came to mean for Cyprian was "I must not interfere with the action of a bishop who still maintains the unity and discipline of the Church" (p. 414). This premise—together with the affirmation of Cyprian that "he must report matters of importance to Rome" (Bévenot 415) is not easily reconcilable with Girardet's picture of the authority of a bishop in the early Church as being, even theoretically, absolute: his authority was conditioned by his relationship to the universal episcopacy and rooted in its implicit doctrinal unanimity. With regard to Tertullian's deficient and rather individualistic concept of a bishop, see Adam, *Der Kirchenbegriff Tertullians*, 41–45. On the essential relationship of a bishop to his fellow bishops (according to Cyprian), see Poschmann, *Ecclesia principalis*, 24–29. See also Bévenot's important article, "Épiscopat et Primatué

within the Imperial Church. Since no one bishop is recognized by the Eusebians as having a primacy or superior authority arising from the specific Apostolic nature of the Church in particular with regard to the specific Petrine Successions within the Apostolic Succession, then they felt justified in considering the synod with its majority principle as the only authority capable of deciding matters of dispute between bishops, i.e., as decided between functionaries of equal status.

It would be worthwhile to examine the parallels in Roman law but that is beyond the scope of our subject. It is sufficient here to note how the synod as an *institution* evolved. According to the Eusebian concept, the synod has thus emerged as an autonomous, collective authority, composed of bishops but also superior to anyone of them. And thus, by the radical application of the principle of (quantitative or functional) equality, they had produced an institution which in fact denied the principle of equality, and which acted according to majority vote, not unanimity based on common conviction. It was an institution which moreover was determined no longer by Apostolic norms but by the imperial boundaries of the various provinces. The fate of the individual bishop was reduced to these accidental and changing borders; if he could not find justice within them, he was forbidden by this superstructure, the Imperial Synod, from seeking redress outside of them. But this contradicts what we saw at the beginning of our examination of Eusebius' *History* as the original concept of a bishop, which was preserved intact up to the opening of the fourth century in the East: his *universal* character as responsible to God, before the entire Church; he was responsible not only for the local Church assigned to him but also for the Church Universal, communion with which he guaranteed (in his office as bishop for this particular local Church). This universal character was expressed and guaranteed by mutual communication, especially between the three major

chez Saint Cyprien," 176–185. See also Demoustier, "Épiscopat et union à Rome selon Saint Cyprien," 337–369. (ii) The distinction proposed by Girardet, and used by him as the hermeneutical-key to interpret both the *Letter of the Eusebians* and Julius' reply, is based on a distinction between theory and practice which was alien to the ancient Church, and which could only arise from the mistake of transforming into absolute norms, the imperfect levels of ecclesiological reflection in the early Church (see Bévenot's comments on Cyprian's inconsistencies, p. 415). The concept of the "altkirchliche Idee" proposed by Girardet is based on an understanding of the nature and functioning of a synod in the early Church, which fails to take cognizance of what theologians have recently described as the process of the "reception" of synodal judgements, and its essential role in determining the validity of such decisions; see in particular Grillmeier, "Konzil und Rezeption," in *Mit ihm und in ihm*, 303–334). I fail to see how Hess could claim in *The Early Development*, 183, that "Twomey accepts without interpretation of the Antiochene canons advanced by Girardet."

Sees,[209] and the exchange of communion letters. Such an exchange of *Letters of Communion* was practiced even by the Eusebians, whose *pro forma* use of this traditional practice, based on the Apostolic and Petrine nature of the Church, paradoxically brought their new, more fundamental, imperial ecclesiology finally into the open—and into open conflict with the Apostolic Church. Moreover, this autonomous synodal institution, with its corollary principle of nonintervention, mitigated against the fundamental demands of justice, which require that the condemnation of any one person be proved in the presence of all parties and open to the scrutiny of all. These two points form the basis of Julius' reply to the Eusebians.

But before we examine the letter of the Bishop of Rome, a final observation must be made about the Synod of Antioch in whose name the Eusebian letter was composed. It is remarkable that the president of that synod was not the Bishop of Antioch but, as it seems, Danius, the Bishop of Caesarea in Cappadocia.[210] This demonstrates not only the low prestige enjoyed by the successor of St. Peter in the East, but the lingering influence of Danius' predecessor, Firmilian of Cappadocia, one of the leading figures at the attempted deposition of Fabius of Antioch and (especially) the successful expulsion of Paul of Samosata from the Eastern Petrine See.[211]

§7 The 4th Letter of Julius, Bishop of Rome, 341

After keeping the contents of the *Letter of the Eusebians* secret as long as possible, Julius sent for Athanasius to return to Rome and reassembled the synod in order to discuss its contents. The Eusebian letter amounted to nothing less than the threat of a schism on the part of the Eusebian-controlled Oriental bishops.[212] Thus, even though Athanasius tells us[213] the Synodal Fathers were indignant

---

[209] See, e.g., Caspar, *Geschichte des Papsttums* I, 119, for examples of this practice shortly before 325.

[210] Cf. *Apol.* 21,1 (Opitz 102,13); see the commentary of Opitz. Danius is mentioned as the first addressee of the *Letter of Julius,* before Flacillus, the Bishop of Antioch. Commenting on this, Jalland, *Church and Papacy*, 214, footnote 4, expresses his surprise in view of Canon V of Nicaea that Flacillus did not preside and draws the (false) conclusion that "it seems to support the view that neither creed nor canons of that council were as yet regarded as finally authoritative."

[211] Cf. Eusebius, *HE* 6,46,3 (Schwartz 628,11); *HE* 7,30,4–5 (Schwartz 706,17–708,3).

[212] Julius warns the addressees of his *letter* not to become the "authors of schism"; cf. *Apol.* 25,4 (Opitz 106,19); *Apol.* 32,3 (Opitz 111,8). See also Sozomen *HE* 3,8,4

with the Eusebians, the tone of Julius' *4th Letter* is on the whole marked by the spirit of reconciliation, despite its firm stand on the issues and principles involved.[214] And yet the letter pulsates with grave concern in the face of the threatened schism,[215] and occasionally betrays a certain undeniable vexation at the grievous accusations made against him by the Eusebian-controlled Oriental Synod of Antioch.

Before we examine the contents of this document, the question as to the influence of Athanasius on its composition must be raised. Fialon suggested on the basis of its Greek style that Athanasius actually wrote the letter[216] while Haller maintains that the pen of Athanasius is clearly discernible in the way the facts are bent to suit the purpose and the main points ignored.[217] Fialon's suggestion was modified by Joannou who held that the letter was translated by Athanasius from the original Latin version,[218] which modification was adopted by one of the most recent commentators on the *Letter of Julius*, Gessel.[219] Haller's opinion is not convincing, even

(Bidez-Hansen 111,9) who described the *Letter of the Eusebians* as not being devoid of "the most terrible threats."

[213] Cf. *Apol.* 20,20 (Opitz 102,9–10).

[214] Cf. Jalland, *Church and Papacy*, 214; see Batiffol, *La paix constantinienne*, 422, 427; The description of the *Letter of Julius* by Schwartz, *NGG* (1911), 497 (= *GS* III, 301–303), as one of embarrassment in the face of the "noble and decisive rejection of his unfriendliness" on the part of the Eusebians (!), has found few supporters.

[215] Cf. Caspar, *Geschichte des Papsttums* I, 153. Caspar, unsurprisingly, is skeptical of Julius' declared charity.

[216] Fialon, *Saint Athanasius*, 146.

[217] Haller, *Das Papsttum*, 67.

[218] Joannou, *Die Ostkirche und die Cathedra Petri*, 66. Joannou evidently rejected the objection of Fialon, who held that a mere translation was improbable since Athanasius expressly referred to his translation of two other Latin documents (the famous letters of Valens and Ursacius), while such an admission is absent in his introduction to the *Letter of Julius*. Indeed, Fialon's objection is not convincing, since the Greek version of the *Letter of Julius*, even if translated by Athanasius, was its official form, while the original letters of Valens and Ursacius were in Latin.

[219] Gessel, "Das primatiale Bewußtsein Julius' I," 73–74. However, Gessel's tentative suggestion that in the translation of the letter, Athanasius (who did not, in the first place, have the primatial activity of the Roman bishops in view, but quotes the letter with the purpose of demonstrating the justification of his own person) polished over all the points which referred to himself in order to placate the Eusebians, cannot be maintained. As we have seen above, the *Apologia* was composed in 354—i.e., after the Eusebian party as such had vanished—and was, at least in part, an attack on their successors, the Neo-Arian party of Valens and Ursacius. Even if Athanasius translated the original letter at Rome in 341, even then he had no cause to placate the

if one were to accept his contention about the falsification of the facts (which one cannot), since any parallel between the contents of Julius' letter and Athanasius' presentation of the case can be explained by the simple fact that on examination of the Eusebian charges and the Athanasian defense, Julius and the Synod of Rome opted for the latter and incorporated it into the letter. The arguments based on the Greek style of the letter are very slender: the most one could maintain is that Athanasius may well indeed have been responsible for the translation. But the literary style and the general presentation of the letter is other than that of Athanasius, as Batiffol observed;[220] they indicate the independent mind of Julius. And yet, since Julius expressly called Athanasius to Rome to attend the synod where the contents of the Eusebian letter were made public, and thus evidently sought his advice, it can be expected that the influence of Athanasius in the composition of the letter was not inconsiderable. We will therefore attempt in the course of our analysis of the *Letter of Julius* to determine as precisely as possible the influence of Athanasius, not in relationship to Julius' presentation of the case of Athanasius as such but rather in the way Julius attempted to come to terms with the more fundamental ecclesiological issues raised by the Eusebians. These are the issues which will primarily occupy our attention here.

In his opening paragraph (Apol. 21), Julius sets the tone of his letter and announces the main lines of his reply to the Eusebians. He gently but firmly calls the Eusebians to task for the contentious way they responded to his previous letters, which he maintains were written "in charity and out of a responsibility for the truth."[221] Then he affirms unambiguously: "in ecclesiastical affairs there is no place for an exhibition of eloquence, but [rather] the Apostolic canons and earnest care not to scandalize any of the little ones in the Church."[222] These two statements form the basis on which Julius builds up the argumentation of his letter with regard

---

Eusebians. The difference in style between the paragraph that deals with Marcellus and the other sections relating to Athanasius, which difference Gessel shrewdly observed, must be otherwise explained. See below, pp. 416–418.

[220] Batiffol, *La paix constantinienne*, 422.

[221] πῶς ἡμεῖς μὲν ἀγάπῃ καὶ συνειδήσει ἀληθείας ἐγράψαμεν (*Apol.* 21,2 = Opitz 102,17).

[222] ἐν γὰρ τοῖς ἐκκλησιαστικοῖς οὐ λόγων ἐπίδειξίς ἐστιν, ἀλλὰ κανόνες ἀποστολικοὶ καὶ σπουδὴ τοῦ μὴ σκανδαλίζειν ἕνα τῶν μικρῶν τῶν ἐν τῇ ἐκκλησίᾳ (*Apol.* 21,5 = Opitz 103,11–12). Gessel, "Das primatiale Bewußtsein Julius' I," 70, aptly comments, "Programmatisch erklärt Julius zu Anfang seines Schreibens: in kirchlichen Angelegenheiten sind nur die apostolischen Satzungen maßgebend."

to his intervention in Eastern affairs. As we will see, the Bishop of Rome
will seek to uncover the contentiousness of the Eusebians by pointing out
to them the blatant contradictions between their statements and their
actions,[223] while at the same time he attempts to lead his readers back to the
Apostolic constitution of the Church, which the Eusebians, by means both
of ironic asides and tendentious interpretations of certain ecclesiastical
principles and customs, clouded and therefore gave scandal to the "little
ones," the faithful of the Church.[224] In the first statement, the Bishop of
Rome refers in very general terms to the motives which he claims justified
his intervention in these disputes: charity and responsibility for the truth.

Julius devotes considerable space to clarifying the motive of charity in
his opening paragraph. He describes the mission of his delegates, Elpidius
and Philoxenus as "characteristic of charity," i.e., "to send presbyters to
sympathize with those who suffer and to exhort those who have written [to
me] to come thither, that it might be possible to set aright all the issues after
a speedy settlement. . . ."[225] In the first place, Julius wishes to contrast the
upright motives which moved him to write to the Eusebians with the contentious spirit that animated their reply. But the passages also gently allude
to the special responsibility which accrued to him as Bishop of Rome with
respect to the universal ἀγάπη (or κοινωνία), and which was his final justification for intervening in the affairs of the Eastern and Egyptian Churches.
Rome is not mentioned explicitly but only implicitly in the mission of
the Roman delegates, and in the expected journey of those summoned to
Rome to have the issues amended. It is of note that Julius does not take
up the Eusebian tendentious summary of the traditional understanding
of Rome's prerogatives, but simply warns his readers not to confuse the
faithful with their sophistry and reminds them to pay attention to the

---

[223] Girardet, *Kaisergericht und Bischofsgericht*, 87–105, interprets this method of
argumentation adopted by Julius to mean: "Julius nun spielt die Praxis gegen die
Idee der geistlichen Verbindlichkeit aus" (90), and this forms the framework of
his detailed commentary on the *Letter of Julius*. We have already criticized his
concept of the "altkirchliche Idee" and the artificial distinction he makes between
idea and custom in the early Church (see footnote 208). It may be added here
that not only Julius but also the Eusebians call on the practice of the earlier
Church history (when, e.g., they refer to the precedents of Novatian and Paul of
Samosata, which, it will be remembered, they interpreted in a one-sided fashion,
as indeed the excellent treatment of these incidents by Girardet in *Kaisergericht
und Bischofsgericht*, 98–100, demonstrates).

[224] Julius refers explicitly to Mt 18,6; cf. *Apol.* 21,5 (Opitz 103,13–14).

[225] *Apol.* 21,3 (Opitz 102,21–23).

Apostolic canons. He himself does not in his letter discuss the theological understanding of his office as Bishop of Rome but is intent on demonstrating how he, at all times, had acted in accordance with the Apostolic canons and with the demands of this office—the nature of which the Eusebians tried to gloss over with their irony, and which demands could be summed up as "charity and responsibility for the Truth."

In his second paragraph (*Apol.* 22), he elucidates the two basic principles which, he maintains, were witnessed to by former ecclesiastical practice, and by which he justified his intervention. The first principle is that concerning the universality of synodal judgements, or rather their transparency. As we have seen, the central argument made by the Eusebians was based on the absolute autonomy of (provincial) synods. They maintained, correctly, that "each synod has unshakable authority" but added that "he who judges is dishonored if his judgement is examined (ἐξετάζηται) by others."[226] The consequences, thus drawn from the traditional understanding of the irreversible authority of synods—a principle which Julius also affirms[227] as we will see—were not in accord with the practice of the Church, even in the case of Novatian (Fabius) and Paul of Samosata, which they gave as precedents. According to the Tradition of the Church, the decisions of a synod became irreversible *once* they were implicitly or explicitly received by the universal Church. Such decisions generally referred to matters of Faith and morals (= customs).

With regard to those cases which relate to the *behavior* of individuals, Canon V of the "Great Synod at Nicaea," as Julius called it,[228] *received* the earlier ruling of the (provincial) synods of Elvira

---

[226] *Apol.* 22,6 (Opitz 104,18–19).

[227] Jalland, *Church and Papacy*, 215, incorrectly maintained that Julius "nowhere suggests that the decisions of Nicaea are final" (whereas the whole argument of *Apol.* 22,1–6 is based on the understanding that they were definitively binding). So also Sieben, "Zur Entwicklung der Konzilsidee," 359–361. Although de Vries, "Die Struktur der Kirche," 64, does not find Sieben's interpretation completely watertight, yet he concludes: "Die völlige Einzigartigkeit der Ökumenischen Synode von Nikaia erscheint jedoch nach allem im Brief von Julius, der sehr wahrscheinlich von Athanasius inspiriert war, nicht klar zu sein." It has been overlooked in this discussion that the principle defended by Julius, regarding the revision of synodal judgements, relates to judgements concerning human behavior and *not* to those relating to doctrinal decisions. This material element is of decisive importance, it seems to me, for a right interpretation of Julius' *letter*. Regarding the formal character of Nicaea, see below, footnote 245.

[228] Cf. *Apol.* 22,2 (Opitz 103,23).

and Arles, which provided that those clerics and laity excommunicated by their bishop should not be readmitted by others,[229] but modified it by ruling that "an inquiry should be made (ἐξεταζέσθω) lest such persons were excluded from the congregation due to pettiness, contention (φιλονικίᾳ) or some such odious behavior on the part of the bishop."[230] For this purpose, the Synod of Nicaea ordered that (provincial) synods be held twice a year (before Lent and in the Autumn) to examine and settle issues. Here, the Nicaean synod applies the same principles as that which determined the reception of synodal decisions concerning Faith and morals. They became irreversible once their transparency was established. The principle of the transparency of truth has been applied to the matter of justice (i.e., the truth regarding human behavior). Canon V therefore, itself, demonstrates the way provincial synodal decisions were given final authority by means of their reception, and how this reception was not uncritical (merely a rubber stamp, as the Eusebians had demanded of Julius with regard to his reception of their decisions), and at the same time it establishes the principle of the necessary (universal) transparency of those judgements which involve the behavior of individuals. According to the letter of the law, Julius had little right to appeal to Canon V,[231] since the it deals with clerics and laity (not bishops) and the revision of individual episcopal judgements by provincial synods; yet he appeals not to the letter but to the *principle of justice implicit in the* canon,[232] and possibly to the example it provides of the reception of provincial synods by the universal episcopacy (a point which has been ignored in the debate up to now). The Bishop of Rome states: "Because of this (= the readiness of the just judge to have his decision examined since he is confident of its justice), the bishops who assembled at the Great Synod of Nicaea agreed, not without the Will of God, that the [decisions] of one Synod be examined (ἐξετάζεσθαι) by another so

---

[229] See Girardet, *Kaisergericht und Bischofsgericht*, 82–83.

[230] Περὶ τῶν ἀκοινωνήτων γενομένων εἴτε τῶν ἐν τῷ κλήρῳ εἴτε τῶν ἐν τῷ λαϊκῷ τάγματι ὑπὸ τῶν καθ᾽ ἑκάστην ἐπαρχίαν ἐπισκόπων κρατείτω ἡ γνώμη κατὰ τὸν κανόνα τὸν διαγορεύοντα τοὺς ὑφ᾽ ἑτέρων ἀποβγηθέντας ὑφ᾽ ἑτέρων μὴ προσίεσθαι. Ἐξεταζέσθω δέ, μὴ μικροψυχίᾳ ἢ φιλονεικίᾳ τινὶ τοιαύτῃ ἀηδίᾳ τοῦ ἐπισκόπου ἀποσυνάγωγοι γεγένηνται·... (*COD* 8).

[231] See Caspar, *Geschichte des Papsttums* I, 149; see also the commentary of Opitz on this text.

[232] See Girardet, *Kaisergericht und Bischofsgericht*, 90, who, however, goes on to propound his theory about the way Julius reportedly justified his ἐξέτασις of the judgements of Tyre and Constantinople, as based on the traditional process of the reception of synods in contradiction to the "altkirchliche Idee" of the autonomous local Church (p. 91).

that those who judge, having before their eyes the second judgement that was
to follow, might examine [each case] with the greatest diligence, and those
who are judged might be confident that they themselves were sentenced,
not through the enmity of the first synod, but according to the dictates of
justice."[233] Further, the Bishop of Rome chides the Eusebians for attempting,
as a small party within the Church, to abolish an ancient custom "that once
obtained in the [entire] Church and has been established by Synods."[234]

The Eusebians affirm the principle of the irreversibility of synodal
judgements but attempt to reinterpret it, according to their new understanding of the provincial synod as an autonomous institution, by excluding
the possibility of its decisions being scrutinized by others. By doing so, they
act contrary to the universal nature of the Church and in contradiction to
the universality of truth and justice on which the Church is founded. The
answer of Julius is to insist, in the first place, on the necessary transparency
of justice, which was enshrined in Canon V of Nicaea. Thus, the Bishop of
Rome unambiguously states that the synod which Julius, on the initiative
of the Eusebian delegates, had summoned,[235] had as its sole object to secure
"that *in the presence of all* a just judgement could be arrived at."[236] Here
Julius makes his own, the plea of the Catholic clergy of Alexandria in their
Letter to the Mareotis Commission (335) where, alluding probably to Acts
25,16, the Alexandrian presbyters and deacons call for a trial where accusers
and accused should face each other.[237] Later Athanasius states that this

---

[233] διὰ τοῦτο καὶ οἱ ἐν τῇ κατὰ Νίκαιαν μεγάλῃ συνόδῳ συνελθόντες ἐπίσκοποι οὐκ ἄνευ
θεοῦ βουλήσεως συνεχώρησαν ἐν ἑτέρᾳ συνόδῳ τὰ τῆς προτέρας ἐξετάζεσθαι, ἵνα
καὶ οἱ κρίνοντες πρὸ ὀφθαλμῶν ἔχοντες τὴν ἐσομένην δευτέραν κρίσιν μετὰ πάσης
ἀσφαλείας ἐξετάζωσι καὶ οἱ κρινόμενοι πιστεύωσι, μὴ κατ᾽ ἔχθραν τῶν προτέρων,
ἀλλὰ κατὰ τὸ δίκαιον ἑαυτοὺς κρίνεσθαι (*Apol.* 22,2 = Opitz 103,23–27).

[234] Cf. *Apol.* 22,2 (Opitz 103,27–30). Against this, Simonetti, *La Crisi Ariana*, 149.

[235] Girardet, *Kaisergericht und Bischofsgericht*, 92, maintains that Julius falsifies the
events of 338: according to Girardet's own reconstruction of those events, Julius'
presentation is indeed seen to be in contradiction—but, as pointed out above,
it is unlikely that Julius would have left himself open to such an accusation in a
letter addressed to those who could easily have contradicted him. Julius, further,
had no *need* to falsify the events of 338; he affirms, a few sentences later, that
even if the Eusebian delegates had not taken the initiative, but that he himself
had done so, then even that would have been in accordance with ecclesiastical
custom (cf. *Apol.* 22,5).

[236] *Apol.* 22,3 (Opitz 104,5–6).

[237] Cf. *Apol.* 73,2 (Opitz 152,14–15).

procedure is demanded by "divine law"[238] and quoted Acts 25,16 in support of his contention.[239] According to the Egyptian bishops at Tyre in their letter to their fellow-bishops there, it was also "divine law" that forbade an enemy from being either a witness or a judge.[240] In the *Letter of the Synod of Alexandria*, 338, they clarify the main source of that enmity, which, they claim, is the Eusebian zeal for the Arian teaching and the opposition they found in Egypt.[241] There the Egyptians allude to Canon V of Nicaea, when they accuse their judges at Tyre of acting out of enmity.[242] This, then, is the ultimate motive of Julius' actual intervention in the Eastern and Egyptian dispute: not only that justice be done but that it should be seen to be done.

Again, in this second paragraph of his letter, Julius lightly indicates his formal right to intervene (the second principle enunciated by Julius). Having pointed out the fact that he summoned the Synod (of Rome) at the request of the Eusebian delegates,[243] i.e., that his intervention did not arise from any initiative of his, the Bishop of Rome goes on to speculate: "Now supposing that the party of Martyrius and Hesychius had not requested that a synod take place, but that I were the person who had persuaded myself to trouble those who had written (= the Eusebians) for the sake of our brethren who claimed to have suffered injustice, then this proposal would have been reasonable and just, since it is ecclesiastical and pleasing to God." Here the Bishop of Rome claims for himself the right to take the initiative "to trouble those who had written," i.e., to summon them to a synod, and he makes this claim on the basis of his responsibility for the brethren who claimed to suffer injustice, i.e., his responsibility for the universal ἀγάπη, a claim which, further, is rooted in the nature of the Church (= "ecclesiastical") and, with respect to the norms of justice, pleasing to God. In principle, the Bishop of Rome maintains, he has the right to intervene on behalf of the suffering brethren *on his own initiative*, which right is ecclesiastically based and in accordance with divine law.

In the following three paragraphs (*Apol.* 23–25), Julius contrasts the practice of the Eusebians with the principle of the absolute autonomy of

---

[238] Cf. *Apol.* 82,2 (Opitz 161,20).
[239] Cf. *Apol.* 82,2 (Opitz 161,20–25). This text is part of Athanasius' narrative in the *Apologia* and thus dated 356.
[240] Cf. *Apol.* 77,9 (Opitz 157,29–30).
[241] Cf. *Apol.* 8,2 (Opitz 94,5–8).
[242] Cf. *Apol.* 8,1 (Opitz 94,3–4).
[243] Cf. *Apol.* 22,3 (Opitz 103,31–104,6).

synodal judgements that they so righteously defend. He cites three examples about the way the Eusebians "dishonoured"[244] the "Great Synod of Nicaea"—whose decisions Julius assumes to be irreversible:[245] (i) by their reception into communion of those whose (Arian) heresy was condemned by the universal Church represented at the Synod of Nicaea;[246] (ii) by their appointment of one (Pistos) who had been excommunicated by Bishop Alexander of Alexandria and by the Synod of Nicaea, one who, moreover, had been ordained by Bishop Secundus, also excommunicated at Nicaea;[247] and (iii) by their disregard for Canon XV, which forbade translations of bishops from one see to another.[248] These three paragraphs also contain another contrast.

Having displayed the serious discrepancies between the theory and the practice of the Eusebians, the Roman bishop compares his own activity with that of the Eusebians. He, suspecting that Athanasius and Marcellus had been judged *ex parte*, summoned all parties to an impartial examination of the cases involved;[249] he refused to enter into communion with one excommunicated by the Great Synod and ordained by an excommunicated bishop,[250] which practice, he concludes, is, unlike the Eusebian practice, completely in accordance with the (ecclesiastical) canons.[251] The third of these passages (*Apol.* 25) introduces

---

[244] In this way Julius also replies to the charge of the Eusebians—that he was guilty of dishonoring their synod (at Tyre); cf. *Apol.* 23,2 (Opitz 104,30) and other references given above in note 201.

[245] Julius refers to the Synod of Nicaea as having assembled "not without the Will of God" (*Apol.* 22,2 = Opitz 103,24). He constantly stresses the universal nature of their anathemas against the Arian heresy (*Apol.* 23,1 = Opitz 104,25; *Apol.* 23,2 = Opitz 104,28; *Apol.* 23,3 = Opitz 104,32; *Apol.* 25,1 = Opitz 105,28). The decrees of the Great Synod, he assures his readers, were framed "with great care and discretion as in the presence of God" (*Apol.* 24,4 = Opitz 105,25). It is noteworthy that the Bishop of Rome does not once refer to the presence of Emperor Constantine.

[246] Cf. *Apol.* 23,1–4 (Opitz 104,23–105,4), particularly *Apol.* 23,2 (Opitz 104,28–31).

[247] Cf. *Apol.* 24,1–4 (Opitz 105,5–25), particularly *Apol.* 24,2 (Opitz 105,11–18).

[248] Cf. *Apol.* 25,1–2 (Opitz 105,26–106,7). It is in this connection that Julius quotes the Eusebian letter where they refer to the precedents of Novatian and Paul of Samosata. He does not examine the two cases as such, but takes the principle enunciated by the Eusebians (the irreversibility of synodal decisions) and illustrated by them in the use of these two incidents, and applies it to the decisions of Nicaea. He also cites the principle of the equality of all bishops (before God) in order to show how the Eusebians deny this principle in practice through their episcopal translations (an allusion to Eusebius of Nicomedia).

[249] Cf. *Apol.* 23,4 (Opitz 104,37–41).

[250] Cf. *Apol.* 24,4 (Opitz 105,23–25).

[251] Cf. *Apol.* 25,1 (Opitz 105,32).

the theme of Church unity, which the Eusebians accused Julius of disturbing.[252] Julius' reply is to point to the activity of the Eusebians which resulted in their becoming the "authors of schism,"[253] since they failed to attend the Synod of Rome, to which he had summoned them, and offered excuses which were totally unconvincing.[256] Here Julius cleverly turns the accusation of the Eusebian-controlled Orientals against themselves, and at the same time points to the ultimate end of his own intervention: the preservation of the universal *unanimitas,* which the Eusebians had brought into jeopardy by their failure to obey his summons to the Synod of Rome.

In the sixth paragraph (*Apol.* 26), the Bishop of Rome now takes up the two objections of the Eusebian-controlled Oriental bishops to his *3rd Letter,* which communicated the decisions of the Synod of Rome: (i) that he wrote only to the Eusebians (and not to all the Oriental bishops) and (ii) that he did so merely in a personal capacity.[257] The first point is easily answered. Julius wrote to those who had first written to him, the Eusebians.[258] The second touches a more fundamental issue, that of Julius' authority. The Bishop of Rome replies that "even though I alone wrote, this is not the judgement of myself alone but of all the bishops in Italy and these parts (= the Synod of Rome)."[259] A little further on, he continues: "By all means, the bishops assembled on the appointed day and came to this decision, which, writing to you again, I signify to you (σημαίνω), so that, beloved, even though I alone write, you [will] perceive that this is the judgement of all."[260] Here the unique relationship between the Bishop of Rome and the synod is somewhat explicitly clarified. On the one hand, his official communication does not simply convey a personal opinion but expresses (signifies) the general opinion of the synod, and yet, on the other hand, when communicating this judgement, the Bishop of Rome is not simply

---

[252] Cf. *Apol.* 25,1 (Opitz 105,30).
[253] Cf. *Apol.* 25,4 (Opitz 106,19). Footnotes 254 and 255 have been deleted after revision.
[256] Cf. *Apol.* 25,3–4 (Opitz 106,7–21).
[257] Cf. *Apol.* 26,1 (Opitz 106,23); the quotation marks given by Opitz are incorrect.
[258] Cf. *Apol.* 26,1–2 (Opitz 106,24–30).
[259] *Apol.* 26,2 (Opitz 106,32–34). See Batiffol, *La paix constantinienne*, 428–429.
[260] *Apol.* 26,3 (Opitz 106,35–38).

the mouthpiece of the synod (its secretary for example)[261] but acts alone
in the first person singular. The unique authority which enables him to
do so (the Petrine Succession) is only mentioned explicitly at the end of
Julius' letter, as we will see.

In the next two paragraphs (*Apol.* 27–28) Julius then goes on to
justify the judgement of the Synod of Rome in receiving Athanasius (and
Marcellus) into communion. Here we need only note how Julius puts into
practice the principle of the transparency of justice he defended at the
outset of his letter. Succinctly, he gives the reasons which persuaded him
and the Synod of Rome to grant communion to Athanasius.[262]

In the light of such evidence, Julius continues *in the ninth paragraph*
(*Apol.* 29), the Synod and Bishop of Rome were compelled by the rule of
the Church (ὁ ἐκκλησιαστικὸς κανών) to receive Athanasius into communion and recognize his episcopal claims.[263] "And nevertheless after these
things, you complained as though we 'had transgressed the canons.'"[264]
As will be remembered from the above analysis of the Eusebian letter, the
canons Julius was accused of violating were most probably the Canons
of Antioch, which gave legal expression to the new Imperial Church
and its institution of completely autonomous provincial synods. Having
demonstrated how the procedure he adopted, with regard to Athanasius,
was in accordance with the ecclesiastical law, Julius rejects the Eusebian
allegation with this rhetorical question and then goes on to demonstrate
how the Eusebians themselves were guilty of "transgressing the [genuine]
canons," devoting two paragraphs to the topic (*Apol.* 30–31).

The first charge *in the tenth and eleventh paragraphs,* which
is brought against the Eusebian-controlled Orientals, is of special
note: "in the first place, if the truth must be told, once we decree
that a synod take place, it is not permitted that anyone anticipate its decisions."[265] This is the strongest indication of Julius'

---

[261] See Caspar, *Geschichte des Papsttums* I, 146. See Roethe, *Synoden*, 81–89, for
correction.

[262] Though mentioned together with Athanasius in *Apol.* 27,1 (Opitz 107,2), the
case of Marcellus of Ancyra is not treated until *Apol.* 32.

[263] Cf. *Apol.* 29.1 (Opitz 108,29–30).

[264] *Apol.* 29,3 (Opitz 108,34–35).

[265] πρῶτον μὲν γάρ, εἰ δεῖ τἀληθὲς εἰπεῖν, οὐκ ἔδει γραψάντων ἡμῶν σύνοδον γενέσθαι
προλαβεῖν τινας τὴν ἐκ τῆς συνόδου κρίσιν (*Apol.* 30,1 = Opitz 109,6–8).

consciousness of his authority as Bishop of Rome we have so far encountered in the letter. We have seen how he claimed the right based on the nature of the Church and the nature of justice (= divine law) to take the initiative if necessary in matters affecting the *unanimitas* of the Church Universal; now he states that, once this initiative was taken, no one had the right to anticipate the judgement of the synod he had summoned; he further implies that this is demanded by the law of the Church (ἔδει). But the Eusebian-controlled Synod of Antioch jumped the gun by appointing Gregory as Bishop of Alexandria. Further, they bypassed all "ecclesiastical law" and "Apostolic Tradition" by sending Gregory to Alexandria at a time when the Church was at peace and when so many bishops (Julius does not say *all* bishops) were in communion with Athanasius: such indeed was an "innovation."[266] The list of objections to Gregory's appointment ends with the charge that he was sent to Alexandria (to be installed there) accompanied not by clergy "but by soldiers."[267] Here we meet the first explicit critical allusion to the Imperial Church. Julius goes on to condemn the actual procedure adopted by the Antiochene synod for the election of Gregory (even presuming that Athanasius were found guilty by the Synod of Rome) as contrary to Church law and amounting to the abrogation of the canons (handed down) from the Apostles.[268] In this paragraph, the Bishop of Rome has touched the nerve of the Eusebian reaction: the new understanding of the Church, which (i) bypassed the central authority of the Bishop of Rome, contrary to the Apostolic Tradition and Church practice; (ii) adopted the novel procedure of sending a bishop to another see, while the occupant was in communion with the other bishops; (iii) arranged to have him installed by the imperial authority; and, finally, (iv) disregarded the clearly defined Apostolic rules for the election of bishops and dared to assume the power to appoint a bishop (as though from a superior authority, the Synod of Antioch) over the heads of the local clergy and neighboring bishops.

This new ecclesiology was, as we saw, given legal expression in the Canons of Antioch in contravention of which Julius was accused of acting. Julius' reply is to demonstrate how this ecclesiology itself was a "*novum*," i.e., a heretical innovation and contrary to the traditional understanding of the Church as handed down from the Apostles and sanctioned by ecclesiastical practice. The Bishop of Rome not only condemns the formal aspect of the action of the Eusebian-

---

[266] Cf. *Apol.* 30,1 (Opitz 109,8–15).
[267] Cf. *Apol.* 30,1 (Opitz 109,11–15).
[268] Cf. *Apol.* 30,2 (Opitz 109,16–21).

controlled Synod of Antioch in no uncertain terms,[269] but he goes on, after expressing his indignation at the disturbances and violence caused by Gregory's arrival in Alexandria,[270] to uncover the source of this new ecclesiology. This is the *identity* of Church and Empire as exemplified in the conduct of the Mareotis Commission, where the imperial forces played a major role and an inquiry into matters concerning the most sacred of mysteries, Christ's Body and His Blood, took place in the presence of the prefect, heathens, and Jews, while the ministers of these mysteries (the presbyters of Mareotis) were not allowed to attend.[271] Here Julius makes no bones about describing the Imperial Officer Philagrius, the Prefect of Egypt, as an "external judge."[272] His imperial status did not entitle him to be involved in the internal affairs of the Church.

A final observation on this is Julius' open attack on the new Imperial Church: "Beloved we speak loud and clear *as in the presence of God* and say with truth: this is neither orthodox (εὐσεβές) nor lawful nor ecclesiastical."[273] What is of special note here is the phrase ὡς θεοῦ παρόντος, which is identical with that used by Julius when he previously described the way the decrees of the Great Synod of Nicaea were drawn up.[274] Now he uses it with respect to his own condemnation of the new Imperial Church, and so draws a parallel between the Nicene decrees and his own judgement (anathema) on the "innovation" in the East.

In the twelfth paragraph (*Apol.* 32), the Bishop of Rome now turns his attention to the case of Marcellus of Ancyra who had been charged with heresy by the Orientals led by Eusebius of Caesarea. Faced with this accusation, the Roman bishop demanded from Marcellus, a written confession of Faith, which on examination proved to be in harmony with that confessed at Nicaea, where Marcellus' opposition to Arianism had been witnessed by the two Roman presbyter-delegates, and which was in fact cleverly formulated so as to disguise his actual heretical opinions.[275] Gessel recently

---

[269] Cf. *Apol.* 30,3 (Opitz 109,21–23).
[270] Cf. *Apol.* 30,3–4 (Opitz 109,23–110,4).
[271] Cf. *Apol.* 31,1–2 (Opitz 110,5–18).
[272] Compare *Apol.* 31,2 (Opitz 110,12–13) with *Apol.* 31,1 (Opitz 110,9).
[273] *Apol.* 30,3 (Opitz 109,21–23).
[274] Cf. *Apol.* 24,4 (Opitz 105,25). See above, note 245.
[275] Cf. *Apol.* 32,1–4 (Opitz 110,19–111,9). See Schwartz, *NGG* (1911), 497–501 (*GS* III, 303–306). However, Schwartz's totally unfounded suggestion (p. 500 = *GS* III, 306) must be finally rejected as absurd—to the effect that it was

pointed out that a stylistic difference can be perceived in this paragraph in comparison with the rest of the *Letter of Julius*.[276] Even though one could argue with his description of this difference (he talks, e.g., about "den Schimmer eines triumphalistischen Untertons") and reject the reasons he proposes to explain this disharmony in the tone of the letter, yet his basic observation remains valid. When discussing the case of Marcellus, Julius is on surer ground than with regard to the charges brought against Athanasius. The latter concerned human behavior—a much more complex and ambiguous entity than doctrinal matters, such as were raised by Marcellus. Also, it must be said that here Julius is on surer ground with regard to his formal authority. The responsibility of Rome to preserve the Apostolic Teaching and reject heresy was not rejected in principle even by the Eusebians in their letter, however much they sought to rob it of its content and effectiveness, whereas his responsibility in matters of justice (and thus jurisdiction), which flowed directly from his responsibility for Faith and morals, was only in the process of coming to the surface and finding articulation in which process this letter itself played a major role. We must return to this point later. For the moment it will suffice to note that, apart from this paragraph dealing with Marcellus, Julius' strongest and most direct language was found in his condemnation of the new "teaching" with regard to the nature of the Church, which had become manifest in the actions of the Eusebians.

Julius next gives brief attention *in the thirteenth paragraph* (*Apol.* 33) to the cases of the other Oriental bishops who had appealed to him to redress the injuries they had received at the hand of the Eusebians. Their accusations against the Eusebians are only treated in summary. They amount to various charges of violence.[277] The Roman bishop does not go into detail on these charges, both because of their dreadful nature[278] and because he wishes to give the Eusebians an opportunity to defend themselves first, and so not prejudge the issue.[279] The latter reason introduces the final two—and the most significant—paragraphs of the *Letter of Julius*.

In the second to last paragraph (*Apol.* 34), Julius returns to the accusation leveled against him by the Eusebians, to the effect that he,

Athanasius and Julius who persuaded Marcellus to conceal his heretical tendencies!
[276] See above, footnote 219.
[277] Cf. *Apol.* 33,1–3 (Opitz 111,10–30).
[278] Cf. *Apol.* 33,3 (Opitz 111,28–30).
[279] Cf. *Apol.* 33,4 (Opitz 111,30–32).

through his intervention in Eastern affairs, had disturbed the unanimity there by lighting up the flames of discord. Referring to the disturbances the Eusebians caused to various Churches in the East and in Egypt, he asks rhetorically: "Who are those who have 'lighted up the flame of discord?' We who grieve about such events and sympathize with the brethren who suffer or they who brought them about?"[280] Here Julius alludes once again to his responsibility for the suffering brethren that marked the opening of his letter. After criticizing the confusion that apparently reigned in the Eastern Churches, he clarifies his motive for intervening:

> On which account, as God the Father of Our Lord Jesus Christ knows, it was out of concern for your reputation and a desire that the Churches not be in a state of disorder, *but remain regulated as [determined] by the Apostles*, that I was led to write thus to you, to the end that you will at length put to shame those who, through their enmity towards one another, have thus afflicted the Churches. For I have heard that they are few in number who are responsible for all these things."[281]

Of note here is, first of all, the witness of God the Father for the truth of his statement—the only such reference in the entire letter. Secondly, this passage informs us of the object of the responsibility that pertains to the Bishop of Rome, which is to ensure that the Churches are regulated as set down by the Apostles: ὥσπερ ὑπὸ τῶν ἀποστόλων ἐκανονίσθη....[282] In other words, to preserve the Apostolic constitution of the Church in the face of the "*novum*"—the Imperial Church. This small party (the Eusebians) had acted contrary to the canon[283]—and here κανών does not refer to the code of written laws but the Church's traditional understanding of her nature, which was at the time in the early stages of being translated into canons, rules, and regulations—while Julius insists that he had acted "canonically and justly"[284] in receiving Athanasius and Marcellus into communion, i.e., he had acted in accordance with the traditional practice of the Church, and in accordance with the demands of justice. But again, Julius announces his readiness to reexamine the cases, should his readers be able to produce

---

[280] *Apol.* 34,1 (Opitz 112.4–6).

[281] *Apol.* 34,2 (Opitz 112,11–16).

[282] The translation suggested by Batiffol, *La paix constantinienne*, 426 ("Il termine par une appel à la paix de l'Église dans le respect des canons que les apôtres lui donnés"), does not quite do justice to the intention of Julius.

[283] Cf. *Apol.* 34,3 (Opitz 112,17).

[284] Cf. *Apol.* 34,4 (Opitz 112,23). See Hess, *The Early Development*, 77.

evidence against those they had accused.[285] With this we arrive at the final paragraph of the *4th Letter of Julius,* which text has been the source of considerable scholarly comment.[286]

The fifteenth and final paragraph (*Apol.* 35) provides (i) an elucidation of the correct procedure to be adopted in matters of dispute between bishops, based both on the principle of justice (its transparency) and on the Apostolic nature of the Church; and (ii) it provides the clearest manifestation of Julius' primatial consciousness in the whole letter. It also contains (iii) a final criticism of the new Imperial Church created by the Eusebians.

Should the Synod of Antioch feel confident that they could produce new evidence to support their indictments against Athanasius, Marcellus, and the other Oriental bishops, then Julius calls on the Eusebian-controlled Oriental bishops to let him know "so that we may write both to them and to the bishops who must needs reassemble so that the accused be condemned in the presence of all and disorder no longer prevail in the Churches."[287] Julius' objective is first and foremost that justice be done and be seen to be done (in the presence of all parties, accused and accusers, and the entire Church). He then turns to summarize his criticisms of the procedures adopted in the East, where "in the presence of bishops, bishops were banished."[288] This is a reference to the new type of synod which functioned as an imperial commission, and so exercised the authority (reserved to the State) of punishing individuals with exile. After referring to the other Eastern bishops and presbyters who had suffered such violence, Julius cries out: "O beloved, the judgements of the Church are no longer in accordance with the Gospel but rather with a view to banishment and death."[289] Then

---

[285] Cf. *Apol.* 34.5 (Opitz 112,27–29).

[286] E.g., Batiffol, *La paix constantinienne,* 426–429. Caspar, *Geschichte des Papsttums* I, 150f.; Jalland, *Church and Papacy,* 216; Girardet, *Kaisergericht und Bischofsgericht,* 96–105; Gessel, "Das primatiale Bewußtsein Julius' I," 72–73.

[287] *Apol.* 35,1 (Opitz 112,30–32).

[288] *Apol.* 35,1 (Opitz 112,33).

[289] *Apol.* 35,3 (Opitz 112,38–113,1). Girardet's comment (*Kaisergericht und Bischofsgericht,* 96, note 294) to the effect that Julius (and Athanasius) could be said to display a double standard of morality since they apparently would not have objected to the banishment of a "heretic" such as Arius, but only objected when an orthodox bishop or presbyter (i.e., of their own party) was exiled, misjudges the intention of Julius here: Arius and his supporters were not banished by the Synod of Nicaea, but by the emperor, just indeed as Athanasius was after Tyre.

follows the most important passage in the entire letter, which attempts to
clarify the formal issues raised by the Eusebians:

> (v. 3) In short, if, as you maintain, some misdeed occurred among
> them, the judgement ought to have been reached according to eccle-
> siastical precept and not in such fashion: all of us ought to have been
> notified so that a just [sentence] might be determined by all. They
> were, namely, bishops who suffered, and the Churches which suffered
> were of no mean significance, but those over whom the Apostles them-
> selves had ruled in their own persons. (v. 4) Above all, why were we
> not notified about the Alexandrian Church? Do you not know that
> it was the custom to notify us first and from here just [sentences] be
> determined? If then any such suspicion rested on the bishop there,
> this Church here ought to have been notified; whereas now, after
> neglecting to inform us, they act themselves as they pleased and desire
> us to ratify [their decisions] though we have not condemned [him].
> (v. 5) Not so did the precepts of Paul, not so did the Fathers, hand
> on: this is another principle, one which has been newly fabricated. I
> exhort [you], bear with me in patience: those things I write are for
> the sake of the common good. Those things we have received from
> Blessed Peter the Apostle, these things I also signify to you. I should
> not have written, as I assume these things to be evident to all, had not
> these events alarmed us.[290]

That which shocked the Bishop and Synod of Rome was, according
to Julius in the above text, the *novum*: that principle (τύπος) foreign

[290] (v.) 3. ὦ ἀγαπητοί, οὐκέτι κατὰ τὸ εὐαγγέλιον, ἀλλὰ λοιπὸν ἐπὶ ἐξορισμῷ καὶ θανάτῳ αἱ
κρίσεις τῆς ἐκκλησίας εἰσίν. εἰ γὰρ καὶ ὅλως, ὡς φατε, γέγονέ τι εἰς αὐτοὺς ἁμάρτημα,
ἔδει κατὰ τὸν ἐκκλησιαστικὸν κανόνα καὶ μὴ οὕτως γεγενῆσθαι τὴν κρίσιν, ἔδει
γραφῆναι πᾶσιν ἡμῖν, ἵνα οὕτως παρὰ πάντων ὁρισθῇ τὸ δίκαιον. ἐπίσκοποι γὰρ
ἦσαν οἱ πάσχοντες καὶ οὐχ αἱ τυχοῦσαι ἐκκλησίαι αἱ πάσχουσαι, ἀλλ᾽ ὧν αὐτοὶ οἱ
ἀπόστολοι δι᾽ ἑαυτῶν καθηγήσαντο.
(v.) 4. διὰ τί δὲ περὶ τῆς Ἀλεξανδρέων ἐκκλησίας μάλιστα οὐκ ἐγράφετο ἡμῖν; ἢ
ἀγνοεῖτε, ὅτι τοῦτο ἔθος ἦν, πρότερον γράφεσθαι ἡμῖν καὶ οὕτως ἔνθεν ὁρίζεσθαι τὰ
δίκαια; εἰ μὲν οὖν τι τοιοῦτον ἦν ὑποπτευθὲν εἰς τὸν ἐπίσκοπον τὸν ἐκεῖ, ἔδει πρὸς
τὴν ἐνταῦθα ἐκκλησίαν γραφῆναι, νῦν δὲ οἱ ἡμᾶς μὴ πληροφορήσαντες, πράξαντες
δὲ αὐτοὶ ὡς ἠθέλησαν, λοιπὸν καὶ ἡμᾶς οὐ καταγνόντας βούλονται συμψήφους εἶναι.
(v.) 5. οὐχ οὕτως αἱ Παύλου διατάξεις, οὐχ οὕτως οἱ πατέρες παραδεδώκασιν· ἄλλος
τύπος ἐστὶν οὗτος καὶ καινὸν τὸ ἐπιτήδευμα. παρακαλῶ, μετὰ μακροθυμίας ἐνέγκατε·
ὑπὲρ τοῦ κοινῇ συμφέροντός ἐστιν ἃ γράφω. ἃ γὰρ παρειλήφαμεν παρὰ τοῦ μακαρίου
Πέτρου τοῦ ἀποστόλου, ταῦτα καὶ ὑμῖν δηλῶ. καὶ οὐκ ἂν ἔγραψα φανερὰ ἡγούμενος
εἶναι ταῦτα παρὰ πᾶσιν, εἰ μὴ τὰ γενόμενα ἡμᾶς ἐτάραξεν (*Apol.* 35,3–5 = Opitz
112,38–113,14).

to the Apostolic Tradition (= Paul and the Fathers),[291] that new fabrication (καινὸν τὸ ἐπιτήδευμα) of the Imperial Church which, as the
immediately foregoing context indicated, and as his earlier exposition
(*Apol.* 30–31) also described, created the autonomous synodal institution that functioned as an imperial commission (v. 5). Against that,
Julius implores the Eusebian-controlled Orientals to return to the procedure which is truly ecclesiastical (v. 3). That procedure was based on
the principle of the transparency of justice and on the basic equality
of all bishops which demanded that the details concerning any charge
brought against one bishop ought to be sent to all (πᾶσιν ἡμῖν) so that the
justice of his sentence could be determined by all (παρὰ παντῶν = other
bishops).[292] Πᾶσιν ἡμῖν could be said to imply that the Bishop of Rome

[291] The phrase αἱ Παύλου διατάξεις does not seem to refer to any collection of
Apostolic ordinances, as has been suggested (cf. Robertson, *Athanasius*, LNPF2,
118, note 4). Neither does Julius (at least in the first place) call on the precepts
of Paul to support his teaching on the correct ecclesiastical procedure as, e.g.,
Batiffol, *La paix constantinienne*, 429, and more recently, Girardet, *Kaisergericht
und Bischofsgericht*, 102, suggest. The negative form of the statement must be
given due attention: Julius quite simply denies that the innovatory procedures
of the Eusebians could call either on the Apostle Paul or on the tradition of
the Fathers for support. It is possible that Julius is here rejecting a claim by the
Eusebian-controlled Orientals in their *letter* to him, that they in the East were
the possessors of an authentic Pauline tradition, more ancient than that of Rome
(cf. the *Letter of the Eusebians*: "Those who introduced the Teaching [to Rome]
came from the East to reside there"), just as the denial of Julius regarding a claim
to the tradition of the Fathers probably has in mind the Eusebian claim that
"those priests who had proceeded them in the East had offered no stiff opposition
when Novatian was deposed by the Roman Church" (*Letter of the Eusebians*,
see note 197 above).

[292] See Jalland, *Church and Papacy*, 216. Caspar's observation remains valid:
"Nicht von einem Urteil (κρίσις), wie im vorangehenden Satz, ist die Rede,
sondern zweimal ist ein anderer Ausdruck, ὁρίζειν τὰ δίκαια, gewählt, womit die
Begutachtung eines gefällten Urteils auf seine Rechtmäßigkeit hin gemeint ist.
Mit anderen Worten: das 'Gewohnheitsrecht,' auf welches sich Julius I. berief,
war der alte Brauch, daß Synodalentscheidungen erst durch die Rezeption auf
dem Weg des zwischenkirchlichen Nachrichtenaustausches in der Gesamtkirche
Kraft erlangten ... " (*Geschichte des Papsttums* I, 150). However, Caspar's application of this principle to the case of Athanasius (pp. 150–151) fails to take
cognizance of other nuances in the text of Julius, as we will see below. Girardet,
Kaisergericht und Bischofsgericht, 97–101, who accepts Caspar's distinction
between κρίσις and ὁρίζειν τὰ δίκαια but rejects his suggested translation, is right
to point out that Julius here attacks the "Alleingang" of those who condemned Athanasius and Marcellus, but draws the unacceptable conclusion from
this insight (which is itself complementary to that of Caspar) that "Ὁρίζειν
τὰ δίκαια ist also die Bezeichnung für Konsultationen vor einer möglichen
Synode" (p. 101). His presentation of the procedure adopted in the cases of

and the Occident should be included, but it would be false to understand this in terms of a projection of the later Occident-Orient division into the situation of the Church in the year 341.[293] Julius here speaks on behalf of *all* bishops, not simply those of the West.

This text is his reply to the Eusebian interpretation of the principle that all bishops are equal (and thus not to be estimated according to the greatness of their cities) to justify the autonomy of their new synodal institution. Julius' interpretation of this principle is that because all bishops are equal, therefore any sentence brought against any one of them must in principle be examined and approved by *all* his brethren. "They are namely *bishops* who suffered," explains Julius and then adds the remark which reflects how this principle, based on the Apostolic nature of the episcopacy, was actually applied in practice: "and the Churches which suffered were of no mean significance, but those over whom the Apostles themselves had ruled in their own person." As we saw in Part One, those bishops who enjoyed direct Apostolic Succession enjoyed on that account greater authority so that communion with one of them was sufficient for an "ordinary" bishop to guarantee his orthodoxy. Julius, we remember, did not deny the principle that the size of cities was of no consequence for the "honor" accorded to them within the Church. He only showed how the Eusebians in fact acted contrary to this principle. What Julius affirms here is, as the original *History* of Eusebius assumed, that *the Apostolic claims of* a Church do affect the standing of its bishop within the universal

Fabius of Antioch and Paul of Samosata (in itself a valuable contribution) in support of his theory fails to convince, since, with regard to Fabius, his deposition resulted from his reluctance to "receive" the judgement of the Synod of Rome, which rejected Novatian and elected Cornelius, while the activities of the Eastern bishops before their final deposition of Paul, at the Synod of Antioch 268 (their warning letters to their fellow bishops), can hardly be understood as constituting what Girardet meant by τὸ δίχαιον: what the latter signified was that which occurred after the synodal deposition in 268, when the Roman Church scrutinized the judgement of the Synod of Antioch which they had communicated to Rome and Alexandria (see above, pp. 129–131).

[293] This is a weakness in the interpretation, e.g., of Lietzmann, *Geschichte* III, 188–190; Caspar, *Geschichte des Papsttums* I, 150, and Opitz's commentary on Opitz 113,1. This separate development of an "Eastern" as distinct from a "Western" Church only begins to manifest itself at this time—not generally in the East or West, but at first confined to the small but influential Eusebian party in the East, whose influence in the East climbed steadily from the Synods of Antioch 328–330 up to the Synods of Ariminum and Seleucia (359), when it suffered its first major setback.

κοινωνία—a generally recognized ecclesiological principle which the Eusebians could only attack by means of irony—and further, that, *a fortiori*, cases affecting any one of these bishops claiming direct Apostolic Succession should have been brought to the attention of the universal episcopate.

"Above all," the Bishop of Rome continues, "why were we not notified about the Alexandrian Church? Do you not know that it was the custom (ἔθος) to notify us first and in this manner just [sentences] be determined? If then any such suspicion rested on the bishop there, this Church here ought to have been notified." Here the special relationship between the preeminent Petrine Sees—Rome, Alexandria, and Antioch— which determined the early ecclesiology of Eusebius of Caesarea, i.e., the ecclesiology generally accepted in the East and West before the Great Persecution, is behind this text, although only Rome and Alexandria are mentioned (as determined by the actual case in question) and not, in the first place at least (Julius speaks in the plural: τὰ δίκαια), the precedent of the controversy concerning the two Dionysii of Rome and Alexandria.[294] (There, however, a similar consciousness may indeed be said to have been present.) The ἔθος, which Julius reminds the Eusebians of, is the practice which had crystalized out of the ancient custom of exchanging *Letters of Communion* between bishops, and which had been formed under those conditions which were determined by the preeminence of Apostolic and, above all, Petrine Sees. According to that custom, communion for any bishop with the universal Church was guaranteed through communion with one of those Petrine Sees, which in turn communicated with each other, so that, for example, the claims of a bishop ratified by a Petrine See were recognized by the other two. Such was the background to the Novatian controversy concerning Fabius of Antioch (who was not inclined to recognize Cornelius of Rome) and, of course, the controversy between the two Dionysii. The later controversy illustrated the primacy of the Roman See (thanks to the martyrdom of Peter) among the three Petrine Sees; the bishops of the Pentapolis, who complained to Dionysius of Rome about his namesake in Alexandria, did not apparently journey to Antioch but to Rome. The corollary of the exchange of *Kommunionbriefe* between the Petrine Sees, which manifested their special relationship with each other, was that (as Julius here points out) any charge affecting those sees must of necessity be reported to the Church of

---

[294] Cf. Caspar, *Geschichte des Papsttums* I, 151 (apparently); Girardet, *Kaisergericht und Bischofsgericht*, 101.

Rome so that the accusation might be scrutinized (and approved or rejected).

The special procedures involving all Churches claiming direct Apostolic Succession is also reflected in the body of the *Letter of Julius*: the case which Julius treats of in greatest detail is that concerning the successor of St. Peter's disciple and interpreter, namely that of Athanasius (*Apol.* 8–31); Marcellus, who occupied the Pauline See of Ancyra, is dealt with in one paragraph (*Apol.* 32), while the other Oriental bishops who appealed to the Bishop of Rome are not even mentioned by name but are treated generally in another paragraph (*Apol.* 33). Likewise, there is no doubt as to who is meant by the first-person plural (ἡμῖν) in v. 4 of the text from the fifteenth paragraph just quoted. The express reference to "the Alexandrian Church" and "the Church here" indicate the personal pronoun refers to Julius, the Bishop of Rome.[295] Above all, in the case of the Bishop of Alexandria, Julius was not prepared to ratify the decisions of an arbitrarily constituted synod without first examining the case himself.[296] The intensification of the argumentation based on the Apostolic nature of the episcopal office and its relationship to the episcopate in general, as well as the Bishop of Rome in particular, is clearly seen in the parallel structure[297] of verses 3 and 4:

v. 3 . . . ἔδει γραφῆναι πᾶσιν ἡμῖν,

       ἵνα οὗτος παρὰ πάντων ὁρισϑῇ τὸ δίκαιον

       (regarding bishops in general, but especially those claiming direct Apostolic Succession);

v. 4 . . . τοῦτο ἔϑος ἦν, πρότερον γράφεσϑαι ἡμῖν

       καὶ οὕτως ἔνϑεν ὁρίζεσϑαι τὰ δίκαια

       (regarding Petrine Sees, in this case Alexandria).

In both cases, the Bishop of Rome demands the right to scrutinize the justice of judgements passed on any one of his fellow-bishops; but this involvement of his is only *implicit* in the case of bishops in

---

[295] Cf. *Apol.* 35,1 (Opitz 112,30), where Julius also speaks in the first-person plural. See Batiffol, *La paix constantinienne*, 428–429.

[296] Opitz's suggestion that Julius rejected the decisions of Tyre, since too few bishops were present there to judge the cases of the bishops of Ancyra and Alexandria (see his commentary in Opitz 113,1f.), fails to take cognizance of the basic concern of Julius: he misinterprets the Bishop of Rome's affirmation of the general principle, based on the equality of all bishops, and the principle of justice, to the effect that judgements concerning bishops must be open to the scrutiny of all other bishops.

[297] I am grateful to the Stephan O. Horn (Regensburg) for drawing my attention to this parallelism.

general, while it is *explicitly* demanded in the case of the Petrine See of Alexandria, corresponding to the ecclesiastical structure and practice which had evolved in the Church up to that point.[298] However, the claims which Julius makes in the name of the generally accepted ecclesiastical norm (κατὰ τὸν ἐκκλησιαστικὸν κανόνα, v. 3) with respect to all bishops, and in the name of ancient practice (ἔθος, v. 4) with regard to Alexandria, contain in germ the principle relating to the right of all bishops to have their claims to justice (and to their sees) examined by other bishops (of another province) and ultimately, if necessary, by the Bishop of Rome, which principle found its first tentative canonical expression in the "Appeal Canons" of the Synod of Sardica, 343.[299]

After outlining in verses 3 and 4 the proper procedure demanded by the ecclesiastical rules and practice to be adopted in the case of bishops, in particular those claiming Apostolic Succession and above all those of (the Petrine See of) Alexandria who were judged (by their fellow-bishops at a provincial synod), Julius at the end of verse 4 attacks the principle of absolute autonomy on the part of provincial synods, adopted in theory and practice by the Eusebians, which demanded that the Bishop of Rome, and the other bishops of the universal episcopacy, simply approve of their decisions without examining the justice of such judgements. Then he goes on to affirm in verse 5, as already mentioned above, that the procedure adopted by the Eusebians (and applied by means of the *illegitimate* agency of the imperial authority), could not appeal to Apostolic Tradition (St. Paul or the Fathers) for support. He continues: "I exhort [you], bear with me in patience; it is for the sake of the common good that I write as such. Those things we have received from the Blessed Peter the Apostle, these things I also signify (δηλῶ) to you."[299a] The special responsibility of the Bishop of Rome for the ἀγάπη and for truth, with which Julius opened his letter, and the cause of his energetic rejection of the most serious accusation of the

---

[298] Though, as Jalland, *Church and Papacy*, 215, pointed out, the mode of expression used by Socrates may be anachronistic, yet his paraphrase of Julius' *letter,* and that of his fellow-historian (and fellow-jurist) at Constantinople, Sozomen, accurately perceived the central point of Julius' argument: τοῦ ἐκκλησιαστικοῦ κανόνος κελεύοντος, μὴ δεῖν παρὰ γνώμην τοῦ ἐπισκόπου Ῥώμης κανονίζειν τὰς ἐκκλησίας (Socrates, *HE* 2,17,7 = Hussey 214); εἶναι γὰρ νόμον ἱερατικόν, ὃς ἄκυρα ἀποφαίνει τὰ παρὰ γνώμην πραττόμενα τοῦ Ῥωμαίων ἐπισκόπου (Sozomen, *HE* 3,10,1 = Bidez-Hansen 113,3–4).

[299] See below, pp. 456–458.

[299a] *Apol.* 35,5 (Opitz 113,11–13): παρακαλῶ, μετὰ μακροθυμίας ἐνέγκατε· ὑπὲρ τοῦ κοινῇ συμφέροντός ἐστιν ἃ γράφω. ἃ γὰρ παρειλήφαμεν παρὰ τοῦ μακαρίου Πέτρου τοῦ ἀποστόλου, ταῦτα καὶ ὑμῖν δηλῶ.

Eusebian-controlled Orientals, to the effect that he had created discord within the unanimity of the Eastern Churches, are here reechoed in this simple, clear statement of the Bishop of Rome's *ultimate motive* for his insistence on the traditional procedure based on the Apostolic nature of the Church. He is moved, Julius tells us, by no other consideration than the good of the entire Church. *Universality* is the keynote which dominates each paragraph of Julius' letter, such as his concern for the suffering brethren, wherever they may be (*Apol.* 21; 33; 34), his defense of the principle of the transparency of just judgements and of the genuine equality of all bishops (*Apol.* 22; 35; passim), and now his fundamental concern for the common good of the Church. The final aim of the Bishop of Rome is to preserve the universal κοινωνία based on the Apostolic Tradition of the Church and the procedures which flow therefrom, and which he had assumed were universally accepted: "I should not have written," he concludes, "as I assume these to be evident to all, had not the events alarmed us." "*These things* we have received from Blessed Peter the Apostle" refer to the procedures which arose from the Apostolic nature of the Church, and which had been established and sanctioned by ecclesiastical rule and custom in opposition to the non-Apostolic innovations of the Eusebians, which arose from the new imperial institutional Church. Julius here calls on the Petrine Tradition of the Church of Rome (note the first-person plural of παρειλήφαμεν) as the *final authority* for the ecclesiological precepts he has outlined in such detail. In this way he counteracts the irony of the Eusebians, who so wished to discredit the primacy of Rome based on her generally accepted renown as the *school of Apostles and capital of orthodoxy since the beginning,* with the only means available to overcome irony: a straightforward, upright affirmation of this authority. Though he mentioned St. Paul immediately before, this was only in the negative context of rejecting the Eusebian innovation as incompatible with any Apostolic or ecclesiastical tradition. Here the Bishop of Rome calls exclusively on the Petrine Tradition of the Church of Rome. "These things," he continues, "I also signify to you." The first-person plural has given way to the first person singular: unambiguously the Bishop of Rome resorts to his personal authority as successor to St. Peter in order to rule out any uncertainty about the significance of the "ecclesiology," or rather ecclesiological principles and precepts, which he has endeavored to spell out for the recalcitrant Eusebians. These precepts are guaranteed by the Petrine Tradition of the Church of Rome, which Julius, as Bishop of Rome and Successor to St. Peter, personally sanctions and which are thus of universal relevance.

The ecclesiology of the esarly Eusebius of Caesarea, which saw in the Bishop of Rome, the preeminent Successor of St. Peter and thus the one whose office was to preserve the Apostolic Tradition and combat all attacks by the successors of Simon Magus, is seen in action in this *Letter of Julius*. It will be remembered that earlier in the letter, the Bishop of Rome flatly and authoritatively rejected the procedures of the new Imperial Church with the magisterial statement: "Beloved! We speak loud and clear as in the presence of God and say with truth: this is neither orthodox nor lawful nor ecclesiastical." This bold sentence, which rejected the *novum* of the Eusebians, was couched as we saw in terms similar to those used to describe the way the decrees of Nicaea are drawn up.[300] The corollary of this anathema-like negative sentence is the above statement calling on the Petrine tradition and spoken in the first person singular in order to give the positive teaching of the Church on matters relating to ecclesiastical procedure and custom its final authority. It is of note that Julius here uses the term δηλῶ in a way similar to the usage he makes of σημαίνω when speaking of the judgement of the Synod of Rome. Referring to the latter, Julius affirmed that "even though I alone write, you [will] perceive that this is the judgement of all." Here he refers to the Petrine tradition preserved in the Church of Rome (and possibly alludes to the Synod of Rome as well) which forms the content of his letter, but the binding force of this teaching is ultimately rooted in the authority invested in the person of the Bishop of Rome himself, Successor to St. Peter par excellence.

The obvious influence of Athanasius on the position taken by Julius, with regard to the former's claim to the See of Alexandria (*Apol.* 27–28), has already been mentioned; having examined the accusations of the Eusebians and the defense of Athanasius, Julius opted for the latter. And yet Julius' presentation of the defense of Athanasius is not a simple report of the arguments of Athanasius. The Bishop of Rome, for example, modifies the contention of Athanasius regarding the conspiracy of the Eusebians (without either denying or explicitly affirming it).[301] It is also possible that the Roman bishop accepted the Bishop of Alexandria's advice with

---

[300] See above, footnote 245.
[301] The conspiracy is mentioned explicitly on three occasions (*Apol.* 27,2 = Opitz 107,12; *Apol.*28,1 = Opitz 107,33; *Apol.*28,3 = Opitz 108,4).

regard to answering the charges brought against Julius himself, to the effect that he, the Bishop of Rome, had "transgressed the canons," namely, that Julius should point out to the Orientals how the Eusebians themselves had "dishonored" the Great Synod of Nicaea (*Apol.* 23–25), though this information as such could have been known independently by Julius. With respect to the basic argumentation of the *Letter of Julius*, it is possible again that it was Athanasius who was ultimately responsible for bringing the attention of Julius to the fundamental ecclesiological issues involved in the controversy, which had ostensibly broken out due to attacks on his personal behavior and his claim to the See of Mark, such as the appearance in the Eusebian-controlled East of an entirely new institution, foreign to the Apostolic nature of the Church. As we have seen in our outline of Athanasius' history, the Alexandrian bishop, after Tyre, was quick to perceive the ecclesiological implications of the actions of those who had achieved his exile to Trier, and responded in his 10th *Festal Letter* by drawing attention to the Apostolic constitution of the Church[302] in order to counteract the new ecclesiology of the Eusebians, who "put forward the name of a synod and ground its proceedings on the authority of the Emperor," as the Synod of Alexandria in 338 protested.[303] On the other hand, the reaction of Miltiades of Rome to the intervention of Constantine in the early stages of the Donatist dispute, as well as Sylvester's refusal to attend either the Synod of Arles or the Synod of Nicaea in person, indicate an independent attitude to the new "Christian" Emperor, one centered on Rome, which is in sharp contrast with the enthusiasm of an Eusebius of Caesarea, even before his definitive "conversion" to the new Imperial Church after Nicaea. Julius had no need of Athanasius' insights on the question of the relationship between Church and State, though it cannot be excluded that the Alexandrian bishop of such exceptional ability did help to stimulate Julius' own reflections.[304]

---

[302] See above, pp. 363–366.

[303] *Apol.* 10,1 (Opitz 95,27).

[304] Jalland, *Church and Papacy*, 216, commenting on the real cause of Julius' anxiety, perceptively observed: "... the eastern solution of the new problem created by the changed relation of Church and State ... involved the replacement of the primitive conception of the *paradosis* as something received from the Apostles and transmitted by their successors in the teaching office by something entirely new, namely, the identification of the *paradosis* with the δόγμα of Augustus." However, Jalland does not do justice to the *Letter of Julius* when he points to the "appeal of Julius to the twofold apostolic *paradosis* the Church of Rome" (216–217) as though this only indicated the possibility that Julius was able to perceive the development

However valuable and significant the influence of Athanasius' penetrating intellect may have been, the *Letter of Julius* bears all the marks of the independent mind of the Bishop of Rome. This is above all illustrated in the way Julius takes up the idea of "Divine Justice," which had been previously used by Athanasius, clarifies it in terms of what we have called the transparency of justice, and demonstrates its sanction by tradition (Nicaea). When he proceeds to answer systematically the objections of the Eusebians, he uses on various occasions, the earlier arguments of Athanasius, but he synthesizes these by means of the principle of the transparency of justice, and demonstrates how all of these were in harmony with traditional practice and the Church's understanding of herself as Apostolic and universal. The internal unity of purpose and the more sharply delineated concepts found in this letter point to an author of independent mind and one of no mean stature:[305] that of Julius of Rome who generally uses the *pluralis majestatis* and, on rare but significant occasions, the first person singular, such as at the climax of the letter (*Apol.* 35) when

which was in progress. As we have seen, the basic thrust of the letter, which climaxes with the appeal to the tradition of Peter, is an attack on the "Eastern solution" so ably summarized by Jalland.

[305] In his evaluation of the *Letter of Julius*, Caspar, *Geschichte des Papsttums* I, 152–154, observes: "Alles an ihm ist überkommenes Ideengut" (p. 154), which up to a point is true and, yet, at the same time, Caspar fails to do justice to the true originality of the letter—its new synthesis of the Church's original understanding of herself, made necessary in view of the attack on her nature by the Eusebians' theory and practice. This synthesis is new, not in the sense of the *novum* of the Eusebians—i.e., something foreign to the nature of the Church—but in the sense of a new insight into the original nature of the Church which was occasioned by the Eusebian attack on the same. Gessel, "Das primatiale Bewußtsein Julius' I," 70–71, admirably expressed this as follows: "Die Rechtfertigung des Athanasius zu Rom erfolgte also durch nichts anderes als durch die genaue Anwendung der kirchlichen Kanones. Genau das wollte Julius bis in die einzelnen Details seiner Darstellung der Untersuchung der römischen Synode beweisen. Daraus erhellt nicht nur das julische Bestreben, selbst gemäß den kirchlichen Bestimmungen vorgegangen zu sein und die Verfahrensweise der römischen Synode als kirchenrechtlich abgesichert darzustellen, sondern auch sein Anspruch, über die Einhaltung gesamtkirchlicher Bestimmungen zu wachen und diese authentisch zu interpretieren. Dieses so verstandene Wächteramt verpflichtet ihn, die korrekte Anwendung der Beschlüsse des Konzils von Nicäa zu garantieren. Seine Sorge gilt, allgemein ausgedrückt, der Bewahrung von Recht und Gerechtigkeit in der Kirche, die wiederum Grundlage der kirchlichen Ordnung ist. Diese Ordnung gewährleistet Frieden und Einheit in der Kirche.... Er wacht darüber, daß in der Kirche keine unbillige Neuerung eingeführt wird, die nicht aufgrund kirchlicher oder apostolischer Tradition gerechtfertigt werden kann."

he clearly speaks as the successor of St. Peter in defense of the Apostolic and "Catholic" (universal) nature of the Church, as witnessed to by the Petrine tradition preserved at Rome.

The question of Athanasius' influence on the composition of Julius' letter already partially answers the separate question, which is of primary interest to us, namely, Athanasius' own attitude to the contents of this letter. What is left unanswered is the important question as to the attitude of Athanasius to the formal character of the letter: the self-consciousness of Julius as successor to St. Peter and thus the final authority in the Church Universal in matters relating to the Church's authentic understanding of herself (i.e., what later became known as his teaching office, which function expresses itself here with regard to his "Teaching" on the correct legal procedures to be adopted in accordance with the Church's Apostolic nature and her truly ecclesiastical practice), and in matters relating to the universal binding force of synodal judgements (i.e., what later developed into his jurisdictional office, which function is in this letter lightly sketched in terms of his special right to examine the justice of synodal sentences passed on bishops, especially those holding Apostolic or Petrine Sees, and, if necessary, to take the initiative to do so and thus come to the aid of the "suffering brethren").

Our examination of Athanasius' appreciation of St. Peter and Mt 16,16–18 demonstrated that he shared the general view of Peter's unique role in the foundation of the Church as the spokesman of the Apostles and his divinely ordained journey to, and death in, Rome, which in the original *History* of Eusebius provided the theological justification for the recognized primacy of the Roman See. The action of Athanasius in having recourse to Rome, 339, could be said to indicate that the Bishop of Alexandria seems to have recognized the jurisdictional dimension of the Bishop of Rome's generally recognized unique authority. The way Athanasius incorporates the *Letter of Julius* into his *Apologia* (356), and the central role the *Letter of Julius* plays in it in order to demonstrate the ecclesiastical nature of his legal claim to the See of Alexandria, both confirm this conclusion. With regard to Athanasius' recognition of the final or universal "teaching" authority of the Bishop of Rome, attention may be drawn to a letter Athanasius wrote to his friend and aide in Egypt, Serapion of Thumis, probably to accompany the 12th *Festal Letter* for Easter, 340 (no longer extant), which letter was most likely written not long after his arrival in Rome, towards the end of the year 339, and is preserved in the Syriac collection of his *Festal Letters*. The 12th

Festal Letter apparently introduced a new liturgical practice into Egypt, the extension of the strict Paschal or Lenten Fast to cover the full forty days and not simply the six days of Holy Week, as had previously been the case.[306] What is of note is the reason Athanasius gives for this change that he introduced soon after his arrival in Rome: ". . . you should proclaim the fast of forty days to the brethren, and persuade them to fast, lest, *while all the world is fasting*, we in Egypt should be derided, as the only people who do not fast. . . ."[307] Thus it appears that, for Athanasius, the traditions preserved at Rome have universal application, which is surely the point of Julius' sentence: "Those things we have received from the Blessed Peter the Apostle, these things I also signify to you. I should not have written, as I assume these to be evident to all, had not these events alarmed us."

§8 The Sequel to the Synod of Rome: The Great Synod of Sardica, 343

The fundamental ecclesiological and canonical issues thrown up by the deposition of Athanasius at Tyre, 335, first perceived by the Bishop of Alexandria during his exile at Trier and articulated in various ways by him in his 10th *Festal Letter* (337), the *Encyclical Letter of the Synod of Alexandria* (338), and in his own *Encyclical* (339), were sifted and evaluated by Julius of Rome in his *4th Letter* (341), according to the norms of ecclesiastical practice which arose from the Apostolic nature of the Church and the divine law of justice. Julius' reply to the letter of the Eusebian-controlled Synod of Antioch, and to the argumentation found therein, based on their new understanding of the Church—which found its expression in the provincial synod as absolutely autonomous, superior to the individual bishop irrespective of the see he held but inferior to the emperor, and which was rooted both

---

[306] The fast of forty days was known previous to this, but, as Lauchert, *Leben*, 54–55, observed, it appears that the strict fast as such was confined to Holy Week, as the *Festal Letters* up to 339 seem to indicate. Lauchert, it should be pointed out, incorrectly dates the *Letter to Serapion* as though it accompanied the 11th *Festal Letter* for the year 341. The supposed reasons for the actual change in this liturgical practice, as given by Schwartz, *NGG* (1911), 502 (= *GS* III, 308), reflect his own prejudice concerning Athanasius and his "political" ambitions, and finds no support in the text of the letter itself. However, Bardy, *Saint Athanase*, 75, accepts the suggestion of Schwartz.

[307] *Festal Letter* XII, Robertson, *Athanasius*, LNPF², 538 (translation by Payne-Smith).

in a one-sided, radicalized interpretation of the history of the Antiochene Church and in the *identity* of the Church with the (Christian) Empire—was clear and firm: that new understanding was a *novum*, foreign to the Apostolic Tradition, i.e., foreign to an understanding of the office of bishop and the function of the synod, based on their Apostolic nature and foreign to the universal (or Catholic) nature of the Church, whose final authority is Petrine and centered on Rome. Expressed in simple terms, the Bishop of Rome rejects the Imperial Church of the two Eusebii and calls on the Synod of Antioch to return to procedures which are based on the Apostolicity and Catholicity of the Church.

But though Julius in effect anathematized the new institution of the Imperial Church, this did not mean that he, or the Bishop of Alexandria, had any intention of attempting to turn the tide of history by ignoring the changed relationship of the empire to the Church which Constantine had inaugurated. As we will see, they respected the benevolence of the emperor and the new (material and legal) opportunities he afforded the Church to fulfil her mission. They did not refuse to seek the cooperation of the "Christian" Emperor—provided he did not interfere directly in the internal affairs of the Church, and they rejected categorically, as we have seen, any attempt (theoretical or practical) to *identify* the Church with the empire, which identity in effect meant the subordination of the Church to the imperial authority. It should also be clear by now that this *novum* of the Imperial Church was not characterized solely by its attempt to absorb the Church into the empire but also by its new principle concerning the absolute autonomy of provincial synods. One could go so far as to say that this second element is the primary characteristic of their Imperial Church, as the letter of the Eusebian-controlled Orientals, and Julius' reply, have shown—which element, though prepared by the unique events which marked the history of the Church of Antioch for a period of over sixty-five years prior to Tyre (335), received its ultimate form due to the way Eusebius of Caesarea and his namesake of Nicomedia (and later Constantinople) interpreted the new relationship of the Church to the empire. It is important to remember that the actual manifestation of the Imperial Church, so clearly rejected by Athanasius and Julius, was this new "institutionalized" synodal structure with its implicit subordination of the Church to the imperial authority, created by a small but influential party *within* the Church, which represented *their interpretation* (and manipulation) of the new situation of the Church after the Great Persecution: it quite obviously was not the new benevolent attitude of the emperor as such.

On the other hand, the rediscovery, as it were, of the Apostolic nature of the Church cannot be adequately described in terms of the reaffirmation of the freedom of the Church. The Apostolic nature of the Church is, at the same time, both more and less than the simple freedom of the Church from the control of the emperor, though such freedom is the necessary condition for her adherence to the truth.[308] It is more insofar as the nature of the Church is not negatively conceived simply in terms of freedom from external interference but is rather understood to be determined by its own internal structure given to her by God from the very beginning of her existence (= "Apostolic") in order to fulfil her Apostolic mission with regard to the redemption of all mankind and all creation. Thus, the authority that accrues to the Apostolic nature of the Church—her Apostolic Authority—is not only necessarily and intrinsically independent of (and thus, free from) all created authority, such as the imperial or civil authority, but is superior to all, as is demanded both by its origin and its mission. The Apostolic nature of the Church is, however, less than that simple freedom of the Church which would conceive the Church as neither of the world nor in the world. The extent of the Church's freedom that flows from her Apostolic nature is in a sense "limited" to the Apostolic mission of the Church and does not "free" her members from the obligations which arise from the created order in which she fulfils her mission, or from the legitimate political authorities that rule the society in which she operates (cf. 1 Tim 2,2; 1 Pet 2,3–16).

The failure to distinguish on the one hand between the attitude to the emperor as such on the part of the orthodox (e.g., Julius and Athanasius), and on the other, their attitude to the *novum* of the Eusebian *Reichskirche*, has naturally resulted in the misinterpretation of the actions and writings of Athanasius. Berkhof maintains, e.g., that even in 335, Athanasius appealed to the emperor while his indignation in 339 was not so much directed against the civil intervention as such, but rather against the fact that the power of the State gave its support to his enemies; it was only in the late fifties (= *Historia Arianorum*)—so Berkhof—that Athanasius clearly rejects the attempt of the State to intervene in Church affairs and affirms the necessity of the freedom of the Church.[309] Hagel claimed to have been able to distinguish four different stages in the attitude of Athanasius to the "emperor:" (i) under Constantine

---

[308] See Berkhof, Kirche und Kaiser, 133, whose study is marred by an overemphasis on the separation between Church and State as the ideal that was first worked out by "western" theologians (including Athanasius) in the fourth century.

[309] Berkhof, *Kirche und Kaiser*, 133–135.

the Great, Athanasius subordinated himself and the other ecclesiastical institutions under the jurisdiction of the emperor; (ii) Tyre caused
him to doubt this arrangement and so this second period is characterized by uncertain criticism of the emperor—during which time, Julius of
Rome tried zealously, by championing his person and cause, to implicate
Athanasius in his own papal ambitions; (iii) seeing the danger posed by
his "protector," Julius, Athanasius now develops "seine geniale Theorie
von der freien Kirche unter dem Schutz des Kaisers," according to which
the rights of both Church and emperor are clearly delineated, which
theory Athanasius (iv) finally abandoned under Constantius when he
demanded the complete separation of Church and Empire.[310] A modified
version of this interpretation is found, e.g., in Setton.[311] We have already
seen how the details of these interpretations fail to find support in either
the writings or the actions of Athanasius. Here it will suffice to point to
our, as yet incomplete, analysis of Athanasius' reaction under Constantius
in order to determine their lack of credibility. It was under Constantius
II (356) that in the composition of the dual legal defense—*Apologia* and
Ad Constantium—Athanasius distinguished most clearly between the
two jurisdictional spheres, acknowledging in the ecclesiastical sphere the
central position of the Bishop of Rome, and in the civil sphere, the rights
and obligations of the imperial authority to give civil effect to genuine
ecclesiastical judgements. But behind this clarity is not a theory relating
to the freedom of the Church but the affirmation of her *Apostolic* nature
in the face of the Eusebian effort to replace it with the imperial authority.
This affirmation was already implicit in Athanasius' reply to the emperor
at the beginning of his episcopacy, when he refused to admit Arius to communion on the order of Constantine the Great; in the year 337, it became
explicit for the first time in the 10th *Festal Letter*. Having first affirmed
the Apostolic nature of the Church, Athanasius then went on to reject the
Eusebian innovation of the Imperial Church (338–339).

Girardet, commenting on the actions of Julius and Athanasius
after the Synod of Rome, to which we must now give our attention, observed that since Constans, the Western emperor, had
clearly sided with the "Anti-Arian" party, the Bishops of Rome
and Alexandria found it easier to modify their earlier rejection
of the *reichskirchliche Gerichtsbarkeit*: ". . . und zwar dahingehend

---

[310]   Hagel, *Kirche und Kaisertum*, especially p. IV.
[311]   Setton, *Christian Attitude Towards the Emperor*, 71–108.

zu modifizieren, daß die 'Rechtgläubigkeit' des Kaisers und seine Haltung gegenüber Athanasius selbst zum Maßstab für die Beurteilung der kaiserlichen Synodalgewalt wird."[312]

Here, as we will see, the failure to distinguish between the *Reichskirche* as the *novum* of the Eusebians, and the legitimate *external* relationship of Church and Empire, in particular that between the ecclesiastically constituted synod and the imperial authority, has, in my opinion, resulted in a rather distorted view of the actual historical situation.

When, in 338, the Eusebians began their new maneuvers to have the deposition of Athanasius at Tyre legally recognized by securing the *Letters of Communion* from Julius of Rome for their successor to the See of Mark, Pistos, they wrote not only to the Bishop of Rome but also to all three rulers:[313] Constantine II, Constans, and Constantius II, among whom the empire was partitioned out[314] after the death of their father Constantine the Great on May 22, 337. These letters have received far less attention than they deserve, though they form, as it were, the backdrop to the entire second exile of Athanasius and in particular the Synod of Sardica. From the first three paragraphs of the *Letter of the Synod of Alexandria,* 338 (*Apol.* 3–6), we gather how important the synod considered the Eusebian letters to the three emperors and how vehemently they repudiate the charges they contain, before the Fathers take up (and answer) the indictments brought against Athanasius at Tyre, which led to his deposition and exile to Trier, and which they maintain were part of an Eusebian conspiracy.

After the eldest of Constantine's sons, Constantine II, granted Athanasius permission to return to his homeland from his exile in Trier, June 17, 337,[315] the Bishop of Alexandria did not immediately set out for Egypt. Though the political situation was still unclear,[316] Constantius, to whom his father Constantine had (335) allotted the entire East (including Egypt), was evidently in control there as Caesar, and so Athanasius needed his approval before he could return to Alexandria. All three Caesars came together at Pannonia and were proclaimed Augusti on September 9, 337.[317]

---

[312] Girardet, *Kaisergericht und Bischofsgericht,* 107.

[313] Cf. *Letter of Synod of Alexandria* (338) = *Apol.* 3,5–7 (Opitz 89,19–90,15); *Hist. Arian.* 9,1 (Opitz 188,3–5), where, however, only Constantine II and Constans are mentioned (see below); *Ad Const.* 4 (*SC* 56, Szymusiak, 92).

[314] See Schwartz, *NGG* (1911), 469–472 (= *GS* III, 265–269).

[315] *Apol.* 87,4–7 (Opitz 166,11–29).

[316] See reference in footnote 314.

[317] Cf. Schwartz, *NGG* (1911), 471 (= *GS* III, 268).

Around this time, most probably shortly before the imperial conference, Athanasius met Constantius II at Viminacium (Upper Moesia) as well as after the conference, i.e., once again at Caesarea in Cappadocia,[318] before he arrived triumphant in Alexandria on 27

---

[318] Cf. *Ad Const.* 5 (*SC* 56, Szymusiak, 93). Cf. Rogala, *Anfänge*, 107, who reports that he journeyed through the Danube valley. The question of the return of Athanasius from his first exile, and in particular its chronology, are discussed in detail by Baynes in his article, "Athanasiana," 65–69. Baynes draws on the imperial history of the time in order to reconstruct the events associated with the return of Athanasius, and comes to the conclusion that the bishop arrived in Alexandria not in the year 337 (as held by the majority of scholars, such as Gwatkin, *Studies*, note CC, 140–141; Lietzmann, "Chronologie," 251–259; Lauchert, *Leben*, 49; Bardy, *Saint Athanase*, 51–56), but on November 23, 338 (cf. also Seeck, *Regesten*, 186). However enlightening his use of imperial history undoubtedly is in order to sketch in the background to the return journey, yet he opts for the year 338 instead of the previous year primarily on the basis of his contention that Athanasius could not have reached Alexandria in November of the same year as the meeting of the three sons of Constantine in "Paeonia," early in September 337, and still have had the time needed to commit all the outrages, of which the Eusebians at Sardica accused him; further, Baynes adduces the fact that the *Festal Letter* for 338 was written during the return journey and not in Alexandria in December 337 as further proof that Athanasius could not have reached Alexandria in 337. But the composition of the *Festal Letter* on his return journey simply demonstrates that Athanasius, unsure of how long it would take him to get the permission of Constantius and arrive back in Alexandria, took no chances and so wrote his letter in advance: when he arrived in Alexandria, he most likely had neither the time or inclination to rewrite it—an exercise that was foreign to his direct and decisive nature. With regard to the accusations of the Eusebians at Sardica, these I find completely untrustworthy (see also Rogala, *Anfänge*, 104) and the similar accusations voiced in the Meletian papyrus, discovered by Bell, cannot be considered as in any way confirmatory. (With regard to Athanasius' apparent silence—and thus implicit admission of guilt—Baynes ignores the explicit denial of such charges by Athanasius and the Synod of Alexandria, 338, and fails to recognize that such charges, since they were of a civil nature, had no place in the other documents preserved in the *Apologia*. He also ignores the fact that Athanasius challenged his accusers to prove these charges before Emperor Constantius in Antioch, 346.) If we posit that Athanasius met the Caesar Constantius before the meeting of the three sons of Constantine early in September, and met the Emperor Constantius in Caesarea (in order to confirm that which has been agreed before in Viminacium before he was declared emperor), then he had sufficient time to reach Alexandria by November 23—i.e., almost three months. Further, once Eusebius of Nicomedia had gained the confidence of Constantius early in the year 338, and once the new accusations of a civil nature were brought before the three emperors at the Synod of Constantinople that same year, it is unlikely that Constantius would have granted Athanasius permission to return to Alexandria, and thus the second meeting between the emperor and the bishop at Caesarea in Cappadocia could not have taken place in 338.

of Athyr (November 23), 337.[319] We possess no details about these meetings with Emperor Constantius II—only the mere fact of their occurrence. However, it seems reasonable to conclude that they were sought by Athanasius with the purpose of securing the approval of the Eastern emperor for his return from the exile imposed on him by his father, the late emperor. Constantius had not yet come under the influence of Eusebius of Nicomedia.

But the bishop of the imperial city of Nicomedia (whose close ties to the court go back to the reign of Licinius) soon ingratiated himself with the young emperor. Early in the year 338, if not earlier,[320] Eusebius was, according to Socrates, declared (ἀναδείκυσι) Bishop of Constantinople by Constantius.[321] Though the historian's mode of expression is most likely anachronistic, it is clear that the role played by the emperor in this translation of Eusebius cannot have been insignificant. Enthroned in the new capital of the (Christian) Empire, Eusebius assembled the Synod of Constantinople that elected Pistos to replace Athanasius in Alexandria, and sent a delegation to Rome to secure the *Letter of Communion* for Pistos. It was the same synod that also wrote to the three Augusti, as just mentioned. Schwartz has suggested that the letter of the Synod was only ostensibly addressed to all three emperors,[322] but was in truth intended only for Constantius. The documentary evidence would suggest that perhaps the very opposite was the case. That Constans, at least, received a copy of the letter, is clearly witnessed to in *Ad Constantium* 4,[323] while in the *Historia Arianorum,* Athanasius informs us that Eusebius and his party wrote to Constantine and Constans—and fails to mention Constantius.[324]

---

[319] *Festal Index* X; see Schwartz, *NGG* (1911), 473 (= *GS* III, 270).

[320] Cf. Schwartz, *NGG* (1911), 479 (= *GS* III, 278).

[321] Socrates, *HE* 2,7,2 (Hussey 188).

[322] Schwartz, *NGG* (1911), 480 (= *GS* III, 279).

[323] Τῷ ἀδελφῷ σου οὐκ ἔγραψα, ἢ μόνον ὅτε οἱ περὶ Εὐσέβιον ἔγραψαν αὐτῷ κατ᾽ ἐμοῦ, καὶ ἀνάγκην ἔσχον ἔτι ἐν τῇ Ἀλεξανδρείᾳ ἀπολογήσασθαι (Szymusiak 92).

[324] *Hist. Arian.* 9,1 (Opitz 188,3–5). Schwartz's comment on this text (*NGG* [1911], 480 = *GS* III, 279, note 2) to the effect that Athanasius only mentioned the two emperors before whom he defended himself does not exactly correspond to the content of the text: Athanasius names those emperors who accepted the defense of his delegates. The fact that he does not mention Constantius cannot be so interpreted to mean: "Er hütete sich wohl, sich an Konstantius zu wenden." The latter observation is out of place at this early stage of Constantius' career, at the most, six months after their last meeting at Caesarea in Cappadocia, where Constantius graciously received Athanasius, and their conversation was free from any controversy (cf. *Ad Const.* 5); even as late as 356, as we saw, Athanasius attempted to plead his case personally before the said emperor.

The contents of the letter are relatively easy to reconstruct from the way the Synodal Fathers at Alexandria refer to it in their *encyclical* of the year 338. The Eusebian letters to the three emperors accused Athanasius of violence and murder on his return to Alexandria the previous year,[325] and of selling the corn set aside by Constantine for the support of certain widows and appropriating the profits for himself;[326] it also contained a list of charges which resulted in his deposition at Tyre, 335 (and his exile to Trier). The list of indictments brought against Athanasius at Tyre was probably mentioned only in connection with the announcement of the newly appointed Pistos. The emphasis in the letter to the three Augusti was clearly on the two new charges—both of a civil nature, and both of which, if proved, would have secured the death penalty for the "deposed" Athanasius, or at least his exile,[327] which was the final object of the letter. Since Constantine the Younger had initially granted Athanasius an amnesty, then it is likely that he was one of the main addressees of the letter, if not the principal recipient; Constantius had probably already been convinced of Athanasius' undesirability by Eusebius, while Constans had at the time no connection whatever with Athanasius.

The Eusebian party were not satisfied with their formal appointment of a successor to Athanasius; as we have seen, they expected Julius of Rome to give his blind approval. Their major problem now was to have Athanasius physically removed from Alexandria, and to achieve this they composed their letters to the three emperors, reminding them of the judgement of Tyre and the indictments brought against Athanasius there, and produced two fresh accusations which carried the death penalty (and did not call for a revision of Tyre or the amnesty of either Constantine II or Constantius II). Athanasius reacted as he had previously done when accused before the emperor by the Meletians: he sent delegates to the emperors—at the same time as he sent delegates to Julius of Rome—who were able to convince the two Western emperors, but

---

[325] Cf. *Apol.* 5,1–5 (Opitz 90,41–91,32).

[326] Cf. *Apol.* 18,1–4 (Opitz 100,25–101,3). Schwartz, regrettably, ignores this most important point completely.

[327] The emphasis in the two new charges is also indicated by the position they secure in the *Encyclical of the Synod of Alexandria*: at the very opening of that letter, and at the end of the actual defense of Athanasius, i.e., providing the framework of the letter where Athanasius and the Egyptian bishops highlight the object of the *Letters of the Eusebians*: to secure the death or, at the very least, the exile of Athanasius (cf. *Apol.* 3,7–4,1 = Opitz 90,15–21; *Apol.* 18,1 = Opitz 100,25–27).

failed, apparently, to win over Constantius.[328] When Julius of Rome unexpectedly called for a synod to reexamine the sentence of Tyre, the Eusebians rushed to Antioch, where Constantius had established his winter quarters, and set up their famous permanent synod there, the first act of which was to appoint a new candidate for the See of Alexandria (Gregory) to replace the obviously unsuitable Pistos. They sent Gregory to Alexandria accompanied by Philagrius and an imperial guard; Gregory's appointment was proclaimed by means of an imperial edict.

After the Alexandrian delegation had convinced the two Western emperors, one of them (Constans), at least, wrote to Athanasius. However, the only thing we know about this letter is that it included a request for Athanasius to send him bound volumes of the Sacred Scriptures.[329] When Athanasius departed for Rome in 339, as he insists in his *Letter of Defense to Constantius* (in the year 356), his object was the Church of Rome and not Constans,[330] now sole emperor in the West, whom he first met personally almost four years after the correspondence with him, which the Eusebian party had necessitated,[331] i.e., three years after his arrival in Rome. With Gregory enthroned in Alexandria and Athanasius "exiled" in Rome, the Eusebians had achieved their objective. They ignored the summons of Julius to the Roman synod and only reacted when the Bishop of Rome granted Athanasius, Marcellus, and the other Oriental bishops his communion and restored them to their sees. We have considered in detail the first part of their violent reaction, which was their famous letter to Julius. We have also mentioned in passing the second element: they had evidently succeeded in getting Constantius to threaten Athanasius with the death penalty

---

[328] Cf. *Hist. Arian.* 9,1 (Opitz 188,5–6). See above, footnote 324.

[329] Cf. *Ad Const.* 4 (Szymusiak 92).

[330] Cf. *Ad Const.* 4 (Szymusiak 92).

[331] Girardet, *Kaisergericht und Bischofsgericht*, 108, correctly insists that the reference in *Ad Const.* 4 refers to the correspondence between Athanasius and Constans, which took place while the former was still in Alexandria (338) and not to Athanasius' arrival in Rome (339), as Hess (*Canons of Sardica,* 142) assumes (likewise Lauchert, *Leben*, 55). However, the computation of the date by Girardet cannot be accepted: if the said correspondence took place in 338 (occupying most of the year) and if Constans, after three years had elapsed, called Athanasius to Milan within the fourth year, as the text states (Τριῶν τοίνυν ἐτῶν παρελθόντων, τῷ ἐνιαυτῷ γράφει κελεύσας ἀπαντῆσαί με πρὸς αὐτόν ... [*Ad Const.* 4]), then the meeting between bishop and emperor took place not in 341, as Girardet states, but early in 342. Schwartz (*NGG*, 1911, 516 = GS III, 326) also seems to posit 342; Seeck, *Regesten*, 191, places Athanasius' audience before Constans sometime around the beginning of December 342, which is too late in the year.

on the charge of selling the corn reserved for widows and appropriating the proceeds for himself.[332] We will return to this shortly. What we have not mentioned is the reaction to the decision of the Synod and Bishop of Rome to grant Marcellus communion, namely, the *Dedication Synod at Antioch* in the summer of 341. This synod, which need not take up too much of our attention here, was not occasioned by the *4th Letter of Julius* (i.e., his reply to the Eusebian letter) as is generally assumed,[333] but by that part of the *3rd Letter of Julius* which communicated the decision of the Synod of Rome (340) to receive Marcellus into communion. The Synod of the Dedication at Antioch assembled around the same time as the second session of the Synod of Rome, which Julius assembled to consider the Eusebian letter, i.e., around the middle of the year 341,[334] and devoted itself exclusively to drawing up a credal formula to counteract the opinions of Marcellus of Ancyra;[335] the case of Athanasius was, apparently, not even mentioned.[336] With this synod, the Christological controversies—dormant since Nicaea, 325—are again brought into the open, not with regard to the Arian

---

[332] See above, footnote 168.

[333] See, e.g., Schwartz, *NGG* (1911), 505 (= *GS* III, 311); more recently Girardet, *Kaisergericht und Bischofsgericht*, 108; Simonetti, *La Crisi Ariana*, 153f.

[334] Regarding the date of the Dedication Synod, see Schwartz, *NGG* (1911), 504 (= *GS* III, 310, note 1). The date of the reassembled Synod of Rome can be ascertained as follows: Julius (*Apol.* 21) informs us that, after he received the Eusebian letter from his delegates, Elpidius and Philoxenus, i.e., late February 341 (at the earliest), he kept the contents to himself in the hope that a delegation from Antioch would arrive to discuss its contents. Once it was clear that no one would come, Julius then recalled Athanasius and reassembled the synod; this means that the synod could not have taken place before early summer of 341 (see also footnote 337).

[335] See Schwartz, *NGG* (1911), 505–510 (= *GS* III, 311–318) for an analysis of the three Creeds actually approved by the synod. Schwartz clearly demonstrates that the prime target of the Synodal Fathers was the teaching of Marcellus of Ancyra. See also Kelly, *Creeds*, 263–274, who is skeptical of Athanasius' interpretation; Bardy, *Saint Athanase*, 77; Caspar, *Geschichte des Papsttums* I, 154–155; Jalland, *Church and Papacy*, 217. See especially Simonetti, *La Crisi Ariana*, 154–160, who maintains that the synod was anti-Nicaean as well as rejected the Monarchian theology of Sabellius and Marcellus of Ancyra; the synod, he claims, tried to find an "intermediate" position between Arius and Nicaea.

[336] Against Batiffol, *La paix constantinienne*, 430–431; Bardy, *Saint Athanase*, 77. This misunderstanding (which arises naturally from the assumption that the Synod of Antioch replied to the *4th Letter of Julius*) also led the ancient historians, Socrates and Sozomen, to confuse the Synod of Antioch, 338/39, which elected Gregory to succeed Athanasius with the Dedication Synod of 341 (see Schwartz reference given in footnote 334). Once one removes the reference to the former synod (Socrates, *HE* 2,8,6–2,10,1 = Hussey 190–193; Sozomen, *HE* 3,5,3–4 = Bidez-Hansen 105,24–106,8), the remaining texts relating to Antioch (341) do not mention Athanasius.

tenets (at least ostensibly) but, in the first place, in opposition to the heresy of Marcellus.[337] Nicaea is not explicitly attacked, it is ignored.

It is the second element of the Eusebian reaction that is of interest to us at the moment. When Elpidius and Philoxenus, the Roman delegates sent to Antioch to announce the date of the proposed Synod of Rome, arrived back in Rome early in the year 341 with the letter containing the legal objections of the Eusebians to the admittance of Athanasius and the other Orientals to communion, they also brought news of the emperor's threat to impose the death penalty on Athanasius for misappropriation of the corn supply for widows in Alexandria.[338] It is of note that the first charge brought against him in the Eusebian letter to the three Augusti, that concerning the violence he was alleged to have caused on his return from his first exile, has been in effect abandoned.[339] It is the second of the new indictments that has been revived. The *4th Letter of Julius* makes no express mention of this accusation—it was of a purely civil nature and so had no place in his letter—although it is probable, it seems to me, that he alluded to it on one occasion. The Bishop of Rome accused the Eusebian-controlled Orientals of inconsistencies in their letters against Athanasius, even to the point of contradiction.[340] It is possible that Julius here refers to the inconsistency between the accusation brought by the Eusebians before Constantine (after Tyre, 335), that "Athanasius

---

[337] The bishops at the Dedication Synod, however, do protest against being called "followers of Arius" and claim that they had examined his faith and found that it accorded with the Faith which they had received "from the beginning" (*De syn.* 22,3–4 = 248,31f.), just as the Synod of Rome had claimed, presumably, with regard to the faith of Marcellus. It may be added that the Dedication Synod here practices in a sense a type of "reexamination" of the decisions of Nicaea with regard to Arius' teaching—in contradiction to their declared policy regarding the scrutiny of synodal judgements: had they received Julius' *4th Letter,* they might have avoided such an admission (*De syn.* 22,3–4 = Opitz 248,29–32). Cf., by comparison, the *Letter of the Synod of Jerusalem,* 335, in which the same bishops affirm that they admitted Arius into communion on the *emperor's* witness to their orthodoxy (*De syn.* 21,4 = Opitz 248,2–6). Jalland, *Church and Papacy,* 217–218, confuses these two documents.

[338] Cf. Socrates, *HE* 2,17,1–3 (Hussey 213). Also, Sozomen, *HE* 3,9,5 (BidezHansen 112,24–28).

[339] This was refuted by the *Letter of the Synod of Alexandria,* 338 = *Apol.* 5,4 (Opitz 91,13–31). Though Sozomen, *HE*, does mention the charge of violence, he makes it clear that the principal charge against Athanasius was that concerning the corn.

[340] Cf. *Letter of Julius* = *Apol.* 27,2 (Opitz 107,5–9).

threatened to hinder the shipment of corn from Alexandria to (the emperor's) home city (= Constantinople),"[341] and the new charge, raised in their letter to the three Augusti, 338, of "selling all the corn (given by the father of the emperors for the sustenance of the widowed) and appropriating the gains for his own ends."[342] As we saw above, this last indictment was very much a live issue in the year 341, when Julius wrote his *4th Letter*, since his delegates to the permanent Synod of Antioch returned to Rome with the news that Constantius II was again threatening Athanasius with the death penalty on its account, for which reason Athanasius went into hiding until he was recalled to Rome for the reassembly of the Synod of Rome which resulted in Julius' reply to the Eusebians.

In any event, though the actual Synod of Rome (340) had granted Athanasius the necessary communion and so recognized his right to the See of Alexandria, and the second session followed this up with a rejection of the legal objections raised by the Eusebian-controlled Synod of Antioch, a major problem remained: the possibility of Athanasius' actual return to his see. Not only did Constantius support the "antipope" in Alexandria and the Eusebian party at Antioch, but he had apparently given credence to the new Eusebian charge of a civil nature with regard to the sale of corn in Alexandria and had threatened Athanasius with the death penalty despite the recognition he found at the Synod of Rome. Athanasius could not return to Alexandria until such time as Constantius gave him permission to do so.

The first attempt to secure this permission seems to me to have been made in connection with Julius' reply to the Eusebians. Athanasius informs us in the *Apologia* that Julius sent this (his *4th Letter*) to the Eusebians not by means of Roman presbyters, as was the case with the *3rd Letter,* but "by means of Gabianus the Comes."[343] No attempt has been made to explain this strange fact, as far as I know. Indeed, it is not the only puzzle connected with the *4th Letter of Julius*. The reception of that letter by the Eastern bishops at Antioch has not, as yet, been satisfactorily explained or even examined.[344]

After Sozomen describes the contents of Julius' letter, he continues: "All these reasons convinced [Julius] of the need to come to

---

[341] *Apol.* 87,1 (Opitz 166,3–4).

[342] *Letter of Synod of Alexandria = Apol.* 18,2 (Opitz 100,31–32).

[343] *Apol.* 20,3 (Opitz 102,11).

[344] Joannou's assumption that the Synod of Antioch (341) was the reply of the Eusebians to the *Letter of Julius* (see pp. 71–77) has been shown above to be untenable.

the rescue of Athanasius and Paul [of Constantinople]; for the latter, who had arrived in Italy not long previously, had lamented bitterly the accusations against him. When, for the said reasons, he [Julius] had written about them [Athanasius and Paul] to the priests in the East and accomplished nothing, he made the indictments against them known to the Emperor Constans. He then wrote to the Emperor Constantius, his brother, to send some bishops of the East to defend their deposition of [Athanasius and Paul]."[345] The chronology of Sozomen, not too good at its best, is here hopelessly confused. Further, he has given a false emphasis to the role played by Paul of Constantinople in the dispute, due possibly to the expected interest of his audience at Constantinople in the first bishop of the new imperial capital, or more likely due to the false information at his disposal;[346] Paul's name does not even occur in the *Letter of Julius*. The two personalities mentioned by name are Athanasius and Marcellus, the second of whom Sozomen (or the source he uses) tendentiously ignores, probably due to Marcellus' heretical tenets. Despite the chronological confusion (e.g., Paul of Constantinople arrived in Rome probably around the same time as Athanasius, i.e., at the end of the year 339 and not a short while previous to Julius' letter written in the middle of 341), and the false substitution of Paul for Marcellus, Sozomen seems to report a fact based on independent evidence, namely that Julius informed Constans about the issues raised in the letter.[347] Sozomen, though his chronology and interpretation may be faulty, does not invent those facts he relates and interprets. His interpretation of the *reason* why Julius contacted Constans is, however, interesting: it was that the *4th Letter* "accomplished nothing." This was probably prompted by the fact that Sozomen could find no trace of the expected, immediate reaction on the part of the Oriental bishops. Considering the fact that Julius sent his letter "by means of Gabianus the Comes," as Athanasius tells us, and the fact that Julius evidently informed Constans of its contents, it seems likely to me that the Bishop of Rome sent his letter to the East *via* Constans, who at the time was apparently in Italy.[348] Julius' reason for doing

---

[345] Sozomen, *HE* 3,10,3 (Bidez-Hansen 113,9–14).

[346] See footnote 352 below.

[347] Athanasius simply informs us in very general terms that Constans and Constantius learned about the disturbances in various Churches caused by the Eusebians (*Apol.* 36,1 = Opitz 114,1–3 and about the decisions of the Synod of Rome (*Hist. Arian.* 15,2 = Opitz 190,8–10).

[348] Cf. Sozomen, *HE* 3,10,5 (Bidez-Hansen 113,17), who reports that the Antiochene bishops, sent by Constantius in reply to his brother's request, arrived in Italy. But Athanasius reports that the Eastern delegates met Constans in

so was obviously to secure the help of the Western emperor which would enable Athanasius, the legitimate claimant to the See of Alexandria according to ecclesiastical law, to return to his city.[349] Three years previously, Constans, together with Constantine II, had dismissed the new charges of a civil nature brought against Athanasius by the Eusebians in their letters to the three Augusti, which indictments his brother Constantius now upheld in order to threaten Athanasius with the death penalty. Since April 340, Constans was sole ruler in the West. It was obvious that he alone could persuade his brother to drop the civil charges, to which he himself did not give credence, and to urge Constantius to recognize the judgement of the Bishop and Synod of Rome regarding the legitimate Bishop of Alexandria. Julius had another reason to enlist the aid of Constans: the danger to peace between the Eastern and Western parts of the empire caused by the threatened schism of the Eusebian-controlled Oriental bishops who had the backing of Constantius.

But Constans did not apparently respond as Julius might have hoped. He must have been aware of a potentially explosive situation. A schism within the Church menaced the political relations between East and West. His brother emperor clearly supported the Eusebian-controlled Orientals, while he himself had previously opted for one of the opposing parties who had meanwhile found support in the West and was now expected to interfere on their behalf. He was at the time but newly in control of the West and was himself about to engage in a campaign against the Franks, and thus could not risk either enmity with his brother nor internal trouble with the Western bishops. He reacted not unlike the way his father had done in the wake of Tyre, and requested his brother to send representatives from the East to explain their stand,[350] while

Gaul (*De syn.* 25,1 = Opitz 250,26). It is likely that the independent evidence used by Sozomen (see footnote 352) referred to Italy as the location of the Western emperor at the time he sent his request to his brother and that he thus (incorrectly) assumed Italy to be the same location for the meeting between Constans and the bishops from Antioch. According to Seeck, *Regesten*, 191, Constans was in Lauriacum (Noricum) on June 24. It is possible that he was at Aquileia or Milan at the time Gabianus conveyed Julius' *letter* to him.

[349] Cf. Sozomen, *HE* 3,11,3 (Bidez-Hansen 114,11–12).

[350] See above, footnote 345; also Socrates, *HE* 2,18,1 (Hussey 216); Schwartz, *NGG* (1911), 513 (= *GS* III, 322–323) claims ". . . daß Konstans die orientalischen Bischöfe zitiert, um sich wegen der Absetzung des Athanasius zu rechtfertigen, ist ein staatsrechtliches Monstrum." But Schwartz ignores the broader context of issues involving Athanasius (the civil charges brought against him) as does Girardet, *Kaisergericht und Bischofsgericht*, 109, who, however, does consider the civil consequences which arose from the Synod of

he also, probably at the same time, sent to Rome for representatives from there.[351] It is even possible that he did not, at this stage, forward the *4th Letter of Julius* so as to avoid appearing to take sides. He moved, apparently, with extreme caution so as not to offend either party—at least initially.

A few months after the Synod of Dedication, i.e., around September 341, the Eusebians dispatched their delegates to Constans: Narcissus of Neronias, Maris of Chalcedon, Theodore of Heraclea, and Marcus of Arethusa.[352] At Trier, they refused to enter deliberations with the representatives of Julius,[353] who were sent to uphold the

Rome, though his interpretation is also unacceptable: there is no evidence that Constans, at this stage, "demanded" any action of his brother apart from requesting him to send delegates from Antioch. Neither did he "cite" the Eastern bishops, as Schwartz maintains. Schwartz's reconstruction of the events (primarily on the basis of his own invalid presuppositions) that led to the convocation of the Synod of Sardica (*NGG*, 1911, 514 = *GS* III, 322) is unconvincing. The reconstruction suggested here attempts to take into consideration all of the evidence available, though the evidence is admittedly not unambiguous. And yet, as will be shown, the evidence is not as confused or valueless as, e.g., de Clercq, *Ossius of Cordova*, 306–311, seems to suggest—provided one attempts to establish its correct chronological sequence. Without such indications, de Clercq is thus forced to such unacceptable conclusions as e.g., his statement that the Eastern mission to Constans was unsolicited (p. 307). The reconstruction offered by Girardet is based on a chronology that is untenable: see below, footnote 361. The interpretation made by Joannou, *Die Ostkirche und die Cathedra Petri*, 78–79, is built upon the assumption (which, as was pointed out above, we do not accept) that the Canons of Antioch were drawn up at the Synod of the Dedication (341).

[351] Socrates, *HE* 2,18,2 (Hussey 216), reports that when the Eusebian delegates arrived (at the Court of Constans at Trier), "they in no way admitted the Athanasian party to enter into discussions (with them)." This clearly presupposes that a delegation was present to represent the case of Athanasius. The Bishop of Alexandria, having been summoned to Milan to meet Constans (for the first time) and having enquired about the reason for such a meeting, informs us "I learned that certain bishops had gone up (to Constans) and requested him to write to Your Piety (= Constantius) so that a synod might take place" (*Ad Const.* 4 = Szymusiak 92). See also Joannou, *Die Ostkirche und die Cathedra Petri*, 80. See Siminotti, *La Crisi Ariana*, 163f., for a discussion of the credal formula presented to Constans by the Eusebians.

[352] Cf. *De syn.* 25,1 (Opitz 250,25–27). See Schwartz, *NGG* (1911), 513 (= *GS* III, 322). Socrates, *HE* 2,18,1 (Hussey 216), and Sozomen, *HE* 3,10,4 (Bidez-Hansen 113,15–17), clearly draw on independent source material (they both confuse Paul of Constantinople with Marcellus and mention *three* bishops, though Socrates corrects his account on the basis of Athanasius' *De syn.* 25,1).

[353] See above, footnote 351. It may be observed that the "Athanasian party" mentioned by Socrates does not necessarily reply that they were sent by Athanasius himself. Athanasius in fact protests that he knew nothing of the delegation to Constans (*Ad Const.* 4).

decision of Rome with regard to Athanasius and Marcellus. Later, the "Eusebian" party at Sardica claimed that Maximin, the Bishop of Trier and friend of Athanasius since the latter's exile on the banks of the Mosel, refused to receive the Eusebians.[354] Though this is not improbable, yet it is more likely that neither party was anxious to enter into communion with the other and so retained their distance. Socrates insists that at this stage there was no official break in the communion between East and West.[355] In any event, the Eusebian delegates achieved nothing and departed Trier, probably at the end of 341.[356]

It was probably after the departure of the Eastern delegates that the Roman delegates, together with Maximin of Trier, persuaded Constans to arrange for the assembly of an "oecumenical" synod (along the lines of Nicaea) at a neutral city on the borders of the Eastern and Western parts of the empire, at Sardica.[357] This must have occurred early in 342, after Constans had peacefully settled his affairs with the Franks.[358] According to Sabinus, as preserved by Socrates, the Eusebian-controlled Orientals pointed to Julius as the one finally responsible for convening the synod.[359] Julius had proposed in his *4th Letter* that he was prepared to convene another

---

[354] *Encyclical of Orientals*, 27,7 (CSEL 65, Feder 66,30f.). See Schwartz, *NGG* (1911), 515 (= *GS* III, 324); Joannou 80.

[355] Cf. Socrates, *HE* 2,18,7 (Hussey 218).

[356] Cf. Socrates, *HE* 2,18,6 (Hussey 218); Sozomen 3,10,6 (Bidez-Hansen 113,22–25).

[357] See Socrates, *HE* 2,20,1–14 (Hussey 229–233). Socrates simply informs us that οἱ περὶ Παῦλον καὶ Ἀθανάσιον were responsible for calling Sardica (Socrates, *HE* 2,20,2 = Hussey 229). The names of the Roman delegates are unknown to us. Ossius of Cordova was probably *not* numbered among them (as, e.g., de Clercq 310, and Joannou, op. cit., suggested). Neither is there any evidence to suggest that Julius *explicitly* requested Constans to convene Sardica: this was proposed by his *delegates,* who, however, may have acted on the advice of Julius, as we will see. As de Clercq (pp. 309–310) rightly pointed out, if Julius had personally suggested the synod, then Athanasius, who was in Rome at the time, would have known about it, but, as Athanasius tells us himself, he knew nothing of the proposal (*Ad Const.* 4). Regarding the initiative of Julius in calling Sardica, see Hefele-Leclercq (1,2) 735, 742; Bardy, "La crise Arienne," 123. It is very doubtful if, as Opitz in his commentary on *Apol.* 36,1 (= Opitz 114,1) suggests, that while they were in Trier (341–342), the Eusebian delegates from the Synod of Antioch to the Emperor Constans took the initiative to request that a synod be convened. The documentary evidence points to a "Western" initiative only.

[358] See Schwartz, *NGG* (1911), 515 (= *GS* III, 325). See also Socrates, *HE* 2,20,6 (Hussey 230), who reports that the synod took place one-and-a-half years after it was summoned.

[359] Socrates, *HE* 2,20,6 (Hussey 230).

synod, if the bishops at Antioch were able to produce fresh evidence to support their accusations against Athanasius, Marcellus, and the other bishops, "so that the accused be condemned *in the presence of all* and disorder no longer prevail in the Church."[360] This seems to have been the reason why his delegates at Trier suggested that a synod be assembled. Though the type of synod, originally conceived by Julius in his *4th Letter,* was not an oecumenical synod in the later technical sense of the term, yet his insistence on the essential universal dimension of all synods (e.g., πάντων παρόντων) was sufficient to suggest to his delegates at Trier, that the only way out of the impasse in which they found themselves was to assemble a synod according to the pattern of Nicaea where the implicit nature of all synods was expressed in the physical assembly itself, with representatives from various provinces present at the deliberations. The model of Nicaea (325) was made necessary both by the Eusebian insistence on the (false) autonomy of the synod as an institution, and by the political implications for the whole empire which arose from the threatened schism within the Church. It may be added in parenthesis that historians who seek to examine the nature of Nicaea should give more attention to Sardica than they have up to now, since it—and not Tyre (335), as is usually suggested, and much less Rome (340)—was apparently organized and run according to the precedent set by Nicaea.

Since one-and-a-half years elapsed between the decision to call the synod and its actual assembly at Sardica, midsummer 343,[361] then it

---

[360] *Letter of Julius—Apol.* 35,1 (Opitz 112,31–32).

[361] See Socrates, *HE* 2,20,6 (Hussey 230). I follow the date suggested by Hess, *Canons of Sardica,* 140–144, who corrects the suggestion of 342 made by Schwartz, *NGG* (1911), 515–522 (= *GS* III, 325–334), although one item of Hess' arguments needs correction (see above, footnote 331). Girardet's recent attempt (*Kaisergericht und Bischofsgericht,* 108) to review the date proposed by Schwartz fails to do justice to all the evidence apart from apparently erring on the very point he criticizes Hess for (see footnote 331). As we will see, the Synod of Sardica could not have taken place in 342, if one takes into consideration the many events that proceeded it: the correspondence between the two Augusti, the correspondence of Constans with Athanasius, the meeting of Athanasius with Constans in Milan, and the bishop's journey some time later to Gaul (Trier?) to meet Ossius of Cordova, and finally their journey to Sardica—it is impossible that all of this occurred within six months, i.e., between the beginning of 342 and midsummer of the same year. For further literature on the controversial question as to the date of Sardica, see de Clercq, *Ossius of Cordova,* 313, note 95. After a thorough examination of all the evidence, and due consideration of the scholarly objections, de Clercq (pp. 313–324) also comes to the conclusion that the synod took place in the year 343. See also Simonetti, *La Crisi Ariana,* 167, note 12.

is clear that Constantius did not as readily acquiesce to his brother's suggestion, as Socrates maintained[362] and Schwartz assumed.[363] However, his reluctance mellowed in the course of the year 342, due to two historical circumstances: (i) The Eusebians had lost their leader. Eusebius of Nicomedia died either at the end of 341 or the beginning of 342,[364] and a suitable successor had not as yet appeared on the scene; the future leaders (Valens and Ursacius in the West, and Acacius in the East, the successor to Eusebius of Caesarea who died about two years previously) would only emerge to succeed Eusebius a decade later. (ii) Constantius found himself in a weak political situation comparable to that which prevented Constans from taking direct action in 341—unrest within the Church (e.g., at Constantinople where Paul reinstated himself on the death of Eusebius and the populace reacted so vehemently against the general, Hermogenes, sent by the emperor to remove Paul, that Constantius was compelled to hasten to the city himself to expel Paul and to suppress the revolt)[365] and the threat of the Persians (who forced the emperor hastily to return from Constantinople to Antioch, around February 342).

Even by the autumn of 342, there was as yet no news, it seems, of Constantius' agreement to allow a synod take place. It was at this stage that Constans summoned Athanasius to meet him (for the first time) at Milan.[366] There, Constans informed him of the suggestion

---

[362] Cf. Socrates, *HE* 2,20,3 (Hussey 230). Sozomen, *HE* 3,11,3 (Bidez-Hansen 114, 12–13), more accurately records the initial reluctance of Constantius.

[363] Cf. Schwartz, *NGG* (1911), 515 (= *GS* III, 325).

[364] The "obituary notice" of Schwartz, *NGG* (1911), 510–511 (= *GS* III, 318–320), where the German scholar attempts to salvage the wreck of Eusebius of Nicomedia from the storm of historians, who from the fifth to the twentieth century have almost universally condemned this extraordinary man, tells us more about Schwartz's own personal preferences than the light it intended to throw on the first of the many bishops who, as opportunists, merely misused the new positive attitude of the State to the Church. In one point, at least, one must agree with Schwartz: Eusebius of Nicomedia was a man of exceptional political talents. It is understandable that Schwartz, at home in profane history, should show his appreciation for such ability. But one must also judge the ends to which he put his talents to use and the means he employed to achieve those ends, namely: the total absorption of the Church into the (Christian) Empire (and so effectively the end of her universal mission) and the conspiracies he conducted against Athanasius and the "orthodox," not to mention the foul means used to bring them to a successful conclusion—calumny, injustice, and violence.

[365] See Socrates, *HE* 2,13,1–7 (Hussey 203–204); Sozomen, *HE* 3,7,4–8 (BidezHansen 109,16–110,11). See Seeck, *Regesten*, 190.

[366] Cf. Athanasius, *Ad Const.* 4. See also Theodoret, *HE* 2,4,4, whose unreliable account probably refers to this meeting. See above, footnote 331.

(made by the Roman delegates at Trier) that a general synod should be assembled and that he had written to Constantius to make arrangements for its assembly. But Constans still had heard nothing from his brother. It was only after the Western emperor had returned to Gaul, that he apparently received the assent of Constantius. Then he summoned Athanasius and Ossius of Cordova to meet him (presumably at Trier) so as to make the necessary preparations for the forthcoming synod at Sardica.[367] This occurred early in the year 343.[368] The synod took place in the summer of that year.

It is beyond the limited scope of this study to examine this important event in any detail.[369] Our only interest in it, at the moment, is to examine the relationship between the empire and the Church as it was reflected in the synod itself. Even this is secondary to our main object, which is to consider the attitude of Athanasius to the imperial authority. Up to now, we have seen how insignificant his initial involvement in the convocation of Sardica was. The initiative was apparently taken by the delegates of Julius to Constans, together with Maximin of Trier. Only after Constantius II had

---

[367] Cf. Athanasius, *Ad Const.* 4. That this journey of Athanasius to Gaul was occasioned by the (probably grudging) consent of Constantius, and was undertaken with the purpose of making final arrangements for Sardica is the only plausible explanation for the meeting of Athanasius and Ossius at Trier. The reasons for inviting Ossius were: (i) the prestige he enjoyed as president of Nicaea and (ii) his experience of that famous synod which was taken as the model for Sardica. Such motives are overseen by de Clercq, *Ossius of Cordova*, 311.

[368] Cf. Seeck, *Regesten*, 193.

[369] A list of the available primary source material—which is very plentiful—is to be found in Girardet, *Kaisergericht und Bischofsgericht*, 111. However, Girardet's presentation of the legal issues raised by the two main groups at Sardica cannot be uncritically accepted, since (i) it is based on his interpretation of the foregoing events and their legal presuppositions (such as his concept of the "altkirchliche Idee" of synodal autonomy) which, as has been shown above, cannot be accepted as doing justice to the issues involved; (ii) it ignores the role which Julius' *4th Letter* played in the assembly of the synod and in the reaction of the "Eusebian" Orientals to the synod, which, as will be seen, was not inconsiderable; he also ignores (iii) the original concern about Athanasius' physical restitution to his see and the abolition of the civil charges (amounting to the death penalty), brought against him by the Eusebians and upheld by Constantius, which concern on the part of Julius was the occasion for calling on the assistance of the Western emperor and so involving him in the controversies that resulted in Sardica. Finally, it seems to me that Girardet is unjustifiably anti-Athanasian (in the spirit of Schwartz) and equally unjustifiably partial to the Orientals who refused to attend the main assembly (e.g., he ignores the evidence of Bishops Arius of Palestine and Asterius of Arabia [*Apol.* 46,3]). See Simonetti, *La Crisi Ariana*, 167–187, for a comprehensive account of the synod, one sympathetic to the position of the Orientals.

given his consent, did Athanasius become actively involved, i.e., when he travelled to Trier to help make the final arrangements for the proposed synod at Sardica. The way the assembly was to be conducted, we can well assume, coincided with his understanding of the relationship between the Church and the imperial authority.

Though the initial suggestion of a general synod was made, it seems by the Roman delegates acting independently though with the basic concern of Julius in mind, the ultimate responsibility was placed on the shoulders of the Bishop of Rome by the "Eusebians"[370] themselves.[371] We have seen how the *4th Letter of Julius* did not rule out another synod—how in fact it proposed to convene on should the Eusebians be able to produce new evidence against their opponents—and how this synod was to be held in the presence of all, i.e., all parties involved, especially accused and accusers, but also their fellow-bishops from the entire Church who would ensure that a just sentence, transparent to all, would be passed. Though the Synod of Sardica was not exactly what Julius originally envisaged, yet in essence it attempted, as will be seen, to fulfil the conditions elaborated by the Bishop of Rome in his letter. As we will see, the Synod of Sardica, as seen from the point of view of the majority—bishops from both East and West, though the latter predominated[372] (as the Eastern bishops had done at Nicaea)—was constituted and conducted according to the principles enunciated by Julius: it was in a sense their "reception" of the *Letter of Julius*. The reaction of the Eusebian party, it will also be seen, reflects their "reception" of the famous letter. The letter is the key to a proper understanding of the Sardican synod, not only the contents of the letter but also the circumstances surrounding its dispatch to the East through Gabianus, namely Julius' apparent attempt to enlist the support of Constans in the unsolved matter concerning

---

[370] Even though the Oriental party, in opposition to Athanasius and Marcellus, ought to no longer to be called "Eusebians" now that their actual political and ideological leaders (Eusebius of Nicomedia and his namesake of Caesarea) are dead, yet the term has been retained in the text since the party, as such, still retained its homogeneity at Sardica (though it was about to disintegrate into splinter groups, such as the extreme Neo-Arians and the "Semi-Arians"), and since the term avoids confusing the party with the Oriental bishops as a whole—many of whom were present with their western counterparts at Sardica—a distinction which is all too rarely made.

[371] Cf. *The Letter of the Orientals at Sardica* 27,6 (CSEL 65, Feder 66,12) calls "Julius of the city of Rome" the *princeps et dux malorum*. See also Socrates, *HE* 2,20,6 (Hussey 230).

[372] Regarding the composition of the Synod of Sardica, see Feder, *Studien zu Hilarius II*, 18–70.

the necessary civil permission from Constantius that would enable Athanasius return to his home-country, which attempt set the convocation of the general synod in motion.

In the *Letter of the Synod of Sardica to Julius*[373] (not preserved by Athanasius), the three issues treated by the synod are briefly outlined by the Synodal Fathers:

> There were three matters which were handled, for the most pious emperors themselves conceded that, concerning the entire [dispute] the divisive [issues] be discussed altogether, especially [those matters] pertaining to the holy Faith and the integrity of the truth, which they [the Eusebians] have injured; secondly concerning those persons, whom they claim to be deposed after an unfair sentence, so that, if they had been able to prove [their accusations], they might be lawfully confirmed; thirdly, in truth an inquiry, which is truly entitled an inquiry, on the ground that they had caused grievous and bitter injuries, even unbearable and abominable outrages, to the Church, when they seized bishops, presbyters and deacons and sent all clerics into exile, transferred them to desert places, put them to death by hunger, thirst and every indigence, destroying other captives in prison, squalor and stink, some with iron chains so that their necks were throttled with the most ingenious bands.[374]

The opening reference to Emperors Constans and Constantius is most revealing: by using the term *"permiserunt,"* the Synodal Fathers most accurately described the relationship of the imperial authority to the synod, since the initiative, with regard to the convocation of the synod, is not attributed to them nor are they said to have determined the subject matter of the assembly, but simply that they conceded that the synod take place[375] to debate the controverted

---

[373] Preserved by St. Hilary (CSEL 65, Feder 126,5–130,18).

[374] Tria fuerunt, quae tractanda erant. nam et ipsi religiossimi imperatores permiserunt, ut de integro uniuersa discussa disputarentur et ante omnia de sancta fide et de integritate ueritatis, quam uiolauerunt. secunda de personis, quos dicebant esse deiectos de iniquo iudicio, ut, si potuissent probare, iusta fieret confirmatio. tertia uero quaestio, quae uere quaestio appellanda est quod graues et acerbas iniurias, intolerabiles etiam et nefarias contumelias ecclesiis fecissent, cum raperent episcopos, presbiteros, diacones et omnes clericos in exilium mitterent, ad deserta loca transducerent, fame, siti, nuditate et omni egestate necarent, alios clausos carcere et squalore et putore conficerent, nonnullos ferreis uinculis, ita ut ceruices eis artissimis circulis strangularentur" (*Letter of Synod to Julius,* 3,1–2 = CSEL 65, Feder 128,4–16).

[375] See also Socrates 2,20,3 (Hussey 230); Sozomen *HE* 3,11,3 (Bidez-Hansen 114,15–17).

issues. Their role is essentially a passive one in allowing the synod to actually take place (and placing the imperial post at the disposal of the bishops).[376] The text, by its general reference to the entire dispute, which also threatened the inner unity of the empire, alludes to the specific interest of the emperors in the occurrence of the synod. But the ultimate "initiator" of the synod, as we have seen, and the one who in effect determined the terms of reference of the oecumenical or general synod was the Bishop of Rome, whom the Sardican bishops, representing both West and East, now address in their letter.

The three issues enumerated by the Fathers at Sardica were those raised by Julius in his *4th Letter* to the Eusebians: (i) The question of the Holy Faith and the integrity of the truth referred to the disregard of the Eusebians for the Faith defined at Nicaea—as shown in their readiness to receive into communion those whose (Arian) heresy was condemned by the Church Universal represented there[377]—and to the threat to the integrity of the truth posed by the appointment of blatant supporters of Arius;[378] but the integrity of the truth was also endangered by the procedures adopted by the Eusebians, which compelled Julius to outline the correct procedures demanded by the divine law of justice (i.e., truth with regard to human behavior) and which resulted in the Sardican bishop's insistence that "probauimus secundum ueritatem et rationem ea, quae ab illis commissa sunt."[379] In their canons, the Synod of Sardica polished and refined the procedures outlined by Julius in his *4th Letter.* We will later take a brief glance at these.

(ii) The second issue concerning those persons who had been deposed by the Eusebians clearly presupposes the sentence of Julius of Rome, which determined that those depositions were as a result of an unjust judgement. The Synod of Sardica did not set itself the exercise of reexamining the sentence passed by the Bishop of Rome,[380] but, as Julius had determined in his letter, should the accusers of Athanasius (and Marcellus) be able to produce fresh evidence to support their charges, then he was prepared to write to the bishops "who must needs reassemble so that the accused be

---

[376] See Caspar, *Geschichte des Papsttums* I, 156.

[377] Cf. *Letter of Julius = Apol.* 23,1–4 (Opitz 104,23–105,4). Compare with *Encyclical Letter of the Synod of Sardica to all Churches* 8 (CSEL 65, Feder 122,10–126,3).

[378] Cf. *Letter of Julius = Apol.* 24,1–4 (Opitz 105,5–25); compare with *Encyclical Letter* 8.

[379] Cf. *Encyclical Letter* 5 (CSEL 65, Feder 114,1–2).

[380] Cf. *Letter of the Synod of Sardica to the Church of Alexandria = Apol.* 37,5 (Opitz 115,32–116,5).

condemned in the presence of all and disorder no longer prevail in the Church."[381] It is absurd to maintain as, e.g., Girardet does,[382] that the "Western" bishops at Sardica prejudiced the possible outcome of the proceedings by refusing to exclude Athanasius (and Marcellus) either from their communion or from the actual assembly, as the Eusebians had demanded.[383] Both parties were considered by the synod to be in principle innocent before they were proven guilty and thus enjoyed the right to be treated equally, i.e., as both accused and accusers, since each party produced indictments against the other. The invitation to the Eusebians to join the synod and to present themselves and their cases before the other bishops, and before those whom they accused,[384] was strictly in accordance with the principles of divine justice outlined by Julius. Further, as the initial summons of Julius to attend the Synod of Rome (340) in his *1st and 2nd Letters to the Eusebians* had made clear, and as his *3rd and 4th Letters* repeated,[385] the Eusebian party itself had to answer the charges brought against them by Athanasius and the other Oriental bishops. As was emphasized in our analysis of the *4th Letter of Julius,* the Bishop of Rome, though evidently deeply troubled by the reports of various outrages attributed to the Eusebian party (apart from their neglect of the Faith and Canons of Nicaea), was extremely careful not to condemn that party in their absence. He gave them every opportunity to defend themselves before their accusers: such an opportunity—their final opportunity—was Sardica.

(iii) Julius was even reluctant to mention the nature of the violent disorders of which the Eusebians were charged by Athanasius and in particular the other Oriental bishops.[386] But now the Sardican bishops, having examined the matter, give a frightening summary. The third issue raised by the synod was, then, a judicial inquiry into the abominable outrages said to have been committed by the

---

[381] *Letter of Julius = Apol.* 35,1 (Opitz 112,31–32).

[382] Girardet, *Kaisergericht und Bischofsgericht*, 112f.

[383] Cf. *Letter of the Orientals at Sardica* 14,1–2 (CSEL 65, Feder 58,1–8).

[384] Cf. *Encyclical Letter of the Synod of Sardica* 2,2–4 (CSEL 65, Feder 107,1–109,6), especially: expectantibus omnibus et cohortantibus eos uenire ad iudicium, ut omnia, quae de consacerdotibus nostris uel dixerunt uel scripserunt, praesentes possent conuincere, uocati non uenerunt, sicut praediximus, ostendentes etiam ex his falsitatem suam et non solum commentatitiam fraudem aut exquisitam uersutiam, quam fecerunt prodentes per excusationem. qui enim habent fiduciam probare ea, quae absentes dicunt, haec presentes parati sunt conuincere.

[385] Cf. *Letter of Julius = Apol.* 33,1–4 (Opitz 111,10–112,2).

[386] Cf. *Letter of Julius = Apol.* 33,1–4 (Opitz 111,10–112,2).

Eusebian party, which inquiry had been suggested by Julius in his *4th Letter*. This, the third point, was evidently the one which most occupied the attention of the synod. The inquiry resulted in the excommunication of the leaders of the Antiochenes—the "Eusebians"—whom the synod clearly distinguishes from those other bishops who came with them to Sardica but who were forcedly prevented from participating in the assembly.[387] The refusal of the Eusebians to attend the synod and their "flight" back to Antioch were interpreted by the synod as the clearest possible evidence of their guilt.[388] It was their *fifth* refusal to face their accusers and prove their charges before the rest of the Church, once one takes into consideration the previous *four Letters of Julius* and the invitations they contained. The Synodal Fathers insist that they had subjected these indictments against the Eusebians to a genuine inquiry. There is no cause to doubt their word.

§9 The Letter of the Orientals at Sardica[389]

In order to keep within the limits of this study, a full analysis of this text cannot be undertaken here. We must confine our attention to the ecclesiological issues raised therein. But first, a short note on the relationship of this letter—explicitly addressed to Gregory of Alexandria, Amfionus of Nicomedia, and Donatus of Carthage (!), among others[390]—and the *4th Letter of Julius*. As has already been mentioned, the Eusebian letter describes Julius as the *princeps et dux malorum*[391]—although the Bishop of Rome was not actually present but was represented by two presbyters, Archidamus and Philoxenus, as at Nicaea. More important than the empirical observation that Julius is mentioned by name on five other occasions[392] is the fact that the letter concludes with the explicit condemnation

---

[387] Cf. *Encyclical Letter of the Synod of Sardica* 7,3–4 (CSEL 65, Feder 119,5–121,9).

[388] Cf. *Encyclical* 7,1 (Feder 118,7–10); see also *Encyclical* 3,1–4,3 (Feder 109,7–113,7); *Letter of Sardica to the Church of Alexandria* = *Apol.* 37,4–5 (Opitz 115,29–33); *Apol.* 38,3 (Opitz 117,7–11).

[389] The text is preserved by St. Hilary (CSEL 65, Feder 48,9–67,20). According to Hess, *Canons of Sardica*, 16–18, the Eusebians' meeting at Philippolis was but a preliminary to their assembly at Sardica.

[390] Cf. *Letter of the Orientals* (Feder 48,11–49,7).

[391] See above, note 371.

[392] *Letter of the Orientals* 11,2 (Feder 56,8); *Letter of the Orientals* 14,1 (Feder 58,1); *Letter of the Orientals* 24,1 (Feder 63,26); *Letter of the Orientals* 27,2 (Feder 65,31); *Letter of the Orientals* 28,1 (Feder 67,9).

of Julius and Ossius.[392a] It is clear that Julius is the chief villain of the piece—ostensibly for his readiness to enter into communion with those condemned by the Eusebian synods. However, the strongest attack on Julius follows an exposition on the legal procedure adopted by the Eusebians and used by them to justify their refusal to attend a synod whose president and members blatantly contravene their concept of the Church's discipline.[393] This tract, which most clearly expounds their ecclesiology, is much more detailed than that which apparently was contained in their original reply to Julius' summons. The elaborations they now provide all indicate that the exposition was prompted by the *4th Letter of Julius,* particularly the way they accuse the Occidentals of trying to impose their will on the Church,[394] and how they describe the claim of Julius to the effect that synodal judgements are in principle open to examination by other synods as a *novum,*[395] thus replying to Julius' condemnation of their innovation. Yet the Eusebians never refer explicitly to the *4th Letter of Julius,* though, as we will see, their entire letter reflects their attempt to meet his main formal arguments (as well as certain of his factual points), though it ignores some central issues raised by Julius and taken up by the Synod of Sardica, such as their support for the Arian heresy.

Whether on account of the nature of the document as a type of encyclical, or by the fact that the skilled author of their earlier reply to Julius was dead, this letter of theirs is markedly lacking in style and irony. The lack of irony could have been due to Julius' severe criticism of same in his letter to them. In its place are to be found pious-sounding general statements, supported by relatively frequent scriptural quotations—which, with two exceptions, are of no great significance. One of these exceptions is a text from 1 Sam 2,25: si pecaverit homo in hominem, orabunt pro eo ad dominum; si autem in deum peccaverit homo, quis orabit pro eo? nos autem talem consuetudinem non habemus nec ecclesia dei.[396] This is applied to the

---

[392a] Propter has igitur causas iustum duxit concilium, ut Iulium urbis Romae et Ossium ceterosque supra memoratos discingeret atque damnaret (Feder 67,8–10).

[393] *Letter of the Orientals* 23,1–26,3 (Feder 63,1–65,25).

[394] E.g., ita autem sceleratorum omnium duces quaerunt ecclesiae principatum quasi aliquod tyrannidis regnum (*Letter of the Orientals* 25,2 [Feder 65,4–6]).

[395] Nec hoc propter bonum quoque iustitiae inquirunt. non enim ecclesiis consulunt, qui leges iuraque diuina (ac) ceterorum decreta dissoluere perconantur. propterea hanc nouitatem moliebantur inducere, quam horret uetus consuetudo ecclesiae, ut, in concilio Orientales episcopi quidquid forte statuissent, ab episcopis Occidentalibus refricaretur, similiter et, quidquid Occidentalium partium episcopi, ab Orientalibus solueretur (*Letter of the Orientals* 26,1 [Feder 65,7–13]).

[396] *Letter of the Orientals* 21,2 (Feder 62,8–12).

cases of Marcellus and Athanasius, who are respectively accused of teaching false doctrine and introducing *novae traditiones,* and is in a sense the scriptural backing for their concept of the irreversibility of synodal judgements. In its crude application, the text is characteristic of the letter's merciless tone and inconsequential argumentation, since their own disregard for the decisions of Nicaea (as manifested in their readmittance of Arius to communion and in ordaining Pistos as successor to Athanasius) blatantly contradicts in practice their pious Old Testament principles. The second scriptural quotation of consequence will be taken up later in the text; it is of greater importance.

The Eusebian *encyclical,* like the *4th Letter of Julius,* concentrates on Marcellus and Athanasius in that order. We can, for the moment, leave the case of Marcellus aside, except to point out that the letter does not enter into the heretical teaching of Marcellus in any detail but rather reports the condemnation of the Bishop of Ancyra by the Synod of Constantinople (336)—*sub praesentia beatissimae memoriae Constantini imperatoris*[397]— as though such a judgement bore irrefutable authority. They refer to the seven-year-old judgement as though it was a witness from tradition, since it was passed *a parentibus nostris in Constantinopoli ciuitate!* Since, even in the case of Marcellus, the Eusebians find refuge in the decisions of former synods, then it is not surprising that the main brunt of their letter is concentrated on the legal or ecclesiological issues raised by Julius in the case of Athanasius.

Evidently cut to the quick by Julius' anathematization of the *novum* constituted by the Eusebian Imperial Church, with its predominant characteristic of the autonomous provincial synod, the *encyclical* responds by describing the legal precedents concerning the reception of synodal judgements expounded by Julius on the basis of the principles of Divine Justice and the Apostolic nature of the Church as themselves being *novae traditiones,*[398] a *nouitas,*[399] and *noua lex.*[400] Further, they insist that it is their own procedures (relating to the absolute autonomy of provincial synods and their principle of nonintervention) that are founded on evangelical precepts

---

[397] *Letter of the Orientals* 3,1 (Feder 50,20–21).

[398] *Letter of the Orientals* 1,1 (Feder 49,16); *Letter of the Orientals* 21,3 (Feder 62,13.

[399] *Letter of the Orientals* 26,1 (Feder 65,9).

[400] nouam legem introducere putauerunt, ut Orientales episcopi ab Occidentalibus iudicarentur. et uolebant ecclesiae iudicium per eos posse constare, qui non tam illorum miserebantur, quam actibus suis. hoc itaque nefas quoniam numquam recepit ecclesiastica disciplina, quaesumus, dilectissimi fratres, ut sceleratam perniciem conatusque mortiferos perditorum nobiscum etiam ipsi damnetis (*Letter of the Orientals* 12,2 = Feder 57,12–17). See also above, note 305.

and handed down from the Apostles to the present times,[401] and that
it is their actions that are truly in accordance with ecclesiastical discipline.[402] In reply to the central argument of Julius—regarding the divine
law of justice—they contend that divine law forbids the reception into
communion of those condemned by a synod: unidentes enim, quod hi,
qui damnatos recipiunt, in offensam crimenque incurrunt et uiolatores
caelestium legum, tali auctoritate iudicum constituere conabantur, ut sese
iudices iudicum dicere uellent atque eorum, qui iam cum deo sunt, si fas
est, sententiam refricare.[403] This, then, is their central argument. It completely ignores their own earlier actions when, e.g., they admitted Arius to
communion though his teaching was condemned by Nicaea.

The Eusebian position articulated in their encyclical most clearly
demonstrates the way they take hold of a genuine ecclesiastical principle—the irreversibility of synodal decisions relating to Faith and customs
(liturgical and disciplinary)—and reinterpret it to suit their own situation.
We have seen how synodal decisions became irreversible once they had
been "received," either implicitly or explicitly by the Church Universal. The
Eusebians insist on the irreversibility of synodal judgements but extend the
content of such to include human behavior, while they reverse the procedure of the "reception:" because a synod so judged, they argue, then it must
be accepted unexamined by the whole Church. Their method of argumentation is well illustrated in the way they use the text from Scripture: nolite
transferre terminos aeternos, quos constituerunt patres uestri (Prov 22,28).
This is the parallel text of Deut 19,14, which, as we saw in our analysis of
Eusebius' History, was used by Dionysius of Alexandria when he appealed
to the Church of Rome (through the presbyter Philemon) to tolerate the
local custom of rebaptizing heretics and schismatics, which was held by
certain Asian Churches and adopted by their synods.[404] Athanasius will use

---

[401] Est quidem nobis omnibus indeficiens oratio, dilectissimi fratres . . . ut ecclesiae
regula sanctaque parentum traditio atque iudicia in perpetuum firma solidaque
permaneant nec nouis emergentibus sectus traditionibusque peruersis, maxime in
constituendis episcopis uel in exponendis, aliquando turbetur, quominus teneat
euangelica atque sancta praecepta et quae sanctis et beatissimis apostolis iussa
sunt et maioribus nostris atque a nobis ipsis in hodiernum usque seruata sunt
et seruantur (*Letter of the Orientals* 1,1 = Feder 49,8–21). See also, *Letter of the
Orientals* 23,3–4 (Feder 63,12–22); *Letter of the Orientals* 17,1 (Feder 59,12–13).

[402] Uerum nos tenentes ecclesiasticae regulae disciplinam . . . (*Letter of the Orientals*
15,1 = Feder 58,14). Here the Eusebians refer to their refusal to communicate
with the condemned Athanasius and the heretic Marcellus. See also, *Letter of the
Orientals* 26,3 (Feder 65,19–25).

[403] *Letter of the Orientals* 17,2 (Feder 59,20–24). See *Letter of the Orientals* 26,1
(Feder 65,8–9); see also *Letter of the Orientals* 23,3 (Feder 63,12–16).

[404] See above, p. 122.

the same text, with respect to the decisions of Nicaea concerning the Faith.[405] The Eusebians use it twice. In the first instance, they quote the text in association with the condemnation of Marcellus and his teaching.[406] The text would have been apposite in that context if the decision of Constantinople (336) had been accepted by the Church Universal. The rejection of this judgement by the Synod of Rome (340), demonstrated that such was not yet the case. On the second occasion, they use the quotation to support their refusal to submit the decision of Tyre, 335 (regarding the behavior of Athanasius), to the scrutiny of another synod.[407] Apart from being inconsistent with the principles of justice, as Julius of Rome pointed out, this application of the principle of the irreversibility of synodal judgements relating to Faith and customs (and its scriptural foundation as suggested by Dionysius), to cover decisions concerning *human behavior,* is completely unjustified and nowhere witnessed to by the Tradition of the Church. The precedents originally given in the Eusebian reply to Julius' summons to attend the Synod of Rome—the case of Paul of Samosata and "Novatian"—are extended to include Sabellius and Valentinus.[408] These two new "precedents" are even less suitable than the previous example to suit the case of Athanasius, since they both refer to heretical opinions (both of which were rejected by the final Petrine authority in the Church) and do not refer to human behavior.

The response of the Eusebians to the criticism of Julius concerning the identity of imperial and ecclesiastical authority—the second element of the Imperial Church of the two Eusebii, now dead and considered by their followers as their "Fathers" who are now with God[409]—is ambiguous. On the one hand, they boast of the Synod of Constantinople (336) that condemned Marcellus: it was

---

[405] Cf. *Ad Afros* 1 (*PG* 26,1032,A12–23).

[406] *Letter of the Orientals* 6,1 (Feder 53,5–7).

[407] quam ob rem, quoniam a parentum traditione discedere non possumus, quia nec talem auctoritatem sumsit ecclesia nec talem potestatem a deo accepit, supradictos ad honorem dignitatemque ecclesiae nec ipsi suscipimus et suscipientes digne damnamus. sed nec alios, qui aut olim aut postea merito damnati sunt, in ecclesia recipimus adhaerentes legibus dei traditionibusque paternis atque ecclesiasticis disciplinis, credentes prophetae dicenti: *noli transgredi terminos aeternos, quos posuerunt patres tui.* quare nos numquam fixa solidaque concutimus, sed magis ea, quae sunt a parentibus constituta, seruamus (*Letter of the Orientals* 23,3–4 = Feder 63,12–22).

[408] num in urbe Roma sub Nouato et Sabellio et Ualentino haereticis factum concilium ab Orientalibus confirmatum est. et iterum in Oriente, sub Paulo a Samosatis quod statutum est, ab omnibus est signatum (*Letter of the Orientals* 26,2 = Feder 65,16–19).

[409] Cf. *Letter of the Orientals* 16,1 (Feder 58,30); *Letter of the Orientals* 17,2 (Feder 59,23–24).

held sub praesentia beatissimae memoriae Constantini imperatoris.[410] They also recognize Sardica as having been *convened* by the emperors,[411] though the orthodox at Sardica only admit to the concession of the emperors who *allowed* the synod to take place. On the other hand, they protest that the "Westerners" thought they could frighten them into communion with the condemned persons by producing the imperial letters,[412] i.e., on the authority of the emperors. By so interpreting the Synod of Sardica (which was not summoned to force any side into communion but to examine the charges brought against both parties), the Eusebians implicitly accuse the majority there of the same kind of misuse with regard to the imperial authority, for which Julius had earlier reproved them. Their most explicit rejection of Julius' censure of their illicit mixture of the ecclesiastical and imperial authority is contained in their indignant repudiation of the Sardican bishops' confusion of human matters with divine matters, i.e., their coupling of the mundane with ecclesiastical affairs as manifested in the revolt of the people of Sardica against them, which disturbance, they claim, was instigated by Ossius of Cordova and Protogenes of Sardica.[413] The criticism of the *Reichskirche* contained in Julius' *4th Letter* must have made a deep impression.

The Eusebian letter never once intimates that they themselves were on trial at Sardica, or that they had been summoned to Sardica to answer accusations about their own Faith and behavior. The object of the letter is to distract the reader from the actual purpose of the synod and to justify their refusal to join the synod on the grounds that, according to ecclesiastical and divine law, the judgements of (provincial) synods were irreversible.

§10 The Documents which Resulted from the Synod of Sardica: the Synod's Rejection of the "Eusebian Heresy"

Again, we can only give our attention to those documents which throw some light on the ecclesiological issues raised by the synod. And, once again, it must be pointed out that the analysis cannot be an exhaustive one. The relationship of the *4th Letter of*

---

[410] Cf. *Letter of the Orientals* 3,1 (Feder 50,20–21).

[411] Cf. *Letter of the Orientals* 16,1 (Feder 58,4).

[412] Cf. *Letter of the Orientals* 22,1 (Feder 62,19–20).

[413] diuinis humana miscentes et ecclesiasticis rebus priuatas adiungentes ciuitatis nobis concentum seditionemque conflarunt dicentes nos grauem schismate ciuitati importasse iniuriam, nisi illis—quod nefas erat—communicaremus, et haec frequenter acclamabant (*Letter of the Orientals* 19,3 = Feder 61,2–6).

Julius to the synod, which has been outlined above in the way the synod
was assembled and its terms of reference were determined, is reflected in
other documents which were issued by the bishops assembled at Sardica.
Apart from the synod's letter to Julius, part of which we have already
examined, *the Letter of the Synod assembled at Sardica to the Presbyters,
Deacons, and all the Holy Church of God in Alexandria*[414] most clearly
reveals the influence of Julius' *4th Letter*. There ἡ κρίσις τοῦ ἀδελφοῦ καὶ
συνεπισκόπου ἡμῶν Ἰουλίου which determined that the bishops should
be in no doubt whatever about receiving Athanasius into communion
was seen to be obvious and just (φανερὰ καὶ δικαία), since their accusers
proved their inability to produce concrete evidence against him by their
refusal to attend the synod.[415] From their insistence that the synod gave
his accusers every opportunity to prove their charges against Athanasius,[416]
one can perceive how strictly the Synodal Fathers adhered to the terms of
reference suggested by Julius: Athanasius was to be considered innocent
until evidence to the contrary should be produced.

The *Encyclical Letter of the Synod to the Entire Church*[417] also mentions
the correspondence of Julius with the Eusebians,[418] though not quite as
explicitly, but for the same purpose as in the previous letter. This letter
further summarizes the findings of the synod with regard to the three issues
it detailed in its letter to Julius[419] as in a sense the agenda of the assembly,
which issues were first raised by Julius' *4th Letter* to the Eusebians: (i)
regarding matters of the Faith, the teaching of Marcellus is upheld—
though their distinction between the theological opinions he proposed
by way of inquiry (*proponens*) and those he approved (*conprobans*)[420]
indicates a growing uncertainty on the part of the Synodal Fathers—
and the Arian tenets of the Western bishops, Valens and Ursacius, were
rejected,[421] though, as the textual tradition and the express testimony

---

[414] Text preserved by Athanasius; see *Apol.* 37,1–40,3 (Opitz 115,13–118,25).
[415] *Apol.* 37,4–5 (Opitz 115,29–33). See Roethe, *Synoden*, 86.
[416] E.g., *Apol.* 37,6 (Opitz 116,5–9) and 38,3 (117,8–11).
[417] Text preserved in Latin by Hilary (CSEL 65, Feder 103,1–126,3) and in *The
       Theodosian Collection* (Turner 645–653). A Greek translation is to be found in
       Athanasius, *Apol.* 119,4–123,25, and Theodoret, *HE* 2,8. The various texts and
       their variations have been collected by Feder.
[418] *Encyclical Letter of the Synod of Sardica* 2,2 (CSEL 65, Feder 107,1–3).
[419] See above, p. 445.
[420] Cf. *Encyclical Letter of the Synod of Sardica* 6,1 (Feder 117,5–118,3).
[421] According to the text preserved in *The Theodosian Collection* (Turner 651–652).

of Athanasius both make clear,[422] the attempt by some of the Fathers to draft a statement of the Faith did not find general approval at the synod; (ii) after it became evident, that the accusers of Athanasius (and Ascelpas of Gaza) could produce no new proof to support their charges, the synod declared them innocent,[423] though not before (iii) the Synodal Fathers had made an inquiry into the allegations of violence, compulsion, and other outrages committed by the Eusebians, which moved the synod to reject the claims of various usurpers to Alexandria and other sees, to excommunicate them,[424] and to condemn their Arian tenets.[425]

The threat to the Church posed by the *novum* of the Imperial Church, as originally conceived by the two Eusebii and condemned by Julius, was dealt with by the Synod of Sardica in the rules for ecclesiastical discipline, which they drew up and passed unanimously. Though practically ignored by historians and theologians alike, this *novum* of the Imperial Church was most probably that described in the documents relating to the actual Synod of Sardica as the *Eusebiana heresis,*[426] whose leaders were *Eusebii duo.*[427]

---

[422] It seems to me that the text rejecting the Arian teaching of Valens and Ursacius was possibly displaced in the textual tradition. The text—which is not so much a creed or confession as an elaboration on the Nicene Faith—possibly formed part of the *Letter of Ossius of Cordova and Protogenes of Sardica to Pope Julius* (Turner 644), a fragment of which has been preserved in the Theodosian collection. In support of this suggestion—here but tentatively made—is the unexpected mention of Valens and Ursacius in the *Letter of the Synod to Julius* (Feder 129,6–130,3) and the later recantation of their heresy to Pope Julius. The reason for this elaboration on the Nicene Faith was probably the growing support for the Arian tenets *in the West,* thanks to the proselytizing efforts of these two strange bishops (see Gwatkin, *Studies,* 127, note 1); see also previous footnote. Athanasius in his *Tomus ad Antiochenos* 5 (*PG* 26,800,C2–801,A2) denies that the synod made any such definition, but that some of those present also held that the Nicene Synod was defective (i.e., not sufficiently clear in its rejection of the Arian tenets) and so attempted to draw up a statement of faith, which, however, was rejected by the Sardican Synod as a whole, which maintained that the Faith confessed by the Nicene Fathers was sufficient. Kelly, *Creeds,* 278–279, argues that the Creed formed an authentic part of the encyclical.

[423] Cf. *Encyclical Letter of the Synod of Sardica* 2,1–5,4 (Feder 106,2–117,4); see also *Encyclical Letter of the Synod of Sardica* 8,1 (Feder 122,4–10).

[424] Cf. *Encyclical* 3,1–3 (Feder 109,7–112,2); *Encyclical* 7,1–2 (Feder 118,7–124,5).

[425] Cf. *Encyclical* 7,2 (Feder 124,5–126,3).

[426] Cf. *Encyclical Letter of the Synod of Sardica* 3,3 (Feder 129,3); see also *Letter of Athanasius (at Sardica) to the Church of Alexandria* (Turner 654,12–13; 22; 29). In his *Letter to the Church of the Mareotis,* also from Sardica, Athanasius writes "Olim itaque latebat hereticorum mores, nunc tamen omnibus expansi sunt et patefacti . . ." (Turner 659,19–21).

[427] Cf. *Encyclical Letter of the Synod of Sardica* 7,3 (Feder 119,6). The *encyclical,*

The way the synod attempted to counteract this new "heresy" is to be found expressed in Canons 3, 4, and 5, the so-called Appeal Canons of Sardica. Their object was to determine, as precisely as possible, the right of appeal from synodal or episcopal judgements in cases relating to the behavior of bishops, presbyters, or deacons. Without examining these canons in detail here,[428] it seems to me that the appeal procedure was, in the first place, hammered out according to the principle of the transparency of justice, as articulated by Julius in his *4th Letter*—which principle is the main concern of the canons and not the definition of the jurisdictional primacy of the Roman bishop—and, secondly, according to the jurisdictional implications which arose from the traditional understanding of the nature of the Church, which understanding implied the equality of all bishops as well as the (as yet not fully defined) primacy of the Bishop of Rome. With regard to the latter, the Sardican Fathers confirm the right of a bishop, condemned by his fellow-bishops in his province, to appeal to the Bishop of Rome *in order to have his judgement reexamined by another synod*. The Bishop of Rome's function was, primarily, to judge whether or not a revision was necessary, not to judge the case himself, which was the function of the other bishops in the universal episcopate, though in certain cases, a condemned bishop could request the presence of a Roman presbyter who could be sent with the delegated authority of the Bishop of Rome to judge together with the bishops of the Revision Synod.

The understanding of the primacy of the Roman bishop as held by the Sardican bishops, of both Eastern and Western provenances, and which was the basis of the procedures outlined in the Appeal Canons, is expressed most clearly in the opening paragraph of their *Letter to Julius*:

> That which we have at all times believed, we still hold; since experience proves and confirms what everyone has heard with his ears. For that which the most blessed Apostle Paul, teacher of the Gentiles, spoke of himself is true, quia experimentum quaeritis eius, qui in me loquitur Christus (2 Cor 13,3), though certainly, because Christ the Lord dwelt in him, there can be no doubt that the Spirit spoke through his mind and resounded

a few lines previously, mentions Eusebius of Caesarea by name in connection with the deposition of Asclepas of Gaza by a synod (presumably conceived as an imperial commission similar to that which deposed Eustathius of Antioch in 328) whose president was the ideological leader of this "heresy" (cf. *Encyclical* 6,2 = Feder 118,5).

[428] For the same, see Hess, *Canons of Sardica*, 109–127; Hess, *The Early Development*, 93f.; see also Simonetti, *La Crisi Ariana*, 175f., especially his comments on p. 177; Troianos, "Der apostolische Stuhl," 245–259; Maccarrone, "Sedes Apostolica," 280.

through the organ of his body. And thus, most beloved brother, though separated in the body, you were present [with us] in a harmony of thought and will; the explanation of your absence was both upright and cogent, lest either schismatic wolves might have attacked and plundered [you] by means of deceits, or heretical curs, provoked by their senseless, raving madness, railed at [you], or the devil, a serpent in very deed, pour forth the poison of his blasphemies. This therefore will seem best and greatly appropriate: if the Lord's bishops, each from his own province, report to the head, that is to the See of Peter the Apostle.[429]

The "presence" of Julius at the synod *mente concordi ac uoluntate* has already become manifest in the influence of his *4th Letter,* both on the reaction of the Eusebians and in the documents and decisions of the synod. In this text, the Synodal Fathers affirm that the truth of what they had heard (about the various ecclesiological and personal issues raised by Julius in his letter) has been confirmed by their own experience at Sardica, so that the bishops draw an analogy between St. Paul's claim with regard to himself—that Christ spoke in him—with that which they "at all times believed and still held," namely, the "general belief that the authentic Christian tradition is to be found at Rome," as Jalland expressed it.[430] Julius' reason for his physical absence is not directly stated. It is likely that the practice of the Bishop of Rome sending delegates, as at Arles (314) and Nicaea, may have been the main reason. However, from the "commentary" of the Sardican bishops, one could conclude that, had he been present, it would have given the Eusebians an opportunity to attack his person as, e.g., they had in fact attacked the president of the synod, Ossius, and Protogenes, the Bishop of the City of Sardica, in the hope of bringing his office into disrepute.[431] The response to whatever reason Julius gave is the affirmation by the Sardican Fathers of his Petrine office and the responsibility of each bishop towards it: hoc enim optimum et ualde congruentissimum esse uidebitur, si ad caput, id est ad Petri apostoli sedem, de singulis quibusque prouinciis domini referant sacerdotes.[432]

---

[429] *Letter of the Synod of Sardica to Julius* 1,1–2 (CSEL 65, Feder 126,7–127,5).
[430] Jalland, *Church and Papacy*, 221, note 6.
[431] See above, footnote 413.
[432] The opinion that this sentence is a later interpolation (not earlier than the period of the decretals of Innocent I) as held, e.g., by Caspar, *Geschichte des Papsttums* I, 587, has not found general support (cf. Jalland, *Church and Papacy*, 222, note 4; Hess, *Canons of Sardica*, 117, note 2; Girardet, *Kaisergericht und Bischofsgericht*, 128–129, note 96).

An interesting echo of the final paragraph of Julius' *letter* (*Apol.* 35) is to be found in the different ways the synodal letter refers in the above text to St. Paul and to St. Peter. The Bishop of Rome, who himself pointed to Peter as the final authority for the legal procedures he had outlined ("those things we have received from Blessed Peter, the Apostle, these things I also signify to you"), is here described as the head (of the Church), that is (the occupant of) "the See of Peter the Apostle." St. Paul is not mentioned by Julius in connection with the tradition he there defends, but only in the negative context of a denial that the Eusebians could claim the support of St. Paul for the traditions they proposed. In the Sardican text, the teacher of the Gentiles is not directly used in connection with the Apostolic Succession at Rome, which gave its bishop the primacy as head of the Church, but is used only in an analogous way to describe the quality of Julius' judgement (on ecclesiastical procedures and the cases involving the unjustly deposed Oriental bishops) as comparable to the inspiration Paul claimed for his teaching.

Finally, a word about the external framework of the synod: its relationship to the imperial authority. From the canons drawn up at Sardica to regulate evident abuses which had arisen out of the new positive attitude of the empire to the Church (Canons 8 to 12), the little that can be gathered about this question is not without significance. "It was the concern of the Synod," Hess correctly states, "to prohibit ambitious or questionable representations by individual bishops, to define causes of petition which should be considered legitimate, and to regulate the way in which admissible representations might be made."[433] Their basic tendency was directed against the "Hofbischöfe," as Girardet pointed out.[434] But they do not question the positive attitude of the empire to the Church; they only attempt to define (in the sense of to limit) the Church's relationship to the imperial authority.

In our reconstruction of the events which led to the assembly of the synod at Sardica by the two emperors, we saw how important the charges initially brought against Athanasius were in the *Letter of the Eusebians to the Three Augusti* (338), and how they were revived in the year 341, when Constantius threatened the "deposed" Bishop of Alexandria with the death penalty, primarily for his reputed appropriation

---

[433] Hess, *Canons of Sardica*, 128.
[434] Girardet, *Kaisergericht und Bischofsgericht*, 135, note 124.

of the proceeds from the sale of corn intended for widows in Egypt. It was this indictment of a purely civil nature that prevented Athanasius' return to his city and that apparently prompted Julius to send his *4th Letter* to the Eusebians through the Court of Constans, requesting him to urge his brother emperor to recognize Athanasius as the legitimate claimant to Alexandria and to drop the civil charges that Constans himself had in the year 339 rejected. We have further pointed out how careful the Sardican Fathers were in their *Letter to Julius* to describe the function of the emperors in arranging that the synod take place: they conceded (*permiserunt*) to the assembly—in contradistinction to the description of the Eusebians who claimed that the emperors summoned the synod (*conuenti*). The Sardican Fathers in their *encyclical* likewise state: denique gratia dei iuuante etiam ipsi clementissimi imperatores congregauerunt ex diuersis prouinciis et ciuitatibus ipsam synodum sanctam in Serdicensium ciuitatem [et] fieri permiserunt.[435] The same neutral, almost pragmatic, attitude of the Synodal Fathers to the role they attributed to the emperors in the assembly of the synod is reflected in Canons 8–12, where certain consequences for the discipline of the Church were drawn (though not exclusively) from the experience of Athanasius (among others) who was frequently cited on civil charges by the Eusebians, and earlier by the Meletians, before the imperial court. This influence of Athanasius' case, with regard to the formulation of the canons, has been generally ignored by commentators.

According to Canon 8, the Synodal Fathers did not conceive the emperor as being in any sense superior to the Church and her concerns, as the Eusebian Synod of Antioch (330) did, but allowed for intercession at the court for the poor, the oppressed, widows, and orphans, though it condemned indiscriminate petitions and those whose object was personal ambition.[436] It also provided that appeals for pardon be made on behalf of those who had suffered injustice and fled to the mercy of the Church, and those found guilty who were exiled or received any kind of sentence.[437] It has been suggested that *ad misericordiam ecclesiae confugiant* is the

---

[435] *Encyclical Letter of the Synod of Sardica* 1,2 (CSEL 65, Feder 104,4–7).

[436] See Hess, *Canons of Sardica*, 131; Girardet, *Kaisergericht und Bischofsgericht*, 134–135.

[437] Sed quoniam saepe contingit, ut ad misericordiam ecclesiae confugiant, qui iniuriam patiuntur aut qui peccantes in exilio vel insulis damnantur aut certe quamcumque sententiam suscipiunt, subveniendum est his et sine dubitatione petenda indulgentia. Hoc ergo si vobis placet? Universi dixerunt: placet et constituatur (Joannou, *Fonti*, 169–170).

earliest known reference to the privilege of sanctuary in Christian Church buildings.[438] However, it is possible that it was prompted by cases such as that of Athanasius, who was repeatedly cited before the imperial court on various unfounded charges by the Meletians and Eusebians and who more recently fled to the Church of Rome after he had been accused of violence and appropriation of the corn provided for widows. Julius' request to Constans, that these charges be dropped by his brother Constantius, was a precedent for other such petitions of pardon envisaged by the Synod of Sardica. A glance at the other canons seems to confirm this suggestion.

The procedures for the presentation to the imperial court of such legitimate petitions, as permitted by Canon 8, are described in Canon 9. Ordinarily such appeals are to be conveyed to the court by a deacon, having been first sent to the provincial metropolitan for his recommendation,[439] while Canon 10a adds: Qui vero Roman uenerint, sicut dictum est (καθὼς προείρηκα) sanctissimo fratri et coepiscopo nostro [Ἰουλίῳ] Romanae ecclesiae praeces quas habent tradant, ut et ipse prius examinet si honestae et iustae sunt et praestet diligentiam adque sollicitudinem ut ad comitatum perferantur.[440] According to Hess,[441] the interpretation of this text seems to depend on the meaning of καθὼς προείρηκα. This phrase probably refers to an earlier proposal, made by Ossius himself (who also proposed this canon), to insert the phrase "et confugerit ad beatissimum ecclesiae Romae episcopum" into Canon 7, which dealt with the case of a bishop who fled to the Bishop of Rome in order to have his unjust sentence reexamined (as in the precedent of Athanasius). "If this is the correct interpretation, the clause provides for those bishops who have been deprived of their sees and who flee to Rome to appeal their cases; they may present petitions for clemency to the emperor, subject to the approval of the Roman bishops."[442] The

[438] See Hess, *Canons of Sardica*, 131. For literature, see his note 4 on p. 131.

[439] Cf. Joannou, *Fonti*, 170–171. Here I follow the interpretation of Hess, *Canons of Sardica*, 132–134; however, I am not fully convinced of his claim that the provincial metropolitan was at the time an exclusively Eastern institution (cf., e.g., *Hist. Arian.* 33,6, where Athanasius speaks of "Paulinus, Bishop of Trier, the metropolis of the Gauls, Lucifer, Bishop of the Metropolis of Sardica, Eusebius of Vercelli in Italy and Dionysius of Milan, that is the metropolis of Italy," unless Athanasius is projecting the Eastern Church order onto the West).

[440] Turner. Following Hess, *Canons of Sardica*, 119–121, 135, I also opt for the Greek reading of "Julius" in place of the Latin "of the Roman Church."

[441] Hess, *Canons of Sardica*, 135.

[442] Hess, *Canons of Sardica*, 135. The interpretation of Caspar, *Geschichte des Papsttums* I, 163, note 2, that Canon 10 deals with the (hypothetical) question as to the procedure to be adopted

interpretation of Hess seems to be confirmed in so far as the provisions of the canon, so understood, perfectly reflect the other historical circumstances—ignored by the American scholar—surrounding the flight of Athanasius to Rome to secure a revision of his sentence at Tyre, namely, his unjust indictment on civil charges before the three emperors and its sequel, Julius' petition for pardon to the emperor, which led to the assembly of the Sardican Synod.

The Canons of Sardica reveal the picture of a Church ready to make as much use as possible of the new positive attitude of the emperor in order to further her mission as advocate of the poor and distressed, as well as of those who suffered injustice at the hands of the State (and who otherwise would have had no hope of redress); even taking the side of the guilty, she was prepared to plea for clemency on their behalf before the emperor. This is a different tone from the self-righteousness that is to be discerned in the Eusebian *"encyclical"* with its pharisaical insistence on the strict observance of incorrectly understood "rules" (regarding the irreversibility of synodal judgements). Further, the Sardican canons make no provision whatever for petitions to the imperial authority, with regard to matters which concerned the internal affairs of the Church. As they indicated, with regard to the "Appeal Canons," such cases were to be dealt with by the Church's own "legal" machinery—then in the initial stages of development—the center of which was the Bishop of Rome, with his authority to cause synodal judgements (relating to the behavior of bishops) to be revised.

Athanasius' threatened condemnation on a civil indictment by Emperor Constantius II, as well as the civil *recognition* of his claim to the See of Alexandria and the like claims of the other bishops, still remained to be settled. To achieve the latter, the bishops at Sardica composed a *letter to Constantius II:*[443] Et hoc obsecramus pietatem tuam, ut eos, qui adhuc—egregii uidelicet sacerdotes, qui tanti nominis praepollent dignitate—aut in exilio aut in desertis

when the imperial court took up residence in Rome is not at all "viel wahrscheinlicher," as Girardet, *Kaisergericht und Bischofsgericht*, 136, suggests (though without giving any reason for his preference). Apart from the fact that at the time of the Synod of Sardica, the possibility that an emperor would again take up residence at Rome was not very likely, the Canons of Sardica show no indication that the Fathers dealt with hypothetical situations, but rather framed regulations as were determined by the actual circumstances surrounding the cases which made the canonical regulations necessary.

[443] Preserved by St. Hilary (CSEL 65, Feder 181,5–184,13).

locis tenentur, iubeas ad sedes suas remeare, ut ubique grata liberatas sit et iucunda laetitia.[444] The letter also makes a general plea for freedom, in the first place, for the orthodox,[445] and concludes with a light warning to the emperor, when it reminds the Eastern emperor that: "Those who imprudently and carelessly mix with the communion of those [who were excommunicated by the synod], since they become associates in their evil deeds, necessarily suffer eternal punishment as sharers in the crimes of those who already in this world are despicable and rejected."[446] Girardet recently drew attention to the significance of this sentence, where Constantius is gently but undeniably threatened with excommunication and eternal damnation, should he fail to distance himself from those Eusebians who were excommunicated by the Synod of Sardica.[447] It is the first sign of a development which reached its completion with St. Ambrose of Milan, who refused to admit Theodosius I to communion after the emperor had caused the death of several thousand citizens in Thessalonica (390), and who also affirmed that the Christian Emperor is Ecclesiae filius.... Imperator enim intra Ecclesiam, non supra Ecclesiam est.[448] This development was anticipated by St. Athanasius, when, at the beginning of his career as a bishop, he refused to obey Constantine and admit Arius with the explanation: "no communion exists with this anti-Christian heresy according to [the law of] the Catholic Church,"[449] and was greatly furthered by the Bishop of Alexandria in his *Historia Arianorum,* to which we will give our attention in the following chapter.

§11 The Civil Restoration of Athanasius to His See

That Constantius was unwilling, even after Sardica, to allow Athanasius return to the city of Alexandria, and only reluctantly acceded to the pressure exerted on him by his brother emperor

---

[444] *Letter of the Synod of Sardica to the Emperor Constantius,* 4,1 (CSEL 65, Feder 183,17–20); see also *Letter to Constantius,* 1,2 (Feder 181,13–182,2) and the *Letter of the Synod to the Church in Alexandria = Apol.* 39,1 (Opitz 117,25–31).

[445] iccirco laboratis et salutaribus consiliis rem publicam regitis, excubatis etiam et uigilatis, ut omnes, quibus imperatis, dulcissima libertate potiantur (*Letter to Constantius* 2,1 = Feder 182,6–18).

[446] *Letter to Constantius* 5,2 (Feder 184,10–13).

[447] Girardet, *Kaisergericht und Bischofsgericht,* 139–140.

[448] Ambrose, *Contra Auxentium* (*PL* 16,1018,B6–9).

[449] μηδεμίαν εἶναι κοινωνίαν τῇ χριστομάχῳ αἱρέσει πρὸς τὴν καθολικὴν ἐκκλησίαν (*Apol.* 140,11–12).

Constans is well attested by our sources.[450] Similarly, the documentary evidence—in particular the three letters of Constantius to Athanasius requesting him to return to his see[451]—reveal Athanasius' caution, indeed his reluctance, to take the Eastern emperor at his word after Constantius had finally agreed to the return of the bishop to Alexandria (most probably after the death of the "antipope" there, Gregory, on June 26, 345). The result was that even though the judgement of Julius regarding his claim had been confirmed by the Synod of Sardica in the summer of 343, Athanasius only returned to his Church on the October 21, 346. The details of the complicated story of his return to Alexandria need not occupy too much of our attention here. Only three points need to be briefly touched on: the nature of Athanasius' restoration by the emperor, the question of the civil indictment (regarding the corn), and Athanasius' final visit to Rome.

a) It should be clear by now, both from the genesis of the Synod of Sardica and the documents which issued from it (i.e., from the actual synod and not the Eusebian gathering), the problem of Athanasius' civil restoration to his see played a major role. His claim to Alexandria, which was vitiated in Tyre, was recognized by the Synod of Sardica; the Eastern emperor was again asked to give it civil recognition by permitting Athanasius return to his city. In what is most probably a fictional dialogue between Constantius and Athanasius at Antioch, September (?) 346, where Athanasius was eventually received by the Eastern emperor and dispatched to Alexandria with the necessary civil documents of recognition, the Eastern emperor is reported to have said: "You have recovered your See according to the decree of the synod and with our approval."[452] This text, attributed to the emperor, accurately reflects the double-authority presupposed and implicitly affirmed by the Synod of Sardica: the ecclesiastical ψῆφος τῆς συνόδου on the one hand,

---

[450] Cf. *Hist. Arian.* 49,2 (Opitz 211,19–20), where Athanasius puts words into the mouth of Constantius which, most probably, accurately describe the expressed sentiments of the emperor after 356: τὴν πρὸς τὸν ἀδελφὸν αἰδούμενος φιλίαν τὸν τῆς θείας καὶ εὐσεβοῦς μνήμης ἐπὶ καιρὸν αὐτῷ τὴν ὡς ὑμᾶς γενέσθαι πάροδον ἠνεσχόμην; cf. Theodoret, *HE* 2,8,53–57 (Parmentier-Scheidweiler 118,5–119,11); Socrates, *HE* 2,22,3–2,24,2 (Hussey 241–242); Sozomen, *HE* 3,20,1–22,6 (Bidez-Hansen 133,29–137,15). See also Lauchert, *Leben*, 57–59; Batiffol, *La paix constantinienne*, 451–455; Bardy, *Saint Athanase*, 87–97; Schwartz, "Zur Kirchengeschichte," 139f. (= *GS* IV, 13f.).

[451] Cf. *Apol.* 54,1–56,3 (Opitz 135,1–137,20).

[452] Socrates, *HE* 2,23,34 (Hussey 253).

and the συναίνεσις of the emperor on the other. Such a clear distinction is essentially other than the identity of Church and Empire, as assumed in the "Eusebian heresy" of the Imperial Church.

Whether or not the same distinction was actually held by Constantius is not clear from the decrees he issued at Antioch (346).[453] It is striking that none of the three documents explicitly refer to the Synod of Sardica as such. The only possible allusions to the synod are to be found in the opening of the *Letter of Constantius to the Bishops and Presbyters of the Catholic Church (in Egypt?)*, where he states: "The most reverend Athanasius has not been abandoned by the grace of God. But, although for a brief period he was subjected to that trial to which man is liable, nevertheless he has obtained the decree (ψῆφον) that is due [to him] from the omniscient providence, when he, according to the will of the Almighty (βουλήσει τοῦ κρείττονος) and our sentence (κρίσει ἡμετέρᾳ) was restored to his fatherland and to the Church over which he presided by divine command."[454] It is possible that both ψῆφος and βούλησις τῆς κρείττονος refer to the decision of the Synod of Sardica, though this has been denied.[455] What is undeniable is that Constantius' evident avoidance of any express mention of the synod indicates his reluctance to admit openly what in effect amounted to his submission to that synod's judgement (ψῆφος), here attributed rather vaguely (though not incorrectly) to Providence.[456] What is also clear from the text just quoted is the limited scope of Constantine's judgement (κρίσις), to which he explicitly draws attention: the civil restoration of Athanasius to his homeland and thus to the Church over which he presides "by divine command"—another possible allusion to Sardica.

b) Constantius' civil recognition of the claim of Athanasius to the Church of Alexandria was not the only object of the bishop's journey to the Court of Constantius at Antioch (346). The civil indictments of the Eusebians—first raised in their letter to the three Augusti (338), and taken up again by them in 341 after

---

[453] The three are preserved by Athanasius in his *Apologia* (see above, note 451).

[454] *Apol.* 54,2 (Opitz 135,3–7).

[455] E.g., Batiffol, *La paix constantinienne*, 455–456.

[456] Caspar, *Geschichte des Papsttums* I, 167, maintains that there was no causal connection between the judgement of Sardica and the restoration to his see by the emperor, and claims that Athanasius' hesitation to accept Constantius' invitation to come to the court was due to his unwillingness to be rehabilitated by the free grace of the emperor. Caspar comes to such a conclusion since he ignores the question of the *civil charges* (for which Athanasius indeed received a type of royal pardon).

news of Athanasius' recognition by the Synod of Rome had reached them by means of Julius' *3rd Letter*—needed to be settled. It is remarkable, as has already been observed, that these charges have been ignored by historians, ancient and modern, although they form an essential part of the background to the entire second exile of Athanasius in particular the Synod of Sardica. They also explain in part why Athanasius was so reluctant to accept the invitation of Constantius to come to the court and be restored to his city. Even as late as 341, Constantius had threatened the bishop with the death penalty on their account. From the *Letter of Ossias of Cordova to the Emperor Constantius* composed ca. 356,[457] we learn about what actually happened when Athanasius arrived in Antioch.

> On another occasion Athanasius came to your Court, when you sent for him by letter, and requested that his enemies, who were at the time in Antioch, be summoned, either altogether or each of them singly, in order that they might either convict [him] or be convicted, and that they might in his presence prove [him to be] the kind of man they asserted, or cease to slander him in his absence. You would not allow this suggestion; but they rejected it.[458]

The calumnies referred to by Ossius in this letter cannot have been the charges of an ecclesiastical nature raised at Tyre and rejected by Julius of Rome, whose judgement was recognized as just by the Synod of Sardica, but only to the accusations of a civil nature, relating to the reputed violence caused by Athanasius on his return from the first exile, and his reputed appropriation of the proceeds from the sale of the corn set aside by imperial decree for the widows in Egypt. It appears, then, that Constantius declined an inquiry into the said charges—though Athanasius had expressly requested one—and simply "ordered that the decrees formerly issued by him (= Constantius) against me (= Athanasius) in consequence of the false accusation of the Eusebian party be cancelled and effaced from the Orders of the Duke and the Prefect of Egypt; and Eusebius the Decurion, who was dispatched [thence], removed them from the Orders."[459] The slander referred to here by Athanasius can only have been the false charge relating to the corn

---

[457] Preserved by Athanasius in *Hist. Arian.* 44,1–11 (Opitz 207,20–209,4).

[458] *Hist. Arian.* 44,4 (Opitz 208,1–5). See also Athanasius' own account of the meeting at Antioch in *Hist. Arian.* 22,1–3 (194,1–13).

[459] *Apol.* 56,1 (Opitz 136,8–11). Cf. fragments of the imperial decree, preserved in *Hist. Arian.* 23,3 (Opitz 195,22–28) and *Apol.* 56,2–3 (136,12–20).

supply for the widows in Egypt and not the ecclesiastical charges raised at Tyre.

c) Schwartz intimated that, after the Synod of Sardica, Athanasius paid little attention to Julius of Rome.[460] A little earlier, Hagel had drawn attention to the brief mention in the *Apologia* of Athanasius' final visit to Rome (June-July? 346) before his journey to the imperial court at Antioch *en route* to Alexandria, and uses its scantiness as one of the five indications which, he claims, point to an important change in the attitude of Athanasius to Julius after the Synod of Rome.[461] (The other four indications, we will shortly see, are based on a misinterpretation of the *Apologia*.) More recently, Piétri drew a similar conclusion.[462] Before we take a closer look at the points raised by Hagel and Piétri, it is necessary to clear the air with regard to the actual historical situation.

From our analysis of the various documents associated with the Synod of Sardica, and from our reconstruction of the events which led up to Sardica, it should be evident that any attempt to depict Athanasius as either turning away from the protection of Julius after the Synod of Rome, or seeking the alternative support of the emperor (Constans and later Constantius) is as unfounded as the opinion that behind such a change of attitude lay the clash of two ecclesiological principles, Papalism and Episcopalism, as has been suggested.[463] We have seen that Julius and Athanasius shared the same ecclesiological principles—indeed it can be said, that in his famous *4th Letter,* Julius in a sense took up and systematically developed the various concepts originally perceived by Athanasius as essential ecclesiological principles to be defended in the face of the "Eusebian heresy," namely, the Church's Apostolic nature and its essential freedom. The documentary evidence further indicates that it was Julius (not Athanasius) who most probably interceded with Constans to secure the necessary civil recognition from his brother Constantius that would permit Athanasius to return to Alexandria.

The immediate outcome of Sardica—an open schism between the majority, based mostly in the West, and the Eusebian party, mostly in the East—did not initially encourage Constantius to comply with the decision of the synod with regard to Athanasius. As we have mentioned, Constantius only conceded to Athanasius' return

---

[460] Schwartz, "Zur Kirchengeschichte," 141 (= *GS* IV, 16).
[461] Hagel, *Kirche und Kaisertum*, 58–59.
[462] Piétri, "La question d'Athanase vue de Rome," 116–117.
[463] Cf. Hagel, *Kirche und Kaisertum*, 59.

after the death of Gregory, the Eusebian candidate in Alexandria (June 26, 345), though it must be added that in August 344 he had already shown signs of a change of attitude, when he granted clemency to the supporters of Athanasius in Alexandria.[464] The uncertainly of the situation after Sardica is reflected in the movements of the Bishop of Alexandria. He remained near the borders of the Eastern provinces that were controlled by Constantius, evidently waiting both for the necessary civil permission to return to Egypt and for his clearance from the civil charges brought against him by the Eusebians. He celebrated Easter (344) at Naissus in Illyricum[465] and only moved to Aquileia early in the year 345 to meet Constans there. Constans had summoned him by letter after the Western emperor had received word from his brother Constantius at the end of 344, most probably to the effect that he was prepared to show leniency to Athanasius.[466] Athanasius, however, was not prepared to risk his life. He was still threatened with the death penalty. He remained at Aquileia and awaited further developments. After the death of Gregory, he received three letters from Constantius requesting him to come to the court and be restored to his see. At the same time as the third letter, i.e., early in the year 346, Constantius again wrote to Constans,[467] exhorting the Western emperor to persuade Athanasius to return. This was a complete reversal of the attitude of Constantius at the beginning of the second exile, and indeed up to and immediately after the year 341. It was also a humiliation for the Eastern emperor, one he did not forget. Once he gained control of the entire empire, he would make Athanasius pay dearly for this loss of face.

On receipt of his brother's letter, Constans again sent for Athanasius to meet him in Gaul (possibly at Trier)[468] where he must have received assurances that his life was no longer in danger. From there he set out for Antioch to meet Constantius and to receive the necessary civil permission for his return to Alexandria.

---

[464] Cf. *Hist. Arian.* 21,1 (Opitz 194,1–5). See Seeck, *Regesten*, 192; Simonetti, *La Crisi Ariana*, 189.

[465] *Festal Index* XVI (Robertson, *Athanasius*, 504; Larsow, *Fest-Briefe*, 31); see Seeck, *Regesten*, 193.

[466] Cf. *Ad Const.* 4 (Szymusiak 93). The *Letter of Constantius to Constans* (no longer extant) coincides chronologically with the change of attitude of Constantius towards the supporters of Athanasius in Alexandria (see above, footnote 464). See also *Ad Const.* 3 = Szymusiak 90); *Apol.* 51,1 (Opitz 132,8–9). See Seeck, *Regesten*, 193.

[467] Cf. *Hist. Arian.* 21,3 (Opitz 194,9–13).

[468] Cf. *Ad Const.* 4 (Szymusiak 93). This meeting between Athanasius and Constans is ignored by Seeck.

But Athanasius first journeyed to Rome to take leave of Julius. The reason for this, his final visit to Rome, can only have been to express his gratitude to the bishop, Julius, whose intervention for him, both in the ecclesiastical and civil spheres, was ultimately responsible for his restoration. The action apparently undertaken by Julius in association with his *4th Letter* to the Eusebians, namely, to secure the support of Constans in getting Constantius to give Athanasius' claim to the See of Alexandria civil recognition, had finally in 346 borne fruit. Julius' *Letter to the Presbyters, Deacons, and People residing at Alexandria*[469] on that occasion is a letter of congratulations to the Church (and to the Bishop of Alexandria himself) on the actual restoration of Athanasius. It is full of joy and thanksgiving for the fulfilment of the prayers of the Alexandrian Church, and abounding in praise for Athanasius, "who, having passed victorious through the perils of so many tribulations, is now restored to you, having been proved innocent not only by us but also by the entire Synod."[470] Here, in what must be the most sublime document that issued from the murky controversies of the second exile, there is not a trace of any tension between the two great men, Julius and Athanasius, nor the slightest vestige on the part of the Bishop of Rome of any attempt to make capital out of the central contribution he made to achieve the desired restoration. Julius does not even hint at his authority as occupant of the See of Peter, newly reaffirmed at Sardica. This letter, which gives us the most authentic picture of Athanasius' character and his intimate paternal relationship to his Church, from which he was forcibly separated for almost seven years, also reveals the ultimate motive of Julius' involvement in the cause of Athanasius: his sympathy for the sufferings of the brethren, i.e., the charity that characterized his office with its specific responsibility for truth, as he expressed it in his *4th Letter* to the Eusebians.[471] As in that letter, so too in this letter of congratulations to the Church of Alexandria, the preeminence of the Bishop of Rome is simply taken for granted.

§12 The *Apologia* in the Light of the Historical Background

With the triumphal entry of Athanasius into Alexandria on October 21, 346, began the ten years of relative calm which has

---

[469] Preserved by Athanasius in *Apol.* 52,1–53,6 (Opitz 133,19–134,30).
[470] *Apol.* 53,1 (Opitz 134,8–9).
[471] See above, p. 400f.

been described in the literature as the "Golden Decade."[472] However, it was only the calm before the worst storm that broke over the Church in the fourth century, one that also almost succeeded in sundering the Bishop of Alexandria from his "spouse," the Church of Alexandria. During the golden decade, Athanasius devoted all his energies to his pastoral and missionary responsibilities and built up the Church so efficiently that she was able to survive the even greater crisis ahead. The first clouds on the horizon appeared early in the year 350, when Constantius II became sole ruler of the empire, after the murder of Constans in consequence of the insurrection of the usurper Magnentius.[473] The news caused alarm in Alexandria. Constantius' *Letter to Athanasius*,[474] reassuring the bishop that he wished him to continue to function as Bishop of Alexandria despite the recent death of Constans, can only have brought cold comfort to the said bishop. The implication of the letter was that he could remain bishop as long as he retained the royal favor.

Two years later (April 12, 352),[475] Julius of Rome died and the Synod of Antioch apparently utilized the exchange of communion letters with his successor Liberius to revive the deposition of Tyre, claiming that Athanasius had been restored not by the law of the Church (= the Synod of the Orientals) but due to the contentiousness of his friends, namely Constantine II (in 337) and Constans (in 346). A synod held by Liberius in Rome (end of 352—beginning of 353) after the delegates from Antioch and Alexandria had presented their cases decided in favor of Athanasius. Due to the objections of the Antiochenes to the Synod of Rome (352–353), Liberius requested Constantius (now in the West attempting to subdue the insurrection of Magnentius) to arrange a synod at Aquileia to reexamine the issue. The synod was assembled, not at Aquileia, but at Arles, and Athanasius was condemned by all, including the Roman delegates, with the exception of Paulinus, the successor of Maximin of Trier. Liberius called for another synod and the emperor permitted it to take place in Milan (355). A handful of bishops, including Liberius' delegates, refused to condemn Athanasius

---

[472] See Bardy, *Saint Athanase*, 98–127.

[473] See Seeck, *Regesten*, 197; Lauchert, *Leben*, 61; Schwartz, "Zur Kirchengeschichte," 149 (= *GS* IV, 27).

[474] A Greek translation of the Latin original is preserved by Athanasius in *Hist. Arian.* 24,1–4 (Opitz 196,3–13). Another translation is to be found in *Ad Const.* 23 (Szymusiak 113).

[475] See above, p. 305f. The following is mostly a paraphrase of our findings there.

and were exiled. Once deposed as Bishop of Alexandria, Constantius indicted Athanasius for offences amounting to lèse majesté, which carried the death penalty.

Having failed in the year 353 to lure Athanasius away from Alexandria to Italy on the pretext of settling the legal doubt with regard to his claim to his see, the Imperial Notary Diogenes was sent to imprison the bishop in August 355. After Diogenes failed to fulfil his mission, the emperor sent the Dux Syrianus to remove Athanasius. By producing the earlier decrees of Constantius, which granted him the civil permission he needed to return to Alexandria at the end of the second exile, Athanasius was able to postpone an arrest; Syrianus deceived the bishop and the faithful by assuring them that he would refer matters to the emperor and await the necessary documents from him. Then unexpectedly, on the eve of February 9, 356, the Dux attacked the Church of Theonas, where the bishop and the faithful celebrated a vigil service. Athanasius dramatically escaped and so began his third exile.

He set out to meet Constantius personally. Then in the desert, while on the way to the West, he heard the news of the bishops who had been banished for not subscribing to his condemnation at Milan—including Liberius of Rome and Ossius of Cordova—and, around the same time, the news that almost ninety bishops of Egypt and Libya had been removed from their sees and their places given to those of Arian tenets. Shortly after this, Athanasius learned that he had been condemned to death by the emperor on various charges amounting to treason. He then went into hiding, where he wrote his *Encyclical to his Fellow-Bishops in Egypt and Libya,* his first prolonged attack on the tenets of the Arians. There he received from an emissary of Paulinus of Trier, the details of the Synods of Arles and Milan, and learned about the treachery of Valens and Ursacius, now undisputed leaders of the Neo-Arian party in the West, as well as received copies of their earlier recantation to Julius of Rome. Then Athanasius sat down to compose two legal defenses: the first, the *Apologia,* was composed for the "ecclesiastical court," the Synod of Milan, while the second, *Ad Constantium,* contained his legal defense before the emperor in the face of accusations of a purely civil nature.

When we compare Athanasius' presentation of the events and documents associated with his second exile and its background with the reconstruction of these events above, which is not based exclusively on the evidence of Athanasius but on a critical review of all the reliable source material at our disposal, then the first observation to be made is with regard to the historical accuracy of

Athanasius. Once one takes into consideration the literary form of the *Apologia* as a legal defense relating to one specific charge, namely that he had not been *declared* innocent by the *competent ecclesiastical authorities,* then we do not expect to find an exhaustive historical account of his condemnation at Tyre and restoration at Rome/Sardica. And yet the detached observer cannot but be impressed by the general accuracy of Athanasius with regard to historical matters. He is in fact more of a genuine historian than the ideologist Eusebius of Caesarea, since he is to an eminent degree aware of the need to uncover the causes and effects, the motives and significance of events that make up the warp and woof of history. His outline of the Eusebian-Meletian conspiracy, which brought him to Tyre, for example, is evidently colored by hindsight but is nevertheless fully in accordance with the facts, though admittedly pointed and presented with the view to highlight the fundamental motive of the Eusebians which was their sympathy for Arius and his teaching. Likewise, his general presentation, including omissions, summaries, and the unusual chronological sequence, which recounts the events leading up to the first exile in Part II of the *Apologia* and the events which took place after the first exile (and during the second exile) in Part I, is admittedly dominated by his overriding object to prove that he had been restored to his see by the competent ecclesiastical authorities. But in no way does he falsify facts or information, nor, despite his emphatic presentation, does he ignore the nuances of the situation. The latter is demonstrated in his presentation of the thorny question of Church-Empire relations.

In Part I of the *Apologia*, Athanasius demonstrates that he was declared innocent by the universal episcopacy at synods which were truly ecclesiastical, i.e., as he points out in his introductory narrative to the documents of Sardica, by a synod such as Sardica, which assembled without counts and where soldiers were not present,[476] in contrast with the Eusebian party who arrived at Sardica accompanied by Counts Musonianus and Hesychius.[477] Athanasius does not deny the role of Constans and Constantius in ordering (ἐκέλευσαν) the Synod of Sardica,[478] but he avoids the term "to summon"

---

[476] Cf. *Apol.* 36,3 (Opitz 114,9f.).

[477] Cf. *Apol.* 36,2 (Opitz 114,7–9). It should be noted that the truth of this statement is guaranteed by the simple fact that Musonianus, at least, was still alive in 356 (according to Seeck, *Regesten*, 475, he was Praefectus praetorio Orientis from July 25, 354 until June 7, 357), and so could have contradicted the report of Athanasius.

[478] Cf. *Apol.* 36,1 (Opitz 114,2–3).

(καλεῖν), which he used to describe the way both he and the Eusebians were called to Rome for the synod there. Neither does he try to hide the fact that Constantius granted him the necessary civil permission to return to Alexandria, but this is clearly shown to be a consequence of his truly ecclesiastical clearance at Rome and Sardica. On the other hand, his presentation in Part II of the events, which led to his deposition at Tyre, including his criticism of that synod, demonstrated how the Eusebians (and thus their successors the Neo-Arians, with Valens and Ursacius, who were active in the Mareotis Commission in 335, at their head) misused the legitimate and limited relationship of the imperial authority to the Church; this misuse was a basic element of what Sardica, following Julius of Rome, condemned as the "Eusebian heresy."[479]

What is of primary interest to us is the significance of the *Apologia* for the attitude of Athanasius to the Bishop of Rome. According to Hagel (and, more recently, Piétri), after 343 at the latest, the relationship between the two Apostolic Sees cooled off considerably. One of the indications given by both scholars has already been proved groundless. Hagel[480] claims that in the "theory" of Athanasius, with regard to the relationship of the Church to the empire that was propounded by the Bishop of Alexandria around the year 350, there was no place for Julius. Hagel based his analysis on the hypothesis of Seiler regarding the composition of the *Apologia* as the product of various revisions made during a period of two decades, which hypothesis, we have seen is untenable. Since the *Apology* was composed (as a unit) in 356 and since, as has been shown, Julius of Rome plays a central role in the text (as in the historical events), then the theory of Hagel must be abandoned. The other three indications used by Hagel to support his theory are likewise based on a misinterpretation of the *Apologia* and its purpose: (i) the fact that Athanasius does not mention the "Appeal Canons," which were based on the acknowledged primacy of the Bishop of Rome, does not mean that he in any way denied their content but simply that they, like many other documents associated with Sardica (such as his own two letters to the Churches of Alexandria and the Mareotis), were irrelevant to the specific object of the *Apologia*; (ii) neither does the insistence of Athanasius that the Eusebians held the final responsibility for the intervention of the Bishop of Rome in any way indicate his attempt to play down the role of Julius, since Julius himself insisted that he became involved

---

[479] See above, p. 340f.
[480] Cf. Hagel, *Kirche und Kaisertum*, 58–59.

in the case of Athanasius, not on his own initiative but in response to the Eusebians' attempt to find his recognition for their sentence at Tyre, and since Athanasius' own emphasis on the responsibility of the Eusebians had a contemporary relevance, namely, to reveal the new conspiracy of Valens and Ursacius; (iii) the fact that Athanasius received the copies of the two letters of repentance, written by Valens and Ursacius, from Paulinus of Trier and not directly from Julius is to be explained in terms of the historical circumstances associated with Arles and Milan, and is of no significance whatsoever for the relationship between Julius and Athanasius.

Piétri[481] draws attention to the decision of the Synod of Sardica, according to which, agreement between Rome and Alexandria about the dates on which Easter should be celebrated for the coming fifty years was reached.[482] As Joannou pointed out,[483] here Athanasius brought the Alexandrian custom in line with the Roman one,[484] which claimed as its authority, the tradition handed down by the Apostle Peter.[485] But the fact that in 350 and 360 (not 349 as Piétri states), the Alexandrian Church apparently reverted to its former custom cannot simply be interpreted as an indication that beginning in 343, the relationship between the two Apostolic Sees began to cool off. The reason for the differences in 350 and 360 cannot be examined in detail here, but we will not go far wrong if we see in them the reluctance of the Egyptian *faithful* to abandon fixed customs, a reluctance that can be felt in Athanasius' *Festal Letter* XXI for 346, where he exhorts his presbyters and deacons not to hesitate or dispute about the date, though it was other than the date customary in Egypt. Since Athanasius wrote thus in the year 346, then there can be no substance to the theory that relations between the Bishops of Rome and Alexandria deteriorated after the Synod of Sardica, 343.

Written in the year 356, Athanasius' *Apologia* set out to demonstrate that he had been pronounced innocent by the competent ecclesiastical authorities "acting justly and in accordance with the ecclesiastical [rules]."[486] Our independent analysis of this legal defense of Athanasius demonstrated that this "ecclesiastical authority" was first and foremost the universal episcopate and its

---

[481] Cf. Piétri, "La question d'Athanase vue de Rome," 117f.
[482] Cf. "Festal Index XV for Easter, 343" (Robertson, *Athanasius*, 504).
[483] Cf. Joannou, *Die Ostkirche und die Cathedra Petri*, 92.
[484] Cf. *Festal Letter* XVIII for Easter, 346 (Robertson, *Athanasius*, 544).
[485] Cf. "Festal Index XXI for Easter, 349" (Robertson, *Athanasius*, 504).
[486] *Apol.* 89,1 (Opitz 167,11); see also *Apol.* 90,3 (168,10–11).

mode of expression was their universal unanimity. However, it was clear that, for Athanasius, the Bishop of Rome occupied a unique position within the universal episcopate and played the most significant role in the establishment of the necessary unanimity. He is singled out from all other bishops as one whose relationship to the universal episcopacy is essential and not accidental, and whose authority includes the right to convene a synod before which bishops from the East (including Alexandria and Antioch) and West could be cited. Further, he recognizes the singular relationship between the Bishop of Rome and the synod as expressed in the way the judgement of the Synod of Rome is ἡ κρίσις τοῦ ἀδελφοῦ καὶ συνεπισκόπου ἡμῖν Ἰουλίου as Sardica described it. In other words, such a decision, when communicated by the Bishop of Rome, rests solely on his authority.

The central function of the Bishop of Rome, within the universal episcopate and its expression of unanimity, was not only of importance to Athanasius for his demonstration of the legality of his claim to the See of Alexandria in the past, but also in the year 356, when he wrote the *Apologia*. This is evident from the conclusion to the *Apologia* (*Apol.* 89–90), an examination of whose contents we have ignored up to now. As will be remembered, Athanasius composed the *Apologia* after news had reached him that, apart from the bishops who refused to subscribe to his condemnation at Arles (353) and Milan (355) and so were sent into exile, Liberius of Rome and Ossius of Cordova had also been banished on his account, i.e., since they preferred to abide by the judgement of Rome and Sardica (340–343) rather than accept his deposition at Tyre. There he reminds his readers (the Synod of Milan) that such bishops were not ordinary men but ἐπισήμων πόλεων καὶ κεφαλαὶ τοσούτων ἐκκλησιῶν,[487] who (unlike the party of Valens and Ursacius, which appropriated for themselves the violent methods of compulsion used by their predecessors, the Eusebians) only attempted to persuade by the power of argument and were prepared to endure banishment, such as Liberius, the Bishop of Rome.[488] Then follows a list of the other bishops: the great Ossius and bishops from Italy, Gaul, Spain, Egypt, Libya, and the Pentapolis,[489] who are not mentioned by name. Again, we note that the Bishop of Rome is singled out from the other bishops and, in a sense, is

---

[487] *Apol.* 89,2 (Opitz 167,16).
[488] Cf. *Apol.* 89,3 (Opitz 167,18–19). See above, p. 304f. for comment on the interpolation in Opitz 167,19–20.
[489] Cf. *Apol.* 89,3 (Opitz 167,20–22). See above, p. 304f. for comment on the interpolation in Opitz 167,22–25.

described as their foremost representative, whose attitude (as one who persuades with arguments and not with external force) is the opposite to that manifested by the Neo-Arians, as also by their ideological and political "fathers," the Eusebians. Behind this contrast lies the earlier battle of Julius and Athanasius against the Eusebians for the freedom of the Church in the face of the "Eusebian heresy" that employed the imperial authority to force its will on the Church and destroy her Apostolicity.

The Apology concludes with a final reference to the party of

> Liberius and Ossius and those with them, who perceiving the attacks on our person submitted to all kinds of suffering rather than betray the truth and the judgement which had been given in our favor. This they did with due deliberation and from a religious motive: since those things they suffered, reveal (δείχνυσι) the violence, which the others (= the bishops at Arles and Milan) suffered. They (= Liberius, Ossius, and their companions in exile) are reminders and exposures of the Arian heresy and the wickedness of calumniators; they are also a model and pattern to those who come after "to contend for the truth until death" (cf. Sir. 4,28), to turn away from the Arian heresy, being as it is at enmity with Christ and a forerunner of the Antichrist, and not to believe those who endeavor to speak against us. For the defense on our behalf and the sentence (ἡ ὑπὲρ ἡνῶν ἀπολογία καὶ ψῆφος) of so many and such bishops, (i.e., bishops of such important Churches), are eminently trustworthy (ἀξιόπιστος) and sufficient testimony.[490]

With these words, Athanasius closes his legal defense. The sufferings and exile of Liberius of Rome, Ossius, and the other bishops are seen by Athanasius to have a fourfold meaning: (i) they reveal the external pressure and violence exercised on the majority at Arles and Milan who subscribed to the condemnation of Athanasius; (ii) they expose the evil nature of the Arian heresy; (iii) they are examples to be imitated by those who contend for the truth; (iv) they are sufficient testimony to the innocence of Athanasius with regard to his claim to Alexandria and, as such, are of greater significance than his condemnation by the Synods of Arles and Milan, which was achieved by the use of external force on the part of Valens, Ursacius, and their party. The first three meanings of the exile undertaken by Liberius and his companions bring to light what we have described in our introductory chapter as the basic motive, the

---

[490] *Apol.* 90,2–3 (Opitz 168,3–11).

driving force of Athanasius' life and writings: his pastoral concern. The fourth underlines the importance which Athanasius attached to the testimony of those in exile with regard to his own claim to Alexandria. All four display the encouragement Athanasius drew from their freely undertaken sufferings on his behalf and on behalf of the Nicene Faith which now for the first time is openly attacked in the West and in the East. All the more, therefore, can one understand the shattering effect on Athanasius and his supporters when, over a year later, news reached Alexandria that Liberius had subscribed to the condemnation of Athanasius, and had accepted an alternative credal formula to that of Nicaea (the second Credal formula of Sirmium, 357). The details of the so-called lapse of Liberius are here of less interest than the significance of the fall on the part of the Bishop of Rome for Athanasius' own understanding of his office as successor to St. Peter. These are to be found in the much-abused work of Athanasius that was born in the trauma of the lapse of Liberius: the so-called *Historia Arianorum*.

CHAPTER TEN

Historia Arianorum ad monachos: Liberius and the Confession of Faith

The *Historia Arianorum ad monachos* (referred to in the following as *Historia*) has been described by one scholar, otherwise generally sympathetic to St. Athanasius, as "the one work which we would gladly believe to have come from any other pen."[1] E. Schwartz dismissed it as "ein von Haß sprühendes Pamphlet"[2] and used it to characterize the general tone of Athanasius' historico-apologetic writings. Although L. Bouyer called it "un roman comique endiable,"[3] the French scholar did insist that the work is

---

[1] Robertson, "Prolegomena," lvii. That Athanasius was the immediate author of the *Historia Arianorum* has been questioned (see Robertson, *Athanasius*, LNPF[2], 267) but this is no longer the subject of dispute. See Bardenhewer, *Geschichte der altkirchlichen Literatur* III, 62; Quasten, *Patrology* III, 37.

[2] See above, Chapter Six, footnote 3.

[3] Bouyer, *L'Incarnation et l'Église*, 19.

devoid of any bitterness.[4] And yet the general opinion of scholars is, that the *Historia* was a secret libel, composed for distribution among his most faithful—if not to say, fanatical—followers, the monks of the Thebaid,[5] a libel directed against the Emperor Constantius.[6] According to my interpretation, the above descriptions fail to do justice to the nature and aim of the document, and tend to forget the historical circumstances that occasioned its composition.

§1 Date of Composition

Towards the end of the year 355,[7] Liberius, who had been summoned to appear before the emperor at Milan, was exiled to Beroia in Trace since he refused to subscribe to the deposition of Athanasius. According to the *Historia*,[8] two years later his resistance broke down and he gave his signature to the condemnation of the Alexandrian bishop. The *terminus a quo* is thus the end of the year 357. There is almost universal agreement among scholars that this work was thus composed around 357–358.[9] Is it possible to establish the date of composition more accurately?

It is probable that Athanasius received news of the so-called lapse of Liberius around the same time as Constantius heard it, which, according to Jalland,[10] took place five months after the emperor's departure from Rome on May 29, 357, i.e., sometime in October

---

4 Bouyer, *L'Incarnation et l'Église*, 31.
5 See, for example, Gwatkin, *Studies*, 157; also, Fialon, *Saint Athanase*, 196–199; Lauchert, *Leben*, 36 (and 74–75); Baynes, "Athanasiana," 64. A less derogatory description of the *Hist. Arian.* is to be found in Bardy, *Saint Athanase*, 142–144.
6 Setton, *Christian Attitude Towards the Emperor*, 78.
7 Cf. Sozomen, *HE* 4,11,3 (Bidez-Hansen 152,26–153,3). See also Jalland, *Church and Papacy*, 228; Caspar, *Geschichte des Papsttums* I, 176.
8 *Hist. Arian.* 41,3 (Opitz 206,9–12).
9 For example, ± 357: Stülcken, *Athanasiana*, 79. The majority of scholars opt for the period between the end of 357 and the beginning of 358; see Lauchert, *Leben*, 73; Hagel, *Kirche und Kaisertum*, 61; Bardenhewer, *Geschichte der altkirchlichen Literatur* III, 62; Batiffol, *La paix constantinienne*, 512. Opitz in his commentary, p. 183, and Quasten, *Patrology* III, 37, opt for 358. Opitz pointed out that the work contains no reference to the insurrection of Athanasius' followers in Alexandria, September 358 (cf. the commentary of Opitz 216,13), which means that the *Historia* could not have been written later than that date.
10 Jalland, *Church and Papacy*, 231. There is no evidence, to the best of my knowledge, to support the contention of Caspar, *Geschichte des Papsttums* I, 186, to the effect that Constantius knew about the fall of Liberius in May 356, during his visit to Rome.

357. The text presumes that Leontius, the Arian Bishop of Antioch, was still alive at the time of composition.[11] But Leontius died in the year 357, though the exact date of his death has long been the subject of debate.[12] His death cannot have taken place before the fall of Liberius as Hefele suggested[13] or in the summer of 357 as Gwatkin proposed,[14] since Athanasius would most certainly have heard of it.[15] Robertson in a well-argued discussion of the question[16] convincingly pointed out that Leontius must have died at the very latest in October 357 in order to gain room for the events which culminated in the Synod of Ancyra (358). Accepting the argumentation of Robertson, it is reasonable to assign the *terminus ad quem* to late October—early November 357. Thus, the *Historia* must have been composed in October 357, after Athanasius had received word about the reputed subscription of Liberius to his deposition and excommunication, but before the news of Leontius' death had trickled through to Egypt. It was composed, therefore, within a comparatively short space of time, as indeed the homogeneity of the work and the consistency of its high-pitched protest both confirm. It is the impassioned, though nonetheless well-argued and carefully written, response of one who has been deeply shocked by recent events. As we will see, it is the answer of Athanasius to his apparent excommunication by the Roman Successor of St. Peter.

---

[11] Cf. *Hist. Arian.* 4,2 (Opitz 185,7–8); *Hist. Arian.* 28,1 (Opitz 198,1–4).

[12] See Hefele-Leclerq 911–912. The documentary evidence for the death of Leontius is to be found in Socrates, *HE* 2,37,7 (Hussey 303), and Sozomen, *HE* 4,12,3f. (Bidez-Hansen 154,23f.). Their accounts are not harmonious. Socrates dates the death of Leontius around the time of the Synod of Ariminum, 359, which is clearly too late; Sozomen simply informs us that the news of Leontius' death arrived while the emperor was in the West.

[13] See previous note.

[14] Gwatkin, *Studies*, 157, footnote 2.

[15] Gwatkin simply takes for granted that the death of Leontius was unknown to Athanasius. Hefele tried to solve the problem by suggesting that the accounts of the acquiescence of Ossius and Liberius to the state-backed Neo-Arian party were later inserted into the text, which, he maintained, was originally composed in 357, while Robertson (*Athanasius*, LNPF[2], 266–267) proposed that the *Historia* was begun at about the time when *De fuga* had been completed and was finished when the lapse of Liberius became known in Egypt. Both of these opinions are difficult to maintain in the face of the closely-knit structure and consistent style of the *Historia*, which would seem to rule out the presence of later additions and interpolations, or the possibility of a long drawn-out period of composition.

[16] Robertson, *Athanasius*, LNPF[2], 254. According to Batiffol, *La paix constantinienne*, 484, footnote 2, Leontius died in the final months of 357 or early 358.

§2 *Sitz im Leben*

Constantius,[17] as we saw above, had been practically coerced by his brother Emperor Constans into recognizing the decrees of the Synod of Sardica and suffered the public humiliation of having to request Athanasius on three separate occasions to return to his see in Alexandria, though he, Constantius, had previously threatened the exiled bishop with the death penalty for lèse majesté. The emperor did not forget this humiliation. After Athanasius was deposed from his see at Milan (355), the emperor brought new charges of a civil nature against the bishop, one of which was that Athanasius had set Constans, his brother, against him.[18] Later that same year, Constantius repeated this assertion in the course of his interview in Milan with bishop Liberius of Rome and added: "No success has meant as much to me, not even the victory over Magnentius and Silvanus (= usurpers), as the removal of that abominable person from Church affairs."[19]

Constans was murdered in 350, but Constantius was too preoccupied with the usurpers Magnentius and Silvanus to be able to take his revenge on Athanasius. Before a decisive victory over Magnentius at Mursa (September 28, 351), Constantius received moral support from the bishop of that city, who happened to be Valens.[20] From that time on, Valens, together with his friend Ursacius, became the emperor's chief advisors in ecclesiastical matters, and thus was formed a fateful alliance between three men, each of whom had been humiliated by Athanasius. But as long as Julius of Rome lived, they could not act openly against the Bishop of Alexandria. Their renewed interference in Church affairs began at the end of the year 351, when the two bishops were present at a synod held in Sirmium, where Constantius had taken up residence in order to depose and excommunicate the bishop of that city, Photinus, who had taken the erroneous teaching of his master Marcellus of Ancyra to its logical and patently heretical conclusion.[21] The credal formula, with its 27 anathemas, that was issued at the time and is generally known as First Sirmium,[22] was not directed against

[17] For a concise, and sympathetic, account of the ecclesiastical policy of Constantius, see Schwartz, "Zur Kirchengeschichte," 152f. (= *GS* IV, 30f.).

[18] Cf. *Ad Const.* 3f. (Szymusiak 90f.).

[19] Theodoret, *HE* 2,16,21 (Parmentier-Scheidweiler 134,24–135,3).

[20] Cf. Sulpicius Severus, *Chron. II*, 38,5 (Halm 91,21–24); see Schwartz, "Zur Kirchengeschichte," 150 (= *GS* IV, 28).

[21] See Sozomen, *HE* 4,6,1–16 (Bidez-Hansen 143,13–146,8); Socrates, *HE* 2,29,1–5 (Hussey 276–277); see Simonetti, *La Crisi Ariana*, 202–206.

[22] The Greek translation is preserved by Athanasius in *De syn.* 27,2–3 (Opitz

the Faith of Nicaea but against the heretical teaching of Photinus; even a few of the anathemas, such as the first one, were ostensibly directed against Arianism. According to Sozomen, this synod was held in the presence of the emperor[23] and was composed solely of Eastern delegates;[24] this report, considering the attendance of the two Western bishops, Valens and Ursacius, cannot be considered completely accurate. The sentence against Photinus caused little stir in the West, since the Synod of Milan (345) was even prepared to condemn his teachings as heretical.[25] Sozomen further informs us that the teaching of Photinus was condemned by East and West alike, by those who favored the Nicene Faith and by those who sympathized with the Arian tenets,[26] while Socrates states that the decision of Sirmium was universally commended both at that time and afterwards,[27] a statement that is confirmed by St. Hilary's favorable interpretation of the creed and its athenamas.[28] Our sources are silent as to the reaction of Julius of Rome to this synod; his silence could well be interpreted to mean his consent.

On April 12 of the following year, 352, Julius died. His successor, Liberius, was ordained Bishop of Rome on May 17.[29] The political and ecclesiastical constellations in the East and in the West are now completely other than in the year 337 when the Eusebians began their second campaign against Athanasius. As we have already seen, with the death of Julius and the election of Liberius, the third campaign as it could be called, was launched against Athanasius by the successors to the Eusebians, the Neo-Arian party, who were led in the West by Valens and Ursacius. But now a new emphasis can be detected in the ecclesiological ideology. The "Eusebian heresy" of the *Reichskirche* was primarily concerned with the autonomy of provincial synods and the irreversibility of synodal decisions, while the actual imperial dimension was, in a sense, secondary since it was confined to the region of presuppositions, mostly to be detected from their actions. But now the element of the imperial authority moves to center stage, while

---

254,17–256,22), while the Latin original is to be found in Hilary, *De syn.* 38 (*PL* 10,509,B7f.). See the commentary of Kelly, *Creeds*, 281–283.

[23] Sozomen, *HE* 4,6,12 (Bidez-Hansen 145,13). See also Batiffol, *La paix constantinienne*, 464; Kelly, *Creeds*, 281.

[24] See, Kelly, *Creeds*, 281.

[25] See Kelly, *Creeds*, 280.

[26] Sozomen, *HE* 4,6,3 (Bidez-Hansen 143,19–24).

[27] Socrates, *HE* 2,29,5 (Hussey 277).

[28] See Kelly, *Creeds*, 282.

[29] See Seeck, *Regesten*, 198–199.

the question of the irreversibility of synodal judgments, though still explicitly adhered to, fades somewhat into the background of the discussion. And yet despite the new emphasis, the battle on the ecclesiological front is essentially the same as that conducted under Julius of Rome. It is on the one hand the attempt of the Imperial Church to supplant the Apostolic Church, an attempt that had been ideologically prepared by Eusebius of Caesarea when he abandoned the Petrine ecclesiology and superimposed his imperial ecclesiology on its ruins. On the other hand, we have the almost futile struggle of the Apostolic Church—led by the principal Petrine Sees, Rome and Alexandria—against the combined forces of this world to preserve its original integrity within the new historical *milieu,* ostensibly so, favorable to the Church and her mission, but in reality, a constant danger and potential obstacle once the legitimate relationship between the Church and the empire broke down or was replaced by another.

To Jalland is due the credit for having been the first to recognize the nature of the issues involved in the period of the Church's history marked by the third exile of Athanasius. With the succession of Liberius, Jalland rightly observes, "the stage was set for a spectacular trial of strength between two powers, the state in the person of Constantius, now sole Augustus, and master of the Roman world, and the Church represented by Liberius, Bishop of Rome and guardian of the 'potior principalitas'; in other words, between two rival conceptions of the source of dogmatic truth, the will of the sovereign and the apostolic *paradosis*."[30]

At the synod held at Antioch (352), most probably to ratify the election of Liberius through the exchange of the *Letters of Communion,* the Neo-Arians elected George of Cappadocia to the See of Alexandria and attempted in turn to secure his recognition from Liberius, again by means of *Letters of Communion,* and thus implicitly Liberius' ratification of Athanasius' deposition at Tyre, 335.[31]

---

[30] Jalland, *Church and Papacy,* 224. In his reconstruction of the events following Liberius' election, Simonetti in *La Crisi Ariana,* 211f., seems unaware of their ecclesiological significance. Neither does he do justice to the initiative taken by Liberius in defense of the Nicaenum.

[31] The following is mostly a resumé of above, p. 305f. Since Jalland is unaware of the Synods of Antioch and of Alexandria, 352, and takes no account of their apparent cause—the exchange of the *Letters of Communion* on the election of Liberius to the See of Rome—then he is forced to conjecture that the reason for the Synod of Arles, and for the invitation of the emperor to Athanasius to travel to Italy, was the news of fresh disorders in Alexandria which had reached the court. Here, again, the influence of Schwartz's rather distorted picture of Athanasius as the ambitious troublemaker may possibly be detected.

The Synod of Alexandria also assembled in 352, either as a result of the decision of Antioch to elect George, or more likely with the purpose of arranging the exchange of the *Letters of Communion* with the newly elected Liberius. The synod demonstrated the legitimacy of Athanasius' claim to Alexandria by referring to the earlier Synods of Alexandria, Rome, Sardica, and Jerusalem. After the delegates from Antioch and Alexandria arrived in Rome and presented the decisions of their respective synods, Liberius held a synod and opted in favor of Athanasius. The Neo-Arians objected on technical grounds to the judgment of Liberius and so, following the procedure decided on by Sardica, the Bishop of Rome called for a synod composed of both parties to reexamine the issue and asked the emperor to arrange for its assembly at Aquileia. The emperor conceded to the synod but convened it at Arles, where he celebrated his *vicennalia* and his final victory over Magnentius. The change of venue and the actual historical circumstances are the first indications of Constantius' new policy of direct involvement in Church affairs.

When Athanasius received word of the synod proposed by Liberius, he sent a large and impressive delegation of five bishops and three presbyters, led by his friend and confidant, Serapion of Thmuis. In *Studens paci,* the first of the four letters signed by Liberius, under the pressure of his "protectors" after two years of exile, we are informed that Liberius had summoned Athanasius himself to Rome after the new Roman bishop had received letters from the Oriental bishops, which had been addressed to his predecessor, Julius, and that Liberius had threatened Athanasius with excommunication if he failed to obey.[32] The protracted debate about the genuineness of these four letters—now accepted by most scholars as genuine[33]—has highlighted one important fact: the great discrepancy between the contents of these documents and the contents of the unquestionably authentic letter, *Obsecro, tranquillissime,*[34] written by Liberius to Constantius after the Synod of Arles (353), with respect to Liberius' attitude to Athanasius. The discrepancy points to the fact that they were written under external compulsion and, thus, their value as historical evidence, concerning events reported

---

[32] Hilary, *Frag. hist.*, series B, III, 1 (Feder 155).

[33] See, for example, Feder, *Studien zu Hilarius*, 123–125 and 153–183. Regarding the details of this debate, see Caspar, *Geschichte des Papsttums* I, 589; see footnote on page 183f.; Jalland, *Church and Papacy*, 229, footnote 3. However, some scholars, such as Joannou in *Die Ostkirche und die Cathedra Petri*, 106, still contend that the letters are Arian forgeries.

[34] Cf. Hilary, *Frag. hist.*, series A VII, 1–6 (Feder 89,1–93,15).

in them, is extremely meagre. Unless there is independent evidence to support their contentions, then they cannot be used in an historical reconstruction, as has been attempted even by such scholars as Jalland[35] and Caspar.[36] When all the other evidence suggests a different series of events than those indicated by these documents,[37] then their value as source material is nil.

There was no reason for the Eastern bishops to write to Julius about Athanasius in the year 352. Their excuse to resurrect the issue of Tyre only came with Julius' death and the election of his successor. But the captors of Liberius had good grounds to invent such a "letter" to Julius, since by doing so, they could suggest that new evidence had been found that would have altered Julius' known attitude of support for Athanasius, had he lived to investigate them; at the same time, Liberius' own change of heart could be made to seem more credible. The historical evidence suggests, at the most, that Liberius had requested Athanasius to send delegates to his proposed synod (at Aquileia), while it was the emperor who personally invited Athanasius to come to Italy to settle the newly revived canonical objections to his claim to the See of Alexandria.[38] There was no need for Liberius to summon Athanasius to Rome in 352. In what can be considered Athanasius' reply to *Studens paci,* the *Historia,* Athanasius stresses what contemporary historians seem to have forgotten, namely that Liberius wrote under compulsion and thus what he wrote is more representative of his captors' intentions than those of the Bishop of Rome. Not only that, but he also indirectly answers the allegation that he failed to obey the summons of Liberius by going to rather extreme lengths to stress that, when he had in fact been summoned to Rome by the bishop there (Julius), he did not hesitate but hastened there without delay.[39] It is clear, therefore, that the contents of *Studens paci* and the three other "letters," though they carry the apparent authority of Liberius' signature and are not later Arian forgeries, cannot really be treated as equal to that of the undeniably genuine letters of Liberius, either in their authority as "papal" documents, or as credible historical sources.

At Arles, the Roman delegates requested that, before the question of Athanasius' condemnation be debated, the disputed questions

[35] See Jalland, *Church and Papacy*, 225.
[36] Caspar, *Geschichte des Papsttums* I, 169–170.
[37] See above, p. 305f. and p. 469f.
[38] See above, pp. 308–309.
[39] Cf. *Hist. Arian.* 11,1 (Opitz 188,29–30).

concerning the Faith be settled.[40] From the consistent attitude of Liberius, up to his exile, it is evident that the disputed subject matter is no longer the heresy of Photinus but the definition of Nicaea. The introduction of the debate on the *Nicaenum* by the Roman delegates at Arles marks, it seems to this writer, a very significant development in the history of the Church in the fourth century.

Up to then, the Synod of Nicaea had been mostly confined to the background of the controversies that were thrown up by the "Eusebian heresy." All parties involved paid lip service, at the very least, to the great synod. Those who favored the Arian tenets or, as was more common, those who felt rather uncomfortable about the Sabellian taste of the Nicene Creed, preferred to ignore it in practice without openly rejecting it. In any event, the Christological debates were primarily preoccupied with the heretical opinions held by Marcellus and Photinus. Athanasius and the Church of Egypt protested against the way the Eusebian-controlled bishops *in practice* contravened the decrees of Nicaea with regard to their admittance to communion of Arius and those who shared his heretical views, but their protest was drowned by the noise of the calumnies flung at Athanasius and the din caused by the legal battles which centered around his claim to the See of Mark. Julius of Rome heard his protest with sympathy, but he did not force the issue in his famous *4th Letter* to the Eusebian-controlled Synod of Antioch, which was aimed at healing the impending schism that the Eusebians had threatened. We remember how in his answer to the charge of the Eusebians, that he had dishonored their synod by reexamining its decrees, Julius simply pointed out that the Eusebians themselves had in fact dishonored the Synod of Nicaea by admitting the Arians to communion.[41] At Sardica, the question of the Nicene Faith as such was first raised in the face of the growing influence, it seems, of the teaching of Valens and Ursacius in the West, but the statement produced at the synod by Ossius and Protogenes did not apparently receive the assent of the participants and was, in any event, quite secondary to the main issues raised at the synod, which were the question of Marcellus' teaching, the claims of Athanasius to the See of Alexandria, and

---

[40] Cf. Sulpicius Severus, *Chron. II,* 39,2 (Halm 92,11–15). See also Caspar, *Geschichte des Papsttums* I, 171.

[41] *4th Letter of Julius = Apol.* 23,1–4 (Opitz 104,23–105,4). Towards the end of his letter, Julius mentions the complaints of presbyters who had more recently come to Rome from Egypt. The presbyters complained that bishops had been exiled because they refused to communicate with Gregory and his Arian associates (cf. *Apol.* 33,2 = Opitz 111,23–25).

the various charges brought against the Eusebian party. Two years later, at a synod held at Milan (345), four Eusebian delegates from Antioch, who tried to explain their interpretation of the Faith with their famous *Ecthesis Macrostichos,*[42] refused to condemn the heretical teaching of Arius—i.e., they most probably refused to subscribe to the Creed and anathemas of Nicaea—and so departed from the synod.[43] But now at Arles, 353, the legates of Liberius demand that before any other business can be transacted, before the case of Athanasius in particular can be examined, the question of the Synodal Fathers' attitude to Nicaea must be clarified. The Bishop of Rome had made the Nicene Creed into an issue for the first time since Nicaea itself, and demanded an explicit profession of the Faith defined there.

In the year 354, Liberius replied to the condemnation of Athanasius at Arles by demanding that another synod be assembled that would examine everything thoroughly. Again, he insisted that such an examination could only be undertaken after general consent, with regard to the *Nicaenum,* had been established.[44] At the proposed synod that was assembled the following year at Milan, Eusebius of Vercelli, acting on instructions from Liberius,[45] produced a copy of the Nicene Creed and requested that all subscribe to it in order to demonstrate the synod's unanimity with regard to matters of the Faith, before the case of Athanasius could be examined.[46] When he was brought before the emperor at Milan at the end of that same year (355), Bishop Liberius persisted in his insistence on the principle that before the question of Athanasius was taken up at a future synod, unanimity regarding the Nicene Faith must first be established. He told Constantius openly and courageously: "You condemn without reason a man, whom we have not judged. But I require that first a general subscription confirming the Faith set out at Nicaea but undertaken, so that thus, after our brothers are recalled from exile and restored to their own positions [in the

---

[42] Translated by Athanasius into Greek in *De syn.* 26,1f. (Opitz 251,22–254,12). See Kelly, *Creeds,* 279f., whose interpretation of the motives of the Western bishops in the stand they adopted is perhaps less than fair.

[43] quae est pax, clementissime imperator, cum sint ex partibus ipsis quattuor episcopi Demofilus, Macedonius, Eudoxius, Martyrius, qui ante annos octo, cum apud Mediolanium Arii hereticam sententiam noluissent damnare, de concilio animis iratis exierunt? (*Obsecro, tranquillissime* 4,1 = Hilary, *Frag. hist.,* Series A, VII, 4 = Feder 91,17–21).

[44] Cf. *Obsecro, tranquillissime* 6,1 (Hillary, *Frag. hist.* = Feder 92,20–93,8).

[45] See the letters of Liberius to Eusebius of Vercelli (*PG* 8,1355).

[46] Cf. Hilary, *Ad Const. Augustum,* 8 (*PL* 10,562,C2–8).

Church], then all should assemble in Alexandria,[47] if it appears that those who are now causing tumult in the Churches assent to the Apostolic Faith, and there, the accused and the accusers together with their defender being present, we might together penetrate behind the issues concerning them when we examine (ἐξετάσαντες) the matter."[48] Liberius had placed the Nicene Faith at the center of the public discussion—for the first time since the great assembly at Nicaea in the year 325—and declared all other questions to be secondary to, or at least dependent on, universal agreement with regard to the *Nicaenum*.

What was the reason for this very significant development? It is unlikely that in 352 Liberius had already heard of the extreme Arian teaching of the Anomoeans, Aëtius, and Eunomius, which was then making its first appearance at Antioch, though the possibility cannot be ruled out. Neither was Liberius directly influenced in his decision by Athanasius. As we saw, the Bishop of Alexandria only wrote his first work specifically aimed at the Arian teaching four years later (in 356), and even there Athanasius is not in the first place concerned with an exposition of the Nicene Creed, but simply instructs his readers to adhere firmly to the Faith they had received from the Fathers, and which had been defined in writing by those who assembled at Nicaea.[49] The reaction of Demofilus, Macedonius, Eudoxius, and Martyrius (the delegates from Antioch at the Synod of Milan, 345) to the request by the synod to condemn the heresy of Arius, apparently left a deep impression on Liberius and probably otherwise in the West: the Antiochene delegation departed angrily from the synod. This reaction probably enabled Liberius to perceive the fundamental importance of the question that had been regulated to the background in the controversies surrounding Athanasius, despite the protests of the latter.[50] But what in all likelihood brought the dogmatic issue to the surface was the exchange of the *Letters of Communion* occasioned by Liberius' succession, which resulted in the Synod of Antioch (352). That synod attempted anew to enforce the deposition of Tyre (335) by appointing the Arian George of Cappadocia to Alexandria (as though Alexandria was technically vacant), and attempting to

---

[47] This was probably due to the suggestion made by the Eusebian party at Sardica in their *Encyclical* 18,1–2 (Hilary, *Frag. hist.* = Feder 60,1–15).

[48] Theodoret, *HE* 2,16,16 (Parmentier-Scheidweiler 133,23–134,8).

[49] Cf. *Ad epp. Aeg. et Lib.* 8 (*PG* 25,566,A14–B2).

[50] Cf. *Obsecro, tranquillissime* 4,1–2 (Hilary, *Frag. hist.* = Feder 91,17–92,2).

secure for him the traditional communion with the Roman bishop, the inexperienced Liberius. Liberius, or the Synod of Rome, clearly examined his case together with that of Athanasius and the documents supplied by the Synod of Alexandria (352). They must have sifted all the evidence at their disposal and made full use of the archives of the Roman Church (where, for example, they found a letter, no longer extant, from Bishop Alexander of Alexandria to Silvester of Rome on the subject of the Arian heresy) and established that George had been in official communion with those placed outside the Church (by the Synod of Nicaea).[51] On the other hand, Liberius established that Athanasius had consistently and unequivocally protested against the Eusebian party's transgressions of the decrees of Nicaea. And so, when the Bishop of Rome was summoned before the Emperor, Liberius called Athanasius: "the present-day defender of the orthodox Faith that was defended at Nicaea."[52] It is of note that in the year 346 Constantius recognized that "union with him (= Athanasius) will be sufficient proof of each person's orthodox disposition;"[53] it is possible that Liberius' may have wished to allude to this statement of the emperor.

To Liberius alone, therefore, must be given the credit for this decisive turn of events in the controversy surrounding Athanasius. There is no historical evidence to suggest that the Athanasian *party*, as such, "provoked by the ascendancy won by their opponents and the increasing extravagance of their views, had decided openly to adopt the Nicene council and its creed as their standard of orthodoxy" as Kelly[54] maintains, since the growing influence of Valens and Ursacius, which, though it had its beginning on the evening of September 27, 351, only manifested itself at Arles in 353, i.e., after Liberius' delegates had demanded that the question of the Nicene Creed be debated previous to any examination of the case of Athanasius, and since it is unlikely that Liberius was at the time aware of the extreme Arian views which were being developed in the East. What finally moved Liberius to insist so strongly on the *Nicaenum* was, as is clear from his letter to Constantius and his defense before the same emperor at Milan, his responsibility for the Apostolic *paradosis* that was laid on him as Bishop of Rome in the face of the threat to its integrity posed by those in the East and

---

[51] Cf. *Obsecro, tranquillissime* 4,2 (Feder 92,2–4).

[52] ὁμόφροντες τοῦ σήμερον ἀντιποιουμένου τῆς κατὰ Νίκαιαν ἐκτεθείσης ὀρθοδόξου πίστεως (Theodoret, *HE* 2,16,22 = Parmentier-Scheidweiler 135,7–8).

[53] *Letter of Constantius to the Bishops and Presbyters of the Catholic Church (in Alexandria)* = *Apol.* 54,5 (Opitz 135,13–14).

[54] Kelly, *Creeds*, 284.

in the West who attempted to place on the Throne of Mark, a man who was in communion with the excommunicated Arian party, and to secure the Bishop of Rome's approval.

"God, however, is my witness," Liberius wrote to Constantius, "the entire Church together with its members is witness to the fact that I, acting with faith and awe towards my God, trample on and have trampled on all worldly considerations, as the evangelical and Apostolic rule so admonished. As far as the law is concerned, I have acted, not out of rash anger, but rather according to the established and recognized divine law; even when I was a cleric in another ministry, I did nothing out of pride or with a desire for honor. I reached this office of mine—my God is my witness—against my will; and indeed, my sole ambition, as long as I am in this world, is to remain in it without giving offence to God. And never have I executed rules of my own but rather those that are Apostolic, that they might always be maintained and observed. Following the custom and commandment of my predecessors, I have suffered no enlargement to the episcopacy of the city of Rome—and no diminution. And watching over that Faith, which was passed on by the succession of such great bishops, among whom there have been many martyrs, I eagerly desire that it be always preserved unimpaired."[55]

In this remarkable passage, the Bishop of Rome opens with a reference to the only authority to which he is responsible: God and His Church, the Church Universal. His actions, he tells the emperor, are not dictated by worldly considerations of any nature, but by his conscience that has God as its object and the rule established by the Gospel and the Apostles as its norm. He then defends his decision with regard to Athanasius' claim to Alexandria (that he should be regarded as the lawful claimant[56] and that, previous to any discussion of the case, the Nicene Faith be expressly confessed so that the true *pax* of the Church might be established[57]), since the emperor had evidently made his own the charge of the Arians to the effect that Liberius, like Julius before him, had tried to impose a new law on the Church and was thus threatening the peace of the (Christian) Empire.

Regarding the question of the ecclesiastical law concerning the authority of the Bishop of Rome to subject the judgment of local synods to reexamination, Liberius affirms that he was motivated

---

[55] *Obsecro, tranquillissime* 3,1–2 (Feder 90,27–91,14).
[56] Cf. *Obsecro, tranquillissime* 2,1–3 (Feder 90,9–25).
[57] Cf. *Obsecro, tranquillissime* 4,1 f. (Feder 91,15f.).

by one thing only—the divine law (i.e., of justice)[58]—and that he had acted in accordance with the Apostolic rules, with a view to their preservation. Further, he rejects any criticism of his exercise of that office entrusted to him as Bishop of Rome, which he neither desired nor willingly accepted, and he protests that he did not permit any increase in the authority that accrued to the See of Rome other than that which was customarily exercised by his predecessors; he adds the slightly threatening reminder that he was not prepared to suffer any diminution of that authority either. And then he indicates the source of that authority, which is the special responsibility of the Bishop of Rome to guard the Faith which had been transmitted to him by his predecessors, and to ensure that it remains intact. His "aside" concerning the numerous martyrs among his predecessors recalls the ironic remarks of the Eusebians in their reply to Julius' *3rd Letter,* where they attempted to disparage the traditional authority, generally attributed to the successors of Peter in Rome, by reminding Julius of the poor behavior of his predecessors during the Great Persecution, and by contrasting the same with the countless martyrs in the East during that reign of terror. It is possible that the criticism of the Roman bishops had been newly championed by Constantius. In reply, Liberius reminds the emperor of the many Bishops of Rome who had in fact suffered martyrdom.

Here Liberius articulates the traditional consciousness of each bishop's responsibility to God and before the Church Universal, as was earlier voiced by Polycrates of Ephesus and Cyprian of Carthage; he also affirms the unique responsibility of the Bishop of Rome to preserve the Apostolic constitution of the Church, as expressed in her customs and rules, and to guard the integrity of her Faith. In this letter, the Bishop of Rome rejects the superficial concept of the Church's *pax* and *unanimitas*, as it was understood by Eusebius of Caesarea and by Constantine, who accepted it as a useful instrument in order to help him achieve his goal of a united empire, namely, by means of external conformity; in its stead, Liberius proposes the traditional concept of peace based on internal assent: ego enim, religiossime imperator, tecum ueram pacem requiro, quae non sit uerbis composita interna dispositione fallaciae, sed praeceptis euangeliorum rationabiliter confirmata.[59]

---

[58] The first recorded words of Liberius at Milan are: τὰ ἐκκλησιαστικὰ κρίματα μετὰ πολλῆς δικαιοκρισίας γίνεσθαι ὀφείλει (Theodoret, *HE* 2,16,2 = Parmentier-Scheidweiler 131,18–19).

[59] *Obsecro, tranquillissime* 1,2 (Feder 89,16–19).

At Arles, the assembled bishops had subscribed to the condemnation of
Athanasius, including the Roman legates, who had acted contrary to the
instruction of Liberius. The one exception at Arles was Paulinus of Trier.
Valens and Ursacius were responsible for the stage-management of this
spectacle, that was executed behind the proscenium of the imperial residence and in front of a small but all-powerful audience of one: the sole
autocrat of the empire. Sad to say, this scene was not to be the last of its kind
in the history of the Church, when a body of bishops bowed to the will of
the prince.[60] Against this background, the attitude of Liberius cannot be
described as anything other than heroic. He was well aware of the danger
he was courting when he wrote the above letter to Constantius. And after
the even more distressing event of the Synod of Milan (355), salvaged only
by the courage and faith of a handful of bishops (this time including the
Roman legates), Liberius wrote to the three exiled bishops—who, with
Paulinus of Trier, refused to conform to the will of the sovereign—that he
too awaited the day when he would also share in their "martyrdom."[61] In the
opening words of that letter, he again demonstrates how well he had perceived the nature of the issues at stake: "under the guise of peace, the enemy
of the human race is seen to attack the members of the Church most furi-
ously."[62] The "peace" referred to is, of course, the attempt by the emperor
to impose his will on the Church and so to create an artificial uniformity.

According to the report of Athanasius, when the bishops Paulinus
of Trier, Lucifer of Cagliari, Eusebius of Vercelli, and Dionysius of Milan
refused to subscribe to Athanasius' condemnation or hold communion
with heretics on the ground that this was a *novum* and not an ecclesiastical law, the Emperor Constantius is said to have replied: ἀλλ᾽ ὅπερ ἐγὼ
βούλομαι, τοῦτο κανών, and added, "Let it be recognized as a custom:
for those who are called bishops of Syria bear with me when I so speak.
Therefore, either obey or go into exile."[63] Though this formulation is undeniably that of Athanasius himself, yet the statement, "my will is law," well
expresses the attitude of the emperor[64] as well as indicating its ideological

---

[60] Caspar, *Geschichte des Papsttums* I, 174, seems to assume that it was an isolated
     incident.
[61] Cf. *Quamvis sub imagine* (*PL* 8,1357,A5f.).
[62] *Quamvis sub imagine* (*PL* 8,1356, C12–1357,A2).
[63] Athanasius, *Hist. Arian.* 33,7 (Opitz 202,2–4).
[64] See Caspar, *Geschichte des Papsttums* I, 174; Jalland, *Church and Papacy*, 228,
     footnote 1. This interpretation has been vigorously contested—though not
     very convincingly—by Klein, *Constantius II. und die christliche Kirche*, 286 and
     passim.

paternity: "those who are called bishops of Syria," i.e., the Eusebians of Antioch.

When Liberius was brought before the emperor at Milan,[65] he displayed the same courage as was evident in the words of his previous letters. Those who had subscribed to Athanasius' condemnation, he accused of cowardice and of servility to the emperor—they cared not for the honor of God.[66] As Constantius defended the earlier Eusebian stance regarding the irreversibility of provincial synods in questions concerning human behaviour,[67] so also Liberius upheld the ecclesiastical principles of Julius concerning the demands of justice, which required that no bishop should condemn another without having first examined the case himself,[68] that the accusers must face the accused and not condemn him in his absence,[69] and, above all, that all matters be conducted according to the law of the Church.[70] What differentiates the stand of Liberius from that taken by Julius is the insistence of Liberius that before the case of Athanasius be examined, all bishops should expressly confess their adherence to the Nicene Faith.

In the argumentation of the emperor, a new element is also to be detected. He can now point to a large number of bishops in the East, and in the West who had confirmed the decision of Tyre, 335: καὶ ἐν τῇ συνόδῳ κατεψηφίσαντο πάντες οἱ ἐπίσκοποι τῆς οἰκουμένης,[71] and he asks Liberius rather sarcastically: "How do you measure [your] portion of the empire (οἰκουμένης), so that you alone might take the part of a wicked man (= Athanasius) and dissolve the peace of the empire, indeed of the whole world?" To this Liberius answered calmly: "The esteem of the Faith will not be diminished on account of my being alone: for according to the Old Testament, only three were found who opposed the order [of

---

[65] See the minutes of the meeting, preserved in Theodoret, *HE* 2,16,1–29 (Parmentier-Scheidweiler 131,12f.). For an account of the event, see Batiffol, *La paix constantinienne*, 478–481; Caspar, *Geschichte des Papsttums* I, 176–178. See also Herrmann, "Ein Streitgespräch mit verfahrensrechtlichen Argumenten," 77–86.

[66] Theodoret, *HE* 2,16,4–6 (Parmentier-Scheidweiler 132,4–10).

[67] Ὁ βασιλεύς· "Τὰ ἤδη τύπον ἐσχηκότα ἀναλύεσθαι οὐ δουνατόν ἐστι· τῶν γὰρ πλειόνων ἐπισκόπων ἡ ψῆφος ἰσχύειν ὀφείλει . . ." (Theodoret, *HE* 2,16,19 = Parmentier-Scheidweiler 134,14–15).

[68] Cf. Theodoret, *HE* 2,16,2 (Parmentier-Scheidweiler 131,18–24); *HE* 2,16,6 (132,8–10); *HE* 2,16,8 (132,14–16).

[69] Cf. Theodoret, *HE* 2,16,8 (Parmentier-Scheidweiler 132,14–16); also, *HE* 2,16,16 (133,23–134,8); *HE* 2,16,22 (135,4–10).

[70] Cf. Theodoret, *HE* 2,16,2 (Parmentier-Scheidweiler 131,18–19); *HE* 2,16,16 (133,23–134,8); *HE* 2,16,22 (135,5–6).

[71] Theodoret, *HE* 2,16,7 (Parmentier-Scheidweiler 132,12–13).

the King].["][72] The Apostolic Church and the Imperial Church had come face to face in the palace at Milan.

Liberius' penalty for his opposition was his banishment to Trace. When the emperor on two separate occasions sent the bishop a considerable sum of money, ostensibly to cover expenses but most probably as an attempt to bribe him,[73] Liberius bluntly rejected the offer.

That was at the end of the year 355. The following summer Athanasius wrote his *Apologia*, where he held up the various bishops who had been exiled on his account and on account of their loyalty to the Nicene Faith as examples to be imitated by those who had contended for the truth. There, Liberius of Rome headed the list of bishops. Less than 18 months later, the news reached Athanasius in his hiding place, that the resistance of Liberius had been broken and that he had finally subscribed to his condemnation. Added to his excommunication by synods in the East and West, the opponents of Athanasius, and so of the Nicene Creed, could now point to his excommunication by the Bishop of Rome, Successor to St. Peter, whose acknowledged primacy had been his strongest and most authoritative support. Proof of his excommunication was provided by the letters of Liberius, which were now in circulation.[74] But of even greater importance to Athanasius than his own personal destiny, or even his claims to the See of Alexandria, was the significance of Liberius' "fall" from the Nicene Faith.

The fact that Liberius seems to have signed the first Sirmium credal formula[75] is of no particular relevance, since, as we saw above, neither in the reign of Julius nor even at a later date was this statement of Faith, which was directed against Photinus, seen to be Anti-Nicene in intent. Further, Athanasius makes no reference to it in the *Historia,* which is remarkable, since he makes no attempt

---

[72] Theodoret, *HE* 2,16,14 (Parmentier-Scheidweiler 133,18–20).

[73] Eusebius the Eunuch was on other occasions used by Constantius to bribe; see Ammianus Marcellinus, *RG* 18,4,3–4 (Clark 141,26–142,9). Earlier, Liberius had referred to certain bishops who did not resist the imperial bounty (cf. Theodoret, *HE* 2,16,6 = Parmentier-Scheidweiler 132,8–9).

[74] Cf. Hilary, *Frag. hist.*, series B, III,1–IV,4 (Feder 155–164). For a description of their contents, see Caspar, *Geschichte des Papsttums* I, 183–186.

[75] The following year, he apparently signed the third Sirmium credal formula; cf. Sozomen, *HE* 4,15,1–6 (Bidez-Hansen 158,1–31). Joannou, *Die Ostkirche und die Cathedra Petri*, 124–130, interprets this subscription as an anticipation of the later doctrinal developments, which thus helped to bridge the differences that were beginning to divide the Church. See also the interpretations of Caspar, *Geschichte des Papsttums* I, 186–188; Jalland, *Church and Papacy*, 232; Simonetti, *La Crisi Ariana*, 236[56].

to hide the fact that Ossius had subscribed to the second Sirmium formula that was clearly Anti-Nicene. The significance of Liberius' apparent excommunication of Athanasius was due to the way Liberius himself had identified the Bishop of Alexandria with the Nicene Faith, as we saw above, so that the excommunication was tantamount to a condemnation of the Faith professed by the Fathers at Nicaea. It seemed to the Church at the time, as it did to Jalland in 1942, that: "Thus the custodian of the Apostolic *paradosis* did obeisance to the δόγμα of Caesar."[76]

This, then, is the main concern of Athanasius in the *Historia:* to interpret the significance of his own excommunication by the Bishop of Rome. The secondary motif that runs through the entire work is to uncover the nature of the forces that were then apparently dominating the Church, namely, the "Eusebian heresy" as adopted and radically applied in practice by the Neo-Arians and their patron, Constantius.

A comment needs to be made on the very obvious change of attitude on the part of Athanasius towards Constantius, which took place between the composition of his legal defense *Ad Constantium,* written immediately after the *Apologia* in the autumn of 356, and the writing of the *Historia* in October 357. In his letter to the emperor in 356, where he offered his defense in the face of false charges of a civil nature, Athanasius was motivated to so act by the conviction that the emperor was being innocently manipulated by the Neo-Arians.[76a] Though he had been removed from the Church on imperial orders executed by the imperial forces, and had been condemned to death by the emperor on the basis of new calumnies, yet Athanasius did not abandon his hope that, should Constantius hear his defense, he would be convinced of his innocence and reject the slanderers. As Paulinus of Trier had evidently informed him Constantius himself seemed to have become a pliable instrument in the hands of Valens and Ursacius. Thus, both in the *Apologia* and in *Ad Constantium,* the chief enemies attacked by Athanasius are these two sinister prelates.

Within six months of his attempt in the summer and early autumn of 356 to counter the ecclesiastical and civil indictments brought against him at the Synod of Milan (355), Athanasius received a copy of a letter written by Ossius of Cordova to Constantius,[77] in reply

---

[76] Jalland, *Church and Papacy,* 229.
[76a] Cf. *Ad Const.* 32 (Szymusiak 126–127); see also *Ad epp. Aeg. et Lib.* 5 (*PG* 25,547,A4–7).
[77] Preserved by Athanasius in *Hist. Arian.* 44,1–11 (Opitz 207,20–209,4). See Caspar, *Geschichte des Papsttums* I, 179–180.

to the various attempts of the emperor to persuade the "Abraham-like" old man to subscribe to Athanasius' condemnation. In this noble letter, the aged confessor of the Great Persecution and one-time president of the Synods of Nicaea and Sardica unambiguously reminded the comparatively young emperor: "Intrude not yourself into ecclesiastical matters, neither give commands unto us concerning them; but learn from us. God has put into your hands the kingdom; to us He has entrusted the affairs of his Church; and as he who would steal the empire from you would resist the ordinance of God, so likewise fear on your part least by taking upon yourself the government of the Church, you become guilty of a great offence. It is written, 'Render unto Caesar the things that are Caesar's, and unto God the things that are God's.'"[78] With regard to the extent of Constantius' own guilt, the attitude of Ossius is similar to that of Athanasius: the emperor had fallen under the evil influence of Valens and Ursacius and their colleagues in the East.[79] But the grey-haired Bishop of Cordova did not underestimate the gravity of the actual situation and the possible effects of Constantius' open support for the Arian party, and so he tells the emperor that he is as ready now as he had been under Constantius' grandfather Maximian to endure any suffering, rather than shed innocent blood and betray the truth.[80] But in the year 357, Ossius, who had been brought to the imperial court at Sirmium, weakened and signed the second Sirmium formula[81]—called the "Blasphemy of Sirmium."[82] This credal formula, which was the first openly Arian creed that was Anti-Nicene in intent, though without expressly attacking the terminology of Nicaea, sent a wave of shock throughout the entire Church.[83] In effect, the Nicene Faith had been outlawed and Ossius, who was present at the Synod of Sirmium, was forced to subscribe. The reverberations of the stir caused by this—the third synod at Sirmium, which was held in the

---

[78] *Hist. Arian.* 44,7 (Opitz 208,18–23). Translation by Newman (in Robertson, *Athanasius*, LNPF2, 286).

[79] Cf. *Hist. Arian.* 44,1 (Opitz 207,23–24). It should be noted that Athanasius did not maintain "that the Arians were completely the tools of the Emperor" as Setton claims in *Christian Attitude Towards the Emperor*, 83, but the very opposite. This latter conviction was also shared by the followers of Athanasius, cf. *Hist. Arian.* 81,3 (Opitz 228,34–229,1).

[80] Cf. *Hist. Arian.* 44,1 (Opitz 207,20–22).

[81] The text is to be found in Athanasius, *De syn.* 28,2–12 (Opitz 256,25–257,27) in a Greek translation. The Latin original is in Hilary, *De syn.* 11 (*PL* 10,487,A12f.).

[82] Hilary, *De syn.* 10 (*PL* 10,487,A8).

[83] See Gwatkin, *Studies*, 161—162; Kelly, *Creeds*, 285–287.

summer or autumn of 357—are to be felt in Athanasius' work *Apologia de fuga sua,* which was penned soon after news of this event had reached him. Here, a new tone is to be detected which is remarkably different from that found in the *Apologia* and in *Ad Constantium:*[84] it is his first document which could be exclusively described as really *Contra Arianos.* Of greater significance for our present subject is the fact that in *De fuga,* Athanasius calls Constantius a heretic and censures the nomination of Leontius of Antioch as one that had been forced on the Church by the emperor.[85] This work of Athanasius, *De fuga,* which of all his writings is the one that comes closest to a truly personal apology, was his reply to the Synod of Sirmium and the lapse of Ossius. In *Ad Constantium,* Athanasius had already replied to the charge of cowardice leveled at him by his enemies.[86] Now he answers the charge more exhaustively, not so much in order to defend his own conduct as rather to reveal the nature of the Neo-Arian party, now in apparent control of the Church, and to uncover the effects of such a control, namely, a new persecution. The persecuted orthodox are recommended to adopt the rule of conduct observed by the earlier martyrs: "When persecuted, they fled, and while concealing themselves, they remained steadfast, but when they were discovered they bore witness."[87] The persecutions in the East and in Egypt,[88] the exile of the western bishops led by Liberius,[89] and, above all, the treatment of the aged Ossius at the hands of the Arians[90] reveal their evil and demonstrate that their authors are not truly Christian. But though Athanasius goes so far as to call the emperor a heretic and accuse him of irregular interference in Church affairs, through his nomination of Leontius and the imposition of this Arian on the Church of Antioch, yet he does not otherwise directly associate Constantius with the Arian-instigated persecutions.

In the *Historia,* however, the emperor is shown to be working hand-in-hand with the enemies of Christ, the Neo-Arians, and indeed he is himself called the forerunner of the Antichrist. Though Athanasius still persists in his conviction that the emperor is an

---

[84] See comments of Batiffol, *La paix constantinienne,* 510–511; Bardy, *Saint Athanase,* 140–142.

[85] Cf. *De fuga* 26,3 (Opitz 86,2–3). Though two (related) MSS (N and W) do not contain this passage, there is reasonable certainty that, since all the other MSS contain it, then it was part of the original text (see Szymusiak 72–77).

[86] Cf. *Ad Const.* 32 (Szymusiak 127–128).

[87] Cf. *De fuga* 22,2 (Opitz 83,19–20).

[88] *De fuga* 3,1–6 (Opitz 69,25–70,15).

[89] *De fuga* 4,1–2 (Opitz 70,16–71,6).

[90] *De fuga* 5,1–3 (Opitz 71,7–18).

instrument in the hands of the Arians,[91] he has abandoned his trust in Constantius' basic goodwill, which hope he had preserved throughout the past one-and-a-half years, despite so much evidence to the contrary, including the persecutions in his own Church,[92] the exile of so many bishops in the East and West, and, finally, the violence done to Ossius. In the *Historia,* the relationship between the Neo-Arians and the emperor is seen to be reciprocal. Constantius is seen to have used the Arians for his own ends as much as they had used him to achieve their desired objectives. What finally tipped the scales against the emperor was the "lapse" of Liberius, the apparent obeisance of the Successor of Peter to the man, in the symbolism of the early Euesbius, who now appeared to be a successor of Nero.

§3 Addressees of the *Historia*

According to the fifth-century compiler of the MSS, this document *"concerning those things undertaken by the Arians under Constantius"* was addressed *"to the monks everywhere."*[93] In his *Letter to Serapion* concerning the death of Arius, Athanasius apparently refers to this document, when he remarks that he had sent his friend, Bishop Serapion, a copy of what he had written to the monks in reply to his friend's request for information concerning the recent events in his life.[94] Another such reference is apparently to be found in a *Letter of Athanasius to the Monks Everywhere,*[95] which letter accompanied a theological tract, possibly the major theological writings of Athanasius—the three *Orationes contra Arianos.*[96] In order to interpret the *Historia,* it is important to keep in mind the nature of his audience—and their expectations, which the author endeavored to meet.

If we simply consider the evidence found in Eusebius' *History* and in the writings of Athanasius himself, the life of these monks was in its essence remarkably similar to that of their spiritual successors

---

[91] See in particular, *Hist. Arian.* 35,1 (Opitz 202,24–28).

[92] For a description, see Bardy, *Saint Athanase*, 129f.

[93] Τοῦ αὐτοῦ πρὸς ἀπανταχοῦ μοναχοὺς περὶ τῶν γεγενημένων παρὰ τῶν Ἀρειανῶν ἐπὶ Κωνσταντίου (Opitz 183,1–2: the commentary of Opitz). Regarding the relationship between Athanasius and the monastic movement, see Loofs, "Athanasius von Alexandria," 197–198.

[94] *De morte Arii* 1,1 (Opitz 178,2–3).

[95] *Ad monach.* 1,1 (Opitz 181,6).

[96] Opitz in his commentary (Opitz 180,1) suggests on the other hand either *Serap. I, II,* or *III.*

down through the century, the early Irish monks, for example, or the early Benedictines, Carthusians, or Dominicans. It was a life of total consecration to God, abstinence from all worldly pursuits, coupled with a dedication to study and the search for a deeper penetration of the truth. The quality of their intellectual niveau can be gathered from the fact that in all probability Athanasius wrote his major theological treatise on the Trinity for these monks. St. Antony's discourses with the philosophers (*Vita Antonii* 72–79), may be but a literary device on the part of Athanasius; and yet they do betray Athanasius' aim to demonstrate how superior the monks were to those who claimed to be lettered. Earlier Eusebius, in the original *History,* found no difficulty in interpreting Philo's *De vita contemplativa* as though it were a description of the Egyptian ascetics. As representatives of those monks, St. Serapion of Thmuis, the friend and protege of Athanasius, or Bishop Dracontius of Hermopolis Parva, could be instanced. Serapion, who was the addressee of Athanasius' treatises on the Holy Spirit, was an author in his own right; he was also considered capable enough to lead the furtive Alexandrian delegation to the synod that Liberius called for in order to defend Athanasius' claim to his see. Dracontius was the abbot of a monastery who, when he was elected bishop, did not wish to leave the contemplative quiet of his monastery for the turbulence of the pastoral scene.

The monks, therefore, whom Sozomen describes as renowned for their virtue and the philosophical tenor of their lives,[97] were in the first place deeply committed to the pursuit of the truth in the silence of the desert. They needed the theological enlightenment of Athanasius' great treatises. They also needed direction in order to understand and interpret the recent events, which had rocked the Barque of Peter. Their daily bread was the awareness of God's Providence. And thus, how should they, who so clearly appreciated the reality of God's intervention in and direction of history, understand the apparent triumph of Arianism? Though Bouyer may have done the *Historia* an injustice when he described it as a furious comic novel,[98] yet he did perceive the true nature of the work when he called it "un ouvrage théologique"[99] in the first place. And it can be thus described because of its addressees, the monks.

---

[97] Cf. Sozomen, *HE* 4,10,2 (Bidez-Hansen 152,15–16). See also the comments of Bardy, *Saint Athanase*, 141.

[98] However, the work is not lacking in irony; see, e.g., *Hist. Arian.* 52,6 (Opitz 213,17–21), though this text cannot be understood as characteristic of the entire composition.

[99] Bouyer, *L'Incarnation et l'Église*, 19.

§4 Literary Genre and Aims

It should be clear by now that there is little evidence to support the contention that the *Historia* is a secret libel. The facts that it was expressly written for the monks and that secret pamphlets were not uncommon at the time[100] are not sufficient evidence to support such a charge. The main ground for the popularity of this description seems to be the marked difference in the way Athanasius speaks about the emperor in the *Historia*, as compared with the apparent show of respect as found in his *Apologia ad Constantium*, written but 12 months earlier. It is generally thought that his tone of respect was occasioned by the public nature of the latter document, whereas the *Historia* reveals the real, private attitude of Athanasius towards the emperor. But, as was pointed out above, already in *De fuga*, which was written in the intervening period and was clearly intended for public circulation, Athanasius did not hesitate to call the emperor a heretic and to criticize him openly for his nomination of Leontius. There is no evidence that the *Historia* was composed for private circulation, but that it was originally written at the request of a specific group of interested people, the monks, just as the *Vita Antonii* was written, most likely, for certain "brethren in foreign parts"[101] and yet went into general circulation, apparently almost immediately.

The different attitudes to the emperor, as displayed in the *Apologia ad Constantium* and the *Historia Arianorum* respectively, are to be explained by the different aims and literary forms of these two documents, as much as by the changed historical circumstances. *Ad Constantium* is a legal defense aimed at convincing the emperor of the author's innocence with regard to the civil accusations brought against him, while the *Historia* is a type of "theological" interpretation of recent historical events for his readers, the monks, which events were common knowledge and generally well-known to his readers—an important point to be kept in mind when we come to interpret the work. Neither is it true to say that the *Historia* is "a derogatory pamphlet directed against Constantius, . . . in which the latter is made the object of all the bitter abuse to which Athanasius could lay his tongue."[102] Though no one can deny that Constantius

---

[100] See Fialon, *Saint Athanase*, 196–199. It should be noted that when Athanasius requested the monks (cf. *Ad monach.* 3,3 = Opitz 182,20–23) and Bishop Serapion (cf. *De morte Arii* 5,2 = Opitz 180,17–24) to return the works he had sent them (and not to have them copied), he referred to his *dogmatic* treatises.

[101] Cf. *PG* 26,835–836.

[102] Setton, *Christian Attitude Towards the Emperor*, 78.

is severely censured in this work, yet, since Athanasius persists in stressing that the emperor is but the weak, though willing, instrument of the Arians, the most severe "abuse" is aimed at the Neo-Arian party in their capacity as executors of the "Eusebian heresy," which attempted to replace the Apostolic, genuinely ecclesiastical, authority with an imperial one.[103]

What is new in the *Historia* is the personal identity of the emperor with the Imperial Church of the two Eusebii. Constantius has made his own the Eusebian heresy and for this he is condemned by Athanasius. The most trenchant attack on the personal misbehavior of the emperor[104] reaches its climax when Athanasius, alluding to Prov 7,22, accuses him of being *willing* to yield himself to others, namely, the Eusebians.[105] Thus, whereas Eusebius of Caesarea had transferred the Petrine authority from the Bishops of Rome, Alexandria, and Antioch on to the emperor, and had almost "re-divinized" the Augustus by making him the supreme instrument of God on earth, Athanasius endeavors in the *Historia* to "demythologize" this exaggerated concept of the emperor by explicitly denying his claim to final authority in the Church (= "my will is law"), and by reminding his readers of the emperor's basic humanity. To achieve the latter, Athanasius abandoned the formal language of the court, such as he had used in the *Apologia ad Constantium,* and even used on occasion a diminutive form of his name: Κωστύλλιος.[106] In the *Vita Antonii,* written soon after the *Historia,* Athanasius continued in the same vein when he recalled the reaction of St. Antony to the letters the hermit had received from the Emperor Constantine and his sons, Constantius and Constans: "Do not be astonished if the Emperor writes to us, since he is a man; but rather marvel at the fact that God wrote to men when he communicated the Law, and has spoken to us through His own Son."[107]

The difference between the "Eusebian heresy" and that version of it attacked by Athanasius in the *Historia* is simple but important for an understanding of Athanasius' attitude to the imperial authority. It can be mentioned here in parenthesis as it were since we will not devote any special attention to this question in our analysis of the document itself. When dealing with the original "Eusebian heresy," neither Julius of Rome nor Athanasius himself

---

[103] Cf., for example, *Hist. Arian.* 66,1–67,4 (Opitz 219,11–220,17).
[104] Cf. *Hist. Arian.* 69,1–70.4 (Opitz 220,34–221,30).
[105] Cf. *Hist. Arian.* 70,2f. (Opitz 221,19f.).
[106] Cf. *Hist. Arian.* 74,1 (Opitz 224,4).
[107] *Vita Ant.* 81 (*PG* 26,956,B7–10).

placed any blame on the emperor as such, but rather on those bishops who in theory and practice invited the imperial authority to interfere in Church-affairs and, indeed, conceived the Roman Emperor as the source of the Church's authority. The activity of Constantius in the new phase of the dispute, which began with his sole rule of the empire and the death of Julius of Rome, manifested its true nature at Milan in 355 and finally revealed itself fully in the forced subscription of Liberius to Athanasius' excommunication around September 357. With the latter event, no doubt was left in the mind of Athanasius but that the emperor himself had made the Eusebian heresy his own. Failure to recognize this has led commentators, such as Berkhof, to interpret the *Historia* as Athanasius' cry for a complete separation of Church and State.[108]

But when Athanasius protests: "When did a judgment of the Church receive its validity (τὸ κῦρος) from an Emperor?"[109] and accuses Constantius of "dissolving the regulation of the Lord handed on by the Apostles, by altering the customs of the Church and thinking up for himself a new method of making appointments."[110] He is not simply attacking the actions of Constantius as such, but rather the ideological principles inherent in those actions: what Athanasius calls "his own heresy,"[111] i.e., Constantius' personal adaptation of the Eusebian concept of the Imperial Church. Neither was Athanasius voicing any new theory on the relationship between Church and Empire since, as our analysis above demonstrates, these ideas had been previously articulated by the Synod of Alexandria (338) and by Julius of Rome (341).

Faced with the apparent universal victory of the imperial ecclesiology—now displaying its nature in all its crassness and apparently in control of the entire Church, including the major sees of Rome, Alexandria, and Antioch—Athanasius had to explain to the monks where the true Apostolic Church was to be found and what were its characteristics. In other words, he set out to enable them all

---

[108]   See, for example, Berkhof, *Kirche und Kaiser*, 133–135; Setton, *Christian Attitude Towards the Emperor*, 78f., and, to a lesser extent, Hagel, *Kirche und Kaisertum*, 61 f.; Hagel did recognize that what Athanasius fought against was not the relationship of the State to the Church as such, but rather the unhealthy connection between both as found in the pro-Arian Church (cf. Hagel 71–72 in particular).

[109]   *Hist. Arian.* 52,3 (Opitz 213,8). See the entire context: *Hist. Arian.* 51,1–52,6 (Opitz 212,10–213,21). See also *Apol.* 10,2 (Opitz 95,33); see above, p. 360.

[110]   *Hist. Arian.* 74,5 (Opitz 224,19–20); see the whole subsection: *Hist. Arian.* 74,1–77,4 (224,1–226,24).

[111]   *Hist. Arian.* 77,3 (Opitz 226,17).

the more easily to test and discern the spirit of their times,[112] once the news had reached them that the Imperial Church had finally crushed the resistance of the final custodian of the Apostolic Church, Liberius, Bishop of Rome.

The *Historia*, thus, is not "history" in any empirical sense of a report of events by a more or less "detached" observer, nor was it so intended.[113] Just as St. Athanasius conceded to relate the story of Arius' death in his letter to Serapion,[114] since that event so clearly manifested (δείκνυμι) the judgment of God on the Arian heresy, so Athanasius pens this account of the historical events in order to highlight the *significance* of these events, which, as such, were well known to his intended readers (the monks of the Thebaid) but which so urgently needed an interpretation: the news of the world-wide episcopal acquiescence to the anti-Nicene party, the subscription of the one-time president of Nicaea, Ossius, to an alternative credal formula, as well as the coarse triumph of the imperial-supported "Arians," nearer home in Egypt and Libya, and above all the apparent lapse of Liberius. These events needed to be interpreted for those who did not doubt the Divine Providence or His intervention in the affairs of men but could be led to doubt the rightness or orthodoxy of their own belief in the face of such a universal "unanimity."

The literary form of the *Historia* could thus be described as dramatic historiography whose object is to interpret recent events by unveiling the motives of the chief protagonists. Athanasius achieves his object both by his selection, arrangement and description of the events he narrates, and by his colorful use of fictional monologue or dialogue, placing into the mouths of the personalities involved, words which disclose their hidden motives—as seen by Athanasius.[115] This work can also be termed a type of "theological"

---

[112] See the final paragraph of the *Historia* (*Hist. Arian.* 80,1–3 = Opitz 228,9–25).

[113] Bardy, "Athanase d'Alexandrie," in *DHGE* IV, col. 1332, observed that the *Historia* could not be called a history in the strict sense of that term. Instead, he calls it "un plaidoyer ou une apologie," which description I find inadequate, as will be seen below.

[114] Cf. *De morte Arii* 1,1f. (Opitz 178,1f.), especially *De morte Arii* 4,1–2 (Opitz 179,29f.).

[115] See *De syn.* 7,1–2 (Opitz 234,31–235,4), where he explicitly acknowledges this method of historical presentation. See Hagel, *Kirche und Kaisertum*, 62, who recognizes this characteristic of Athanasius, though he goes a little too far in his estimate of the subjective element in these dialogues. The basic objectivity of these texts can be judged from the faithfulness of Athanasius regarding the contents of the dialogues between Liberius and the Eunuch Eusebius (representing the emperor) when compared with the minutes of the meeting between the Bishop of Rome and Constantius at Milan (see below, p. 488f.). The historiographical

history. More complete with historical details than the legal defense of the *Apologia*,[116] it is only interested in the actual historical process insofar as events, documents, and reconstructed dialogue uncover basic motives, while these motives are themselves in turn x-rayed to discover their theological validity and relevance. It is the latter that is of primary interest to us: more precisely, our object is to establish what are the theological or ecclesiological principles that shaped Athanasius' rhetoric aimed at discerning the Apostolic Church's Faith, despite the apparent triumph of the Imperial Church.

This work certainly betrays the author's righteous passion. It has been described as polemical and that is correct. The language is at times startlingly blunt, but hardly such as to merit, for their author, the charge that "he fully condescends to the coarse brutality of the age, mingling it unpardonably with holy things."[117] Athanasius speaks, rather, like a full-blooded Old Testament prophet with the stature of an Elijah.[118] Polemics get their force from commonly accepted assumptions—in this case, assumptions about the Apostolic nature of the Church and, more specifically, about the role of the Bishop of Rome in the contemporary struggle against the Eusebian ecclesiology in defense of the Nicene Creed. It is these assumptions that concern us here.

Despite the heat of the controversy in which nothing less than the Apostolic Faith of the Church was at stake, and despite the short space of time in which it was composed, the *Historia* was written with extreme care and attention. Athanasius is crystal clear as to the significance of recent events. His estimate of the Eusebian *Reichskirche* had been tested and sharpened during the events that marked his first and second exile, and a little over twelve months previously, he had an opportunity to review those events in the *Apologia*. The events and documents were fresh in his mind; Athanasius' aims were clear and so he went like a rocket to his target. Thus, by working through the structure of the text as a whole, then back into the individual sections and subsections, and by comparing his presentation with the events we have

---

method employed here by Athanasius is that of Thucydides, as found in the famous *Orations*, which method was so well described by Schwartz, *Das Geschichtswerk des Thukydides*, 25–28 (see also Syme, "Thucydides," 114f.; Milburn, *Christian Interpretations of History*, 62–63). One can only record one's astonishment that Schwartz, who defended Thucydides so eloquently, could not appreciate Athanasius' use of a similar style but dismissed the *Historia* so disparagingly, but then prejudice does affect one's judgement.

[116] See Hagel, *Kirche und Kaisertum*, 61–62.

[117] Robertson, *Athanasius*, LNPF[2], 267.

[118] Cf. *Hist. Arian.* 47,3 (Opitz 210,26); *Hist. Arian.* 53,2 (Opitz 213,29); *Hist. Arian.* 68,1 (Opitz 220,20).

already examined in our various historical reconstructions, we can trace the direction of his thought and the concept of the Church that he here defends in the face of the imperial ecclesiology adopted by the emperor Constantius.

The title by which this work is known, *Historia Arianorum ad monachos* (Montfaucon's translation into Latin of the Greek description by the fifth-century compiler of Athanasius' writings), has in my opinion been largely responsible for the general misinterpretation of this work. This in turn coupled with the equally unfortunate title given to the *Apologia,* as though it too were *contra Arianos,* has left its mark on the attempts of historians and theologians alike to reconstruct the history of the fourth century, since it gave the impression that the dogmatic issues raised by the Arians were the primary focus of attention in the controversies of the second quarter of that epoch-making century. The *Historia* is not concerned with the Arian heresy as such, but rather with the Eusebian party that adopted the Arian tenets and, after 352, their successors, the Neo-Arians, whose extreme adherents were the first to develop the Christological and Trinitarian views of Arius. The *Historia* does not deal with the Christological opinions of the early protagonists of Athanasius, the Eusebians, apart from the vaguest allusions, and only refers to the extreme Arian views of the Neo-Arians in the broadest way. The work is, as the fifth-century compiler indicated, a description of events that were caused by those who, indeed, subscribed to the Arian heresy but who were primarily distinguished by their appeal to the imperial authority.

§5 The Internal Structure of the *Historia Arianorum*

We have already seen, with respect to the *Apologia,* how the external structure and form of presentation can be of singular importance in uncovering the mind of St. Athanasius. This is even more so, with regard to the *Historia.* Here, another aspect of his method of theologizing—already recognized with regard to his dogmatic writings, but as yet ignored in studies of his "apologetic" or "historic" works to the best of my knowledge—can, with certain variations, be discerned: namely, an attempt to develop concepts or themes in pairs so that each theme stands in a relationship of reciprocal enlightenment with reference to the other. In the *Historia* we find a form of parallelism whereby one part, unit, section, subsection, or even paragraph is dependent on the preceding one for its meaning and vice versa. The structure of the *Historia,* insofar as our immediate purpose is served, may be broken down as follows:

Part II   Ch. 47–80 (the persecution in Egypt by the Imperial
                                  Church) receives its meaning from
                                  Part I, Ch. 1–46 (the nature of orthodoxy and heresy)

Within Part I:
Unit II   Ch. 28–46 (the persecution of the orthodox)
                                  receives its meaning from
                                  Unit I, Ch. 1–27 (the triumph of the orthodox)

Within Unit II:
Section II   Ch. 35–46 (the stories of Liberius and Ossius)
                                  receives its meaning from
                                  Section I, Ch. 28–35 (new form of confessing the Faith)

Within Section II:
Subsection II   Ch. 42–45 (the "Fall" of Ossius)
                                  receives its meaning from
                                  Subsection I, Ch. 35–41 (the "Fall" of Pope Liberius)
                                          Ch. 46 acts as an epilogue to Part I

This breakdown of the structure of the text confirms that which our examination of the date and immediate cause of the *Historia Arianorum* brought to light: the lapse of Liberius is its *raison d'être.* We will therefore concentrate our analysis on that text: what proceeds it will be treated in a summary fashion in order to establish the general context of that passage, while the rest of the book can be left aside, since it primarily deals with the Imperial Church and its manifestation in Egypt without contributing anything new to the description of same, as found in the earlier documents,[119] apart from the new emphasis already referred to, namely, the way the emperor had made the Eusebian heresy his own.

§6 Analysis

The specific object of our study is not to present an exhaustive commentary on the *Historia Arianorum ad monachos,* but to examine the way Athanasius presents the lapse of Liberius in

---

[119] Part II of the *Historia* does, however, provide a control for the ideas worked out in Chapter Eight.

order, thereby, to understand the theological significance he attached to that traumatic event. We will begin our analysis, however, with a brief consideration of Unit I of Part I, which is itself composed of two sections in order to appreciate the background to this event as seen by Athanasius and described by him for his readers.

a) Part I, Unit I: The Universal Unanimity (Hist. Arian. 1–27)

The span of historical events covered by this Unit corresponds approximately to that covered by the *Apologia* (335–357). Unlike the *Apologia,* the broad outline of Unit I roughly follows the chronological order of the events. However, in the first Section of this Unit, the chronological sequence is of secondary importance; there the theological themes are clarified. On the other hand, in the second Section, the priorities of the author are reversed and so the theological significance of the chronological events reported there can only be gleaned indirectly from the way Athanasius presents the events themselves.

aa) Section I: The Nature of the [Eusebian] Heresy (Hist. Arian. 1–8)

This Section is concerned with a similar sequence of events as found in the second half of the *Apologia* (59–88), namely those which climaxed in the first exile of Athanasius.[120] It is framed by the readmission of Arius to communion at Jerusalem after the Synod of Trye,[121] which event opens the document as we have it today,[122]

---

[120] The chronological correspondence is, indeed, very crude since most of *Apol.* 59–88 concentrates on the events which led up to the Synod of Tyre; only the final three chapters of the *Apologia* mention those events which are described in relative detail in *Hist. Arian.* 1–8. This discrepancy may be due in part to the mutilated text, which indicates that a section of the opening has been lost. It is possible that the lost text treated those events which led up to the Synod of Tyre, though probably only in a very summary fashion, since they were not completely *ad rem* to his main topic; they were in any case well-known to his readers. The internal balance between the various parts, units, and sections seems to confirm the impression that nothing very substantial has been lost. See below, footnote 122.

[121] *Hist. Arian.* 1,1 (Opitz 183,3–4).

[122] Based on a consideration of the internal structure and content of Section I, it is my opinion that the missing text opened with a brief mention of the unanimity which Nicaea witnessed to and followed this up with a concise account of the conspiracies which led to Tyre, thus showing how Tyre marked the beginning of the breakup of the former unanimity and legitimate relationship between Church and State. In its present form, the text opens with the aftermath of Tyre: the readmission of Arius into communion at Jerusalem—itself an apt opening, even if not originally so intended.

and the letter of Constantine II (June 17, 337) restoring Athanasius
to Alexandria after his exile in Trier, which brings the Section to its
close.[123] But there is no attempt to relate these two events, as was the
case in the *Apologia*. The connection is presumed to be known to his
readers and is simply hinted at in various rather general references in
the third person,[123a] to the early history of Athanasius.[124] In point of fact,
the intervening narrative either consists of some general descriptions
of the "Eusebian heresy" as such, and not the Arian heresy as is generally believed (*Hist. Arian.* 1–3), or cameo descriptions of other bishops
(Eustathius of Antioch, Eutropius of Adrianople, Marcellus of Ancyra, and
Paul of Constantinople) who had suffered at the hands of the Eusebian
party and who, with one exception (Marcellus), are not mentioned in
the *Apologia*. Athanasius' purpose in recalling the case histories of these
bishops, who had suffered at the hand of the Eusebians,[125] is to illustrate
the true character of those who oppose the orthodox.[126] The three opening
paragraphs characterize the heresy of the Eusebians as that which had
adopted the tenets of Arius (as illustrated by their readmittance of the
heresiarch to communion) and, moreover, which is dependent on the
authority of the emperor for its existence.[127] This theme, but implicit in the
Apologia, is here clearly and explicitly enunciated: the Eusebians persecute
Athanasius and the other bishops "not on the authority of an ecclesiastical

---

[123] *Hist. Arian.* 8,1–2 (Opitz 187,20–188,2).

[123a] In this work, Athanasius generally refers to himself in the third person (cf. *Hist.
   Arian.* 8,1; 9,1; 11,1) and only occasionally in the first. As the document is not a
   type of *historia arcana,* there is no reason to posit with Setton in his *Christian
   Attitude Towards the Emperor*, 78, that Athanasius was anxious not to identify
   himself with the work and so published it anonymously. The third person singular may have been due to the use of an amanuensis (see Robertson, *Athanasius*,
   LNPF², 266), but since the use of an amanuensis cannot be ruled out for his
   other works—where he uses the first person singular—then another reason
   must be found for this peculiar style. Such a reason seems to be suggested by the
   nature of the composition as a type of "theological" history; there Athanasius
   is concerned with the theological significance of the events he relates, in which
   he is one of the principal participants, and thus is anxious to downplay his own
   personal and subjective involvement in order to highlight the theological issues
   involved.

[124] See *Hist. Arian.* 2,1–3,5 (Opitz 183,17–184,30).

[125] These descriptions, which likewise constitute a subsection (*Hist. Arian.* 4–8),
   refer also to events that occurred at later dates, such as the mention of Rome/
   Sardica in the case-history of Marcellus of Ancyra (*Hist. Arian.* 6,2 = Opitz
   186,3–8).

[126] *Hist. Arian.* 1,2 (Opitz 183,11); *Hist. Arian.* 2,1 (Opitz 183,17); *Hist. Arian.* 3,5
   (Opitz 184,27–28).

[127] *Hist. Arian.* 1,1 (Opitz 183,7–8); also *Hist. Arian.* 1,1 (Opitz 183,5).

sentence, but on the strength of the emperor's threats."[128] The nature of this new understanding of Church is such that a man of criminal character can be approved by them[129] and so become a friend of the emperor,[130] who then authorizes his imposition (as bishop) on an unwilling Church,[131] while the one who espouses the cause of Christ and exposes the nature of their heresy is sent into banishment by the emperor, though he knows himself to be innocent.[132] "Like some great beast (cf. Dan 7,5), this heresy has emerged on the earth: since it not only corrupts the innocent with its words as though with teeth, but it has hired an external authority (τὴν ἔξοθεν ἐξουσίαν) to assist it in its treachery."[133]

Four cameo-biographies of the orthodox bishops are sketched, which illustrate the dire consequences of this unholy alliance between the Arian teaching and the imperial authority: their persecution of the orthodox, which is the most obvious manifestation of the evil of the Eusebian ecclesiology. This Section ends on a dramatic note that helps to underline this, since it depicts the imperial authorities (the three youthful Caesars—Constantine II, Constans, and Constantius II) as being themselves appalled by the "murderous disposition" of the Eusebian party, which manifested itself in their handling of the orthodox: even they (the Caesars) perceived the real nature of the Eusebians and thus permitted the persecuted to return to their sees.[134]

The last reference to the restoration of the orthodox after the death of Constantine also serves to indicate the conviction of Athanasius: that the imperial authority, as such, is not intrinsically hostile, but only the civil authority of the empire when put at the service of wickedness and heresy— or rather when heretics misuse the clearly defined, limited, and external relationship of the empire to the Church.[135] This attitude is consistently upheld by Athanasius throughout this entire work.[136]

---

[128] *Hist. Arian.* 1,2 (Opitz 183,11–12).

[129] Cf. *Hist. Arian.* 2,1 (Opitz 183,18f.). Athanasius probably refers to Gregory of Cappadocia who was the first "antipope" to be sent to Alexandria.

[130] Cf. *Hist. Arian.* 2,1 (Opitz 183,20).

[131] Cf. *Hist. Arian.* 2,3–4 (Opitz 184,3–11).

[132] Cf. *Hist. Arian.* 2,2 (Opitz 183,22–184,3); *Hist. Arian.* 2,4 (Opitz 184,6–7). This is clearly a reference to Athanasius himself.

[133] *Hist. Arian.* 3,3 (Opitz 184,18–20).

[134] Cf. *Hist. Arian.* 8,1 (Opitz 187,20–24).

[135] Cf. *Hist. Arian.* 2,1–4 (Opitz 183,17–184,11).

[136] Apart from *Hist. Arian.* 80,1 (Opitz 228,9–11), we note that on two other occasions Constantius is called the *precursor* of the Antichrist (*Hist. Arian.* 46,3 = Opitz 210,14–15; *Hist. Arian.* 77,2 = Opitz 226,15–16) while his actions are described as part of the preparation for his coming (*Hist. Arian.* 70,4 = Opitz 221,29–30; *Hist. Arian.* 71,1 = Opitz 222,2; *Hist. Arian.* 79,1 = Opitz 227,16–21). However, Athanasius also identifies Constantius with the

There is but one mention of Rome in Section I, which occurs in *Hist. Arian.* 6, the story of Marcellus of Ancyra; it is very significant. The story belongs chronologically to the following Section II, concerning, as it does, the Synods of Rome and Sardica; its mention here serves to illustrate the orthodox approach to authority in comparison with the attitude of the Eusebians. Thus the "orthodox" confessor Marcellus is depicted as turning to "Rome" for justice and confirmation of his orthodoxy while Eusebius and his party show no interest in justice but place their hopes on winning over the support (authority) of the emperor through the influence of ladies at court.[137] Here we notice that "Rome" has become synonymous with the Church there—a usage which reoccurs systematically in the *Historia*.[138] A second observation is even more worthy of attention. Here Athanasius does not emphasize the alternative pope-emperor, faintly outlined in the *Apologia,* but is more concerned with the two general principles of authority: ecclesiastical (= Rome) and civil (= the emperor and his court).

Summing up, we can say that Section I is mainly preoccupied with enabling its readers to discern the character of the Eusebian heresy[139] by clearly pointing out to them its agreement with the opinions of Arius and, above all, its most characteristic hallmarks: (1) its dependence on the imperial as distinct from purely ecclesiastical authority, and (2) its propensity to persecute those who do not uphold its tenets. These negative criteria already imply the positive criteria by which the readers are helped to discern the orthodox bishops: (1) those who rely solely on ecclesiastical authority, and (2) those whose witness has been tested by persecution, the confessors. These themes are now taken up and developed by Athanasius.

bb) Section II: The Traditional Concept of Ecclesiastical Authority
     (*Hist. Arian.* 9–27)

The contents of Section II, which deal with the events that marked the second exile of Athanasius, broadly correspond to the subject

---

Antichrist (*Hist. Arian.* 67,3 = Opitz 220,5; *Hist. Arian.* 74,1 = Opitz 224,4; *Hist. Arian.* 74,2 = Opitz 224,9; *Hist. Arian.* 76,1 = Opitz 225,13), and his actions with those of the Antichrist (*Hist. Arian.* 75,2 = Opitz 225,6–7; *Hist. Arian.* 77,1 = Opitz 226,4–5). The characteristic actions of the emperor, which earned for him this derogatory title, were his willing and violent interference in Church affairs and his blasphemous arrogation of ecclesiastical authority.

[137] Cf. *Hist. Arian.* 6,2 (Opitz 186,3–8).

[138] Cf. *Hist. Arian.* 9,1 (Opitz 188,3); *Hist. Arian.* 11,1 (Opitz 188,30); *Hist. Arian.* 15,1 (Opitz 190,5); *Hist. Arian.* 26,1 (Opitz 197,7); *Hist. Arian.* 28,2 (Opitz 198,7); *Hist. Arian.* 29,2 (Opitz 198,25).

[139] It should be noted that the term "heresy," as used in this context, is almost

matter of Part I of the *Apologia,* where the history of the period 338–347 was on the whole covered by the lengthy documents quoted there. Here Athanasius ignores the actual documents, apart from brief references to their existence, and gives us his own historical reconstruction of the events. It is a concise, generally accurate description of the triumph of the orthodox over the intrigues of the Eusebian party.

The account begins with the report of how the Eusebians (in the year 338) perceived the serious set-back to their faction's influence caused by the return of Athanasius and the other Nicene bishops, and so took up their earlier charges against Athanasius by writing to "Rome" as well as to the emperor.[140] The Section concludes with a description of the defeat of the heretic and the triumph of the orthodox, as expressed in the universal concord and communion which existed between Athanasius and the universal episcopate:[141] in other words, Section II describes how Athanasius, by reason of this concord and universal communion, had his claim to the See of Alexandria ratified in the traditional authoritative way: first at "Rome,"[142] then at the Synod of Sardica,[143] and later at Palestine,[144] while "bishops from all parts" wrote the customary letters of peace (= communion letters),[145] and the arch-enemies, Ursacius and Valens, repented of their misdeeds by acknowledging their conspiracy.[146] The silence about the Synod of Alexandria (338), which preceded that of Rome, is noteworthy since, by leaving it out, Athanasius could more clearly outline his concept of the traditional universal authority: union with the Church of Rome (the center) together with the West (= Sardica) and the East (= Palestine); or, as he himself expressed it in summary fashion, communion with bishops of the whole Church.

As in the previous Section, so too in Section II we do not find Athanasius developing, at this stage, the pope-emperor alternative. If anything, we find the role of Pope Julius underplayed. Continuing the tendency of Section I, it is the synodal character of "Rome" that is given the main emphasis in Section II; however, there

interchangeable with the term "party" or sect and was so conceived by the early Church.

[140] Cf. *Hist. Arian.* 9,1 (Opitz 188,3–45).
[141] Cf. *Hist. Arian.* 27,1–2 (Opitz 197,24–32).
[142] Cf. *Hist. Arian.* 15,1 (Opitz 190,5).
[143] Cf. *Hist. Arian.* 17,1 (Opitz 191,24–25).
[144] Cf. *Hist. Arian.* 25,2 (Opitz 196,17–20).
[145] Cf. *Hist. Arian.* 25,5 (Opitz 197,2–4).
[146] Cf. *Hist. Arian.* 26,1–5 (Opitz 197,5–23).

is explicit mention of Julius, Bishop of Rome, who took the initiative that "a synod ought to take place,"[147] whose decision Athanasius obeyed,[148] and who wrote to the Eusebians, having decided on the date of the synod.[149] Yet Athanasius prefers to speak of "Rome" and not its bishop as the authority to which the Eusebians first appealed,[150] and to which Athanasius had recourse.[151] It is likewise the synodal character of his acquittal at Rome which Athanasius here emphasizes.[152] Finally, we notice the significant absence of any reference to Athanasius' journey to Pope Julius after Sardica and before he went to the court of Constantius at Antioch to receive his (civil) *placet*.

This concept of "Rome," i.e., the Church of Rome, while it retains a clear awareness of the pope's role vis-à-vis the synod, with regard to summoning it, clearly emphasizes the synodal character of its authority. This raises the question: why? And the answer which suggests itself at this stage is that in the whole of Section II, Athanasius is clearly resolved to demonstrate his communion with the universal episcopate, within which, however, the Church of Rome enjoys a unique, central, though not clearly-defined position. He takes every opportunity to underline the *scope* of this communion. Thus, apart from the references given above, we find Athanasius drawing attention to the near universal representative character of the Synod of Sardica: "the holy Synod which had been assembled out of more than thirty-five provinces."[153] And as if to counteract any uncertainties on this score, which may have arisen due to the sizeable schism of Eusebian-controlled Oriental bishops at Sardica, Athanasius states emphatically that "*all* the Bishops of Palestine, apart from one or two and those who are viewed with suspicion, thus welcomed Athanasius and embraced communion with him."[154] It is this general tendency of Athanasius to highlight the broad extent of the universal communion he enjoyed at the end of the second exile, which is responsible for his emphasis on the synodal ("collective") character of the Church of Rome and his apparent lack of specific attention to the *Bishop of Rome* as such. However, the central role played by Rome within this universal communion is

---

[147] Cf. *Hist. Arian.* 9,1 (Opitz 188,6–7).
[148] Cf. *Hist. Arian.* 11,1 (Opitz 188,29–30).
[149] Cf. *Hist. Arian.* 11,1. (Opitz 188,30–32).
[150] Cf. *Hist. Arian.* 9,1 (Opitz 188,3–4).
[151] Cf. *Hist. Arian.* 11,1 (Opitz 188,29–30).
[152] Cf. *Hist. Arian.* 15,1 (Opitz 190,5–8).
[153] *Hist. Arian.* 17,1 (Opitz 191,23–24); cf. also *Hist. Arian.* 15,3 (Opitz 190,13–14).
[154] Cf. *Hist. Arian.* 25,2 (Opitz 196,16–19).

clear: the Church of Rome is treated as though it were synonymous with ecclesiastical authority.

The picture Athanasius sketches is really that of the pre-Nicene era: it is an over-simplified presentation of the traditionally accepted form of universal authority. Within this framework, the orthodoxy or legitimate claim of a bishop to his see was expressed through communion with the universal episcopate, though as we saw in Eusebius' *History*, the form of this expression varied. Such a concept was basic to the ecclesiology behind his *encyclical* of the year 339, written before he departed for Rome and the synod called by Julius, as it was the final presupposition which determined his demonstration of the canonicity of his claim to the See of Alexandria in the *Apologia* (356). This communion was the expression of that unanimity, which springs from her Apostolicity and which, for example, was considered by St. Cyprian to be an essential mark of the Church itself.[155] When we come to examine *Unit II*, we will see that Athanasius' main consideration there (and in the book as a whole) is to review the traditional ecclesiastical principles in the light of a totally new situation in which this unanimity can no longer find its traditional expression due to the active intervention of a non-ecclesiastical power: the State. Unit I, then, serves to prepare the reader to revise his thinking on this issue by recalling the traditional expression of universal authority in the Church.

b) Part I, Unit II: The Alternative to Universal Unanimity (Hist. Arian. 28–41)

This Unit covers the events that took place in the universal Church, and which led to the third exile of Athanasius. Those events that marked the history of the Church in Egypt during the same period are reserved for detailed treatment in Part II. Due to the limits of our study, we must ignore them.

aa) Section I: The Prelude to the "Fall of Liberius" (Hist. Arian. 28–34)

Describing the ecclesiastical situation at the time of his return to Alexandria (346) in the wake of Rome-Sardica, Athanasius informs his readers that unanimity and peace (συμφονία καὶ εἰρήνη) prevailed between him and the universal episcopate.[156] This unanimity is one of the essential manifestations of genuine ecclesiastical

---

[155] Cf. *De ecclesiae unitate* 6 and 25 (Hartel 214,17–215,10 and 232,3–11).
[156] Cf. *Hist. Arian.* 28,2 (Opitz 198,6).

authority, as Athanasius will further develop in *De synodis*. In Ch. 28 he is satisfied to indicate the fact itself, which he does by listing the ecclesiastical provinces, and their countries, whose bishops had signed the encyclical letter of the Council of Sardica[157] and so accepted him into their communion. We note, however, that unlike the list of signatures given in the *Apologia*,[158] where the president of the Synod, Ossius, heads the list (as also at Nicaea) followed by the Roman delegates, this summary list in the *Historia* is headed by "the great Rome." On examining the occasions when Athanasius has cause to list bishops or their Churches (other than direct quotations of lists of signatures), we find that on five other occasions, Rome or its bishop heads the list.[159] On the two occasions when Rome does not appear at the top of the list, we note that there Athanasius draws attention to the *personal* character or prestige of the office-holders being listed (in particular Ossius).[160] Apart from the prominence thus given to Rome and its bishop, this distinction between office and person is of fundamental importance to Athanasius, as we will see when we come to examine his treatment of Liberius and Ossius.[161] Here in Ch. 28, the distinction is lightly but clearly sketched: Rome heads the list, while the only bishop to be mentioned by name is Ossius. Further Athanasius singles out Rome with the adjective "great" and applies the same to Ossius. To understand the significance of the reference to μεγάλη 'Ρώμη, we must first recall the principle enunciated by the Eusebians in reply to Julius' summons to attend a synod: the size (or political importance) of a city ought not affect the authority of its bishop. Apart from pointing out to the Eusebians that they denied this in practice, Julius accepted the principle, yet he did not hesitate to point out that theological or ecclesiastical factors do affect its authority: namely, the claims of a see to direct Apostolic Succession.[162] Such was the traditional understanding of the Church's nature, as our analysis of Eusebius' original *History* brought to light. A brief look at the use of the term μέγας by Athanasius will

---

[157] Cf. *Hist. Arian.* 28,2 (Opitz 198,7–13).

[158] Cf. *Apol.* 48,2f. (Opitz 123,29f.).

[159] Cf. *Apol.* 89,3 (Opitz 167,18f.); *Ad Const.* 27 (Szymusiak 118–119); *De fuga 4,2* (Opitz 71,1f.); *Ad Afros* 1 (*PG* 26,1029,A1f.); *Hist. Arian.* 46,2 (Opitz 210,4f.).

[160] Cf. Ad epp. Aeg. et Lib. 8 (PG 25,556,C1f.); De fuga 9,4 (Opitz 74,24f.).

[161] Gwatkin observes in Studies, 154–155: "The grandeur of Hosius was merely personal, but Liberius claimed the universal reverence due to the Apostolic and Imperial See of Rome." However, it was not the see's imperial character that mattered for Athanasius (or the early Eusebius) but its Apostolic character.

[162] See above, pp. 414–419.

show that the Bishop of Alexandria shared this traditional assumption.

According to the article in the *Lexicon Athanasianum*,[163] μέγας, though frequently used in the generally undifferentiated sense of "large," is also used by Athanasius almost in a technical sense as an *epitheton honoris*, as e.g., with reference to the prophets of the Old Testament—Daniel[164] and Samuel,[165] but especially Elijah[166] and Moses.[167] Both Moses and Elijah are on occasion singled out as "great" in contexts which refer to their functions as teaching authorities[168] and as leaders of the People of God.[169] Apart from one reference to "the great martyr Stephan,"[170] the only saint of the New Testament to receive this title is, significantly, St. Peter, and this occurs on five occassions.[171] Otherwise the term is regularly applied to Ossius,[172] once to other orthodox bishops as a group,[173] as well as to Bishop Achillas of Alexandria[174] who was revered as a saint and known for his decisive action against the schismatic Meletians. It might be added that the epithet is frequently used when speaking of each of the three Divine Persons.[175] The only persona who, despite the lack of either orthodoxy or sanctity, is honored with this term is Plato, though with a remarkable restriction: ὁ μέγας παρ᾽ Ἕλλεσι Πλάτων.[176]

Thus we can conclude that, generally speaking, the term is used by Athanasius to connote the presence of the "Holy." When the

---

[163] Müller, *Lexicon*, col. 880–882.

[164] *Hist. Arian.* 79,4 (Opitz 228,2).

[165] *De incarn.* 35,8 (Kannengiesser 390–391).

[166] *De fuga* 10,6 (Opitz 75,18); *De fuga* 18,4 (Opitz 81,3); *De fuga* 20,4 (Opitz 82,6); *Vita Ant.* 7 (*PG* 26,853,C1); *Hist. Arian.* 53,2 (Opitz 213,29).

[167] *C. Gentes* 46 (Thompson 128); *De incarn.* 33,4 (Kannengiesser 384); *De fuga* 18,2 (Opitz 80,26); *Serap. I,* 12 (*PG* 26,561,B7); *Ad Dracont.* 5 (*PG* 25,520,A3); *Or. c. Ar. II,* 51 (*PG* 26,256,B4); *Or. c. Ar. II,* 59 (*PG* 26.273,C7).

[168] Cf. *De incarn.* 33,4 (Kannengiesser 384), re. Moses, and *Vita Ant.* 7 (*PG* 26,855,C1), where Elijah is considered to be the exemplar or model of perfection for the hermit. See above, p. 258.

[169] Moses was entrusted with the government of the people (*Or. c. Ar. I,* 51 = *PG* 26,256,B4) while the great Elijah established his leadership when he destroyed the prophets of Baal (*De fuga* 20,4 = Opitz 82,6).

[170] *De sent. Dion.* 7,3 (Opitz 51,1).

[171] See above, Chapter Seven, footnote 1.

[172] *Apol.* 89,3 (Opitz 167,20); *Ad epp. Aeg. et Lib.* 8 (*PG* 25,556,C1); *Ad Const.* 27 (Szymusiak 118); *De fuga* 5,1 (Opitz 71,7); *Hist. Arian.* 16,3 (Opitz 191,16); *Hist. Arian.* 28,2 (Opitz 198,9); *Hist. Arian.* 42,1 (Opitz 206,20); *Hist. Arian.* 46,2 (Opitz 210,4–5); *Hist. Arian.* 49,1 (Opitz 211,17).

[173] *Ad epp. Aeg. et Lib.* 8 (*PG* 25,557,A6).

[174] *Ad epp. Aeg. et Lib.* 23 (PG 25,592,B15).

[175] See Müller, *Lexicon*, col. 882.

[176] *De incarn.* 2,3 (Kannengiesser 264).

adjective is made to qualify human beings we find in addition that the
term receives two further nuances: that of leadership in witnessing to the
Faith or truth and that of orthodoxy—as we may deduce from the color
reflected on the term by the personalities so singled out. Then we are not
surprised to find Athanasius limiting the term to the two synods, which he
could alone describe as holy and orthodox: Nicaea[177] and Sardica.[178] Rome
is the only city, see, or province to receive the epitheton μέγας—and this
occurs on six different occasions.[179] Therefore, we are led to conclude that
with the term, μέγας, Athanasius did not intend to refer to Rome's size,
ancient glory or political importance, but rather wished to give expression
to Rome's significance in the history of salvation: she is the holy city, whose
greatness lies in her being the "capital of orthodoxy from the beginning,"
as even the Eusebians admitted in their letter to Julius[180]—whence came
her leading role in witnessing to the truth. The source of this "greatness" is
to be found in her unique Apostolic Tradition, the tradition of St. Peter,
who as we saw is the only N.T. saint, apart from the confessor and martyr
Stephan, to receive the title "great," and whose martyrdom at Rome was
understood by Athanasius, like Eusebius before him, to be part of the
Divine Dispensation.

     To return to *Hist. Arian.* 28 and recapitulate: At the opening of the
section of *Hist. Arian.,* which leads directly into the detailed accounts
of the fall of Liberius, Bishop of Rome, and that of Ossius (i.e., *Hist.
Arian.,* Ch. 28–34), the importance and unique position of "Rome," its
Church and bishop (the name of the city is again used here as a synonym
for both), as distinct from the importance attached to the personality
of Ossius, is brought to the reader's attention both by their position in
the list of bishops and by attributing to both the term μέγας with its
specific nuances of orthodoxy and even holiness. Rome is given prominence among the universal episcopacy with whom Athanasius enjoys
communion. This communion is a witness to that unanimity, which is
an essential characteristic of ecclesiastical authority—and thus where
orthodoxy is to be found. The aim of the rest of this Section is to
show how, when (as a result of the intrigues of the heretics) external

---

[177] *De syn.* 39,5 (Opitz 265,28); *De decr. Nic.* 26,1 (Opitz 21,31); *Ad Afros* 4 (*PG*
26,1036,A5); *Ad Afros* 5 (*PG* 26,1037,A12).

[178] *Ad epp. Aeg. et Lib.* 7 (*PG* 25,553,B4); *De fuga* 26,4 (Opitz 86,6).

[179] *Hist. Arian.* 28,2 (Opitz 198,7); *Ad Afros* 1 (*PG* 26,1029,A3); *Ad Afros* 6
(*PG* 26,1039,B13); *Ad Afros* 10 (*PG* 26,1045,C12 and D5); *Ad Epict.* 1 (*PG*
26,1052,A7).

[180] Sozomen, *HE* 3,8,5 (Bidez-Hansen 111,11).

violence is done to the participants of this communion and the unanimity is externally shattered, then the sufferings endured by them are themselves witnesses to the inner depth of that unanimity, whose source is God.

It is also of note to observe how, again at the opening of this prelude to the fall of Liberius, Rome is further singled out as the place where freedom of conscience reigns supreme. Reporting on the events which led to the Synods of Arles and Milan, Athanasius points out that these were set in motion by the relapse of Valens and Ursacius. There he recalls their earlier repentance, when "they voluntarily went up to Rome, and there, where there was no fear from without, but where there is only fear of God and each one has freedom of conscience, they repented and signed of their own accord."[181] "Rome" is thus presented as the haven of liberty of conscience. This passage receives its particular significance due to the contrast Athanasius wishes to make between the beginning of this new phase in the history of the "Eusebian heresy," and its climax when the Bishop of Rome is torn away from that Church, where true freedom is preserved, and is forced against his will to subscribe to Athanasius' condemnation by the party of Valens and Ursacius, who had previously been able to act freely at Rome.

At Arles (353), the synod that Liberius had originally requested the emperor to hold at Aquileia met and condemned Athanasius. The one voice of dissent was that of Paulinus of Trier, who was immediately banished. Liberius, shattered at the news, endeavored to have the matter handled again. The emperor agreed and called a synod at Milan in 355. Here again the imperial pressure to conform broke whatever resistance there might have been in the majority and they condemned Athanasius, with the notable exception of the Bishops Eusebius of Vercelli, Dionysius of Milan, Lucifer of Cagliari, and the two Roman delegates—the priest Pancratius[182] and the deacon Hilarius.

Consistent with the aims of his writing, Athanasius, however, gives no details regarding the synods (which may be presumed to have been known to his readers) but instead treats both as one event,[183] and is content to highlight the threats of violence on the part of the Neo-Arians and the imperial power, before which the synodal

---

[181] *Hist. Arian.* 29,2 (Opitz 198,25–26).

[182] Cf. *Ep. Liberii ad Eusebium episcopum Vercellensem* (*PG* 8,1355,C10). Athanasius errs when he gives his name as Eutropius (*Hist. Arian.* 41,1 = Opitz 205,32).

[183] Cf. *Hist. Arian.* 31,1f. (Opitz 199,21f.); see also *Hist. Arian.* 33,6 (201,28–34).

Fathers weakened and signed the condemnation. His real concern is to
point out the theological significance of such compulsion:[184] it is evil and
belongs to the enemies of Christ, whereas "persuasion and counsel" characterize Our Lord.[185] The weight of authority he attached to such synods is
nil: the procedure according to which the emperor's wishes must be taken
as law ("whatever I will, that is law")[186] is a *novum* and thus not binding as
far as the law of the Church is concerned.

The attentive reader will notice that in his description of the synods,
Athanasius makes no mention of the Roman delegates, neither those
who signed at Arles nor those who refused to sign at Milan. That Liberius
dissociated himself from the former was common knowledge, neither
had Athanasius any reason to refer to them. But the banishment of the
Roman presbyter Pancratius and the scouring of the deacon Hilarius
for their refusal to condemn Athanasius certainly merited the attention
of the writer. Yet he reserves any mention of them until he reaches the
conclusion of his treatment of Liberius, and does so for a very specific
purpose, as we will see.

The Synods of Arles and Milan were, however, of major significance as far as the traditional concept of ecclesiastical authority, which
found its expression in universal unanimity, was concerned. According
to Athanasius, the unanimity established at those synods was merely
a conformity that had been achieved by means of external pressure. In
the new situation created by the positive attitude of the State towards
the Church, the possibility has also been created whereby the synod, as
an institution, could be misused (= the Eusebian ecclesiology), and an
apparent unanimity could be produced by the application of the external
force at the disposal of the emperor (= the later Neo-Arian version of the
Eusebian concept as adopted by Constantius). In such a situation, the
questions arose: where was the genuine unanimity to be found and under
what form did it manifest itself?

At the end of this "prelude" (Ch. 34), Athanasius takes up the
theme of banishment as a new form of persecution and martyrdom,
which, more effectively than words, preaches the Gospel in every
place and city, and so proclaims the orthodox faith.[187] This extension

---

[184] Cf. *Hist. Arian.* 33,1–7 (Opitz 201,13–202,4).

[185] οὐ γὰρ ξίφεσιν ἢ βέλεσιν οὐδὲ διὰ στρατιωτῶν ἡ ἀλήθεια καταγγέλεται, ἀλλὰ πειθοῖ
καὶ συμβουλίᾳ (*Hist. Arian.* 33,3 = Opitz 201,20–21).

[186] *Hist. Arian.* 33,7 = Opitz 202,2.

[187] The extension of the term "martyrdom" to cover those persecuted for the
orthodox faith by their (heretical) brethren was already made by Liberius in

of the term "martyrdom" to cover "suffering for the Faith at the hands of heretical brethren" was formulated by Athanasius at the very beginning of his third exile: "Not only the refusal to offer incense is proof of martyrdom, but also not to deny the faith effects the martyrdom of the clear conscience."[188] We have seen how the theme was announced at the conclusion of the *Apologia*, where the orthodox bishops—exiled after Arles and Milan, and led by Liberius of Rome—were held up to his readers as models and patterns for their successors "to contend for the truth until death."[189] The following year he developed the same theme in the *Apologia de fuga sua,* where he described the function which, according to God's wonderful dispensation, is given to those who are persecuted, and so are either banished or forced to flee into exile among the trackless wastes, namely to preach the Gospel, to warn us of the wickedness of the conspirators, and to confirm the faithful.[190] In a *letter* to Lucifer of Cagliari, one of the three bishops exiled after Milan (355), Athanasius states his belief that, by means of such confessors and servants of God, God is renewing the Catholic Church and reuniting (at a more profound level) that which the heretics were tearing asunder on the surface.[191]

Following this train of thought, Athanasius is at pains here[192] to show that the bishops who were exiled for their protest against the emperor's attempt to mingle Roman sovereignty with the constitution of the Church (= the Eusebian heresy) (and against his introduction of the Arian teaching),[193] accepted their banishment as a ministry of service to proclaim the orthodox Faith and anathematized the heretics wherever they went.[194] The more distant the banishment, the more effective was the witness to the truth, so that all who saw them considered them to be confessors.[195] This

his letter to Eusebius of Vercelli, Dionysius of Milan, and Lucifer of Cagliari, upon hearing of their exile on account of their stand for the Faith at the Synod of Milan in 355 (cf. Hilary, *Frag. hist.*, series B, VII, 2 = Feder 164–165). St. Hilary later develops this theme in his *Lib. c. Const. Imp.* (*PL* 10,577f.).

[188] *Ad epp. Aeg. et Lib.* 21 (*PG* 25,588,A7–10).
[189] See above, pp. 475–476.
[190] Cf. *De fuga* 21,2 (Opitz 82,24–25); re. the theme of God's dispensation, see *De fuga* 17,1–20,5 (Opitz 79,29–82,16).
[191] Cf. *Ad Lucif. I* (*PG* 26,1182,D3–4).
[192] *Hist. Arian.* 34,1–4 (Opitz 202,5–23).
[193] Cf. *Hist. Arian.* 34,1 (Opitz 202,8–10) after the translation of Atkinson in Robertson, *Athanasius*, LNPF[2], 281.
[194] *Hist. Arian.* 34,3 (202,13–15).
[195] *Hist. Arian.* 34,4 (202,21).

coupling of the idea of banishment with the confession of the Faith now becomes the *leitmotiv* of Athanasius' description and evaluation of the subscription of Liberius that follows.

It should be noted that the "confessors" who went into exile protested not only against Constantius' application in practice of the earlier Eusebian heresy, and the unjust condemnation of Athanasius by a provincial synod that derived its authority from the emperor, but also against the emperor's support for the Neo-Arian heresy. Here the Blasphemy of Sirmium is most likely in the mind of Athanasius since it forms the content of the lapse of Ossius, which he will treat at the end of the following section. This shorthand reportage, however, reminds his readers that the controversy surrounding his claim to Alexandria had taken on a new dimension since the Synods of Arles and Milan. It is no longer a relatively simple dispute about the constitution of the Church, but one that concerns the Apostolic Faith. As we have seen, it was Liberius of Rome who, it seems, was primarily responsible for the transformation of the question of Athanasius' claim to the See of Alexandria into an issue of the Faith, so that communion with Athanasius could be treated by him as equivalent to a confession of the Nicene Faith. Here Athanasius takes full cognizance of the development, which in 355 was so encouraging, but in October 357, with the apparent subscription of Liberius to Athanasius' deposition and excommunication, so potentially dangerous for the integrity of the Faith.

bb) Section II: The Lapse of Liberius and the Petrine Office of the
     Bishop of Rome; the Fall of Ossius (*Hist. Arian.* 35–46)

In accordance with the epistemology of Athanasius, whereby the intention takes precedence over the mere term or expression,[196] the capitulation of Liberius (like that of Ossius) before Constantius' violent abuse of his power is interpreted by Athanasius not as a "fall," but as a clear expression of the orthodoxy which the pope "proclaimed as a free man": ". . . For those things which are produced by torture, contrary to their original judgment, are not the willing deeds of those who are in fear, but rather of their tormentors. . . ."[197] Athanasius is not concerned with the letter but

---

[196] As seen, for example, especially in *De synodis*.

[197] *Hist. Arian.* 41,4 (Opitz 206,14–15). We note that this sentence is rarely quoted, thus giving a false impression of Athanasius' intention in this passage. See Caspar, *Geschichte des Papsttums* I, 190, who simply remarks on the absence of the "usual polemical style" and finds in its place an "undertone of compassionate contempt." When one considers the reference "hac ego libenti animo suscepi" in the letter to the Oriental bishops attributed to Liberius (Hilary,

with the spirit of it—or rather, here, the *intention of it*. The two years of banishment—which led to Liberius weakening and ultimately, under the pressure of external violence, subscribing to the condemnation of Athanasius—and the sufferings the Bishop of Rome endured are, for Athanasius, all the weightier *confessions of his true belief*, since they constitute his martyrdom. This then is the main point of Ch. 35–41, which deals with the story of Liberius. But its full significance, regarding the attitude of Athanasius to the Bishop of Rome's preeminence, is not readily apparent when taken as a mere cold statement outside its context within the entire literary subsection of Ch. 35–41.

A comparison with the subsection, which follows and which deals with the lapse of Ossius,[198] shows first of all how clearly Athanasius wishes to emphasize that the importance of Ossius (his greatness, which was such a source of annoyance to the heretics until they could conquer him) lay in his personal prestige as "father of the bishops"—referring to his old age and his presidency of the Councils of Nicaea and Sardica, as well as his reputation as a confessor, and as having ruled his see for over 60 years;[199] so too Ossius' ability to argue and defend the Faith and his role in formulating the Nicene Creed are cited.[200] The importance of Liberius on the other hand derives exclusively from his *office* as Bishop of Rome. This contrast was already apparent (*Hist. Arian.* 28) in the opening paragraph of Section I (the "Prelude" to this Section), where the two authorities were given prominence among the universal episcopate, whose communion guaranteed their orthodoxy since it witnessed to their unanimity. Before moving on to consider the cases of Liberius and Ossius in detail, Athanasius had already introduced the concept of martyrdom through exile as the new form of confession of the truth and as the new alternative to that other hallmark of orthodoxy (i.e., the truth), namely, the unanimity of universal communion, which unanimity was being destroyed by external violence. Thus, we can understand how the description of the banishment and sufferings of Liberius and Ossius will have

---

Frag. hist., series B, VII, 8,2 = Feder 169,2), Athanasius' interpretation seems to be generous—but the very explicit reference to Liberius' "free subscription" would lead the critical observer to suspect the opposite, as indeed Athanasius did—possibly on receiving a copy of the said letter. Hilary (?) apparently thought otherwise.

[198] *Hist. Arian.* 42,1–45,5 (Opitz 206,19–209,29).

[199] See *Hist. Arian.* 42,1 (Opitz 206,19–25).

[200] Cf. *Hist. Arian.* 42,3 (Opitz 206,30–34). The Synod of Sardica also pays tribute to the age and confessional status of Ossius (cf. *Apol.* 32,7). Caspar describes Ossius as "eine moralische Macht ersten Ranges" (*Geschichte des Papsttums* I, 179).

this aim: to show how they were as prominent in this alternative form of witnessing to the truth as in the original form of external unanimity, as befitted the unique office of Liberius (itself based on the Confession of St. Peter) and the unique personal status of Ossius (the Confessor of the Diocletian Persecution). For the purposes of this study, we must limit ourselves to the office of Liberius, Bishop of Rome, as presented in *Hist. Arian.*, Ch. 35–41.

Within this subsection dealing with Pope Liberius, we find a further "parallelism:" each paragraph is so related to the paragraph immediately following, so that within its presentation of certain "historical" events and by means of fictional dialogue, the basic conception of the pope's office is developed, elaborated, and clarified in ever narrowing circles which focus in on the actual "fall" of Liberius, so as to illuminate the significance of that event. And so, we will examine this section by section, commenting briefly on this development of the basic idea as it occurs from paragraph to paragraph.

Attention must also be paid to the reception and development of those seminal concepts regarding the primacy of Rome, which were found in the *Apologia* and its background.

i)   The Office of the Bishop of Rome (*Hist. Arian.* 35)
The paragraph opens as follows:

1. Now it would have been better if from the beginning Constantius had not been so associated with this heresy, or being associated, had not become so entangled with the godless, or being entangled, if he [only] had stood by them up to these events (sc. the banishment of the orthodox at Arles and Milan) so that they might but deserve the usual condemnation which these [atrocities] merit. However, it would seem that, as befits the demented, chaining themselves ever tighter to their godlessness, they are drawing down a much greater judgement on their heads.

2. [This is so] since from the beginning they did not even spare Liberius the Bishop of Rome but extended their madness even into those parts and showed no respect for [its] Apostolic Throne; neither did they honor [the fact] that it is [the] metropolis, the Rome of the Roman territory, nor did they remember that, when they previously wrote, they said "[the] men [are] themselves apostolic."[201]

---

[201] 1. Βέλτιον μὲν οὖν ἦν κατὰ τὴν ἀρχὴν Κωνστάντιον μηδ᾽ ὅλως τῆς αἱρέσεως ταύτης γενέσθαι ἢ γενόμενον μὴ τοσοῦτον ἐνδοῦναι τοῖς ἀσεβέσιν ἢ ἐνδόντα

The opening sentence confirms the initial findings, which resulted from our analysis of the *Sitz im Leben,* and the structure of the *Historia,* namely, how the report of the fall of Liberius was the work's *raison d'être* and so occupies a central position (if not *the* central position) in this presentation of the Eusebian and Neo-Arian controversies. With a typical economy of words, the author recalls the direct involvement of the empire (in the person of Constantius) from the beginning of this new phase up to the present time, and so sums up in a few terse clauses the basic thrust of the *Historia.* The style of the sentence highlights the dramatic element: the mounting involvement of the imperial authority in the ever increasing iniquity of the successors of the Eusebians reaches its climax with the attack on Pope Liberius: if, Athanasius says, the Neo-Arian party had but ceased their iniquitous activity with the forced submission of the West at Milan (the East being long since under their control), they would have merited the condemnation of all—but the condemnation they now deserve, by attacking Rome, is beyond description.

When we compare the first and second sentence we note that (reechoing the *Apologia*) where the function of the Bishop of Rome, as the ecclesiastical counterpart to the emperor was first hinted at in the writings of Athanasius, Constantius, and Liberius, is presented here as though their confrontation was inevitable: κατὰ τὴν ἀρχήν. This phrase has been translated: "from the beginning," which could be understood to refer quite simply to the beginning of the respective reigns of Liberius as pope and Constantius as sole ruler. On the other hand, the phrase may well have been intended to imply "in principle," so that the text could be read: direct state intervention in Church affairs could not *in principle* tolerate an independent ecclesiastical authority, as incorporated in the universal function of the Bishop of Rome's office, and so must of necessity result in the attempt to subdue "Rome," which name, as we saw in our earlier analysis, was almost synonymous with independent ecclesiastical authority, and was identified as the Church where freedom of conscience was preserved and the fear of God reigned supreme (an interpretation which W. Gessel, *Theol. Revue* 81 [1985] 287, rejects).

μέχρι τούτων στῆναι μετ' αὐτῶν, ἵνα κἂν ἕως τούτων ἔχωσι κοινὴν τὴν κρίσιν. ὡς δὲ ἔοικε, κατὰ τοὺς ἄφρονας δεσμοῖς τῆς ἀσεβείας ἑαυτοὺς περιπείροντες μείζονα καθ' ἑαυτῶν τὴν κρίσιν ἐπιστῶνται.

2. καὶ γὰρ οὐδὲ Λιβερίου τοῦ ἐπισκόπου Ῥώμης κατὰ τὴν ἀρχὴν ἐφείσαντο, ἀλλὰ καὶ μέχρι τῶν ἐκεῖ τὴν μανίαν ἐξέτειναν καὶ οὐχ ὅτι ἀποστολικός ἐστι θρόνος ᾐδέσθησαν, οὐδ' ὅτι μητρόπολις ἡ Ῥώμη τῆς Ῥωμανίας ἐστὶν ηὐλαβήθησαν, οὐδ' ὅτι πρότερον 'ἀποστολικοὺς αὐτοὺς ἄνδρας' γράφοντες εἰρήκασιν ἐμνημόνευσαν (*Hist. Arian.* 35,1–2 = Opitz 202,24–31).

At the conclusion of this paragraph, Athanasius reports how the Eunuch Eusebius was sent from the imperial court to Liberius to secure the submission of the pope to the imperial authority by means of bribery and threats. Eusebius orders the Bishop of Rome to excommunicate Athanasius and to enter into communion with the Neo-Arians with the statement: "This the Emperor wishes and commands you to do."[202] Thus, in the opening paragraph, the emperor and the Bishop of Rome are presented as representing two different ecclesiologies, whose basic tendencies are in principle mutually exclusive and thus, from the beginning, the spectacular trial of strength between Constantius and Liberius[203] was, according to Athanasius, unavoidable.

The attack on Pope Liberius was not, according to Athanasius, to be considered merely at the level of the atrocities committed against the other bishops but, as the author repeats at the end of this subsection, "from the beginning," the aim of the Arians was to corrupt the Church of the Romans with their heresy (*Hist. Ar.* 41,3). The motive of the Neo-Arians is more precisely stated by Athanasius in the fictional soliloquy he put into their mouths: "If we can prevail upon Liberius, we shall quickly rule over all."[204] We must return shortly to this phrase in order to examine its implications.

Corresponding to the phrase κατὰ τὴν ἀρχήν, which projects the attack on Pope Liberius back to the very origins of the Neo-Arian attacks on the Church, Athanasius selects the phrase ἀλλὰ καὶ μέχρι τῶν ἐκεῖ to describe the extremity of all possible enmity against the Church and the orthodox in the execution of this aim: "but even into those parts."[205] The language of Athanasius here records his shock in the

---

[202] *Hist. Arian.* 35,5 (Opitz 203,4). Commenting on the motives of Constantius, Ammianus Marcellinus reports that the emperor, who was always hostile to Athanasius, endeavored to have his condemnation ratified by the Bishop of Rome: id . . . tamen auctoritate quoque potiore aeternae urbis episcopi firmari desiderio nitebatur ardenti (*RG* 15,7,10 = Clark 57,24–26). For a description of the Eunuch Eusebius, see Ammianus Marcellinus, *RG* 18,4,3–4 (Clark 141,26–142,9); see also *RG* 14,10,5 (Clark 28,21–22) and *RG* 14,11,2 (Clark 31,11–15), regarding his bribery and flattery. See the article by Schwartz on "Eusebios" in *PWK* VI, col. 1367f.

[203] See Jalland, *Church and Papacy*, 224.

[204] εἰ τὸν Λιβέριον πείσαιμεν, πάντων ταχέως κρατήσομεν (*Hist. Arian.* 35,3 = Opitz 203,1).

[205] Hilary describes the action of Constantius in similar terms: Vertisti deinde usque ad Romam bellum tuum, eripuisit illinc (*Liberius*) episcopum . . . (*Lib. c. Const. Imp.* 11 = *PL* 10,589,A6–8).

face of such a great sacrilege—that the enemy should dare to enter such a sanctuary, i.e., that the Arians failed to show reverence towards the *Apostolic Throne* of Rome.

This is the only reference in the writings of St. Athanasius to the term "Apostolic Throne." According to Batiffol, Athanasius did not say that Rome is the Apostolic Throne *par excellence*;[206] however, the question may be posed whether or not Athanasius may have intended this to be his meaning. The fact that the term is not otherwise used by Athanasius would at least suggest that he regarded no other Church as worthy of such a title—and it would seem indeed to be used by Athanasius precisely as a title: ἀποστολικός ἐστι θρόνος.[207] So too the absence of the definite article can hardly be taken to signify an indefinite but rather an absolute sense. These tentative interpretations are based on *ex silentio* arguments and are not conclusive. However, Athanasius himself goes on to draw out the implications of such a title by rephrasing this final atrocity of the Arians in a type of parallelism: "neither did they honor [the fact] that it is [the] metropolis, the Rome of the Romania, nor did they remember that, when they wrote previously, they said "the men [are] themselves apostolic."

Of itself, this parallelism is at first glance no less difficult to interpret as the phrase ἀποστολικός ἐστι θρόνος. The title μητρόπολις ἡ Ῥώμη τῆς Ῥωμανίας could refer to the political importance of Rome,[208] but such an interpretation fails to convince due both to the immediate context, which sharply contrasts the ecclesiastical and imperial authorities, and the mind of St. Athanasius who,

---

[206] Batiffol, *Cathedra Petri*, 155.

[207] Julius of Rome (in his *4th Letter to the Eusebians*) spoke of the Churches of those bishops who had taken refuge in Rome as Churches which had been ruled by the Apostles. He evidently wished to refer to the special standing of Apostolic Sees, which claimed direct Apostolic Succession (see above, p. 416f.). The Synod of Sardica referred (in their *Letter to Julius*) to the Head of the Church as *Petri apostoli sedes* (see above, pp. 456–457). However, the first appearance of the term *sedes apostolica,* used to signify the *Cathedra Petri* as *the* seat of the Petrine Succession that guarantees the authentic Apostolic Tradition, is to be found in the *Letter of Liberius to Eusebius of Vercelli* (*PL* 8,1350,B1–4), dated 354. The technical—or, at least, the semitechnical—use of this terminology by Liberius and Athanasius within three years of each other is significant: the "Apostolic" nature of the Church and her tradition was, at the time, under its most severe attack since the beginning of the Church, and this attack had finally made its way into the Church of Rome, the final guarantor of that tradition in the Church, and so forced the Church to declare its true nature in a technical language. See Maccarrone, "'Cathedra Petri' und die Idee der Entwicklung des päpstlichen Primates," especially 291–292; Krömer, *Die Sedes Apostolica der Stadt Rome*, especially 106–108.

[208] See Batiffol, *Cathedra Petri*, 155.

following the thought of his predecessor Alexander,[209] and that of Pope Julius,[210] attaches no importance to quantity as such,[211] or to the size or importance of a city, be it economic or political, as also our analysis of the term μέγας confirmed. In a work which most categorically rejects the Eusebian ecclesiology and its application of imperial norms to regulate Church-affairs, we would indeed be surprised to find Athanasius calling on the political importance of Rome as the basis of her authority. Finally, if we may mention the obvious, Constantinople and not Rome was the chief civil metropolis of the empire since May 11, 330. The new capital on the Bosporus, it may be added, is described in a general way by Athanasius as one of the illustrious cities (ἐπιφανής), whose bishops were attacked by the Eusebian party.[212]

Two paragraphs earlier,[213] Athanasius uses the term μητρόπολις in his list of orthodox bishops exiled after Arles and Milan: "Paulinus Bishop of Trier, the Metropolis of the Gauls, Lucifer, Bishop of Trier, the Metropolis of the Gauls, Lucifer, Bishop of the Metropolis of Sardinia, Eusebius of Vercelli in Italy, and Dionysius of Milan which is also the Metropolis of Italy." Here the term μητρόπολις is used as in Canon VII of Nicaea, where it refers to the chief Church or see of a province. Thus, it is possible to interpret the unique term Ῥωμανία as the Roman Province[214] and understand our present reference to Rome as to the Metropolis of the Province of Rome. However, a comparison of the different ways Athanasius uses the term when he refers to the other bishops and when he refers to the Bishop of Rome shows how Athanasius did not consider the Metropolis Rome to be on the same level as the other sees.[215]

---

[209] Cf. *Depositio Arii = Urkunde* 4b,4 (Opitz 7,5).

[210] *Apol.* 25,2 (Opitz 106,2–7).

[211] See *De syn.* 43,2 (Opitz 268,22–24).

[212] Cf. *Hist. Arian.* 7,1 (Opitz 186,10). Regarding the political situation of the city of Rome under Constantine, see Jalland, *Church and Papacy*, 207.

[213] *Hist. Arian.* 33,6 (Opitz 201,31–34).

[214] See Müller, *Lexicon*, col. 1317.

[215] In *Hist. Arian.* 33,6, Athanasius refers to each city, or rather each Church, as being simply the μετρόπολις of a province (e.g., "Paulinus of Trier, the metropolis of the Gauls"), but in *Hist. Arian.* 35,2, he speaks of the "metropolis, the Rome of the Romania," and not, as we might expect, "Rome, metropolis of the Romania." There is an interesting text in *De fuga* 4,2 (Opitz 71,1), where the bishops exiled after Arles and Milan are listed: Liberius, who heads the list (as is usual in Athanasius, although his exile was chronologically later), is described as ὁ ἐπίσκοπος τῆς Ῥώμης, whereas the others are listed as ὁ τῆς μετροπόλεως τῶν Γαλλίων . . . τῆς Ἰταλίας . . . etc., perhaps indicating that "Bishop of Rome" was almost a technical term due to the uniqueness of that see.

If we are prepared to accept the interpretation of Ῥωμανία as "Roman territory,"[216] then we may transcribe μητρόπολις ἡ Ῥώμη τῆς Ῥωμανίας as the chief See (and thus authority) of the whole (Roman) Empire, which, according to the foregoing clause, derives its authority from the "Apostolic Throne." This interpretation of μητρόπολις receives a not insignificant confirmation from an unexpected source: the Eusebians.

In the second part of the parallelism, Athanasius explicitly calls attention to a previous letter of the "Arians." This is most likely the infamous reply of the Eusebians to Julius early in the year 341, which we analyzed above;[217] we note that in the excerpt (or paraphrase) recorded by Sozomen, the Eusebians acknowledge the Church of the Romans as εὐσεβείας μητρόπολις ἐξ ἀρχῆς γεγενημένην . . . the metropolis of orthodoxy from the beginning.[218] It is probable that Athanasius has this, the original passage from the Eusebian reply, in mind when he now speaks of Rome as *the* Metropolis.

The second section of the parallelism, which draws attention to the basis of the authority enjoyed by the Chief See of the Empire, refers to the admission by the Arians that "the men are themselves apostolic," as they wrote formerly in their letters. If we are correct in assuming that Athanasius is quoting (or paraphrasing) the Eusebian letter to Julius just mentioned, then the most likely reference is to the same text as that which Athanasius had in mind when speaking of Rome as the Metropolis: the Eusebians confessed (ὡμολόγουν) that they honored the Church of the Romans as ἀποστόλων φροντιστήριον.[219] The term φροντιστήριον has been translated as "house of refuge,"[220] which would suggest that the Eusebians acknowledged Rome as the Refuge of Apostles. This, however, is not the primary meaning of the term, as has already been indicated in the previous chapter, but rather "a place for hard thinking"[221] (an academy or a school), as derived from φροντίζω, or even "a place for meditation, a monastery."[222] Thus, we may

---

[216] Lampe who in *Lexicon*, 1219, gives this text of Athanasius as the first reference to the term, translates it as "Roman empire, Roman territory." The same translation is used by Ortiz de Urbina in "Patres graeci," 113. The term is not to be found in Liddell-Scott, which suggests that it probably does not occur in profane literature. See von Ivánka, *Rhömerreich und Gottesvolk*, 75.

[217] See above, pp. 381–398.

[218] Sozomen, *HE* 3,8,5 (Bidez-Hansen 111,11).

[219] See the discussion of these terms above, pp. 388–389.

[220] Lampe, *Lexicon*, 1491.

[221] According to Liddell-Scott, *Lexicon*, col. 1957, the school of Socrates was so designated by Aristophanes.

[222] Cf. Theodoret, *HE* 3,24,2 (Parmentier-Scheidweiler 203,6).

tentatively translate the term (as used by the Eusebians) to mean "school of Apostles," which closely resembles the paraphrase of Athanasius: "the men are themselves apostolic," i.e., their teaching carries the weight of Apostolic Authority. Atkinson's translation of the phrase in *Hist. Arian.* 35,2 would seem to be quite accurate: "they had spoken of her bishops as Apostolic men."[223]

The reference of Athanasius to the *Letter of the Eusebians* is the key to a correct understanding of the passage: the Neo-Arians "showed no respect for its Apostolic throne, neither did they honor the fact that it is the Metropolis, the Rome of the Romania, nor did they remember that, when they previously wrote, they said "the men are themselves apostolic." In that letter, the Eusebians confessed "that, according to the general opinion, the Church of Rome held a position of honor [though one not untinged with ambition] as it was the school of Apostles and capital of orthodoxy from the beginning. . . ." As our analysis uncovered, that letter, while witnessing to the commonly accepted understanding of the Roman bishop's primacy based on the Petrine Succession, which Eusebius of Caesarea took for granted in his original *History*, attempted to neutralize its significance with its ironic reminder of the behavior of the Roman bishops during and after the Great Persecution, and denied its present relevance for the universal communion. The reaction of the Synod of Rome, at whose second session in 341 Athanasius was also present, is the famous *4th Letter of Julius,* which Athanasius preserved for us in his *Apologia.* There Julius rejects the *novum* of the Eusebian party, who had adopted the middle and later ecclesiological ideas of Eusebius of Caesarea, and translated them into the canons and practice of the Imperial Church. In order to counteract the influence of what they called the "Eusebian heresy," the Synodal Fathers at Sardica reaffirmed the truly ecclesiastical procedures, originally outlined by Julius, and expressly affirm what the Eusebians wished to deny, namely, the effective primacy of the Roman bishop, even in "jurisdictional" matters, since it is *Petri apostoli sedes.* Now Athanasius, who we remember was also an active participant at the Synod of Sardica, takes up this reaction to the Eusebian endeavor to negate Rome's traditional significance, by affirming its central authority, which is based on its singular Apostolic Succession. It is the θρόνος ἀποστολικός

---

[223] See Robertson, *Athanasius*, LNPF², 282. However, Batiffol in *Cathedra Petri*, 155, paraphrases the text as follows: "Les ariens ont traité les membres de l'Église de Rome d'hommes apostoliques."

in an exclusive sense, peculiar to Rome itself, such as was used by Liberius
of Rome but three years previously.[224]

The extent of Rome's authority is part of the subject treated in the two
sentences of *Hist. Arian.* 35,3–4, which now follow. Central to these two
sentences is the "quotation" from the fictional soliloquy of the Arians: "If
we prevail upon (πείσαιμεν) Liberius, we shall quickly rule over *all*.[225] This
quotation is framed by a description of Liberius as zealously persuading *all*
to renounce the heresy and, following up on the "quotation," a description
of the emperor's motives: he expected to "draw *all* [men] quickly to himself
by means of Liberius (διὰ Λιβερίου)."[226] Both the Arians and Constantius
realize that, if they get the support of Liberius' authority, this would
enable them to rule over *all*—with *immediate* effect (ταχέως). According
to Athanasius, since what we are studying are, in the first place, his ideas
projected on to his adversaries, the authority of the Bishop of Rome is
universal in extent and immediate in effect.[227]

The paragraph ends with a mention of the mission which
Constantius entrusted to the Eunuch Eusebius: namely, he must
"persuade" Liberius using bribery and threats[228] to subscribe against
Athanasius and hold communion with the Arians.[229] The gifts (τὰ δῶρα)
would seem to have a double purpose: to bribe and to act as "offerings,"
the reception of which would signify not only the obeisance of the

---

[224] See above, footnote 207.

[225] *Hist. Arian.* 35,3 (Opitz 203,1).

[226] κἀκεῖνος ταχέως προσδοκήσας διὰ Λιβερίου πάντες ἕλκειν πρὸς ἑαυτὸν γράφει (*Hist. Arian.* 35,4 = Opitz 203,2–3). The basic truth of this assertion is confirmed by Ammianus Marcellinus (see above, footnote 202).

[227] Grisar, *Geschichte Roms und der Päpste im Mittelalter*, 255, correctly draws attention to the "gewaltige Bedeutung des Primates Petri," which is implied in the statement we have just considered. Grisar attributes this to the Arians, but it is more accurately a reflection of the mind of Athanasius.

[228] *Hist. Arian.* 35,4 (Opitz 203,3–4).

[229] ἀπελθὼν τοίνυν ὁ σπάδων εἰς τὴν Ῥώμην πρῶτον παρακάλει τὸν Λιβέριον κατὰ Ἀθανασίου μὲν ὑπογράψαι, τοῖς δὲ Ἀρειανοῖς κοινωνῆσαι, λέγων· 'τοῦτο βασιλεὺς βούλεται καὶ κελεύει σε ποιῆσαι.' εἶτα ἐπιδεικνὺς τὰ δῶρα παρεκάλει καὶ χειρῶν ἥπτετο λέγων· 'πείσθητι βασιλεῖ καὶ ταῦτα δέξαι' (*Hist. Arian.* 35,5 = Opitz 203,4–8). The (fictional) speech of the Eunuch reiterates the first principle of the Eusebian imperial ecclesiology adopted by Constantius and formulated but two chapters previously, when Athanasius put into the emperor's mouth the words: ὅπερ ἐγὼ βούλομαι, τοῦτο κανών (*Hist. Arian.* 33,7 = Opitz 202,2). With regard to Constantius' reputation for bribery, see Hilary, *Lib. c. Const. Imp.* 5 (*PL* 10,581,B14–15). Cf. also the account of the emperor's attempt to bribe Liberius after their encounter in Milan, where Eusebius the Eunuch was also employed (cf. Theodoret, *HE* 2,26,27 = Parmentier-Scheidweiler 136,1–3).

final ecclesiastical authority before the totalitarian imperial power but also, as (sacrificial) offerings, communion with the Arians.

One final observation concerns the two ways Athanasius uses the term πείθω: when used with regard to Liberius, it has the straightforward meaning of "to persuade by means of argumentation"[230] but when used in connection with the Arians it conveys rather the derogatory connotation of persuasion by means of force and compulsion. We remember how the comparison between these two basic attitudes was the subject of *Hist. Arian.* 33—compulsion is of the devil, while persuasion by means of argumentation characterizes Christ.[231] This is the key to that discernment of spirits which enables Athanasius to interpret the fall of Liberius in such a positive fashion, as already briefly mentioned.

To summarize our findings, we may say that Athanasius singles out the attack on Pope Liberius as the inevitable confrontation between pope and emperor, Church and sacral empire, caused by the inordinate intervention of the empire in ecclesiastical affairs (= the Eusebian heresy), and as the final exposure of the fundamental aims and ultimate extent of the Neo-Arian atrocities: the attack on Liberius was an attack on the highest ecclesiastical authority, the Apostolic Throne—the source both of her authority as the chief see of the whole empire and of the living Apostolic Tradition present in her bishops.

In examining the following paragraphs, we will note how the various ideas mentioned in this paragraph (*Hist. Arian.* 35) will be taken up and developed by Athanasius against the background of his narrative describing the events leading up to the subscription of Liberius.

ii)   The way the Bishop of Rome exercises his responsibility
      (*Hist. Arian.* 36)

The second paragraph consists almost exclusively of a speech attributed to Liberius, but which is a literary composition of Athanasius, even if the basic statement of the speech does in fact correspond essentially to the record of the dialogue between the pope and the emperor at Milan (355) as preserved by Theodoret[232] and

---

[230]   Cf. *Hist. Arian.* 35,3 (Opitz 202,34); *Hist. Arian.* 36,1 (Opitz 203,9). Cf. Eusebius, *HE* 7,24,6–9 (Schwartz 688,9–690,8), where Dionysius of Alexandria is portrayed in a similar fashion.

[231]   Cf. *Hist. Arian.* 33,2 (Opitz 201,15–20); see also *Hist. Arian.* 67,1–2 (Opitz 219,35–220,3).

[232]   Theodoret, *HE* 2,16,1–27 (Parmentier-Scheidweiler 131,10f.). See above, pp. 450–451.

so accurately reflects the attitude of Liberius. It is conceivable that a verbal
and not completely accurate report of this interview between Liberius
and Constantine had gained wide circulation. Otherwise, it is difficult to
account for the basic agreement of both accounts. That Athanasius had at
his disposal a written account, such as a copy of the minutes preserved for
us by Theodoret, seems to be ruled out by the considerable discrepancy
in some details which cannot simply be accounted for by Athanasius'
free and creative use of his source material. Here the speech is addressed
not to the emperor but to his delegate, the eunuch, and is situated not at
Milan but Rome. However, our interest here does not concern us with
the attitude of Liberius[233] but that of Athanasius and so our examination
will concentrate on the accidentals, that is, those elements not found in
the dialogue between Liberius and Constantius at Milan, but which are
highlighted here by Athanasius in order to draw attention to various
theological nuances.

First a word about the opening sentence which introduces the speech:
Ὁ δὲ ἐπίσκοπος λόγῳ πείθων ἐδίδασκε. This may be literally translated: "The
bishop who persuades with reason taught. . . ." The speech which follows
is thus evaluated as the *teaching* of one, who as bishop speaks the truth as
Christ did since he does not use physical force but the gentle persuasive
power of truth's intelligibility.[234] The "teaching" contained therein concerns the correct procedure with regard to the exercise of ecclesiastical
jurisdiction, as did the *4th Letter to Julius to the Eusebians* and the Appeal
Canons of Sardica; it was in fact the core of Liberius' *defensio* before
Constantius at Milan.

The fictional speech of Liberius to the Eunuch Eusebius begins as
follows:

1. How could one do such a thing to Athanasius (sc. = excommunicate him)? How could we condemn him, whom not only one
   but a second synod gathered from all parts justly cleared [of all
   false charges] and whom the Church of the Romans dismissed
   in peace? Who will approve of our conduct if we reject in his absence one whom, while present, we welcomed and admitted to
   communion? This is not ecclesiastical canon nor have we ever
   received such a tradition from the Fathers which they [in turn]
   received from the blessed and great Apostle Peter.

[233] See above, pp. 484–492.
[234] Cf. *Hist. Arian.* 33,2–3 (Opitz 201,15–22).

2. But if the emperor has the peace of the Church at heart, if he orders that our letters regarding Athanasius be annulled, then let
their proceedings against him be cancelled, as also their proceedings against the others, and then allow an ecclesiastical synod take
place at a distance from the court, at which the emperor shall not
be present, nor a Comes be admitted, nor a imperial judge threat-
en the participants, but only the fear of God be of any influence
and the regulation of the Apostles, so that first of all the ecclesiastical Faith as the Fathers defined at the Council of Nicaea may be
thus preserved, [then] those who think like Arius be cast out [of
the Church] and [finally] their heresy be anathematized.

3. Then, when these matters have been judged, let Athanasius and
any other person accused on such charges be indited, so that they
who are guilty might be thrown out and the innocent might
enjoy freedom: since it does not behoove a synod to reckon
among its numbers those who deny the Faith, nor is it fit that
an enquiry regarding conduct be given preference to an enquiry concerning Faith.[235]

Athanasius puts into the mouth of Liberius three reasons for
his refusal to obey the emperor and enter into communion with
the Arians. Two of these reasons are in essence the main arguments of the *Apologia:* i) the innocence of Athanasius has been justly

[235] 1. Ὁ δὲ ἐπίσκοπος λόλῳ πείθων ἐδίδασκε· 'πῶς οἷόν τε τοῦτο γενέσθαι κατὰ
Ἀθανασίου; ὃν γὰρ οὐ μόνον μία, ἀλλὰ καὶ δευτέρα σύνοδος πανταχόθεν συναχθεῖσα
καλῶς ἐκαθάρισε καὶ ἡ Ῥωμανίων δὲ ἐκκλησία μετ' εἰρήνης ἀπέλυσε, πῶς δυνάμεθα
κατακρῖναι; ἢ τίς ἡμᾶς ἀποδέξεται, εἰ ὃν παρόντα ἠγαπήσαμεν καὶ εἴχομεν τῇ
κοινωνίᾳ, τοῦτον ἐὰν ἀποστραφῶμεν ἀπόντα; οὐκ ἔστιν οὗτος ἐκκλησιαστικὸς
κανὼν οὐδὲ τοιαύτην πώποτε παράδοσιν ἔσχομεν παρὰ τῶν πατέρων τῶν καὶ αὐτῶν
παραλαβόντων παρὰ τοῦ μακαρίου καὶ μεγάλου ἀποστόλου Πέτρου.
2. ἀλλ' εἴπερ ἄρα μέλει τῷ βασιλεῖ περὶ τῆς ἐκκλησιαστικῆς εἰρήνης, εἰ κελεύει
λυθῆναι τὰ παρ' ἡμῖν περὶ Ἀθανασίου γραφέντα, λυέσθω καὶ τὰ παρ' ἐκείνων κατ'
αὐτοῦ γενόμενα, λυέσθω δὲ καὶ τὰ κατὰ πάντων καὶ γενέσθω λοιπὸν ἐκκλησιαστικὴ
σύνοδος μακρὰν τοῦ παλατίου, ἐν ᾗ βασιλεὺς οὐ πάρεστιν, οὐ κόμης παραγίνεται, οὐ
δικαστὴς ἀπειλεῖ, ἀλλὰ μόνον ὁ τοῦ θεοῦ φόβος ἀρκεῖ καὶ ἡ τῶν ἀποστόλων διάταξις,
ἵν' οὕτως προηγουμένως ἡ μὲν ἐκκλησιαστικὴ πίστις σώζηται, καθὼς οἱ πατέρες
ὥρισαν ἐν τῇ κατὰ Νίκαιαν συνόδῳ, οἱ δὲ τὰ Ἀρείου φρονοῦντες ἐκβάλλωνται καὶ ἡ
αἵρεσις αὐτῶν ἀναθεματισθῇ.
3. καὶ τότε λοιπὸν κρίσεως γενομένης περὶ ὧν Ἀθανάσιος καὶ εἴ τις ἕτερος
ἐγκαλεῖται καὶ περὶ ὧν ἐγκαλοῦνται καὶ αὐτοί, οἱ μὲν ὑπεύθυνοι ἐκβάλλωνται, οἱ
δὲ καθαροὶ παρρησίαν ἔχωσιν. οὐ γὰρ οἷόν τε συνόδῳ συναριθμηθῆναι τοὺς περὶ
πίστιν ἀσεβοῦντας οὐδὲ πρέπει προκρίνεσθαι πράγματος ἐξέτασιν τῆς περὶ πίστεως
ἐξετάσεως (*Hist. Arian.* 36,1–3, Opitz 203,9–25).

established according to ecclesiastical law as acknowledged by his communion with the universal Episcopate including the Church of the Romans;[236]
ii) the judgment of Athanasius can consequently be revised only by an
ecclesiastical authority in accordance with ecclesiastical law.[237] The third
point made by Liberius is by far the most important: iii) behind the controversies concerning Athanasius' legal claim to Alexandria are concealed
issues concerning the Faith; questions regarding the Faith, however, must
receive precedence before questions of conduct.[238]

Contrasting the points attributed to Liberius in the first verse of this
fictional dialogue with the contents of the *Apologia,* the following differences are to be noted. Whereas in the introductory paragraphs (*Apol.* 1–2)
which stem from Athanasius' pen, the three main bodies which acquitted
Athanasius are given in the order: Synod of Alexandria—Rome—Synod
of Sardica. This trio is presented in the "speech of Liberius" in this order:
Synod (of Alexandria)—Synod (of Sardica)—Church of the Romans.
These two synods, whose names are not mentioned, are said to have
"cleared" Athanasius from the false charges (ἐκαθάρισε), but it was the
"Church of the Romans" who "dismissed him in peace" (μετ' εἰρήνης
ἀπέλυσε)—i.e., authoritatively granted him full communion. This important point was merely suggested by Athanasius in the *Apologia* 52,1[239] while
it is here unequivocally stated. Athanasius makes Liberius speak of the
authoritative actions of his predecessor as though they were his own decisions, and so outlining the fact that the decisions received their authority
from the *office* of the Bishop of Rome.

In the second verse, we find the thought of Athanasius on the limits of
legitimate State involvement in Church Affairs, found scattered throughout the *Apologia,*[240] here succinctly summarized: the emperor is requested
(i) not to *summon* a synod but to make it (physically) possible for one to
take place, and (ii) to refrain from directly interfering in the actual working
of the same synod. In contrast, the Bishop of Rome declares that the criteria for an authentic synod are freedom, where the only fear is the fear of

---

[236] *Hist. Arian.* 36,1; compare with Theodoret, *HE* 2,16,2 (Parmentier-Scheidweiler
131,18–23) and *HE* 2,16,11 (133,1–10).

[237] *Hist. Arian.* 36,2; cf. Theodoret, *HE* 2,16,2 (Parmentier-Scheidweiler 131,18–19)
and *HE* 2,16,16 (Schwartz 133,23–134,8).

[238] *Hist. Arian.* 36,3; cf. Theodoret, *HE* 2,16,16 (Parmentier-Scheidweiler 134,1–6)
and *HE* 2,16,22 (Schwartz 135,6–10).

[239] See above, pp. 388–389; also p. 468.

[240] See above, pp. 333, 337–8, and 341–5. Cf. also *Ad Const.* 26 (Szymusiak 117–118).

God, and adherence to the Apostolic regulations. We also note in the first line of verse 2 a re-echo of that specific pope/emperor relationship first outlined in the *Apologia* together with the implicit affirmation of the universal effect of the pope's authority in the suggestion that the peace of the Church depended on the pope's *Letter of Communion*. In verse 3, we note that the author seems to draw attention to the duty of the emperor to execute the civil consequences of the decisions arrived at by the independent ecclesiastical authority.

More striking than the reoccurrence and development of ideas found in the *Apologia* is the reappearance in the first two verses of ideas central to the *4th Letter of Julius,* with minor variations. Liberius is said to have informed the emperor's delegates that he, as Bishop of Rome, would only be prepared to excommunicate the Bishop of Alexandria on the basis of his own judgment of the case, and not on that of another authority.[241] For another authority to try to impose its decisions on Rome would in fact mean a serious breach of the ecclesiastical canon and the traditions of the Fathers which they received from "the great and blessed Apostle Peter." In contrast with the *Letter of Julius*, where the "other authority" is the "Eusebian" institution of the autonomous provincial synod, here the unmediated authority of the emperor seems to be intended. This, however, is but a matter of emphasis, and one, moreover, that accurately corresponds to the development at the time of Liberius when Constantius adopted as his own the Eusebian *ecclesiology* that was rooted in the later concept of Eusebius of Caesarea who saw the emperor as the final source of the Church's authority which normally manifested itself in the decisions of the synodal institution. More striking is the way Athanasius explicates what is more or less implicit in the *Letter of Julius,*[242] that is, the Petrine tradition as the formal justification for the Roman bishop's insistence on his right to judge the case of an excommunicated bishop, or in other words, his right to review the judgments of provincial synods. This clear statement of Athanasius is even more explicit than that of the Synod of Sardica.[243]

When we compare this paragraph with the foregoing one (*Hist. Arian.* 35), we find a certain development of ideas originally introduced there, namely the mention of the Apostolic Throne and the clarification of what was meant by calling Rome the Chief See of

---

[241] *Hist. Arian.* 36,1; cf. Theodoret, *HE* 2,16,2 (131,22–23).
[242] See above, pp. 414–421.
[243] See above, pp. 456–458.

the Empire, by demonstrating this jurisdictional authority in action (i.e., acting according to the norms laid down by the Petrine tradition) and highlighting its specific ecclesiastical method of functioning (i.e., free from external pressure). So too, the sharp definition of the State's legitimate though limited function in affairs of the Church, as found in this "speech" of Liberius, is a development in a more positive fashion of the negative criticism previously meted out to the totalitarian ambitions of Constantius in the foregoing paragraph. The importance of Liberius' speech, however, lies in the way the Nicene Faith is connected with the charges against Athanasius. Here the actual speech reported by Theodoret and the fictional one we are considering overlap in essentials: Liberius did in fact demand that any examination of the new charges brought against Athanasius ought to be preceded by the express testimony by all parties to the Faith defined at Nicaea.[244] This Athanasius compresses into the formula: "all disagreement concerning the Faith must first be eradicated and then the enquiry concerning conduct take place."[245] The πράγματα referred to here are the disputes concerning the claims of Athanasius to the See of Alexandria and the accusations of the Eusebians brought against Athanasius with regard to his supposed misbehavior. Before an examination of such issues be undertaken, Liberius, both through the agency of his legates at Arles and Milan and personally in the presence of Constantius at Milan, insisted that the adherence to the Faith defined at Nicaea be established among the members of a synod. This emphasis on unanimity with regard to the Faith as the *conditio sine qua non* for a legitimate synod is the *Regulation of the Apostles*, a phrase used by Athanasius but not found in the actual speech.

Since Athanasius presented Liberius as teaching in the manner which characterizes Our Lord, i.e., persuading his opponents by means of arguments, we must concentrate our attention on the *arguments* which Liberius is said to give for this procedure regarding the reexamination of the judgment on the Bishop of Alexandria. The arguments are fundamentally arguments from authority—Apostolic Authority. Verse 1 states that Liberius is not prepared to act contrary to the procedure dictated by ecclesiastical canon and the tradition which "we" (sc. = the Bishops of Rome) have received

---

[244] See Theodoret, *HE* 2,16,16 (Parmentier-Scheidweiler 134,1–4) and *HE* 2,16,22 (Parmentier-Scheidweiler 135,7–9).

[245] χρὴ γὰρ πρῶτον πᾶσαν περὶ τῆς πίστεως διαφωνίαν ἐκκόπτεσθαι καὶ τότε τὴν περὶ τῶν πραγμάτων ἔρευναν ποιεῖσθαι (*Hist. Arian.* 36,4 = Opitz 203,26–27).

from St. Peter through the *Fathers*. Then he goes on to "teach" what this procedure is: it is the Regulation of the Apostles whereby agreement regarding the Faith (defined by the *Fathers* at Nicaea) must be achieved (verse 2) before examining matters of conduct (verse 3). This regulation is rooted in the example of Our Lord, who demanded faith before he healed the afflicted (verse 4). In the final verse 5, the statement of verse 1 is taken up (and developed) by Liberius when he states: "These things we have learned from the *Fathers*, these you are to announce to the emperor since they are conducive to his real advantage and build up the Church."[246] In verse 1, "the Fathers" signify the authoritative tradition which is explicitly rooted in St. Peter. In verse 2, they guarantee the authority of the Nicene Faith. Here in the final verse, the mention of "the Fathers" would seem to have the purpose of drawing attention to Liberius as the *receiver* of this authoritative tradition, and *so* as the disciple of the Lord (ἐμάθομεν cf. Mt. 16,13) who now authoritatively hands it on (ἀπάγγειλον) for the instruction of the empire *and* for the "building up" of the Church. The phrase τὴν ἐκκλησίαν οἰκοδομεῖ recalls to mind Mt. 16,18. It is the first announcement of a theme which Athanasius begins to weave into the story from now on. One may not deduce too much from this first faint reference to the Confession of St. Peter at Caesarea; its full significance will only be apparent when one has considered the way Athanasius so consistently develops it.

Considering this "speech" of Liberius to the imperial delegate, we could say in summary fashion that Athanasius puts into the mouth of the Bishop of Rome his reasons for rejecting the attempts of the Neo-Arians and the emperor to have the Bishop of Alexandria deposed: he did not wish to judge Athanasius in his absence, or to ignore the earlier synodal judgments which had cleared Athanasius, or to forget that the Church of the Romans had previously dismissed him in peace, since to do so would be to act contrary to the tradition he represented, that of St. Peter. From the fictive speech we learn how ecclesiastical authority ought to operate. It must be free from all external influence or imperial control and function according to the Apostolic regulations, which first and foremost demand that unanimity with regard to questions of the Faith be established. The authority called upon by "Liberius" to support his interpretation of the Apostolic regulations is the Petrine tradition

---

[246] ταῦτα παρὰ τῶν πατέρων ἐμάθομεν, ταῦτα ἀπάγγειλον τῷ βασιλεῖ, ταῦτα γὰρ καὶ αὐτῷ συμφέρει καὶ τὴν ἐκκλησίαν οἰκοδομεῖ (*Hist. Arian.* 36,5 = Opitz 203,29–30).

preserved (at Rome) by his predecessors, the Fathers. The object of his teaching with regard to these regulations is both the spiritual good of his addressee (in this case, the emperor) and the building up of the Church (cf. Mt. 16,18).

iii) The misuse of the imperial authority: its interference in Church affairs (*Hist. Arian.* 37)

The third paragraph continues the narrative of events which were said to have taken place in Rome and which lead up to the actual meeting between pope and emperor at Milan (355). In sharp contrast with Liberius (who was presented in the previous paragraph as persuading as Christ did), the imperial delegate Eusebius is here seen as one who persuades with the methods of the devil, using threats and bribes—and failing dramatically. As already mentioned, the gifts he offers the pope serve not only the purpose of bribery[247] but are meant to symbolize Rome's acceptance of the Arian party into communion.[248] Athanasius goes on to develop the full implications of the second purpose attached to the gifts as sacrificial offerings for the Eucharist.

The Eunuch Eusebius, "recalling to mind Saul's transgression, goes to the *Confessio* of the Apostle and offers the gifts to him."[249] Saul's transgression most probably refers to 1 Sam 13,7f., the invalid sacrifice of Saul at Gilgal and his subsequent rejection by God as pronounced by Samuel. In the parallel situation depicted by Athanasius, Saul's place is taken by Constantius (as represented by his delegate Eusebius) while the role of Samuel is taken by Liberius, who like Samuel at Gilgal arrives after the attempted "sacrifice" and rejects the emperor in the person of his delegate and his gifts. What gives this incident its special coloring is the mention of τὸ μαρτύριον Πέτρου τοῦ ἀποστόλου, namely, the Church erected by Constantine over the apostle's tomb.[250] The text may thus be taken

---

[247] See Seppelt, *Geschichte der Päpste*, bd. I, 97; Jalland, *Church and Papacy*, 229. Casper does not consider these "gifts" as though they were a bribe, but rather as a special courtesy demanded by the ceremony surrounding the official meetings of persons of rank (see *Geschichte des Papsttums* I, 175).

[248] See Hefele-Leclerq, *Histoire de Conciles* I, 878; Joannou, *Die Ostkirche und die Cathedra Petri*, 122.

[249] πράττει δὲ τι παράνομον Χριστιανῶν μὲν ἀλλότριον, σπαδόντων δὲ τολμηρότερον. τὴν γὰρ παράβασιν τοῦ Σαοὺλ μιμησάμενος ἀπελθὼν εἰς τὸ μαρτύριον Πέτρου τοῦ ἀποστόλου τὰ δῶρα αὐτῷ ἀνέθηκεν (Hist. Arian. 37,1 = Opitz 204,1–3).

[250] See Jalland, *Church and Papacy*, 67f. and 205. The only other reference to a Church as τὸ μαρτύριον in the writings of Athanasius is to be found in the *Letter of the Synod of Jerusalem, Sept. 335 (Apol.* 84,3), where it refers to the

to mean: the emperor's delegate endeavored to establish an invalid communion with the source of Rome's authority, St. Peter, as a substitute for his failure to gain communion with his actual successor (which term, of course, does not occur, even though the fact is affirmed). Liberius' rejection of Eusebius and his gifts ("he threw them out as an unacceptable sacrifice") thus receives the nuance of excommunication,[251] and the reason for the excommunication is given in the following verse (verse 2), which is a fictional speech of the Arians: "What concerns us is no longer the question of Liberius' subscription (sc. to the deposition of Athanasius) but that he is so disposed against the Arians so as to anathematize the Arians by name." Any doubts that the doctrinal issues are not basic to the controversies concerning Athanasius are removed; Liberius has pitted the full force of his (Petrine) authority against the heretics (and the imperial power), instead of granting them his much sought-after official support. This, at least, is how Athanasius interprets the reported events.

The historical kernel of this paragraph is that described by Theodoret,[252] who reports that after Liberius of Rome has been banished to Beroia in Trace by the emperor, i.e., after their meeting in Milan, three attempts were made to bribe Liberius. The first was made by the emperor himself, the second by the empress, and finally there was a third attempt by the Eunuch Eusebius (who had a reputation for such transactions). Athanasius, however, has located the incident in Rome and so the chronology has been altered accordingly. It is possible that this was the version of the story that had made its way to Egypt. In any event, Athanasius made full use of the incident and, perhaps exercising a certain literary license, uses it to uncover the underlying significance of the confrontation between Liberius and Constantius. His intention is (a) to sum up the main concepts worked out in the foregoing paragraphs by means of a vivid and concrete picture, and (b) thus explicitly introduce the central idea of this entire subsection, namely the confession of the Nicene Faith by Liberius as the contemporary realization of the Confession of Peter. He achieves both his aims (i) by drawing attention to the tomb of St. Peter as the source of Rome's authority:

occasion of the synod there, namely the consecration of the Church of the Holy Sepulcher (see Eusebius, *VC* 3,29).

[251] Cf. *Hist. Arian.* 37,1 (Opitz 204,4–5). By refusing to accept the offerings, the Bishop of Rome thus manifested the unsuitability of the donor to participate in the Eucharistic communion and so automatically signified his exclusion from the *Communio* of the Church.

[252] Theodoret, *HE* 2,16,27–29 (Parmentier-Scheidweiler 136,1f.).

hers is the Apostolic Throne, the Chief Sedes of the Empire, the Throne
of Peter whose tradition Liberius calls upon to justify his actions; (ii) by
using the technical term τὸ μαρτύριον (otherwise not used by Athanasius)
rather than ἡ ἐκκλησία or even τὸ μνημεῖον, the author of this text is able
to introduce the concept of St. Peter's Confession, which he had merely
hinted at in the foregoing but will develop in the next paragraph, and apply
it to Liberius' stand for the Nicene Faith and Athanasius.

In this paragraph, Athanasius has clarified the motive of the Neo-Arian
inspired imperial intervention, which motive had been merely hinted at
earlier in the first paragraph (Ch. 35), namely, that the Neo-Arians sought
not the personal support of Liberius, but rather the authority of Peter.

iv) The Petrine Authority of the Teaching of the Roman Bishop (Mt
     16,16–17) (*Hist. Arian.* 38)
The fourth paragraph describes the situation in Rome after Liberius' rejection of the Arians and the representative of Constantius: the "persuasion"
of the Neo-Arians turns to persecution. Verse 1–2 recounts the various
methods used by the Arians to gain the submission of the Roman Church.
In verse 3, Athanasius traces the origins of the persecution back to the
eunuchs at the court (Constantius is seen as a mere instrument in their
hands—cf. verse 5 fin.). This is not intended to convey mere factual or
historical information; it must be understood in accordance with the
literary genre of the *Historia*, which has as its purpose the detection and
clarification of the real motives behind the historical events themselves.
Whereas in the former paragraphs, the Eunuch Eusebius is seen not simply
as a representative of the emperor, but as a spokesman for the Eusebian
heresy—the association of ideas conjured up by his actual name must have
been welcome to Athanasius—now our author latches on to Eusebius' personal characteristic as a eunuch to make him seem a fitting representative
of the Christological heresy that the Neo-Arians embraced. With stinging
irony—but also with a definite theological purpose—Athanasius uses the
eunuchs to symbolize the Arians: "what is astonishing about such treachery
is this: the Arian heresy which denies the Son of God receives its support
from eunuchs, who are by nature impotent and whose souls are barren of
virtue, and thus cannot even bear to hear about a son."[253]

[253] *Hist. Arian.* 38,3 (Opitz 204,23–25).

In the light of this, Athanasius takes up the incident of the Eunuch Eusebius at the *Confessio* of St. Peter mentioned in the last paragraph and interprets it accordingly in verse 4: Eusebius is now seen as representative of the theological eunuchs (= the Arians who cannot generate and so deny the Generation of the Son of God). And Liberius' action in rejecting the "offerings" at the Confessio of St. Peter and so anathematizing and excommunicating the representative of the Neo-Arians—which was the effective outcome of the latter's refusal to accept the pope's teaching regarding the *Regulation of the Apostles*—is now interpreted in terms of Mt 16,16–17, the Confession of Peter at Caesarea.

4. The Eunuch of Ethiopia indeed, who did not understand what he read, allowed himself to be persuaded by Philip and by what he taught concerning the Savior, yet the eunuchs of Constantius refuse to consent to that which is being confessed by Peter but even turn away from the Father when He manifests the Son and rave against those who say that he is genuinely the Son of God, thus championing a heresy of eunuchs who deny Him to be genuinely and truly "of the Father."[254]

"(They) refuse to consent to that which is being confessed by Peter" (οὔτε τοῦ Πέτρου ὁμολογοῦντος ἀνέχονται) is, as indicated by the use of the present tense, clearly a reference to the refusal of Eusebius the Eunuch to consent to the teaching of Liberius on the Regulation of the Apostles—i.e., (i) the ecclesiastical procedure, based on the regulations of the Apostles, with regard to synodal judgements, which procedures (ii) demand, as the *conditio sine qua non* for a genuine synodal authority, that unanimity concerning the Faith be first of all established among its member-bishops. We recall that Julius in his *4th Letter* formulated his rejection of the new procedures that arose from the "Eusebian heresy" in terms which approximated to a formal anathema and expressed his teaching on the ecclesiastical procedure that arose from the Apostolic Tradition and ecclesiastical practice by having recourse to the Petrine authority of his office. Again, we saw how the Synod of Sardica gave explicit recognition to the Petrine authority that was the source of

---

[254] ὁ μὲν οὖν ἐκ τῆς Αἰθιοπίας εὐνοῦχος μὴ νοῶν ἃ ἀνεγίνωσκεν ἐπείθη τῷ Φιλίππῳ διδάσκοντι περὶ τοῦ σωτῆρος, οἱ δὲ τοῦ Κωνσταντίου σπάδοντες οὔτε τοῦ Πέτρου ὁμολογοῦντες ἀνέχονται, ἀλλὰ καὶ τὸν πατέρα δεικνύντα τὸν υἱὸν ἀποστρέφονται καὶ μαίνονται καὶ κατὰ τῶν λεγόντων γνήσιον εἶναι τὸν υἱὸν τοῦ θεοῦ ἐκδικοῦντες σπαδόντων αἵρεσιν, μηδὲν εἶναι γνήσιον καὶ ἀληθινὸν ἐκ τοῦ πατρός (*Hist. Arian.* 38,4 = Opitz 204,25–30).

Julius' defense of the Apostolic and customary procedures. Here Athanasius describes Liberius' teaching on the ecclesiastical procedure, whose content has been extended to include unanimity concerning the Faith, specifically the Nicene Creed, as the contemporary Confession of St. Peter. This new emphasis reflects the new development in the controversies since the Synods of Arles and Milan due to the fact that Liberius had brought the dogmatic issue to the surface and identified the cause of Athanasius with the Faith of Nicaea.[254a]

In this way, Athanasius has unambiguously focused the attention of the reader on the center of the entire controversy: the Apostolic Faith in the Divinity Christ. As Liberius once called Athanasius the Defender of the Faith, so now Athanasius describes Liberius as the Confessor of the Faith, whose refusal to enter into communion with the Neo-Arians (as represented by the eunuch) is seen to be a contemporary realization of St. Peter's Confession at Caesarea Philippi. In verse 4, Athanasius affirms that the "teaching" of Liberius ought to have been more convincing than the instruction of St. Philip to the Ethiopian Eunuch on the grounds that this "teaching" carried the weight of a contemporary Confession of St. Peter. Just to what extent Athanasius considered the teaching of Liberius on the Nicene Creed to be a contemporary Confession of St. Peter is unambiguously stated by our author in the phrase: ἀλλὰ καὶ τὸν πατέρα δεικνύντα τὸν υἱὸν ἀποστρέφονται . . . "but (they) even turn away from the Father when He *manifests* the Son. . . ." This is meant to refer in the first place to the turning away of Eusebius from the "teaching" of Liberius, but emblematically represents to the turning away of the Neo-Arians (= theological eunuchs) from the Nicene Creed. The "teaching" of Liberius, his confession of the Faith defined at Nicaea which affirmed the divinity of the Son of God, is thus seen to be a contemporary realization of that original revelation to St. Peter at Caesarea: ὅτι σὰρξ καὶ αἷμα οὐκ ἀπεκάλυψέν σοι ἀλλ᾽ ὁ πατήρ μου ὁ ἐν τοῖς οὐρανοῖς. Instead of ἀπεκάλυψέν, our text uses the present tense of δείκνυμι—a term which needs to be noted here, since it will be taken up by Athanasius in the succeeding paragraphs.

With this use of Mt. 16,17b, Athanasius has illustrated what he himself understood by the quote from the *Letter of the Eusebians*: "[the] men [are] themselves apostolic."[255] Athanasius affirms that the Apostolic Tradition[256] attributed to the Church of Rome, capital

---

[254a] See above, p. 484f.
[255] *Hist. Arian.* 35,2. See above, p. 526.
[256] Cf. *Hist. Arian.* 36; see commentary above pp. 528–535.

of orthodoxy,[257] which rests on her claim to the Apostolic Throne[258] and which she traces back to St. Peter[259] becomes actualized in the confession of Faith proclaimed[260] by the Bishop of Rome, through whom the Father reveals the nature of His Son as He did to Peter at Caesarea.

The paragraph ends (verse 5) with an attack on the "eunuchs" (in fact the Neo-Arians) and their usurpation of authority in Church and Empire. In the final sentence, the emperor is depicted as a puppet in the hands of the (theological) eunuchs: "Submitting to them, Constantius conspired against *all* and banished Liberius." Here the reader is reminded of the Arians' motive mentioned by Athanasius at the opening of this sub-section: "If we prevail upon Liberius we shall quickly rule over *all*[261]—an indirect but clear indication of the universal extent of the pope's authority. This reminder serves the literary purpose of introducing the scene to be described in the next paragraph in such a way as to provide the reader with the hermeneutical key to understand it, namely Athanasius' version of the confrontation between the pope and the emperor at Milan (355) as a confrontation between the two universal authorities, of Church and Empire, a confrontation which ought not to have taken place but which was the consequence of the evil inherent in the Neo-Arian heresy of the Imperial Church (and not in the empire as such).

v)   The Successor of St. Peter opposes the successor of Nero (*Hist. Arian.* 39)

The fifth paragraph recounts how, dragged before the emperor (at Milan, 355), Liberius defends himself in language which reminds one, as Athanasius intends, of the speeches made by the martyrs before their pagan persecutors. This second "speech" of Liberius deserves more careful attention than, e.g., the curt dismissal of Opitz to the effect that it merely contains a "wertlose rhetorische Mitteilung."[262] We have seen how the actual speech of Liberius (his part of the dialogue at Milan) appears to have been worked into the fictional speech of the pope before the emperor's delegate, the Eunuch Eusebius (Ch. 36), to suit the literary and theological purpose of the author. Here it must be noted that the attitude of

---

[257]   Cf. *Hist. Arian.* 35,2; see commentary above p. 523–527.
[258]   Cf. *Hist. Arian.* 35,2; see commentary above p. 523f.
[259]   Cf. *Hist. Arian.* 36,1; see commentary above p. 533–534.
[260]   Cf. *Hist. Arian.* 36,5; see commentary above p. 534.
[261]   Cf. *Hist. Arian.* 35,3; see commentary, above pp. 522, 527.
[262]   See the commentary of Opitz on *Hist. Arian.* 39,2 (205,3).

Liberius depicted in this present fictional speech is identical with the sentiments expressed by the pope in his letter of consolation to the orthodox bishops exiled at Milan.[263] There Liberius professes his own longing to suffer martyrdom for the faith; here Athanasius draws the reader's attention to those same sentiments of the pope so as to underline the fact that, although dragged before the emperor by force (verse 1), Liberius himself was no reluctant or powerless prisoner, but a martyr of independent stature—"we *hastened* here, knowing that exile awaits us at your hands" (verse 4). What Athanasius above all wishes to depict here is that "authoritative support (of Liberius for Athanasius and so for the Nicene Creed) when he was able to exercise free choice" (*Hist. Arian.* 41,3)—the description of the actual fall).

The theme of persecution, heralded in the foregoing paragraph, becomes explicit in this one. Athanasius (verse 1) dates the incident at Milan as occurring at the time of the persecution in Alexandria—referring probably to the attack on the Church of Theonas on February 8–9, 356. This reference to the Alexandrian Church is not only of chronological interest but is above all intended to draw attention to the intrinsic relationship between the destiny of Rome and that of Alexandria—both Churches being mentioned in this verse, since both endured the one persecution for the sake of the same cause: the Faith as defined at Nicaea.

The fictional speech of Liberius is as follows:

2. Cease persecuting the Christians! Do not attempt to introduce this heresy into the Church by means of us! We are prepared to endure all rather than be called Arian maniacs. Do not compel us who are Christians to become enemies of Christ.

3. This then we counsel you: do not wage war against Him who gave you this office, nor act profanely towards Him who deserves your gratitude, nor persecute those who believe in Him, lest you also should hear: ". . . it is hard for you to kick against the goad." Would that you might hear, so that you too might be persuaded as St. Paul [was].

4. Behold, we have arrived, we came before they might invent some pretext. Then for this reason we have hastened here, knowing that exile awaits us at your hands: that before we

---

263 Hilary, *Frag. hist.*, series B, VII, 2 (Feder 164–166). See also in this context, Theodoret, *HE* 2,16,24 (Parmentier-Scheidweiler 135,15–16). The literary dependence of Athanasius on the actual letter cannot be completely ruled out.

might suffer on some pretext, it might be clearly manifested to all,
that all [the confessors] have suffered as we [are about to suffer],
the charges brought against them were invented by their enemies,
and [that] all things [said] about them are calumnies and lies."[264]

The ambiguity inherent in the "persuasion" of Constantius is now unveiled
by Liberius, who is here presented as speaking clearly of the present *persecution* whose object is to *compel* the Christians to become enemies of Christ
(verse 2). Here we are reminded of the antithesis between the two types
of persuasion, which antithesis runs through the *Historia*: i.e., between
compulsion by force, which is a mark of the devil, and persuasion by way of
argumentation, which is characteristic of the true representative of Christ
Our Lord. Athanasius had previously identified these contrary methods of
persuasion with the "Eusebians" (and their successors) and with Liberius
respectively. Now they are contrasted in the different attitudes displayed by
the emperor, who persecutes in order to compel assent (verse 2), and by the
Bishop of Rome, who tries to convince through his counsel to Constantius
(verse 3). Taking up the theme mentioned in the final verse of the previous
paragraph,[265] Liberius further accuses Constantius of trying to achieve his
object "by means of us" (δι' ἡμῶν), i.e., by means of the pope, the emperor
would try to introduce heresy into the Church and so "quickly rule over
all." The use of the term "to introduce" (εἰσάξαι) can hardly be intended in a
chronological sense (to introduce for the first time) but rather as connoting
an authoritative sense: to definitively introduce the heresy by means of the
pope's (universal) authority.

The second part of verse 3 explicitly refers to the conversion of
St. Paul on the road to Damascus (Acts 26,14) and draws a parallel

---

[264] 2. παῦσαι ... διώκων Χριστιανούς· μὴ πείραζε δι' ἡμῶν εἰσάξαι τὴν ἀσέβειαν εἰς τὴν
ἐκκλησίαν. πάντα ὑπομένειν ἐσμὲν ἕτοιμοι ἢ Ἀρειομανῖται κληθῆναι. Χριστιανοὺς
ὄντας ἡμᾶς μὴ ἀνάγκαζε χριστομάχους γενέσθαι.
3. τοῦτο καὶ σοὶ συμβουλεύομεν· μὴ μάχου πρὸς τὸν δεδωκότα σοι τὴν ἀρχὴν ταύτην·
μὴ ἀντ' εὐχαριστίας ἀσεβήσῃς εἰς αὐτόν· μὴ δίωκε τοὺς πιστεύοντας εἰς αὐτόν· μὴ
ἀκούσῃς καὶ σύ· "σκληρόν σοι πρὸς κέντρα λακτίζειν." ἀλλ' εἴθε κἂν ἀκούσῃς, ἵνα
καὶ οὐ πεισθῇς ὡς ὁ ἅγιος Παῦλος.
4. ἰδοὺ πάρεσμεν, ἤλθομεν, πρὶν πλάσωνται πρόφασιν· διὰ τοῦτο γὰρ ἐσπεύσαμεν
εἰδότες ὅτι ἐξορισμὸς ἡμᾶς μένει παρὰ σοῦ, ἵνα, πρὶν προφάσεως πάθωμεν, καὶ πᾶσι
δειχθῇ φανερῶς ὅτι καὶ οἱ ἄλλοι πάντες οὕτω πεπόνθασιν ὡς ἡμεῖς καὶ αἱ λεχθεῖσαι
κατ' αὐτῶν προφάσεις ἐπλάσθησαν παρὰ τῶν ἐχθρῶν καὶ πάντα τὰ κατ' αὐτούς ἐστι
συκοφαντία καὶ ψευδῆ (Hist. Arian. 39,2–4 = Opitz 205,3–13).
[265] καὶ τούτοις ὑποπίπτων Κωνστάντιος πᾶσιν ἐπεβούλευσε καὶ Λιβέριον ἐξώρισεν (*Hist.
Arian.* 38,5 = Opitz 204,37).

between Saul's persecution of the Christians and that of the emperor. Parallel to the voice of Christ to Saul, is the "counsel" of the pope to Constantius: "do not wage war against Him who gave you this office." The very terms of this "counsel" just quoted recall the reply of Our Lord to Pilate in St. John's account of His Trial (Jo 19,11). Thus, in verse 4, "Liberius," using the pluralis maiestatis, speaks as the representative of all persecuted Christians ("we have arrived, we are come"), and in this sense speaks as Vicar of the mystical Body of Christ now being persecuted whose function is to manifest (δείκνυμι) to all (the world) the cause of the confessors' suffering—namely their defense of the Nicene Faith.

With regard to the latter affirmation, one is struck by the way Athanasius does not say "to manifest to all that we are going to suffer in solidarity (as it were) with all the other Confessors," but, reversing the chronological order, affirms: "for this reason, we have hastened here ... that before we might suffer on some pretext it might be clearly manifest (δειχθῇ) to all that the Confessors have suffered as we [are about to suffer]." Here Athanasius explicitly states that which we have already seen to be the purpose behind the Historia, namely, to shed light on the theological significance of the present persecution, whereby the lesson to be learned from the fall of Liberius is of paramount importance for the understanding of the destiny of the other confessors in particular Ossius.

The parallel between the pope's warning to the emperor and the voice of Christ to Saul together with the "self-consciousness" of Liberius as Vicar of the persecuted mystical Body of Christ in the foregoing verse, considered in conjunction with the use of δείκνυμι in verse 4, all show how Athanasius develops the concept of the pope's confession as a contemporary realization of the original Confession of Peter: the sufferings of the pope (his martyrdom) due to his courageous stand for the Nicene Faith are themselves a type of wordless revelation of Christ's nature as Son of God and thus a manifestation "to all" of the ultimate cause of the present persecution (hatred of Christ that was articulated in the Arian denial of His Divinity).

vi) The object of the emperor's persecution: destruction of the universal unanimity (*Hist. Arian.* 40)

The sixth paragraph, first of all, serves the literary purpose of reinserting the story of Liberius into the general "history" of the "confessors" according to that theological emphasis which we have seen was the concern of *Hist. Arian.* 39,4; there the chronologically earlier exiles of the orthodox bishops were shown to be "theologically" subsequent to (or causally dependent on) Liberius' refusal to obey the Arianizing demands of the emperor. Verse 1 of this paragraph presents the exile of the various bishops as though it were the consequence of Liberius' refusal at Milan. Whereas this is chronologically incorrect—yet it essentially corresponds to the facts, insofar as the "confessors" (Paulinus of Trier, Lucifer of Cagliari, Eusebius of Vercelli, and Dionysius of Milan) were banished at the Synod of Milan for supporting the line adopted by the pope's delegates and so refusing to obey the emperor. This is another incident where Athanasius adjusts the superficial or empirical facts (known to his readers) in order to bring out their ultimate or inner significance.

In verse 2, Athanasius recalls the theme of banishment for the sake of the Faith as a new form of martyrdom which, more effectively than words, preaches the Gospel in every place and so proclaims the orthodox Faith; this theme was introduced at the end of the "Prelude" to the subsection we are at present considering.[266] Here the theme is developed by drawing a parallel between the persecution of Constantius and that of his predecessor Maximian. The present persecution, Athanasius claims, is worse than that caused by the pagan emperor, since Constantius went so far as to *separate* the confessors from each other. Both this verse and the following one place great emphasis on the savage cruelty of Constantius who so "*separated* the Confessors from each other," an emphasis which must seem rather exaggerated to the impartial reader but which has a very specific theological purpose: this exaggeration is meant to draw the reader's attention to the concept of martyrdom through exile as the new form of confession to the truth and the *present alternative* to that other hallmark of orthodoxy, *concord* and *unanimity*[267] (ὁμοφροσύνη καὶ ὁμοψυχία).

In other words, Athanasius here describes the motives of the persecution: to destroy the unanimity of the true confessors of the Faith by means of their separation from each other. But Athanasius points out, this is a futile hope since the bond of this unity is the Lord himself. Here Athanasius picks up the threads of the main theological concepts which dominate Part I of the *Historia*: the

---

[266] Cf. *Hist. Arian.* 34 (see above, p. 516f.).
[267] Cf. *Hist. Arian.* 40,2 (Opitz 205,23). This theme was introduced by Athanasius already at the opening of the entire work: *Hist. Arian.* 1,2 (Opitz 183,12–16).

limits of the customary criterion of ecclesiastical authority understood as universal unanimity (Unit I) and the alternative necessitated by its breakdown, namely the witness of the individual confessors (Unit II). Section I of Unit II demonstrated the breakdown of the traditional possibility of establishing this unanimity through the Synod of Bishops, due to the external interference of the imperial authority, and indicated the form that an alternative authority would take, that is, the confession of the martyrs. Section II of Unit II, which we are at present considering, points to the confession of the Bishop of Rome as the confession *par excellence,* which springs from the Petrine source of his office and which gives to the witness of the other bishops, who were also exiled for their Faith, its necessary and *authoritative* confirmation—since not all who suffer exile need necessarily be witnesses to the truth. At the same time the final cause of the Church's unanimity is brought to light: the Lord Himself, who unites the true confessors with each other. The more the confessors suffer and the greater the distance they are separated from one another, the more they are dawn into union with Christ and the more effectively does their witness spread throughout the world.[268]

vii) The Fall of Liberius: the contemporary Confession of St. Peter
     (Matt. 16,18) (*Hist. Arian.* 41)

The seventh paragraph. In the earlier description of the Synod of Milan and its aftermath (*Hist. Arian.* 33) we drew attention to the unexpected silence of our author regarding the destiny of the two Roman legates who refused to obey the emperor and condemn Athanasius. The explanation is to be found here: their story was reserved for this paragraph, where it now introduces (verses 1 and 2) the fall of Liberius and where it is intended to vividly illustrate the true confession of the Bishop and Church of Rome. The account of the exile of the Priest-Legate Pancratius (whom Athanasius incorrectly names as Eutropius) and especially the description of the scourging and banishment of the Deacon-Legate Hilary, who both faithfully represented the attitude of the pope towards Athanasius and his profession of Faith, are used here by Athanasius to effectively and vividly recall to his readers' mind the "original judgment" of Liberius (verse 4) "when he was able to exercise free-choice" (verse 3), and so to illustrate the affirmation implicit in the foregoing paragraph, namely that Liberius ought to be considered the confessor *par excellence.* Athanasius'

[268] Cf. *Hist. Arian.* 40,2–3 (Opitz 205,19–30).

narrow description of the sufferings of the papal legates recalls the two "kinds
of persuasion," which he has been consistently using to help his reader dis-
criminate between the supporters of truth and justice on the one hand and
the advocates of error and injustice on the other: the Neo-Arians scourge
Hilary the Deacon and so attempt to force him to turn against Liberius, while
Hilary for his part remains firm and praises God, "since it is a characteristic of
Christians to endure the lash, but to scourge Christians is the stock-in-trade of
a Pilate or Caiaphas" (end of verse 2). Then follows the relatively brief mention
of the actual lapse of Liberius—a text which is all too often misquoted and
completely detached from its context, which we have been considering.

3.   Thus, also while they [sc. = the Neo-Arians] endeavored from the
      beginning to destroy the Church of the Romans, wishing to infil-
      trate their heresy into it, yet [only] after two years' exile did Liberius
      slacken and, frightened by the threat of death, subscribe. But this
      only manifests on the one hand their violence, and on the other the
      hatred of Liberius towards the heresy and his authoritative support
      for Athanasius when he was able to exercise free choice.

4.   Since those things which occur under torture, contrary to one's
      original judgment, are not the resolutions of those being fright-
      ened but of those who torture.[269]

The main affirmation here is that Liberius' original resolute defense of Nicaea
and Athanasius was only broken after two years' violent exile and the threat
of immanent death[270]—a fact which most clearly demonstrates to all the
real *intention* of the pope, the clarification of which, as mentioned above, is
the decisive point in Athanasius' hermeneutics either of Scripture, the statements of the Fathers, or those of his opponents (verse 4). Athanasius is no

---

[269] 3. οὕτω μὲν οὖν καὶ τὴν Ῥωμαίων ἐκκλησίαν καὶ κατὰ τὴν ἀρχὴν ἐπεχείρησαν
      διαφθεῖραι θελήσαντες ἐγκαταμίξαι καὶ ἐν αὐτῇ τὴν ἀσέβειαν, ὁ δὲ Λιβέριος ἐξορισθεὶς
      ὕστερον μετὰ διετῆ χρόνον ὤκλασε καὶ φοβηθεὶς τὸν ἀπειλούμενον θάνατον
      ὑπέγραψεν. ἀλλὰ καὶ τοῦτο δείκνυσιν ἐκείνων μὲν τὴν βίαν, Λιβερίου δὲ τὸ κατὰ τῆς
      αἱρέσεως μῖσος καὶ τὴν ὑπὲρ Ἀθανασίου ψῆφον, ὅτε τὴν προαίρεσιν εἶχεν ἐλευθέραν.
      4. τὰ γὰρ ἐκ βασάνων παρὰ τὴν ἐξ ἀρχῆς γνώμην γιγνόμενα, ταῦτα οὐ τῶν
      φοβηθέντων, ἀλλὰ τῶν βασανιζόντων ἐστὶ βουλήματα (Hist. Arian. 41,3–4 =
      Opitz 206,9–15).
[270] See Goermans, "L'exil du Pape Libère," 184–189, for a description of the severe
      conditions under which the exiled bishops suffered—and thus presumably
      Liberius. More attention might to be paid to this aspect by scholars who examine
      the history of the event.

narrow legalist[271] but treats the weakening of Liberius most sympathetically as befitted one who could appreciate his own providential fortune
in escaping actual persecution due to his timely flight.[272] This attitude is
far removed from that "undertone of compassionate contempt" which
Caspar unjustly attributed to Athanasius in his interpretation of this text.[273]

One is struck by the reoccurrence in verse 3 of the phrase κατὰ τὴν
ἀρχήν which figured so prominently at the very opening of this subsection
dealing with Liberius.[274] The theme, so fully treated there, is here summarily
recalled: the attack on Rome, her Church and bishop, though chronologically later was in fact *from the beginning* the final aim of the Arians. By
the use of this type of cross-reference we are also reminded of the reason
given there for this attack[275]—the universal authority due to the Bishop of
Rome's Apostolic Throne,[276] which authority Liberius had granted to the
Nicene Faith through his whole-hearted support for Athanasius.

But the term which most surprises the observer in this very
compact text is the verb δείκνυμι: "the lapse of Liberius only *manifests*
on the one hand their violence and on the other the hatred of Liberius
towards the heresy. . . ." The sentence is a parallel text to the foregoing
sentence (also in verse 3) as can be seen by the use of μέν . . . δέ and the
conjunction ἀλλά and is intended to highlight the theological significance of the foregoing sentence with its mention of Liberius' fall. The
term δείκνυμι was used to paraphrase the verb ἀπακαλύπτω found in
Mt. 16,17b when Athanasius described the confession of Liberius before
the imperial delegate in terms of the Confession of Peter at Caesarea.[277]
Again in Athanasius' version of Liberius' *defensio* at Milan in the presence of the emperor, where the counsel of the pope to Constantius is
paralleled to the voice of Our Lord to Saul on the road to Damascus, and
the pope himself is depicted as the representative of the persecuted mystical Body of Christ,[278] the verb δείκνυμι is used to designate the specific

---

[271] See Athanasius' 19th *Festal Letter* (for Easter, 347), where he severely censures the
legalism of the Jews (see Robertson, *Athanasius*, LNPF², 545; Larsow, *Fest-Briefe*,
142–143).

[272] See also *Ad Rufin* (*PG* 26,1180–1181) for further proof of the magnanimity of
Athanasius.

[273] Caspar, *Geschichte des Papsttums* I, 190.

[274] *Hist. Arian.* 35,1–2.

[275] *Hist. Arian.* 35,3.

[276] *Hist. Arian.* 35,2.

[277] *Hist. Arian.* 38,4.

[278] *Hist. Arian.* 39,4.

function which the pope's sufferings would have (sc. his exile and torture), namely, to *manifest* the true nature of the persecution and the sufferings of the confessors. A similar use of δείκνυμι is to be found in the *Letter to Serapion* describing the death of Arius, which letter is particularly relevant to our analysis, since it was written as an accompanying letter to the *Historia*. Interpreting the death of Arius, Athanasius uses the term δείκνυμι no less than three times to describe that event as a revelation of God's judgment on Arius and his heresy, which had been *"manifested* in a manner transcending the judgment of men."[279]

In our text, Athanasius uses δείκνυμι to affirm that the lapse of Liberius in no way lessens the authority of his previous confession but rather manifests (or reveals) it to the world in a new and definitive way, since the evil of the Neo-Arians that caused the persecutions of the orthodox had thereby readied the extremity of its wickedness: "since from the beginning they did not even spare Liberius the Bishop of Rome but extended their madness even into those parts and showed no respect for [its] Apostolic throne; neither did they honor the fact that it is the metropolis of orthodoxy, the Rome of the Romania, nor did they remember that, when they previously wrote, they said 'the men are themselves apostolic.'"[280] To use the symbolism of Eusebius' original ecclesiology, the Successor of Nero spurned on and motivated by the Successors of Simon Magus, had attempted to conquer the Successor of Peter and failed, since their apparent victory itself became the means used by the Father to transform it into a definitive confession of the Faith of Nicaea which defined the Divinity of the Son. In other words, the lapse of Liberius was a contemporary form of the original confession at Caesarea Philippi, where Peter, acting as spokesman for the other apostles, confessed the Divine Nature of the Son, through the sole means of the Father's revelation.

The paragraph concludes with a statement that evokes the final nuance of Mt 16,18:

4.   In fact, they attempted everything to further the cause of their heresy. While in every Church, those who guarded the

---

[279] ὅτι τοῦτο ὑπὲρ τὰς ἀνθρώπων κρίσεις ἐδείχθη (*De morte Arii* 4,1 = Opitz 179,33–34). There is also a description of the death of Arius in *Ad epp. Aeg. et Lib.* 19 (*PG* 25,581,C6f.), where the same terminological usage is to be found in order to describe the theological significance of his death. See also *Hist. Arian.* 57,1 (Opitz 215,9) and *De fuga* 5,3 (Opitz 71,14–18) for other examples of the use this term.

[280] *Hist. Arian.* 35,2.

Faith, which they had learned [from the Fathers], awaited their teachers, cast off the heresy which is at enmity with Christ and all avoided [it as they would] a serpent.[281]

This summarizes succinctly the preceding narrative. The Neo-Arians stopped at nothing to advance their cause, even to the extent of attacking the Bishop of Rome. But the effect was the opposite to what they had intended. They had hoped to definitively establish their heretical teaching by means of the Bishop of Rome's unique Petrine authority. Through him they wished, as Athanasius told us at the opening of this Section, "to draw all men quickly"[282] to the heresy that was supported by the emperor and so to enable them to "quickly rule over all."[283] And what did they actually achieve? "In every Church" the faithful hold fast to the Faith handed down to them by the Fathers and they await the return of their true teachers, the exiled confessors: all reject the heresy. The final phrase: "all avoided [it] like a serpent" is possibly an allusion to Mt 16,18b ("the gates of hell will not prevail against it"), since the mention of the serpent here refers to the devil,[284] and as far as Athanasius is concerned, the real author of the heresy[285] and of the persecution.[286]

§7 Conclusion

The main themes interwoven into the prelude to and description of the fall of Liberius in the *Historia* were already sounded by Athanasius in his *Encyclical to his Fellow-Bishops of Egypt and Libya* (356), namely, (i) the essential freedom of the Church that arose from her Apostolic nature, (ii) the Apostolicity of the Faith handed on to the bishops to preserve and authoritatively proclaim, (iii) the readiness to bear witness to this Faith, if necessary

---

281 πάντα μέντοι ποιεῖν ὑπὲρ τῆς αἱρέσεως ἐπεχείρησαν. καθ' ἑκάστην δὲ ἐκκλησίαν τηροῦντες ἣν ἔμαθον πίστιν, τοὺς μὲν διδασκάλους προσδοκῶσι, τὴν δὲ χριστομάχον αἵρεσιν κατέβαλον καὶ κάντες ὡς ὄφιν ἐκτρέπονται (*Hist. Arian.* 41,4 = Opitz 206,15–18).

282 *Hist. Arian.* 35,4 (Opitz 203,2).

283 *Hist. Arian.* 35,3 (Opitz 203,1).

284 Cf. *Ad epp. Aeg. et Lib.* 1 & 2 (*PG* 25,540,B8–9; 541,C1).

285 Athanasius compares Eusebius and Arius to serpents who emerged from their pits to vomit forth their poisonous heresy (cf. *Hist. Arian.* 66,2 = Opitz 219,13–15). See *Hist. Arian.* 3,3 (Opitz 184,18), where the heresy is described as the great beast of the Book of Daniel; see also *Hist. Arian.* 20,1 (Opitz 193,1–6).

286 Cf. *Hist. Arian.* 33,2 (Opitz 201,15–16).

with one's blood, and (iv) the description of the heresy as a serpent.[287]
The first two were the products of his reflection on the ecclesiastical
issues involved in the controversies which initially surrounded his person
and his claim to the See of Mark. The third concept was rooted in his
understanding of the Cross, which is central to his theology[288] and in his
appreciation of the fundamental importance of our participation in the
salvific suffering of Christ.[289] The fourth concept, very common to the
early Church, is to be found already at the beginning of his Episcopacy
(329–330).[290] It was the third theme that enabled Athanasius rediscover
the original meaning of Mt 16,16–18 and its intrinsic relationship to the
Petrine Succession at Rome.

   We have seen that the unifying motif common to the seven paragraphs,
which describe the events which led up to the traumatic excommunication of Athanasius by Liberius of Rome, was the Confession of Peter at
Caesarea Philippi. The fact that Athanasius only alludes to Mt 16,16–18
is of greatest importance. It indicated that for his readers, the monks of
Egypt, the unique association between the Bishop of Rome and St. Peter,
and so with this passage, was taken for granted, since an allusion receives
power of evocation due to its familiarity. Indeed, the reference to the
Letter of the Eusebians to Julius (341), which itself admitted to the generally recognized primacy of Rome based on its Petrine origins, confirms
this assumption. It was the same understanding of Rome's primacy that
provided Eusebius of Caesarea with the conceptual framework for his
original *History*. In our examination of the place St. Peter played in the
thought of Athanasius and of the way he used and understood the text
of Mt 16,16–18 in his other writings, we have also seen how the concepts
of the early Eusebius were presupposed by Athanasius. He understood
St. Peter to be the "originator of the primary teaching" concerning our
Salvation (the economic theology of Athanasius), while his Confession
at Caesarea Philippi is for him "the sovereign principle of our Faith"
(his ontological theology), which is representative of the basic thrust

---

[287] Cf. *Ad epp. Aeg. et Lib.* 20 (*PG* 25,585).

[288] See, for example, the central position occupied by the Cross in his earlier theological works (cf. *C. Gentes* 1 = Thomson 2–4 and *De incarn.* 8 = Kannengiesser
288f.). See also the 6th *Festal Letter* (Robertson, *Athanasius*, LNPF2, 519–520);
Ad Const. 33 (Szymusiak 128); *Vita Ant.* 79–80 (*PG* 26,952,C9–956,A13); *Or.
c. Ar. I*, 43–45 (*PG* 26,100,C1f.).

[289] See the "7th" *Festal Letter*, in Robertson, *Athanasius*, LNPF2, 523–524; Larsow,
Fest-Briefe, 95–99.

[290] See the 2nd *Festal Letter* for 330 (Robertson 511; Larsow 67–68).

of Scripture, the *Regula Fidei*. At Caesarea Philippi, Peter is expressly seen to be the spokesman for the Apostles. His Confession alone is representative of the Apostolic Faith and, as such, is the Rock on which the Church is built. But his Confession at Caesarea was itself brought to its completion through his martyrdom at Rome. His martyrdom there was the climax of his mission (to found the Church) and as such part of the Divine Dispensation.

In order to interpret the significance of Liberals' lapse, Athanasius in the *Historia* draws on the intrinsic connection between Peter's Confession at Caesarea and the Petrine Succession in Rome, where Peter definitively crowned his verbal confession with his blood. The Apostolic Throne of St. Peter was attacked by all the forces of hell, i.e., heresy and Antichrist (the intrusion of an external authority into the Church), so Athanasius informs the monks, but could not prevail against the confession of the Apostolic man, Liberius, who had freely undertaken the suffering of exile rather than abandon his support for the man he had identified with the Nicene Faith. Even the apparent lapse of Liberius, whose human weakness seemed to highlight the Divine source of his office's authority, Athanasius appears to suggest, only served to manifest to the whole Church the extreme hatred of the Neo-Arians for that which the Successor of Peter officially professed when he had the necessary freedom to make his intention known, namely the confession of the sovereign principle of our Faith.

The Church of Rome itself was depicted by Athanasius in his concise review of the events that led up to and followed from his own recourse to Liberius' predecessor, Julius as the center of the universal unanimity and was synonymous with ecclesiastical authority. It was thus contrasted with the Eusebian Imperial Church that relied on the external force of the imperial authority. In the prelude to the fall of Liberius, Rome is thus alone described as "great," i.e., holy and orthodox, where liberty of conscience reigns supreme, i.e., where the Church is free from external force. The cause of Rome's greatness, articulated briefly at the opening of the section that specifically deals with Liberius, is her Apostolic Throne, which made her the capital of orthodoxy and even compelled her enemies to admit that her "men," i.e., her bishops, were Apostolic. Consequently, the contemporary supporters of the Eusebian heresy, the Neo-Arians, were in principle opposed to it and from the beginning attempted to subdue it.

The Bishop of Rome is presented by Athanasius as the spokesman for the Church in particular the exiled "confessor-bishops" in opposition to the emperor Constantius, who does not simply represent the empire but the Eusebian heresy of the Imperial Church, which he had made his own and thus became the forerunner of Antichrist if not actually the Antichrist himself. As spokesman for the suffering bishops and the whole Church, the Bishop of Rome reflects the role of Peter as spokesman for the Apostles. The Roman bishop's authority is seen to be universal in extent and immediate in effect, and its source is the Petrine tradition of Rome which arose from Peter's martyrdom there. In his account of Liberius' opposition to the Imperial Church as represented aptly by the Eunuch Eusebius, Athanasius thus draws his reader's attention to the permanent memorial of that martyrdom, τὸ μαρτύριον—the Church built over the tomb of Peter in Rome. As spokesman for the persecuted Apostolic Church, Liberius is also depicted as Vicar of the mystical Body of Christ, who exercises his authority like Christ, i.e., without the threat of force he persuades solely on the basis of argumentation; his argumentation is characterized by his appeal to the Fathers (Tradition). And so, his authoritative words can be compared to the voice of Christ to Saul who persecuted the Church. What he teaches is for the spiritual good of the individual and the building up of the Church, which makes his teaching comparable to the Confession of Peter on which the Church is built. Basic to his teaching is his insistence on adherence to the Apostolic regulations, which in turn demand the establishment of unanimity with regard to the Faith most recently defined at Nicaea.

Liberius' own intervention which placed the Nicene Faith at the center of the controversies surrounding Athanasius (for the first time since the year 325) resulted in his own identification with that Faith and thus his identification with the Confession made by Peter at Caesarea Philippi. When the universal unanimity of the bishops was destroyed by the external power of the imperial authority, the attention of the monks is directed to the few "confessor-bishops" who alone witness to the Apostolic Faith, among whom the Bishop of Rome enjoys a primacy which corresponds to his normal primacy in the universal communion, and which gives to the witness of the other bishops its authoritative stamp. His fall is thus paradoxically interpreted as the ultimate witness to that which he stood for as a free man and a manifestation of the extremes to which the enemies of Christ are prepared to go. But Athanasius seems to say, due to the promise of the Lord to Peter, the forces of evil cannot prevail over the Church founded on Peter's Confession, since even in his weakness, the Father continues to manifest His Son and the whole Church remains firm in the Faith and rejects the heresy.

Note III
THE EPISCOPAL ELECTION AND ORDINATION
OF SAINT ATHANASIUS

The legality of Athanasius' election was first questioned by the Eusebians at the Synod of Tyre.[1] Basing his account on the information to be gleaned from the rejection of this charge by the Synod of Alexandria (338),[2] Socrates repeats the charge.[3] But Sozomen[4] draws on an Arian source for his version of the accusation, while another, almost contradictory version of the supposed illegal election is graphically painted by Philostorgius.[5] Modern historians tend to give more and more credence to this indictment. This is in part due to the influence of Seeck and Schwartz, who *a priori* distrusted orthodox sources—recently described by Girardet[6] as characterized by a "one-sided pro-Athanasian" view—and thus tend to give Arian sources more credence than perhaps they deserve.[7] Let us therefore examine the evidence.

Alexander of Alexandria died on April 17, three days after Easter (328), and Athanasius was ordained bishop on June 8 of the same year, i.e., on the first day of the week, following Pentecost.[8] Does this interval of seven and a half weeks—and not three months as Telfer suggests[9]— indicate that something irregular occurred about this time? According to Telfer, a change in the procedure of electing and ordaining the Bishop of Alexandria took place at this time, whereby the earlier procedure, by which the presbyters of Alexandria elected one of their own rank to the See of Alexandria, was changed by order of Bishop Alexander in accordance with the provisions of Canon IV of Nicaea. Here Telfer bases his argument primarily on a text of Eutchyius, Melchite Patriarch of Alexandria (933–943), whom Kemp[10] in his criticism of Telfer maintains was an ignorant and blundering writer, whose evidence cannot be relied

1   Cf. *Apol.* 6,4 (Opitz 92,17–19).
2   Cf. *Apol.* 6,5–6 (Opitz 92,20–29).
3   Socrates, *HE* 1,23,3 (Hussey 130).
4   Sozomen, *HE* 2,17,4 (Bidez-Hansen 72,17f.).
5   Philostorgius, *HE* 2,11 (Bidez 22,9–23,10).
6   Girardet, *Kaisergericht und Bischofsgericht*, 54.
7   See, e.g., Girardet, *Kaisergericht und Bischofsgericht*, 55 on Philostorgius.
8   Cf. Festal Index (Robertson, *Athanasius*, LNPF, 503; Larsow, *Fest-Briefe*, 26–27; 49).
9   Telfer, "Episcopal Succession in Egypt," 11. Telfer follows Epiphanius (see comments below).
10 Kemp, "Bishops and Presbyters at Alexandria," 138.

upon with any degree of certainty.[11] However, allowing for the possible reliability of references to the reputed earlier practice concerning the ordination by presbyters at Alexandria to be found in Jerome, Severus of Antioch, and Eutchyius, Kemp does not rule out the possibility that "we may have in them evidence of the survival at Alexandria to a later date than elsewhere of a presbyteral college with episcopal powers...."[12] But he also admits the plausibility of the arguments made by Gore and Turner to the effect that "we have in these writers traces of what was originally an Arian calumny about Athanasius."[13] The latter solution was also recommended by Lécuyer[14] as worthy of consideration. It is the explanation which seems the most likely to this writer.

After the death of Alexander, Athanasius informs us in a text which has been the subject of some debate,[15] that the Meletians once again began to trouble the Church though but five months previously they had been finally reconciled to the Catholic Church in accordance with the provisions of the Nicene Synod.[16] What did Athanasius mean when he said that five months after their reconciliation with Bishop Alexander,[17] the Meletians πάλιν τὰς ἐκκλησίας ἐτάραττον? From the preceding phrase οἱ δὲ κατὰ τοὺς κύνας οὐκ ἐπιλαθόμενοι ὧν ἐξήρασαν (probably an allusion to 2 Pet 2,21–22),

---

[11] The theory of Telfer has also been rejected by Lécuyer, "Le problème des consécrations épiscopales," 241f.

[12] Kemp, "Bishops and Presbyters at Alexandria," 140.

[13] Kemp, "Bishops and Presbyters at Alexandria," 139–140.

[14] Lécuyer, "Le problème des consécrations épiscopales," 256–257.

[15] The text is from the *Apologia contra Arianos*, as it was previously called (see Chapter Eight); *Apol.* 59,3 (Opitz 139,15–18).

[16] Here I accept the interpretation of Montfaucon (*PG* 25,1vii) adopted by Robertson, "Prolegomena," xxi, and more recently by Telfer, "Meletius of Lycopolis and Episcopal Succession," 234. But according to the hypothesis of Seeck, "Untersuchungen," 36 and Schwartz, *Nachrichten*, 1911, 380f. (= *GS* III,205) a second session of the Synod of Nicaea was summoned by the emperor at the end of the year 327 (to reconcile the Arians—in particular Eusebius of Nicomedia and Theognis of Nicaea—with the Church); it was five months after this event that Alexander died, claims Schwartz. This theory, originally proposed by Seeck and more recently accepted by Opitz (who included the document on which it is based in his Urkundensammlung, as though it was genuine), as also by Lietzmann, *Geschichte* III, 111–112, Joannou, *Die Ostkirche und die Cathedra Petri*, 37–38, and Girardet, *Kaisergericht und Bischofsgericht*, 53–54, is based on Urkunde 31 (Opitz 65–66) which Rogala, *Anfänge*, 78–85, clearly proved to be an Arian forgery (See also Baynes, "Athanasiana," 58). For further literature on the subject, as well as an independent argument against the credibility of such a theory, see Szymusiak, *Apologie a l'empereur*, Appendice I, 169–173.

[17] Cf. *Apol.* 71,5–72,1 (Opitz 149,13f.).

it is clear that the Meletians again went back into schism, presumably since they had ignored the conditions for communion imposed on them by Nicaea.[18]

Epiphanius reports,[19] that, after Alexander's death, Athanasius, whom he had delegated to become his successor, was at the imperial court on business and so the Meletians elected a certain Theonas who died after a three-month reign; soon after, according to Epiphanius, Athanasius arrived back in Alexandria and was elected by an orthodox synod. That Epiphanius is notoriously unreliable as an historian is in itself sufficient to treat this text with extreme caution. One's skepticism is confirmed by such assertions as the absence of Athanasius from Alexandria at the time of Bishop Alexander's death, which is not otherwise documented, the mention of a "Theonas," otherwise unknown, and especially the false chronology of a three-month interregnum. And yet Epiphanius seems to be so confident of the existence of "a certain Theonas" that he refers to him a second time in connection with the election of Athanasius,[20] this time in a discussion of the Arian heresy. In this account we notice yet another detail that destroys any faith one may have in the reliability of Epiphanius: he relates in the same context the election of Achillas as the successor to Alexander, although Achillas was his predecessor. Is it possible that Epiphanius is here reporting a garbled version of a Meletian tradition to the effect that, after the death of Alexander, the Meletians attempted to place a successor on the throne of Mark? We are in the dark as to what extent Epiphanius was true to his source, nor have we any indication of how long such a tradition could have been in existence. All we can say is that the story was in circulation ca. 375–377, which is an important fact to be noted. Further, it is clear that the tradition is at variance with the other versions about Athanasius' election which were held by his opponents.

According to the version preserved by Sozomen,[21] it was claimed that after the death of Alexander, fifty-four followers of both Alexander and the Meletians assembled together and agreed to choose a successor by common vote but that seven bishops separated themselves from the majority and ordained Athanasius surreptitiously. This is a variation of the charge brought against Athanasius at Tyre, where the Eusebians accused him of being unworthy of the office and of having been clandestinely elected by six or

---

[18] Cf. *Urkunde* 23,6–10 (Opitz 48,15–50,9).
[19] Epiphanius, *Panarion* 68,7,2–4 (Holl 147,5–17).
[20] Epiphanius, *Panarion* 69,11,4 (Holl 161,8–18).
[21] Sozomen, *HE* 2,17,4 (Bidez-Hansen 72,17f.).

seven other bishops in a secret place.[22] The account of Sozomen shows signs of later embellishments: originally there was no mention of the "assembly" of orthodox and Meletians, but only of a secret election. Further, the Sozomen version, which is probably based on the collection of Sabinus (ca. 375) and of Arian provenance, shows an ignorance of the prescriptions of Nicaea with regard to elections. According to Nicaea, only those who had not been found in schism could nominate or ordain those worthy to hold sacred office.[23]

It is possible that yet another version of this story is to be found in *Apophthegmata Patrum* 78,[24] which is also dated around 375. There it is reported that two Arians accuse a bishop, who is generally recognized as Athanasius, of having been ordained by *presbyters*.[25]

Philostorgius (between 425 and 433) finally shows how the original story had taken on legendary proportions within the late Arian camp. There is no mention of any assembly of bishops, as had been reported by Sozomen (= Sabinus?) and Epiphanius, each in his own way, nor is it six or seven orthodox bishops who clandestinely elect and ordain Athanasius, as the Eusebians alleged at Tyre and as is later taken up by the Arians at the end of the fourth century, but rather it is "the impious instrument of falsehood," Athanasius himself, who is now accused of having taken the initiative. He is reported to have seized the Church of St. Dionysius and forced *two* bishops he found there to ordain him against their will; consequently, so Philostorgius, he was anathematized by all the bishops but was able to strengthen his position by writing to the emperor and receiving the imperial confirmation.[26] The fact that such a legend was nourished and developed is not in itself sufficient proof, as e.g., Barnard assumes,[27] of an authentic historical tradition,

22 Cf. *Apol.* 6,5–6 (Opitz 92,20–29).

23 Cf. *Urkunde* 23,8 (Opitz 49,10–50,2). Girardet, *Kaisergericht und Bischofsgericht*, 54, apparently ignores this text since he claims that those supporters of Meletius who were not ordained by him could have legally participated in an election. Nicaea clearly excluded all who had been found in schism, whether they had been ordained by Meletius or not. As Martin, "Athanase et les Mélitiens," 40–44, points out, Athanasius would have interpreted the stipulations laid down by Nicaea according to their strict sense (p. 43).

24 *PG* 65,341,B8–15.

25 See Kemp, "Bishops and Presbyters at Alexandria," 136–137, where he refers, with some reserve, to the theory of Gore and Turner. See also Lécuyer, "Le problème des consécrations épiscopales," 256–257.

26 Philostorgius, *HE* 2,11 (Bidez 22,9–23,10).

27 Barnard, "Two Notes," 349.

even though the actual story is reported in both orthodox and Arian sources.[28] That Athanasius sought and received the confirmation of the emperor, as Girardet affirms on the sole authority of Philostorgius,[29] is clearly an Arian fabrication, since it is an anachronism to speak about an imperial confirmation in the year 328.

The inconsistencies, indeed the blatant contradictions in this Meletian/Arian tradition, are themselves the strongest indication that it contains little if any historical substance. However, we must examine the origins of this accusation about the irregularity of Athanasius' election and ordination to see how it arose and what was the cause of its continued relevance to the later Meletians and Arians.

It has been suggested recently that Athanasius described the origins of the Meletian disturbances in the Alexandrian Church—in the much debated text from the *Apologia* already mentioned above[30]—in a deliberately vague way so as to conceal something of embarrassment regarding his own election to the See of Alexandria after the death of Alexander.[31] This interpretation is based on a false understanding of the purpose for which the *Apologia* was written (namely that it was Athanasius' reply to the various slanders and charges levelled at him by his enemies). As we have seen in Chapter Eight, the *Apologia* was composed in the latter half of 356 and had at its object the demonstration of his canonical claim to the See of Alexandria on the basis of his *restoration* to his Church by the competent ecclesiastical authorities. That was the precise issue at stake in the years 352–356. *The question of his election or the validity of his ordination were not raised at that time.* The object of Athanasius in the *Apologia*, where he describes the Meletian disturbances in Alexandria, which began with their relapse into schism but five months after their reconciliation under Alexander, was, as we saw,[32] to explain to an audience ignorant of the details of the Meletian schism how it arose and developed.

---

28 Likewise, there is no proof that the reason for Athanasius' journey within his province after his consecration was politically motivated, i.e., "to consolidate his rather shaky position," as Barnard assumes in "Two Notes," 349. It is more likely that Athanasius' visitation of his Church was motivated quite simply by pastoral reasons.

29 This text is a reputed *Letter of Constantine*, now preserved in the anonymous *Vita Constantini* (cf. *Philostorgius* = Bidez 23,31f.) and most probably also the product of the Arian historian (see Bidez, *Einleitung*, xci).

30 *Apol.* 59,3 (Opitz 139,15–18). See above, footnotes 15 and 16.

31 See Orlandi, "Sull'Apologia secunda," 60f.

32 See above, p. 320f.

We cannot rule out the possibility that the Meletians made some attempt to elect their own successor to Alexander. And yet it is of note that the first attack of the Meletians on Athanasius—in the year 330—was not to question the regularity of his election but to accuse him before the emperor of having imposed a tax on the Egyptians.[33] When they did object to his ordination—ca. 330–331—they protested, again to the emperor, of his youth.[34] This earned them the ridicule of Constantine.[35] It was around three years later that the first accusation about his election as such was made,[36] which charge was finally brought against Athanasius at Tyre, 335, as mentioned above. This indictment was answered so effectively by the Synod of Alexandria, 338,[37] that it was never again raised during the lifetime of Athanasius.

It is of note that the next document, which, to the best of my knowledge, reports this accusation is the *Panarion of Epiphanius*,[38] written circa 375–377, i.e., two to four years after the death of Athanasius. Epiphanius is evidently embarrassed about the interregnum between Alexander and Athanasius—which covered seven-and-a-half weeks but which he understood to have lasted three months.[39] To account for this unusually long period, Epiphanius most probably had recourse to a Meletian tradition, which was at the time again in circulation, concerning the election of a successor to Alexander. As we noted above, it was around the year 375 that the two other documents that apparently record other versions of the story (that of the Arian Sabinus, which presumably Sozomen used, and that of the *Apophthegmata Patrum*). It seems, then, that the Meletians and Arians resurrected this old charge after the death of Athanasius; but what could have been the reason for this? It could have been quite simply part of a *damnatio memoriae* of

---

[33] Cf. *Apol.* 60,2 (Opitz 140,15–18). See also Socrates, *HE* 1,27,8a (Hussey 145); Sozomen, *HE* 2,22,7 (Bidez-Hansen 79,22–24); and Theodoret, *HE* 1,26,4–5 (Parmentier-Scheidweiler 81,11–22).

[34] *Chronicon* III (*PG* 26,1352,A14–15 = Larsow, *Fest-Briefe*, 27).

[35] *Apol.* 62,3 (Opitz 142,3–8) = *Letter of Constantine to People of the Catholic Church at Alexandria*.

[36] See above, p. 350f.

[37] Cf. *Letter of the Synod of Alexandria*, 338 (*Apol.* 6,4–6 = Opitz 92,12f.).

[38] Epiphanius, *Panarion* 69,11,5 (Holl 161,10–12).

[39] It is possible that a similar embarrassment may have caused Severus, Bishop of El-Aschmounein, in his tenth-century *History of the Coptic Church of Alexandria*, to remark: "So when the blessed Father Alexander went to his rest, the Church was widowed for a few days" (*POr* I, 403; see Telfer, "Episcopal Succession in Egypt," 11).

an opponent whom both parties failed to destroy in his lifetime. However, it seems to me that the Meletians and Arians in Egypt had another vested interest in questioning the election and ordination of Athanasius even after his death. Since "the successors of St. Mark were, directly or at one remove, the source of all ministry in the Egyptian Church,"[40] then any proof of the irregularity of Athanasius' election or ordination would automatically cast doubts on the legality or even validity of the orthodox bishops and clerics of Egypt.

The historical question that remains concerns the seven-and-a-half weeks which elapsed between the death of Alexander and the ordination of Athanasius as his successor. It is possible that the delay was due to the time needed to summon the bishops of Egypt and allow them sufficient time to arrive in Alexandria.[41] It is also possible that the electors and ordaining bishops could only journey to Alexandria after the Easter celebrations, over which they presided, had been completed with the Feast of Pentecost, as is suggested by the *Festal Index* (= *Chronicon Athanasianum*).[42] On the first Sunday after Pentecost, June 8, 328, Athanasius was ordained by the orthodox bishops who alone were competent to do so.[43] He mounted the throne of St. Mark to the general acclamation of the people.[44]

---

[40] Telfer, "Episcopal Succession in Egypt," 3.
[41] Cf. Martin, "Athanase et les Mélitiens," 41–42, in particular footnote 25.
[42] See Robertson, *Athanasius*, LNPF, 503: Larsow 26–27.
[43] The judgement of Loofs, "Athanasius von Alexandria," (1897), 196, remains valid: "die Wahl ist durchaus ordnungsmäßig erfolgt."
[44] Cf. *Apol.* 6,5–6 (Opitz 92,20–29).

GENERAL CONCLUSION

St. Athanasius and his readers shared an understanding of the significance of the Petrine Succession in Rome similar to that which characterized the original ecclesiology of Eusebius, the Father of Church History. The function of the Roman succession-lists was to provide the original *History* with its basic structure or framework into which the events and personalities of the Church's early history were fitted according to the stated aims of his pioneering work. This corresponded to the function of the Petrine Successions in Eusebius' understanding of the Church as Apostolic by nature: the Petrine Succession, primarily at Rome (but also at Alexandria and Antioch), guaranteed in a definitive, authoritative way the Apostolicity of the Church. As Peter was spokesman for the Apostles, so too the Bishop of Rome was not conceived as though he occupied a position in the Church which separated him from the other bishops who participated in the Apostolic Succession but was rather seen to be their preeminent representative. Among the other sees, Alexandria and Antioch (whose succession-lists were also included in the *History*) likewise participated in the Petrine function of being the guarantor for the authentic preservation and transmission of the Apostolic Tradition of teaching from generation to generation. This participation corresponded to the nature of the particular relationship of those sees to St. Peter. But it was the specific "office" of the Bishop of Rome to detect heresy and excommunicate the heretics, as Peter had originally detected and destroyed the errors of the founder of all heresies, Simon Magus, and to authoritatively approve the teaching of the orthodox writers, as Peter had once sanctioned the Gospel of Mark for reading in the Churches. It was the definitive aspect of the Bishop of Rome's authority which apparently distinguished his Petrine Succession from that of either Alexandria or Antioch. This characteristic of the authority attributed to the Roman Successor of St. Peter was in all probability seen by Eusebius to have been due to the fact that Rome was the location of the final witness to the Faith by St. Peter: his martyrdom with St. Paul at the hands of Nero, the first persecutor of the Church. Thus, the Petrine Successor in Rome was expected to give final witness to the Faith.

561

Eusebius' disillusionment with the behavior of the preeminent Successor of St. Peter during the Great Persecution is itself an indirect testimony to the central importance the Church historian attributed to the Bishop of Rome, since that unexpected manifestation of Peter's human weakness led to Eusebius' eventual abandonment of the traditional concept of the Church as Apostolic by nature. The original Apostolic Church, founded on St. Peter and preserved down through the centuries by the Petrine "dynasty," was raised to the ground by the longest and most severe of all the persecutions endured by the Church in her early history, one moreover which fell upon the Church—and Eusebius in particular—like a thief in the night.

The later imperial ecclesiology of Eusebius transferred the Petrine Succession on to the shoulders of the first "Christian Emperor" who in the new dispensation inaugurated by Constantine replaced in Eusebius' mind the old Apostolic Successions and thus attributed to the Christian Emperor the source of all authority in the Church. Eusebius' so-called political theology melded his earlier Petrine ecclesiology with traditional concepts of a sacral imperial authority such as that of the Pontifex Maximus. It was not without reason that earlier generations called Eusebius the author of "Caesaropapism," though the unfortunate appellation may well be an inaccurate description of later Byzantine theocracy first manifested in Emperor Theodosius I.

The significance of what was uncovered from a close analysis of Athanasius historico-apologetical writings about his attitude to the position of the Bishop of Rome within the Church is twofold. In the first place, it confirms that the preeminence of the Successor of Peter in Rome (based on Peter's definitive Confession of the Faith in his martyrdom, as reflected in the early Eusebius) was simply assumed by Athanasius and his readers in the East and West, though differences of understanding were emerging thanks to Constantine's new dispensation. But the analysis also revealed how profoundly Athanasius had come to appreciate the theological meaning of Rome's preeminence. Like every insight, it was the product of years of reflection. His reflection was provoked by his own personal confrontation with the reality of the Eusebian imperial ecclesiology, which confrontation occupied the first half of his long episcopate and forced him to spend almost as much time away from his Church as in it. His personal sufferings, however, enabled him to perceive the true nature of the Eusebian Imperial Church as a very real and dangerous threat to the Apostolic nature of the Church, to her autonomy and universality, and thus to her freedom. Here he was ahead of his fellow-bishops, a prophetic voice, like

Elijah, with only a few supporters. He was also among the first to recognize that in the new situation in which the Church found herself, it was the Petrine Succession in Rome which ultimately could guarantee the preservation of the Church's Apostolicity and universality and thus her freedom to proclaim the Apostolic Faith to all. Accordingly, Rome was seen by Athanasius to be the Apostolic See *par excellence*. His reflection on the traditional understanding of the Petrine Succession in the light of the most severe attack of the Neo-Arians on the Apostolic See enabled him to perceive for the first time the implications of the Lord's promise to Peter (Mt 16,16–18), which were only partially and incorrectly understood by Eusebius of Caesarea.

The controversies which surrounded the person of Athanasius and his claims to the See of Mark introduced a new problem for the Church. Up to the fourth century, it appears that no bishop had been excommunicated solely on the grounds of personal misbehavior. Even Paul of Samosata was deposed and expelled from his Church on account of his heretical views and not, in the first place at least, for his infamous style of life. The first bishop to be deposed on charges relating to personal misbehavior was Eustathius of Antioch. There the Eusebians, led by Eusebius of Caesarea, were completely victorious. But when they tried to remove the Bishop of Alexandria from the See of Mark, Athanasius challenged both the material content of their accusations and the formal grounds on which they based their case against him. Since the accusations of the Eusebians included charges of a civil nature, Athanasius had recourse to the emperor—before *and* after Tyre (335). But once he became aware of the new ecclesiological principles which were based on an understanding of the Christianized Sacral Emperor as the final authority in the Church, Athanasius had recourse to Rome. Confronted with the case of Athanasius and the cases of the other Oriental bishops who had recourse to Rome, Julius of Rome drew the necessary consequences from the universal nature of truth when applied to matters concerning human behavior: justice must be transparent—it must not only be done, but it must be seen to be done. Motivated by charity and his responsibility for the truth and speaking in the name of the Petrine Succession of Rome, Julius rejected the claims to absolute autonomy on the part of provincial synods. The Bishop of Rome refused to recognize the principle of non-intervention, which distinguished the Imperial Church of the two Eusebii in its early stages, and insisted on the need for the scrutiny and possible revision of synodal judgements by the rest of the episcopacy and ultimately, if necessary, by the See of Rome. For sees of direct Apostolic origin, and above all for sees of Petrine origin, he claimed the right to reexamine such judgements as affected their occupants. In doing so, Julius was applying the same basic principle as that which held good for the "reception" of synodal judgements on matters of teaching and liturgical custom. The way he applied this principle, i.e., his recognition of a certain hierarchy within the universal episcopate, reflects the incipient patriarchal system which, we saw, determined the structure of the first draft of Eusebius' *History* and was ultimately based on his Petrine/Apostolic ecclesiology. The fifth-century Church historian in Constantinople, Sozomen, accurately described the final motive which moved the Bishop of Rome to intervene in the controversies of the East (in particular Alexandria and Antioch) as his "solicitude for all, which becomes him due to the dignity of his throne."

The extent of Athanasius' influence on the composition of Julius' reply to the Eusebian-controlled Synod of Antioch, in which he justified his rejection of the judgement of the Synod of Tyre, 335, and his acceptance of Athanasius and the other Orientals into the communion of the Church, is difficult to determine. Both men saw the *novum* of the Eusebian Imperial Church as a threat to the Church's basic constitution. Julius, like Athanasius four years previously, reminded his readers of the Apostolic nature of the Church and the implications this had for the regulation of Church discipline. But the synthesis of Julius, based on the idea of the transparency of justice and the traditional Apostolic ecclesiology, is the work of an independent mind. The sympathy of Athanasius for the primatial self-consciousness of Julius, which is lightly but undeniably present in Julius' letter, can be gathered from the central importance which the Bishop of Alexandria attached to this document in his *Apologia*. At the Great Synod of Sardica, Athanasius was present and evidently approved when the Synodal Fathers rejected the *novum* of the two Eusebii. It can also be assumed that he gave his *placet* to the Appeal Canons where the "Great Synod of Sardica," which he put on a par with Nicaea, translated the principles worked out by Julius into canonical form.

At that stage in the history of Athanasius, the significance of the Petrine See was seen in terms of its role to preserve the universality or Catholicity of the Church in the face of the Eusebian attempt to "provincialize" the Catholic Church according to political or geographical divisions. Its function was, further, to ensure that the law of Divine Justice be universally applied and to protect the universal dimension of the Apostolic office of each bishop, i.e., the equality of those who, as men responsible also for the whole Church and not simply for their local Church, therefore had the right to be judged not only by some bishops or by any collective institution but by all their fellow-bishops.

The Synod of Sardica is generally recognized as an event of major importance in the history of the Church, and the development of the papacy in particular, since it marked the initial stage in the translation of the traditional preeminence of the Roman bishop relating to the Apostolic Teaching into what was later termed his Primacy of Jurisdiction. What is not commonly appreciated is that this development was necessitated by the threat to her *Apostolic* nature which was posed by the innovation of the Eusebian Imperial Church. It is, further, important to stress that this development was a logical one, since the roots of the Church's jurisdictional authority are to be ultimately traced back to that unique responsibility of the Successors of the Apostles, the bishops, for the Apostolic Faith, which responsibility has as its corollary the power to grant or to refuse admittance to the communion of the Church. Such responsibility was to a preeminent degree entrusted to the Roman bishop as Successor of St. Peter.

In the year 356, Athanasius wrote the *Apologia* in order to demonstrate to the bishops assembled at Milan that he had been restored to his see by the competent ecclesiastical authority. To do so, he pointed to his restoration by Julius of Rome and its confirmation by the Synod of Sardica and other synods such as that of Jerusalem. But he also went a step further and proved that the legal procedure according to which he was restored was both free from that external pressure (which was one of the distinguishing characteristics of the Imperial Church) and was fully in accordance with the autonomous nature of the Church. Here again Athanasius drew attention to the central role in this procedure which was played by the Bishop of Rome. This document also revealed the nuanced attitude of Athanasius to the legitimate imperial authority as well as his recognition of the function of the Bishop of Rome as the ecclesiastical counterweight, as it were, to the central authority of the emperor in civil affairs.

The *Historia Arianorum* reflected the changes which occurred after the death of Julius, 352. The Eusebian heresy of the Imperial Church was then adopted by Emperor Constantius II as his own, thereby bringing to light the other side of that ecclesiology, namely its replacement of the Apostolic Authority with that of the emperor: ὅπερ ἐγὼ βούλομαι, τοῦτο κανών. This much abused work also records

the new emphasis in the subject matter of the controversies surrounding
Athanasius thanks to the intervention of Liberius of Rome who placed the
Faith of Nicaea in the foreground—up to 353 it was confined to the background—of the debate. Faced with the apparent triumph of the Imperial
Church in securing under pressure the subscription of the exiled Liberius
to the excommunication and deposition of the man whom he had previously supported as the Defender of the Nicene Faith, even to the extent
of suffering exile on his account, Athanasius spelt out the significance of
this and other related events for his readers, the monks of the Thebaid.
There he drew on the latent understanding of the Roman primacy which
was based on the Petrine Succession in order to interpret the true meaning
of his own recent excommunication by Liberius and Ossius of Cordoba.

The Antichrist had appeared in the Church. A new authority was
present which usurped the Church's authority and refused to recognize her
Apostolic Faith. As the precursor of the Antichrist, if not the Antichrist
himself, Constantius had the physical power to create the semblance of
the normal manifestation of the Church's own authority, the unanimity
of her bishops. But true to the understanding of that concept as shared by
Irenaeus, Hegesippus, and Cyprian, Athanasius did not understand this
unanimity in terms of superficial uniformity or mere conformity which
could be forced on the Church by external pressure and accepted by her
at the cost of compromising the truth. As he indicates in *De synodis* (361–
62), he saw it as the manifestation of that unity of Faith which is preserved
and confessed in a harmony of word *and thought* by the bishops and which
must of necessity be unanimous since its source is their oneness with the
Apostolic Tradition of the Church and their oneness with God in Christ.
As the confession of the Successor of St. Peter in Rome was acknowledged
by the rest of the Church as definitive, it was not sufficient to force the
bishops of East and West to subscribe to the Neo-Arian demands but, as
Athanasius pointed out in the *Historia,* Constantius needed the authority
of the Apostolic See *par excellence* before he could claim complete victory.

When the traditional form of establishing the universal unanimity (through the reciprocal exchange of *Letters of Communion*
and a freely determined synodal judgement) was usurped and thus
rendered null and void by the misuse of the imperial authority, then
Athanasius singled out for his readers the alternative expression of
that pre-given concord: the "martyrdom" of the confessor-bishops,
among whom Liberius enjoyed a clear primacy, due not

to his personal merit but to his office as Bishop of Rome. His presence among them was seen to give the personal witness of the handful of bishops its ultimate meaning. It was the contemporary Confession of St. Peter whose original Confession at Caesarea Philippi, which Athanasius had previously indicated in his letter to Bishop Dracontius, had been crowned by his martyrdom in Rome. The bold teaching of Liberius in response to the attempts by the imperial delegate and representative of the Neo-Arians to condemn Athanasius (and so the Nicene Creed) was expressly compared to the revelation of the Father to Peter. At Milan, the Bishop of Rome was depicted as the spokesman for the confessor-bishops, who on their behalf and in the name of the whole Church opposed the Eusebian Imperial Church incorporated in the person of Constantius. The entire presentation of the fall of Liberius was intent on showing that the Eusebian Imperial Church, with which the emperor now identified, was in principle opposed to the Apostolic Church and that consequently it necessarily had to come into conflict with that see which, of all Apostolic Sees, is the Apostolic See *par excellence* due to its association with St. Peter and his martyrdom there. It was equally intent on demonstrating that the forces of the Antichrist could not prevail against the Church since even the temporary weakness of the occupant of that see was itself the most powerful manifestation of the contemporary Confession of Peter's Successor, on which Confession the Church is founded, namely that Christ is the Son of God, consubstantial with the Father.

Athanasius must, therefore, be given the credit for being the first known writer to have perceived and described, however tentatively, the vast implications of the Dominical Promise to St. Peter as applied to the Petrine Succession of the Roman bishop. He was the first to perceive that, should the ordinary magisterium (the bishops in communion with the Bishop of Rome) be unable to fulfil its teaching function, then the Bishop of Rome alone, as Successor of St. Peter, could and must give final witness to the Apostolic Faith, and that this witness was guaranteed to the Church irrespective of the "flesh and blood," the human weakness of its occupant. His appreciation of Rome as the Apostolic See *par excellence* made St. Athanasius the Great the forerunner of those who, beginning with Pope Damasus (see the decree of the Synod of Rome (382) in reply to the 3rd Canon of Constantinople (381) and the claims of Theodosius I), had recourse to the *traditional* understanding of the Church as reflected in the original *Church History of Eusebius* in order to defend the Church's autonomous and *Apostolic* nature in the face of those bishops and emperors who, in one form or another, adopted the "heresy of the two

Eusebii" as their own. Following the example of the Bishop of Alexandria, Successor of St. Mark, those who pointed to the Petrine Succession at Rome as the divinely established guarantor of the Church's Apostolicity were also necessarily compelled to plumb the depth of the Church's mystery and through their reflection bring to light the full significance of the Lord's promise to St. Peter at Caesarea Philippi.

SOURCES AND LITERATURE

1. ABBREVIATIONS

i. *The Writings of Eusebius of Caesarea*

Chronicle	The Armenian version of the Chronicle (translated into German)
CM	Contra Marcellum
Comm. in Ps.	Commentaria in Psalmos
DE	Demonstratio Evangelica
De mart. Pal.	De martyribus Palaestinae
Ecl	Eclogae Propheticae
ET	De ecclesiastica theologia
HE	Historia Ecclesiastica
LC	Laus Constantini
PE	Praeparatio Evangelica
Theoph	Theophania
VC	Vita Constantini

ii. *The Writings of St. Athanasius of Alexandria*

Ad Adelph.	Epistola ad Adelphium episcopum
Ad Afros	Epistola ad Afros
Ad Const.	Apologia ad imperatorem Constantium
Ad Dracont.	Epistola ad Dracontium
Ad epp. Aeg. et Lib.	Epistola encyclica ad episcopos Aegypti et Libyae
Ad Joan. et Ant.	Epistola ad Joannem et Antiochum presbyteros
Ad Lucif. I–II	Epistolae duae ad Luciferum episcopum
Ad monach.	Epistola ad monachos
Apol.	Apologia secunda = Apologia contra Arianos
C. Gentes	Oratio contra Gentes
De decr. Nic.	Epistola de decretis Nicaenae synodi
De fuga	Apologia de fuga sua
De incarn.	Oratio de incarnatione
De morte Arii	Epistola de morte Arii
De sent. Dion.	Epistola de sententia Dionysii episcopi
De syn.	Epistola de synodis Arimini in Italia et Seleuciae in Isauria celebratis
De virgin.	De virginitate
Ep. encycl.	Epistola ad episcopos encyclica
Exp. in Ps.	Expositiones in Psalmos
Festal Letters	Easter Letters (preserved in Syriac and Coptic and translated into English and German)
Hist. Arian.	Historia Arianorum ad monachos
Or. c. Ar. I–III	Orationes contra Arianos I–III

Or. c. Ar. IV	Orationes contra Arianos IV (Pseudo-Athanasius)
Serap. I–III	Epistolae ad Serapion I–III
Tom. ad Ant.	Tomus ad Antiochenos
Vita Ant.	Vita Antonii

iii. *Other Abbreviations*

A.D.	anno Domini
AHP	Archivum Historiae Pontificum
ANL	Ante-Nicene Fathers, Buffalo and New York
ca.	circa
cf.	confer
col.	Column
e.g.	exempli gratia
Ep.	Epistola
f.	and following
GS III–IV	E. Schwartz. *Gesammelte Schriften*. Bande III und IV. Berlin, 1959–1960.
Ibid.	ibidem
i.e.	id est
Intervention	List of interventions by See of Rome in the affairs of the Churches of the East in the fourth century compiled by P.-P. Joannou (see below, 3, ii.)
LNPF²	A Select Library of Nicene and Post-Nicene Fathers of the Christian Church. Ed. by Ph. Schaff and H. Wace. Buffalo and New York, 1889–1900. Reprinted: Grand Rapids, 1952f.
MS (S)	manuscript(s)
N.T.	New Testament
O.T.	Old Testament
p(p)	page(s)
SC	*Sources Chrétiennes*. Ed. by H. de Lubac and J. Daniélou. Paris, 1941f.
Stud. Pat.	Studia Patristica: Papers presented to the International Conference on Patristic Studies held at Christ Church, Oxford.
Transl.	translated by

Apart from the abbreviations listed below (under 2.iii–iv and 3.ii), all other abbreviations have been taken from the *Lexicon für Theologie und Kirche,* Band I, Freiburg, ²1957, 16*—48*.

2. PRIMARY SOURCES (EDITIONS)

i. *Eusebius of Caesarea*

Eclogae Propheticae. Ed. by T. Gaisford (PG 22,1021–1261). Paris, 1857.
Commentaria in Psalmos. Ed. by B. de Montfaucon (PG 23). Paris, 1857.
Vita Constantini. Ed. by F. Winkelmann (GCS 7, *Eusebius Werke* 1,1). Berlin, 1975.
Laus Constantini. Ed. by I. Heikel (GCS 7, *Eusebius Werke* 1). Leipzig, 1902.
Historia Ecclesiastica (including *De mart. Pal.*). Ed. by E. Schwartz (GCS 9, *Eusebius Werke* 2,1 and 2). Leipzig, 1903 and 1908.
Theophania. Die griechischen Brückstücke und Übersetzung der syrischen Überlieferung. Ed. by H. Gressmann (GCS 11, *Eusebius Werke* 3,2). Leipzig, 1904.

Contra Marcellum and *De ecclesiastica theologia*. Ed. by E. Klostermann (GCS 14, *Eusebius Werke* 4). Leipzig, 1906.

Die Chronik aus dem Armenischen übersetzt, by J. Karst (GCS 20, *Eusebius Werke* 5). Leipzig, 1911.

Demonstratio Evangelica. Ed. by I. Heikel (GCS 23, *Eusebius Werke* 6). Leipzig, 1913.

Praeparatio Evangelica. Ed. by K. Mras (GCS 43, *Eusebius Werke* 8., vol. 1 and 2). Berlin, 1954 and 1956.

ii. *St. Athanasius of Alexandria*

Opera omnia quae exstant. Ed. by B. de Montfaucon (PG 25–28). Paris, 1857.

Athanasius Werke. Hrsg. im Auftrage der Kirchenväter-Kommission der Preußischen Akademie der Wissenschaften von H.G. Opitz, II/1, 1–280: *Die Apologien*. Berlin-Leipzig, 1945.

Apologie a l'Empereur Constance; Apologie pour sa fuite. Introduction, texte critique, traduction et notes de Jan-M. Szymusiak, SJ (SC 56). Paris, 1958.

Athanasius. *Contra Gentes and De Incarnatione*. Ed. and transl. by R. W. Thompson (Oxford Early Christian Texts). Oxford, 1971.

Sur l'incarnation du Verbe. Introduction, texte critique, traduction, notes, et index par Ch. Kannengiesser (*SC* 199). Paris, 1973.

Die Fest-Briefe des Heiligen Athanasius Bischofs von Alexandria. Aus dem Syrischen übersetzt und durch Anmerkungen erläutert von F. Larsow. Leipzig-Göttingen, 1852.

Festal or Easter Letters. The Oxford translation. Revised by Miss Payne-Smith. Edited, with Introduction (including the *Historia Acephala* and *Index*) and revised notes by Rev. A. Robertson in Robertson, *Athanasius*, LNPF[2]. Buffalo and New York, 1891 (reprint 1971), 495f.

Osterfestbriefe des Apa Athanasius. Aus dem Koptischen übersetzt und erlautert von P. Merendino, OSB. Düsseldorf, 1965.

iii. *Other Ancient Sources*

Acta Petri	Vouaux, L. *Les Actes de Pierre*. Paris, 1922.
Ammianus Marcellinus RG	*Ammiani Marcellini Rerum Gestarum*. Ed. by C. U. Clark. Vol. I and II. Berlin, 1963.
Arnobius. Adv. Gentes	*Arnobii Afri Disputationum adversus Gentes libri septem* (PL 5, 713f.).
St. Augustine	*Sancti Aureli Augustini scripta contra Donatistas*, Pars II (CSEL 52). Vienna-Leipzig, 1909. Pars III (CSEL 53). Vienna-Leipzig, 1910.
Clemens	S. Clementis Romani. *Epistula ad Corinthios quae vocatur prima graece et latine*. Recensuit, apparata critico instruxit C. Th. Schaefer. Bonn, 1941.
(*Clementina*) Hom.	Clementina. *Homiliae*. Ed. by B. Rehm. Prepared for printing by J.Irmscher. Second improved edition by F. Paschke (GCS 42). Berlin, 1969.
Recog.	Clementina. *Recognitiones* (Rufino interprete). Ed. by B. Rehm and prepared for printing by F. Paschke (GCS 51). Berlin, 1965.
St. Cyprian	*S. Thasci Caecili Cypriani Opera Omnia*. Recensuit et commentario critico instruxit G. Hartel (CSEL 3). Vienna, 1868.

Epiphanius Panarion   *Ancoratus und Panarion haer.* Hrsg. von K. Holl
(GCS 25,153–464: *Haer.* 1–33), Leipzig, 1915; (GCS 31:
Haer. 34–64), Leipzig, 1922; (GCS 37: *Haer.* 65–80),
Leipzig, 1933.

St. Hilary   *Liber ad Constantium Imperatorem* (PL 10,577–606). Paris,
Ad Const. Aug.   1845.

Frag. hist.   S. Hilarii. *Episcopi Pictaviensis Opera.* Pars Quarta (including *Fragmenta historica*). Ed. A. Feder SJ (CSEL 65).
Vienna-Leipzig, 1916.

St. Hippolytus   *Hippolytus Werke,* 3. Band: *Refutatio omnium haeresium.*
Philosophumena   Hrsg. von P. Wendland (GCS 26). Leipzig, 1916.

St. Irenaeus   *Adversus haereses* I–V. Ed. by R. Massuet (PG 7). Paris, 1882.
Adv. haer.   *Adversus haereses* III. Ed. by A. Rousseau and L. Doutreleau,
SJ (SC 211). Paris, 1974.

Josephus Antiq.   *Flavii Iosephi Opera.* Edidit et aparatu critico instruxit, B.
Niese. Vol. IV: *Antiquitatum Iudaicarum Libri XVI—XX et
vita.* Berlin, 1890.

St. Justin M. Apol.   *Apologia prima pro Christianis* (*PG* 6), 327–440. Paris, 1884.

Lactantius   *De mortibus persecutorum.* Ed. by S. Brandt and G. Laub-
mann,
De mort. per.   CSEL 27. Prague-Vienna-Leipzig, 1897.

St. Liberius   Liberius papa. *Epistolae, dicta et gesta.* In: PL 8, 1351–1410.

St. Optatus   *S. Optati Mileuitani Libri VII: Accedunt Decem Monumenta
Vetera ad Donatistarum historiam pertinentia.* Ed. by C. Zwisa
(CSEL 26). Prague-Vienna-Leipzig, 1893.

Origen c. Cel.   *Origenes Werke,* 1. Band: *Gegen Celsus.* Hrsg. von P. Koetschau
(GCS 2–3). Leipzig, 1899.

Comm. in Matt.   *Origenes Werke,* 10. Band: *Origenes Matthäuserklärung* I.
Hrsg. von E. Klostermann (GCS 40,1). Leipzig, 1935.

Philostorgius HE   *Philostorgius Kirchengeschichte.* Hrsg. von J. Bidez, 2,
überarbeitete Auflage besorgt von F. Winkelmann (GCS).
Berlin, 1972.

Severus of   *The History of the Patriarchs of the Coptic Church of*
El-Aschmounein   *Alexandria.* Arabic text edited, translated, and annotated by
B. Evetts (*POr* 1, fasc. 3 and 4).

Socrates HE   *Socrates Scholasticus. Ecclesiastica Historia.* Ed. by R. Hussey
in three volumes. Oxford, 1853. (Note: where the volume
number is not indicated in the footnotes, then the reference is
to vol. I.)

Sozomen HE   *Sozomenus Kirchengeschichte.* Hrsg. von J. Bidez und G. C.
Hansen (GCS 50). Berlin, 1960.

Sulpicius Severus   *Chronicorum libri duo.* Ed. by C. Halm (CSEL 1).
Chron.   Vienna, 1866.

Tertullian Apol.   *Tertullien: Apologétique.* Texte établi et traduit par J.P.
Waltzing avec la collaboration de A. Severyns. Paris, 1971.

Theodoret HE   *Historia ecclesiastica.* Ed. by L. Parmentier, second edition.
Revised by F. Scheidweiler (GCS 14). Berlin, 1954.

iv. *Collections of Documents*

COD   *Conciliorum Oecumenicorum Decreta.* Edidit Instituto per le
                Scienze Religiose. Bologna, [3]1973.

Duchesne   *Le Liber Pontificalis,* par l'Abbé L. Duchesne (Bibliotheque
                des Écoles Francaises d'Athènes et de Rome, 2e Sér. iii). Paris,
                1886–1892.

Joannou   Pontificia Commissione per la Redazione del Codice di
Fonti   Diritto Canonico Orientale. Fonti, fasc. IX, *Discipline générale*
                antique (IVe–IXe s.), par P.-P. Joannou, t. I,2: *Les canons des*
                Synodes. Particuliers, Rome, 1962.

Mansi   *Sacrorum conciliorum nova et amplissima collection.* Ed. J. D.
                Mansi, vol. VIII. Florence, 1762.

Mommsen   *Monumenta Germaniae Historica: Auctorum antiquissimo-*
Monumenta   *rum,* Tom. IX: *Chronicorum minorum saec. IV, V, VI, VII.* Vol.
                I. Berlin, 1892.

Opitz   *Athanasius Werke.* Hrsg. im Auftrag der Kirchenväter-
Urkunde(n)   Kommission der Preußischen Akademie der Wissenschaften
                von H. G. Opitz. Band III/1, 1–76: *Urkunden zur Geschichte*
                des Arianischen Streites, 318–328. Berlin-Leipzig, 1934.

Turner   *Ecclesiae Occidentals Monumenta Iuris Antiquissima.* Ed. by
                Ch. Turner. Oxford, 1899f. (References are to tom. I, fasc. II,
                pars IV.)

3. OTHER SOURCES

i. *Translations and Commentaries*

Cleveland Coxe, A., MacMahon, J. H., Wallis, E., Salmond, S. D. F. *Fathers of the*
    Third Century: Hippolytus, Cyprian, Caius, Novatian, Appendix (ANF Vol. V).
    Grand Rapids (Reprint), 1975.

Ferrar, W. J., *The Proof of the Gospel being the Demonstratio Evangelica of Eusebius of*
    Caesarea. London and New York, 1920 (2 vols.).

Fisch, J. *Ausgewählte Schriften des heiligen Athanasius* (BKV1). Kempten, 1872–1875
    (2 vols.).

Gifford, E. H. *Eusebii Pamphili Evangelicae praeparationis libri XV.* Oxford, 1903 (4
    vols).

Hartranft, C. D., and Zenos, A. C. *Socrates and Sozomen* (LNPF[2], Vol. II.). Buffalo
    and New York, 1890 (reprinted in 1952).

Lake, K., and Oulton, J. E. L. *Eusebius: The Ecclesiastical History* (The Loeb Clas-
    sics). London-New York, 1926–1932 (2 vols.).

Legge, F. *St. Hippolytus: Philosophumena or the Refutation of all Heresies* (2 vols.).
    Translated from the text of Cruice. London, 1921.

Lippl, J., Stegmann, A., und Mertel, H. *Des heiligen Athanasius ausgewählte Schriften*
    aus dem Griechischen übersetzt (BKV[2], Bande 13 und 31). Kempten-München,
    Band I: 1913, Band II: 1917.

Lawlor, H. J., and Oulton, J. E. L. *Eusebius Bishop of Caesarea: The Ecclesiastical*
    History and the Martyrs of Palestine. London, Vol. I: 1927, Vol. II: 1928.

Lightfoot, J. B. *The Apostolic Fathers.* Part I: *S. Clement of Rome,* vols. I and II.
    London-New York, 1890.

McGiffert, A.C., and Richardson, E.C. *Church History of Eusebius: The Life of Constantine by Eusebius together with the Oration of Constantine to the Assembly of the Saints and the Oration of Eusebius in praise of Constantine* (LNPF[2], Vol. I). Oxford-New York, 1890 (Reprinted 1952).

Roberts, A., and Rambaut, W.H. *The Writings of Irenaeus* (ANCL Vol. I). Edinburgh, 1868.

Robertson, A. *Select Writings and Letters of Athanasius, Bishop of Alexandria* (LNPF[2], Vol. IV). Oxford-New York, 1892 (Reprinted 1971).

Shapland, C. R. B. *The Letters of Saint Athanasius concerning the Holy Spirit.* London, 1951.

Thelwall, S., Holmes, etc. *The Writings of Quintus Sept. Flor. Tertullianus*, vol. I (ANF, Vol. XI). Edinburgh, 1869.

Violet, B. *Die palästinischen Märtyrer des Eusebius von Cäsarea* (TU 14,4). Leipzig, 1896.

Whiston, W. *The Works of Flavius Josephus.* London, 1879 (2 vols.).

ii. *Dictionaries and Lexicons*

DCB	*Dictionary of Christian Biography, Literature, Sects and Doctrines.* Ed. by W. Smith and H. Wace. London, 1877–1887 (4 vols.).
DHGE	*Dictionnaire d'Histoire et de Geographie Ecclésiastique.* Ed. by A. Baudrillart. Paris, 1912f.
Lampe, Lexicon	*A Patristic Greek Lexicon.* Ed. by G. W. H. Lampe. Oxford, 1961.
Liddell-Scott	*A Greek-English Lexicon*, Oxford, [9]1940.
[1]LThK	*Lexikon für Theologie und Kirche.* Hrsg. v. M. Buchberger. Freiburg/Br., 1930–1938.
[2]LThK	*Lexikon für Theologie und Kirche.* Hrsg. v. J. Hofer u. K. Rahner. Freiburg/Br., 1957f.
Müller, Lexicon	*Lexicon Athanasianum.* Ed. by G. Müller. Berlin, 1952.
NCE	*New Catholic Encyclopedia.* Ed. by W. J. McDonald. New York, St. Louis, San Francisco, Toronto, London, Sydney, 1967.
ODCC	*The Oxford Dictionary of the Christian Church.* Ed. by F. L. Cross and E. A. Livingstone. London, New York, Toronto, [2]1974.
PWK	*Paulys Realenzyklopädie der klassischen Altertumswissenschaft.* Neue Bearb. v. G. Wissowa u. W. Kroll (mit K. Mittelhaus). Stuttgart, 1893f.
RAC	*Reallexikon für Antike und Christentum.* Hrsg. v. Th. Klauser. Stuttgart, 1941 (1950f).
RE	*Realenzyklopädie für protestantische Theologie und Kirche.* Begr. J. J. Herzog. Hrsg. v. A. Hauck. Leipzig,[3] 1896–1913.

iii. *Bibliography*

Archivum Historiae Pontificum. Vol. 1–15. Rome, 1963–1977.

Bibliographie de la Revue d'histoire ecclésiastique. Louvain.

Geerard, M. *Clavis Patrum Graecorum.* Vol. II: *Ab Athanasio ad Chrysostomum.* Brepols-Turnhout, 1974.

Quasten, J. *Patrology.* Utrecht-Westminster/Md. Vol. I: 1950 (Reprint 1975). Vol. II: 1953 (Reprint 1964). Vol. III: 1960 (Reprint 1963).

Schneemelcher, W. *Bibliographia Patristica.* Bde. I–XVIII (1956–1972). Berlin, 1959–1978.

4. SECONDARY LITERATURE
The list of secondary literature is divided into three sections corresponding to Part One (including the General Introduction), Part Two, and Part Three (additions from the Revised edition).

Part One

Abramowski, L. "Die Synode von Antiochien 324/25 und ihr Symbol." In ZKG 86 (1975), 356–366.

Aland, K. "Kaiser und Kirche von Konstantin bis Byzanz." In Aland, K., *Kirchengeschichtliche Entwürfe*, 257–279. Gütersloh, 1960. Reprinted in: Ruhbach, G. *Die Kirche angesichts der konstantinischen Wende*, 42–73. Darmstadt, 1976.

Alberigo, G. et al. *Conciliorum Oecumenicorum Generaliumque Decreta*. Turnhout, 2006.

Altaner, B. "Der 1. Clemensbrief und der römische Primat." In *Kleine patristischen Schriften*, 534–539. Hrsg. von G. Glockmann (TU 83). Berlin, 1967.

Andresen, C. "Der Erlaß des Gallienus an die Bischofe Ägyptens" (Euseb, *HE* VII, 13). In *Stud. Pat.* XII (TU 115). Berlin, 1975: 385–398.

Azkoul, M., SJ. "Sacerdotium et Imperium: The Constantinian Renovatio According to the Greek Fathers." In *ThSt* 32 (1971): 431–464.

Bardenhewer, O. *Geschichte der altkirchlichen Literatur*. Band. II. Freiburg, ²1914.

Bardy, G. *Paul de Samosate*. Louvain, 1929.

Bardy, G. "Alexandrie, Antioche, Constantinople (325–451)." In *L'Église et les Églises*, Tome I, 183–207. Edited by O. Rousseau. Chevetogne, 1954.

Bardy, G. "La theologie d'Eusèbe de Césarée d'après l' 'histoire ecclesiastique.'" In *RHE* 50 (1955): 5–20.

Bardy, G. *Eusèbe de Césarée: Histoire ecclésiastique*, Tome I, Introduction (SC 73). Paris, 1960.

Batiffol, P. See below: Secondary Literature. Part Two.

Baur, F. Ch. *Die Epochen der kirchlichen Geschichtsschreibung*. Tübingen, 1852.

Baus, K., and E. Ewig. *Die Reichskirche nach Konstantin dem Großen. Von Nikaia bis Chalkedon*. Handbuch der Kirchengeschichte, vol. II/1. Edited by Herbert Jedin. Freiburg-Basel-Vienna, 1985.

Baynes, N. H. "Eusebius and the Christian Empire." In *Mélanges Bidez*, Tome II. Brussels, 1933, 13–18. (Reprinted in his collection: *Byzantine Studies and other Essays*, 168–172. See below.)

Baynes, N. H. *Constantine the Great and the Christian Church* (The British Academy Raleigh Lecture on History, 1929). 2nd Edition, with preface by H. Chadwick. London, 1972.

Baynes, N. H. *Byzantine Studies and Other Essays*. London, 1955.

Bebis, G. "Eusebius and his Theology of History." In "Πόνημα εὐγνῶμον" πρὸς τιμὴν τοῦ κατηγητοῦ Βασιλείον Βέλλα, 70–94. Athens, 1969.

Berkhof, H. *Die Theologie des Eusebius von Caesarea*. Amsterdam, 1939.

Berkhof, H. *Kirche und Kaiser*. Translated by G. W. Lorcher. Zürich, 1947.

Bévenot, M. "A Bishop is Responsible to God Alone (St. Cyprian)." In *RSE* 39 (1951): 397–415.

Botte, Dorn B., OSB. "Die Kollegialität im Neuen Testament und bei den apostolischen Vätern." In *Das Konzil und die Konzile*, 1–22. Edited by B. Botte, etc. Stuttgart, 1962.

Brox, N. "Tendenzen und Parteilichkeiten im Osterfeststreit des zweiten Jahrhunderts." In *ZKG* 83 (1972): 291–324.

Burke, J. "Eusebius on Paul of Samosata: A New Image." In Κληρονομία 7 (1975): 8–20.

Campenhausen, H. Freiherr von. *Kirchliches Amt und Geistliche Vollmacht in den ersten drei Jahrhunderten*. Beiträge zur historischen Theologie, 14. Tübingen, 1953.

Campenhausen, H. Freiherr von. *Griechische Kirchenväter*. Stuttgart, ³1961.

Campenhausen, H. Freiherr von. "Ostertermin oder Osterfasten? Zum Verständnis des Irenäusbriefs an Viktor (Euseb. Hist. Eccl. 5,24,12–17)." In *VigChr* 28 (1974): 114–138.

Caspar, E. *Die älteste römische Bischofsliste: Kritische Studien zum Formproblem des eusebianischen Kanons sowie zur Geschichte der ältesten Bischofslisten und ihrer Entstehung aus apostolischen Sukzessionenreihen*. Schriften der Königsberger Gelehrten Gesellschaft, 2.Jahr., Geisteswissenschaftliche Klasse, Heft 2. Berlin, 1926.

Caspar, E. "Kleine Beiträge zur älteren Papstgeschichte." In *ZKG* 46 (1927): 321–355.

Caspar, E. *Geschichte des Papsttums*. Band I. Tübingen, 1930.

Chadwick, H. "Ossius of Cordova and the Presidency of the Council of Antioch, 325." In *JThS* 9 (1958): 292–304.

Chapman, J. H. *Studies on the Early Papacy*. London, 1928.

Clercq, V. C. de. *Ossius of Cordova: A Contribution to the History of the Constantinian Period*. Washington, 1954.

Connolly, R. H. "Eusebius H. E. v. 28." In *JThS* 49 (1948): 73–79.

Cranz, F. E. "Kingdom and Polity in Eusebius of Caesarea." In *HThR* 45 (1952): 47–66.

Cullmann, O. *Petrus: Jünger, Apostel, Märtyrer*. Zürich, 1952.

Daniélou, J., and Marrou, H. *The First Six Hundred Years. The Christian Centuries*, vol. I. Translated by V. Cronin. London, 1964.

Downey, G. *A History of Antioch in Syria*. Princeton, 1961.

Drake, H. A. *Constantine and the Bishops: The Politics of Intolerance*. Baltimore and London, 2000.

Duchesne, L. *Histoire Ancienne de l'Église*. Tome II. Paris, ⁵1911.

Dvornik, F. *The Idea of Apostolicity in Byzantium*. Cambridge, Mass., 1958.

Dvornik, F. "Byzantium and the Roman Primacy." In *AER* 144 (1961): 289–312.

Eger, H. "Kaiser und Kirche in der Geschichtstheologie Eusebs von Cäsarea." In *ZNW* 38 (1939): 97–115.

Emonds, H. *Zweite Auflage im Altertum*. Leipzig, 1941.

Eno, R. B. "Origen and the Church of Rome." In *AER* 167 (1973): 41–50.

Farina, Raffaele. *L'impero e l'imperatore Cristiano in Eusebio di Caesarea: La prima teologia politica del Cristianesimo*. Zürich, 1966.

Finkenzeller, J. "Ketzertaufe." In *LThK*² VI, col. 131–133.

Foakes-Jackson, F. J. *Eusebius Pamphili. Bishop of Caesarea in Palestine and the first Christian Historian. A Study of the Man and his Writings. Five Essays*. Cambridge, 1933.

Giles, E. *Documents Illustrating Papal Authority, AD 96–454*. London, 1952.

Girardet, Klaus M. *Der Kaiser und sein Gott: Das Christentum im Denken und in der Religionspolitik Konstantins des Großen*. Berlin-New York, 2010.

Girardet, K. M. See Secondary Literature. Part Two.

Grant, R. M. "Eusebius and his Church History." In *Understanding the Sacred Texts: Essays in Honour of Morton S. Enslin*, 235–247. Edited by J. Reumann. Valley Forge (Judson), 1972.

Grant, R. M. "Papias in Eusebius' Church History." In *Mélanges d'histoire des religions offerts à Henri-Charles Puech*, 209–213. Paris, 1974.

Grant, R. M. "The Case against Eusebius or, Did the Father of Church History write History?" In *Stud. Pat.*, vol. XII (TU 115), 413–421. Berlin, 1975.

Grapin, É. *Eusèbe: Histoire écclesiastique*. Tome III. Paris, 1913.

Grillmeier, A., SJ. *Christ in Christian Tradition*. Translated by J. Bowden. London and Oxford, ²1975.

Grotz, H., SJ. *Die Hauptkirchen des Ostens von den Anfängen bis zum Konzil von Nikaia (325)*. OrChrA 169. Rome, 1964.

Grotz, H., SJ. "Die Stellung der römischen Kirche anhand frühchristlicher Quellen." In *AHP* 13 (1975): 7–64.

Hadrill, D. S. Wallace. See under Wallace-Hadrill.

Haller, J. *Das Papsttum: Idee und Wirklichkeit.* Band I, Die Grundlagen. Urach und Stuttgart, 1950.

Harnack, A. von. *Lehrbuch der Dogmengeschichte.* Vol. I, II, and III. Freiburg/ Br.-Leipzg, ³1894–1897.

Harnack, A. von. *Die Chronologie der altkirchlichen Literatur bis Eusebius.* Band II. Leipzig, 1904.

Hastings, A. "The Papacy and Rome's Civil Greatness." In *DR*, vol. 75 (1957): 359–382.

Hefele, C. J. *Conciliengeschichte.* Band I. Freiburg/Br., 1835.

Heiler, F. *Altkirchliche Autonomie und päpstlicher Zentralismus (Die Katholische Kirche des Ostens und Westens.* Bd. II: *Die römisch-katholische Kirche, Teil).* Munich, 1941.

Hertling, L., SJ. "Communio und Primat: Kirche und Papsttum in der christlichen Antike." In *Una Sancta* 17 (1962): 91–125. Originally in *Miscellanea Historiae Pontificiae,* 1943.

Hertling, L., SJ. *A History of the Catholic Church.* Translated from the German by A. G. Biggs. Westminster/Md., 1957.

Hess, H. *The Canons of the Council of Sardica AD 343: A Landmark in the Early Development of Canon Law.* Oxford, 1958.

Higgins, M. J. See Secondary Literature. Part Two.

Hofstetter, K. "Das Petrusamt in der Kirche des 1.–2. Jahrhunderts: Jerusalem-Rom." In *Begegnung der Christen: Studien evangelischer und katholischer Theologen,* 373–389. Hrsg. v. M. Roesle u. O. Cullmann. Stuttgart, ²1960.

Holland, D. L. "Die Synode von Antiochien (324/25) und ihre Bedeutung für Eusebius von Caesarea und das Konzil von Nizäa." In *ZKG* 81 (1970): 163–181.

Huber, W. *Passa und Ostern.* Beiheft zur ZNW 35. Berlin, 1969.

Instinsky, H. U. *Bischofsstuhl und Kaiserthron.* Munich, 1955.

Jackson, F. J. Foakes-. See under Foakes-Jackson.

Jalland, T. G. See Secondary Literature. Part Two.

Jaskowski, F. "Die Kirchengeschichte des Eusebius und der Primat." In *IKZ* (1909): 104–110 and 322–362.

Javierre Ortas, Antonio M. "Successione e apostolica e successione primaziale." In *Il Primatto del vescovo di Roma nel primo millennio,* 53–138. Edited by Michele Maccarone. Vatican, 1991.

Jedin, H. "Einleitung in die Kirchengeschichte." In *Handbuch der Kirchengeschichte.* Band I, 1–55. Hrsg. v. H. Jedin. Freiburg-Basel-Vienna, 1963.

Kaethler, Andrew. See Mitralexis.

Karrer, O. "Das Petrusamt in der Frühkirche." In *Festgabe J. Lortz.* Band I, 507–525. Hrsg. von. E. Iserloh u. P. Manns. Baden-Baden.

Kartaschow, A. "Die Entstehung der kaiserlichen Synodalgewalt unter Konstantin dem Großen, ihre theologische Begründung und ihre kirchliche Rezeption." In *Kirche und Kosmos: Orthodoxie und evangelisches Christentum,* 137–153. Studien Heft Nr. 2. Hrsg. vom Kirchlichen Außenamt der EKD. Witten-Ruhr, 1950.

Katzenmayer, H. "Petrus und der Primat des römischen Bischofs in der ἐϰϰλησιαστιϰὴ ἱστορία des Bischofs Eusebius von Caesarea." In *IKZ* 38 (1948), 158–171.

Kelly, J. N. D. *Early Christian Doctrines.* London, ⁴1968.

Kelly, J. N. D. See Secondary Literature. Part Two.

Klauser, Th. *Der Ursprung der bischöflichen Insignien und Ehrenrechte: Rede gehalten beim Antritt des Rektorats der Rheinischen Friedrich-WilhelmUniversität zu Bonn am 11. Dezember 1948.* Krefeld, ²1953.

Kohlmeyer, E. "Zur Ideologie des ältesten Papsttums: Succession und Tradition." In *ThStK* 103 (1931), 230–243.

Kraft, H. "Einleitung: Eusebius von Caesarea." In *Eusebius Kirchengeschichte*, 11–74. Hrsg. v. H. Kraft, Munich, 1967.

Kretschmar, G. "Der Weg zur Reichskirche." In *Verkündigung und Forschung*, vol. 13 (1968): 3–44.

Krömer, A. *Die Sedes apostolica der Stadt Rom in ihrer theologischen Relevanz innerhalb der abendländischen Kirchengeschichte bis Leo I.*, Dissertation. Freiburg/ Br., 1973.

Lanne, E., OSB. "Partikularkirchen und Patriarchate zur Zeit der großen Konzilien." In *ThJ* (1965): 459–484.

La Piana, G. "The Roman Church at the End of the Second Century." In *HThR* 18 (1925), 201–277.

Laqueur, R. *Eusebius als Historiker seiner Zeit*. Berlin-Leipzig, 1929.

Lawlor, H.J. *Eusebiana: Essays on the Ecclesiastical History of Eusebius*. New York, 1912.

Lee, G. M. "Eusebius on St. Mark and the Beginnings of Christianity in Egypt." In *Stud. Pat.* XII (TU 115), 422–431. Berlin, 1975.

L'Huillier, Peter. *The Church of the Ancient Councils: The Disciplinary Work of the First Four Ecumenical Councils*. Crestwood, NY, 1996.

Lietzmann, H. "Simon Magus." In *PWK* III, A. 1, col. 180–184.

Lietzmann, H. *Geschichte der Alten Kirche*. Bd. I: Berlin-Leipzig: 1932. Bd. II: 1936. Bd. III: 1938.

Lightfoot, J. B. "Eusebius." In *DCB*, vol. II: 308–348.

Lohse, B. *Das Passafest der Quartodecimianer*. Gütersloh, 1953.

Loofs, Fr. *Paulus von Samosata* (TU 44,5). Leipzig, 1924.

Ludwig, J. *Die Primatworte Mt 16,18–19 in der altkirchlichen Exegese*. Münster/ Westf., 1952.

Maccarone, M. "'Cathedra Petri' und die Idee der Entwicklung des päpstlichen Primates vom 2. bis 4. Jahrhundert." In *Saeculum* 13 (1962), 278–292.

McCue, J. F., SJ. "The Roman Primacy in the Second Century and the Problem of the Development of Dogma." In *ThSt* 25 (1964): 161–196.

McCue, J. F. "The Roman Primacy in the Patristic Era, 1: The Beginnings through Nicaea." In *Papal Primacy in the Universal Church*, 43–72. Cd. by P. C. Empie and bishop T. A. Murphy. Lutherans and Catholics in Dialogue V. Minneapolis/ Minn., 1974.

McDermott, M., SJ. "The Biblical Doctrine of KOINΩNIA." In *BZ* 19 (1975): 64–77 and 219–233.

McGiffert, A. C. Prolegomena to *Eusebius: The Church History*. LNPF². Vol. I, 1–72.

Meyendorff, J. *Byzantine Theology: Historical Trends and Doctrinal Themes*. London-Oxford, 1974.

Milburn, R. L. P. *Early Christian Interpretations of History*. The Bampton Lectures of 1952. London, 1954.

Minnerath, Roland. "La position de l'Elgise de Rome aux trois premiers siècles." In *Il Primatto del vescovo di Roma nel primo millennio*, 1139–1171. Edited by Michele Maccarone. Vatican 1991.

Mitralexis, Sotiris, and Andrew Kaethler, eds. *Mapping the Una Sancta: Eastern and Western Ecclesiology in the Twenty-First Century*. Winchester [to be published in 2022].

Mohrmann, Ch. "Le conflit pascal au IIe siècle." In *VigChr* 16 (1962): 154–171.

Monachino, V., SJ. "Communio E Primato Nella Controversia Ariana." In *AHP* 7 (1969): 43–78.

Moreau, J. "Eusèbe de Césarée de Palestine." In *DHGE* XV, col. 1437–1460.

Moreau, J. "Eusebius." In *RAC* VI: 1052–1088.

Nigg, W. *Die Kirchengeschichtsschreibung*. Munich, 1934.

Nordberg, H. *Athanasius and the Emperor*. Commentationes Humanarum Litterarum XXX, 3. Helsinki, 1963.

Nyman, J. R. *The Arian Controversy from its beginnings to the Council of Nicaea*. Theol. Fac. D. Phil. Diss. Oxford, 1960.

Nyman, J. R. "The Synod at Antioch (324–325) and the Council of Nicaea." In *Stud. Pat.* IV (TU 79), 483–489. Berlin, 1961.

O'Connor, D. W. *Peter in Rome: The Literary, Liturgical, and Archeological Evidence*. New York-London, 1969.

O'Connor, D. W. "Peter in Rome: A Review and Position." In *Christianity, Judaism and other Graeco-Roman Cults: Studies for Morton Smith at Sixty*. Part Two, "Early Christianity," 146–160. Edited by J. Neusner. Leiden, 1975.

Opitz, H. G. "Euseb von Caesarea als Theologe." In *ZNW* 34 (1935): 1–19.

Opitz, H. G. "Dionys von Alexandrien und die Libyer." In *Quantulacumque*, 41–53. Studies presented to Kirsopp Lake. Edited by R. P. Casey, S. Lake, and A. K. Lake. London, 1937.

Ortiz de Urbina, I. "Patres graeci de sede romana." In *OrChrP* 29 (1963): 95–154.

Overbeck, F. *Über die Anfänge der Kirchengeschichtsschreibung*. Basel, 1892.

Overbeck, F. *Die Bischofslisten und die Apostolische Nachfolge in der Kirchengeschichte des Eusebius*. Basel, 1898.

Percival, H. R., ed. *The Seven Ecumenical Councils of the Undivided Church: Their Canons and Dogmatic Decrees, Together with all the Canons of all the Local Synods Which Have Received Ecumenical Acceptance*. Edited, with notes gathered from the writings of the greatest Scholars (LNPF ²XIV). Grand Rapids, 1974 (Reprint).

Peterson, E. *Der Monotheismus als politisches Problem*. In E. Peterson, *Theologische Traktate*, 45–147. Munich, 1951.

Peterson, E. "Das Martyrium des Hl. Petrus nach der Petrus-Apokalypse." In E. Peterson, *Frühkirche, Judentum und Gnosis. Studien und Untersuchungen*, 88–91. Rome-Freiburg-Vienna, 1959.

Places, É. Des. "Numénius et Eusèbe de Césarée." In *Stud. Pat.* XIII (TU 116), 19–28. Berlin, 1975.

Ratzinger, J. "Primat, Episkopat und Successio Apostolica." In K. Rahner-J. Ratzinger, *Episkopat und Primat*, 37–59. Quaestiones Disputatae 11. Freiburg-Basel-Vienna, 1961.

Ratzinger, J. *Das neue Volk Gottes. Entwürfe zur Ekklesiologie*. Düsseldorf, 1969.

Richardson, E. C. Prolegomena to *Eusebius: Life of Constantine, Oration in Praise of Constantine*, 411–469. LNPF², vol. I.

Ricken, F., SJ. "Die Logoslehre des Eusebios von Caesarea und der Mittelplatonismus." In *Theologie und Philosophie* 42 (1967): 341–358.

Rimoldi. A. *L'Apostolo san Pietro: Fondamento della Chiesa, principe delgi apostoli ed ostiario celeste nella Chiesa primitiva dalle origini al Concilio di Calcedonia*. Rome, 1958.

Roethe, G. *Zur Geschichte der römischen Synoden im 3. und 4. Jahrhundert*. Stuttgart, 1937.

Rousseau, A., and Doutreleau, L., SJ. *Irénée de Lyon: Contre les hérésies, livre III, Edition critique. Tome I: Introduction, Notes justificatives, Tables* (SC 210). Paris, 1974.

Ruhbach, G. *Apologetik und Geschichte: Untersuchungen zur Theologie Eusebs von Caesarea*. Diss. Heidelberg, 1962.

Ruhbach, G. "Die politische Theologie Eusebs von Caesarea." In *Die Kirche angesichts der konstantinischen Wende*, 236–258. Darmstadt, 1976.

Ruhbach, G., ed. *Die Kirche angesichts der konstantinischen Wende*. Darmstadt, 1976.

Sansterre, J.-M. "Eusèbe de Césarée et la naissance de théorie 'Césaropapiste.'" In *Byzantion* 42 (1972): 131–195 and 532–594.

Scheffczyk, L. *Das Unwandelbare im Petrusamt*. Berlin, 1971.

Schelkle, K. H. "Jerusalem und Rom im Neuen Testament." In *Wort und Schrift: Beiträge zur Auslegung und Auslesungsgeschichte des Neuen Testaments*, 126–144. Düsseldorf, 1966.

Schmidt, C. "Exkurs III: Die Passahfeier in der kleinasiatischen Kirche." In C. Schmidt, *Gespräche Jesu mit seinen Jüngern nach der Auferstehung* (TU 43), 577–725. Leipzig, 1919 (Reprint).

Schmitt, C. "Eusebius als der Prototyp Politischer Theologie." In G. Ruhbach, *Die Kirche angesichts der konstantinischen Wende*, 220–235. Darmstadt, 1976 (originally published in 1970).

Schneemelcher, W. "Das konstantinische Zeitalter: kritisch-historische Bemerkungen zu einem modernen Schlagwort." In Κληρονομία 6 (1974): 37–60.

Schneemelcher, W. "Kirche und Staat im 4. Jahrhundert." In G. Ruhbach, *Die Kirche angesichts der konstantinischen Wende*, 122–148. Darmstadt, 1976.

Schultze, B. "Der Primat Petri und seiner Nachfolger nach den Grundsätzen der universellen und der eucharistischen Ekklesiologie." In *OrChrP* 31 (1965): 21–52 and 277–294.

Schwartz, E. "Eusebios von Caesarea." In *PWK* VI: col. 1370–1439.

Schwartz, E. *Eusebius Werke* 2–3 (GCS 9). Einleitung, Leipzig, 1909.

Schwartz, E. *Zur Geschichte des Athanasius* (= GS III). Berlin, 1959 (see secondary literature, part two).

Schwartz, E. *Die Synode von Antiochien im Jahr 324/325: Ein Beitrag zur Geschichte des Konzils von Nicäa*. Berlin, 1913 (Reprint, 1973).

Schwartz, Ed. "Zum Decretum Gelasianum." In *Zeitschrift für neutestamentliche Wissenschaft* 33 (1930): 161–167.

Seeberg, R. *Lehrbuch der Dogmengeschichte*. Vol. I and II. Leipzig-Erlangen, ³1922–1923.

Sellers, R. V. *Eustathius of Antioch and His Place in the Early History of Christian Doctrine*. Cambridge, 1928.

Seppelt, F. X. *Geschichte der Päpste*. Bd I: *Der Aufstieg des Papsttums von den Anfängen bis zum Ausgang des sechsten Jahrhunderts*. Munich, ²1954.

Setton, K. M. *Christian Attitude Towards the Emperor in the Fourth Century, Especially as Shown in Addresses to the Emperor*. New York, 1941 (Reprint, 1967).

Simonetti, Manlio. *La crisi ariana nel IV Secolo*. Rome, 1965.

Stadler, K. "Apostolische Sukzession und Eucharistie bei Clemens Romanus, Irenäus und Ignatius von Antiochien." In *IKZ* 62 (1972): 231–244, and *IKZ* 63 (1973): 100–128.

Stauffer, E. "Petrus und Jakobus in Jerusalem." In M. Roesle and O. Cullmann, *Begegnung der Christen*, 361–372. Stuttgart-Frankfurt/M., ²1960.

Stead, G. C. "Eusebius and the Council of Nicaea." In *JThS* 24 (1973): 85–100.

Stevenson, J. *Studies in Eusebius*. Cambridge, 1929.

Stevenson, J. "Eusebius of Caesarea." In *NCE* V: 633–636.

Stockmeier, P. "Primat und Kollegialität im Licht der alten Kirche." In *ThPQ* 121 (1973): 318–328.

Strathmann, H. "Die Stellung des Petrus in der Urkirche: zu Frühgeschichte des Wortes an Petrus Matthäus 16,17–19." In *ZSTh* 20 (1943): 223–282.

Straub, J. A. "Kaiser Konstantin als ἐπίσκοπος τῶν ἐκτός." In *Stud. Pat.* I (TU 63), 678–695. Berlin, 1957.

Straub, J. A. "Constantine as ΚΟΙΝΟΣ ΕΠΙΣΚΟΠΟΣ: Tradition and Innovation in the Representation of the First Christian Emperor's Majesty." In *DOP* 21 (1967): 39–55.

Tailliez, F., SJ. "Notes conjointes sur un passage fameux d'Eusèbe." In *OrChrP* 9 (1943): 431–436.

Tetz, Martin. "Christenvolk und Abrahamsverheißung." In *Jenseitsvorstellung in Antike und Christentum: Gedenkschrift für Alfred Stuiber.* Jahrbuch für Antike und Christentum, Ergänzungsband 9. Münste, 1982.

Timofejeff, Bischof German. "Die Idee des Stuhles Petri in ihrer Entwicklung in vornikäischer Zeit." In *Pro Oriente, Konziliarität und Kollegialität als Strukturprinzipien der Kirche. Das Petrusamt, Christus und seine Kirche*, 131–135. Innsbruck-Vienna-Munich, 1975.

The Abbot of Downside. "Eusebius and St. Victor." In *DR* 69 (1951): 393–410.

Thomson, Stuart R. "Apostolic Authority: Reading and Writing in Clement of Alexandria." In *Studia Patristica*, vol. LXVI: 19–32. Papers presented at the Sixteenth International Conference held in Oxford, 2011. Leuven-Paris-Walpole MA, 2013.

Torrey, C. C. "James the Just and his Name 'Oblias.'" In *JBL* 63 (1944): 93–98.

Trevijano, R. "The Early Christian Church of Alexandria." In *Stud. Pat.* XII (TU 115), 471–477. Berlin, 1975.

Troianos, Spyros N. "Der apostolische Stuhl im Früh-und Mittelbyzantinischen Kanonischen Recht." In *Il Primato del vescovo di Roma*, 245–259. By Michele Maccarrone. Città del Vaticano, 1991.

Turner, C. H. *Studies in Early Church History*. Oxford, 1912.

Turner, C. H. "Apostolic Succession: A. The Original Conception." Essay III, in *Essays on the Early History of the Church and the Ministry*, 95–142. Edited by H. B. Swete. London, 1918.

Völker, W. "von welchen Tendenzen ließ sich Eusebius bei der Abfassung seiner Kirchengeschichte leiten?" In *VigChr* 4 (1950): 157–180.

von Ivánke, Endre. *Rhomäerrich und Gottesvolk*. Freiburg-Munich, 1968.

Wallace-Hadrill, D. S. *Eusebius of Caesarea*. London, 1960.

Wallace-Hadrill, D. S. "Eusebius of Caesarea's *Commentary on Luke*: Its Origin and Early History." In *HThR* 67 (1974), 55–63.

Wallace-Hadrill, D. S. "Eusebius of Caesarea and the Testimonium Flavianum (Josephus, *Antiquities*, XVIII, 63f.)," In *JEH* 25 (1974): 353–362.

Wallace-Hadrill, D. S. *Eusebius' Handlung of his Josephan Sources* (Unpublished, 1974).

Wenham, J. "Did Peter go to Rome in AD 42 [Acts 12:17]." In *Tyndale Bulletin* 23, 94–102. Cambridge, 1972.

Wicks, J., SJ. Introduction to his English translation of *Communio: Church and Papacy in Early Christianity*, by L. Hertling. Chicago, 1972.

Williams, Rowan. *Arius: Heresy and Tradition*. London, 1987.

Wolf, E. "Zur Entstehung der kaiserlichen Synodalgewalt, zu ihrer theologischen Begründung und kirchlichen Rezeption." In *Kirche und Kosmos*, 153–168 (see above, under Kartaschow, A.).

Zernov, N. "Eusebius and the Paschal Controversy." In *ChQR* 116 (1933): 24–41.

Part Two

Adam. K. *Der Kirchenbegriff Tertullians*. Paderborn, 1907.

Altendorf, H.-D. See under Schwartz, E., *Gesammelte Schriften* III and IV.

Aubineau, M. "La tunique sans couture du Christ. Exégèse patristique de Jean 19, 23–24." In *Kyriakon: Festschrift Johannes Quasten*. Vol. I, 100–127. Hrsg. v. P. Grainfield and J. A. Jungmann. Münster/Westf., 1970.

Bardenhewer, O. See Secondary Literature. Part One.

Bardy, G. "Athanase d'Alexandrie (Saint)." In *DHGE* IV (Paris, 1912f.): col. 1313–1340.

Bardy, G. *Saint Athanase (296–373)*. Paris, ²1914.

Bardy, G. "La politique religieuse de Constantin après le concile de Nicée." In *RSR* 8 (1928): 516–551.

Bardy, G. "La crise Arienne." In Fliche-Martin III, 69f.

Bardy, G. See also Secondary Literature. Part One.

Barnard, L. W. "The Date of S. Athanasius' Vita Antonii." In *VigChr* 28 (1974): 169–175.

Barnard, L. W. "Some Notes on the Meletian Schism in Egypt." In *Stud. Pat.* XII (TU 115), 399–405. Berlin, 1975.

Barnard, L. W. "Two Notes on Athanasius. 1. Athanasius Election as Archbishop of Alexandria. 2. The Circumstances surrounding the *Encyclical Letter of the Egyptian Bishops (Apologia contra Arianos.* 3,1–19,5)." In *OrChrP* 41 (1975): 344–356.

Batiffol, P. *Cathedra Petri*. Unam Sanctam 4. Paris, 1938.

Batiffol, P. See also Secondary Literature. Part One.

Baynes, N. H. "Athanasiana." In *JEA* 11 (1925): 58–69.

Baynes, N. H. "Athanasius." From a review of F. L. Cross, *The Study of St. Athanasius*. Oxford, 1945. In *Journal of Roman Studies* 35 (1945): 121–124.

Baynes, N. H. See also Secondary Literature. Part One.

Bell, H. I. *Jews and Christians in Egypt*. Oxford, 1924.

Berkhof, H. See Secondary Literature. Part One.

Bévenot, M. "Épiscopat et Primauté chez Saint Cyprien." In *EThL* 42 (1966): 176–185.

Bévenot, M. See also Secondary Literature. Part One.

Bouyer, L. *L'Incarnation et l'Église-Corps du Christ dans la théologie de saint Athanase*. Paris, 1943.

Brennan, B. R. "Dating Athanasius' Vita Antonii." In *VigChr* 30 (1976): 52–54.

Brennecke, Hanns Christof. *Hilarius von Poitiers und die Bischofsopposition gegen Konstantius II*. Berlin, 1984.

Bright, W. "Athanasius." In *DCB*, vol. I: 179–203.

Campenhausen, H. Freiherr von. See Secondary Literature. Part One.

Caspar, E. See Secondary Literature. Part One.

Češka, J. "Die politischen Hintergründe der Homousios-Lehre des Athanasius." In *Die Kirche angesichts der konstantinischen Wende*, 297–321. Edited by G. Ruhbach. Darmstadt, 1976.

Clercq, V. C. de. See Secondary Literature. Part One.

Cross, F. L. "The Study of St. Athanasius." In *An Inaugural Lecture Delivered Before the University of Oxford on 1 December 1944*. Oxford, 1945.

Demoustier, A., SJ. "Épiscopat et union à Rome selon Saint Cyprien." In *RSR* 52 (1964): 337–369.

Demoustier, A., SJ. "L'ontologie de L'église selon Saint Cyprien." In *RSR* 52 (1964): 554–587.

Duane, W. H. Arnold. *The Early Episcopal Career of Athanasius of Alexandria*. Notre Dame, 1991.

Dvornik, F. See Secondary Literature. Part One.

Duchesne, L. See Secondary Literature. Part One.

Eltester, W. See Schwartz, E., *Gesammelte Schriften* III and IV.

Feder, A. L., SJ. *Studien zu Hilarius von Poitiers I*. In *Sitzungsberichte der Kaiserlichen Akademie der Wissenschaften in Wien. Philosophisch-Historische Klasse 162*. Band 4. Abhandlung, Vienna, 1910.

Feder, A. L., SJ. "Studien zu Hilarius von Poitiers II." In *Sitzungsberichte der Kaiserlichen Akademie der Wissenschaften in Wien. Philosophisch-Historische Klasse 162*. Band 4. Abhandlung, Vienna, 1911.

Fialon, F. *Saint Athanase, Étude littéraire: Suivie de l'Apologie a l'Empereur Constance et de l'Apologie de Sa Fuite, Traduites en Français.* Paris, 1877.

Florovsky, G. "The Concept of Creation in Saint Athanasius." In *Stud. Pat.* IV (TU 81): 36–57.

Gessel, W. "Das primatiale Bewußtsein Julius' I. im Lichte der Interaktionen zwischen der Cathedra Petri und den zeitgenössischen Synoden." In *Konzil und Papst: Festgabe für Herman Tüchle*, 63–74. Hrsg. v. G. Schwaiger. Munich-Paderborn-Vienna, 1975.

Gibbon, E. *Decline and Fall of the Roman Empire*, vol. II. Everyman's Library Edition. London-New York, 1976.

Girardet, K. M. "Appellatio: Ein Kapitel kirchlicher Rechtsgeschichte in den Kanones des vierten Jahrhunderts." In *Historia*, vol. 23 (1974): 98–127.

Girardet, K. M. *Kaisergericht und Bischofsgericht: Studien zu den Anfängen des Donatistenstreites (313–315) und zum Prozeß des Athanasius von Alexandrien (328–346).* Antiquitas Reihe 1, Abhandlung zur alten Geschichte, Band 21. Bonn, 1975.

Goermans, M. "L'exil du Pape Libère." In *Mélanges offerts à Mademoiselle Christine Mohrmann*, 184–189. Utrecht, 1963.

Grillmeier, A., SJ. "Konzil und Rezeption." In A. Grillmeier, SJ., *Mit ihm und in ihm. Christologische Forschungen und Perspektiven*, 303–412. Freiburg-Basel-Vienna, 1975.

Grisar, H., SJ. *Geschichte Roms und der Päpste im Mittelalter.* 1. Band: *Rom beim Ausgang der Antiken Welt.* Freiburg/Br., 1901.

Gummerus, J. *Die Homöusianische Partei bis zum Tode des Konstantins.* Leipzig, 1900.

Gwatkin, H. M. *Studies of Arianism.* Cambridge, ²1900.

Hagel, K. F. *Kirche und Kaisertum in Lehre und Leben des Athanasius.* Borna-Leipzig, 1933.

Haller, J. See Secondary Literature. Part One.

Hefele, Charles-Joseph. *Histoire des Conciles d'après les documents originaux. Nouvelle traduction française corrigee et augmentee par L. Leclerq.* Vol. I, parts I and II. Paris, 1907.
(Quoted: Hefele-Leclerq.)

Hertling, L. von. *Antonius der Einsiedler.* Forschungen zur Geschichte des innerkirchlichen Lebens, 1. Heft. Innsbruck, 1929.

Herrmann, J. "Ein Streitgespräch mit verfahrensrechtlichen Argumenten zwischen Kaiser Konstantius und Bischof Liberius." In *Festschrift für Hans Liermann*, 77–86. Hrsg. v. K. Obermayer u. H. R. Hagemann. Erlangen, 1964.

Hess, Hamilton. *The Early Development of Canon Law and the Council of Serdica.* Oxford, 2002.

Hess, H. See Secondary Literature. Part One.

Higgins, M. J. "Two Notes: 1. Athanasius and Eusebius on the Council of Nicaea; 2. The Pope's Right to try Patriarch on Disciplinary Charge." In *Polychronion: Festschrift Franz Dölger*, 238–243. Heidelberg, 1966.

Hoss, K. *Studien über das Schrifttum und die Theologie des Athanasius auf Grund einer Echtheitsuntersuchung von Athanasius contra gentes und de incarnatione.* Freiburg, 1899.

Hugger, V. "Des hl. Athanasius Traktat in Mt. 11,27." In *ZKTh 42* (1918): 437–441.

Jalland, T. G. *The Church and the Papacy: A Historical Study.* London 1944.

Joannou, P.-P. *Die Ostkirche und die Cathedra Petri im 4. Jahrhundert.* Bearbeitet von G. Denzler, Päpste, und Papsttum. Band 3. Stuttgart, 1972.

Jones, A. H. M. "The Date of the *Apologia contra Arianos* of Athanasius." In *JThS* 5 (1954): 224–227.

Kannengiesser, C. "La date de l'Apologie d'Athanase 'Contre les Païens' et 'Sur l'Incarnation du Verbe'" In *RSR* 58 (1970): 383–428.

Kannengiesser, C. "Athanasius von Alexandrien. Seine Beziehungen zu Trier und seine Rolle in der *Geschichte* der christlichen Theologie." In *TThZ* 82 (1973): 141–153.

Kannengiesser, C. "Athanasius of Alexandria and the Foundations of Traditional Christology." In *ThSt* 34 (1973): 103–113.

Kannengiesser, C., ed. *Politique et Théologie chez Athanase d'Alexandrie. Actes due Colloque de Chantilly 23–25 Septembre 1973*. Théologie historique 27. Paris, 1974.

Kehrhahn, T. *De sancti Athanasii quae fertur Contra Gentes oration*. Berlin, 1913.

Kelly, J. N. D. *Early Christian Creeds*. London, ²1967.

Kemp, E. W. "Bishops and Presbyters at Alexandria." In *JEH* 6 (1955): 125–142.

Klein, R. *Constantius II. und die christliche Kirche*. Darmstadt, 1977.

Kraft, H. See Secondary Literature. Part One.

Kreilkamp, H. *The Origin of the Patriarchate of Constantinople and the first Roman Recognition of its Patriarchal Jurisdiction*. PhD Dissertation. The Catholic University of America, 1964.

Krömer, A. See Secondary Literature. Part One.

Laminski, A. *Der Heilige Geist als Geist Christi und Geist der Gläubigen: Der Beitrag des Athanasios von Alexandria zur Formulierung des Trinitarischen Dogmas im vierten Jahrhundert*. Erfurter theologische Studien, band 23. Leipzig, 1969.

Lanne, E., OSB. See Secondary Literature. Part One.

Larentzakis, G. "Einige Aspekte des hl. Athanasios zur Einheit der Kirche." In Κληρονομία 6 (1974): 242–259.

Lauchert, Fr. *Leben des heiligen Athanasius des Großen*. Cologne, 1911.

Lécuyer, J. "Le problem des consecrations épiscopales dans l'Église d'Alexandrie." In *BLE* 65 (1964): 241–257.

Lécuyer, J. "La succession des évêques d'Alexandrie aux premiers siècles." In *BLE* 70 (1969): 81–99.

Lietzmann, H. "Chronologie der ersten und zweiten Verbannung des Athanasius." In *ZWTh* 44 (1901): 380–390, quoted from the reprint in *Kleine Schriften*, vol. I, *Studien zur spätantiken Religionsgeschichte*, 251–259. Hrsg. v. K. Aland (TU 67). Berlin, 1958.

Lietzmann, H. "Die Anfänge des Problems Kirche und Staat." In *Die Kirche angesichts der konstantinischen Wende*, 1–13. Hrsg. v. G. Ruhbach. Darmstadt, 1976 (originally published in *Sitzungsberichte der Preuß. Akademie der Wissenschaften*, XXXVII–XLVI, 1938).

Lietzmann, H. See also Secondary Literature. Part One.

Loofs, F. "Athanasius von Alexandrien." In *RE* III (1897): 194–205.

Loofs, F. "Die chronologischen Angaben des sog. 'Vorbericht' zu den Festbriefen der Athanasius." In *Sitzungsberichte der königlich preußischen Akademie der Wissenschaften*, 1013–1022. 1908.

Ludwig, J. See Secondary Literature. Part One.

Maccarrone, Michele, ed. *Il Primato del vescovo di Roma nel primo millennio. Richerche e testimonianze. Atti del symposium storico-teologico*, Roma, 9–13 Octobre 1989. Vatican City, 1991.

Maccarrone, Michele. "'Sedes Apostolica—Vicarius Pietri.' La perpetuità del Primato nella sede e nel vescovo di Roma (Secoli III-VIII)." In *Il Primato del vescovo di Roma*, 275–362. Città del Vaticano, 1991.

Maccarrone, M. See Secondary Literature. Part One.

Marot, Dom H., OSB. "Les conciles romains des IVe et Ve siècles et le développement de la primauté." In *Istina* 4 (1957): 435–462.

Marot, Dom H., OSB. "Vornicäische und ökumenische Konzile." In *Das Konzil und die Konzile*, 23–41. Hrsg. v. B. Botte u. a. Stuttgart, 1962.

Martin, A. "Athanase et les Mélitiens." In *Politique et théologie chez Athanase d'Alexandrie*, 31–61. Edited by C. Kannengiesser. Paris, 1974.

Meijering, E. P. *Orthodoxy and Platonism in Athanasius. Synthesis or Antithesis?* Leiden, 1974.

Merendino, P. *Paschale Sacramentum: Eine Untersuchung über die Osterkatechese des hl. Athanasius von Alexandrien in ihrer Beziehung zu den frühchristlichen exegetisch-theologischen Überlieferungen.* Liturgiewissenschaftliche Quellen und Forschungen, Heft 42. Münster/Westf., 1964.

Michel, A. "Der Kampf um das politische oder Petrinische Prinzip der Kirchenführung." In *Konzil von Chalkedon*, 491–562. Edited by A. Grillmeier and H. Bacht. Würzburg, 1953.

Möhler, J. A. *Athanasius der Große und die Kirche seiner Zeit, besonders im Kampfe mit dem Arianismus.* Minz, [2]1844.

Newman, J. H. *Select Treatises of St. Athanasius in Controversy with the Arians.* Vol. II, 250–253. London, Pickering, 1881.

Nordberg, H. "Athanasius' Tractates Contra gentes and De incarnatione: an Attempt at Redating." In *Commentationes Humanarum Litterarum XXVIII*, 2 (1961): 1–30.

Nordberg, H. See also Secondary Literature. Part One.

Opitz, H.-G. *Untersuchungen zur Überlieferung der Schriften des Athanasius.* Arbeiten zur Kirchengeschichte 23. Berlin und Leipzig, 1935.

Orlandi, T. "Sull'Apologia secunda (contra Arianos) di Atanasio di Alessandria." In *Augustinianum* 15 (1975): 49–79.

Ortiz de Urbina, I. *Nizäa und Konstantinopel.* Geschichte der ökumenischen Konzilien, band I. Mainz, 1964.

Ortiz de Urbina, I. See also Secondary Literature. Part One.

Peeters, P. "Comment S. Athanase s'enfuit de Tyr en 335." In *Académie royale de Belgique: Bulletin de la classe des lettres et des sciences morales et politiques*, 131–177. 5 Série. Tome XXX. Brussels, 1945.

Peeters, P. "L'épilogue du Synode de Tyr en 335." In *AnBoll* 63 (1945): 131–144.

Pelikan, J. *The Light of the World.* New York, 1962.

Piétri, Ch. "La question d'Athanase vue de Rome (338–360)." In *Politique et Théologie chez Athanase d'Alexandrie*, 93–126. Edited by C. Kannengiesser. Paris, 1974.

Poschmann, B. *Ecclesia principalis: Ein kritischer Beitrag zur Frage des Primats bei Cyprian.* Breslau, 1933.

Rahner, H. *Kirche und Staat im frühen Christentum.* Munich, 1961.

Rimoldi, A. See Secondary Literature. Part One.

Ritschl, D. *Athanasius: Versuch einer Interpretation.* Theologische Studien, heft 76. Zürich, 1964.

Ritter, A. M. *Das Konzil von Konstantinopel und Sein Symbol.* Göttingen, 1965.

Robertson, A. Prolegomena to his edition of *Select Writings and Letters of Athanasius, Bishop of Alexandria.* LNPF[2], vol. IV (1891).

Roethe, G. See Secondary Literature. Part One.

Rogala, S. *Die Anfänge des arianischen Streites.* Forschungen zur christlichen Literatur und Dogmengeschichte, bd. VII, 1. Paderborn, 1907.

Roldanus, J. *Le Christ et l'homme dans la theologie d'Alexandrie. Étude de la conjunction de sa conception de l'homme avec sa christologie.* Studies in the History of Christian Thought, vol. 4. Leiden, 1968.

Rondeau, M.-J. "Une nouvelle prevue de l'influence littéraire d'Eusèbe de Césarée sur Athanase: l'interprétation de psaumes." In *RSR* 56 (1968): 385–434.

Ruhbach, G. See Secondary Literature. Part One.

Scheidweiler, F. "Zur neuen Ausgabe des Athanasius." In *ByZ* 47 (1954): 73–94.

Schlier, H. *Der Römerbrief.* Herders Kommentar zum Neuen Testament, band VI. Freiburg-Basel-Vienna, 1977.

Schneemelcher, W. "Athanasius von Alexandrien als Theologe und als Kirchenpolitiker." In *ZNW* 43 (1950/51): 242–256.

Schneemelcher, W. "Zur Chronologie des arianischen Streites." In *ThLZ* 79 (1954): col. 393–400.

Schwartz, E. "Die Quellen über den melitianischen Streit." In *Nachrichten* (= *NGG*), 1905: 164–187 (= *GS* III, 87–116).

Schwartz, E. "Die Dokumente des arianischen Streites bis 352." In *Nachrichten* (1905): 257–299 (= *GS* III, 117–168).

Schwartz, E. "Das antiochenische Synodalschreiben von 325." In *Nachrichten* (1908): 305–374 (= *GS* III, 169–187).

Schwartz, E. "von Nicaea bis zu Konstantins Tod." In *Nachrichten* (1911): 367–426 (= *GS* III, 188–264).

Schwartz, E. "von Konstantins Tod bis Sardica 342." In *Nachrichten* (1911): 469–522 (= *GS* III, 265–334).

Schwartz, E. "Der s.g. Sermo major de fide des Athanasius." In *SAM* (Jahrg. 1924, 6. Abh.). Munich, 1925.

Schwartz, E. "Zur Kirchengeschichte des 4. Jahrhunderts." In *ZNW* 34 (1935): 129–213 (= *GS* IV, 1–110).

Schwartz, E. *Zur Geschichte des Athanasius* (Gesammelte Schriften = GS III. Edited by W. Eltester and H.-D. Altendorf). Berlin, 1959.

Schwartz, E. *Zur Geschichte der alten Kirche und ihres Rechtes* (Gesammelte Schriften = *GS* IV. Edited by W. Eltester and H.-D. Altendorf). Berlin, 1960.

Schwartz, E. *Das Geschichtswerk des Thukydides.* Hildesheim (Reprint) 1969 (from the third, unchanged edition of 1929).

Seeck, O. "Untersuchungen zur *Geschichte* des Nicänischen Konzils." In *ZKG* 17 (1896): 1–71 and 319–362.

Seeck, O. *Regesten der Kaiser und Papste für die Jahre 311 bis 476 n. Chr: Vorarbeit zu einer Prosopographie der christlichen Kaiserzeit.* Frankfurt/M., 1964 (reprint from Stuttgart, 1919).

Seeck, O. *Geschichte des Untergangs der antiken Welt.* Stuttgart, 1920–1923.

Seiler, R. *Athanasius' Apologia contra Arianos* (Ihre Entstehung und Datierung). Diss. Tübingen, Düsseldorf, 1932.

Sellers, R. V. See Secondary Literature. Part One.

Seppelt, F. X. See Secondary Literature. Part One.

Setton, K. M. See Secondary Literature. Part One.

Sieben, H.J., SJ. "Zur Entwicklung der Konzilsidee: Werden und Eigenart der Konzilsidee des Athanasius von Alexandrien." In *Theologie und Philosophie* 45 (1970): 353–389.

Simonetti, Manlio. *La crisi ariana nel IV Secolo.* Rome, 1965.

Simonetti, M. *La crisi ariana nel IV Secolo.* Studia Ephemeridis "Augustinianum" 11. Rome, 1975.

Steidle, B., OSB. "'Homo Dei Antonius.' Zum Bild des 'Mannes Gottes' im Alten Mönchtum." In *SA* 38 (1956): 148–200.

Straub, J. A. See Secondary Literature. Part One.

Stülcken, A. *Athanasiana. Literaturund Dogmengeschichliche Untersuchungen* (TU 19,4). Leipzig, 1899.

Syme, R. Thucydides. Lecture on a Master Mind. From *The Proceedings of the British Academy*, vol. XLVIII, 39–56. Oxford University Press, 1963.

Szymusiak, Jan-M. SJ. *Apologie a l'empereur Constance. Apologie pour sa fuite* (SC 56). Paris, 1958.

Telfer, W. Review of Cross' Inaugural Lecture, "The Study of St. Athanasius." In *JThS* 47 (1946): 88–90.

Telfer, W. "Episcopal Succession in Egypt." In *JEA* 3 (1952): 1–13.

Tetz, Martin. "Athanasius und die Vita Antonii. Literarische und theologische Relationen." In *ZNW* 73 (1982): 1–30.

Tetz, Martin. "Athanasius und die Einheit der Kirche: Zur ökumenischen Bedeutung des Kirchenvaters." In *ZThK* 81/2 (1984): 196–219.

Tillemont, L. S. *Le Nain de, Mémoires pour servir à l'histoire ecclesiastique des six premiers siècles.* Tome VIII: *Histoire de S. Athanase.* Paris, 1693–1712 (16 Vols).

Torrance, T. F. "Spiritus Creator: A Consideration of the Teaching of St. Athanasius and St. Basil." In T. F. Torrance, *Theology in Reconstruction,* 209–228. London, 1965.

Voelkl, L. *Der Kaiser Konstantin. Annalen einer Zeitenwende, 306–337.* Munich, 1957.

Vries, W. de, SJ. "Die Struktur der Kirche gemäß dem ersten Konzil von Nikaia und seiner Zeit." In *Wegzeichen. Festgabe zum 60. Geburtstag von Prof. Dr. Hermenegild M. Biedermann OSA,* 55–82. Hrsg. v. E. Chr. Suttner u. C. Patock OSA (Das östliche Christentum, N. F., Heft 25). Würzburg, 1971.

Vries, W. de, SJ. "Die Ostkirche und die Cathedra Petri im IV. Jahrhundert." In *OrChrPer* 40 (1974): 114–144.

van Winden, J. C. M. "On the Date of Athanasius' Apologetical Treatises." In *VigChr* 29 (1975): 291–295.

Winter, H. "Recourse to Rome: Batiffol's Argument." In *Revue de l'Université d'Ottawa* 37 (1967): 477–509.

Part Three (from the revised edition)

Alberigo, G. et al. *Conciliorum Oecumenicorum Generaliumque Decreta.* Turnhout, Belgium: Brepols, 2006.

Anatolios, Khalad. *Athanasius.* London and New York: Routledge, 2004.

Anatolios, Khaled. *Retrieving Nicaea: The Development and Meaning of Trinitarian Doctrine.* Grand Rapids, MI: Baker Academic, 2018.

Arnold, Duane W.-H. *The Early Episcopal Career of Athanasius of Alexandria.* Notre Dame, IN: University of Notre Dame Press, 1991.

Ayres, Lewis. *Nicaea and its Legacy: An Approach to Fourth Century Trinitarian Theology.* Oxford: Oxford University Press, 2004.

Barnes, Timothy D. *Constantine and Eusebius.* Cambridge, MA: Harvard University Press, 1981.

Barnes, Timothy D. *Athanasius and Constantius: Theology and Politics in the Constantinian Empire.* Cambridge, MA: Harvard University Press, 1993.

Butterweck, Christel, ed. *Athanasius von Alexandrien: Bibliographie.* Opladen: Westdeutscher Verlag, 1995.

Colish, Marcia L. *Medieval Foundations of the Western Intellectual Tradition, 400–1400.* New Haven and London: Yale University Press, 1997.

Dassmann, Ernst. *Kirchengeschichte II/1: Konstantinische Wende und spätantike Reichskirche.* Stuttgart: Kohlhammer, 1996.

Dawson, Christopher. *The Making of Europe: An Introduction to the History of European Unity.* London: Sheed & Ward, 1939.

Drake, Harold A. *Constantine and the Bishops: The Politics of Intolerance.* Baltimore and London: The John Hopkins University Press, 2000.

Farina, Raffaele. *L'impero e l'imperatore Cristiano in Eusebio di Cesarea: La prima teologia politica del cristianismo.* Zürich: Pas-Verlag, 1966.

Girardet, Klaus M. *Die Konstantinische Wende: Voraussetzung und geistige Grundlagen der Religionspolitik Konstantins des Großen.* Darmstadt: Wissenschaftliche Buchgesellschaft, 2007.

Gottlieb, Gunther. See Lehmeier.

Hanson, R.P.C. *The Search for the Christian Doctrine of God: The Arian Controversy, 318–381.* Edinburgh: T. and T. Clark, 1988.

Hess, Hamilton. *The Early Development of Canon Law and the Council of Serdica.* Oxford: University Press, 2002.

Kraft, Heinrich. *Einführung in die Patrologie.* Darmstadt: Wissenschaftliche Buchgesellschaft, 1991.

Lattey, C., ed. *The Papacy: Papers from the Summer School of Catholic Studies Held at Cambridge, August 7–10, 1923.* London: Burns Oates & Washbourne, 1924.

Lehmeier, Eve and Gunther Gottlieb. "Kaiser Konstantin und die Kirche. Zur Anfänglichkeit eines Verhältnisses." In Schlange-Schöningen, *Konstantin und das Christentum*, 150–170.

Luibhéid, Colm. *Eusebius of Caesarea and the Arian Crisis.* Dublin: Irish Academic Press, 1981.

Peterson, Eric. *Der Monotheismus als politisches Problem.* In *Theologische Traktate.* Munich: Kösel-Verlag, 1951.

Ratzinger, Joseph. *Die Einheit der Nationen. Eine Vision der Kirchenväter.* Salzburg: Anton Pustet, 1971 [=Joseph Ratzinger, *Gesammelte Schriften*, vol. 1, 557–563].

Ray, Stephen K. *Upon This Rock.* San Francisco: Ignatius Press, 1999.

Rebenich, Stefan. "Vom dreizehnten Gott zum dreizehnten Apostel? Der tote Kaiser in der Spätantike." In Schlange-Schöningen, *Konstantin und das Christentum*, 216–244.

Roldanus, Johannes. *The Church in the Age of Constantine: The Theological Challenges.* London and New York: Routledge, 2006.

Schlange-Schöningen, Heinrich, ed. *Konstantin und das Christentum* (Neue Wege der Forschung). Darmstadt: Wissenschaftliche Buchgesellschaft, 2007.

Schwartz, Eduard. "Zum Decretum Gelasianum." *Zeitschrift für neutestamentliche Wissenschaft* 33 (1930): 161–168.

Seeliger, H. R. "Konstantin I., Kaiser (der Grosse)." In *Lexikon der antiken christlichen Literatur*, edited by Siegmar Döpp and Wilhelm Geerlings. Freiburg-Basel-Vienna: Herder, 2002.

Studer, Basil. *Schola Christiana: Die Theologie zwischen Nizäa (325) und Chalzedon (451).* Paderborn-Munich, Vienna, Zürich: F. Schöningh, 1998.

Timpe, Dieter. "Was ist Kirchengeschichte? Zum Gattungscharaker der Historia Ecclesiastica des Eusebius." In *Festschrift Robert Werner zu seinem 65. Geburtstag*, edited by W. Dahlheim et al., 171–204. Konstanz: Univ.-Verl. Konstanz, 1989.

Winkelmann, Friedhelm. *Euseb von Kaisareia: Der Vater der Kirchengeschichte.* Berlin: Verlags-Anstalt Union, 1991.

Tetz, Martin. *Athanasiana.* Edited by W. Geerlings et al. Berlin: Walter de Gruyter Gmbh US SR, 1995.

Twomey, D. Vincent. "The Political Implications of Faith in a Triune God: Erik Peterson Revisited." In D. V. Twomey and L. Ayres, *The Mystery of the Holy Trinity in the Fathers of the Church.* Dublin: Four Courts Press, 2007.

Twomey, D. Vincent. "Concluding Reflection: The Perennial Importance of the Great Persecution for Politics and Religion." In *The Great Persecution.* Edited by D. V. Twomey, S.V.D., and Mark Humphries. Dublin: Four Courts Press, 2009.

Voegelin, Eric. *The New Science of Politics.* Chicago & London: University of Chicago Press, 1952.

von Ivánka, Endre. *Rhomäerreich und Gottesvolk.* Alber: Freiburg/München, 1968.

Williams, Rowan. *Arius: Heresy and Tradition.* London: Darton, Longman & Todd, 1987.

APPENDIX

A number of important monographs and articles on Eusebius and Athanasius were published after the completion of the above study. Though they do not actually deal with the main subject—the Primacy of Rome—yet all are of significance either for one or other related topic, or with regard to my interpretation of the writings of Eusebius and Athanasius. Within the limits of this Appendix, it will not be possible to discuss these recent studies as thoroughly as they deserve. Instead, I will confine my comments to a brief review of the recent literature in relationship to some of the issues raised in my discussion of Eusebius and Athanasius. First of all, I should like to mention a most important contribution to the study of Eusebius: *Jean Sirinelli, Les vues historique d'Eusèbe de Césarée durant la periode prénicéenne*, Dakar, 1961 (Université de Dakar, Faculté des Lettres et Science Humaines, Publications de la section de Langues et Literatures No. 10). Though published over twenty years ago, this study has not in my opinion received the attention it deserves. Though I knew of its existence previously, yet it was only recently that I had the opportunity to read it—thanks to the kind assistance of Alois Grillmeier SJ and Stephan O. Horn SDS.

This remarkable work is nothing less than an attempt to establish some form within the apparently amorphous mass of ideas found in Eusebius. That he succeeds to a great extent is due in no small way to his fundamental insight, namely, that the thought of the erudite academic of Caesarea underwent an evolution in the pre-Nicene period.[1] Thus many otherwise confusing inconsistencies in Eusebius can be accounted for, since they fit into a certain pattern. This discovery of the evolution in Eusebius' thought-process is perhaps his most important contribution to Eusebian studies, as has

---

[1] Sirinelli was wise to limit his study to the pre-Nicene period, since Nicaea seems to have marked the turning-point in Eusebius' life and in his thought (see my comments above, Chapter Five, note 41). After Nicaea, Eusebius certainly expands on his ideas but his basic concepts would seem to have been fixed—fixed on the emperor—as his life became more and more embroiled in Church politics.

recently been acknowledged by R. M. Grant.[2] My own findings with regard to Eusebius' *History* in Chapter Five above confirm the basic insight of Sirinelli.

Sirinelli manages to achieve what almost amounts to a synthesis of Eusebius' main concepts—or rather, to be more accurate, his preoccupations. This he does more by the way he allows the development in Eusebius' preoccupations (such as chronology, synchronisms, Providence, Divine Economy, divine interventions, civilization, persecution, Second Coming) to unfold than by any overt attempt to synthesize them. From his presentation, it becomes clear that there is a basic consistency in the thought of Eusebius and that one idea flows into the other. But also, the basic flaws and weaknesses of Eusebius' theology come to the surface, which the author deals with sympathetically but not uncritically.

Of particular interest to our investigations are Sirinelli's analysis of the *Chronicle* and its synchronisms (pp. 31–134),[3] his presentation of Eusebius' concept of civilization (pp. 208–246),[4] and the latter's understanding of the Church's triumphant march through history as seen in his chapter on the Second Parousia. The author also provides an extensive treatment of Eusebius' ambivalent attitude to the persecutions (pp. 412–454)[5] and what must be the most comprehensive account of the evolution in Eusebius' understanding of the Pax Romana and its significance as seen within his overall *Weltanschauung* (pp. 387–411).[6] And like Ruhbach (who came to the same conclusion independent of Sirinelli it would seem), the uniqueness and centrality of Eusebius' concept of Providence is brought out (cf. especially p. 365f.). As we saw above, this concept determines to a great extent the historiography of Eusebius. Of particular value within this context is Sirinelli's discussion of Eusebius' sincere endeavor (and ultimate failure) on the theoretical level to counter Hellenistic fatalism with a Christian concept of Providence which would take free will into account (pp. 339–363). In the light of Sirinelli's analysis, my own comments on Eusebius' failure to take free will into account[7] may need slight modification. But here another recent publication needs to be consulted.

---

[2] See the discussion on Grant below, p. 592.
[3] Cf. above pp. 46–48, 53, 63, 97, 108 (synchronism of events); pp. 29, 85–86 (synchronism of heretics); pp. 29, 75–76, 86–90, 113, 136 (synchronism of orthodox writers).
[4] See above, pp. 150–151.
[5] Cf. above, p. 148f.
[6] Cf. above, p. 170f.
[7] See above, p. 201f.

The philosophy of history of the first Christian historians is the subject of an illuminating study by *Glenn F. Chesnut, The First Christian Histories: Eusebius, Socrates, Sozomen, Theodoret and Evagrius*, Paris, 1977 (Théologie Historique 46).[8] Limiting our comments to his treatment of Eusebius, it must be said that Chesnut's main contribution is to draw attention to the Graeco-Roman historiography which formed the background out of which Eusebius developed his understanding of history. Thus, for example, he demonstrates how Eusebius reinterpreted the Pagan concept of Fortune (τύχη), which idea he built into the heart of his philosophy of history (p. 69). Though Chesnut clarifies the originality and real achievement of Eusebius as well as showing how deeply indebted he was to his cultural background, he does not devote too much attention to a critical assessment of the final outcome of Eusebius' effort. However, this study contains a wealth of ideas which could help develop and clarify some of the arguments found in Chapters One and Five above. Thus, it is possible to argue that since Eusebius considers the universal Logos to be the structure of human history and since he adopted and modified the Graeco-Roman concept of the power of Fortune, then he assumed a priori that a *pattern* can be detected in the flow of historical events; such a pattern we have tried to uncover for the early Eusebius. I would question on the other hand whether Eusebius' adaptation of his Hellenistic concepts was as radical as that required by the Christian Faith and its philosophical consequences. The attempt by Augustine (mentioned on pp. 123–124) would seem more apt. It is a pity that the work of Sirinelli was not taken into account by the American scholar, since, apart from providing an alternative understanding of many concepts of Eusebius (such as Providence and free will), it would have drawn attention to the evolution in Eusebius' thought, which Chesnut ignores. I am not fully convinced by all the parallels drawn between the Pagan background and Eusebius' world of thought, as when, for example, Chesnut argues that φθόνος signified for Eusebius more than mere subjective envy: it was rather the demonic personification of one of the three psychological forces πλάνη, ἀπάτη, and φθόνος, which, as in Greek tragedy, moved men to act contrary to their better nature (p. 128, cf. also pp. 58–60, 78, 103). But this interpretation, like many other stimulating ideas contained in this book, could, if proved acceptable, shed interesting light on my own analysis of Eusebius.[9]

8   This monograph I had originally overlooked. I am grateful to Norbert Brox for drawing my attention to it.
9   Cf. above p. 177f.

A study devoted to Eusebius' *History* from the point of view of the Church historian's own aims and the way Eusebius achieves them is long overdue. *Robert M. Grant, Eusebius as Church Historian*, Oxford, 1980 provides such a study. Opting for a date of composition even earlier than that proposed originally by Laqueur, though on the basis of independent evidence, Grant demonstrates that the evolution in Eusebius' thought, which Sirinelli stresses, can also be traced in the *History*. He shows that changes in the text undertaken by Eusebius were not limited to those uncovered by Laqueur in Books 8–10: Eusebius also revised the text of Books 1–7, as we indicated above. Grant examines the *History* primarily under the headings of the themes given in the aims set down by Eusebius in Book 1.[10] But he seems unaware of the overriding purpose of the original *History* as conceived by Eusebius: the Church considered as the "Apostolic Succession," its origins and the way it spread the Christian Religion throughout the world and handed it down through the centuries by means of the bishops, orthodox writers and martyrs, despite the opposition of the pagan nations (the emperors), the Jews, and the heretics. Thus, we get no idea of the organic unity of the original work and its subsidiary aims, nor any appreciation of the subsequent development in the later revisions with their inner consistency. For this reason, Grant's study, though it offers a host of important insights on individual topics, lacks a certain inner cohesion. That his interpretation on many topics—such as the role of the Bishops of Rome, Alexandria, Antioch, and Jerusalem—differs considerably from that given above, is to be expected.

With regard to recent Athanasian studies, the most important contribution by far must surely be that of *Martin Tetz*, "Zur Biographie des Athanasius von Alexandrien," in *ZKG* 90 (1979) 304–338 (= von Konstantin zu Theodosius, Wilhelm Schneemelcher zum 65. Geburtstag, pp. 158–192). This impressive piece of scholarship amply demonstrates from the writings of Athanasius not only that the modifications in the picture of Athanasius painted by J. Burckhardt and E. Schwartz, as suggested by Lietzmann, Vogt, Schneemelcher, and von Campenhausen, are well-founded but, as indicated above in Chapter Five, that a radical revision of that false legend is called for. Such a revision Tetz also provides by means of a detailed and incisive analysis of some of the writings of Athanasius, paying special attention to the Athanasian concept of the *Imitatio sanctorum*. He concludes that for Athanasius, Scripture is the

---

[10]   See above, p. 21f.

criterion he used to determine both his "religious concerns" (to quote Schwartz) and the way he fulfilled his episcopal duties.

In a similar vein, Wilhelm Schneemelcher in his article, "Der Schriftgebrauch in den 'Apologien' des Athanasius," in M. Brecht (Editor), *Text—Wort—Glaube* (= Arbeiten zur Kirchengeschichte 50), Berlin-New York, 1980, pp. 209–219, comes to the conclusion that the motivating force in Athanasius' "politics" and the basic thrust of his "polemical pamphlets," as Schwartz described the historico-apologetic writings, is rooted in the Alexandrian bishop's vibrant faith in the Incarnate Word. He appeals for a more positive approach to the historico-apologetic writings on the basis of his examination of Athanasius' use of Scripture in same. On the basis of the hermeneutics of Athanasius as presented by H.J. Sieben, "Herméneutique de l'exégèse dogmatique d'Athanase," in *Politique et Théologie chez Athanase d'Alexandrie*, ed. par Ch. Kannengiesser, Paris, 1974, pp. 195–214, he examines the "Apologien" and demonstrates that a similar use of Scripture is to be found there (even in the *Historia Arianorum*) as in the "dogmatic" writings of Athanasius analyzed by Sieben. Contrary to the opinion of Schwartz, Athanasius did not unscrupulously use Scripture for his own questionable ends but, as Tetz also indicated, found in Scripture the norm and end of his life and writings.

Of particular importance is the recent interest shown in the place of the Cross in the writings of Athanasius,[11] the centrality of which[12] has not always been taken into account.

With regard to the historical events and their interpretation as outlined above (especially in Chapter Nine), an alternative interpretation is supplied by Myron Wojtowytsch, *Papsttum und Konzile von den Anfängen bis zu Leo I (440–461)*: Studien zur Entstehung der Überordnung des Papstes über Konzile, Stuttgart, 1981 (*Päpste und Papsttum*, hrsg. v. G. Denzler, Band 17). Characterized by its broad scope, detailed knowledge of the sources and attention to the mass of secondary literature, it is a valuable contribution to the study of this disputed topic, though—at least with regard to

---

[11] See especially M. Tetz, "Das kritische Wort vom Kreuz und die Christologie bei Athanasius von Alexandrien," in: *Theologia Crucis—Signum Crucis, Festschrift für Erich Dinkler*, zum 70. Geburtstag, hrsg. v. C. Andresen und G. Klein, Tübingen, 1979, pp. 447–465. Also: W. Schneemelcher, "Das Kreuz Christi und die Dämonen. Bemerkungen zur Vita Antonii des Athanasius," in *Pietas, Festschrift für Bernhard Kötting*, hrsg. v. E. Dassmann und K. Suso Frank, Münster, 1980, pp. 381–389. See also: G. T. Armstrong, "The Cross in the Old Testament according to Athanasius, Cyril of Jerusalem and the Cappadocian Fathers," in: *Theologia Crucis—Signum Crucis*, 17–38.

[12] See above, p. 550.

the first half of the fourth century—it does not differ too much from the generally accepted views discussed above.

Finally, a word about the Habilitationsschrift of *Gregor Larentzakis, Einheit der Menschheit. Einheit der Kirche bei Athanasius: Vorund nach- christliche Soteriologie und Ekklesiologie bei Athanasius von Alexandrien,* Graz 1978 (= Grazer theologische Studien I). Larentzakis attempts a reconstruction of Athanasius' ecclesiology on the basis of the latter's soteriology, thereby stressing the relationship of the Church to the sal- vation of mankind. The author stresses the continuity between the ante and post-Christian stages of Salvation History (O.T. und N.T.)—perhaps too much in view of the centrality of the Cross in Athanasius—and sees in this continuity the primacy of holiness (sanctification) as basic to the constitution of the Church. In the light of such a (more mystical) concept of Church unity rooted in the Unity of the Triune God, the external struc- tures—such as dogmatic formulations—are for Athanasius secondary and "ergänzungsbedürftig." No attention is given to the concrete structures of the Church. This study is of value in particular for drawing attention both to the more theological understanding of the Church's nature as founded in grace and to Athanasius' treatment of the same. Yet I am not convinced that Athanasius who spent a greater part of his life in exile for the sake of her "external" structures saw them as being secondary in any way, nor am I quite sure that he considered her dogmatic formulations as "ergänzu- ngsbedürftig"—except in a very limited way indeed. Yet Larentzakis' study is an important reminder that there is more to Athanasius' ecclesiology than external structures.

INDEX OF BIBLICAL REFERENCES

INDEX OF ANCIENT AUTHORS

INDEX OF NAMES AND TOPICS

INDEX OF GREEK TERMS (SELECTION)

INDEX OF MODERN AUTHORS